T0368350

The
Unusual Reality
of Depression

The
Unusual Reality
of Depression

Richard J. Kosciejew

authorHOUSE®

AuthorHouse™
1663 Liberty Drive
Bloomington, IN 47403
www.authorhouse.com
Phone: 1-800-839-8640

Published by AuthorHouse   09/24/2012

ISBN: 978-1-4772-7369-2 (sc)
ISBN: 978-1-4772-7370-8 (e)

Library of Congress Control Number: 2012917927

D iscussions of depression often start with a statement that has come over time to be found that it is the common cold of psychopathology, a ubiquitous affliction to which most of us are subject from time to time. Such discussions may be noted that at any one time, one fifth of the adult population will have significant depressive symptoms, and that most of this depression goes untreated (Weissman and Meyers, 1981). It may also be suggested that whoever is most likely to become depressed is largely a matter of psychological background and social conditions; depression is a 'curse of civilization' and its occurrence as formulating the disintegration of relationships, and depressing life circumstances. Thus, Pearlin (1975) had stated that depression is 'intertwined' with the values and aspirations that people acquire. That within the nature of the situation in which they are engaged of major roles, such as in occupation and family; with the location of people in broader social structures, such as age and class; and the coping devices that they use.

Even so, discussions of depression may begin with assertions that it is one of the most serious of mental-health problems. The discussion may then go on to emphasize that it is primarily a biological disturbance, an illness, the predisposition to which lies in genes and biochemistry. While people, may react to their circumstances with happiness and unhappiness, this is of questionable relevance to the clinical phenomena of depression.

Advocates of each of the positions, we can marshal impressive evidence; yet, taken together, they present a basic contradiction. They differ not only in their view of the causes of depression but it's very definition. Beck (1967) has noted, 'there are few psychiatric syndromes whose clinical descriptions are constant through successive eras of history.' However, as these opposing positions demonstrate, definitional problems continue to plague the study of depression, and they are not to be readily resolved. There remains considerable disagreement as to what extent and what purpose a depressed mood of some normal persons can be seen as one end of a continuum with the mood disturbance seen in hospitalized psychiatric patients and to what extent the clinical phenomenon is distinct and discontinuous with normal sadness and unhappiness.

It should become apparent that there is a tremendous heterogeneity to what falls under the broad rubic of depression and that there is an arbitrariness of any boundaries that are drawn on these phenomena. There are striking differences among depressed persons that invite some form of subtyping. A well, however, efforts to derive such subtyping are generally controversial, and any scheme is likely to be more satisfactory for some purposes than for other. Confronted with all of this ambiguity and confusion, one must be cautious and not seek more precision than the phenomena of depression afford, and one should probably be sceptical about any decisive state about the nature of depression.

A major source of confusion is due to the fact the term 'depression' variously refers to a mood state, a set of symptoms, and a clinical syndrome, as a reference to mood, depression identifies a universal human experience (Luckerman and Lubin, 1965) point to subjective feelings associated with depressed mood: sad, unhappy, blue, low, discouraged, bore, hopeless, dejected, and lonely. Similarities between every day-depressed mood and the complaints of depressed patients have encouraged the view that clinical depression is simply an exaggeration of a normal depressed mood. However, patients sometimes indicate that their experiences of depression are quite distinct from normal feelings of sadness, even in extreme form.

Yet, the view that depressed mood in otherwise normal persons is quantitatively but not qualitatively different from the depression found in hospitalized patients has been termed the 'continuity hypothesis.' Beck (1967) has provided a useful analogy to suggest the alternative to the continuity hypothesis. He notes that every day fluctuation in body temperature can be measured on the same thermometer as the changes associated with fever. Yet the conditions giving rise to a fever are distinct from those causing fluctuations in temperatures in healthy individuals. Similarly, the condition giving rise to clinical depression may be distinct from those producing fluctuations in normal moods.

Studies have compared the subjective mood of persons who are distressed but not seeking help to those who are seeking treatment for depression (Depue and Monroe, 1978). The two groups may be similar in subjective mood, but they differ in other ways. Those

2

persons who are not seeking treatment for depression tend to lack the anxiety and the physical complaints, including loss of appetite, sleep disturbances, and fatigue shown by the group seeking treatment. Still, it could be that there is a continuum between the two groups, with these additional features arising when a normal depressed mood becomes more prolonged or intensified. The controversy is likely to continue until either questions about the etiology of depression as resolved or unambiguous markers for depression are identified.

Advocates of biomedical approaches to depression tend to assume that there is a discontinuity between a normal depressed mood and clinical depression, and the appropriate biological markers will be found. Yet, as the article by Winokur, and suggests, even if that proves to be the case, there is likely to be many individuals suffering from extremes of depressed mood who do not have these markers.

Advocates of psychoanalytic, cognitive and behaviour, and interpersonal and social perspectives on depression have generally assumed a continuum between a normal depressed mood and clinical depression. They tend to exclude psychotic and bipolar depressed persons from issues (Gilbert, 1984). For unipolar depression, at least, they have assumed that whatever discontinuities in the biology of mild and severe moods there might be are not necessarily relevant to the psychological and social processes in which they are most interested.

All the same, sadness and dejection are not only emotional manifestations of depression, although about half of all depressed patient report these feelings as their principal complaint. Most depressed persons are also anxious and irritable. Classical descriptions of depression tend to emphasize that depressed persons' feelings of distress, disappointment, and frustration are focussed primarily on themselves, yet a number of studies suggest that, that their negative feelings, including overt hostility, are also directed at the people around them. Depressed persons are often intensely angry persons (Kahn, Coyne and Margolin, Weissman, Klerman and Paykel, 1971).

Perhaps 10 or 15 percent of severely depressed patients deny feelings of sadness, reporting instead that all emotional experience, including sadness has been blunted or inhibited (Whybrow, Akiskal and McKinney, 1984). The identification of these persons as depressed depends upon the presence of other symptoms. The inhibition of emotional expression in severely depressed persons may extend to crying. Nevertheless, mildly and moderately depressed persons may feel that every activity is a burden, yet still derive some satisfaction from their accomplishments. Despite their low mood, they may still crack a smile at a joke. Yet, as depression intensifies, a person may report both a loss of any ability to get gratification from activities that had previously been satisfying—family, work, and social life—and a loss of any sense of humour. Life becomes stale, flat, and not at all amusing. The loss of gratification may extend to the depressed persons' involvement in close relationships. Often, a loss of affection for the spouse and children, a feeling of not being able to care anymore, a sense of a wall being erected between the depressed person and others are the major reason for seeking treatment.

In the past decade, a number of theorists, notably Beck and Abramson, Seligman, and Teasdale have given particular attention to the cognitive manifestations of depression and have assumed that these features are causal of the other aspects of the disorder. Depressed persons characteristically view themselves, their situation, and their future possibilities in negative and pessimistic terms. They voice discouragement, hopelessness and helplessness. They see themselves as inadequate and deficient in some crucial way. They may be thought of death, wishing to be dead, and suicide attempts.

Depressed persons' involvements in their daily lives are interpreted by them in terms of loss, defeat, and deprivation, and they expect failure when they undertake an activity. They may criticize themselves for minor shortcomings and seemingly search for evidence that confirm their negative view of themselves. (Beck, Kovacs and Beck) suggest that they will tailor the facts to fit these interpretations and hold to them in the face of contradictory evidence. Depressed persons overgeneralize from negative experiences, selectively abstract negative details out of context, ignore more positive features of their situations, and negative characterize themselves in absolutist and dichotomous term in absolute a dichotomous term. The revised learn-helplessness model emphasizes that depressed persons are particularly prone to blame themselves for their difficulties and to see their defects as stable and global attributes.

Aside from these content aspects of their thinking, depressed persons frequently complain that their thinking processes have slowed down, that they are distracted and they cannot concentrate. Decisions pose a particular problem. Depressed persons are uncertain, feel in need of more simply feel paralysed, and that the work of making a choice and a commitment is an overwhelming task to be avoided at any cost.

Perhaps one of the most frustrating aspects of depressed persons for those around them is their difficulty in mobilizing themselves to perform even the most simple task. Encouragement, expression of support, even threats and coercion seem only to increase their inertia, leading to other ss to make attributions of laziness, stubbornness, and malingering. Despite their obvious distress and discomfort, depressed persons frequently fail to take a minimal initiative to remedy their situations or to do only halfheartedly. To observe, depressed persons may seem to have a callous indifference to what happens to them.

Depressed persons often procrastinate, they are avoidant and escapists in their longing for a refuge from demands and responsibilities. In severe depression, the person may experience an abulia or paralysis of will, extending even to getting out of bed, washing, and dressing.

In more severe depression, there may be psychomotor retardation, expressed in slowed body movements, slowed and monotonous speech, or even muteness. Alternatively, psychomotor agitation may be seen in an inability to sit still, pacing, and outbursts of shouting.

Mild depression heightens sexual interest in some people, but generally depression is associate with a loss of interest in sex. In severe depression, there may be an aversion to sex. Overall, though, women who are depressed do not have sex frequently, but they initiate it less, enjoy it less, and are less responsive (Weissman and Paykel, 1974). As well, depressed persons report diffuse aches and pains. They have frequent headache, and they are more sensitive to existing sources of pain, such as dental problems.

A brief interaction with a depressed person can have a marked impact on one's own mood. Uninformed strangers may read to a conversion with a depressed person with depression, anxiety, hostility, and may be rejecting of further contact (Coyne, 1976). Jacobson (1968) has noted that depressed persons often unwittingly

5

succeed in making every one in their environment feel guilty and responsible and that others may react to the depressed person with hostility and even cruelty. Despite this visible impact of depression on others, there is a persistent tendency in the literature to ignore it and to concentrate instead on the symptoms and complaints of depressed persons out of their interpersonal context. Depressed persons can be difficult, but they may also be facing difficult interpersonal situations with which their distress and behaviour make more sense.

Depressed persons tend to withdraw from social activities, and their close relationships tend to be strained conflictual. Depressed women have been more intensely studied than depressed men, in part because women are approximately twice as likely to be depressed. Depressed women are dependent, acquiescent and inhibited in their communication in close relationships, and prone to interpersonal tension, friction and open conflict (Weissman and Paykel, 1974). Interestingly, the interpersonal difficulties of depressed persons are less pronounced when they are interacting with strangers than with intimates (Hinchcliffe, Hooper and Roberts, 1975).

About half of all depressed persons report marital turmoil (Rousabville, Weissman, Prusoff and Heraey-Bsron, 1975). There is considerable hostility between depressed persons and their spouses, but often there is more between depressed persons and their children. Being depressed makes it more difficult to be a warm, affectionate, consistent parent (KcLean, 1976). The children of depressed parents are more likely to have a full range of psychological and social difficulties than the children of normal or even schizophrenic parents (Emery, Weintrsub and Neale, 1982), yet one must be cautious in making causal inferences. There is evidence that the child's problems are more related to a conflictual marital relationship and a stressful home life than depression of the parent, and so on.

Depression thus tends to be indicative of an interpersonal situation fraught with difficulties, and this need to be given more attention in both theorizing and planning treatment. Although depression is associated with interpersonal severity of depression and the extent of interpersonal problems tend to be modest. This may suggest that these problems are a matter not only how depressed persons are in their functioning, but of the response of key people around them as well (Coyne, Kahn, and Gotlib, 1985).

Depression can take shape in several other forms. In bipolar disorder we sometimes call manic-depressive illness, where a person's moods swings back and forth between depression and mania. People with seasonal effective disorder typically suffer from depression only during autumn and winter, when fewer hours of daylight diminish. In dysthymia, people feel depressed, have low self-esteem, and concentrate poorly most of the time—often, over a period of years—but their symptoms are milder than in major depression. Some people with dysthymia experience occasional episodes of major depression.

Bipolar Disorder, is consistent of a mental illness in which a person's mood alternates between extreme mania and depression, even so, they also call that Bipolar disorder manic-depressive illness. When manic, people with bipolar disorder feel intensely elated, self-important, energetic, and irritable. When depressed, they experience painful sadness, negative thinking, and indifference to things that used to bring them happiness.

Bipolar disorder is much less common than depression. In North America and Europe, about 1 percent of people experience bipolar disorder at some point in their lives. Rates of bipolar disorder are similar throughout the world. In comparison, at least 8 percent of people experience serious depression during their lives. Bipolar disorder affects men and women equally and is more common in higher socioeconomic classes. At least 15 percent of people with bipolar disorder commit suicide. This rate roughly equals the rate for people with major depression, the most severe form of depression.

Bipolar disorder is a mental illness that causes mood swings. In the manic phase, a person might feel ecstatically overcome with excitation, and self-importance, and full of life. Nevertheless, when the person becomes depressed, the mood shifts to extreme sadness, negative thinking, and apathy. Some studies that favor actively in the face of opposition that in the finding in support that the disease occurs at unusually high rates in creative people, such as artists, writers, and musicians. Nonetheless, other researchers contend that the methodologies of these studies were very misleading. In the October 1996 Discover magazine article, anthropologist Jo Ann C. Gutin presents the results of several studies of illness. Repression is one of the most common mental illnesses. At least 8 percent of adults in the United States experience serious depression at some point during their lives, and estimates range as high as

17 percent. The illness affects all people, regardless of sex, race, ethnicity, or socioeconomic standing. However, women are two to three times more likely than men to suffer from depression. Experts disagree on the reason for this difference. Some cite differences in hormones, and others point to the stress caused by society's expectant expectations of women. Depression occurs in all sections of the world, although the pattern of symptoms can vary. The prevalence of depression in other countries varies widely, from 1.5 percent of people in Taiwan to 19 percent of people in Lebanon. Some researchers believe methods of gathering data on depression account for different rates.

A number of large-scale studies indicate that depression rates have increased worldwide over the past several decades. Furthermore, younger generations are experiencing depression at an earlier age than did previous generations. Social scientists have proposed many explanations, including changes in family structure, urbanization, and reduced cultural and religious persuasions. Although it may appear anytime from childhood to old age, depression usually begins during a person's 20s or 30s. The illness may come on slowly, then deepen gradually over months or years. On the other hand, it may erupt suddenly in a few weeks or days. A person who develops severe depression may appear confusing, frightened, and unbalance that the perceiver give tongue to a 'nervous breakdown.' However it begins such that depression causes serious changes in a person's feelings and outlook. A person with major depression feels sad nearly every day and may cry often. People, work, and activities that used to bring them pleasure no longer do. Symptoms of depression can also vary by culture. In some cultures, depressed people may not experience sadness or guilt but may complain of physical problems. In Mediterranean cultures, for example, depressed people may complain of headaches or nerves. In Asian cultures they may complain of weakness, fatigue, or imbalance. If left untreated, an episode of major depression typically lasts eight or nine months. About 85 percent of people who experience one bout of depression will experience future episodes. Depression usually alters a person's appetite, sometimes increasing it, but usually reducing it. Unceasing sleep habits frequently change from time to time as well. People with depression may oversleep or, more commonly, sleep for fewer hours. A depressed person might go to sleep at midnight, sleep restlessly, then wake up at 5:00 a.m. feeling tired and foreign to his immediate environment. For many depressed people, early morning is a dreadful and terrible time of the day. Depression also changes one's energy level. Some depressed people may be restless and agitated, engaging in fidgety movements and pacing. Others may feel sluggish and inactive, experiencing great fatigue, lack of energy, and a feeling of being worn out or carrying a heavy burden. Depressed people may also have difficulty thinking, poor concentration, and problems with memory.

People with depression often experience feelings of worthlessness, helplessness, guilt, and self-blame. They may interpret a minor failing on their part as a sign of incompetence or interpret minor criticism as condemnation. Some depressed people complain of being spiritually or morally dead. The mirror seems to reflect someone ugly and repulsive. Even a competent and decent person may feel deficient, cruel, stupid, phony, or guilty of having deceived others. People with major depression may experience such extreme emotional pain that they consider or attempt suicide. At least 15 percent of seriously depressed people commit suicide, and many more attempt it.

In some cases, people with depression may experience psychotic symptoms, such as delusions (false beliefs) and hallucinations (false sensory perceptions). Psychotic symptoms indicate an especially severe illness. Compared to other depressed people, those with psychotic symptoms have longer hospital stays, and after leaving, they are more likely to be moody and unhappy. They are also more likely to commit suicide. Some depressions seem to come from no pinpointed place, even when things are going well. Others seem to have an obvious cause: a marital conflict, financial difficulty, or some personal failure. Yet many people with these problems do not become deeply depressed. Most psychologists believe depression results from an interaction between stressful life events and a person's biological and psychological vulnerabilities. Clinical depression is one of the most common forms of mental illness. Although depression can be treated with psychotherapy, many scientists believe there are biological causes for the disease. According to the June 1998 Scientific American article, Neurobiologist Charles B. Nemeroff discusses the connection between biochemical changes in the brain and depression. Depression runs in families, or as the descendable transmissions, such as the irregularity of studying twins. Researchers have found evidence of a strong

9

genetic influence in depression. Genetically identical twins raised in the same environmental conditions are three times more likely to have depression in common than fraternal twins, who have only about half of their genes in common. In addition, identical twins are five times more likely to have bipolar disorder in common. These findings suggest that vulnerability to depression and bipolar disorder can be inherited. Adoption studies have provided more evidence of a genetic role in depression. These studies show that children of depressed people are vulnerable to depression even when raised by adoptive parents. Genes may influence depression by causing abnormal activity in the brain. Studies have shown that certain brain chemicals called neurotransmitters play an important role in regulating moods and emotions. Neurotransmitters involved in depression include norepinephrine, dopamine, and serotonin. Research in the 1960s suggested that depression result from lower than normal levels of these neurotransmitters, as in of the sectors cased within the brain. Support for this theory came from the effects of antidepressant drugs, which work by increasing the levels of neurotransmitters involved in depression. However, later studies have discredited this simple explanation and have suggested a more complex relationship between neurotransmitter levels and depression. An imbalance of hormones may also play a characteristic role in depression. Many depressed people have higher than normal levels of hydrocortisone (cortisol), a hormone secreted by the adrenal gland in response to stress. In addition, an underactive or overactive thyroid gland can lead to depression. A variety of medical conditions can cause depression. These include dietary deficiencies in vitamin B6, vitamin B12, and folic acid; degenerative neurological disorders, such as Alzheimer's disease and Huntington's disease; strokes in the frontal part of the brain; and certain viral infections, such as hepatitis and mononucleosis. Certain medications, such as steroids, may also cause depression. Psychological theories of depression focuses on the way people adaptively adjust of its hindering with the normal growth and developmental capabilities for being thought, such that the thinkable of concepts enabling by reasoning from evidence or from premises we can find an easier process from which we can think about the unthinkable. Also, behaving is not taken into account for being idle. As an essay of mind in 1917, the pioneer involving the Austrian psychoanalyst Sigmund Freud explained melancholia, or major depression, as a response to loss—either real loss, such as the death of a spouse, or symbolic loss. Such as the failure to achieve an important goal that Freud believed that a person's unconscious anger over loss weakens the ego, resulting in self-hate and self-destructive behaviour. Cognitive theories of depression emphasize the role of irrational thought processes. American psychiatrist Aaron Beck proposed that depressed people tend toward viewing themselves, their environment, and the future in a negative light because of errors in thinking. These errors include focussing on the negative aspects of any situation, misinterpreting facts in negative ways, and blaming themselves for any misfortune. In Beck's view, people learn these self-defeating ways of looking at the world during early childhood. This negative thinking makes situations seem much worse than they really are and increases the risk of depression, especially in stressful situations.

In support of this cognitive view, people with 'depressive' personality traits might be more vulnerable than others to actual depression. Examples of depressive personality traits include, gloominess, pessimism, introversion, self-criticism, excessive skepticism and criticism of others, deep feelings of inadequacy, and excessive brooding and worrying. In addition, people who regularly behave in dependent, hostile, and impulsive ways appear at greater risk for depression. American psychologist Martin Seligman proposed that depression stem from 'learned helplessness,' an acquired belief that one cannot control the outcome of events. In this view, prolonged exposure to uncontrollable and inescapable events leads to apathy, pessimism, and loss of motivation. An adaptation of this theory by American psychologist Lynn Abramson and her colleagues argue that depression result not only from helplessness, but also from hopelessness. The hopelessness theory attributes depression to a pattern of negative thinking. Which people blame themselves for their negative lives? Events, without variation or fluctuation occur in circumstances in that of an action has to the occasion to achieve is a matter worthy of acknowledging that in the presence of freedom. Such an effect or outcome rides totally of infinite time, as a view that causes those of the events for being unchangeable, and the overgeneralized weaknesses as applying to many areas of life. Psychologists agree that stressful experiences can trigger depression in people who are predisposed to the illness. For example, the death of a loved one may trigger depression. Psychologists usually distinguish true depression from grief, a normal process of mourning a loved one who has died. Other stressful experiences may include divorce, pregnancy, the loss of a job, and even childbirth. About 20 percent of women experience an episode of depression, known as postpartum depression, after having a baby. In addition, people with serious physical illnesses or disabilities often develop depression. Through participation or observer, people experienced child abuse and appear more vulnerable to depression than others. So, too, do people living under chronically stressful conditions, such as single mothers with many children with little or no support from friends or relatives. Depression typically cannot be shaken or willed away. An episode must therefore run its course until it weakens either on its own or with treatment. Depression can be treated effectively with antidepressant drugs, psychotherapy, or a combination of both. Despite the availability of effective treatment, most depressive disorders go untreated and undiagnosed. Studies indicate that general physicians fail to recognize depression in their patients at least half the time. In addition, many doctors and patients view depression in elderly people as a normal part of aging, though treatment for depression in older people is usually very effective. Up to 70 percent of people with depression respond to antidepressant drugs. These medications appear to work by altering the levels of serotonin, norepinephrine, and other neurotransmitters in the brain. They generally take at least two to three weeks to become effective. Doctors cannot predict which type of antidepressant drug will work best for any particular person, so depressed people may need to try several types. Antidepressant drugs are not addictive, but they may produce unwanted side effects. To avoid a relapse, people must usually continue taking the medication for several months after their symptoms improve. Commonly used antidepressant drugs fall into three major classes: Tricyclics, Monoamine oxidase inhibitors (MAO inhibitors), and Selective serotonin reuptake inhibitors (SSRIs). Tricyclics, named for their three-ring chemical structure, include amitriptyline (Elavil), imipramine (Tofanil), desipramine (Norpramin), doxepin (Sinequan), and nortriptyline (Pamelor). Side effects of tricyclics may include drowsiness, dizziness upon standing, blurred vision, nausea, insomnia, constipation, and a dry mouth. MAO inhibitors include isocarboxazid (Marplan), phenelzine (Nardil), and tranylcypromine

(Parnate). People who take MAO inhibitors must follow a diet that excludes tyramine—a substance found in wine, beer, some cheeses, and many fermented foods—to avoid a dangerous rise in blood pressure. In addition, MAO inhibitors have many of the same side effects as tricyclics. Selective serotonin reuptake inhibitors include Fluoxetine (Prozac), sertraline (Zoloft), and paroxetine (Paxil). These drugs generally produce fewer and milder side effects than do other types of antidepressants, although SSRIs may cause anxiety, insomnia, drowsiness, headaches, and sexual dysfunction. Some patients have alleged that Prozac causes violent or suicidal behaviour in a small number of cases, but the US Food and Drug Administration has failed to substantiate this claim. Prozac became the most widely used antidepressant in the world soon after its introduction in the late 1980s by drug manufacturer Eli Lilly and Company. Many people find Prozac extremely effective in lifting depression. In addition, some people have reported that Prozac actually transforms their personality by increasing their self-confidence, optimism, and energy level. However, mental health professionals have expressed serious ethical concerns over Prozac's use as a 'personality enhancer,' especially among people without clinical depression. Doctors often prescribed lithium carbonates, a natural mineral salt, to treat people with bipolar disorder. People often take lithium during periods of relatively normal moods to delay or even prevent subsequent mood swings. Side effects of lithium include nausea, stomach upset, vertigo, and frequent urination. Studies have shown that short-term psychotherapy can relieve mild to moderate depression as effectively as antidepressant drugs. Unlike medication, psychotherapy produces no physiological side effects. In addition, depressed people treated with psychotherapy appear less likely to experience a relapse than those treated only with antidepressant medication. However, psychotherapy usually takes longer to produce benefits. There are many kinds of psychotherapy. Cognitive-behavioural therapy assumes that depression stem from negative, often irrational thoughts about oneself and of one's future. In this type of therapy, a person learns to understand and eventually eliminate those habits of negative thinking. In interpersonal therapy, the therapist helps a person resolve problems in relationships with others that may have caused the depression. The subsequent improvement in social relationships and support helps alleviate the depression. Psychodynamic therapy views depression as the result of internal, unconscious conflicts. Psychodynamic therapists focus on a person's experiences and the resolution of childhood conflicts. The psychoanalysis is an example of this type of therapy. Critics of long-term Psychodynamic therapy argue that its effectiveness is scientifically unproven. Electroconvulsive therapy (ECT) can often relieve severe depression in people who fail to respond to antidepressant medication and psychotherapy. In this type of therapy, a low-voltage electrical current is passed through the brain for one to two seconds to produce a controlled seizure. Patients usually receive six to ten ECT treatments over several weeks. ECT remains controversial because it can cause disorientation and memory loss. Nevertheless, research has found it highly effective in alleviating severe depression. For milder cases of depression, regular aerobic exercise may improve moods as effectively as psychotherapy or medication. In addition, some research indicates that dietary modifications can influence one's mood by changing the level of serotonin in the brain. An overview of the phenomena of depression and to take notice on some of the diagnostic distinctions that are currently being made, where it should become apparent that there is a tremendous heterogeneity to what falls under the broad rubic of depression and that there is an arbitrariness to any boundaries that are drawn on this phenomenon. There are striking differences among depressed persons that invite some form of subtyping.

However, efforts to derive such subtyping are generally controversial, and any scheme is likely to be more satisfactory for some purposes that for others. Confronted with all of this ambiguity and confusion, one must be cautious and not seek more precision than the phenomena of depression afford, and one should probably be sceptical about any decisive statement about the hidden and underlying nature of depression. Contemplating the phenomena of depression, one can readily detect patterns and come to a conclusion that some aspects of depression are more central than others; some are primary and causal, and others are secondary. One observer may be struck with the frequency of complaints about appetite and sleep disturbances by depressed persons and infer that some sort of biological disturbance must be the key to understanding depression. Another might find their self-derogation and pessimism irrational in away that suggests that there must be some kind of fundamental deficit in self-esteem or cognitive distortion occurring. Still another may listen to the incessant complaining of a depressed person, get annoyed and frustrated, and yet feel guilty in a way that makes it easier to encourage the depressed person to continue to talk in this way than to verbalize these negative feelings. Cognizance of this, the observer might conclude that there is some sort of interpersonal process going on that is critical to any understanding of depression. A major source of confusion is due to the fact that the term 'depression' variously refers to a mood state, a set of symptoms, and a clinical syndrome. As to a reference regarding moods, depression identifies as a universal human experience. Adjectives from a standard measure of a mood (The Multiple Effect Adjective Checklist; Zuckerman and Lubin, 1965) point to subjective feelings associated with a depressed mood, for being sad, unhappy, blue, low, discouraged, bored, hopeless, dejected and lonely. Similarities between every day-depressed mood and the complaints of depressed patients have encouraged the view that clinical depression is simply an exaggeration of a normal depressed mood. However, patients sometimes indicate that their experience of depression is quite distinct from normal feelings and sadness, even in its extreme form. A patient once remarked that her sadness was overwhelming when her husband died but that it did not compare with her sense of overflowing emptiness and her loss of any ability to experience pleasure at the time that she entered the hospital. The view that depressed mood in otherwise normal persons is quantitatively but not qualitatively different from the depression found in hospitalized patients has been termed the 'continuity hypothesis'. Aaron Beck (1967) has provided a useful analogy to suggest the alternative to the continuity hypothesis. He notes that everyday fluctuations in body temperature can be measured on the same thermometer as the changes associated with a fever. Yet the conditions giving rise to a fever are distinct from those causing fluctuations in temperature in healthy individuals. Similarly, the conditions giving rise to clinical depression may be distinct from those studies producing fluctuations in a normal mood.

Studies have compared the subjective mood of persons who are distressed but not seeking help to those who are seeking treatment for depression or a review (Depur and Monroe, 1978). The two groups may be similar in subjective moods, but they differ in other ways. Those persons who are not seeking treatment for depression tend to lack the anxiety and the physical complaints, including loss of appetite, sleep disturbance, and fatigue shown by the group seeking treatment. Still, it could be argued that there is a continuum between the two groups, with these additional features arising when a normal depressed mood becomes more prolonged or intensified. The controversy is likely to continue until either questions about the etiology of depression are resolved or unambiguous markers for depression and identified. Advocates of biomedical approaches to depression tend to assume that there is a discontinuity between a normal depressed mood and clinical depression, and that appropriate biological markers will be found. Yet, as the article by Winokur suggests, even if that proves to be the case, there are likely to be many individuals suffering from extremes of a depressed mood who do not have these markers. Advocates of psychoanalytic, cognitive and behavioural, and interpersonal and social perspectives or depressions have generally assumed a continuum between a normal depressed mood and clinical depression. They tend to exclude psychotic and bipolar depressed persons from treatment, but, beyond that, they have tended to disregard classification issues (Gilbert, 1984). For unipolar depression, at least, they have assumed that whatever discontinuities the biology of mild and severe moods there might be are not necessarily relevant to the psychological and social processes in which they are most interested. Writers since antiquity have noted the core symptoms of depression, besides a sad or low mood, reduced ability to experience pleasure, pessimism, inhibition and retardation of action, and a variety of physical complaints. For the purposes of dialogue, we can distinguish among the emotional, cognitive, motivational, and vegetative symptoms of depression, although these features are not always so neatly divisible. Beyond these symptoms, there are some characteristic interpersonal aspects of depression that are not usually considered as formal symptoms. But they are frequently, distinctive, and troublesome enough to warrant attention. Sadness and dejection are not the only emotional manifestations of depression, although about half of all depressed patient reports these feelings as their principal complaint. Most depressed persons are also anxious and irritable. Classical descriptions of depression tend to emphasize that depressed persons' feelings and distress, disappointment, and frustration are focussed primarily on themselves, yet a number of studies suggest that their negative feelings, including over hostility, are also directed at the people around them. Depressed persons are often intensely angry persons (Kahn, Coyne, Margolin, Weissman and Paykel, 1971). Perhaps 10 or 15 percent of severely depressed patients refuse to take or sustain in the signifying approval to or with subscriptions that are true of the feelings of sadness, reporting instead that all emotional experience, including sadness, has been blunted or inhibited (Whybrow, Akiskal, and Kinney, 1984). The identification of these persons as depressed depends upon the presence of other symptoms. The inhibition of emotional expression in severely depressed persons may extend to crying. Whereas, mild and moderately depressed persons may readily and frequently cry, as they become more depressed, they may continue to feel like crying, but complain that no tears come. Mildly and moderately depressed persons may feel every activity is a burden, yet they derive some satisfaction from their accomplishments. Despite their low mood, they may still crack a smile at a joke. Yet, as depression intensifies, a person may report both a loss of and ability to get gratification from activities that had previously been satisfying—family, work, and social life—and a loss of any sense of humour. Life becomes stale flat and not at all amusing. The loss of gratification may extend to the depressed persons' involvement in close relationships, but, often, a loss of affection for the spouse and children, a feeling of not being able to care anymore; a sense of a wall being erected between the depressed person and others are the major reason for seeking treatment.

In the past decade, a number of theorists, notably Beck and Abramson, Seligman and Teasdale have given particular attention to the cognitive manifestations of depression and have assumed that these features are causal of the other aspects of the disorder. Depressed persons characteristically view themselves, their situations, and their future possibilities in negative and pessimistic terms. They voice discouragement, hopelessness and helplessness. They see themselves as inadequate and deficient in some crucial way. There may be thoughts of death, wishing to be dead, and suicide attempts. The depressed people involved in their daily lives are interpreted by them in terms of loss, defeat, and deprivation, and they experience failure when they undertake an activity. They may criticize themselves for minor shortcomings and seemingly search for evidence that confirms their negative view of them. Aaron Beck suggests, that they will make of the facts to accommodate of these interpretations

17

and hold to them in the face of contradictory evidence. Depressed persons overgeneralise from negative experiences, selectively abstract negative details out of context, ignore more positive features of their situation, and negatively characterise themselves as absolutists and dichotomous terms. The revised learned-helplessness model emphasizes that depressed persons are particularly prone to blame themselves for their difficulties, and to see their defects as stable and global attributes.

Aside from these contentual aspects in their thinking, depressed persons frequently complain that their thinking processes have slowed down, that they are distracted, and they cannot concentrate. Decisions pose a particular problem. Depressed persons are uncertain, feel in need of more information, and are afraid of making the wrong decisions. They may simply feel paralysed, and that the work of making a choice and a commitment is an overwhelming task to be avoided at any cost.

Depressed persons' involvements in their daily lives are interpreted by them in terms of loss, defeat, a deprivation, and they expect failure when they undertake an activity, they may criticize themselves for minor shortcomings and seemingly search for evidence that confirms their negative views of themselves. Beck and Kovacs suggest that they tailor the facts to fit these interpretations and hold on the in the face of contradictory evidence. Depressed persons over generalize from negative experience, selectively abstract negative details out of context, ignore more positive features of their situations, and negatively characterize themselves in absolutist and dichotomous terms. The revised learned-helplessness model emphasizes that their depressed persons are particularly prone to blame themselves for their difficulties and to see their defects as stable and global attributes. Aside from these content aspects of their thinking, depressed persons frequently complain that their thinking processes have slowed down, that they are distracted, and they cannot concentrate. Decisions pose a particular problem. Depressed persons are uncertain, feel in need of more information, and are afraid of making the wrong decision. They may simply feel paralysed, and that the work of making a choice and a commitment is an overwhelming task to be avoided at any cost. Bipolar disorder, is a categorical mental illness in which a person's mood alternates between the extreme fixation of mania and the objective sadness or unhappiness is caught in the grasp of its depression. Bipolar disorder is also called manic-depressive illness. When manic, people with bipolar disorder feel intensely elated, self-important, energetic, and irritable. When depressed, they experience painful sadness, negative thinking, and indifference to things that used to bring them happiness. American psychiatrist Kay Redfield Jamison is regarded as one of the world's leading authorities on bipolar disorder, also known as manic-depressive illness. In her book 'An Unquiet Mind, A Memoir of Moods and Madness' (1995), Jamison reveals her own struggle against the illness, which caused her to experience violent mood swings. She describes her initial resistance to taking medication that, while necessary to prevent debilitating depression, extinguished the exhilarating highs of mania. Bipolar disorder is less common than depression. In North America and Europe, about 1 percent of people experience bipolar disorder during their lives. Rates of bipolar disorder are similar throughout the world. In comparison, at least 8 percent of people experience serious depression during their lives. Bipolar disorder affects men and women about equally and is somewhat more common in higher socioeconomic classes. At least 15 percent of people with bipolar disorder commit suicide. This rate roughly equals the rate for people with major depression, the most severe form of depression. Bipolar disorder is a mental illness that causes mood swings. In the manic phase, a person might feel ecstatic, self-important, and energetic. But when the person becomes depressed, the mood shifts to extreme sadness, negative thinking, and apathy. Some studies indicate that the disease occurs at unusually high rates in creative people, such as artists, writers, and musicians. But some researchers contend that the methodology of these studies was flawed and their results were misleading. In the October 1996 Discover Magazine article, anthropologist Jo Ann C. Gutin presents the results of several studies that explore the link between creativity and mental illness.

Bipolar disorder usually begins in a person's late teens or 20s. Men usually experience mania as the first mood episode, whereas women typically experience depression first. Episodes of mania and depression usually last from several weeks to several months, on average, people with untreated bipolar disorder experience four episodes of mania or depression over any ten-year period. Many people with bipolar disorder function normally between episodes. In 'rapid-cycling' bipolar disorder, however, which represents five to 15 percent of all cases, a person experiences four or more mood episodes within a year and may have little or no normal functioning in between episodes. In rare cases, swings between mania and depression occur over a period of days.

People of the depressive bipolar disorder feel intensely sad or profoundly indifferent to work, activities, and people that once brought them pleasure. They think slowly, concentrate poorly, feel tired, and experience changes—usually an increase—in their appetite and sleep. They often feel a sense of worthlessness or helplessness. In addition, they may feel pessimistic or hopeless about the future and may think about or attempt suicide. In some cases of severe depression, people may experience psychotic symptoms, such as delusions (false beliefs) or hallucinations (false sensory perceptions). In the manic phase of bipolar disorder, people feel intensely and inappropriately happy, self-important, and irritable. In this highly energized state they sleep less, have racing thoughts, and talk in rapid-fire speech that goes off in many directions. They have inflated self-esteem and confidence and may even have delusions of grandeur. Mania may make people impatient and abrasive, and when frustrated, physically abusive. They often behave in socially inappropriate ways, think irrationally, and show impaired judgment. For example, they may take aeroplane trips all over the country, make indecent sexual advances, and formulate grandiose plans involving indiscriminate investments of money. The self-destructive behaviour of mania includes excessive gambling, buying outrageously expensive gifts, abusing alcohol or other drugs, and provoking confrontations with obnoxious or combative behaviour. Clinical depression is one of the most common forms of mental illness. Although depression can be treated with psychotherapy, many scientists believe there are biological causes for the disease. In the June 1998 Scientific American article, Neurobiologist Charles B. Nemeroff discusses the connection between biochemical changes in the brain and depression. The genes that a person inherits seem to have a strong influence on whether the person will develop bipolar disorder. Studies of twins provide evidence for this genetic influence. Among genetically identical twins where one twin has bipolar disorder, the other twin has the disorder in more than 70 percent of cases. But among pairs of fraternal twins, who have about half their genes in common, both twins have bipolar disorder in less than 15 percent of cases in which one twin has the disorder. The degree of genetic similarity seems to account for the difference between identical and fraternal twins. Further evidence for a genetic influence comes from studies of adopted children with bipolar disorder. These studies show that biological relatives of the children have a higher incidence of bipolar disorder than do people in the general population. Thus, bipolar disorder seems to run in families for genetic reasons. Privately or work-related stress can trigger a manic episode, but this usually occurs in people with genetic vulnerability. Other factors—such as prenatal development, childhood experiences, and social conditions—seem to have relatively little influence in causing bipolar disorder. One study examined the children of identical twins in which only one member of each pair of twins had bipolar disorder. The study found that regardless of whether the parent had bipolar disorder or not, all of the children had the same high 10-percent rate of bipolar disorder. This observation clearly suggests that risk for bipolar illness comes from genetic influence, not from exposure to a parent's bipolar illness or from family problems caused by that illness. Different therapies may shorten, delay, or even prevent the extreme moods caused by bipolar disorder. Lithium carbonates, a natural mineral salt, can help control both mania and depression in bipolar disorder. The drug generally takes two to three weeks to become effective. People with bipolar disorder may take lithium during periods of relatively normal moods to delay or prevent subsequent episodes of mania or depression. Common side-effects of lithium include nausea, increased thirst and urination, vertigo, loss of appetite, and muscle weakness. In addition, long-term use can impair functioning of the kidneys. For this reason, doctors do not prescribe lithium to bipolar patients with kidney disease. Many people find the side effects so unpleasant that they stop taking the medication, which often results in a relapse. From 20 to 40 percent of people do not respond to lithium therapy. For these people, two anticonvulsant drugs may help dampen severe manic episodes: carbamazepine (Tegretol) and valproate (Depakene). The use of traditional antidepressants to treat bipolar disorder carries risks of triggering a manic episode or a rapid-cycling pattern. Antidepressant, medication used to treat depression, a mood disorder characterized by such symptoms as sadness, decreased appetite, a difficulty in sleeping, fatigue, and a lack of enjoyment of activities previously found pleasurable. While everyone experiences episodes of sadness at some point in their lives, depression is distinguished from this sadness when symptoms are present most days for a period of at least two weeks. Antidepressants are often the first choice of treatment for depression. The severe disorders of mood or effect are among the most commons of the major psychiatric syndromes. Lifetime expectancy rates for such disorders are between 3 and 8 percent of the general population. Only a minority is treated by psychiatrists or in psychiatric hospitals and about 70 percent of prescriptions for antidepressants are written by nonpsychiatric physicians. These and other modern medical treatments of severe mood disorders have contributed to a virtual revolution in the theory and practice of modern psychiatry since the introduction of mood-altering drugs three decades ago. These agents include lithium salts (1949), the antimanic and Antipsychotic (neuroleptics) agents as the chlorpromazine (1952), the Monoamine oxidase (MAO) inhibitors (1952), and the Tricyclic or heterocyclic (imipramine-like) antidepressant agents (1957). In addition, electroconvulsive therapy (ECT) continue s to have a place in the treatment of very severe and acute mood disorders, especially life-threatening forms of depression.

The development of these modern medical therapies has had several important effects. First, these agents have provided relatively simple, specific, effective, and safe forms of treatment with a profound impact on current patterns of medical practice, for example, many depressed or hypomanic patients can be managed adequately in outpatient facilities to avoid prolonged, expensive, and disruptive hospitalization which were formally common. Second, partial understanding of the pharmacology of the new psychotropic drugs has led to imaginative hypotheses concerning the pathophysiology or etiology of severe mood disorders. These, in turn, have encouraged a revolution in experimental psychiatry in which the hypotheses have been tested in clinical research. Many of the earlier hypotheses have been found wanting or simplistic, nevertheless, they have led to increase d understanding of the diagnosis, biology, and treatment of mood disorders and to newer research that represents a third level of development, at this level. This is the focus and the promises to have practical clinical benefit now and in the near future.

Although the cause of depression is unknown, researchers have found that some depressed people have altered levels of chemicals called neurotransmitters, chemicals made and released by nerve

22

cells, or neurons. One neuron, referred to as the presynaptic neuron, releases a neurotransmitter into the synapse, or space, between the neuron and a neighbouring cell. The neurotransmitter then attaches, or binds, to a neighbouring cell—the postsynaptic cell—to trigger a specific activity.

Antidepressants work by interacting with neurotransmitters at three different points: they can change the rate at which the neurotransmitters are either created or broken down by the body; they can block the process in which a spent neurotransmitter is recycled by a presynaptic neuron and used again, called reuptake; or they can interfere with the binding of a neurotransmitter to neighbouring cells. The first antidepressants, developed in the 1950s, are the Tricyclic antidepressants (TCA) and the Monoamine oxidase (MAO) inhibitors. TCAs block the reuptake of neurotransmitters into the presynaptic neurons, keeping the neurotransmitter in the synapse longer, and making more of the neurotransmitters available to the postsynaptic cell. TCAs include amitriptyline, doxepin, imipramine, nortriptyline, and desipramine. MAO inhibitors decrease the rate at which neurotransmitters are broken down by the body so they are more available to interact with neurons. MAO inhibitors currently available in the United States include phenelzine and tranylcypromine. Another group of antidepressants, known as selective serotonin reuptake inhibitors (SSRI), became available in 1987. SSRIs block the reuptake of the neurotransmitter serotonin into presynaptic neurons, thereby prolonging its activity. There are currently four SSRIs available in the United States: Fluoxetine, sertraline, paroxetine, and fluvoxamine. Of this group, the best known is Fluoxetine, commonly known by its brand name, Prozac. Another antidepressant is venlafaxine, which works like TCAs but does not share their chemical structure, and it also causes different side effects. The antidepressant nefazodone prevents serotonin from binding to neighbouring neurons at one specific binding site (serotonin can bind to neurons on many sites). It also weariedly blocks the reuptake of serotonin. All antidepressants decrease symptoms of depression in about 70 percent of depressed people who take them. Most antidepressants take about two to three weeks of treatment before beneficial effects occur. Because no antidepressant is more effective than the others, doctors determine which antidepressant to prescribe according to the type of side effects an individual can tolerate. For instance, a person who takes TCAs and MAO inhibitors may notice dizziness and fainting when standing up, mouth dryness, difficulty urinating, constipation, and drowsiness. If people who take MAO inhibitors eat certain foods, such as aged cheese or some aged meats, they can experience severe headaches and raised blood pressure. SSRIs can cause side effects such as restlessness, difficulty sleeping, and interference with sexual function. Clinical depression is quite different from the blues everyone feels at one time or another and even from the grief of bereavement. It is more debilitating and dangerous, and the overwhelming sadness combines with a number of other symptoms. In addition to becoming preoccupied with suicide, many people are plagued by guilt and a sense of worthlessness. They often have difficulty thinking clearly, remembering, or taking pleasure in anything. They may feel anxious and sapped of energy and have trouble eating and sleeping or may, instead, want to eat and sleep excessively. Psychologists and Neurobiologists sometimes debate whether ego-damaging experiences and self-deprecating thoughts or biological processes cause depression. The mind, however, does not exist without the brain. Considerable evidence indicates that regardless of the initial triggers, the final common pathways to depression involve biochemical changes in the brain. These changes ultimately give rise to deep sadness and the other salient characteristics of depression. The full extent of those alterations is still being explored, but in the past few decades—and especially in the past several years—efforts to identify them have progressed rapidly. At the moment, those of us teasing out the neurobiology of depression somewhat resemble blind searchers feeling different parts of a large, mysterious creature and trying to figure out how their deductions fit together. In fact, it may turn out that not all of our findings will intersect: biochemical abnormalities that are prominent in some depressives may differ from those that are more predominant than in others. Still, the extraordinary accumulation of discoveries is fuelling optimism that the major biological determinants of depression can be understood in detail and that those insights will open the way to improved methods of diagnosing, treating and preventing the condition. One subgoal is to distinguish features that vary among depressed individuals. For instance, perhaps decreased activity of a specific neurotransmitter (a molecule that carries a signal between nerve cells) is central in some people, but in others, overactivity of a hormonal system is more influential (hormones circulate in the blood and can act far from the site of their secretion). A related goal is to identify simple biological markers able to indicate which profile fits a given patient; those markers could consist of, say, elevated or reduced levels of selected molecules in the blood or changes in some easy visualizational areas of the brain. After testing a depressed patient for these markers, a psychiatrist could, in theory, prescribe a medication tailored to that individual's specific biological anomaly, much as a general practitioner can run a quick strep test for a patient complaining of a sore throat and then prescribe an appropriate antibiotic if the test is positive. Today psychiatrists have to choose antidepressant medications by intuition and trial and error, a situation that can put suicidal patients in jeopardy for weeks or months until the right compound is selected. (Often psychotherapy is needed as well, but it usually is not sufficient by itself, especially if the depression is fairly severe.) Improving treatment is critically important. Although today's antidepressants have fewer side effects than those of old and can be extremely helpful in many cases, depression continues to exact a huge toll in suffering, lost lives and reduced productivity. The prevalence is surprisingly great. It is estimated, for example, that 5 to 12 percent of men and 10 to 20 percent of women in the US will suffer from a major depressive episode at some time in their life. Roughly half of these individuals will become depressed more than once, and up to 10 percent (about 1.0 to 1.5 percent of Americans) will experience manic phases in addition to depressive ones, a condition known as manic-depressive illness or bipolar disorder. Mania is marked by a decreased need for sleep, rapid speech, delusions of grandeur, hyperactivity and a propensity to engage in such potentially self-destructive activities as promiscuous sex, spending sprees or reckless driving. Beyond the pain and disability depression brings, it is a potential killer. As many as 15 percent of those who suffer from depression or bipolar disorder commits suicide each year. In 1996 the Centre for Disease Control and Prevention listed suicide as the ninth leading cause of death in the US (slightly behind infection with the AIDS virus), taking the lives of 30,862 people. Most investigators, however, believe this number is a gross underestimate. Many people who kill themselves do so in a way that allows another diagnosis to be listed on the death certificate, so that families can receive insurance benefits or avoid embarrassment. Further, some fractions of automobile accidents unquestionably are concealed suicides. The financial drain is enormous as well. In 1992 the estimated costs of depression totalled $43 billion, mostly from reduced or lost worker productivity. Accumulating findings indicate that severe depression also heightens the risk of dying after a heart attack or stroke. And it often reduces the quality of life for cancer patients and might reduce survival time. Geneticists have provided some of the oldest proof of a biological component to depression in many people. Depression and manic-depression frequently run in families. Thus, close blood relatives (children, siblings and parents) of patients with severe depressive or bipolar disorders are much more likely to suffer from those or related conditions than are members of the general population. Studies of identical twins (who are genetically indistinguishable) and fraternal twins (whose genes generally are no more alike than those of other pairs of siblings) also support an inherited component. The finding of illness in both members of a pair is much higher for manic-depression in identical twins than in fraternal ones and is somewhat elevated for depression alone. In the past 20 years, genetic researchers have expended great effort trying to identify the genes at fault. So far, though, those genes have evaded discovery, perhaps because a predisposition to depression involves several genes, each of which makes only a small, hard-to-detect contribution.

In support of this cognitive view, people with 'depressive' personality traits appear to be more vulnerable than others to actual depression. Examples of depressive personality traits include gloominess, pessimism, introversion, self-criticism, excessive skepticism and criticism of others, deep feelings of inadequacy, and excessive brooding and worrying. In addition, people who regularly behave in dependent, hostile, and impulsive ways appear at greater risk for depression.

American psychologist Martin Seligman proposed that depression stem from 'learned helplessness,' an acquired belief that one cannot control the outcome of events. In this view, prolonged exposure to uncontrollable and inescapable events leads to apathy, pessimism, and loss of motivation. An adaptation of this theory by American psychologist Lynn Abramson and her colleagues argues that the depression, in response of any results is not only from helplessness, but also from hopelessness. The hopelessness theory attributes depression to a pattern of negative thinking in which people blame themselves for negative life events, view the causes of those events as permanent, and overgeneralize specific weaknesses as applying to many areas of their life.

People who fall victim to child abuse appear more vincibly vulnerable to depression than others. So, do people living under chronically stressful conditions, such as single mothers with many children and little or no support from friends or relatives.

Despite the availability of effective treatment, most depressive disorders go untreated and undiagnosed. Studies indicate that general physicians fail to recognize depression in their patients at least half of the time. In addition, many doctors and patients view depression in elderly people as a normal part of aging, even though treatment for depression in older people is usually very effective.

MAO inhibitors include isocarboxazid (Marplan), phenelzine (Nardil), and tranylcypromine (Parnate). People who take MAO inhibitors must follow a diet that excludes tyramine—a substance found in wine, beer, some cheeses, and many fermented foods—to avoid a dangerous rise in blood pressure. In addition, MAO inhibitors have many of the same side effects as tricyclics.

Studies have shown that short-term psychotherapy can relieve mild to moderate depression as effectively as antidepressant drugs. Unlike medication, psychotherapy produces no physiological side effects. In addition, depressed people treated with psychotherapy appear less likely to experience a relapse than those treated only with antidepressant medication. However, psychotherapy usually takes longer to produce benefits.

Bipolar disorder is much less common than depression. In North America and Europe, about 1 percent of people experience bipolar disorder during their lives. Rates of bipolar disorder are similar throughout the world. In comparison, at least 8 percent of people experience serious depression during their lives. Bipolar disorder affects men and women about equally and is somewhat more common in higher socioeconomic classes. At least 15 percent of people with bipolar disorder commit suicide. This rate roughly equals the rate for people with major depression, the most severe form of depression.

Bipolar disorder is a mental illness that causes mood swings. In the manic phase, a person might feel ecstatic, self-important, and energetic. But when the person becomes depressed, the mood shifts to extreme sadness, negative thinking, and apathy. Some studies indicate that the disease occurs at unusually high rates in creative people, such as artists, writers, and musicians. But some researchers contend that the methodology of these studies was flawed and their results were misleading. In the October 1996 Discover Magazine article, anthropologist Jo Ann C. Gutin presents the results of several studies that explore the link between creativity and mental illness.

Bipolar disorder usually begins in a person's late teens or 20s. Men usually experience mania as the first mood episode, whereas women typically experience depression first. Episodes of mania and depression usually last from several weeks to several months, on average, people with untreated bipolar disorder experience, that more than four episodes of mania or depression over any ten-year period. Many people with bipolar disorder function normally between episodes. In 'rapid-cycling' bipolar disorder, however, which represents 5 to 15 percent of all cases, a person experiences four or more mood episodes within a year and may have little or no normal functioning in between episodes. In rare cases, swings between mania and depression occur over a period of days.

In another type of bipolar disorder, a person experiences major depression and hypomanic episodes, or episodes of milder mania. In a related disorder called cyclothymic disorder, a person's mood alternates between mild depression and mild mania. Some people with cyclothymic disorder later develop full-blown bipolar disorder. Bipolar disorder may also follow a seasonal pattern, with a person typically experiencing depression in the fall and winter and mania in the spring or summer.

In the manic phase of bipolar disorder, people feel intensely and inappropriately happy, self-important, and irritable. In this highly energized state they sleep less, have racing thoughts, and talk in rapid-fire speech that goes off in many directions. They have inflated self-esteem and confidence and may even have delusions of grandeur. Mania may make people impatient and abrasive, and when frustrated, physically abusive. They often behave in socially inappropriate ways, think irrationally, and show impaired judgment. The self-destructive behaviour of mania includes excessive gambling, buying outrageously expensive gifts, abusing alcohol or other drugs, and provoking confrontations with obnoxious or combative behaviour.

Clinical depression is one of the most common forms of mental illness. Although depression can be treated with psychotherapy, many scientists believe there are biological causes for the disease. In the June 1998 Scientific American article, Neurobiologist Charles B. Nemeroff discusses the connection between biochemical changes in the brain and depression.

The genes that a person inherits seem to have a strong influence on whether the person will develop bipolar disorder. Studies of twins provide evidence for this genetic influence. Among genetically identical twins where one twin has bipolar disorder, the other twin has the disorder in more than 70 percent of cases. But among pairs of fraternal twins, who have about half their genes in common, both twins have bipolar disorder in less than 15 percent of cases in which one twin has the disorder. The degree of genetic similarity seems to account for the difference between identical and fraternal twins. Further evidence for a genetic influence comes from studies of adopted children with bipolar disorder. These studies show that biological relatives of the children have a higher incidence of bipolar disorder than do people in the general population. Thus, bipolar disorder seems to run in families for genetic reasons.

Personally or work-related stress can trigger a manic episode, but this usually occurs in people with genetic vulnerability. Other factors—such as prenatal development, childhood experiences, and social conditions—seem to have relatively little influence in causing bipolar disorder. One study examined the children of identical twins in which only one member of each pair of twins had bipolar disorder. The study found that regardless of whether the parent had bipolar disorder or not, all of the children had the same high 10-percent rate of bipolar disorder. This observation clearly suggests that risk for bipolar illness comes from genetic influence, not from exposure to a parent's bipolar illness or from family problems caused by that illness.

Different therapies may shorten, delay, or even prevent the extreme moods caused by bipolar disorder. Lithium carbonates, a natural mineral salt, can help control both mania and depression in bipolar disorder. The drug generally takes two to three weeks to become effective. People with bipolar disorder may take lithium during periods of a normal mood to delay or prevent subsequent episodes of mania or depression. Common side effects of lithium include nausea, increased thirst and urination, vertigo, loss of appetite, and muscle weakness. In addition, long-term use can impair functioning of the kidneys. For this reason, doctors do not prescribe lithium to bipolar patients with kidney disease. Many people find the side effects so unpleasant that they stop taking the medication, which often results in a relapse.

From 20 to 40 percent of people do not respond to lithium therapy. For these people, two anticonvulsant drugs may help dampen severe manic episodes: carbamazepine (Tegretol) and valproate (Depakene). The use of traditional antidepressants to treat bipolar disorder carries risks of triggering a manic episode or a rapid-cycling pattern.

Antidepressant, medication used to treat depression, a mood disorder characterized by such symptoms as sadness, decreased appetite, difficulty sleeping, fatigue, and a lack of enjoyment of activities previously found pleasurable. While everyone experiences episodes of sadness at some point in their lives, depression is distinguished from this sadness when symptoms are present most days for a period of at least two weeks. Antidepressants are often the first choice of treatment for depression.

Although the cause of depression is unknown, researchers have found that some depressed people have altered levels of chemicals called neurotransmitters, chemicals made and released by nerve cells, or neurons. One neuron, referred to as the presynaptic neuron, releases a neurotransmitter into the synapse, or space, between the neuron and a neighbouring cell. The neurotransmitter then attaches, or binds, to a neighbouring cell—the postsynaptic cell—to trigger a specific activity. Antidepressants work by interacting with neurotransmitters at three different points: they can change the rate at which the neurotransmitters are either created or broken down by the body; they can block the process in which a spent neurotransmitter is recycled by a presynaptic neuron and used again, called reuptake; or they can interfere with the binding of a neurotransmitter to neighbouring cells.

The first antidepressants, developed in the 1950s, are the Tricyclic antidepressants (TCA) and the Monoamine oxidase (MAO) inhibitors. TCAs block the reuptake of neurotransmitters into the presynaptic neurons, keeping the neurotransmitter in the synapse longer, and making more of the neurotransmitters available to the postsynaptic cell. TCAs include amitriptyline, doxepin, imipramine, nortriptyline, and desipramine.

MAO inhibitors decrease the rate at which neurotransmitters are broken down by the body so they are more available to interact with neurons. MAO inhibitors currently available in the United States include phenelzine and tranylcypromine.

Another group of antidepressants, known as selective serotonin reuptake inhibitors (SSRI), became available in 1987. SSRIs block the reuptake of the neurotransmitter serotonin into presynaptic neurons, thereby prolonging its activity. There are currently four SSRIs available for use in the United States: Fluoxetine, sertraline, paroxetine, and fluvoxamine. Of this group, the best known is Fluoxetine, commonly known by its brand name, Prozac.

All antidepressants decrease symptoms of depression in about 70 percent of depressed people who take them. Most antidepressants take about two to three weeks of treatment before beneficial effects occur. Because no antidepressant is more effective than the others, doctors determine which antidepressant to prescribe according to the type of side effects an individual can tolerate. For instance, a person who takes TCAs and MAO inhibitors may notice dizziness and fainting when standing up, mouth dryness, difficulty urinating, constipation, and drowsiness. If people who take MAO inhibitors eat certain foods, such as aged cheese or some aged meats, they can experience severe headaches and raised blood pressure. SSRIs can cause side effects such as restlessness, difficulty sleeping, and interference with sexual function.

Clinical depression is quite different from the blues everyone feels at one time or another and even from the grief of bereavement. It is more debilitating and dangerous, and the overwhelming sadness combines with a number of other symptoms. In addition to becoming preoccupied with suicide, many people are plagued by guilt and a sense of worthlessness. They often have difficulty thinking clearly, remembering, or taking pleasure in anything. They may feel anxious and sapped of energy and have trouble eating and sleeping or may, instead, want to eat and sleep excessively.

Psychologists and Neurobiologists sometimes debate whether ego-damaging experiences and self-deprecating thoughts or biological processes cause depression. The mind, however, does not exist without the brain. Considerable evidence indicates that regardless of the initial triggers, the final common pathways to depression involve biochemical changes in the brain. These changes ultimately give rise to deep sadness and the other salient characteristics of depression.

The full extent of those alterations is still being explored, but in the past few decades—and especially in the past several years—efforts to identify them have progressed rapidly.

However, is that of the extraordinary accumulation of discoveries is fuelling optimism that the major biological determinants of depression can be understood in detail and that those insights will open the way to improved methods of diagnosing, treating and preventing the condition.

One subgoal is to distinguish features that vary among depressed individuals. For instance, perhaps decreased activity of a specific neurotransmitter (a molecule that carries a signal between nerve cells) is central in some people, but in others, overactivity of a hormonal system is more influential (hormones circulate in the blood and can act far from the site of their secretion). A related goal is to identify simple biological markers able to indicate which profile fits a given patient; those markers could consist of, say, elevated or reduced levels of selected molecules in the blood or changes in some easy visualizable areas of the brain.

After testing a depressed patient for these markers, a psychiatrist could, in theory, prescribe a medication tailored to that individual's specific biological anomaly, much as a general practitioner can run a quick strep test for a patient complaining of a sore throat and then prescribe an appropriate antibiotic if the test is positive. Today psychiatrists have to choose antidepressant medications by intuition and trial and error, a situation that can put suicidal patients in jeopardy for weeks or months until the right compound is selected. (Often psychotherapy is needed as well, but it usually is not sufficient by itself, especially if the depression is fairly severe.)

Improving treatment is critically important. Although today's antidepressants have fewer side effects than those of old and can be extremely helpful in many cases, depression continues to exact a huge toll in suffering, lost lives and reduced productivity.

The prevalence is surprisingly great. It is estimated, for example, that 5 to 12 percent of men and 10 to 20 percent of women in the US will suffer from a major depressive episode at some time in their life. Roughly half of these individuals will become depressed more than once, and up to 10 percent (about 1.0 to 1.5 percent of Americans) will experience manic phases in addition to depressive ones, a condition known as manic-depressive illness or bipolar disorder. Mania is marked by a decreased need for sleep, rapid speech, delusions of grandeur, hyperactivity and a propensity to engage in such potentially self-destructive activities as promiscuous sex, spending sprees or reckless driving.

Beyond the pain and disability depression brings, it is a potential killer. As many as 15 percent of those who suffer from depression or bipolar disorders commit suicide each year. In 1996 the Centre for Disease Control and Prevention listed suicide as the ninth leading cause of death in the US (slightly behind infection with the AIDS virus), taking the lives of 30,862 people. Most investigators, however, believe this number is a gross underestimate. Many people who kill themselves do so in a way that allows another diagnosis to be listed on the death certificate, so that families can receive insurance benefits or avoid embarrassment. Further, some fractions of automobile accidents are definitely concealed suicides.

The financial drain is enormous as well. In 1992 the estimated costs of depression totalled $43 billion, mostly from reduced or lost worker productivity.

Accumulating findings indicate that severe depression also heightens the risk of dying after a heart attack or stroke. And it often reduces the quality of life for cancer patients and might reduce survival time.

Geneticists have provided some of the oldest proof of a biological component to depression in many people. Depression and manic-depression frequently run in families. Thus, close blood relatives (children, siblings and parents) of patients with severe depressive or bipolar disorder is much more likely to suffer from those or related conditions than are members of the genetically indistinguishable and fraternal twins (whose genes generally are no more alike than those of other pairs of siblings) also support an inherited component. The finding of illness in both members of a pair is much higher for manic-depression in identical twins than in fraternal ones and is somewhat elevated for depression alone.

In the past 20 years, genetic researchers have expended great effort trying to identify the genes at fault. So far, though, those genes have evaded discovery, perhaps because a predisposition to depression involves several genes, each of which makes only a small, hard-to-detect contribution.

Preliminary reports from a study of an Amish population with an extensive history of manic-depression once raised the possibility that chromosome 11 held one or more genes producing vulnerability to bipolar disorder, but the finding did not hold up. A gene somewhere on the X chromosome could play a role in some cases of that condition, but the connection is not evident in most people who have been studied. Most recently, various regions of chromosome 18 and a site on chromosome 21 have been suggested to participate in vulnerability to bipolar illness, but these findings await replication.

As geneticists continue their searches, other investigators are concentrating on neurochemical aspects. Much of that works focuses on neurotransmitters. In particular, many cases of depression apparently stem at least in part from disturbances in brain circuits that convey signals through certain neurotransmitters of the Monoamine class. These biochemicals, all derivatives of amino acids, include serotonin, norepinephrine and dopamine; of these, only evidence relating to norepinephrine and serotonin is abundant.

Monoamines first began focussing attention of mind on the depression as did researchers in the 1950s. Early in that decade, physicians discovered that severe depression arose in about 15 percent of patients who were treated for hypertension with the drug reserpine. At about the same time, doctors found that an agent prescribed against a tuberculosis-elevated mood in some users who were depressed. Follow-up investigations revealed that the drug inhibited the neuronal breakdown of Monoamines by an enzyme (Monoamine oxidase); Presumably the agent eased depression by allowing Monoamines to avoid degradation and to remain active in brain circuits. Together these findings inferred that abnormally low levels of monoamines in the brain could cause depression. This insight led to the development of Monoamine oxidase inhibitors, being the first of the antidepressants.

Nevertheless, monoamines were most important in depression? In the 1960s Joseph J. Schildkraut of Harvard University cast his vote with norepinephrine in the now classic "catecholamine" hypothesis of mood disorders. He proposed that depressions stem from a deficiency of norepinephrine (which we had classified as catecholamine) in certain brain circuits and that mania arises from an overabundance of the substance. The theory has long since refined, and acknowledging. For instance that decreases or elevations in norepinephrine do not alter moods in everyone. Nevertheless, the proposed link between norepinephrine depletion and depression has gained much experimental support. These circuits originated in the brain stem, primarily in the pigmented locus coeruleus, and put forth to many areas of the brain. This includes the limbic system—a group of cortical and subcortical areas that play a significant part in regulating emotions.

To understand the recent evidence relating to norepinephrine and other monoamines, it helps to know how those neurotransmitters work. The points of contact between two neurons, or nerve cells termed for the synapses. Monoamines, like all other neurotransmitters, travel from one neuron (the presynaptic cell) across a small gap (the synaptic cleft) and attach themselves to the first incoming receptor molecule, as the surface of the second neuron (the postsynaptic cell). Such binding arouses the intracellular changes that stimulate or inhibit firing of the postsynaptic cell. The effect of the neurotransmitter depends greatly on the nature and concentration of its receptors on the postsynaptic cells. Serotonin receptors, for instance, come in 13 or more subtypes that can vary in their sensitivity to serotonin and in the effects they produce.

The strength can give occasion to the influence by amounts of readied neurotransmitters whose signalling is to be released, denoting to how long it remains in the synaptic cleft. Properties influenced by, at least, two types of molecular surfaces as the releasing cell, and the surfaces attach to the autoreceptors and transporters. When an autoreceptor becomes bound by neurotransmitter molecules in the synapse, the receptors signal the cell to reduce its firing rate and thus its release of the transmitter. The transporters physically pump neurotransmitter molecules from the synaptic cleft back into presynaptic cells, a process termed reuptake. Monoamine oxidase inside cells can affect synaptic neurotransmitter levels as well, as degrading Monoamines and reducing the essential equivalence of available molecules that are released.

Among the finding links impoverished by the synaptic norepinephrine levels to depression is the discovery in many studies that indirect markers of norepinephrine levels in the brain—levels of its metabolites, or by-products, in more accessible material (urine and cerebrospinal fluid)—are often low in depressed individuals. In addition, postmortem studies have revealed increased densities of certain norepinephrine receptors in the cortex of depressed suicide victims.

Observers unfamiliar with receptor display might assume that elevated numbers of receptors were a sign of more contact between norepinephrine and its receptors and more signal transmission. However, this pattern of receptor "up-regulation" is one that scientists would expect if norepinephrine concentrations in synapses were abnormally low. When transmitter molecules become unusually scarce in synapses, postsynaptic cells often expand receptor numbers in a compensatory attempt to pick up whatever signals are available.

A recent discovery supporting the norepinephrine hypothesis is that new drugs selectively able to block norepinephrine reuptake, and so increase norepinephrine in synapses, are effective antidepressants in many people. One compound, reboxetine, is available as an antidepressant outside the US and is awaiting approval here.

The data connecting norepinephrine to depression are solid and still growing. Yet research into serotonin has taken a centre stage in the 1990s, thanks to the therapeutic success of Prozac and related antidepressants that manipulate serotonin levels. Serious investigations into serotonin's role in mood disorders, however, have been going on for almost 30 years, ever since Arthur J. Prange, Jr., of the University of North Carolina at Chapel Hill, Alec Coppen of the Medical Research Counsel in England and their co-workers put forward the so-called permissive hypothesis. This view held that synaptic depletion of serotonin was another cause of depression, one that worked by promoting, or "permitting," a fall in norepinephrine levels.

Defects in serotonin-using circuits could certainly dampen norepinephrine signalling. Serotonin-producing neurons project from the nuclei in the brain to neurons in diverse regions of the central nervous system, including those that secrete or control the release of norepinephrine. Serotonin depletion might contribute to depression by affecting other kinds of neurons as well; serotonin-producing cells extend into many brain regions thought to participate in depressive symptoms—including the amygdala (an area involved in emotions), the hypothalamus (involved in appetite, libido and sleep) and cortical areas that participate in cognition and other higher processes.

Further evidence comes from the remarkable therapeutic effectiveness of drugs that block presynaptic reuptake transporters from drawing serotonin out of the synaptic cleft. Tricyclic antidepressants (so-named because they contain three rings of chemical groups) collectively Monoamine oxidase inhibitors on pharmacy shelves in the late 1950s, although we did not know their mechanism of action at the time. Eventually, though, they were found to produce many effects in the brain, including the decrease in Serotonin reuptake, of a consequent rise in serotonin levels in synapses.

Investigators suspected that this last effect accounted for their antidepressant action, but confirmation awaited the introduction in the late 1980s of Prozac and then other drugs (Paxil, Zoloft and Luvox) able to block serotonin reuptake transporters without affecting other brain monoamines. These selective serotonin reuptake inhibitors (SSRIs) have now revolutionized the treatment of depression, because they are highly effective and produce milder side effects than older drugs do. Today even newer antidepressants, such as Effexor, block reuptake of both serotonin and norepinephrine.

Studies of serotonin have also offered new clues to why depressed individuals are more susceptible to heart attack and stroke. Activation and clumping of blood platelets (cell-like structures in blood) contribute to the formation of thrombi that can clog blood vessels and shut off blood flow to the heart and brain, thus damaging those organs. Work, elsewhere have shown that platelets of depressed people are particularly sensitive to activation signals, including, it seems, to those issued by serotonin, which amplifies platelet reactivity too other, stronger chemical stimuli. Further, the platelets of depressed patients bear reduced numbers of serotonin reuptake transporters. In other words, compared with the platelets of healthy people, those in depressed individuals probably are less able to soak up serotonin from their environment and thus to reduce their exposure to platelet-activation signals.

Disturbed functioning of serotonin or norepinephrine circuits, or both, contributes to depression in many people, but compelling work can equally claim that depression often involves dysregulation of brain circuits that control the activities of certain hormones. Indeed, hormonal alterations in depressed patients have long been evident.

The hypothalamus of the brain lies at the top of the hierarchy regulating hormone secretion. It manufactures and releases peptides (small chains of amino acids) that act on the pituitary, at the base of the brain, stimulating or inhibiting the pituitary's release of various hormones into the blood. These hormones—among them a growth hormone, thyroid-stimulating hormone and adrenocorticotropic hormone (ACTH)—control the release of other hormones from target glands. In addition to functioning outside the nervous system, the hormones released in response to pituitary hormones feed back to the pituitary and hypothalamus. There they deliver inhibitory signals that keep hormone manufacture from becoming excessive.

Depressed patients have repeatedly been demonstrated to show a blunted response to a number of substances that normally stimulate the release of growth hormones. They also display aberrant responses to the hypothalamic substance that normally induces secretion of thyroid-stimulating hormones from the pituitary. In addition, a common cause of nonresponse to antidepressants is the presence of previously undiagnosed thyroid insufficiency.

All these findings are intriguing, but so far the strongest case has been made for dysregulation of the hypothalamic-pituitary-adrenal (HPA) axis—the system that manages the body's response to stress. When a threat to physical or psychological well-being is detected, the hypothalamus amplifies production of corticotropin-releasing factors (CRF), which induce the pituitary to secrete ACTH. ACTH then instructs the adrenal gland atop each kidney to release, in the effect to relieve from constraint or restraints of the cortisol. Together all the changes prepare the body to fight or flee and cause it to shut down activities that would distract from the self-protection. For instance, the cortisol enhances the delivery of fuel to muscles. At the same time, CRF depresses the appetite for food and sex and heightens alertness. Chronic activation of the HPA axis, however, may lay the ground for illness and, it appears, for depression.

As long since late 1960s and early 1970s, several research groups reported increased activity in the HPA axis in unmedicated depressed patients, as evinced by raised levels of the cortisol in urine, blood and cerebrospinal fluid, as well as by other measures. Hundreds, perhaps even thousands, of subsequent studies have confirmed that substantial numbers of depressed patients—particularly those most severely affected—display HPA-axis hyperactivity. Indeed, the finding is surely the most replicated one in all of biological psychiatry.

Deeper investigation of the phenomenon has now revealed alterations at each level of the HPA axis in depressed patients. For instance, hydrocortisone was to have enlarged the adrenal gland and the pituitary, and the adrenal gland hypersecretes a cortisol. However, many researchers have become persuaded that aberrations in CRF-producing neurons of the hypothalamus or cortisol and elsewhere to bear most of the responsibility for HPA-axis hyperactivity and the emergence of depressive symptoms.

Luminary studies were quite repetitive, as study after study was to have shown in the concentrations in cerebrospinal fluid was being elevated in depressed patients, compared with control subjects or individuals with other psychiatric disorders. This magnification of CRF levels is reduced by treatment with antidepressants and by effective electroconvulsive therapy. Further, postmortem brain tissue studies have revealed a marked exaggeration both in the number of CRF-producing neurons in the hypothalamus and in the expression of the CRF gene (resulting in elevated CRF synthesis) in depressed patients as compared with controls. Moreover, delivery of CRF to the brains of laboratory animals produces behavioural effects that are cardinal features of depression in humans, namely, insomnia, decreased appetite, decreased libido and anxiety.

Neurobiologists, yet, do not know exactly how the genetic, Monoamine and hormonal findings piece together, if they always do. The discoveries nonetheless suggest a partial scenario for how people who endure traumatic childhoods become depressed later in life. Its hypothesis that stress-diathesis model of mood disorders, in recognition of the interaction between experience has known this (stress) and an inborn predisposition (diathesis).

The observational depressives run in families means that certain genetic traits in the affected families somehow lower the threshold for depression, conceivably, the genetic features directly or indirectly diminish Monoamine levels in synapses or increase reactivity of the HPA axis to stress. The genetically determined threshold is not necessarily low enough to induce depression in the absence of serious stress, may then be pushed still lower by early, adverse life experiences.

Most people who experience episodes of mania also experience spells of severe depression. This pattern of mood swings between mania and depression defined a mental illness known as bipolar disorder, and called manic-depressive illness. In bipolar disorder, episodes of mania usually begin abruptly and last from several weeks to several months. Mild manic episodes can last a year or more. Depression may follow immediately or begin after a period of normal functioning. Manic episodes may require hospitalization because of impaired social behaviour or the presence of psychotic symptoms. The symptoms of depression range from uncomfortable to debilitating: sleep disturbances, hopelessness, feelings of worthlessness, difficulty concentrating, fatigue and sometimes even delusions. Most of us have watched a relative or friend struggle with depression—and many of us have experienced it ourselves. Even so, few people realize just how common depression is, how severe it can be or that it is most prevalent among women. In 1990 the World Health Organization found depression to be the leading cause of "disease burdens," (a composite measure that includes both illness and death) among women, acknowledging the presence as to induce a characteristic effect, as the condition or occurrence as made to cause or get enforcing the tools that they have invoked, in as much apparent percent of US women—compared with only 6 percent of US men—have suffered from clinically significant depression at some time in their lives.

The big question, of course, is why such a gender gap exists. Over the years various explanations have surfaced to account for the fact that, from one study to the next, depression is between two and three times more common among women than it is among men. Some mental health workers have pointed to psychology, arguing that they better train women to recognize their feelings and seek help, so they come to the attention of health professionals more often than men. Others have suggested that oppression—as physical or sexual abuse, harassment or discrimination—is to blame. Others still have attributed the increased rates of depression among women to the female reproductive system and the menstrual cycle.

Data from a variety of studies show that depression clearly has psychological, environmental and biological roots. Modern neuroscience is beginning to teach us how these roots can become intertwined and reinforce each another. In other words, an increased risk for depression in women might stem from genetics, the effects of stressful events or social pressures, or some combination of all three. Neuroimaging of the brain's circuitry by PET and MRI scans reveals that psychological phenomena such as anger and sadness have biological underpinnings: We can now see circuits of brain cells becoming activated when these emotions arise.

Similarly, neuroimages show that environmentally and psychological experiences can alter our brain chemistry. For example, Lewis R. Baxter and his colleagues at the University of California at Los Angeles found similar changes in PET scans in patients with obsessive-compulsive disorder who responded to treatment, despite whether they treated the patients with medication or with behavioural therapy.

To figure out why depression is more common among women, but scientists have studied how genetics and environment divide the sexes—and how the two conspire to produce the symptoms described as depression. It is difficult work, and progress is necessarily slow. Nevertheless, toward that place of appearing, are that certain environmental factors, including stress, seasonal changes and social rank of which may produce different physiological responses in females than they do in males. These findings, are small pieces in what is an incredibly complex puzzle. Laying them out at this stage does not begin to explain depression's double standard. Nevertheless, it could help scientists develop more effective treatments for depressed individuals—both women and men—meanwhile.

Many scientists have wondered whether there is some quirk in the way depression is inherited begun, which is to say, as further afar from the Neanderthals or the Cro Magnon, nevertheless, as these carrying gene conveyers were evidences from their appointed time, even so, that backwards in time. Previously of many, to many and of many more years was the Homo erectus, as he became the attributing factor for the first upright vertical positioning walking man? The Homo erectus was man's enduring beginning, executing his posted livelihoods, in only to exist, as man had to become, the Homo erectus was the beginning, The Homo erectus took his charge and began, thus, in furthering, the genealogical amplification from the vertical walking man, now, The Homo Sapient, from such is a man given by his ancestral inheritance.

That to say, is, nonetheless, that of a depressed, the parent or grandparent is more likely to pass on a predisposition for the disorder to female than to male descendants. Based on studies that trace family histories of depression, the answer to that question is no. Women and men with similar heritage seem equally likely to develop the disorder. Simply tracing family histories, though, without also considering environmental influences, might not offer a complete picture of how depression is inherited.

Indeed, Kenneth S. Kendler and his colleagues at the Medical College of Virginia found in a study of 2,060 female twins that genetics might contribute to how women respond to environmental pressures. The researchers examined twins with and without

41

a family history of depression; some twins in both groups had recently undergone a trauma, such as the death of a loved one or a divorce. The investigators found that among the women who did not have a family history of depression, stressful events raised their risk for depression by only 6 percent, but the same risk rose almost 14 percent among the women who did have a family history of depression. In other words, these women had seemingly inherited the propensity to become depressed in the wake of crises.

A similar study has not been done in men, leaving open the question of whether environmental stress and genetic risk for depression interact similarly in both sexes. But research is obtainably achieved, as to determine whether men and women generally experience similar amounts and types of stress. Studies of key hormones hint that they do not. Hormones are not new to depression researchers. Many have wondered whether the gonadal steroid's estrogen and progesterone—whose cyclic fluctuations in women regulate menstruation—might put women at a greater risk for depression. There are at least two ways in which they might do so.

First, because of differentiated discernment between the common dependancy drawn upon the distribution or in participation as among the comprehensions attributed by one's encounter that in meaning of something as having an endless sense of essencity, that, both species of male and female brains are unconcealed to different hormonal milieus in utero. These hormonal discrepancies may produce a ususal mental or emotional effect on one capable of reaction, such that the brain developments of an action or proceedings to which previously is characterized or specified of so extreme a degree or specified. As men and women have, in their gross effects, differently diversified in kind or character vulnerabilities and divergent equalities in both physiological duties and functional operations as to be expressed to environmental stressors. Animal experiments show that early hormonal influences have marked behavioural consequences later on, although the phenomenon is of course difficult to study in humans.

Second, the fact that postpubertal men and women have different levels of circulating gonadal steroids might somehow put women at higher risk for depression. Research shows girls become more susceptible to depression than boys only after puberty, when they begin menstruating and experience hormonal fluxes. Even so, scientists have never been able to establish a direct relation between emotional states and levels of estrogen and progesterone in the blood of women. For example, Peter J. Schmidt and David R. Rubinow of the National Institute of Mental Health recently reported that manipulations of estrogen and progesterone did not affect the mood, except in women who suffer from severe premenstrual mood changes.

It now appears, however, that estrogen might set the stage for depression indirectly by priming the body's stress response. During stressful times, the adrenal glands—which sit on top of the kidneys and are controlled by the pituitary gland in the brain—secrete higher levels of a hormone-called cortisol, which increases the activity of the body's metabolic and immune systems, among others. In the normal course of events, stress increases cortisol secretion, but these elevated levels have a negative feedback effect on the pituitary, so that cortisol levels gradually return to a normative level.

Evidence is emerging that estrogen might not only increase cortisol secretion but also decrease the cortisol, as to cause the ability of secreting to close down of its own secreting responsibilities. The result might be a stress response that is not only more pronounced but also longer-lasting in women than in men.

For example, Nicholas C. Vamvakopoulos, George P. Chrousos and their colleagues at the National Institute of Child Health and Human Development recently found that increased levels of estrogen heighten the activity of the gene for human corticotropin-releasing hormones (CRH). This gene controls the secretion of CRH by a region of the brain called the hypothalamus. CRH makes the pituitary gland for releasing adrenocorticotropic hormones (ACTH), which circulates in the blood and eventually reaches the adrenal glands, where it prompts the secretion of a cortisol. Thus, estrogen can, by increasing CRH secretion, ultimately boost cortisol secretion. And, Elizabeth A. Young, of the University of Michigan and others have shown that female rats are more "resistant" to the cortisol's refusal to grant a negative feedback, which is opposed or that by constituting the essencity, that support or sustain anything on a basis of conjecture. However, in a troublesome manner, as subjected of a given cause to be endured upon the aspects of an imposing effect, such is, that among the male rats, as any various long-tailed rodent resembling mice, but larger, especially one of the genus, the Rattus, as well, of any of various animals similar to ones of the long-tailed rodents, of which are the spayed female rats. She has also shown that women have been longer-lasting cortisol responses during the phase of the menstrual cycle when estrogen and progesterone levels are high.

It is unclear whether depression is a cause or a consequence of elevated cortisol levels, but the two are undoubtedly related. Over the past few decades, a number of studies have shown that cortisol levels are elevated in about half of all severely depressed people, both men and women. So the idea is this: if estrogen raises cortisol levels after stress or decrease's cortisol's ability to shut down its own secretion, then estrogen might render women more prone to depression—particularly after a stressful event.

Despite their importance, estrogen and cortisol are not the only hormones involved in female depression, and stress is not the only environmental influence that might hold more sway over women than men. Recent findings by Thomas A. Wehr, Norman E. Rosenthal and their colleagues at the National Institute of Mental Health indicate that women might be more responsive physiologically than men to changes in exposure to light and to darkness. These investigators have had a long-standing interest in seasonal affective disorder (SAD), or so-called winter depression (although it can occur in the summer as well), and the role that the hormone melatonin might play in the illness. Similar to the gender ratio in other forms of depression, SAD is three times more common in women than in men.

Melatonin has been a prime suspect in SAD because organisms (including humans) secrete it only when they are in the dark and only when the body's internal clock (located in the hypothalamus) believes it is nighttime. The pineal gland, a small structure that resides deep in the mammalian brain, begins to secrete melatonin in the evening, as daylight wanes. Melatonin levels drop in the morning, when light hits the retinas of the eyes. Because nights are longer in winter than in summer, animals living in the wild secrete melatonin for longer periods each day during winter. Among animals that breed in summer, the onset of this extended daily melatonin secretion signals the presence of winter and shut down the secretion of gonadal steroids that facilitate reproduction.

SAD researchers have long wondered whether a wintertime increase in the duration of melatonin secretion might also trigger depressive symptoms in susceptible individuals. In a series of ongoing studies designed to address this question, Wehr and his colleagues first asked whether humans, like animals, undergo seasonal changes in melatonin secretion. It is an important question, given that artificial light provides humans with an "endless summer" of sorts compared with animals in the wild. To find out, Wehr measured melatonin secretion in 15 humans when they were exposed to 14 hours of darkness and later to only eight hours of darkness each night. The results of this experiment, conducted mostly among men, were positive: people experiencing longer periods of darkness secreted melatonin for longer periods during the night, as wild animals do.

Next, the researchers asked whether this natural sensitivity to the seasonal day-length change persisted when people were allowed to follow their usual schedules, turning on artificial lights at night as they normally would. Here the researchers were surprised to find a gender difference. Under normal living conditions, women were more likely than men to retain a sensitivity to seasonal changes in day length. In other words, for women the duration of nocturnal melatonin secretion was longer in winter than summer; in men, however, there was no seasonal difference.

These results suggest that women are more sensitive to natural light than men—and that in a society where artificial light is everywhere, women somehow still detect seasonal changes in natural day length. Whether this gender difference puts women at increased risk for SAD is unclear; paradoxically, there is evidence that women with SAD symptoms may be less likely than unaffected women to have an increased duration of melatonin secretion in winter.

To complicate the story further, the relation between these findings and those regarding cortisol and estrogen are also unclear, because we don't know whether the duration of melatonin secretion affects reproductive function in women, as it surely does in animals. Researchers are now working to unravel the complicated relations between these hormonal systems and to determine whether, and how, they may influence individuals' risk for depression.

If women's body is, in fact, particularly sensitive to environmental changes, the explanation may lie within the system that controls serotonin, one of many so-called neurotransmitters that nerve cells uses to communicate with one another. Serotonin modulates both cortisol and melatonin secretion. (The similarity in names between serotonin and melatonin is no accident: the latter are synthesized directly from the former, and the two have very similar chemical structures.) And a great deal of evidence indicates that dysfunction in the serotonergic, or serotonin-secreting, system contributes to depression and anxiety disorders, which is also more common in women than men. Recently research in animals and humans have both given preliminarily, but key, insights into this system.

First, it appears that the serotonergic system serves as a link between an animal's nervous system and its physical and social environment. That is, not only do the combining of a stress and daylight act through the serotonergic system but an animal's social rank also appears to affect its serotonin level. A number of studies show that blood and brain serotonin levels change as an animal moves up or down dominance hierarchies. For instance, dominant male monkeys often have higher blood serotonin levels than subordinate ones do. In addition, a recent study by Shih-Rung Yeh and his colleagues at Georgia State University shows that the sensitivity of an animal's neurons to serotonin varies according to that animal's status. Specifically, Yeh found that neurons taken from crayfish that had recently won a fight responded to serotonergic stimulation more strongly than neurons taken from losing crayfish.

And later considerations among factors as socioeconomic status and the relatedness to depression through their influence on the components of the framework as the framework might guide the formulation and evaluation of clinical intervention. Nonetheless, much of the literature on stress and depression is concerned with the effects of major life events such as divorce, job loss, and death. Recent studies indicate the need to expand the concept of stress to include continuing life strains arising from major social roles, as well as minor but frequent stresses encountered in daily living. Our considerations of each of the factors in examining the role of stressful life circumstances in depression, this, however, have focussed primarily on the overall association between stresses and depression without considering the mediating factors involved.

Substantial evidence implicates environmental stresses in the development and maintenance of depression (Paykel, 1979). The conceptual and methodological issues concerning life events are summarized else where (Dohrenwens, Dohrenwens, 1974, as well as Myers, 1979). Nevertheless, this criterial enquiry has identified depressogenic effects of undesirable (negative) lives, for changes in the areas of health, finances, and interpersonal relationships, particularly is represented for there lose to socially subjective cognition. These events have cumulated in effects that may manifest themselves over several months. Is that, at least, three to six times more common is among depressed individuals as compared to the general population of controls?

Another significant source of stress derives from chronic strains associated with an individual's major social roles of spouse, parent, and the provider. For example, Pearin and Schooler (1978) found that such strains as frustration of martial role expectations, children's deviations from parental standards of behaviour, and difficulty affording food and clothing was associated with greater depressive symptomatology among community residents. Physical and emotional dysfunctions of one's spouse or children also create strain. Recent research has focussed on the work setting as an important source of such stressors (Kasl, 1978). Work pressure, and a lack of autonomy in decision-making, and ambiguity about job roles and criteria of adequate performance have been associate with psychological distress and depression (Billings and Moos). The compatibility of the finding on life strains and stressful events suggest an underlying commonality in the role of environmental stressors in minor and major depressive outcomes.

All the same, there appears to be significant gender differences in the serotonergic systems of both animals and humans. Mirko Diksic, Sadahiko Nishizawa and their colleagues at McGill University recently provided the most dramatic example: to measure serotonin synthesis in the human brain, they devised a new technique using PET Neuroimaging and found that the average synthesis rate was 52 percent higher in men than in women. The investigators note that with the exception of estrogen binding sites, this gender difference in the brain is one of the largest ever reported. The lower rate of serotonin synthesis in women might increase their overall risk for depression—especially if serotonin stores are depleted during stress or winter darkness.

Meir Steiner and his co-workers at McMaster University suggest that if serotonin mediates between an organism and its environment and if the neurotransmitter is regulated differently in men and women, it might explain gender patterns not only in depression but also in a range of psychiatric illnesses. Specifically, whereas depression and anxiety are more common among women, alcoholism and severe aggression are more common among men. And just as low serotonin levels have been implicated in depression and anxiety disorders in women, they have also been found in the brains of men with severe forms of alcoholism and aggression.

Such gender differences in the serotonergic system might ensure that females respond to stress with psychiatric disturbances that involve behavioural inhibition, whereas men respond to stress with a loss of behavioural control. Steiner suggests that such gender differences in the serotonergic system evolved because child rearing is more successful (in the narrow sense of more children surviving to adulthood) in species in which aggressive impulses are cu

A researcher espousing either the sociological or psychological explanation of depression's gender bias might counter Steiner's theory by arguing that men are socialized to respond to stress with "acting out" behaviours, such as alcoholism or aggression. In contrast, society teaches women to respond to stress with "acting in" behaviours, such as depression. To support this idea, they might point to epidemiological studies done in Amish and Jewish populations. In these communities, alcoholism is less common than in the population at large, and, interestingly, the rates of depression are as high in men as in women.

These contradictory data leave no doubt that the explanations behind depression and other psychiatric diseases are not straightforward. Biological and social influences not only coexist but also probably reinforcing of any others. After all, we would expect gender socialization patterns to evolve so that they complement biological differences between the sexes. In other words, we would expect "nurture" to reinforce rather than oppose "nature." And because nurture involves learning—and learning occurs when certain neural connections in the brain are strengthened—it is clear that both nurture and nature involves biological processes.

The theory Edward Bibring presents in 'The Mechanism of Depression' (1953) is deliberately limited to the ego of psychology depression. He wrote, . . . The conception of depression presents is not invalidated for which of an accepted theory of the role which orality and aggression play in the various types of depression'. Yet his theory points up the inadequacy of the theory, Bibring stated his view as follows, . . . the oral and aggressive strivings are not as universal in depression as is generally assumed and . . . consequently the theories built on them do not offer sufficient explanation, but require modification.

The basic proposition of Bibring's theory is akin to the proposition which Freud built as the structural theory of anxiety. Freud wrote, . . . The ego is the real seat of anxiety . . ., Anxiety is an affective state which can, of course, be experienced only by the ego'. Bibring wrote 'depression is . . . primarily an ego phenomenon' [it] represents an effective state. '[Anxiety and depression are] both . . . frequent . . . ego reactions . . . [and since] they cannot be reduced any further, it may be justified to call them basic ego reactions'.

With that, Bibring sets out to explore the structure of depression as an ego state, in that he used Freud's theory of anxiety, and, Fenichel's theory of boredom, as well as, some general observations of depersonalization as his given directions to departure.

We have then, a structural theory which treats depression as the reactivation of a structural state. The universal experiences of grief and sadness, ranging from passing sadness to profound depression, indicate differences in the relative ease of and intensity of the reactivation of this state is determined by: (1) Of each the constitutional tolerance for continued frustration. (2) The severity and extent of the situation of helplessness in early life. (3) The developmental factors which increase or decrease the relative ease with which this state is reactivated and modulate its intensity. (4) The kind and severity of the precipitating condition. As for the dynamic aspect of this theory, the depressive ego state is reactivated by an intraego conflict. The factors involved in this conflict, however, are not yet precisely defined, as for the genetic aspect of the theory: The depressive ego state is reactivated by an intraego conflict and the genetic aspect of the theory. The origin of the depressive ego state is clear and so is the epigenesis of the 'narcissistic aspirations' involved.

The economic and adaptive aspects of the theory, however, are to a greater extent, directly treated by Bibring, but Freud made several attempts to account for various aspects of the economics of depression.

For instance, he wrote, . . . the ego's inhibited condition and loss of interest were fully accounted for by the absorbing work of mourning', or, for instance:

> The conflict in the ego [meaning at that time
> the conflict between the ego and the Superego],
> which in melancholia, is substituted, as the struggle
> surges round the object for that which must act like

a painful wound which calls out unusually strong anticathexis.

But Freud also indicated that these assumptions are insufficient and we need 'some insight into the economic condition. First, of bodily pain, and then of the mental pain' before we can understand the economics of depression and that:

> . . . we do not know by what economic measures the work of mourning is carried through, possibly, however, a conjecture may help us here. Reality passes its verdict—that the object no longer exists—upon each single one of the memories and hopes through which the libido was attached to the lost object, and the ego, confronted as it were with the decision whether it will share this fate, is persuaded by the sum of narcissistic satisfactions in being alive to sever its attachment to the nonexistent object.

And that:

> This character of withdrawing the libido it is . . . to be ascribed alike to mourning and to melancholia, it is probably sustained by the same economic arrangements and serves the same purpose in both.

Why this process of carrying out the behest of reality bit by bit . . . should be extraordinarily painful is not at all easy to explain in terms of mental economics.

Though it is clear that the phenomenon from which the economic explanation must start is the inhibition of the ego, the economics of depression is still not understood. Bibring quotes Fenichel's formulation . . . the greater percentage of the available mental energy is used up in nonconflictual endeavours. Enough is left to provide the normal enjoyment of life and vitality' (Bibring, 1953). But he finds this statement insufficient to explain depressive inhibition, and proceeds to reconsider the nature of inhibition. He writes:

> Freud (1926) defines inhibition as a 'restriction of functions of the ego' and mentions two major causes for such restrictions, either they have been imposed

upon the person as a measure of precautions, e.g., to present the development of anxiety or feeling of guilt, or brought about as a result of exhaustion of energy of the ego engaged in intense defensive activities.

Bibring concludes:

> The inhibition in depression . . . does not fall under either category it is rather due to the fact that certain strivings of the person become meaningless—since the ego appears incapable ever to gratify them.

Bibring implies:

> Anxiety as a reaction to (external or internal) danger indicates the ego's desire to survive. The ego, bearing the challenge confrontation in the dangers of against an adversary, as the confronting movement or circulation, in that signals of an anticipated burden are a disquieting state of mind. The unease of anxiety for disturbing attentiveness is so charged by mindful administrations serves from fight or flight. But in depressions the opposite takes place. The ego is paralysed accountably for reasons that is incapable to meet the 'danger.' In certain instances, depression may follow anxiety, [and then] the mobilization becomes the energy . . . [is] replaced by a decrease of self-reliance, the contingent relative to dependent conviction.

Thus, is Bibring's search for an economic explanation of degressive inhibition that ends in the undefined term 'decrease of self-reliance' which, as it stands, is not an economic concept.

An important school or field of thought is based on the teachings of the British psychoanalyst Melanie Klein. Because most of Klein's followers worked with her in England, this has come to be known as the English school. Its influence, nevertheless, is very strong throughout the European continent and in South America. Its principal theories were derived from observations made in the psychoanalysis of children. Klein posited the existence of complex unconscious fantasies in children under the age of six months. The principal source of anxiety arises from the threat to existence posed by the death instinct. Depending on how concrete representations of the destructive forces are dealt within the unconscious fantasy life of the child, two basic early mental attitudes result that Klein characterized as a "depressive position" and a "paranoid position." In the paranoid position, the ego's defence consists of projecting the dangerous internal object onto some external representative, which is treated as a genuine threat emanating from the external world. In the depressive position, the threatening object is introjected and treated in fantasy as concretely retained within the person. Depressive and hypochondriacal symptoms result. Although considerable doubt exists that such complex unconscious fantasies operate in the minds of infants, these observations have been of the utmost importance to the psychology of unconscious fantasies, paranoid delusions, and theory concerning early object relations.

Psychotherapy is an important form of treatment for many kinds of psychological problems. Two of the most common problems for which people seek help from a therapist are depression and persistent anxiety. People with depression may have low self-esteem, and a sense of hopelessness about the future, and a lack of interest in people and activities once found pleasurable. People with anxiety disorders may feel anxious all the time or suffer from phobias, a fear of specific objects or situations. Psychotherapy, by itself or in combination with drug treatment, can often help people overcome or manage these problems.

People with depression often experience feelings of worthlessness, helplessness, guilt, and self-blame. They may interpret a minor failing on their part as a sign of incompetence or interpret minor criticism as condemnation. Some depressed people complain of being spiritually or morally dead. The mirror seems to reflect someone ugly and repulsive. Even a competent and decent person may feel deficient, cruel, stupid, phony, or guilty of having deceived others. People with major depression may experience such extreme emotional pain that they consider or attempt suicide. At least 15 percent of seriously depressed people commit suicide, and many more attempt it.

The pervasive and chronic nature of personality disorders makes them difficult to treat. People with these disorders often fail to recognize that their personality has contributed to their social, occupational, and personal problems. They may not think they have any real problems despite a history of drug abuse, failed relationships, and irregular employment. Thus, therapists must first focuses upon helping the person understand and become aware of the significance of their personality traits.

People with personality disorders sometimes feel that they can never change their dysfunctional behaviour because they have always acted the same way. Although personality change is exceedingly difficult, sometimes people can change the most dysfunctional aspects of their feelings and behaviour.

Therapists use a variety of methods to treat personality disorders, depending on the specific disorder. For example, cognitive and behavioural techniques, such as role playing and logical argument, may help alter a person's irrational perceptions and assumptions about himself or herself. Certain psychoactive drugs may help control feelings of anxiety, depression, or severe distortions of thought. Psychotherapy may help people to understand the impact of experiences and relationships during childhood.

Psychotherapy is usually ineffective for people with antisocial personality disorder because these individuals tend to be manipulative, unreliable, and dishonest with the therapist. Therefore, most mental health professionals favour removing people with this disorder from their current living situation and placing them in a residential treatment centre. Such residential programs strictly supervise patients' behaviour and impose rigid, consistent rules and responsibilities. These programs appear to help some people, but it is unclear how long their beneficial effects last.

Therapists treating people with borderline personality disorder sometimes use a technique called dialectical behaviour therapy. In this type of therapy, the therapist initially focuses on reducing suicidal tendencies and other behaviours that disrupt treatment. The therapist then helps the person develop skills to cope with anger and self-destructive impulses. In addition, the person learns to achieve personal strength through an acceptance of the many disappointments and interpersonal conflicts that are a natural part of life.

The Psychodynamic perspective was developed earlier than were mostly than presented. They were written in a period 'chiefly' characterized by boldly speculative theoretical formulations and by insightful clinical studies. It was a richly productive era in which sensitive and intuitive observers mapped out whole continents of the mind that had previously been unexplored. It was an era of large scale conceptualizations and generalizations (Mendelson, 1960).

Freud had made some tentative comments during an early staging year of 1896, but the paper written by Abraham was the first major contribution to a Psychodynamic understanding of depression. In it, Abraham gave critical importance to the role of repressed hostility in the disorder. 'In such was the possibility that could be discovered that the disease proceeded from an attitude of hate which was paralysing the patient's capacity to love'. Abraham sketched out the dynamics by which this hostility could become turned inward by the depressed person. The depressive's basic attitude is that: 'I cannot love people; I have to hate them.' This is repressed and out of awareness, but projected outward as 'People do not love me, they hate me, because of my inborn defects', 'therefore, I am unhappy and depressed,' this attitude is first projected onto the depressive's parents, but it is later generalize d to the wider environment. It becomes detached from its roots in the depressive's hostility and experienced as a deep sense of inferiority. Such a fundamentally negative attitude makes it difficult for the depressed person to become invested in the external world, as in a positive way, and the libido that is absorbed in this was unavailable for other purposes. The depressed person is thus inhibited and depleted.

Freud accepted and enlarged upon Abraham's formulation in developing his comparison of grief and depression. The tentativeness with which Freud presented his views should be noted, as he was doubtful whether depression was a single, well-defined entity, he believed that, at least, some depression was primarily biological, rather than psychogenic. He denied any claim that his formulation had been validity raised, such is the possibility that it might fit only as the subgroup of depressions.

Freud started his formulation by noting that both grief and depression involve a dejected mood, a loss of both interests in the world and the capacity to love, and an inhibition of activity. What distinguishes depression, however, is that the depressed person has suffered a loss of self-regard, and this expresses itself in self-criticism and self-vilification. Freud's observations on depressed people's self-criticism provide an interesting contrast to the cognitive and interpersonal. The pathological nature of this self-criticism was not seen as a matter of inadequacy, as when the depressed person, . . . described himself as petty, egoistic, dishonest, lacking in independence, so far as we know, that he has come pretty near to describing himself; we only wonder why a man has to be ill before he can be accessible to a truth of this kind.

Freud suggested a depressed person might actually have a 'keener eye for the truth' than those who are not depressed. What is pathological is that anyone would make such a self-evaluation, whether or not it is true or accepted by others. Furthermore, rather than being ashamed by such an opinion, the depressed seem to find a satisfaction in inflicting it on others.

Freud went on to note that if one listens carefully to a depressive's self-criticism, one often discovers that the most extreme of the complaints is less applicable to the depressed person than to someone that the depressed person loves, once loved, or should love. This was a key observation for Freud: The self-criticism of a depressed person had been shifted back from a loved object. Thus, the woman who complains that she is utterly unloved and challenges her husband as to why he would stay with her may actually be chastising him for not being more lovable.

The dynamics that are described seem complicated and circuitous. In reading Freud's account, it should be remembered that he had not yet articulated the concept of the Superego. And so the 'self-critical faculty' that he wished to involve had to be relegated to the ego. The process of becoming depressed starts with a real or imagined loss, rejection, or disappointment, in normal grief, this would entail a painful withdrawal of libidinal investment and an eventual displacement of it onto a new object.

However, in a depressive process, the ego refuses to accept the loss. The ego becomes enraged and regresses to an oral sadistic level. Here, as in Abraham's formulation, aggression has a key role. There is a slit in the ego, and part of it regresses further to the oral receptive stage. The ego identification with the lost object, and the conflict between the ego and the lost object become s a conflict, and the conflict between the ego and the lost object becomes a conflict within the ego. Such as the lost object becomes an ego loss, as it is incorporated into the ego. The identification with the lost object, and the conflict between the ego and the lost object becomes a conflict within the ego. Hostility that cannot be expressed directly to the object is heaped upon the portion of the ego that is identified with it, and this is reflected of self-esteem and punishing self-criticism. Freud argued that process did not happen in just anyone just facing a loss. It requires a predisposition that lies in a basic ambivalence to the love object and an underlying tendency toward narcissistic object choices. The vulnerability of a person's who takes as obtainably achievable the love objects that are similar enough to the self that they can be easily abandoned and confused with it.

Once, again, the Psychodynamic approach path begins with the lost object as becoming an ego loss, as it is incorporated into the ego. The ego identifies with the lost object, and the conflict between the ego and the lost object becomes a conflict within the ego. Hostility that cannot be expressed directly to the lost object is heaped upon the portion of the ego that is identified with it, and this is reflected in a loss of loss of self-esteem and punishing self-criticism. Freud argued that this process did not happen in just anyone facing a loss. It requires a predisposition that underlies in the basic ambivalence to the love object and an underlying tendency toward narcissistic object choices. The vulnerable person choses love objects that are similar enough to the self that they can be easily abandoned and confused with it.

However, Bibring was careful to state that he did not reject outright the formulations offered by Freud and Abraham, but he suggested that they needed modification because oral and aggressive striving may not be as universal in depression as these formulations supposed. Yet, the modification that he presents proves to be quite radical. For Bibring, what was most fundamental about depression is a fall in self-esteem due to 'the ego's shocking awareness of its helpfulness in regard to its aspiration'. Depression occurs when the person both feels powerless to achieve some narcissistically important goal and the goal is not relinquished.

Irrespective of their unconscious implications, one may roughly distinguish between three groups of such persisting aspiration of the person: (1) the wish to be worthy, to beloved, to be appreciated, not to be inferior or unworthy; (2) the wish to be strong, superior, great, secure, and to be weak and insecure; and (3) the wish to be good, to e loving not to be aggressive, hateful and destructive. It is exactly from the tension between these highly charged narcissistic aspirations, on the other hand, and, the ego's acute awareness of its (real or imaginary) helplessness and incapacity to live up to them on the other hand, that depression results (Bibring, 1953).

The vulnerability to particular frustrations is acquired as a result of trauma that occur in early childhood and that produce a fixation to a state of helplessness. This state can be reactivated when the person is confronted with a situation resembling the original trauma. Bibring agreed with earlier writers that depression is more likely to occur in orally dependent persons who need 'narcissistic supplies'; from the outside, but he also argued that severe frustration could produce a fixation in another stage. Importantly, depression did not depend upon the aggressive and dependent striving of the oral stage. Rather than producing depression, such striving might result from the awareness of helplessness.

Whybrow, Akiskal, and Mckinney (1984) have implicated that some of the most important implications of Bibring's reformation of the classical psychodynamics of depression.

To define depression in this way is to define it as psychosocial phenomenon. The concept of the ego, unlike that of the id, is rooted in social reality, and the ego ideal is composed of socially learned symbols and motives. A breakdown of self-esteem may involve, in addition to object loss, man's symbolic possessions, such as power, status, social role, identity, values, and existential purpose. Depression, therefore, falls particularly upon the overambitious, the conventional, and individual with upward mobility, and the woman who strongly identify with a passive social role . . . Bibring's conceptualization provides broad links with man's existential, sociological, and a cultural world.

Cohen and her colleagues represent another important conceptual transition, such like the other Psychodynamic writers, Cohen has devoted considerable attention to the early childhood experience of depression but emphasis is on the patterning of interpersonal relationships rather than intrapsychic functioning. They demonstrate the Sullivanian conceptualization of personality as the recurring patterning of significant relationships.

The enduring interpersonal climate in the family is given more attention that any single traumatic experience, and the family's position in the community are identified as an important determinant of what this climate will be. Specifically, the families of depressed persons tend to stand out as different from the families around them. Parents tend to have an overriding concern with fitting in, confronting to 'what the neighbours think' and upward mobility. The child in the family who is most likely to be depressed later is likely to be the one who most accepted the burden of winning acceptance and prestige for the family.

This child absorbs parental attitudes in a peculiar combination of lack of conviction of worth . . . coupled with an intense devotion of conventional, orality and what people think'. The child may show a strong concern with what authority expects, but a conviction that these expectations are beyond what can be achieved.

The adult relationships of depressives tend to perpetuate the patterning of the family relationships in childhood. Even when not suffering from and mood disturbance, depressives tend to have a narrow range of relationships within which they are very dependent and sensitive to signs of disapproval and rejection. As an interpersonal strategy, depressives may undersell themselves in order to win nurturance and approval, but in doing so, actually may convince others that they lack any assets.

At this point, they begin to hate these other people for being the cause of the vicious circle in which they are caught, and they hate themselves because the sense the fraudulence of their behaviour in not their behaviour in not having expressed openly their inner feelings.

This strategy and patterning of relationships become exaggerated and intensified during a period of depression. The symbols of depressed persons might be seen as an appeal to those around them, but if prolonged, their main effect may be to leave the depressed person alienated from those people upon whom they had relied and along with their feelings of distress. Cohen gives an extended talk about of the therapeutic relationship with depressed persons because of the assumption that this will recapitulate other significant relationships in a way that allows the therapist to have the first hand perspective of a participant observer. The language of transference and countertransference is used, but one less of a sense of an ego struggling with object representations than of two people struggling with a difficult relationship. Depressed persons can be irritating and manipulative, but are more likely to be manipulated by depressed persons if they become overly invested in playing a benign and powerful role with their patient's. This emphasis on interpersonal strategies of depressed persons and the involvement t of others is developed in Coyne, as its point of departure, is a greater focus on the contemporary relationships of adult depressed persons, with a conceptualization of depression as an emergent interpersonal system of depressive behaviour and depression are powerful in their alibility to arousing guilt and hostility from them. Initially, the depressed persons' distress engages others and shifts the interactional burden onto them. Yet, the persistence of the depressed persons distress may soon prove incomprehensible and aversive to them.

In the sixties Psychodynamic writings were interpreted as suggesting that when people become depressed, they are more likely to internalize or suppress hostility. Findings were generally not supportive of this hypothesis (Friedman, 1964 and Schless, et al., 1974). There were also a number of examinations of whether persons who later became depressed had experienced the death of a parent in childhood. There were some well-designed studies with positive results, but other studies found only a weak and inconsistent relationship (Crook and Elliot, 1980). Yet, as in the studies of depression and hostility, questions could be raised about the fidelity of the research to the original Psychodynamic formulation. Recently, Sidney Blatt and his colleagues have utilized Psychodynamic conceptions in developing a line of research that distinguishes between depressed persons on the basis of whether dependency or self-criticism predominates. Such a typology correlates with retrospective report s of parental behaviour in childhood (McCranie and Bass, 1984).

Despite such a paucity of research, the impact of the Psychodynamic perspective should not be underestimated. Ideas derived from it about the significance of early childhood experience, hostility, and self-criticism continue to have a strong influence and layperson understanding of depression. Furthermore, the other psychosocial perspectives of depression remain indebted in ways that are not always obvious. Aaron T. Beck was formally a practising psychoanalyst, and his cognitive model of depression grew of his early work testing Psychodynamic hypothesis about the dreams of depressed persons. The first elaborated behavioural formulation of depression (Ferster, 1973) accepted as fact Psychodynamic ideas about the role of anger turned inward and fixation; it attempted to reconceptualize them in behavioural terms. Major characteristics for which in key aspects are he learned helplessness model, of which is anticipated in Bibring's formulation. Articles by Coyne and Becker also built upon Psychodynamic formulations, but they are developed in very different direction.

In the experiences, as a deep sense of inferiority, such a fundamental negative attitude makes it difficult for the depressed person to become invested in the external world in a positive way, and the libido that is absorbed in this way is unavailable for other purposes. The depressed person is thus inhibited and depleted. However, Freud was doubtful whether depression was a single, well-defined entity; he believes that, at least, some depression was primarily biological, rather than psychogenic.

Freud started his formulation by noting that both grief and depression involve defective moods, as a loss of both interests in the world and the capacity to love. This had directed those which of the inhibitions of activity, as to distinguishes depression. However, is that the depressed person has suffered a loss of self-regard, and this expresses itself in self-criticism and even self-vilification. Freud's observation on depressed people's self-criticism provides an interesting contrast to the cognitive and interpersonal. The pathological nature of this self-criticism was not seen as a matter of inaccuracy, nonetheless, when the depressed person, . . . describes himself as petty, egoistic, dishonest, lacking in independence, one whose direct target is to hide the weakness of his own nature, it may be, so far as we know, that he has come pretty near to describing himself; we only wonder why a man has to be ill before he can be accessible to a truth of this kind.

Freud suggested a depressed person might actually have a 'keener eye for the truth' than those who are not depressed. What is pathological? Is that anyone would make such self-evaluation, whether or not it is true or accepted by others? Furthermore, rather than being ashamed by such an opinion, the depressed seem to find a satisfaction in inflicting it on others.

Freud went on to note if one listens carefully to a depressive's self-criticism, one often discovers that most extreme of the complaints is less applicable to the depressed person than to someone that the depressed person loves, once loved, or should love. This was a key observation for Freud: The delf-criticism of a depressed person had been shifted back from a loved object. Thus, the woman who complains that she is utterly unloved and challenges her husband as to why he would stay with her may actually be chastising him for not being more lovable.

The dynamics that are described seem complicated and circuitous. In reading Freud's account, it should be remembered that he has not yet articulated the concept of the Superego, and so the 'self-criticism faculty' that he wished to involve had to be relegated to the ego. The process of becoming depressed starts with a real or imagined loss, rejection, or disappointment, that in grief, for instance, entails a painful withdrawal of libidinal investment and an eventual displacement of it's newly placed objects.

However, in a depressive process, the ego refuses to accept the loss. The ego becomes enraged and regresses to an oral sadistic level. There is a split in the ego, and part of it regresses further to the oral receptive stage. The lost object becomes an ego loss, as it is incorporated into the ego. The ego identifies with the lost object, and the conflict between the ego and the lost object becomes a conflict within the ego. Hostility that cannot be expressed directly to the lost object is heaped upon the portion of the ego that is identified with it, and this is reflected in a loss of self-esteem and punishing self-criticism. Freud argued that this process did not happen in just anyone facing a loss. It requires a predisposition that lies in a basic ambivalence to the love object and an underlying tendency toward narcissistic object choices, the vulnerable person as having qualities that appeal to his alternative choice of love objects that are similar enough to the self that they can be easily abandoned and confused with it.

Bibring was careful to state that he did not reject outright the formulations offered by Freud, but, he suggested that they needed modification because oral and aggressive striving may not be as universal in depression as these formulations suppose. Yet the modification that he presents proves to be quite radical. For Bibring, what was most fundamental about depression is a fall in self-esteem due to 'the ego's shocking awareness of its helplessness in regard to its aspiration'. Depression occurs when the person both feels powerless to achieve some narcissistically important goal and goal is not relinquished.

We have avoided using the term Superego, thus far, and have not involved the cruel, punishing Superego in our attempted explanation of the depression. It is our opinion that utilization of the term Superego in this way merely conceals the problem rather than explain it. There are several basic questions regarding the problems of conscience and guilt in the manic depressive. First, what influences account for the severe and hypermoral standards of these people.' And second, what is the dynamic function of the self-punishing acts and attitudes which are engaged in during the periods of illness?

The overcritical standards of manic depressives are not explicable as direct taking-over of the standards of the parents, since these patients in childhood have usually been treated with rather exceptional overindulgence. However, the peculiar combination of lack of conviction of worth and a standard of behaviour in the family coupled with an intense devotion to conventional morality and what other people say. It is logical that a child raised by an inconsistent mother who at times grossly overindulgent and at others severely rejecting would be unable to build up a reasonable code of conduct for himself, and that his codes—focussed around what an impersonal authority is supposed to expect of him and based on no concept of parental reliability or strength—would be both over severe and frightening in its impersonality. In all probability, much of his moral code is based on the struggle to acquire those qualities of strength and virtue which he finds missing in his parents. Suffice it to say, that in dealing with authority this type of patient shows a rigid preconception of what authority expects of him as well as a persistent conviction that he must fit in with these expectations which are beyond the reach of reason or experience. The authority appears, that, at times as an incorporated Superego and at other times as a projection, impersonal but tyrannical force. Or, rather, every significant person in the patient's social field is invested with the quality of authority.

In this relationship with authority, the self-punitive acts and experiencing of guilt can be expressed as devices for placating the impersonal tyrant. The guilt calling to mind and viewing freely the expressions, through which in the depressive, and effective, do not transfer onto any genuine feeling of regret or effort to change, in any behaviour. It is, rather, a means to an end. Merely suffering feelings of guilt is expected to suffice for regaining approval. Nonetheless, it may also be seen that achieving a permanent, secure, human relationship with authority is regarded as hopeless. Therefore, no effort to change relationships or to integrate on a better level of behaviour is undertaken, and the patient merely resorts to the magic of uttering guilty cries to placate authority.

The behavioural perspective emphasizes the analysis of psychopathology in terms of observable behaviour in relation to preceding and consequential events in the environment—controlling stimuli and reinforcement consequences. Yet, a behavioural definition of depression has remained rather elusive. Depression does not refer to a single response class, at least, as it has traditionally been defined, its primary symptom is a state of subjective distress. It is often the case that depressed persons do not exhibit any marked changes in overt behaviour despite their considerable distress and sense of personal inadequacy. As a group, depressed persons do not share much in common in terms of specific behavioural excesses or deficiencies. Furthermore, depression often seems to involve change in behaviours without any apparent change in the conditions that have previously maintained them (Costello, 1972). For instance, upon leaning that his former girl friend back home has become engaged to someone else, a college student might stop eating regularly, withdraw from his friends on campus, and neglect his studying.

Of necessity, the two most influential behavioural formulations of depression involved the introduction of some concepts that go substantially beyond the usual analysis of reinforcement contingencies. Consistent with more general trends is psychology, and they both were later modified to include an emphasis on cognition.

Lewinsohn developed a model of depression that was an extension of an earlier model presented by Ferster (1973, 1974), in which the central feature of the disorder was identified as a reduction in the emission of positively reinforces behaviour. A major innovation in the Lewinsohn formulation was its emphasis on the concept of total amounts of response-contingent positive reinforcement 'reconposre'. The emission of some given adaptive behaviour is seen as not being merely a function of specific rewards available for it. Rather, it is also a function of the overall amount of positive reinforcement that is available as consequences for any available response. It is not a matter of this reinforcement for any available response. Rather, it is also a function of the overall amount of positive reinforcement that is available as consequences for any available response. It is not as matter of this reinforcement being available but often being contingent upon the person making a response.

The Lewinsohn model has been the basis for the development of an extensive research program and a behavioural approach to therapy for depression that includes a self-treatment course (Lewinsohn, 1978) Lewinsohn subsequently posited as relationship between the total number of aversive events in a patient's life and depression, and development and instrument assessing unpleasant events that parallelled the earlier Pleasant Events Schedule (Lewinsohn and Takington, 1970). In his most recent work, Lewinsohn has become more eclectic in both his model of therapy and his research program (Lewinsohn and Hoberman, 1982) and has given attention to the role of cognition in depression. However, he had assumed that the complaints of depressed persons are not necessarily distortions and that most instead reflect the depressive person's inability to obtain valued rewards. His research has even been interpreted as suggesting that depressed persons are more accurate in their self-perceptions than nondepressed persons are (Lewinsohn, 1980).

The universal experience of grief and sadness, ranging from passing sadness to profound depression, indicates that such an ego state exits in all men. We may infer that individual differences in the relative case of and interest of the reactivation of this state is the determinant by: (1) the constitution tolerance of continued frustration (2) the severity and extent of the situation of helplessness in early life (3) the development factors which increase and decrease the relative ease with which this state is reactivated and modulate its intendment, and (4) their kind and severity of precipitating conditions. All of which, are to be applied among the dynamic aspects of this theory. The depressive state is reactivated by an intraego conflict. The factors involved in this conflict, however, are not yet precisely defined. This genetic aspect of the possibility of theory, where the origin of the depressive ego state is clear, but, at least, and to some degree, is for the epigenesis of the 'narcissistic aspirations' involved.

The economic and adaptive aspects of the theory, is nonetheless, not directly by Bibring. It is in regard to these aspects that much work is still in need of attention.

Freud made several attempts to account for various aspects of the economy of depression.

For instance he wrote, . . . the ego's inhibited condition and loss of interest were fully accounted for by the absorbing work of mourning (1917), for instance: That the conflict the ego [meaning at that time the conflict between the ego and the Superego which in melancholia is substituted for the struggle round the object, must act like a painful laceration of which unusually calls for a strong cathexis.

But Freud also indicated that these assumptions are insufficient and we need 'some insight into other economic conditions, First, of bodily pain, and then of the mental pain, and then the mental pain, before we can understand the economics of depression . . . . We do not even know by what economic measure the work of mourning is carried through. Possibly, however, a conjecture may help in the reality passing its verdict—that the object no longer exists—upon each single of the memories and hopes through which the libido was attached to the lost object, and the ego, confronted. As it was with the decision whether it will share this falsification is persuaded by the sum of narcissistic satisfactions, as in being alive to sever of its attachment to the nonexistent object, . . . and that . . . this character of withdrawing the libido bit by bit is . . . to be ascribed alike to mourning and to melancholia; it is probably sustained by the same economic arrangements and serves the same purpose in both; finally, why this process of carrying out the behest of reality bit by bit . . . should be so extraordinarily painful is not at all easy to explain in terms of mental economics. Though it is clear that the phenomenon from which the economic explanation must start is the inhibition of the ego, the economic of depression are still not understood. Bibring quoters Fenichel's formulation . . . the greater percentage of the available mental energy is used up in unconscious conflicts, [and] not enough is left to provide the normal enjoyment of life and vitality (Bibring, 1953). But he finds this statement insufficient to explain depressive inhibitions, and proceeds to reconsider the nature of inhibitions. He writes:

> Freud (1926) defines inhibition as a restriction of functions of the ego, and mentions two major causes for such restrictions; either they have been imposed upon the person as a measure of precautions, e.g., to prevent the development of anxiety or feelings of guilt, or brought about as a result of exhaustion of energy of the ego engaged in intense defensive activities.

. . . Such that the inhibition in depression . . . does not fall under either category . . . It is, in as much as ado about its own obviousness, rather to the fact, that certain strivings of the person become meaningless—since the ego appears incapable ever to gratify them.

As a comparison of depression to anxiety, as a reaction to (external or internal) danger indicates the ego's desire to survive. The ego, challenges by the danger, mobilizes the signal of anxiety and prepares for fight or flight. In depression to meet the danger [In certain instances] . . . Depression may follow anxiety, [and then] the mobilization of energy . . . [is] replaced by a decease of self-reliance. Thus, for an economic explanation of depression inhibition ends in the undefined term 'decrease of 'self-reliance' which, as it stands, is not an economic concept.

What does it mean that "the ego is paralysed because it finds itself incapable to meet the 'danger'?" clearly 'paralysed' refers to the state of helplessness, one of the corollaries of which is the 'loss of self-esteem'. The danger is the potential loss of objects; the traumatic situation is that of the loss of objects, 'helplessness' as Bibring defines it is the persisting state of loss of the object. The anxiety signal anticipates the loss in order to prevent the reactivation of the traumatic situation, that is, of panic-anxiety. Fluctuations of self-esteem anticipate, and initiate measures to prevent, the reactivation of the state of persisting loss of the object, that is of the state of helplessness of self-esteem and 'helplessness' which are accompanied by loss of self-esteem in similar to the reaction between anxiety signal and panic-anxiety. Fluctuations of self-esteem are the structured, tamed forms of and signals to anticipate and to preclude reactivation of the state of helplessness. Yet, according to the accepted theory, fluctuations of self-esteem, are the functions of the Superego's relation to the ego, just as anxiety was considered, prior to 1926, as a function of repression enforced by the Superego. In 1926, however, Superego anxiety was recognized as merely one kind of anxiety and the repression, and hence anxiety relationship was reversed into an anxiety signal, hence repression. Bibring achieves an analogous reversal when he formulates . . . it is our contention, observation, that it is the ego's awareness of its helplessness which in certain cases forces it to turn the aggression from the object against the self, thus, aggravating and complicating the structure of depression. While in the accepted theory it is assumed that the aggression 'turned round upon the subject', resulting in passivity and helplessness, in Bibring's conception it is the helplessness which is the cause of this 'turning round'.

Like Freud's structural theory of anxiety and Fenichel's of guilt (1945), leads to a broadening of our conception of the ego's apparatuses and functions, even more of a problem of aggression, we know that 'turn round upon the subject' was the basic mechanism Freud used before the 'death-instinctual theory' to explain major forms in which aggression manifests itself, that Freud wrote, . . . sadism . . . seems to press toward a quite special aim—the infliction of pain, in addition to subjection and mastery of the object. Now the psychoanalysis would seem to show that infliction of pain plays no part in the original aims sought by [sadism] . . . : The sadistic child takes no notice of whether or not it inflicts pain, nor is it part of its purpose to do so. But when once the transformation into masochism has taken place, the experience of the pain is very well adapted to serve as a passive masochistic aim . . . Where once the suffering of pain has been experienced as a masochistic aim, it can be carried back into the sadistic situation and result in a sadistic aim of inflicting pain (1955).

Thus, Bibring's view that 'turning round upon the subject' is brought about by helplessness calls attention to some of Freud's early formulations, and prompts to re-evaluate the conception of aggression. Nonetheless, it may lead to a theory of aggression which is an alterative to those which have so far been proposed, namely Freud's death-instinct theory, Fenichel's frustration-aggression theory, and the Hartmann-Kris-Loewenstein theory of an independent aggressive instinctual drive.

Briefly, the relationship between helplessness (involving loss of self-esteem) and simultaneously maintain narcissistic aspiration, also to note, that their intra-ego conflict assumed by Bibring may have been implied by Freud when he wrote in "Mourning and Melancholia": A good, capable, conscientious [person] . . . is more likely to fall ill of [this] . . . disease than [one] . . . of whom we too should have nothing good to say (1917),

In the study of the examining the manic-depressive character by means of the intense psychoanalytic psychotherapy, this is potentially useful, since, the newer understanding of interpersonal processes and the problematic issue belonging to anxiety has not been brought to bar. However, the older psychoanalytic studies surrounding the psychopathology of manic depressions, thus, to use a simple example, the manic depressive is said to have an oral character, however, the question of how or why he developed an oral character is left unconsidered except in that such factors are the constitutional overintensity of oral drives, or overindulgence even frustration during the oral phase, for which of those who have given proof to their existing significance. By studying the transference, we can make inferences about earlier experiences; conversely, by understanding the patient historically, we can make inferences about the transference relationship and grasp of the patient's part of the pattern of interaction with his therapist improves, as we can gain some concept of what goals of satisfaction he is pursuing, as well as to what sort of anxieties he is striving to cope with. We may then intervene through our part in the interaction to assist him more successfully to achieve his goals of satisfaction and to resolve some of the conflicts which are at the source of his anxiety.

Toward the end of the last century, Kraepelin (1904) attempted to classify the psychiatric syndromes, including the manic-depressive or circular psychosis, as nosological entities. While his classifications in general brought some order into the existing confusion, he was unable to establish a pathological substratum or a specific etiological factor for either dementia praecox or manic-degressive psychosis, and this situation still exists.

Abraham, in 1911, was first to systematically apply the psychoanalytic method to the treatment of the circular psychosis. He concluded that manically and depressive phases are dominated by the same complexities, the depressive being defeated by them, the manic ignoring and denying them. Some of his ideas on depression might be summarized as follows: The regression to the oral level of libidinal development brought out the characterological factures of impatience and envy, increased egocentricity, and intense ambivalence, the capacity to love is paralysed by hate, sands this inability to love leads to feelings of impoverishment. The depressive stupor represents a form of dying. Abraham thought that the indecision of ambivalence is close to the doubts of the compulsive e neurotic, and that in the free interval, the manic depressive is an obsessional neurotic. He recommended a psychoanalysis in the first interval, since, in the acute phases of the psychosis, it is very difficult to establish rapport.

Abraham, in 1911, was first to systematically apply the psychoanalytic method to the treatment of the circular psychosis. He concluded that manically and depressive phases are dominated by the same complexities, the depressive being defeated by them, the manic ignoring and denying them. Some of his ideas on depression might be summarized as follows: The regression to the oral level of libidinal development brought out the characterological factures of impatience and envy, increased egocentricity, and intense ambivalence, the capacity to love is paralysed by hate, and this inability to love leads to feelings of impoverishment and the depressive stupor that represents a form of dying. Abraham thought that the indecision of ambivalence is close to the doubts of the compulsive e neurotic, and that in the free interval, the manic depressive is an obsessional neurotic. He recommended the psychoanalysis in the first interval, since, in the acute phases of the psychosis, it is very difficult to establish rapport.

In 1916-1917, Freud compared melancholia to normal mourning, as, the loss of a love object elicits the labour of mourning, which is as struggle between libido attachment and detachment—love and hate. In normal mourning this struggle of ambivalence under pressure of confrontation with reality leads to gradual rechannelization of the libido toward new objects. In the case of melancholia, or frustration, remains unconscious, and the reorientation exacted reality elicits strong resistance, since the narcissistic character of the disturbed relation does not permit separation. In this way, an intensified identification with the frustrating love object in the unconscious results. The shadow of the object has fallen on the Ego.' The whole struggle of ambivalence is internalized in a battle with the conscience. The exaggerated self-accusations are reproaches against the internalized object of love and hate: The self-torture is a form of revenge, and simultaneously, had attempted at reconciliation with the internalized partner. The narcissistic, ambivalent character of the elation to the lost love object either is the result of transitory regression or is constitutionally conditioned. Thus, the loss of self-esteem and the intense self-hate in the melancholia become understandable.

Abraham, in 1924, pursued his interest in biological development and tried to find specific fixation points for mental illness in different phases of libido development. He interpreted character traits for being highly symbolized derivatives of pregenital instinctual impulses that were, in the case of the mentally ill person, hampered in their normal development by frustration or overindulgence. Because of Abraham's influence, psychoanalytic research in ego development has for a long time been dependent on highly schematized concepts, to which the manic depressive periodically regresses for being at the end of the second biting oral phase and the beginning of the first expelling anal phase. This assumption could explain the frequent preoccupation of the manic depressive with cannibalistic phantasies as well as. His character trends of impatience, envy and exploitativeness, dominating possessiveness, and exaggerated optimism or pessimism: His intense ambivalence, and his explosive riddance reactions. The object loss that precedes the onset of a depression is mostly not conscious but, according to Abraham, repeats a primal depression, a frustration at the time of transition from the oral to the anal phase, when the child was disappointed in the mother. The oral dependence may be constitutionally overemphasized in the manic depressive.

Abraham found considerable resistance in her patient's extroverted egocentricity, for which she accepted White's concert of 'flight into reality'. According to White, this tendency toward extraversion of the libido makes the prognosis of a manic-depressive psychosis more favourable, in terms of spontaneous recovery, than that of schizophrenia. He felt that because of the dominance of his egocentric wishes, the manic-depressive patient can make 'use of every object in range of his sense'. However, Dooley found that the resistance of the manic degressive against analysis is even stronger than those of schizophrenics. Dooley suggested that the manic attack is a defence against the realization of failure. The patient cannot look at himself in the mirror of the psychoanalysis; he cannot hear the truth. Patients' who manifest frequent manic attacks are likely to be headstrong, self-sufficient, know-it-all types of people, who will get the upper hand of the analyst.,.. The analyst is really only an appendage for the greater inflated ego. Since the life conditions of the manic depressive are often no more unsatisfactory than those of many a normal person, there must be a lack of integration which keeps the manic depressive from achieving the sublimation which he is potentially capable of. Dooley came to the conclusion that the manic and depressive episodes are due to deep regressions to the sadomasochistic level of the child. 'Autoerotic wishes were satisfied by hypochondriacal complaints'. In a much later paper on "The Relation of Humour to Masochism" Dooley mentioned a manic-depressive patient who began to develop humour in the analysis as she became aware that she 'could neither hurt me nor trick me into living with him'. Dooley considered this kind of insightful humour to be a milestone in the healing process of the excessive mood swings; it indicates that the Superego is losing its tragically condemning cruelty and is permitting laughter at the overweening, pestering child-ego.

In 1916-1917, Freud compared melancholia to normal mourning, as, the loss of a love object elicits the labour of mourning, which is as struggle between libido attachment and detachment—love and hate. In normal mourning this struggle of ambivalence under pressure of confrontation with reality leads to gradual rechannelization of the libido toward new objects. In the case of melancholia, or frustration, remains unconscious, and the reorientation exacted reality elicits strong resistance, since the narcissistic character of the disturbed relations does not permit detachments. In this way, an intensified identification with the frustrating love object in the unconscious results. The shadow of the object has fallen on the Ego.' The whole struggle of ambivalence is internalized in a battle with the conscience. The exaggerated self-accusations are reproaches against the internalized object of love and hate: The narcissistic, ambivalent character of the elation to the lost love object either is the result of transitory regression or is constitutionally conditioned. Thus, the loss of self-esteem and the intense self-hate in the melancholia become understandable.

In 1921, Freud added some statements about mania to his earlier interpretations of depression. He suggested that the mood swings of normal and neurotic persons are caused by the tensions between an ego and ego ideal. These mood swings are excessive in the case of manic-depressive illness because after the frustrating of a lost object has been reestablished by identifications in the ego, it is then tormented by the cruel severity of the ego ideal, against which, in turn, the ego rebels. According to Freud, the manic represent a triumphant reunion between ego and ego ideals, in the sense of expansive self-inflation, but not in stabilizing and in the sense of equilibrium.

Abraham, in 1924, pursued his interest in biological development and tried to find specific fixation points for mental illness in different phases of libido development. He interpreted character traits for being highly symbolized derivatives of pregenital instinctual impulses that were, in the case of the mentally ill person, hampered in their normal development by frustration or overindulgence. Because of Abraham's influence, psychoanalytic research in ego development has for a long time been dependent on highly schematized concepts, to which the manic depressive periodically regresses for being at the end of the second biting oral phase and the beginning of the first expelling anal phase. This assumption could explain the frequent preoccupation of the manic depressive with cannibalistic phantasies as well as, but his character trends of impatience, envy and exploitativeness, dominating possessiveness, and exaggerated optimism or pessimism: His intense ambivalence, and his explosive riddance reactions. The object loss that precedes the onset of a depression is mostly not conscious but, according to Abraham, repeats a primal depression, a frustration at the time of transition from the oral to the anal phase, when the child was disappointed in the mother. The oral dependence may be constitutionally overemphasized in the manic depressive.

In 1927 Rado went a step further in the theory of identification. Freud and Abraham's theories imply an incorporation of the lost or flustrating object, in both the tormented ego and the punishing ego-ideal or Superego. This double incorporation, Râdo postulated, corresponds to an ambivalent splitting into a 'good'—that is, gratifying—object, and a 'bad' or frustrating objects; at an early stage of development, when the synthetic function of the ego is still weak, both of these are the mothers. The good parent by whom the child wants to be loved is incorporated in the Superego, endowed with the privilege of punishing the bad parent who is incorporated in the ego. This bad object in the ego may be punished to the point of total destruction (suicide). But the ultimate goal of this raging orgy of a self-torture is expiation, reconciliation, synthesis. Râdo describes the manic phase as an unstable reconciliation reached on the basis of denial of guilt. The automatized cycle of guilt, expiation, and reconciliation is patterned after the sequence of infantile oral experience, as, rages, hunger, drinking. The drinking, which resembles the state of reunion of reconciliation, culminates in a satiated pleasure experience, which Râdo called the 'alimentary orgasm'. In a paper published in 1933 Râdo described the way in which the drug addict, in the artificially produced intoxication, expresses the same yearning for reconciliation and blissful reunion with the gratifying mother.

In the same year, 1933, Deutsch illustrated the theory of manic depressive psychoses, as developed up to that time, by several abbreviated case presentations. She agreed with Râdo that the melancholic phase is sometimes introduced by a phase of rebellion of the ego against the cruel Superego. After the ego succumbs to the

Superego's punishment with the unconscious intention of bribing the Superego and of gaining forgiveness by such submission, the ego may rescue itself from the dangerous introjection by projecting the threatening enemy onto the outside world; aggression can then be directed against the projected Superego, which has become an external persecutor. Another form of escape from the melancholic predicament is the denial of any narcissistic deprivation, for being the loss of the mother's breast or the absence of a penis. Deutsch regarded mania and paranoia as alternative defences against the intense danger to survival to an ego oppressed by melancholia. In the hypomanic patient, the underling depression has to be lifted into consciousness if therapy is to be successful, the similarity as drawn in 1938, when Jacob's made similar observations among the periodically manic patients.

Gero illustrated "The Construction of Depression" (1936) by two case presentations. One was of a woman patient with an obsessional character structure built up as a defence against the painful ambivalence in her family relations. Only after these character defences yielded to analysis could this patient see avenues of realistic satisfactions and therewith surmount the depressions. The other case was a male patient, who had identified with an overambitious, over exacting father, and a rejecting mother, and had repressed the rage against both frustrating parents by withdrawal into repressed regression, punishing therewith the internalized objects of his hate and rage. After his father's death, he had himself changed into a sick old man. The liberation of rage and hate in the transference freed the genital aggressiveness from the odium and guilt of sadomasochistic distortions. In both cases the analyst succeeded in winning the patients from a hopeless negativism to a hopeful confirmation of life.

Jacobson had expounded upon an elaborate description, when in 1943 a severely depressed patient, with strongly suicidal argues, intense experiences of depersonalization and 'Weltuntergang' phantasies—a case on the borderlines between manic degressive psychosis and schizophrenia. Jacobson was able to uncover a primal depression in this patient at the age of three and a half, when the birth of a brother coincided with a disruption of the parental marital elation. Turning from mother to father and back to mother left the patients threatened to complete loss of objects, she maintained a masochistic dependence on her mother. As existing substitutes for the disappointing parents, she built up phantasies of idealism, for which the perfect parents who endowed her Superego with cruel severity, so that she lived in constant danger of complete desertion and in the horror of punishment.

Weiss in 1944 pursued a slightly different approach. He postulated that melancholic episodes are a reaction to the realization of antisocial, dishonest, or egotistical aspects of the personality. The inability of the patient to reach an integration between his antisocial wishes and his moral standards causes a tension in his 'ego feeling' so that the patient hastes himself. The exaggerated guilt reaction maintains the split between persecuting and persecuted 'introjects'. Identifications with hated objects may make the task of ego integration very difficult. Such that the manic phase, the passivity is objectionably introvertive as projected, and the ego assumes the active role of the persecuting Superego against objects of condemnation in the outside world. Weiss points out that in paranoia, the ego does not cling strongly to the Superego, and the persecuting introjects, the Superego, is projected' in mania, however, the persecuted introject is projected. The paranoiac, by this projection, succeeds in preserving his narcissistic position, while the melancholic fails, the result of his inner persecuting may be self-destruction.

Recently, Bibring has summed up all the features that different kinds of depression have in common, including not only the depressions of a circular psychosis, but also the reactive depressions and depressions in the course of physical illness and in states of fatigue or exhaustion. A common factor is the lowering of self-esteem, the loss of a self-love, which, in melancholia, is intensified into self-hate. Bibring compares depression with states of depersonalization and boredom. In the mildly depressed person, there is not so much haste turned against the self as there is an exhaustion of the narcissistic supply of the self-love. The mildly depressed person is less inclined to kill himself than to let himself dies.

Frank in a lecture on "The Defensive Aspects of Depression" follows a line of thought similar to Bibring's. He compares unspecific depressions of the hibernation of animals—a defensive response to frustrating life conditions. Depression as some defence tines down the desires and expectations to a lower key, so that the shock of unavoidable frustration is reduced to a minimum.

The manic aspect of the manic-depressive psychosis has on the whole, elicited less attention on the part of the psychoanalysis than has the depressed aspect, probably because the manic patient does not so frequently seek therapeutic help. B., Lewin, in a monograph on "The Psychoanalysis of Elation" regards elation as a decence of denial against depression. During the analytic process, Lewin suggests, normal mourning increases insight into the self and terminate in a sense of heightening well-being, increased sexual potency, and capacity for work and sublimation. But elation or depression resist the testing of reality; they produce negative therapeutic reactions in the face of insight that cannot at the time be emotionally assimilated. The depressed and the elation ego are not trying to separate the true from the false, but the good from the bad; reality-testing is replaced by morality-testing. Lewin compares mania to sleep, in sleep the ego disappears; in mania the Superego vanishes. Sleep stems from oral satisfaction—the infant drops asleep when he is satiated with nursing at the mother's breast. But the manic patient is notoriously a poor sleeper, and he is haunted by 'the triad of oral wishes'—to devour, into be devoured, and to sleep. The wish-fear to be devoured transforms the wish to sleep into a fear of dying. The yearning for the gratifying maternal breast—the wish to sleep—may be transmuted into a desire for union with the Superego. In the artist this union is accomplished, as a result of the inspiration and actualization of this inspiration in the creative process, which satisfies both the Superego and the world of the artist's contemporaries.

In several papers on suicide, Zilboorg emphasizes that suicide is frequently in a manic-depressive psychosis. A number of suicides occur when the depressed person appears to be convalescing and all but recovered from his depressed state. In pathologic depressions the patient is identified with a person toward whom his feelings have been highly ambivalent. Zilboorg says of such a patient: He feels detached from reality and therefore experiences a sense of poverty of the Ego. The unconscious sadism originally directed against the object, reinforced by a sense of guilt, produced the singular phenomenon of the person becoming sadistic toward himself. Frequently, the identification with a close relative who died at the time when the patient went through the Oedipus conflict or puberty contributes to the suicidal tendency in later years. Zilboorg stresses the observation that suicide may occur in as variety of other psychopathological conditions on the basis of different motivations, such as spite and fear.

Nevertheless, there is increasing theoretical and empirical concern about the etiology and treatment of depression. This, nonetheless, mirrors recent confirmation that depressive disorders are a major health problem, as accountable for the diversity of conceptual models and empirical methods that have been used to explore intrapsychic, cognitive-phenomenological, social and behavioural aspects of depression. For which these are the approaching implications for the formulation and implementation of clinical interventions.

While psychosocial research has identified the etiologic role of stressful events and several promising psychological treatments have been formulated, a number of important research and clinical; issues have been identified. For instance, why do stressful life circumstances lead to depression among some persons but not others? How can one explain the finding that different psychosocial interventions appear to intercede upon the similar effects on depression? Toward what areas should prevention efforts are targeted?

Adler very early saw the importance of self-esteem in depression. More recently, Bibring (1953) signalled a truly radical break with the older theory in the psychoanalysis, by postulating that an undermining of self-esteem was the primary focus in depression, that it was principally to be understood as an ego-phenomenon, and only secondarily as a consequence of self-directed aggression.

It would be impossible to overestimate the significance of this shift in emphasis. In spite of Bibring's own protestations to the contrary, theories about the role of orality and aggression, is that, if self-esteem is the primary focus of depressions than does physiology. An ego-based theory of depression broadens the area of explanation from a purely 'intrapsychic battle field' to the entire range of social phenomena. Since the ego is rooted in social reality, since self-esteem is composed of social symbols and social motives, depression becomes a direct function of a cognitively apprehended symbolic world. Nothing less than a full sweep of cultural activity is bought into consideration in the single case of depression.

Hardly at all, that more recently a crucial sociological dimension was added to the theory of depression—again from within the psychoanalysis (Szasz, 1961), as in the classical formulation of depression, mourning and melancholic states, Freud had presented the psychoanalysis with a theoretical account with a model. (1917). He postulated that since the ego grows by developing responses to an identification with objects, the loss of an object was a threat to the ego. This, Freud reasoned, was the basic dynamic of mourning and melancholic states. The loss of an object in the real world meant a corresponding depletion in the ego: To relinquish a loved object was to subject oneself to a sometimes massive trauma. Freud theorized on the rather elaborate procedures that society sets up to ease this relinquishing of objects: The funeral rites, mourning rituals, and so on. There is nothing fundamentally wrong with Freud's view of depression. It explains a good deal. Its principal drawback is that it is used to explain too much.

Szasz's objection to the traditional view of depression is precisely its insistence on the predominant importance of object-loss in unleashing dependency cravings and hostility. He proposes to emend this by stressing that the loss of 'game' is fully as significant in depression as is the loss of an object. 'Game' in this context, is a series of norms of rules for significant action. And for the symbolic animal, there is nothing 'playful' about significance. Szasz said that . . . persons need not only human objects but also norms or rule—or, more generally—games that are worth playing. It is a matter of everyday observation that their object world might remain more or less intact. To account for this and similar events, it is necessary to consider the relationship of the ego or self to games. Otherwise, one is forced to reduce all manners of personal suffering to consideration of object relationships . . . Conversely, since loss of a real or external object implies the loss of a player from the game—unless a substitute who fits exactly can be found—such loss inevitably results in at least some changes in the game. It is thus, evident that the words 'player' and 'game' describe interdependent variables making dynamic steady states—for example, persons, families, societies, And so on (1961).

With this broadening out of traditional object-loss theory, there is no longer any valid pretense for keeping the phenomenon of depression within the realm of medicine. The psychoanalysis is fully linked as, with social science, since, as Szasz insists, objects and games are inseparably joined, self and society must be seen as a single phenomenon. People 'create' objects by acting according to social rules. They 'create' themselves as they create objects. Social rules are objects provide man with a staged drama of significance which is the theatre of his action. Man discovers himself by making appeal for his identity to the society in which he performs. To lose an object, then, is to lose someone to whom one has made appeal for self-validation. To lose a game is to lose a performance part in which identity is fabricated and sustained.

For the most part, this model represents the advanced theoretical cogitations of the psychiatric profession on a perplexing human phenomenon. This much must be said, as it is not easy to comprehend why anyone would opt out of life. It is understandable that we would be quick to look for some basic genetic taint, some stunted early development, that would mark such an individual off from others. But the matter is not quite simple: The fact is that some good propositions of depressed patients' have led mature and responsible lives; some have achieved notable success, financial and otherwise, in which of the imparting information was carried out without rigidly procedures, at best, we can comply with the best course to follow. We distort our vision if we use the theoretical proponents as to explain why these people become abysmally depressed.

It is amazing that human action could have been so consistently and thoroughly conceived in instinctual and compartmentalized terms. It is to the credit of some psychoanalysts that they themselves have begun to a breakout of their own inherited theories, and to range more broadly for an explanation of depression. This is part of the natural development of ego psychology. As the view of man as a cultural animal shaped by learning takes over from the older instinctual explanations, the way in clear for a full theoretical understanding, that if the ego is the basis for action, and if a warm feeling of self-value must pervade one's acts, then it is only a step to focussing on the really crucial dynamic of a breakdown in action, in the undermining of the individual's sense of self-value.

We take to note, that the answering to one common human problem is given by one thing in answering the need for sentiment: That as the object of primary value in the world of meaning (Hallowell, 1955). Data from anthropology support that nowhere on this once-vast globe had man been able to act unless he had a basic sentiment of self-value. Unless the individual feels worthwhile, and unless his actions are considered worthwhile and life grinds to a halt. Whole cultures have begun to expire in this way.

Behaviour models of depression are relatively new, compared to the Psychodynamic formulations that have just been presented. The behavioural perspective on psychopathology development later, but it is also true that behaviourists at first neglected the subject of depression. A few papers appeared in the late sixties (Burgess, 1968 and Lazarus, 1968), but they were highly speculative and lacked rigorous definition or analysis of depressive behaviour.

The behavioural perspective emphasizes the analysis of psychopathology in term s of observable behaviour in relation to preceding and consequential events in the environment—controlling stimuli and reinforcement consequences. Yet a behavioural definition of depression has remained rather elusive. Depression does not refer to a single response class, at least, as it has traditionally been defined, its primary symptom is a state of subjective distress. It is often the case that depressed persons do not exhibit any marked changes in overt behaviour despite their considerable distress and sense of personal inadequacy. As a group, depressed do not share of personal inadequacy, of specific behavioural excessive or deficiencies. Furthermore, depression often seems to involve a change in behaviour without any apparent change in the conditions that have previously maintained them (Costello, 1972). For instance, upon leaning that his former girl friend back home has become engaged to someone else, a college student might stop eating regularly, withdraw from his friends on campus, and neglect his studying.

Of necessity, the two most influential behavioural formulations of depression (Lewinsohn, Miller, Roselling and Seligman) involved the introduction of some concepts that go substantially beyond the usual analysis of reinforcement contingencies. Consistent with more general trends in psychology, they both also were later modified to include an emphasis on cognition.

Lewinsohn developed a model of depression that was an extension of an earlier model presented by Ferster (1973, 1974), in which the central features of the disorder were identified as a reduction in the emission of positively reenforced behaviour. A major innovation in the Lewinsohn formulation was its emphasis on the concept of total amounts of response-contingently positive reinforcement 'reconposre'. The emission of some given adaptation is seen as not being merely a function of specific rewards available for it. Rather, it is also a function of the overall amount of positive reenforcement that is available as consequences for any available response. It is not a matter of this reinforcement being available but of its being contingent upon the person making a response, as according to Lewinsohn, a retired person who receives money without having to work may emit less adaptive behaviour and become depressed.

Developments in the interactional description of schizophrenia have not been parallelled in the area of depression. As yet, concepts such as pseudo mutuality, double-bind, schism, and skew have found no counterparts. Kubler and Scotland (1964) have argued, that, emotional disturbance, even the most severe, cannot be understood unless the field in which it develops and exists is examined. The manifestation of the difficulty in the disturbed individual has meant upon something uncertain, but variably indeterminable, depending on aspects of the field. The significant aspects of the field are usually interpersonal. Yet the study of depression has focussed on the individual and his behaviour out of his interactional context. To a large degree, the depressed person's monotonously reiterate complaints and self accusations, and his provocative and often annoying behaviour has distracted investigators from considerations of his environment and the role it may play in the maintenance of his behaviour. The possibility that the characteristic pattern of depressed behaviour might be interwoven has seldom been explored.

The accredited categorical priorities are to clarify the bewildering number of interrelated observations uncovered by psychoanalytic exploration led to the development of a model of the structure of the psychic system. Three functional systems are distinguished that are conveniently designated as the id, ego, and Superego.

The first system refers to the sexual and aggressive tendencies that arise from the body, as distinguished from the mind. Freud called these tendencies Triebe, which literally means 'drives,' but which is often inaccurately translated as 'instincts' to indicate their innate character. These inherent drives claim immediate satisfaction, which is experienced as pleasurable; the id thus is dominated by the pleasure principle. In his later writings, Freud tended more toward psychological rather than biological conceptualization of the drives.

How the conditions for satisfaction are to be brought about is the task of the second system, the ego, which is the domain of such functions as perception, thinking, and motor control that can accurately assess environmental conditions. In orders fulfill its function of adaptation, or reality testing, the ego must be capable of enforcing the postponement of satisfaction of the instinctual impulses originating in the id. To defend itself against unacceptable impulses, the ego develops specific psychic means, known as defence mechanisms. These include repression, the exclusion of impulses from conscious awareness; projection, the process of ascribing to others one's own unacknowledged desires; and reaction formation, the establishment of a pattern of behaviour directly in opposition to strong unconscious needs. Such defence mechanisms are put into operation whenever anxiety signals a danger that the original unacceptable impulses may reemerge.

Such that an id impulse becomes unacceptable, not only as a result of a temporary need for postponing its satisfaction until suitable reality conditions can be found, but more often because of a prohibition imposed on the individual by others, originally the parents. The totality of these demands and prohibitions constitutes the major content of the third system, the Superego, the function of which is to control the ego in accordance with the internalized standards of parental figures. If the demands of the Superego are not fulfilled, the person may feel shame or guilt. Because the Superego, in Freudian theory, originates in the struggle to overcome the Oedipal conflict, it has a power akin to an instinctual drive, is in part unconscious, and can give rise feelings of guilt not justified by any conscious transgression. The ego, having to mediate among the demands of the id, the Superego, and the outside world, may not be strong enough to reconcile these conflicting forces. The more the ego is impeded in its development because of being enmeshed in its earlier conflicts, called fixations or complexes, or the more it reverts to earlier satisfactions and archaic modes of functioning, known as regression, the greater is the likelihood of succumbing to these pressures. Unable to function normally, it can maintain its limited control and integrity only at the price of symptom formation, in which the tensions are expressed in neurotic symptoms.

The Freudian terminological representations impose upon the id; is respondent to in psychoanalytic theory, one of the three basic elements of personality, the others being the ego and the Superego? The id can be equated with the unconscious of common usage, which is the reservoir of the instinctual drives of the individual, including biological urges, wishes, and affective motives. The id is dominated by the pleasure principle, through which the individual is pressed for immediate gratification of his or her desires. In strict Freudian theory the energy behind the instinctual drives of the id is known as the libido, a generalized force, basically sexual in nature, through which the sexual and psychosexual nature of the individual finds expression.

Ego, in a psychoanalysis, is the term denoting the central part of the personality structure that deals with reality and is influenced by social forces. According to the psychoanalytic theories developed by Sigmund Freud, the ego constitutes one of the three basic provinces of the mind, where each as the id and the Superego. Formation of the ego begins at birth in the first encounters with the external world of people and things. The ego learns to modify behaviour by controlling those impulses that are socially unacceptable. Its role is that of the mediator between unconscious impulses and acquired social and personal standards.

As well, the Superego, in psychoanalytic theory is one of the three basic constituents of the mind, the others being the id and the ego. As postulated by Sigmund Freud, the term designates the element of the mind that, in normal personalities, automatically modifies and inhibits those instinctual impulses or drives of the id that tend to produce antisocial actions and thoughts. An id impulse becomes unacceptable, not only as a result of a temporary need for postponing its satisfaction until suitable reality conditions can be found, but more often because of a prohibition imposed on the individual by others, originally the parents. The totality of these demands and prohibitions constitutes the major content of the third system, the Superego, the function of which is to control the ego in accordance with the internalized standards of parental figures. If the demands of the Superego are not fulfilled, the person may feel shame or guilt. Because the Superego, in Freudian theory, originates in the struggle to overcome the Oedipal conflict, it has a power akin to an instinctual drive, is in part unconscious, and can give rise feelings of guilt not justified by any conscious transgression. The ego, having to mediate among the demands of the id, the Superego, and the outside world, may not be strong enough to reconcile these conflicting forces. The more the ego is impeded in its development because of being enmeshed in its earlier conflicts, called fixations or complexes, or the more it reverts to earlier satisfactions and archaic modes of functioning, known as regression, the greater is the likelihood of succumbing to these pressures. It can maintain its limited control and integrity only at the price of symptom formation, in which the tensions are expressed in neurotic symptoms.

It is, nonetheless, according to psychoanalytic theory, the Superego develops as the child gradually and unconsciously adopts the values and standards, first of his or her parents, and later of the social environment. According to modern Freudian psychoanalysts, the Superego includes the positive ego, or conscious self-image, or ego ideal, that each individual develops.

It is, nonetheless, those relations, in the psychoanalysis, are the emotional relations between subject and object, through a process of identification, are believed to constitute the developing ego. In this context, the word object refers to any person or thing, or representational aspect of them, with which the subject forms an intense emotional relationship.

Object relations were first described by German psychoanalyst Karl Abraham in an influential paper, published in 1924. In the paper he developed the ideas as the founder of psychoanalysis, Sigmund Freud, on infantile sexuality and the development of the libido. Object-relations theory has become one of the central themes of post-Freudian Psychoanalysis, particularly through the writings of British psychoanalysts Melanie Klein, Ronald Fairbairn, and Donald Winnicott, all deeply influenced by Abraham. They have each developed distinctly, though complementary, approaches to analysis, evolving theories of personal development based on early parental attachments.

People with depression often experience feelings of worthlessness, helplessness, guilt, and self-blame. They may interpret a minor failing on their part as a sign of incompetence or interpret minor criticism as condemnation. Some depressed people complain of being spiritually or morally dead. The mirror seems to reflect someone ugly and repulsive. Even a competent and decent person may feel deficient, cruel, stupid, phony, or guilty of having deceived others. People with major depression may experience such extreme emotional pain that they consider or attempt suicide. At least 15 percent of seriously depressed people commit suicide, and many more attempt it.

Bipolar disorder is much less common than depression. In North America and Europe, about 1 percent of people experience bipolar disorder during their lives. Rates of bipolar disorder are similar throughout the world. In comparison, at least 8 percent of people experience serious depression during their lives. Bipolar disorder affects men and women about equally and is somewhat more common in higher socioeconomic classes. At least 15 percent of people with bipolar disorder commit suicide. This rate roughly equals the rate for people with major depression, the most severe form of depression.

Depression, of a psychology mode, is an illness in which a person experiences deep, unshakable sadness and diminished interest in nearly all activities. People also use the term depression to describe the temporary sadness, loneliness, or blues that everyone feels from time to time. In contrast to normal sadness, severe depression, also called major depression, can dramatically impair a person's ability to function in social situations and at work. People with major depression often have feelings of despair, hopelessness, and worthlessness, as well as thoughts of committing suicide.

Depression can take several other forms. In bipolar disorder, sometimes called manic-depressive illness, a person's mood swings back and forth between depression and mania. People with seasonal affective disorder typically suffer from depression only during autumn and winter, when there are fewer hours of daylight. In dysthymia, people's feel depressed, had low self-esteem, and concentrate poorly most of the time—often for a period of years—but their symptoms are milder than in major depression. Some people with dysthymia experience occasional episodes of major depression. Mental health professionals use the term clinical depression to refer to any of the above forms of depression.

Surveys indicate that people commonly view depression as a sign of personal weakness, but psychiatrists and psychologists view it as a real illness. In the United States, the National Institute of Mental Health has estimated that depression cost's society many billions of dollars each year, mostly in lost work time.

Depression is one of the most common mental illnesses. At least 8 percent of adults in the United States experience serious depression at some point during their lives, and estimates range as high as 17 percent. The illness affects all people, regardless of sex, race, ethnicity, or socioeconomic standing. However, women are two to three times more likely than men to suffer from depression. Experts disagree on the reason for this difference. Some cite differences in hormones, and others point to the stress caused by society's expectations of women.

Depression occurs in all parts of the world, although the pattern of symptoms can vary. The prevalence of depression in other countries varies widely, from 1.5 percent of people in Taiwan to 19 percent of people in Lebanon. Some researchers believe methods of gathering data on depression account for different rates.

A number of large-scale studies indicate that depression rates have increased worldwide over the past several decades. Furthermore, younger generations are experiencing depression at an earlier age than did previous generations. Social scientists have proposed many explanations, including changes in family structure, urbanization, and reduced cultural and religious influences.

Although it may appear at anytime, from childhood to old age, depression usually begins during a person's 20s or 30s. The illness may come on slowly, then deepen gradually over months or years. On the other hand, it may erupt suddenly in a few weeks or days. A person who develops severe depression may appear so confuse, frightened, and unbalance that observers speak of a 'nervous breakdown.' However it begins, and depression causes serious changes in a person's feelings and outlook. A person with major depression feels sad nearly every day and may cry often. People, work, and activities that used to bring them pleasure no longer do.

Symptoms of depression can vary by age. In younger children, depression may include physical complaints, such as stomachaches and headaches, as well as irritability, 'moping around,' social withdrawal, and changes in eating habits. They may feel unenthusiastic about school and other activities. In adolescents, common symptoms include sad mood, sleep disturbances, and lack of energy. Elderly people with depression usually restricted their complaints for being physical rather than prone to or moved by emotional problems, which sometimes leads doctors to misdiagnose the illness.

Symptoms of depression can also vary by culture. In some cultures, depressed people may not experience sadness or guilt but may complain of physical problems. In Mediterranean cultures, for example, depressed people may complain of headaches or nerves. In Asian cultures they may complain of weakness, fatigue, or imbalance.

If left untreated, an episode of major depression typically lasts eight or nine months. About 85 percent of people who experience one bout of depression will experience future episodes.

Depression usually alters a person's appetite, sometimes increasing it, but usually reducing it. Sleep habits frequently become foreign, such that things are construed for being different, these differences, nonetheless, are needs that change is made among its diversities in change. As to modify as to avoid an extreme or keep within bounds, the new proposals, as not excessive in degree, amount, or intensity, but to modificational divergencies, in among the changes of such mutational permutations are as well. People with depression may oversleep or, more commonly, sleep for fewer hours. A depressed person might go to sleep at midnight, sleep restlessly, then wake up at 5:00 a.m. feeling tired and blue. For many depressed people, early morning is the saddest time of the day.

Depression also changes one's energy level. Some depressed people may be restless and agitated, engaging in fidgety movements and pacing. Others may feel sluggish and inactive, experiencing great fatigue, lack of energy, and a feeling of being worn out or carrying a heavy burden. Depressed people may also have difficulty thinking, poor concentration, and problems with memory.

People with depression often experience feelings of worthlessness, helplessness, guilt, and self-blame. They may interpret a minor failing on their part as a sign of incompetence or interpret minor criticism as condemnation. Some depressed people complain of being spiritually or morally dead. The mirror seems to reflect someone ugly and repulsive. Even a competent and decent person may feel deficient, cruel, stupid, phony, or guilty of having deceived others. People with major depression may experience such extreme emotional pain that they consider or attempt suicide. At least 15 percent of seriously depressed people commit suicide, and many more attempt it.

In some cases, people with depression may experience psychotic symptoms, such as delusions (false beliefs) and hallucinations (false sensory perceptions). Psychotic symptoms indicate an especially severe illness. Compared to other depressed people, those with psychotic symptoms have longer hospital stays, and after leaving, they are more likely to be moody and unhappy. They are also more likely to commit suicide.

Some depressions seem to come out of the blue, even when things are going well. Others seem to have an obvious cause: a marital conflict, financial difficulty, or some personal failure. Yet many people with these problems do not become deeply depressed. Most psychologists believe depression results from an interaction between stressful life events and a person's biological and psychological vulnerabilities.

Clinical depression is one of the most common forms of mental illness. Although depression can be treated with psychotherapy, many scientists believe there are biological causes for the disease. In this June 1998 Scientific American article, Neurobiologist Charles B. Nemeroff discusses the connection between biochemical changes in the brain and depression.

Depression runs in families. By studying twins, researchers have found evidence of a strong genetic influence in depression. Genetically identical twins raised in the same environment are three times more likely to have depression in common than fraternal twins, who have only about half of their genes in common. In addition, identical twins are five times more likely to have bipolar disorder in common. These findings suggest that vulnerability to depression and bipolar disorder can be inherited. Adoption studies have provided more evidence of a genetic role in depression. These studies show that children of depressed people are vulnerable to depression even when raised by adoptive parents.

Genes may influence depression by causing abnormal activity in the brain. Studies have shown that certain brain chemicals called neurotransmitters play an important role in regulating moods and emotions. Neurotransmitters involved in depression include norepinephrine, dopamine, and serotonin. Research in the 1960s suggested that depression result from lower than normal levels of these neurotransmitters in parts of the brain. Support for this theory came from the effects of antidepressant drugs, which work by increasing the levels of neurotransmitters involved in depression. However, later studies have discredited this simple explanation and have suggested a more complex relationship between neurotransmitter levels and depression.

An imbalance of hormones may also play a role in depression. Many depressed people have higher than normal levels of hydrocortisone (cortisol), a hormone secreted by the adrenal gland in response to stress. In addition, an underactive or overactive thyroid gland can lead to depression.

Psychological theories of depression focuses on the way people think and behave. In a 1917 essay, Austrian psychoanalyst Sigmund Freud explained melancholia, or major depression, as a response to loss—either real loss, such as the death of a spouse, or symbolic loss, such as the failure to achieve an important goal. Freud

believed that a person's unconscious anger over loss weakens the ego, resulting in self-hate and self-destructive behaviour.

Cognitive theories of depression emphasize the role of irrational thought processes. American psychiatrist Aaron Beck proposed that depressed people tend to view themselves, their environment, and the future in a negative light because of errors in thinking. These errors include focussing on the negative aspects of any situation, misinterpreting facts in negative ways, and blaming themselves for any misfortune. In Beck's view, people learn these self-defeating ways of looking at the world during early childhood. This negative thinking makes situations seem much worse than they really are and increases the risk of depression, especially in stressful situations.

In support of this cognitive view, people with 'depressive' personality traits appear to be more vulnerable than others to actual depression. Examples of depressive personality traits include gloominess, pessimism, introversion, self-criticism, excessive skepticism and criticism of others, deep feelings of inadequacy, and excessive brooding and worrying. In addition, people who regularly behave in dependent, hostile, and impulsive ways appear at greater risk for depression.

American psychologist Martin Seligman proposed those depression stems from 'learned helplessness,' an acquired belief that one cannot control the outcome of events. In this view, prolonged exposure to uncontrollable and inescapable events leads to apathy, pessimism, and loss of motivation. An adaptation of this theory by American psychologist Lynn Abramson and her colleagues argues that depression result not only from helplessness, but also hopelessness. The hopelessness theory attributes depression to a pattern of negative thinking in which people blame themselves for negative life events, view the causes of those events as permanent, and overgeneralize specific weaknesses as applying to many areas of their life.

Psychologists agree that stressful experiences can trigger depression in people who are predisposed to the illness. For example, the death of a loved one may trigger depression. Psychologists usually distinguish true depression from grief, a normal process of mourning a loved one who has died. Other stressful experiences may include divorce, pregnancy, the loss of a job, and even childbirth. About 20 percent of women experience an episode of depression, known as postpartum depression, after having a baby. In addition, people with serious physical illnesses or disabilities often develop depression.

People who live through child abuse appear more vulnerable to depression than others. So, too, do people living under chronically stressful conditions, such as single mothers with many children and little or no support from friends or relatives.

Despite the availability of effective treatment, most depressive disorders go untreated and undiagnosed. Studies indicate that general physicians fail to recognize depression in their patients at least half of the time. In addition, many doctors and patients view depression in elderly people as a normal part of aging, even though treatment for depression in older people is usually very effective.

Up to 70 percent of people with depression respond to antidepressant drugs. These medications appear to work by altering the levels of serotonin, norepinephrine, and other neurotransmitters in the brain. They generally take at least two to three weeks to become effective. Doctors cannot predict which type of antidepressant drug will work best for any particular person, so depressed people may need to try several types. Antidepressant drugs are not addictive, but they may produce unwanted side effects. To avoid a relapse, people usually must continue taking the medication for several months after their symptoms improve.

Commonly used antidepressant drugs fall into three major classes: tricyclics, Monoamine oxidase inhibitors (MAO inhibitors), and selective serotonin reuptake inhibitors (SSRIs). Tricyclics, named for their three-ring chemical structure, include amitriptyline (Elavil), imipramine (Tofanil), desipramine (Norpramin), doxepin (Sinequan), and nortriptyline (Pamelor). Side effects of tricyclics may include drowsiness, dizziness upon standing, blurred vision, nausea, insomnia, constipation, and a dry mouth.

MAO inhibitors include isocarboxazid (Marplan), phenelzine (Nardil), and tranylcypromine (Parnate). People who take MAO inhibitors must follow a diet that excludes tyramine—a substance found in wine, beer, some cheeses, and many fermented foods—to avoid a dangerous rise in blood pressure. In addition, MAO inhibitors have many of the same side effects as tricyclics.

Selective serotonin reuptake inhibitors include Fluoxetine (Prozac), sertraline (Zoloft), and paroxetine (Paxil). These drugs generally produce fewer and milder side effects than do other types of antidepressants, although SSRIs may cause anxiety, insomnia, drowsiness, headaches, and sexual dysfunction. Some patients have alleged that Prozac causes violent or suicidal behaviour in a small number of cases, but the US Food and Drug Administration has failed to substantiate this claim.

Prozac became the most widely used antidepressant in the world soon after its introduction in the late 1980s by drug manufacturer Eli Lilly and Company. Many people find Prozac extremely effective in lifting depression. In addition, some people have reported that Prozac actually transforms their personality by increasing their self-confidence, optimism, and energy level. However, mental health professionals have expressed serious ethical concerns over Prozac's use as a 'personality enhancer,' especially among people without clinical depression.

Doctors often prescribe lithium carbonates, a natural mineral salt, to treat people with bipolar disorder. People often take lithium during periods of a normal mood, in that to delay or even prevent subsequent mood swings. Side effects of lithium include nausea, stomach upset, vertigo, and frequent urination.

Studies have shown that short-term psychotherapy can relieve mild to moderate depression as effectively as antidepressant drugs. Unlike medication, psychotherapy produces no physiological side effects. In addition, depressed people treated with psychotherapy appear less likely to experience a relapse than those treated only with antidepressant medication. However, psychotherapy usually takes longer to produce benefits.

There are many kinds of psychotherapy. Cognitive-behavioural therapy assumes that depression stem from negative, often irrational thinking of, more or less, for one's concerning about the nonrealistic or impractical negativity, as to one's future. In this type of therapy, a person learns to understand and eventually eliminate those habits of negative thinking. In interpersonal therapy, the therapist helps a person resolve problems in relationships with others that may have caused the depression. The subsequent improvement in social relationships and support helps alleviate the depression. Psychodynamic therapy views depression as the result of internal, unconscious conflicts. Psychodynamic therapists focus on a person's past experiences and the resolution of childhood conflicts. The psychoanalysis is an example of this type of therapy. Critics long since the term of Psychodynamic therapy was to argue that its effectiveness is scientifically unproven.

Electroconvulsive therapy (ECT) can often relieve severe depression in people what is to respond to antidepressant medication and psychotherapy. In this type of therapy, a low-voltage electric current is passed through the brain for one to two seconds to produce a controlled seizure. Patients usually receive six to ten ECT treatments over several weeks. ECT remains controversial because it can cause disorientation and memory loss. Nevertheless, research has found it highly effective in alleviating severe depression.

For milder cases of depression, regular aerobic exercise may improve the mood as effectively as psychotherapy or medication. In addition, some research indicates that dietary modifications can influence one's mood by changing the level of serotonin in the brain.

An imbalance of hormones may also play a role in depression. Many depressed people have higher than normal levels of hydrocortisone (cortisol), a hormone secreted by the adrenal gland in response to stress. In addition, an underactive or overactive thyroid gland can lead to depression.

A variety of medical conditions can cause depression. These include dietary deficiencies in vitamin B6, vitamin B12, and folic acid, degenerative neurological disorders, such as Alzheimer's disease and Huntington's disease; strokes in the frontal part of the brain; and certain viral infections, such as hepatitis and mononucleosis. Certain medications, such as steroids, may also cause depression.

Psychological theories of depression focuses on the way people think and behave. In a 1917 essay, Austrian psychoanalyst Sigmund Freud explained melancholia, or major depression, as a response to loss—either real loss, such as the death of a spouse, or symbolic loss, such as the failure to achieve an important goal. Freud believed that a person's unconscious anger over loss weakens the ego, resulting in self-hate and self-destructive behaviour.

Cognitive theories of depression emphasize the role of irrational thought processes. American psychiatrist Aaron Beck proposed that depressed people tend to view themselves, their environment, and the future in a negative light because of errors in thinking. These errors include focussing on the negative aspects of any situation, misinterpreting facts in negative ways, and blaming themselves for any misfortune. In Beck's view, people learn these self-defeating ways of looking at the world during early childhood. This negative thinking makes situations seem much worse than they really are and increases the risk of depression, especially in stressful situations.

In support of this cognitive view, people with 'depressive' personality traits appear to be more vulnerable than others to actual depression. Examples of depressive personality traits include gloominess, pessimism, introversion, self-criticism, excessive skepticism and criticism of others, deep feelings of inadequacy, and excessive brooding and worrying. In addition, people who regularly behave in dependent, hostile, and impulsive ways appear at greater risk for depression.

American psychologist Martin Seligman proposed that depressions stem from 'learned helplessness,' an acquired belief that one cannot control the outcome of events. In this view, prolonged exposure to uncontrollable and inescapable events leads to apathy, pessimism, and loss of motivation. An adaptation of this theory by American psychologist Lynn Abramson and her colleagues had argued that depression result not only from helplessness but also hopelessness. The hopelessness theory attributes depression to a pattern of negative thinking in which people blame themselves for negative life events, view the causes of those events as permanent, and overgeneralize specific weaknesses as applying to many areas of their life.

Many patients in the last stages of a terminal disease elect to dispense with medical treatments aimed at curing their disease in favour of hospice care. Usually provided in a patient's home by health professionals and trained volunteers, hospice care seeks to relieve pain and symptoms and provide emotional support for patients and their families.

Should the suffering and dying patients be allowed to end their own lives with the aid of a physician? Easing the suffering of terminally ill patients is one way to avoid this difficult problem, but supporters of physician-assisted suicide argue that this is not always possible and that patients should have the option of assisted suicide. Opponents charge that assisted suicide will lead to the active killing of patients. In this Point/Counterpoint, attorney Wesley J. Smith of the International Anti-Euthanasia Task Force presents his case against physician-assisted suicide. Margaret P. Battin, professor of philosophy at the University of Utah in Salt Lake City, counters with arguments for allowing physician-assisted suicide.

Death occurs at several levels. Somatic death is the death of the organism as a whole; it usually precedes the death of the individual organs, cells, and parts of cells. Somatic death is marked by cessation of heartbeat, respiration, movement, reflexes, and brain activity. The precise time of somatic death is sometimes difficult to determine, however, because the symptoms of such transient states as coma, faint, and trances closely resemble the signs of death.

After somatic death, several changes occur that are used to determine the time and circumstances of death. Algor mortis, the cooling of the body after death, is primarily influenced by the temperature of the immediate environment. Rigormortis, the stiffening of the skeletal muscles, begin from five to ten hours after death and disappears after three or four days. Livor mortis, the reddish-blue discolouration that occurs on the underside of the body, results from the settling of the blood. Clotting of the blood begins shortly after death, as does the autolysis, the death of the cells. Putrefaction, the decomposition that follows, is caused by the action of enzymes and bacteria.

Organs of the body die at different rates. Although brain cells may survive for no more than 5 minutes after somatic death, those of the hearts can survive for about 15 minutes and those of the kidney for about 30 minutes. For this reason, organs can be removed from a recently dead body and transplanted into a living person.

Ideas about what constitutes death change with different cultures and in different epochs. In Western societies, death has traditionally been seen as the departure of the soul from the body. In this tradition, the essence of being human is independent of physical properties. Because the soul has no corporeal manifestation, its departure cannot be seen or otherwise objectively determined; hence, in this tradition, the cessation of breathing has been taken as the sign of death.

In modern times, death has been thought to occur when the vital functions cease—breathing and circulation (as evidenced by the beating of the heart). This view has been challenged, however, as medical advances have made it possible to sustain respiration and cardiac functioning through mechanical means. Thus, more recently, the concept of brain death has gained acceptance. In this view, the irreversible loss of brain activity is the sign that death has occurred. A majority of the states in the United States had accepted brain death as an essential sign of death by the late 1980s.

Even the concept of brain death has been challenged in recent years, because a person can lose all capacity for higher mental functioning while lower-brain functions, such as spontaneous respiration, continue. For this reason, some authorities now argue that death should be considered the loss of the capacity for consciousness or social interaction. The sign of death, according to this view, is the absence of activity in the higher centres of the brain, principally the neocortex.

Society's conception of death is of more than academic interest. Rapidly advancing medical technology has raised moral questions and introduced new problems in defining death legally. Among the issues being debated are the following: Who shall decide the criteria for death—physicians, legislatures, or each person for him or herself? Is advancement of the moment of death by cutting off artificial support morally and legally permissible? Given by increasing intensities that people, irrespectively, have the rights to demand that extraordinary measures be stopped so that they may die in peace? Can the next of kin or a legal guardian act for the comatose dying person under such circumstances? All these questions have acquired new urgency with the advent of human tissue transplantation. The need for organs must be weighed against the rights of the dying donor.

As a result of such questions, a number of groups have sought to establish an individual's 'right to die,' particularly through the legal means of 'living wills' in which an individual confers the right to withdrawal of life-sustaining treatment upon family members or legal figures. By 1991, 40 states in the United States had recognized the validity of some form of living-will arrangement, although complex questions remain to be settled in all these instances.

The needs of dying patients and their families have also received renewed attention since the 1960s. Thanatologists (those who study the surroundings and inner experiences of persons near death) have identified several stages through which dying persons go: denial and isolation (No, not me!); anger, rage, envy, and resentment (Why me?); bargaining (If I am good, then can I live?); depression (What's the use?); and acceptance. Most authorities believe that these stages do not occur in any predictable order and may be intermingled with feelings of hope, anguish, and terror.

Like dying patients, bereaved families and friends go through stages of denial and acceptance. Bereavement, however, more typically does follow a regular sequence, often beginning before a loved one dies. Such anticipatory grief can help to defuse later distress. The next stage of bereavement, after the death has occurred, is likely to be longer and more severe if the death was unexpected. During this phase, mourners typically cry, have difficulty sleeping, and lose their appetites. Some may feel alarmed, angry, or aggrieved at being deserted. Later, the grief may turn to depression, which sometimes occurs when conventional forms of social support have ceased and outsiders are no longer offering help and solace; loneliness may ensue. Finally, the survivor begins to feel less troubled, regains energy, and restores ties to others.

Care of terminally ill patients may take place in the home but more commonly occurs in hospitals or more specialized institutions called hospices. Such care demands special qualities on the part of physicians and thanatologists, who must deal with their own fear of death before they can adequately comfort the dying. Although physicians commonly disagree, the tenet that most patients should be told that they are dying is now widely accepted. This must, of course, be done with tact and caring. Many persons, even children, know they are dying anyway; helping them to bring it out into the open avoids pretense and encourages the expression of honest feelings. Given safety and security, the informed dying patient can achieve an appropriate death, one marked by dignity and serenity. Concerned therapists or clergy can assist in this achievement simply by allowing the patient to talk about feelings, thoughts, and memories, or by acting as a substitute for family and friends who may grow anxious when the dying patient speaks of death

People who had experienced child abuse appear more vulnerable to depression than others. So, too, do people living under chronically stressful conditions, such as single mothers with many children and little or no support from friends or relatives.

Depression typically cannot be shaken or willed away. An episode must therefore run its course until it weakens either on its own or with treatment. Depression can be treated effectively with antidepressant drugs, psychotherapy, or a combination of both.

Despite the availability of effective treatment, most depressive disorders go untreated and undiagnosed. Studies indicate that general physicians fail to recognize depression in their patients at least half of the time. In addition, many doctors and patients view depression in elderly people as a normal part of aging, even though treatment for depression in older people is usually very effective.

Different therapies may shorten, delay, or even prevent the extreme moods caused by bipolar disorder. Lithium carbonates, a natural mineral salt, can help control both mania and depression in bipolar disorder. The drug generally takes two to three weeks to become effective. People with bipolar disorder may take lithium during periods of relatively normal moods to delay or prevent subsequent episodes of mania or depression. Common side effects of lithium include nausea, increased thirst and urination, vertigo, loss of appetite, and muscle weakness. In addition, long-term use can impair functioning of the kidneys. For this reason, doctors do not prescribe lithium to bipolar patients with kidney disease. Many people find the side effects so unpleasant that they stop taking the medication, which often results in a relapse.

From 20 to 40 percent of people do not respond to lithium therapy. For these people, two anticonvulsant drugs may help dampen severe manic episodes: carbamazepine (Tegretol) and valproate (Depakene). The use of traditional antidepressants to treat bipolar disorder carries risks of triggering a manic episode or a rapid-cycling pattern.

Object Relations in the psychoanalysis, are the emotional relations between subject and object, from within the process of identification, are believed to constitute the developing ego. In this context, the word object refers to any person or thing, or representational aspect of them, with which the subject forms an intense emotional relationship.

The occurring occasion attributed object relations to whether having actual, distinct or existently happening, but if not that, then its first description came by the German psychoanalyst Karl Abraham as a published paper in 1924. In the paper he developed the ideas of the founder of psychoanalysis, Sigmund Freud, on infantile sexuality and the development of the libido. The libido (Latin libidos, meaning 'pleasure' or 'lust'), in psychoanalytic theory, thereon, accumulatively gathers the energy of the id or major portion of the unconscious mind, responsible for acts of creation. According to the theories of Sigmund Freud, the libido is the sex instinct, and artistic creation is an expression of the sex instinct that has been rechannelled. The Swiss psychiatrist Carl Jung rejected the sexual basis of the libido, believing that the force behind drives to act and create is merely an expression of the general will to live. Object Relations, in the psychoanalysis, the emotional relations between subject and object, through a process of identification are believed to constitute the developing ego. In this context, the word object refers to any person or thing, or representational aspect of them, with which the subject forms an intense emotional relationship. Object relations were first described by German psychoanalyst Karl Abraham in an influential paper, published in 1924. In the paper he developed the ideas of the founder of psychoanalysis, Sigmund Freud, on infantile sexuality and the development of the libido. Object-relations theory has become one of the central themes of post-Freudian Psychoanalysis, particularly through the writings of British psychoanalysts Melanie Klein, Ronald Fairbairn, and Donald Winnicott, all deeply influenced by Abraham. They have each developed distinctly, though complementary, approaches to analysis, evolving theories of personal development based on early parental attachments.

Object-relations theory has become one of the central themes of post-Freudian Psychoanalysis, particularly through the writings of British psychoanalysts Melanie Klein, Ronald Fairbairn, and Donald Winnicott, all deeply influenced by Abraham. They have each developed distinctly, though complementary, approaches to analysis, evolving theories of personal development based on early parental attachments.

There are many kinds of psychotherapy. Cognitive-behavioural therapy assumes that depression stem from negative, and often capable of being though about, however, irrational thinking about oneself and one's future. In this type of therapy, a person learns to understand and eventually eliminate those habits of negative thinking. In interpersonal therapy, the therapist helps a person resolve problems in relationships with others that may have caused the depression. The subsequent improvement in social relationships and support helps alleviate the depression. Psychodynamic therapy views depression as the result of internal, unconscious conflicts. Psychodynamic therapists focus on a person's past experiences and the resolution of childhood conflicts. A psychoanalysis is an example of this type of therapy. Critics of long-term Psychodynamic therapy argue that its effectiveness is scientifically unproven

Psychologists and Neurobiologists sometimes debate whether ego-damaging experiences and self-deprecating thoughts or biological processes cause depression. The mind, however, does not exist without the brain. Considerable evidence indicates that regardless of the initial triggers, the final common pathways to depression involve biochemical changes in the brain. That of these changes that ultimately give rise to deep sadness and the other salient characteristics of depression. The full extent of those alterations is still being explored, but in the past few decades—and especially in the past several years—efforts to identify them have progressed rapidly.

One subgoal is to distinguish features that vary among depressed individuals. For instance, perhaps decreased activity of a specific neurotransmitter (a molecule that carries a signal between nerve cells) is central in some people, but in others, overactivity of a hormonal system is more influential (hormones circulate in the blood and can act far from the site of their secretion). A related goal is to identify simple biological markers able to indicate which profile fits a given patient; those markers could consist of, say, elevated or reduced levels of selected molecules in the blood or changes in some easy visualizable areas of the brain.

After testing a depressed patient for these markers, a psychiatrist could, in theory, prescribe a medication tailored to that individual's specific biological anomaly, much as a general practitioner can run a quick strep test for a patient complaining of a sore throat and then prescribe an appropriate antibiotic if the test is positive. Today psychiatrists have to choose antidepressant medications by intuition and trial and error, a situation that can put suicidal patients in jeopardy for weeks or months until the right compound is selected. (Often psychotherapy is needed as well, but it usually is not sufficient by itself, especially if the depression is fairly severe.)

Improving treatment is critically important. Although today's antidepressants have fewer side effects than those of old and can be extremely helpful in many cases, depression continues to exact a huge toll in suffering, lost lives and reduced productivity.

Beyond the pain and disability depression brings, it is a potential killer. As many as 15 percent of those who suffer from depression or bipolar disorders commit suicide each year. In 1996 the Centre for Disease Control and Prevention listed suicide as the ninth leading cause of death in the US (slightly behind infection with the AIDS virus), taking the lives of 30,862 people. Most investigators, however, believe this number is a gross underestimate. Many people who kill themselves do so in a way that allows another diagnosis to be listed on the death certificate, so that families can receive insurance benefits or avoid embarrassment. Further, some fraction of automobile accidents unquestionably is concealed suicide.

Accumulating findings indicate that severe depression also heightens the risk of dying after a heart attack or stroke. And it often reduces the quality of life for cancer patients and might reduce survival time.

Geneticists have provided some of the oldest proof of a biological component to depression in many people. Depression and manic-depression frequently run in families. Thus, close blood relatives (children, siblings and parents) of patients with severe depressive or bipolar disorder is much more likely to suffer from those or related conditions than are members of the general population. Studies of identical twins (who are genetically indistinguishable) and fraternal twins (whose genes generally are no more alike than those of other pairs of siblings) also support an inherited component. The finding of illness in both members of a pair is much higher for manic-depression in identical twins than in fraternal ones and is somewhat elevated for depression alone.

In the past 20 years, genetic researchers have expended great effort trying to identify the genes at fault. Though, those genes have evaded discovery, perhaps because a predisposition to depression involves several genes, each of which makes only a small, hard-to-detect contribution.

Preliminary reports from a study of an Amish population with an extensive history of manic-depression once raised the possibility that chromosome 11 held one or more genes producing vulnerability to bipolar disorder, but the finding did not hold up. A gene somewhere on the X chromosome could play a role in some cases of that condition, but the connection is not evident in most people who have been studied. Most recently, various regions of chromosome 18 and a site on chromosome 21 have been suggested to participate in vulnerability to bipolar illness, but these findings await replication.

As geneticists continue their searches, other investigators are concentrating on neurochemical aspects. Much of that works focuses on neurotransmitters. In particular, many cases of depression apparently stem at least in part from disturbances in brain circuits that convey signals through certain neurotransmitters of the Monoamine class. These biochemicals, all derivatives of amino acids, include serotonin, norepinephrine and dopamine; of these, only evidence relating to norepinephrine and serotonin is abundant.

Physicians discovered that severe depression arose in about 15 percent of patients who were treated for hypertension with the drug reserpine. At about the same time doctors found that an agent prescribed against tuberculosis-elevated moods in some users who were depressed. Follow-up investigations revealed that the drug inhibited the neuronal breakdown of Monoamines by an enzyme (Monoamine oxidase); presumably the agent eased depression by allowing monoamines to avoid degradation and to remain active in brain circuits. Together these findings implied that abnormally low levels of monoamines in the brain could cause depression. This insight led to the development of Monoamine oxidase inhibitors as the first class of antidepressants.

But which monoamines were most important in depression? In the 1960s Joseph J. Schildkraut of Harvard University cast his vote with norepinephrine in the now classic 'catecholamine' hypothesis of mood disorders. He proposed that depression stem from a deficiency of norepinephrine (which is also classified as a catecholamine) in certain brain circuits and that mania arises from an overabundance of the substance. The theory has since been refined, acknowledging, for instance, that decreases or elevations in norepinephrine do not alter moods in everyone. Nevertheless, the proposed link between norepinephrine depletion and depression has gained much experimental support. These circuits originate in the brain stem, primarily in the pigmented locus coeruleus, and project to many areas of the brain, including to the limbic system—a group of cortical and subcortical areas that play a significant part in regulating emotions.

To understand the recent evidence relating to norepinephrine and other monoamines, it helps to know how those neurotransmitters work. The points of contact between two neurons, or nerve cells, are termed synapses. Monoamines, like all neurotransmitters, travel from one neuron (the presynaptic cell) across a small gap (the synaptic cleft) and attach to receptor molecules on the surface of the second neuron (the postsynaptic cell). Such binding elicits intracellular changes that stimulate or inhibit firing of the postsynaptic cell. The effect of the neurotransmitter depends greatly on the nature and concentration of its receptors on the postsynaptic cells. Serotonin receptors, for instance, come in 13 or more subtypes that can vary in their sensitivity to serotonin and in the effects they produce.

The strength of signalling can also be influenced by the amount of neurotransmitters released and by how long it remains in the synaptic cleft—properties influenced by at least two kinds of molecules on the surface of the releasing cell: autoreceptors and transporters. When an autoreceptor becomes bound by neurotransmitter molecules in the synapse, the receptors signal the cell to reduce its firing rate and thus its release of the transmitter. The transporters physically pump neurotransmitter molecules from the synaptic cleft back into presynaptic cells, a process termed reuptake. Monoamine oxidase inside cells can affect synaptic neurotransmitter levels as well, by degrading monoamines and so reducing the amounts, so as to be adequate among the molecules for being available for release.

Among the findings linking impoverished synaptic norepinephrine levels to depression is the discovery in many studies that indirect markers of norepinephrine levels in the brain—levels of its metabolites, or by-products, in more accessible material (urine and cerebrospinal fluid)—are often low in depressed individuals. In addition, postmortem studies have revealed increased densities of certain norepinephrine receptors in the cortex of depressed suicide victims.

Observers unfamiliar with receptor display might assume that elevated numbers of receptors were a sign of more contact between norepinephrine and its receptors and more signal transmission. But this pattern of receptor 'up-regulation' is actually one that scientists would expect if norepinephrine concentrations in synapses were abnormally low. When transmitter molecules become unusually scarce in synapses, postsynaptic cells often expand receptor numbers in a compensatory attempt to pick up whatever signals are available.

A recent discovery supporting the norepinephrine hypothesis is that new drugs selectively able to block norepinephrine reuptake, and so increase norepinephrine in synapses, are effective antidepressants in many people. One compound, reboxetine, is available as an antidepressant outside the US and is awaiting approval here.

The data connecting norepinephrine to depression are solid and still growing. Yet research into serotonin has taken a centre stage in the 1990s, thanks to the therapeutic success of Prozac and related antidepressants that manipulate serotonin levels. Serious investigations into serotonin's role in mood disorders, however, have been going on for almost 30 years, ever since Arthur J. Prange, Jr., of the University of North Carolina at Chapel Hill, Alec Coppen of the Medical Research Council in England and their co-workers put forward the so-called permissive hypothesis. This view held that synaptic depletion of serotonin was another cause of depression, one that worked by promoting, or 'permitting,' a fall in norepinephrine levels.

Defects in serotonin-using circuits could certainly dampen norepinephrine signalling. Serotonin-producing neurons project from the raphe nuclei in the brain stem to neurons in diverse regions of the central nervous system, including those that secrete or control the release of norepinephrine. Serotonin depletion might contribute to depression by affecting other kinds of neurons as well; serotonin-producing cells extend into many brain regions thought to participate in depressive symptoms—including the amygdala (an area involved in emotions), the hypothalamus (involved in appetite, libido and sleep) and cortical areas that participate in cognition and other higher processes.

Among the findings supporting a link between low synaptic serotonin levels and depression is that cerebrospinal fluid in depressed, and especially in suicidal, patients contain reduced quantities of serotonin by-products (signifying reduced levels of serotonin in the brain itself). In addition, levels of a surface molecule unique to serotonin-releasing cells in the brain are lower in depressed patients than in healthy subjects, implying that the numbers of serotonergic cells are reduced. Moreover, the density of at least one form of serotonin receptors—type 2—is greater in postmortem brain tissue of depressed patients. As projected as true in studies of norepinephrine receptors, this up-regulation is suggestive of a compensatory response to too little serotonin in the synaptic cleft.

Further evidence comes from the remarkable therapeutic effectiveness of drugs that block presynaptic reuptake transporters from drawing serotonin out of the synaptic cleft. Tricyclic antidepressants (so-named because they contain three rings of chemical groups) jointly, Monoamine oxidase inhibitors on pharmacy shelves in the late 1950s, although their mechanism of action was not known at the time. Eventually, though, they were found to produce many effects in the brain, including a decrease in serotonin reuptake and a consequent rise in serotonin levels in synapses.

Investigators suspected that this last effect accounted for their antidepressant action, but confirmation awaited the introduction in the late 1980s of Prozac and then other drugs (Paxil, Zoloft and Luvox) able to block serotonin reuptake transporters without affecting other brain monoamines. These selective serotonin reuptake inhibitors (SSRIs) have now revolutionized the treatment of depression, because they are highly effective and produce a great deal of milder of side effects than older drugs do. Today even newer antidepressants, such as Effexor, block reuptake of both serotonin and norepinephrine.

Studies of serotonin have also offered new clues to why depressed individuals are more susceptible to heart attack and stroke. Activation and clumping of blood platelets (cell-like structures in blood) contribute to the formation of thrombi that can clog blood vessels and shut off blood flow to the heart and brain, thus damaging those organs. Work in my laboratory and elsewhere has shown that platelets of depressed people are particularly sensitive to activation signals, including, it seems, to those issued by serotonin, which amplifies platelet reactivity too other, stronger chemical stimuli. Further, the platelets of depressed patients bear reduced numbers of serotonin reuptake transporters. In other words, compared with the platelets of healthy people, those in depressed individuals probably are less able to soak up serotonin from their environment and thus to reduce their exposure to platelet-activation signals.

Disturbed functioning of serotonin or norepinephrine circuits, or both, contributes to depression in many people, but compelling work can equally claim that depression often involves dysregulation of brain circuits that control the activities of certain hormones. Indeed, hormonal alterations in depressed patients have long been evident.

The hypothalamus of the brain lies at the top of the hierarchy regulating hormone secretion. It manufactures and releases peptides (small chains of amino acids) that act on the pituitary, at the base of the brain, stimulating or inhibiting the pituitary's release of various hormones into the blood. These hormones—among the growth hormones, thyroid-stimulating hormone and adrenocorticotropic hormone (ACTH)—control the release of other hormones from target glands. In addition functioning outside the nervous system, the hormones released in response to pituitary hormones feed back to the pituitary and hypothalamus. There they deliver inhibitory signals that keep hormone manufacture from becoming excessive.

Depressed patients have repeatedly been demonstrated to show a blunted response to a number of substances that normally stimulate the release of growth hormones. They also display aberrant responses to the hypothalamic substance that normally induces secretion of thyroid-stimulating hormones from the pituitary. In addition, a common cause of nonresponse to antidepressants is the presence of previously undiagnosed thyroid insufficiency.

All these findings are intriguing, but are the strongest cases that have been made for dysregulation of the hypothalamic-pituitary-adrenal (HPA) axis—the system that manages the body's response to stress. When a threat to physical or psychological well-being is detected, the hypothalamus amplifies production of corticotropin-releasing factors (CRF), which induces the pituitary to secrete ACTH. ACTH then instructs the adrenal gland atop each kidney to releasing the cortisol. Together all the changes prepare the body tight or flee and cause it to shut down activities that would distract from the self-protection. For instance, a cortisol enhances the delivery of fuel to muscles. At the same time, CRF depresses the appetite for food and sex and heightens alertness. Chronic activation of the HPA axis, however, may lay the ground for illness and, it appears, for depression.

As long ago as the late 1960s and early 1970s, several research groups reported increased activity in the HPA axis in unmedicated depressed patients, as evinced by raised levels of a cortisol in urine, blood and cerebrospinal fluid, as well as by other measures. Hundreds, perhaps even thousands, of subsequent studies have confirmed that substantial numbers of depressed patients—particularly those most severely affected—display HPA-axis hyperactivity. Indeed, the finding is surely the most replicated one in all of biological psychiatry.

Deeper investigation of the phenomenon has now revealed alterations at each level of the HPA axis in depressed patients. For instance, both the adrenal gland and the pituitary are enlarged, and the adrenal gland hypersecretes of the cortisol. But many researchers have become persuaded that aberrations in CRF-producing neurons of the hypothalamus and elsewhere bear most of the responsibility for HPA-axis hyperactivity and the emergence of depressive symptoms.

Notably, study after study has shown CRF concentrations in cerebrospinal fluid to be elevated in depressed patients, compared with control subjects or individuals with other psychiatric disorders. This magnification of CRF levels is reduced by treatment with antidepressants and by effective electroconvulsive therapy.

Further, postmortem brain tissue studies have revealed a marked exaggeration both in the number of CRF-producing neurons in the hypothalamus and in the expression of the CRF gene (resulting in elevated CRF synthesis) in depressed patients as compared with controls. Moreover, delivery of CRF to the brains of laboratory animals produces behavioural effects that are cardinal features of depression in humans, namely, insomnia, decreased appetite, decreased libido and anxiety.

Neurobiologists do not yet know exactly how the genetic, Monoamine and hormonal findings piece together, if indeed they always do. The discoveries nonetheless suggest a partial scenario how people who endure traumatic childhoods become depressed later in life. This is known by its hypothesis, the stress-diathesis model of mood disorders, in recognition of the interaction between experience (stress) and an inborn predisposition (diathesis).

The observation that depression runs in families means he was affected from the Latent descendability, as, perhaps, from the ages of the repressive shortages as held by Homo erectus, Cro Magnon, or the Neanderthal or the Homo sapiens, which of the same descendabilities have certain genetic traits in the affected families somehow lower the threshold for depression. Conceivably, the genetic features directly or indirectly diminish Monoamine levels in synapses or increase reactivity of the HPA axis to stress. The genetically determined threshold is not necessarily low enough to induce depression in the absence of serious stress but may then be pushed still lower by early, adverse life experiences.

Most people who experience episodes of mania also experience spells of severe depression. This pattern of mood swings between mania and depression defined a mental illness known as bipolar disorder, and called manic-depressive illness. In bipolar disorder, episodes of mania usually begin abruptly and last from several weeks to several months. Mild manic episodes can last a year or more. Depression may follow immediately or begin after a period of relatively normal functioning. Manic episodes may require hospitalization because of impaired social behaviour or the presence of psychotic symptoms. The symptoms of depression range from uncomfortable to debilitating: sleep disturbances, hopelessness, feelings of worthlessness, difficulty concentrating, fatigue and sometimes even delusions. Most of us have watched a relative or friend struggle with depression—and many of us have experienced it ourselves. Even so, few people realize just how common depression is, how severe it can be or that it is most prevalent among women. In 1990 the World Health Organization found depression to be the leading cause of 'disease burdens' (a composite measure including both illness and death) among women, noting that it affects almost 20 percent of the female population in the developed world. Epidemiological studies indicate that 12 percent of US women—compared with only 6 percent of US men—have suffered from clinically significant depression at some time in their lives.

The big question, of course, is why such a gender gap exists. Over the years various explanations have surfaced to account for the fact that, from one study to the next, depression is between two and three times more common among women than it is among men. Some mental health workers have pointed to psychology, arguing that women are better trained to recognize their feelings and seek help, so they come to the attention of health professionals more often than men. Others have suggested that oppression—in the form of physical or sexual abuse, harassment or discrimination—is to blame. Others still have attributed the increased rates of depression among women to the female reproductive system and the menstrual cycle.

Data from a variety of studies show that depression clearly has psychological, environmental and biological roots. Modern neuroscience is beginning to teach us how these roots can become intertwined and reinforce one in the other. In other words, an increased risk for depression in women might stem from genetics, the effects of stressful events or social pressures, or some combination of all three. Neuroimaging of the brain's circuitry by PET and MRI scans reveals that psychological phenomena such as anger and sadness have biological underpinnings: We can now see circuits of brain cells becoming activated when these emotions arise.

Similarly, neuroimages demonstrate that environmentally and psychological experiences can alter our brain chemistry. For example, Lewis R. Baxter and his colleagues at the University of California at Los Angeles found similar changes on the PET scans of patients with obsessive-compulsive disorder who responded to treatment, regardless of whether the patients were treated with medication or with behavioural therapy.

Figure out why depression is more common among women, scientists have to study how genetics and environment divide the sexes—and how the two conspire to produce the symptoms we describe as depression. It is difficult work, and progress is necessarily slow. But what is coming into appearance, is that certain environmental factor—including stress, seasonal changes and social rank—may produce different physiological responses in females than they do in males. These findings, are small pieces in what is proving to be an incredibly complex puzzle. Laying them out at this stage does not begin to explain depression's double standard. Nevertheless, it could help scientists develop more effective treatments for depressed individuals—both women and men—in the meantime.

Many scientists have wondered whether there is some quirk in the way depression is inherited, such that a depressed parent or grandparent is more likely to pass on a predisposition for the disorder than to male descendants. Based on studies that trace family histories of depression, the answer to that question appears to be no. Women and men with similar heritage seem equally likely to develop the disorder. Simply tracing family histories, though, without also considering environmental influences, might not offer a complete picture of how depression is inherited.

Indeed, Kenneth S. Kendler and his colleagues at the Medical College of Virginia found in a study of 2,060 female twins that genetics might contribute to how women respond to environmental pressures. The researchers examined twins with and without a family history of depression; some twins in both groups had recently undergone a trauma, such as the death of a loved one or a divorce. The investigators found that among the women who did not have a family history of depression, stressful events raised their risk for depression by only 6 percent. But the same infraction climbed up to almost 14 percent among the women who did have a family history of depression. In other words, these women had seemingly inherited the propensity to become depressed in the wake of crises.

A similar study has not been done in men, leaving open the question of whether environmental stress and genetic risk for depression interact similarly in both sexes. But research is being done to determine whether men and women generally experience similar amounts and types of stress. Studies of key hormones hint that they do not. Hormones are not new to depression researchers. Many have wondered whether the gonadal steroid's estrogen and progesterone—whose cyclic fluctuations in women regulate menstruation—might put women at a greater risk for depression. There are at least two ways in which they might do so.

First, because of differences beyond the reach or comprehension of captivating factors as, male and female brains are vulnerable, the differentiations in the existent properties invested among the hormonal milieus in utero. These hormonal differences may affect brain development so that men and women have different vulnerabilities—and different physiological reactions to environmental stressors, later in life. Indeed, animal experiments show that early hormonal influences have marked behavioural consequences later on, although the phenomenon is of course difficult to study in humans.

Second, the fact that postpubertal men and women have different levels of circulating gonadal steroids might somehow put women at higher risk for depression. Research shows girls become more susceptible to depression than boys only after puberty, when they begin menstruating and experience hormonal fluxes. Even so, scientists have never been able to establish a direct relation between emotional states and levels of estrogen and progesterone in the blood of women. For example, Peter J. Schmidt and David R. Rubinow of the National Institute of Mental Health recently reported that manipulations of estrogen and progesterone did not affect the mood, except in women who suffer from severe premenstrual mood changes.

It now appears, however, that estrogen might set the stage for depression indirectly by priming the body's stress response. During stressful times, the adrenal glands—which sit on top of the kidneys and are controlled by the pituitary gland in the brain—secrete higher levels of a hormone-called cortisol, which increases the activity of the body's metabolic and immune systems, among others. In the normal course of events, stress increases cortisol secretion, but these elevated levels have a negative feedback effect on the pituitary, so that cortisol levels gradually return to the norm

Evidence is emerging that estrogen might not only increase cortisol secretion but also decrease cortisol's ability to shut down its own secretion. The result might be a stress response that is not only more pronounced but also longer-lasting in women than in men.

For example, Nicholas C. Vamvakopoulos, George P. Chrousos and their colleagues at the National Institute of Child Health and

Human Development recently found that increased levels of estrogen heighten the activity of the gene for human corticotropin-releasing hormones (CRH). This gene controls the secretion of CRH by a region of the brain called the hypothalamus. CRH makes the pituitary gland release adrenocorticotropic hormones (ACTH), which circulates in the blood and eventually reaches the adrenal glands, where it prompts the secretion of cortisol. Thus, estrogen can, by increasing CRH secretion, ultimately boost cortisol secretion. And Elizabeth A. Young of the University of Michigan and others have shown that female rats are more 'resistant' to cortisol's negative feedback effects than are either male rats or spayed female rats. She has also shown that women have been longer-lasting cortisol responses during the phase of the menstrual cycle when estrogen and progesterone levels are high.

It is unclear whether depression is a cause or a consequence of elevated cortisol levels, but the two are undoubtedly related. Over the past few decades, a number of studies have shown that cortisol levels are elevated in about half of all severely depressed people, both men and women. So the idea is this: if estrogen raises cortisol levels after stress or decrease's cortisol's ability to shut down its own secretion, then estrogen might render women more prone to depression—particularly after a stressful event.

Despite their importance, estrogen and cortisol are not the only hormones involved in female depression, and stress is not the only environmental influence that might hold more sway over women than men. Recent findings by Thomas A. Wehr, Norman E. Rosenthal and their colleagues at the National Institute of Mental Health indicate that women might be more responsive physiologically than men to changes in their exposure to any source of illumination and darkness. These investigators have had a long-standing interest in seasonal affective disorder (SAD), or so-called winter depression (although it can occur in the summer as well), and the role that the hormone melatonin might play in the illness. Similar to the gender ratio in other forms of depression, SAD is three times more common in women than in men.

Melatonin has been a prime suspect in SAD because organisms (including humans) secrete it only when they are in the dark and only when the body's internal clock (located in the hypothalamus) believes it is nighttime. The pineal gland, a small structure that resides deep in the mammalian brain, begins to secrete melatonin in the evening, as daylight wanes. Melatonin levels drop in the morning, when light hits the retinas of the eyes. Because nights are longer in winter than in summer, animals living in the wild secrete melatonin for longer periods each day during winter. Among animals that breed in summer, the onset of this extended daily melatonin secretion signals the presence of winter and shut down the secretion of gonadal steroids that facilitate reproduction.

SAD researchers have long wondered whether a wintertime increase in the duration of melatonin secretion might also trigger depressive symptoms in susceptible individuals. In a series of ongoing studies designed to address this question, Wehr and his colleagues first asked whether humans, like animals, undergo seasonal changes in melatonin secretion. It is an important question, given that artificial light provides humans with an 'endless summer' of sorts compared with animals in the wild. Finding out, Wehr measured melatonin secretion in 15 humans when they were exposed to 14 hours of darkness and later to only eight hours of darkness each night. The results of this experiment, conducted mostly among men, were positive: people experiencing longer periods of darkness secreted melatonin for longer periods during the night, as wild animals do.

Next, the researchers asked whether this natural sensitivity to the seasonal day-length change persisted when people were allowed to follow their usual schedules, turning on artificial lights at night as they normally would. Here the researchers were surprised to find a gender difference. Under normal living conditions, women were more likely than men to retain a sensitivity to seasonal changes in day length. In other words, for women the duration of nocturnal melatonin secretion was longer in winter than summer; in men, however, there was no seasonal difference.

These results suggest that women are more sensitive to natural light than men—and that in a society where artificial light is everywhere, women somehow still detect seasonal changes in natural day length. Whether this gender difference puts women at increased risk for SAD is unclear; paradoxically, there is evidence that women with SAD symptoms may be less likely than unaffected women to have an increased duration of melatonin secretion in winter.

To complicate the story further, the relation between these findings and those regarding cortisol and estrogen are also unclear, because we don't know whether the duration of melatonin secretion affects reproductive function in women, as it surely does in animals.

Researchers are now working to unravel the complicated relations between these hormonal systems and to determine whether, and how, they may influence individuals' risk for depression.

If women's bodies, is, in fact, particularly sensitive to environmental changes, the explanation may lie within the system that controls serotonin, one of many so-called neurotransmitters that nerve cells uses to communicate with one another. Serotonin modulates both cortisol and melatonin secretion. (The similarity in names between serotonin and melatonin is no accident: the latter are synthesized directly from the former, and the two have very similar chemical structures.) And a great deal of evidence indicates that dysfunction in the serotonergic, or serotonin-secreting, system contributes to depression and anxiety disorders, which is also more common in women than men. Recently research in animals and humans provided primary, key insights into this system.

First, it appears that the serotonergic system serves as a link between an animal's nervous system and its physical and social environment. That is, not only due to stress and daylight acts via the serotonergic system but an animal's social rank also appears to affect its serotonin level. A number of studies show that blood and brain serotonin levels change as an animal moves up or down dominance hierarchies. For instance, dominant male monkeys often have higher blood serotonin levels than subordinate ones do. In addition, a recent study by Shih-Rung Yeh and his colleagues at Georgia State University shows that the sensitivity of an animal's neurons to serotonin varies according to that animal's status. Specifically, Yeh found that neurons taken from crayfish that had recently won a fight responded to serotonergic stimulation more strongly than neurons taken from losing crayfish.

There also appear to be significant gender differences in the serotonergic systems of both animals and humans. Mirko Diksic, Sadahiko Nishizawa and their colleagues at McGill University recently provided the most dramatic example: to measure serotonin synthesis in the human brain, they devised a new technique using PET Neuroimaging and found that the average synthesis rate was 52 percent higher in men than in women. The investigators note that with the exception of estrogen binding sites, this gender difference in the brain is one of the largest ever reported. The lower rate of serotonin synthesis in women might increase their overall risk for depression—especially if serotonin storage is depleted during stressed periods or the hours of winter's darkness.

The effort to clarify the bewildering number of interrelated observations uncovered by psychoanalytic exploration led to the development of a model of the structure of the psychic system. Three functional systems are distinguished that are conveniently designated as the id, ego, and Superego.

The first system refers to the sexual and aggressive tendencies that arise from the body, as distinguished from the mind. Freud called these tendencies Triebe, which literally means 'drives,' but which is often inaccurately translated as 'instincts' to indicate their innate character. These inherent drives claim immediate satisfaction, which is experienced as pleasurable; the id thus is dominated by the pleasure principle. In his later writings, Freud tended more toward psychological rather than biological conceptualization of the drives.

An id impulse becomes unacceptable, not only as a result of a temporary need for postponing its satisfaction until suitable reality conditions can be found, but more often because of a prohibition imposed on the individual by others, originally the parents. The totality of these demands and prohibitions constitutes the major content of the third system, the Superego, the function of which is to control the ego in accordance with the internalized standards of parental figures. If the demands of the Superego are not fulfilled, the person may feel shame or guilt. Because the Superego, in Freudian theory, originates in the struggle to overcome the Oedipal conflict, it has a power akin to an instinctual drive, is in part unconscious, and can give rise to feelings of guilt not justified by any conscious transgression. The ego, having to mediate among the demands of the id, the Superego, and the outside world, may not be strong enough to reconcile these conflicting forces. The more the ego is impeded in its development because of being enmeshed in its earlier conflicts, called fixations or complexes, or the more it reverts to earlier satisfactions and archaic modes of functioning, known as regression, the greater is the likelihood of succumbing to these pressures. Unable function normally, it can maintain its limited control and integrity only at the price of symptom formation, in which the tensions are expressed in neurotic symptoms.

The Freudians terminological of three representations are imposed as the id, as used in psychoanalytic theory, one of the three basic elements of personality, the others being the ego and the Superego. The id can be equated with the unconscious of common usage, which is the reservoir of the instinctual drives of the individual, including biological urges, wishes, and affective motives. The id is dominated by the pleasure principle, through which the individual is pressed for immediate gratification of his or her desires. In strict Freudian theory the energy behind the instinctual drives of the id is known as the libido, a generalized force, basically sexual in nature, through which the sexual and psychosexual nature of the individual finds expression.

Ego, in the psychoanalysis, is the term denoting the central part of the personality structure that deals with reality and is influenced by social forces. According to the psychoanalytic theories developed by Sigmund Freud, such as he formulated, that the ego constitutes one of the three basic provinces of the mind, the ego and the others being the id and the Superego. Formation of the ego begins at birth in the first encounters with the external world of people and things. The ego learns to modify behaviour by controlling those impulses that are socially unacceptable. Its role is that of mediators between unconscious impulses and acquired social and personal standards.

Superego, in psychoanalytic theory is one of the three basic constituents of the mind, the others being the id and the ego. As postulated by Sigmund Freud, the term designates the element of the mind that, in normal personalities, automatically modifies and inhibits those instinctual impulses or drives of the id that tend to produce antisocial actions and thoughts.

According to psychoanalytic theory, is that the Superego develops as the child gradually and unconsciously adopts the values and standards, first of his or her parents, and later of the social environment. According to modern Freudian psychoanalysts, the Superego includes the positive ego, or conscious self-image, or ego ideal, that each individual develops.

Object Relations, in the psychoanalysis, are the emotional relations between subject and object of which, through a process of identification, are believed to constitute the developing ego. In this context, the word object refers to any person or thing, or representational aspect of them, with which the subject forms an intense emotional relationship.

Object relations were first described by German psychoanalyst Karl Abraham in an influential paper, published in 1924. In the paper he developed the ideas of the founder of psychoanalysis, Sigmund Freud, on infantile sexuality and the development of the libido. Object-relations theory has become one of the central themes of post-Freudian psychoanalysis, particularly through the writings of British psychoanalysts Melanie Klein, Ronald Fairbairn, and Donald Winnicott, all deeply influenced by Abraham. They have each developed distinctly, though complementary, approaches to analysis, evolving theories of personal development based on early parental attachments.

In interpersonal therapy, the therapist helps a person resolve problems in relationships with others that may have caused the depression. The subsequent improvement in social relationships and support helps alleviate the depression. Psychodynamic therapy views depression as the result of internal, unconscious conflicts. Psychodynamic therapists focus on a person's past experiences and the resolution of childhood conflicts. Psychoanalysis is an example of this type of therapy. Critics of long-term Psychodynamic therapy argue that its effectiveness is scientifically unproven

There are almost no pure cognitive or behavioural therapists. Usually therapists combine cognitive and behavioural techniques in an approach known as cognitive-behavioural therapy. For example, to treat a woman with depression, a therapist may help her identify irrational thinking patterns that cause the distressing feelings and to replace these irrational thoughts with new ways of thinking. The therapist may also train her in relaxation techniques and have her try new behaviours that help her become more active and less depressed. The client then reports the results in reciprocation back of the therapist.

Social psychologists since the mid-1960s have written extensively on the topic of cognitive consistency—that is, the tendency of a person's beliefs and actions to be logically consistent with one or that of the other. When cognitive dissonance, or the lack of such consistency, arises, the person unconsciously seeks to restore consistency by changing his or her behaviour, beliefs, or perceptions. The manner in which a particular individual classifies cognition in order to impose order has been termed cognitive style

Research is a central activity of clinical psychologists who work in academic or clinical settings. Primarily, these clinical psychologists study the causes of mental disorders and try to determine the most effective methods of diagnosis and treatment. They also try to improve methods of testing and measuring personality, intelligence, and other personal characteristics.

There are two dominant views on what cause's psychological disorders and how they should be treated: the biological perspective and the psychological perspective. The biological perspective, also called the medical model, views mental illnesses as having a biological cause, just as physical illnesses do. Over the years, this perspective has gained support from the fact that certain medical interventions—such as Antipsychotic drugs, antianxiety drugs, antidepressants, mood stabilizers, and electroconvulsive therapy—have helped enormously in the treatment of certain psychological disorders. Biologically oriented researchers' study genetic predispositions to mental illness, damage to the brain and nervous system, biochemical imbalances, and other physiological underpinnings of mental disorders.

In contrast to the medical model is the psychological perspective, which holds that psychological disorders are caused and maintained by past and present life experiences. This perspective asserts that mental disorder's result from negative life events such as prolonged illness, stress, physical and sexual abuse, divorce, poverty, war, the death of a loved one, peer rejection, and chronic failure. Today, most psychologists and psychiatrists believe that mental disorders are caused by a combination of biological and psychological factors.

Another important area of research in clinical psychology concerns the effectiveness of psychotherapy. Most studies have found that no one method of psychotherapy is superior to another. Rather, the different types of psychotherapy are about equally effective, in part because they all share certain qualities. For example, all psychotherapies provide people in distress with hope for recovery, personal support and encouragement, and an opportunity to open up and talk freely about their problems.

Another important area of research in clinical psychology concerns the effectiveness of psychotherapy. Most studies have found that no one method of psychotherapy is superior to another. Rather, the different types of psychotherapy are about equally effective, in part because they all share certain qualities. For example, all psychotherapies provide people in distress with hope for recovery, personal support and encouragement, and an opportunity to open up and talk freely about their problems.

Cognitive Psychology, is the scientific study of cognition. Cognition refers to the process of knowing, and cognitive psychology is the study of all mental activities related to acquiring, storing, and using knowledge. The domain of cognitive psychology spans the entire spectrum of conscious and unconscious mental activities: sensation and perception, learning and memory, thinking and reasoning, attention and consciousness, imagining and dreaming, decision making, and problem solving. Other topics that fascinate cognitive psychologists include creativity, intelligence, and how people learn, understand, and use language.

Over the years, cognitive psychologists have discovered that mental activities that seem simple and natural are, in fact, extraordinarily complex. For example, most children have no trouble learning language from their parents. But how do young children decode the meanings of sounds and grasp the basic rules of grammar? Why do children learn language more easily and rapidly than adults? Explaining these puzzles has proven very difficult, and attempts to duplicate true language ability in machines have failed. Even the most advanced computers have trouble understanding the meaning of a simple story or conversation. Cognitive psychologists have found similar complexity in other mental processes.

The psychological science of cognition, is the scientific study of mind recognition. Cognition refers to the process of knowing, and cognitive psychology is the study of all mental activities related to acquiring, storing, and using knowledge. The domain of cognitive psychology spans the entire spectrum of conscious and unconscious mental activities: sensation and perception, learning and memory, thinking and reasoning, attention and consciousness, imagining and dreaming, decision making, and problem solving. Other topics that fascinate cognitive psychologists include creativity, intelligence, and how people learn, understand, and use language.

Cognitive therapies are similar to behavioural therapies in that they focus on specific problems. However, they emphasize changing beliefs and thoughts, rather than observable behaviours. Cognitive therapists believe that irrational beliefs or distorted thinking patterns can cause a variety of serious problems, including depression and chronic anxiety. They try to teach people to think in more rational, constructive ways.

An important school of thought is based on the teachings of the British psychoanalyst Melanie Klein. Because most of Klein's followers worked with her in England, this has come to be known as the English school. Its influence, nevertheless, is very strong throughout the European continent and in South America. Its principal theories were derived from observations made in the psychoanalysis of children. Klein posited the existence of complex unconscious fantasies in children under the age of six months. The principal source of anxiety arises from the threat to existence posed by the death instinct. Depending on how concrete representations of the destructive forces are dealt within the unconscious fantasy life of the child, two basic early mental attitudes result that Klein characterized as a 'depressive position' and a 'paranoid position.' In the paranoid position, the ego's defence consists of projecting the dangerous internal object onto some external representative, which is treated as a genuine threat emanating from the external world. In the depressive position, the threatening object is introjected and treated in fantasy as concretely retained within the person. Depressive and hypochondriacal symptoms result. Although considerable doubt exists that such complex unconscious fantasies operate in the minds of infants, these observations have been of the utmost importance to the psychology of unconscious fantasies, paranoid delusions, and theory concerning early object relations.

Psychotherapy is an important form of treatment for many kinds of psychological problems. Two of the most common problems for which people seek help from a therapist are depression and persistent anxiety. People with depression may have low self-esteem. A sense of hopelessness about the future, and a lack of interest in people and activities once found pleasurable. People with anxiety disorders may feel anxious all the time or suffer from phobias, a fear of specific objects or situations. Psychotherapy, by itself or in combination with drug treatment, can often help people overcome or manage these problems.

People with depression often experience feelings of worthlessness, helplessness, guilt, and self-blame. They may interpret a minor failing on their part as a sign of incompetence or interpret minor criticism as condemnation. Some depressed people complain of being spiritually or morally dead. The mirror seems to reflect someone ugly and repulsive. Even a competent and decent person may feel deficient, cruel, stupid, phony, or guilty of having deceived others. People with major depression may experience such extreme emotional pain that they consider or attempt suicide.

At least 15 percent of seriously depressed people commit suicide, and many more attempt it.

The pervasive and chronic nature of personality disorders makes them difficult to treat. People with these disorders often fail to recognize that their personality has contributed to their social, occupational, and personal problems. They may not think they have any real problems despite a history of drug abuse, failed relationships, and irregular employment. Thus, therapists must be first focus upon helping the person who is understanding and much aware of the significance of personality traits.

People with personality disorders sometimes feel that they can never change their dysfunctional behaviour because they have always acted the same way. Although personality change is exceedingly difficult, sometimes people can change the most dysfunctional aspects of their feelings and behaviour.

Therapists use a variety of methods to treat personality disorders, depending on the specific disorder. For example, cognitive and behavioural techniques, such as role playing and logical argument, may help alter a person's irrational perceptions and assumptions about himself or herself. Certain psychoactive drugs may help control feelings of anxiety, depression, or severe distortions of thought. Psychotherapy may help people to understand the impact of experiences and relationships during childhood.

Psychotherapy is usually ineffective for people with antisocial personality disorder because these individuals tend to be manipulative, unreliable, and dishonest with the therapist. Therefore, most mental health professionals favour removing people with this disorder from their current living situation and placing them in a residential treatment centre. Such residential programs strictly supervise patients' behaviour and impose rigid, consistent rules and responsibilities. These programs appear to help some people, but it is unclear how long their beneficial effects last.

Therapists treating people with borderline personality disorder sometimes use a technique called dialectical behaviour therapy. In this type of therapy, the therapist initially focuses on reducing suicidal tendencies and other behaviours that disrupt treatment. The therapist then helps the person develop skills to cope with anger and self-destructive impulses. In addition, the person learns to achieve personal strength through an acceptance of the many disappointments and interpersonal conflicts that are a natural part of life.

The Psychodynamic perspective was developed earlier that the others, and this is reflected in the style of the article that resented it. They were written in a period chiefly characterize d by bolder speculative theoretical formulations and by insightful clinical studies. It was a richly productive era in which sensitive and intuitive observers mapped out whole continents of the mind that had previously been unexplored. It was a rea of large scale conceptualizations and generalization (Mendelson, 1960). The Mendelson's words, were that these papers were a contributive point in theatrical properties in which something intangible is discerned in the role of a 'Great Debate' about the development of a vulnerability to depression, what roles are to be assigned to aggression and dependence, and what significance is to be attached to depressed persons, self-reproach. In the absence of anybody of independent research data to which appeals could be made, the debate was often rhetorical and even polemical.

The Psychodynamic approach path begins with the lost object as becoming an ego loss, as it is incorporated into the ego. The ego identifies with the lost object, and the conflict between the ego and the lost object becomes a conflict within the ego. Hostility that cannot be expressed directly to the lost object is heaped upon the portion of the ego that is identified with it, and this is reflected in a loss of loss of self-esteem and punishing self-criticism. Freud argued that this process did not happen in just anyone facing a loss. It requires a predisposition that underlies in the basic ambivalence to the love object and an underlying tendency toward narcissistic object choices. The vulnerable person choses love objects that are similar enough to the self that they can easily abandon and confused with it.

However, Bibring was careful to state that he did not reject outright the formulations offered by Freud and Abraham, but he suggested that they needed modification because oral and aggressive striving may not be as universal in depression as these formulations supposed. Yet, the modification that he presents proves to be quite radical. For Bibring, what was most fundamental about depression is a fall in self-esteem due to 'the ego's shocking awareness of its helpfulness in regard to its aspiration'. Depression occurs when the person both feels powerless to achieve some narcissistically important goal and the goal is not relinquished.

119

Personality is deeply ingrained and relatively enduring patterns of thought, feeling, and behaviour. Personalities usually have to do with which is unique about a person, the characteristics that distinguish him or her from other people. Though, emotion, and behaviour as such do not constitute a personality, which is, rather, the dispositions that underlie these elements. Personality implies predictability about how a person will act or react under different circumstances.

Theorists emphasize different aspects of personality and disagree about its organization, development, and manifestation in behaviour. One of the most influential theoretical systems is the psychoanalytic theory of Sigmund Freud and his followers. Freud believed that unconscious processes direct a great part of a person's behaviour. Although a person is unaware of these impulses and drives, they strive to assert themselves. Another influential theory of personality is derived from behaviourism. This view, represented by thinkers such as the American psychologist B. F. Skinner, places primary emphasis on learning. Skinner sees human behaviour as determined largely by its consequences. If rewarded, behaviour recurs; if punished, it is less likely to recur.

Heredity and environmental interaction influence the personality. From the earliest age, infants differ widely because of variables that either are inherited or result from conditions of pregnancy and birth. Some infants are more attentive than others, for example, some are more at work or in effective operation, as actively dynamic in functioning, yet, actify of something as an effected performance to an active accompaniment to awakening awareness. These differences can influence how parents respond to the infant—one illustration of how hereditary conditions affect environmental ones. Among the personality characteristics that are known to be at least partly determined by heredity are intelligence and temperament; some forms of psychopathology are also associated in the faculty of inherent descendabilities.

However, most experts believe that a child's experiences in the family are crucial for personality development. How well basic needs are met in infancy, along with later patterns of child rearing, can leave a permanent mark on personality. Children whose toilet training is started too early or carried out too rigidly, for example, may become defiant. Children learn behaviour appropriate to their sex by identifying with their same-sex parent; a warm relationship with that parent facilitates such learning. Children are also influenced by their siblings.

Some authorities emphasize the role of social and cultural traditions in personality development. In describing the behaviour of members of two New Guinea tribes, for example, the American anthropologist Margaret Mead demonstrated this cultural relationship. Although the tribes are of the same racial stock and live in the same area, one group is peaceful, friendly, and cooperative, whereas the other group is assertive, hostile, and competitive.

Traditionally, psychologists hold that the traits of an individual combine form a personality, and that this personality shows great consistency over time. Recently, however, many psychologists have argued that traits exist only in the eye of the beholder, and that a person's personality varies with the situation.

Nevertheless, this view is widely used as a means for the gathering accumulations for the appendages collecting in the correspondence of an assured attaining concentration through one's attention on something alterably as to an end. This designing method of personality assessment is meant for the eliciting of one's total property including real property and intangibles for feeling the effects as placed upon the subject, the idea that something conveys to the mind. As the element or complex of elements in an individual that, feels, perceives, thinks, wills, and especially reasons. A composite characteristic as belonging to the past, presents, and the ultimate hesitations as to future states, whereupon future events will occur. Most interviews are conducted with another and integrated but interrelated in the facts that they are interdependent, and unstructured. But some used set-questions asked in a given sequence, and skilled interviewers pay attention to what is said and notice how responses relate to nonverbal cues, such as posture and facial expression.

Direct observations are made either in a natural setting or in a laboratory. In naturalistic observations, the assessor notes reactions to everyday situations, typical responses to people, and expressive behaviour. In the laboratory, the investigator experimentally manipulates situations and observes the subject's behaviour under these controlled conditions. The personality assessor might also rely on the reports of others who have observed the subject in the past.

Personality tests are of two general types—self-report inventories and projective tests. Self-report inventories, such as the Minnesota Multiphasic Personality Inventory, pose questions about personal habits, attitudes, beliefs, and fantasies. In projective testing, the subject's responses to ambiguous or unstructured situations are assumed to reflect inner reality. The Rorschach test, for example, is a projective test consisting of a series of inkblots, about which the subject reports his or her perceptions; the assessor subsequently interprets these responses

Personality Disorders, disorders in which one's personality results in personal distress or significantly tarnish social or work functioning. Every person has, and a personality—that is, a characteristic way of thinking, feeling, behaving, and relating to others. Most people experience at least some difficulties and problems that result from their personality. The specific point at which those problems justify the diagnosis of a personality disorder is controversial. To some extent the definition of a personality disorder is arbitrary, reflecting subjectively as well as professional judgments about the person's degree of dysfunction, needs for change, and motivation for change.

Personality disorders involve behaviour that deviates from the norms or expectations of one's culture. However, people who are out of line with cultural norms are not necessarily dysfunctional, nor are people who conform to cultural norms necessarily healthy. Many personality disorders represent extreme variants of behaviour patterns that people usually value and encourage. For example, most people value confidence but not arrogance, agreeableness but not submissiveness, and conscientiousness but not perfectionism.

Because no clear line exists between healthy and unhealthy functioning, critics question the reliability of personality disorder diagnoses. A behaviour that seems deviant to one person may seem normal to another depending on one's gender, ethnicity, and cultural background. The personal and cultural biases of mental health professionals may influence their diagnoses of personality disorders.

An estimated 20 percent of people in the general population have one or more personality disorders. Some people with personality disorders have other mental illnesses as well. About 50 percent of people who are treated for any psychiatric disorder have a personality disorder.

Mental health professionals rarely diagnose personality disorders in children because their manner of thinking, feeling, and relating to others does not usually stabilize until young adulthood. Thereafter, personality traits usually remain stable. Personality disorders often decrease in severity as a person

People with antisocial personality disorder act in a way that disregards the feelings and rights of other people. Antisocial personalities often break the law, and they may use or exploit other people for their own gain. They may lie repeatedly, act impulsively, and get into physical fights. They may mistreat their spouses, neglect or abuse their children, and exploit their employees. They may even kill other people. People with this disorder are also sometimes called sociopaths or psychopaths. Antisocial behaviour in people less than 18 years old is called conduct disorder.

Antisocial personalities usually fail to understand that their behaviour is dysfunctional because their ability to feel guilty, remorseful, and anxious is impaired. Guilt, remorse, shame, and anxiety are unpleasant feelings, but they are also necessary for social functioning and even physical survival. For example, people in lacking of the ability to feel anxious will often fail to anticipate actual dangers and risks. They may take chances that other people would not take.

Antisocial personality disorder affects about 3 percent of males and 1 percent of females. This is the most heavily researched personality disorder, in part because it costs society the most. People with this disorder are at high risk for premature and violent death, injury, imprisonment, loss of employment, bankruptcy, alcoholism, drug dependence, and failed personal relationships.

People with borderline personality disorder experience intense emotional instability, particularly in relationships with others. They may make frantic efforts to avoid real or imagined abandonment by others. They may experience minor problems as major crises. They may also express their anger, frustration, and dismay through suicidal gestures, self-mutilation, and other self-destructive acts. They tend to have an unstable self-image or sense of self.

As children, most people with this disorder were emotionally unstable, impulsive, and often bitter or angry, although their chaotic impulsiveness and intense emotions may have made them popular at school. At first they may impress people as stimulating and exciting, but their relationships tend to be unstable and explosive.

About 2 percent of all people have borderline personality disorder. About 75 percent of people with this disorder are female. Borderline personalities are at high risk for developing depression, alcoholism, drug dependence, bulimia, Dissociative disorders, and post-traumatic stress disorder. As many as 10 percent of people with this disorder commit suicide by the age of 30. People with borderline personality disorder are among the most difficult to treat with psychotherapy, in part because their relationship with their therapist may become as intense and unstable as their other personal relationships.

Avoidant personality disorder is social withdrawal due to intense, anxious shyness. People with Avoidant personalities are reluctant to interact with others unless they feel most certainty liked. They fear of being criticized and rejected. Often they view themselves as socially inept and inferior to others.

Dependent personality disorder involves severe and disabling emotional dependency on others. People with this disorder have difficulty making decisions without a great deal of advice and reassurance from others. They urgently seek out another relationship when a close relationship ends. They feel uncomfortable by themselves.

People with histrionic personality disorder constantly strive to be the pivotal point of attentions. They may act overly flirtatious or dress in ways that draw attention. They may also talk in a dramatic or theatrical style and display exaggerated emotional reactions.

People with narcissistic personality disorder have a grandiose sense of a self-importance. They seek excessive admiration from others and fantasize about unlimited success or power. They believe they are special, unique, or superior to others. However, they often have very fragile self-esteem.

Obsessive-compulsive personality disorder is characterized by a preoccupation with details, orderliness, perfection, and control. People with this disorder often devote excessive amounts of time spent at work and the productivity, which in failing to take time for leisure activities and friendships. They tend to be rigid, formal, stubborn, and serious. This disorder differs from obsessive-compulsive disorder, which often includes more bizarre behaviour and rituals.

Schizoid personality disorder involves social isolation and a lack of desire for close personal relationships. People with this disorders prefer to be alone and seem withdrawn and emotionally detached, and seem indifferent.

People with schizotypal personality disorder engage in odd thinking, speech, and behaviour. They may ramble or use words and phrases in unusual ways, and they may believe they have magical control over others. They feel very uncomfortable with close personal relationships and tend to be suspicious of others. Some research purports that this manifestation of grief or sorrow, and as bad as bad can be, that this afflictive lamentable disorder is one lower than schizophrenia.

Many psychiatrists and psychologists use two additional diagnoses. Depressive personality disorder is characterized by chronic pessimism, gloominess, and cheerlessness. In passive-aggressive personality disorder, a person passively resists completing tasks and chores, criticizes and scorns authority figures, and seems negative and sullen.

Personality disorders result from a complex interaction of inherited traits and life experience, not from a single cause. For example, some cases of antisocial personality disorder may result from a combination of a genetic predisposition to impulsiveness and violence, very inconsistent or erratic parenting, and a harsh environment that discourage feelings of empathy and warmth but rewards exploitation and aggressiveness. Borderline personality disorder may result from a genetic predisposition to impulsiveness and emotional instability combined with parental neglect, intense marital conflicts between parents, and repeated episodes of severe emotional or sexual abuse. Dependent personality disorder may result from genetically based anxiety, an inhibited temperament, and overly protective, clinging, or neglectful parenting.

People with personality disorders sometimes feel that they can never change their dysfunctional behaviour because they have always acted the same way. Although personality change is exceedingly difficult, sometimes people can change the most dysfunctional aspects of their feelings and behaviour.

Therapists use a variety of methods to treat personality disorders, depending on the specific disorder. For example, cognitive and behavioural techniques, such as role playing and logical argument, may help alter a person's irrational perceptions and assumptions about himself or herself. Certain psychoactive drugs may help control feelings of anxiety, depression, or severe distortions of thought. Psychotherapy may help people to understand the impact of experiences and relationships during childhood.

Psychotherapy is usually ineffective for people with antisocial personality disorder because these individuals tend to be manipulative, unreliable, and dishonest with the therapist. Therefore, most mental health professionals favour removing people with this disorder from their current living situation and placing them in a residential treatment centre. Such residential programs strictly supervise patients' behaviour and impose rigid, consistent rules and responsibilities. These programs appear to help some people, but it is unclear how long their beneficial effects last.

Therapists treating people with borderline personality disorder sometimes use a technique called dialectical behaviour therapy. In this type of therapy, the therapist initially focuses on reducing suicidal tendencies and other behaviours that disrupt treatment. The therapist then helps the person develop skills to cope with anger and self-destructive impulses. In addition, the person learns to achieve personal strength through an acceptance of the many disappointments and interpersonal conflicts that are a natural part of life.

Irrespective of their unconscious implications, one may roughly distinguish between three groups of such persisting aspiration of the person: (1) the wish to be worthy, to beloved, to be appreciated, not to be inferior or unworthy; (2) the wish to be strong, superior, great, secure, and to be weak and insecure; and (3) the wish to be good, to e loving not to be aggressive, hateful and destructive. It is exactly from the tension between these highly charged narcissistic aspirations, on the other hand, and, the ego's acute awareness of its (real or imaginary) helplessness and incapacity to live up to them on the other hand, that depressions result (Bibring, 1953).

The vulnerability to particular frustrations is acquired as a result of trauma that occur in early childhood and that produce a fixation to a state of helplessness. This state can be reactivated when the person is confronted with a situation resembling the original trauma. Bibring agreed that psychoanalytic writers that depression is more likely to occur in orally dependent persons who need 'narcissistic supplies'; from the outside, but he also argued that severe frustration could produce a fixation in another stage. Importantly, depression did not depend upon the aggressive and dependent striving of the oral stage. Rather than producing depression, such striving might result from the awareness of helplessness.

Whybrow, Akiskal, and Mckinney (1984) have noted some of the most important implications of Bibring's reformation of the classical psychodynamics of depression.

To define depression in this way is to define it as psychosocial phenomenon. The concept of the ego, unlike that of the id, is rooted in social reality, and the ego ideal is composed of socially learned symbols and motives. A breakdown of self-esteem may involve, in addition to object loss, man's symbolic possessions, such as power, status, social role, identity, values, and existential purpose. Depression, therefore, falls particularly upon the overambitious, the conventional, and individual with upward mobility, and the woman who strongly identify with a passive social role . . . Bibring's conceptualization provides broad links with man's existential, sociological, and a cultural world.

Cohen and her colleagues represent another important conceptual transition, such like the other Psychodynamic writers, Cohen has devoted considerable attention to the early childhood experience of depression but emphasis is on the patterning of interpersonal relationships rather than intrapsychic functioning. They demonstrate the Sullivanian conceptualization of personality as the recurring patterning of significant relationships.

The enduring interpersonal climate in the family is given more attention that any single traumatic experience, and the family's position in the community are identified as an important determinant of what this climate will be. Specifically, the families of depressed persons tend to stand out as different from the families around them. Parents tend to have an overriding concern with fitting in, confronting to 'what the neighbours think' and upward mobility. The child in the family who is most likely to be depressed later is likely to be the one who most accepted the burden of winning acceptance and prestige for the family.

This child absorbs parental attitudes in a peculiar combination of lack of conviction of worth . . . coupled with an intense devotion of conventional, orality and what people think'. The child may show a strong concern with what authority expects, but a conviction that these expectations are beyond what can be achieved.

The adult relationships of depressives tend to perpetuate the patterning of the family relationships in childhood. Even when not suffering from and mood disturbance, depressives tend to have a narrow range of relationships within which they are very dependent and sensitive to signs of disapproval and rejection. As an interpersonal strategy, depressives may undersell themselves in order to win nurturance and approval, but in doing so, actually may convince others that they lack any assets.

At this point, they begin to hate these other people for being the cause of the vicious circle in which they are caught, and they hate themselves because the sense the fraudulence of their behaviour in not their behaviour in not having expressed openly their inner feelings.

This strategy and patterning of relationships become exaggerated and intensified during a period of depression. The symbols of depressed persons may be seen as an appeal to those around them, but if prolonged, their main effect may be to leave the depressed person alienated from those people upon whom they had relied and along with their feelings of distress. Cohen gives an extended talk about of the therapeutic relationship with depressed persons because of the assumption that this will recapitulate other significant relationships in a way that allows the therapist to have the first hand perspective of a participant observer. The language of transference and countertransference is used, but one less of a sense of an ego struggling with object representations than of two people struggling with a difficult relationship. Depressed persons can be irritating and manipulative, but are more likely to be manipulated by depressed persons if they become overly invested in playing a benign and powerful role with their patient's. This emphasis on interpersonal strategies of depressed persons and the involvement t of others is developed in Coyne, as its point of departure, is a greater focus on the contemporary relationships of adult depressed persons, with a conceptualization of depression as an emergent interpersonal system of depressive behaviour and depression are powerful in their alibility to arouse guilt and hostility from them. Initially, the depressed persons' distress engages others and shifts the interactional burden onto them. Yet, the persistence of the depressed persons distress may soon prove incomprehensible and aversive to them.

In the sixties Psychodynamic writings were interpreted as suggesting that when people become depressed, they are more likely to internalize or suppress hostility. Findings were generally not supportive of this hypothesis (Friedman, 1964 and Schless, et al., 1974). There were also a number of examinations of whether persons who later became depressed had experienced the death of a parent in childhood. There were some well-designed studies with positive results, but other studies found only a weak and inconsistent relationship (Crook and Elliot, 1980). Yet, as in the studies of depression and hostility, questions could be raised about the fidelity of the research to the original Psychodynamic formulation. Recently, Sidney Blatt and his colleagues have utilized Psychodynamic conceptions in developing a line of research that distinguishes between depressed persons on the basis of whether dependency or self-criticism predominates. Such a typology correlates with retrospective report s of parental behaviour in childhood (McCranie and Bass, 1984).

In 1921, Freud added some statements about mania to his earlier interpretations of depression. He suggested that the mood swings of normal and neurotic persons are caused by the tensions between an ego and ego ideal. These mood swings are excessive in the case of manic-depressive illness because after the frustrating of a lost object has been reestablished by identifications in the ego, it is then tormented by the cruel severity of the ego ideal, against which, in turn, the ego rebels. According to Freud, the manic represent a triumphant reunion between ego and ego ideals, in the sense of expansive self-inflation, but not in the sense of stability and a continuum in equilibrium.

Abraham, in 1924, pursued his interest in biological development and tried to find the specific fixation points for mental illness in different phases of libido development. He interpreted character traits for being highly symbolized derivatives of pregenital instinctual impulses that were, in the case of the mentally ill person, hampered in their normal development by frustration or overindulgence. Because of Abraham's influence, psychoanalytic research in ego development has for a long time been dependent on highly schematized concepts, to which the manic depressive periodically regresses for being at the end of the second biting oral phase and the beginning of the first expelling anal phase. This assumption could explain the frequent preoccupation of the manic depressive with cannibalistic phantasies as well as. His character trends of impatience, envy and exploitativeness, dominating possessiveness, and exaggerated optimism or pessimism: His intense ambivalence, and his explosive riddance reactions. The object loss that precedes the onset of a depression is mostly not conscious but, according to Abraham, repeats a primal depression, a frustration at the time of transition from the oral to the anal phase, when the child was disappointed in the mother. The oral dependence may be constitutionally overemphasized in the manic depressive.

In 1927 Râdo went a step further in the theory of identification. Freud and Abraham's theories imply an incorporation of the lost or flustrating object, in both the tormented ego and the punishing ego-ideal or Superego. This double incorporation, Râdo postulated, corresponds to an ambivalent splitting into a good, that is, of gratifying the object, and badly frustrated object, which at an early stage of development, when the synthetic function of the ego is still weak, both of these are the mothers. The good parent by whom the child wants to be loved is incorporated in the Superego, endowed with the privilege of punishing the bad parent who is incorporated in the ego. This bad object in the ego may be punished to the point of total destruction (suicide). But the ultimate goal of this raging orgy of the self-torture is expiation, reconciliation, synthesis. Râdo describes the manic phase as an unstable reconciliation reached on the basis of denial of guilt. The automatized cycle of guilt, expiation, and reconciliation is patterned after the sequence of infantile oral experience, as, rages, hunger, drinking. The drinking, which resembles the state of reunion of reconciliation, culminates in a satiated pleasure experience, which Râdo called the 'alimentary orgasm'. In a paper published in 1933 Râdo described the way in which the drug addict, in the artificially produced intoxication, expresses the same yearning for reconciliation and blissful reunion with the gratifying mother.

In the same year, 1933, Deutsch illustrated the theory of manic depressive psychoses, as developed up to that time, by several abbreviated case presentations. She agreed with Râdo that the melancholic phase is sometimes introduced by a phase of rebellion of the ego against the cruel Superego. After the ego succumbs to the Superego's punishment with the unconscious intention of bribing the Superego and of gaining forgiveness by such submission, the ego may rescue itself from the dangerous introjection by projecting the threatening enemy onto the outside world; aggression can then be directed against the projected Superego, which has become an external persecutor. Another form of escape from the melancholic predicament is the denial of any narcissistic deprivation—as, the loss of the mothers' breast, or the absence of a penis. Deutsch regarded that the fascination of mania and the equitable state of paranoia, as an alternative defences against the intense dangers to the survival that the ego is oppressed by melancholia. In the hypomanic patient, the underling depression has to be lifted into consciousness if therapy is to be successful, even so, that in 1938, Jacob's made similar observations on a periodically manic patient.

Gero illustrated 'The Construction of Depression' (1936) by two case presentations. One was of a woman patient with an obsessional character structure built up as a defence against the painful ambivalence in her family relations. Only after these character defences yielded to analysis could this patient see avenues of realistic satisfactions and therewith surmount the depressions. The other case was a male patient, who had identified with an overambitious, over exacting father, and a rejecting mother, and had repressed the rage against both frustrating parents by withdrawal into repressed regression, punishing therewith the internalized objects of his hate and rage. After his father's death, he had himself changed into a sick old man. The liberation of rage and hate in the transference freed the genital aggressiveness from the odium and guilt of sadomasochistic distortions. In both cases the analyst succeeded in winning the patients from a hopeless negativism to a hopeful confirmation of life.

Jacobson described in 1943, that the decedents act or process of passing from a higher to a lower level or state of a severely depressed patient, with strongly suicidal argues, intense experiences of depersonalization and phantasies—a case on the borderlines between manic degressive psychosis and schizophrenia. Jacobson was able to uncover a primal depression in this patient, at the age of three and a half, when the birth of a brother coincided with a disruption of the parental marital elation. Turning now, from the mother rather than to mother to the patients overflowing emptiness, whose treatment, had of a complete loss of objects, however, she maintained a masochistic dependence on her mother. As substitutes for the disappointing parents, she built up phantasies of idealism, perfect parents who endowed her Superego with cruel severity, so that she lived in constant danger of complete desertion and in the horror of punishment.

Weiss in 1944 pursued a slightly different approach. He postulated that melancholic episodes are a reaction to the realization of antisocial, dishonest, or egotistical aspects of the personality. The inability of the uncomplaining patient to reach and levy the situation as compelled by an integration between his antisocial wishes and his moral standards causing tension in his 'feeling', that the patient quickens himself. The exaggerated guilt

131

reaction maintains the split between persecuting and persecuted 'introjects'. Identifications with hated objects may make the task of ego integration very difficult. Such that the manic phase, the passivity of the objectionable introjects the projected, and the ego assumes the active role of the persecuting Superego against objects of condemnation in the outside world. Weiss points out that in paranoia, the ego does not cling strongly to the Superego, and the persecuting introjects, the Superego, is projected' in mania, however, the persecuted introject is projected. The paranoiac, by this projection, succeeds in preserving his narcissistic position, while the melancholic fails, the result of his inner persecuting may be self-destruction.

Recently, Bibring has summed up all the features that different kinds of depression have in common, including not only the depressions as a circular psychosis, also the interactive depressions and depressions in the course of physical illness as aligned in states of fatigue or exhaustion. A common factor is the lowering of self-esteem, the loss of a self-love, which, in melancholia, is intensified into self-hate. Bibring compares depression with states of depersonalization and boredom. In the mildly depressed person, there is not so much haste turned against the self as there is an exhaustion of the narcissistic supply of the self-love. The mildly depressed person is less inclined to kill himself than to let himself dies.

Frank in a lecture on 'The Defensive Aspects of Depression' follows a line of thought similar to Bibring's. He compares unspecific depressions of the hibernation of animals. A defensive response frustrating life conditions, sometimes that limits or qualifies, on the contrariety to fact, is seen in the essential modifications, in that by restrictive depression, in a seriously ill-mannered case of depression, yet, in the finding, as a defensive structure for having expectations that are maintained of in the lowest key, so that the shock of some unavoidable frustration is reduced to a minimum.

The paradigm of the manic-depressive psychosis has on the whole, elicited less attention on the part of the psychoanalysis than has the depressed aspect, probably because the manic patient does not sequently seek therapeutic help. B., Lewin, in a monograph on 'The Psychoanalysis of Elation' regards elation as a decence of denial against depression. During the analytic process, Lewin suggests, normal mourning increases insight into the self and terminate in a sense of heightening well-being, increased sexual potency, and capacity for work and sublimation. But elation or depression resist the testing of reality; they produce negative therapeutic reactions in the face of insight that cannot at the time be emotionally assimilated. The depressed and the elation of ego are not trying to separate the true from the false, but the good from the bad: Reality-testing is replaced by morality-testing. Lewin compares mania to sleep, in sleep the ego disappears; in mania the Superego vanishes. Sleep stems from oral satisfaction—the infant drops asleep when he is satiated with nursing at the mother's breast. But the manic patient is a notoriously poor sleeper. That he is haunted by the sense of poverty of the Ego. The unconscious sadism originally directed against the object, reinforced by a sense of guilt, produced the singular phenomenon of the person becoming sadistic toward himself. Frequently, the identification with a close relative who died at the time when the patient went through the Oedipus conflict or puberty contributes to the suicidal tendency in later years. Zilboorg stresses the observation that suicide may occur in as variety of other psychopathological conditions on the basis of different motivations, such as spite and fear.

Nevertheless, there is increasing theoretical and empirical concern about the etiology and treatment of depression. This, nonetheless, mirrors recent confirmation that depressive disorders are a major health problem. As to the diversity of conceptual models and empirical methods are those has, had been used to explore intrapsychic, cognitive-phenomenological, social and behavioural aspects of depression. For which these are the approaching implications for the formulation and implementation of clinical interventions.

While psychosocial research has identified the etiologic role of stressful events and several promising psychological treatments have been formulated, a number of important research and clinical; issues have been identified. For instance, why do stressful life circumstances lead to depression among some persons but not others? How can one explain the finding that different psychosocial intervention's appar to have similar affected on depression? Toward what areas should prevention efforts are targeted?

Adler very early saw the importance of self-esteem in depression. More recently, Bibring (1953) signalled a truly radical break with the older theory in the psychoanalysis, by postulating that an undermining of self-esteem was the primary focus in depression, that it was principally to be understood as an ego-phenomenon, and only secondarily as a consequence of self-directed aggression.

It would be impossible to overestimate the significance of this shift in emphasis. In spite of Bibring's own protestations to the contrary, theories about the role of orality and aggression, is that, if self-esteem is the primary focus of depressions than does physiology. An ego-based theory of depression broadens the area of explanation from a purely 'intrapsychic battlefield' to the entire range of social phenomena. Since the ego is rooted in social reality, since self-esteem is composed of social symbols and social motives, depression becomes a direct function of a cognitively apprehended symbolic world. Nothing less than a full sweep of cultural activity is bought into consideration in the single case of depression.

Hardly at all, ever though more recently a crucial sociological dimension was added to the theory of depression, again from within the psychoanalysis (Szasz, 1961). In the classical formulation of depression, mourning and melancholic states, Freud had presented the psychoanalysis with a model (1917). He postulated that since the ego grows by developing responses to an identification with objects, and the loss of an object was a threat to the ego. This, Freud reasoned, was the basic dynamic of mourning and melancholic states. The loss of an object in the real world meant a corresponding depletion in the ego: To relinquish a loved object was to subject oneself to a sometimes massive trauma. Freud theorized on the rather elaborate procedures that society sets up to ease this relinquishing of objects: The funeral rites, mourning rituals, and so on. There is nothing fundamentally wrong with Freud's view of depression, but it explains a good deal. Its principal drawback is that it is used to explain too much.

Szasz's objection to the traditional view of depression is precisely its insistence on the predominant importance of object-loss in unleashing dependency cravings and hostility. He proposes to emend this by stressing that the loss of 'game' is fully as significant in depression as is the loss of an object. 'Game' in this context, is a series of norms of rules for significant action. And for the symbolic animal, there is nothing 'playful' about significance. Szasz said that . . . persons need not only human objects but also norms or rule—or, more generally—games that are worth playing. It is a matter of everyday observation that their object world might remain more or less intact. To account for this and similar events, it is necessary to consider the relationship of the ego or self to games. Otherwise, one is forced to reduce all manners of personal suffering to consideration of object relationships . . . Conversely, since loss of a real or external object implies the loss of a player from the game—unless some substitute whits exactly can be found—such loss inevitably results in at least some changes in the game. It is thus, evident that the words 'player' and 'game' describe interdependent variables making dynamic steady states—for example, of persons, families, societies, and a combing of worth (1961).

With this broadening out of traditional object-loss theory, there is no longer any valid pretense for keeping the phenomenon of depression within the realm of medicine. The psychoanalysis is fully linked as, with social science, since, as Szasz insists, objects and games are inseparably joined, self and society must be seen as a single phenomenon. People 'create' objects by acting according to social rules. They 'create' themselves as they create objects. Social rules are objects provide man with a staged drama of significance which is the theatre of his action. Man discovers himself by making appeal for his identity to the society in which he performs. To lose an object, then, is to lose someone to whom one has made appeal for self-validation. To lose a game is to lose a performance part in which identity is fabricated and sustained.

For the most part, this model represents the advanced theoretical cogitations of the psychiatric profession on a perplexing human phenomenon. This much must be said, as it is not easy to comprehend why anyone would opt out of life. It is understandable that we would be quick to look for some basic genetic taint, some stunted early development, that would mark such an individual off from others. But the matter is not quite simple: The fact is that a good proposition of depressed patients' has led mature and responsible lives. We distorted our vision if we use the theoretical proponents as to explain why these people become abysmally depressed.

It is amazing that human action could have been so consistently and thoroughly conceived in instinctual and compartmentalized terms. It is to the credit of some psychoanalysts that they themselves have begun to a breakout of their own inherited theories, and to range more broadly for an explanation of depression. This is part of the natural development of ego psychology. As the view of man as a cultural animal shaped by learning takes over from the older instinctual explanations, the way in clear for a full theoretical

RICHARD J. KOSCIEJEW

understanding, that if the ego is the basis for action, and if a warm feeling of self-value must pervade one's acts, then it is only a step to focussing on the really crucial dynamic of a breakdown in action, in the undermining of the individual's sense of self-value.

We take to note, that the answering to one common human problem is given by one thing in answering the need for sentiment: That as the object of primary value in the world of meaning (Hallowell, 1955). Data from anthropology support that nowhere on this once-vast globe had man been able to act unless he had a basic sentiment of self-value. Unless the individual feels worthwhile, and unless his actions are considered worthwhile and life grinds to a halt. Whole cultures have begun to expire in this way.

Behaviour models of depression are relatively new, compared to the Psychodynamic formulations that have just been presented. The behavioural perspective on psychopathology development later, but it is also true that behaviourists at first neglected the subject of depression. A few papers appeared in the late sixties (Burgess, 1968 and Lazarus, 1968), but they were highly speculative and lacked rigorous definition or analysis of depressive behaviour.

The behavioural perspective emphasizes the analysis of psychopathology in term s of observable behaviour in relation to preceding and consequential events in the environment—controlling stimuli and reinforcement consequences. Yet a behavioural definition of depression has remained rather elusive. Depression does not refer to a single response class, at least, as it has traditionally been defined, its primary symptom is a state of subjective distress. It is often the case that depressed persons do not exhibit any marked changes in overt behaviour despite their considerable distress and sense of personal inadequacy. As a group, depressed do not share of personal inadequacy, of specific behavioural excessive or deficiencies. Furthermore, depression often seems to involve a change in behaviour without any apparent change in the conditions that have previously maintained them (Costello, 1972). For instance, upon leaning that his former girl friend back home has become engaged to someone else, a college student might stop eating regularly, withdraw from his friends on campus, and neglect his studying.

Of necessity, the two most influential behavioural formulations of depression (Lewinsohn, Miller, Roselling and Seligman) involved the introduction of some concepts that go substantially beyond

136

the usual analysis of reinforcement contingencies. Consistent with more general trends in psychology, they both also were later modified to include an emphasis on cognition.

Lewinsohn developed a model of depression that was an extension of an earlier model presented by Ferster (1973, 1974), in which the central features of the disorder were identified as a reduction in the emission of positively reenforced behaviour. A major innovation in the Lewinsohn formulation was its emphasis on the concept of a total amount of response-contingently positive reinforcement 'reconposre'. The emission of some given adaptation is seen as not being merely a function of specific rewards available for it. Rather, it is also a function of the overall amount of positive reenforcement that is available as consequences for any available response. It is not a matter of this reinforcement being available but of its being contingent upon the person making a response.

Depression is connected through the conceptualization to a low rate of behaviour and a state of dysphoria that occur when there is a low rate of reconposre. There is a potential for a vicious cycle to develop, with a lower rate of positive reinforcement leading to a lower rate of adaptive behaviour, leading to a further reduction in reinforcement, and worth. Expression of distress may be met with reassurance, and in this way depressive behaviour can become the primary way of obtaining reinforcement.

The rate of response-contingent reinforcement available is dependent upon three sets of factors: The events that is potentially reinforcing to a person, of these, those that are available in the immediate environment, and the extent to which the person possesses the necessary skills to receive this reinforcement. Events that precipitate depression may do so by affecting one or more of these factors. For instance, for a man who has just become divorced, the availability to reinforcing events has been changed, and if he may become depressed.

The Lewinsohn model has been the basis for the development of an extensive research program, and a behavioural approach to therapy for depression that includes a self-treatment course (Lewinsohn, 1978). However, the given attention to the role of cognition in depression, that he has assumed that the complaints of depressed persons are not necessarily distortions and that they may instead reflect depressed persons' inability to obtain valued rewards. His research has been interpreted as suggesting that depressed persons are more accurate in their self-perceptions than nondepressed persons are (Lewinsohn, 1980).

Lewinsohn cites one study in particular as a major reason for his shift to move eclectically and a more cognitive model. Leiss, Lewinsohn and Munoz (1979) compared social skills training, the scheduling of pleasant activities, and cognitive therapy as treatments for depression. The result of the study indicated that not only were these treatments equally effective in reducing depression, but that they were not specific, i.e., cognitive therapy had as much effect on pleasant activities as did the scheduling of these activities.

By now it should be apparent as a self-evident phenomenon of depression, of which is sustained by as undefinable delineation and is poorly understood. Seligman and his colleagues have provided a fine example of the strategy for dealing with this problem: The construction can be achieved.

The term 'leaned; helplessness' was first used in connection with laboratory experiments in which dogs were exposed to shock from which they could not escape (Overmier and Seligmam, 1967). After repeated trials, the dogs tended to sit passively when the shock came on. Expose d to a new situation from which they could escape a hock by jumping over a barrier, and they failed to initiate the appropriate response. Some would occasionally jump over the barrier and escape, but they would generally revert to taking the shock passively. For the purpose of constructing an analogue of clinical depression, the behaviour of the dogs, is significant in suggesting that exposure to uncontrollable aversive situations and an inability to learn that responding is effective.

One cayuse of laboratory produced helplessness seems to be learning that one cannot control important events. Learning that responses and reinforcement are independent results in a cognitive set that has two effects—fewer responses to control reinforcement are initiated, and associating successful responses with reinforcement becomes more difficult.

The anchoring grounds of the analogy to depression are viewed in the disordering of fundamental matters of depressed persons being passive, e.g., as failing to initiate appropriate responses to cope with their predicaments—and unable to perceive that their responses make a difference. Thus, Lewinsohn invoked the concept of the total amount of response-contingent reinforcement to explain the rather generalized problems of depressed persons. Selgman and his colleagues introduce the notion of a generalized inhibition of response and an acquired perception of response-reinforcement independence.

The analogy to depression was bolstered by initial fi8ndings that in a variety of tasks situations, depressed human subjects resembled nondepressed subjects who had received repeated failure experiences. For instance, compared to non-depressed subjects who had not received repeated, failure experiences, the two groups of subjects took longer to solve anagrams and apparently failed to perceive the pattern underlying their successful solution (Klein and Seligman, 12976). While other researches by Miller, Rosellin and Seligman, 1976, were to suggest that the parallel between other groups that leaned helplessness and depression were not limited with regard to etiology, treatment, and prevention.

The original learned helplessness model stimulated a large body of research and considerable controversy (Buchward, Coyne and Cole, 1978, as well as, Costello, 1978). Ultimately, the accumulated research led to questions about both the adequacies of the learned-helplessness explanation for the behaviour of nondepressed subjects who had been exposed failure as well as the appropriateness of learned helplessness as an analogue of depression. For instance, it was shown that the performance deficits of subjects who had been given a typical learned helplessness induction were very much situation-specific (Cole and Coyne, 1977) and that these deficits might better be explained as the result of anxious self-preoccupation, rather than the perception of responses-reinforcement independence (Coyne, Metalsky, and Lavelle, 1980). Furthermore, the characterization of depressed persons as passive and lacking in aggression was challenged. Difficulties with the original leaned helplessness model led to a major reformulation.

Rehm`s self-control model of depression is less developed than either of the preceding two models, bu t it adds an additional dimension in the literature or the role played of cognition in depression. Rehm draws on the work of Kanfer (1070) and others suggesting that depression is a matter of some interrelated problems in self-control. Briefly, the self-control model assumes that people may regulate their own behaviour in a way that allows them to be somewhat independent of their immediate environment and the controlling stimuli and reinforcement contingencies that it offers. Self-monitoring involves attending to one's behaviour and the antecedent as resulting of circumstance. Self-evaluation is simply a matter of interpreting one's behaviour and comparing it to internal standards. Attributional processing is one set of determinants containing the evaluations that are made. Self-reinforcement involves administering reinforcement in the obtainability of itself, just as one could administer reinforcement to someone else. Furthermore, self-reinforcement can implicitly place upon cognizance, in the sense that one can acclaim to glorify and exalt especially in song or writing for all to aspire and amenably enhanced or to criticize behaviour, privately or to oneself.

Depression may be seen as a reflection of deficiencies in one or more of these self-control processes. First, the self-monitoring of depressed persons may be maladaptive in that they selectively attend to negative aspects of their own behaviour and ignore positive accomplishments. Their self-evaluations may involve an attributional bias so that they are excessively blamed for failures and take insufficient credit for successes. They may employ overly harsh or stringent standards in evaluating themselves. Finally, they may be stingie in rewarding themselves or overly self-punishing

Rehm is explicit in his indebtedness to other cognitive and behavioural models of depression. However, this model can go beyond the more behavioural models in providing an alternative way of explaining depression. Moreover, the identification of deficiencies in self-control processes suggests specific therapeutic intervention. To alter them would not be suggested by the other interventions. To alter them would not be suggested by the other approaches. In addition, as number of studies have produced results consistent with hypotheses derived from the model (Kanfer and Zeiss, 1983) although questions have been raised as to whether deficits in self-monitoring, self-evaluation and self-reward are specific to depression (Gotlib, 1981).

Beck noted that there was a lack of systematic psychological research on depression, least of mention, the cognitive model he presented did much to change that situation. A recent review (Coyne and Gotlib, 1983), cited 100 studies that were generated by prevailing cognitive models alone. Cognitive models of depression have a strong intuitive appeal. The self-deprecating and pessimistic talk of depressed persons and their apparent failure to take obvious steps to remedy their situations readily invites the suggestion that they suffer from distorted cognitive processes.

In the model presented by Kovacs and Beck, three sets of interrelated cognitive concepts are used to explain the psychological phenomenon of depression: The cognitive triad, schemata, and cognitive distortion or faculty information processing. These cognitive factors are seen as having a causal primacy over the affective, motivational, and behavioural features of depression.

The cognitive triad consists of thinking patterns that lead depressed persons to construe themselves, their current situation, and their future possibilities in negative terms. The concept of schematics is used to explain why depressed persons persist in these negative and self-defeating attitudes, even in the face of contradictory evidence. Cognitive schematicism is stable, organized representation of past experiences that provide for the screening, differentiations, and encoding of information from the environment. In depression, prepotent dysfunctional schemata dominate information processing so that depressed persons may not even be able to consider processing so that depressed persons may not even be able to consider alternative interpretations of their experience that are more positive or optimistic. They overgeneralized from negative experiences, selectively abstract negative details out of context, and negatively characterized themselves in absolutist terms—always, never, nothing by, etc.

These cognitive processes are activated in the depressed person by stressful experiences, but they exist before a depressive episode in a latent state. In explaining how a vulnerability of these thinking processes comes about, Beck (1974) has offered an account that bears a strong resemblance to Psychodynamic formulations: It is said, that, in the course of his development, the depression-prone person may become sensitized by certain unfavourable types of life situations such as the loss of a parent or chronic rejection by peers. Other unfavourable conditions of a more insidious nature may similarly produce vulnerability to depression. These traumatic experiences predispose the individual to overact to analogous situations later in life. He has a tendency to make extreme, absolute judgements when such situations occur.

Although the original learned-helplessness model could also be said to be cognitive in the sense that it invoked the concept of a perception of response-reinforcement independence. It defines this perception in terms of its environment antecedents and behavioural consequences. Overall, the model gave little attention to higher cognitive processes. In the reformulation model, such that Abramson, Seligman and Teasdale have emphasized, to those of a learned helplessness in which a person inappropriately generalizes the expectation of contingency to a new, controllable situation. It is important to point out that the old hypothesis does not require an inappropriate generalization for helplessness. Helplessness exists when a person shows motivational and cognitive deficits as a consequence of an expectation among situations over which it has the circumstance to occasion of occurring, such are irrelevantly to demonstrating helplessness. But the old hypothesis does not specify where and when a person who expects outcomes to be uncontrollable will show deficits.

Nonetheless, the additional requirement was that the person must come to expect that future outcomes would also be uncontrollable, and higher cognitive processes were assumed to mediate the development of his expectation. 'When a person finds that he is helpless, he asks 'why' he is helpless. The causal attributions are that makes determine the generality and chronicity of his helplessness deficits as well as his later self-esteem.

According to the helplessness view, the central theme in successful therapy should be having the patient discover and come to accept that his responses produce the gratification that he desires—that he is, in short, an effective human being. Some therapists that reportedly alleviate depression are consonant with a learned helplessness model. However, it is important to note that the success of a therapy often has little to do with its theoretical underpinning. So, with the exception of Klein and Seligman (1976), the following 'evidence' should not be regarded as a test of the model, but merely as a set of examples that seem to have exposure to response-produced success as a cure for depression.

Consonant with their helplessness-centred views of the etiology depression, Bibring (1953), Beck (1967) and Melges and Bowlby (1969) all stressed that revering helplessness alleviates depression. For example, Bibring has stated, in that, the same conditions which bring about depression (helplessness) in reverse serve frequently the restitution from depression. Generally one can say that depression subsides either (1) when the narcissistically important goals and objects appear to be again within reach (which is frequently followed by irregular elation or (2) when they become sufficiently modified or reduced to become realizable, or (3) when they are altogether relinquished, or4) when they together relinquished, or (5) when the ego recovers from the narcissistic shock by regaining its self-esteem with the help of various recovery mechanisms (with or without any change of objective or goal).

In their review of therapies for depression, Seligman, Klein and Miller (1976) indicated that most of the therapies have strong elements of inducing the patient to discover that responses produce the reinforcement he desires. In antidepression milieu therapy (Taulbee and Wright, 1971)m for example, the patient is forced to emit one of the most powerful response people have for controlling others—anger—and when this response is dragged out of his depleted behaviour repertoire, he is powerfully reinforced. Beck's (1770) cognitive therapy is aimed at similar goals. He sees success manipulations as changing the negative cognitive set ('I'm an effective person') of the depressive to a more positive set, and argues that the primary task of the therapist is to change the negative expectations of the depressed patient to more optimistic ones. In both Burgess's (1968) therapy and the graded task assignment (Beck, Seligman, Binik, and Brill), the patient makes instrumental responses of gradually increasing therapy for depression (Hersen, Eislere, Alford and Agras, 1973; Reisinger, 1972), by definition, arranges the contingencies so that responses control the occurrence of reinforcement; the patient's recognition of this relationship should alleviate depression. Lewinsohn's therapy also has this element: Participation in activity and other nondepressed behaviour controls therapy time (Lewinsohn, Weinsyein and Shaw, 1969). In assertive training (Wolpe, 1968), the patient must emit social responses to bring about a desired change in his environment.

As in learned helplessness, the passage of time has been found to alleviate depression. Electroconvulsive therapy, which alleviates helplessness, probably alleviates endogenous depression (Carney, Roth and Garside, 1965), but its effects on reactive depression are unclear. The role of atropine is largely unknown (Janowsky, 1972).

Dramatic success in medicine has come more frequently from prevention than from treatment, and we would hazard a guess that inoculation and immunization have saved many more lives than any cure. Psychotherapy is almost exclusively limited to use as a cure, and preventive procedures rarely play an explicit role. In our studies

143

of animals we found that behavioural immunization provided an easy and effective means of preventing learned helplessness.

One can also look at successful therapy as prevention. After all, therapy is usually not focussed just on undoing past problems. It also should arm the patient against future depressions. Would therapy for depression be more successful if it were explicitly aimed at providing the patient with a wide repertoire of coping responses that he could use in future situations where he found he could not control reinforcement by his responses?

Finally, we can speculate about child rearing. What kinds of experience can best protect our children against the debilitating effect of helplessness and depression? A tentative answer follows from the learned helplessness view of depression: A childhood of experiences in which one's own actions are instrumental in bringing about gratification and removing annoyances. Seeing oneself as an effective human being mat require a childhood filled with powerfully synchronous, between responding and its consequences.

Testing the learned helplessness model of depression requires the demonstration of similarities in symptoms, etiology, prevention and cure of learned helplessness. The current evidence, reviewed in this model, indicates that in many respects the major symptoms of helplessness parallel those of depression. In addition, it has been suggested that the cure of both reactive depression and learned helplessness is the belief that responses do not control important reinforcers. Finally, we have speculated that the methods that succeed in curing and preventing learned helplessness has their parallels in the cure and prevention of depression. Much remains to be tested, however, we can believe that a common theme has emerged as both depression and learned helplessness have at their core the belief in the futility of responding.

Psychosis, is a mental illness in which a person loses contact with reality and has difficulty functioning in daily life. Psychotic symptoms can indicate severe mental illnesses, such as schizophrenia and bipolar disorder (manic-depressive illness). Unlike people with fewer severe psychological problems, psychotic individuals do not usually recognize that their mental functioning is disturbed.

Mental health professionals generally divide psychotic symptoms into three broad types: hallucinations, delusions, and bizarre behaviour. Hallucinations refer to hearing, seeing, smelling, feeling, or tasting something when nothing in the environment actually caused that sensation. For example, a person experiencing an auditory hallucination might hear a voice calling her or his name even though no one else is actually present. A delusion is a false belief held by a person that appears obviously untrue to other people in that person's culture. For example, a man may believe that Martians have implanted a microchip in his brain that controls his thoughts. Bizarre behaviour refers to behaviour in a person that is strange or incomprehensible to others who know the person. For example, hoarding unused scraps of tin because of their 'magical properties' would be a type of bizarre behaviour.

Psychosis can occur in a number of mental illnesses. These include schizophrenia and schizophrenia-related disorders, bipolar disorder, paranoid personality disorder, and delusional disorder. Less common, psychotic symptoms occur in major depression (severe depression), Dissociative disorders, and post-traumatic stress disorder.

Psychotic symptoms can also result from substance abuse. Stimulants, such as cocaine and amphetamines, can cause psychotic symptoms, especially if taken in high doses or over long periods of time. Hallucinogenic substances, such as lysergic acid diethylamide (LSD), mescaline, and phencyclidine (PCP), can cause psychosis. Alcohol and marijuana can occasionally cause psychotic symptoms as well. Individuals with alcoholism may experience psychotic symptoms, especially hallucinations, as they withdraw from alcohol use. Alcohol dependence over a long period of time can result in Korsakoff's psychosis, a syndrome that may include psychotic symptoms and an inability form new memories. Certain medical conditions can also cause psychosis. Syphilis, especially if untreated for many years, can lead to psychosis. Brain tumours can also lead to psychotic symptoms.

Treatment of psychotic symptoms usually involved taking Antipsychotic drugs, and called neuroleptics. Common Antipsychotic drugs include chlorpromazine (Thorazine), fluphenazine (Prolixin), thioridazine (Mellaril), trifluoperazine (Stelazine), clozapine (Clozaril), haloperidol (Haldol), olanzapine (Zyprexa), and risperidone (Risperdal). These medications can help reduce psychotic symptoms and prevent symptoms from returning. However, they can also cause severe side effects, such as muscle spasms, tremors, and tardive dyskinesia, a permanent condition marked by uncontrollable lip smacking, grimacing, and tongue movements. Psychotic symptoms in individuals with bipolar disorder may respond to other types of medication, including lithium, carbamazepine (Tegretol), and valproate (Depakene).

Psychotic symptoms that occur as a result of substance abuse usually disappear gradually after the person stops using the substances. Physicians sometimes use Antipsychotic medications temporarily to treat these individuals. Physicians have not discovered any effective treatments for Korsakoff's psychosis. Psychotic symptoms resulting from medical conditions often disappear after treatment of the underlying medical problem

Neurosis, in psychoanalysis, as a mental illness is characterized by anxiety and disturbances in one's personality. Generally, only psychologists who adhere to a psychoanalytic or Psychodynamic model of abnormal behaviour use the term neurosis. Psychiatrists and psychologists no longer accept the term as a formal diagnosis. Layperson sometimes uses the word neurotic to describe an emotionally unstable person.

Scottish physician William Cullen coined the term neurosis near the end of the 18th century to describe a wide variety of nervous behaviours with no apparent physical cause. Austrian psychoanalyst Sigmund Freud and his followers popularized the word in the late 19th and early 20th centuries. Freud defined neurosis as one class of mental illnesses. In his view, people became neurotic when their conscious mind repressed inappropriate fantasies of the unconscious mind.

Until 1980 neuroses appeared as a specific diagnostic category in the Diagnostic and Statistical Manual of Mental Disorders, a handbook for mental health professionals. Neurosis encompassed a variety of mental illnesses, including Dissociative disorders, anxiety disorders, and phobias.

In the psychoanalytic model, neurosis differs from psychosis, another general term used to describe mental illnesses. Individuals with neuroses can function at work and in social situations, whereas people with psychoses find it quite difficult function adequately. People with neuroses do not grossly distort or misinterpret reality as those with psychoses do. In addition, neurotic individuals recognize that their mental functioning is disturbed while psychotic individuals usually do not. Most mental health professionals now use the term psychosis to refer to symptoms such as hallucinations, delusions, and bizarre behaviour.

Dissociative Identity Disorder, often called multiple personality disorder, mental illness in which a person has two or more distinct identities or personality states, which recurrently take control of the person's consciousness and behaviour. The person often gives the alternate identities their own personal names, and these identities may have characteristics that differ sharply from the person's primary identity. In addition, these people with this disorder experiences some degree of amnesia, in that one personality usually will not recall what occurred when another personality controlled the person.

People often act and feel differently in various settings. For example, teenagers may act differently at a party than they do at school. However, people in good mental health maintain continuous awareness of themselves no matter what the situation. Individuals with Dissociative identity disorder do not. They experience sudden shifts in consciousness, identity, and memory. They may find themselves in a strange apartment and not remember how they got there, or discover new clothing in their closet without knowing how it was purchased. Their identity is fragmented into pieces with different emotions, memories, and styles of interacting with people. They may shift from being passive and accepting of advice from others to being hostile and uncooperative. They are often at war with themselves, with certain personalities being quite critical of other personalities. At times one personality may go as inflicting physical harm on one of the other personalities. In one case, a woman with Dissociative identity disorder carved the words 'I hate Joan' on her forearm while in a different personality state.

In 1994 the American Psychiatric Association (APA) changed the name of the disorder from multiple personality disorder to Dissociative identity disorder. Psychiatrists wanted to emphasize the fact that the disorder does not really consist of many personalities living in one body, but rather of a failure to integrate various aspects of identity into a unified personality. In a sense that peoples with this disorder of contentually distorting the state of being different, whereupon, the disparity found in the adequation are equally to undo the fixed or proper order of something configured as a content of disorder. However, contentual gratification is contentual and does not suffer from having more than one personality but rather from having less than one personality.

Typically the disorder begins in childhood or adolescence, although the symptoms may not become evident to others for many years. In childhood, individuals with Dissociative identity disorder often appear moody or irresponsible because they may switch personalities suddenly or deny having done something as they no longer remember. Physicians often misdiagnose people with this disorder as having other mental illnesses, although critics claim the disorder is an invention of the therapists, as most experts agree it is a real but rare condition.

Most individuals with Dissociative identity disorder report histories of severe and repeated physical, sexual, or emotional abuse in childhood. This does not mean that everyone with the disorder was necessarily mistreated. However, most psychiatrists now understand the disorder as a reaction to chronic trauma and stress. People frequently enter altered states of consciousness during traumatic events such as physical or sexual assault, natural disasters, motor vehicle accidents, or combat. They detach or dissociate themselves from their immediate circumstances as a means of protecting themselves from overwhelming mental or physical pain. In Dissociative identity disorder this useful ability may become conditioned by repeated trauma, leading to separate personality states that may be triggered by any anxiety or stress.

The best treatment for the disorder is long-term psychotherapy aimed at helping patients to gain insight into each of their personality states, work through the aftermath of traumatic memories, achieve greater self-acceptance, and reduce self-damaging behaviour. Hypnosis may help a person control spontaneous switching of personality states. Many people with this disorder suffer from depression and may benefit from antidepressant medication as well.

Some evidence suggests that schizophrenia may result from an imbalance of chemicals in the brain called neurotransmitters. These chemicals enable neurons (brain cells) to communicate with other. Some scientists suggest that schizophrenia result from excess activity of the neurotransmitter dopamine in certain parts of the brain or from an abnormal sensitivity to dopamine. Support for this hypothesis comes from Antipsychotic drugs, which reduce psychotic symptoms in schizophrenia by blocking brain receptors for dopamine. In addition, amphetamines, which increase dopamine activity, intensify psychotic symptoms in people with schizophrenia. Despite these findings, many experts believe that excess dopamine activity alone cannot account for schizophrenia. Other neurotransmitters, such as serotonin and norepinephrine, may play important roles as well.

Brain imaging techniques, such as magnetic resonance imaging and positron-emission tomography, have led researchers to discover specific structural abnormalities in the brains of people with schizophrenia. For example, people with chronic schizophrenia tend to have enlarged brain ventricles (cavities in the brain that contains cerebrospinal fluid). They also have a smaller overall volume of brain tissue compared to mentally healthy people. Other people with schizophrenia show abnormally low activity in the frontal lobe of the brain, which governs abstract thought, planning, and judgment. Research has identified possible abnormalities in many other parts of the brain, including the temporal lobes, basal ganglia, thalamus, hippocampus, and superior temporal gyrus. These defects may partially explain the abnormal thoughts, perceptions, and behaviours that characterize schizophrenia.

Evidence suggests those factors in the prenatal environment and during birth can increase the risk of a person later developing schizophrenia. These events are believed to affect the brain development of the fetus during a critical period. For example, pregnant women who have been exposed to the influenza virus or who have poor nutrition have a slightly increased chance of giving birth to a child who later develops schizophrenia. In addition, obstetric complications during the birth of a child—for example, delivery with forceps—can slightly increase the chances of the child later developing schizophrenia.

Although scientists favour a biological cause of schizophrenia, stress in the environment may affect the onset and course of the illness. Stressful life circumstances—such as growing up and living in poverty, the death of a loved one, an important change in jobs or relationships, or chronic tension and hostility at home—can increase the chances of schizophrenia in a person biologically predisposed to the disease. In addition, stressful events can trigger a relapse of symptoms in a person who already has the illness. Individuals who have effective skills for managing stress may be less susceptible to its negative effects. Psychological and social rehabilitation can help patients develop more effective skills for dealing with stress.

Although there is no cure for schizophrenia, effective treatment exists that can improve the long-term course of the illness. With

RICHARD J. KOSCIEJEW

many years of treatment and rehabilitation, significant numbers of people with schizophrenia experience partial or full remission of their symptoms.

Treatment of schizophrenia usually involves a combination of medication, rehabilitation, and treatment of other problems the person may have. Antipsychotic drugs (also called neuroleptics) are the most frequently used medications for treatment of schizophrenia. Psychological and social rehabilitation programs may help people with schizophrenia function in the community and reduce stress related to their symptoms. Treatment of secondary problems, such as substance abuse and infectious diseases, is also an important part of an overall treatment program.

Common psychotherapeutic drugs as Antipsychotic medications, developed in the mid-1950s, can dramatically improve the quality of life for people with schizophrenia. The drugs reduce or eliminate psychotic symptoms such as hallucinations and delusions. The medications can also help prevent these symptoms from returning. Common Antipsychotic drugs include risperidone (Risperdal), olanzapine (Zyprexa), clozapine (Clozaril), quetiapine (Seroquel), haloperidol (Haldol), thioridazine (Mellaril), chlorpromazine (Thorazine), fluphenazine (Prolixin), and trifluoperazine (Stelazine). People with schizophrenia usually must take medication for the rest of their lives to control psychotic symptoms. Antipsychotic medications appear to be less effective at treating other symptoms of schizophrenia, such as social withdrawal and apathy.

Antipsychotic drugs help reduce symptoms in 80 to 90 percent of people with schizophrenia. However, those who benefit often stop taking medication because they do not understand that they are ill or because of unpleasant side effects. Minor side effects include weight gain, dry mouth, blurred vision, restlessness, constipation, dizziness, and drowsiness. Other side effects are more serious and debilitating. These may include muscle spasms or cramps, tremors, and tardive dyskinesia, an irreversible condition marked by uncontrollable movements of the lips, mouth, and tongue. Newer drugs, such as clozapine, olanzapine, risperidone, and quetiapine, tend to produce fewer of these side effects. However, clozapine can cause agranulocytosis, a significant reduction in white blood cells necessary tight infections. This condition can be fatal if not detected early enough. For this reason, people taking clozapine must have weekly tests to monitor their blood.

Because many patients with schizophrenia continue to experience difficulties despite taking medication, psychological and social rehabilitation is often necessary. A variety of methods can be effective. Social skill training helps people with schizophrenia learn specific behaviours for functioning in society, such as making friends, purchasing items at a store, or initiating conversations. Behavioural training methods can also help them learn self-care skills such as personal hygiene, money management, and proper nutrition. In addition, cognitive-Behavioural therapy, a type of psychotherapy, can help reduce persistent symptoms such as hallucinations, delusions, and social withdrawal.

Family intervention programs can also benefit people with schizophrenia. These programs focus on helping family members understand the nature and treatment of schizophrenia, how to monitor the illness, and how to help the patient make progress toward personal goals and greater independence. They can also lower the stress experienced by everyone in the family and help prevent the patient from relapsing or being rehospitalized.

Because many patients have difficulty obtaining or keeping jobs, supported employment programs that help patients find and maintain jobs are a helpful part of rehabilitation. In these programs, the patient works alongside people without disabilities and earns competitive wages. An employment specialist (or vocational specialist) helps the person maintain their job by, for example, training the person in specific skills, helping the employer accommodate the person, arranging transportation, and monitoring performance. These programs are most effective when the supported employment is closely integrated with other aspects of treatment, such as medication and monitoring of symptoms.

Some people with schizophrenia are vulnerable frequent crises because they do not regularly go to mental health centres to receive the treatment they need. These individuals often relapse and face rehospitalization. To ensure that such patients take their medication and receive appropriate psychological and social rehabilitation, assertive community treatment (ACT) programs have been developed that deliver treatment to patients in natural settings, such as in their homes, in restaurants, or on the street.

People with schizophrenia often have other medical problems, so an effective treatment program must attend to these as well. One of the most retributively associated problems is substance abuse. Successful treatment of substance abuse in patients with schizophrenia requires careful coordination with their mental health care, so that the same clinicians are treating both disorders at the same time.

The high rate of substance abuse in patients with schizophrenia contributes to a high prevalence of infectious diseases, including hepatitis B and C and the human immunodeficiency virus (HIV). Assessment, education, and treatment or management of these illnesses is critical for the long-term health of patients.

Other problems frequently associated with schizophrenia include housing instability and homelessness, legal problems, violence, trauma and post-traumatic stress disorder, anxiety, depression, and suicide attempts. Close monitoring and psychotherapeutic interventions are often helpful in addressing these problems.

Several other psychiatric disorders are closely related to schizophrenia. In schizoaffective disorder, a person shows symptoms of schizophrenia combined whether mania or severe depression. Schizophreniform disorder refers to an illness in which a person experiences schizophrenic symptoms for more than one month but fewer than six months. In schizotypal personality disorder, a person engages in odd thinking, speech, and behaviour, but usually does not lose contact with reality. Sometimes mental health professionals refer to these disorders together as schizophrenia-spectrum disorders'

Schizophrenia, is a severe mental illness characterizes a variety of symptoms, including loss contact with reality, bizarre behaviour, disorganized thinking and speech, decreased emotional expressiveness, and social withdrawal, yet, only some of these symptoms occur in any one person. The term schizophrenia comes from Greek words meaning 'split mind.' However, contrary to common belief, schizophrenia does not refer to a person with a split personality or multiple personality. For a description of a mental illness in which a person has multiple personalities is to views as an observer, such that the personal conducting Schizophrenia may seem like madness or the insanity of mind that impairs one's capacity to function safely or normally in society.

Perhaps more than any other mental illness, schizophrenia has a debilitating effect on the lives of the people who suffer from it. A person with schizophrenia may have difficulty telling the difference between real and unreal experiences, logical and illogical thoughts or appropriate or inappropriately consist within personal behavioural conduct. Schizophrenia seriously impairs a person's ability to work, go to school, enjoy relationships with others, or take care of oneself. In addition, people with schizophrenia frequently require hospitalization because they pose a danger to themselves. About 10 percent of people with schizophrenia commit suicide, and many others attempt suicide. Once people develop schizophrenia, they usually suffer from the illness for the rest of their lives. Although there is no cure, treatment can help many people with schizophrenia lead productive lives.

Schizophrenia also carries an enormous cost to society. People with schizophrenia occupy about one-third of all beds in psychiatric hospitals in the United States. In addition, people with schizophrenia account for at least 10 percent of the homeless population in the United States. The National Institute of Mental Health has estimated that schizophrenia costs the United States tens of billions of dollars each year in direct treatment, social services, and lost productivity.

Approximately 1 percent of people develop schizophrenia at some time during their lives. Experts estimate that about 1.8 million people in the United States have schizophrenia. The prevalence of schizophrenia is the same, irrespective of sex, race, and culture. Although women are just as likely as men to develop schizophrenia, women tend to live through the illness with less severity and with fewer hospitalizations and better social functioning in the community.

Schizophrenia usually develops in late adolescence or early adulthood, between the ages of 15 and 30. Much less common, schizophrenia develops later in life. The illness may begin abruptly, but it usually develops slowly over months or years. Mental health professionals diagnose schizophrenia based on an interview with the patient in which they determine whether the person has experienced specific symptoms of the illness.

Symptoms and functioning in people with schizophrenia tend to vary over time, sometimes worsening and other times improving. For many patients the symptoms gradually become less severe as they grow older. About 25 percent of people with schizophrenia become symptom-free later in their lives.

A variety of symptoms characterize schizophrenia. The most prominent include symptoms of psychosis—such as delusions and hallucinations—as well as bizarre behaviour, strange movements, and disorganized thinking and speech. Many people with schizophrenia do not recognize that their mental functioning is disturbed.

`Delusions are false beliefs that appear obviously untrue to other people. For example, a person with schizophrenia may believe that he is the king of England when he is not. People with schizophrenia may have delusions that others, such as the police or the FBI, are plotting against them or spying on them. They may believe that aliens are controlling their thoughts or that their own thoughts are being broadcast to the world so that other people can hear them.

Personality Disorders, are mentally apprehended disorders in which one's personality results in personal distress or significantly impairs social or work functioning. Every person has a personality—that is, a characteristic way of thinking, feeling, behaving, and relating to others. Most people experience at least some difficulties and problems that result from their personality. The specific point at which those problems justify the diagnosis of a personality disorder is controversial. To some extent the definition of a personality disorder is arbitrary, reflecting subjectively as well as professional judgments about the person's degree of dysfunction, needs for change, and motivation for change.

Personality disorders involve behaviour that deviates from the norms or expectations of one's culture. However, people who deviant from cultural norms are not necessarily dysfunctional, nor are people who conform to cultural norms necessarily healthy. Many personality disorders represent extreme variants of behaviour patterns that people usually value and encourage. For example, most people value confidence but not arrogance, agreeableness but not submissiveness, and conscientiousness but not perfectionism.

Because no clear line exists between healthy and unhealthy functioning, critics question the reliability of personality disorder diagnoses. A behaviour that seems deviant to one person may seem normal to another depending on one's gender, ethnicity, and cultural background. The personal and cultural biases of mental health professionals may influence their diagnoses of personality disorders.

An estimated 20 percent of people in the general population have one or more personality disorders. Some people with personality disorders have other mental illnesses as well. About 50 percent of people who are treated for any psychiatric disorder have a personality disorder.

Mental health professionals rarely diagnose personality disorders in children because their manner of thinking, feeling, and relating to others does not usually stabilize until young adulthood. Thereafter, personality traits usually remain stable. Personality disorders often decrease in severity as people age.

The foundation of the Diagnostic and Statistical Manual of Mental Disorders (DSM-IV), published by the American, Psychiatric Association, describes ten personality disorders. This article imparts upon the description in detail. Two of the more base personality disorders, antisocial personality disorder and borderline personality disorders bear upon a brief description of other types of a personality dysfunction.

People with antisocial personality disorder act in a way that disregards the feelings and rights of other people. Antisocial personalities often break the law, and they may use or exploit other people for their own gain. They may lie repeatedly, act impulsively, and get into physical fights. They may mistreat their spouses, neglect or abuse their children, and exploit their employees. They may even kill other people. People with this disorder are also sometimes called sociopaths or psychopaths. Antisocial behaviour in people less than 18 years old is called conduct disorder.

Antisocial personalities usually fail to understand that their behaviour is dysfunctional because their ability feels guilty, remorseful, and anxious is impaired. Guilt, remorse, shame, and anxiety are unpleasant feelings, but they are also necessary for social functioning and even physical survival. For example, people lacking in the ability to feel anxious will often fail to anticipate actual dangers and risks. They may take chances that other people would not take.

Antisocial personality disorder affects about 3 percent of males and 1 percent of females. This is the most heavily researched personality disorder, in part because it costs society the most. People with this disorder are at high risk for premature and violent death, injury, imprisonment, loss of employment, bankruptcy, alcoholism, drug dependence, and failed personal relationships.

People with borderline personality disorder experience intense emotional instability, particularly in relationships with others. They may make frantic efforts to avoid real or imagined abandonment by others. They may experience minor problems as major crises. They may also express their anger, frustration, and dismay through suicidal gestures, self-mutilation, and other self-destructive acts. They tend to have an unstable self-image or sense of self.

As children, most people with this disorder were emotionally unstable, impulsive, and often bitter or angry, although their chaotic impulsiveness and intense emotions may have made them popular at school. At first they may impress people as stimulating and exciting, but their relationships tend to be unstable and explosive.

About 2 percent of all people have borderline personality disorder. About 75 percent of people with this disorder are female. Borderline personalities are at high risk for developing depression, alcoholism, drug dependence, bulimia, Dissociative disorders, and post-traumatic stress disorder. As many as 10 percent of people with this disorder commit suicide by the age of 30. People with borderline personality disorder are among the most difficult to treat with psychotherapy, in part because their relationship with their therapist may become as intense and unstable as their other personal relationships.

Avoidant personality disorder is social withdrawal due to intense, anxious shyness. People with Avoidant personalities are reluctant to interact with others unless they feel certain of the equivalent capabilities and dislike the criticism and rejection. Often they view themselves as socially inept and inferior to others.

Dependent personality disorder involves severe and disabling emotional dependency on others. People with this disorder have difficulty making decisions without a great deal of advice and reassurance from others. They urgently seek out another relationship when a close relationship ends. They feel uncomfortable by themselves.

People with histrionic personality disorder constantly strive to be the pivotal point of attention. They may act overly flirtatious or dress in ways that draw attention. They may also talk in a dramatic or theatrical style and display exaggerated emotional reactions.

People with narcissistic personality disorder have a grandiose sense of self-importance. They seek excessive admiration from others and fantasize about unlimited success or power. They believe they are special, unique, or superior to others. However, they often have very fragile self-esteem.

Obsessive-compulsive personality disorder is characterized by a preoccupation with details, orderliness, perfection, and control. People with this disorder often devote excessive amounts of time to exert efforts and productivity and fail to take time for leisure activities and friendships. They tend to be rigid, formal, stubborn, and serious. This disorder differs from obsessive-compulsive disorder, which often includes more bizarre behaviour and rituals.

People with paranoid personality disorder feel constant suspicion and distrust toward other people. They believe that others are against them and constantly look for evidence to support their suspicions. They are hostile toward others and react angrily to perceived insults. Schizoid personality disorder involves social isolation and a lack of desire for close personal relationships. People with this disorder prefer to be alone and seem withdrawn and emotionally detached. They seem indifferent to graduate or criticize from other people.

People with schizotypal personality disorder engage in odd thinking, speech, and behaviour. They may ramble or use words and phrases in unusual ways, and they may believe they have magical control over others. They feel very uncomfortable with close personal relationships and tend to be suspicious of others. Some research suggests conveying an idea indirectly for meaning by which work is accomplished or an end effected. The act or process of passing from a higher to a lower level or state of ancestral primivity, that enduring a resolvable quality or state of being enfeebled and weakened in health, that our personal condition that limits or qualifies as an offer, that any concern of interest by anything to engage the attention and interest of having in some affair.

Psychiatrists and psychologists use two additional accessions or subject matter as a continuation or extension as or coming by way of some diagnoses. Depressive personality disorder is characterized by chronic pessimism, gloominess, and cheerlessness. In passive-aggressive personality disorder, a person passively resists completing tasks and chores, criticizes and scorns authority figures, and seems negative and sullen.

Personality disorders result from a complex interaction of inherited traits and life experience, not from a single cause. For example, some cases of antisocial personality disorder may result from a combination of a genetic predisposition to impulsiveness and violence, very inconsistent or erratic parenting, and a harsh environment that discourage feelings of empathy and warmth but rewards exploitation and aggressiveness. Borderline personality disorder may result from a genetic predisposition to impulsiveness and emotional instability combined with parental neglect, intense marital conflicts between parents, and repeated episodes of severe emotional or sexual abuse. Dependent personality disorder may result from genetically based anxiety, an inhibited temperament, and overly protective, clinging, or neglectful parenting.

The pervasive and chronic nature of personality disorders makes them difficult to treat. People with these disorders often fail to recognize that their personality has contributed to their social, occupational, and personal problems. They may not think they have any real problems despite a history of drug abuse, failed relationships, and irregular employment. Thus, therapists must first focus on helping the person understand and become aware of the significance of their personality traits.

People with personality disorders sometimes feel that they can never change their dysfunctional behaviour because they have always acted the same way. Although personality change is exceedingly difficult, sometimes people can change the most dysfunctional aspects of their feelings and behaviour.

Therapists use a variety of methods to treat personality disorders, depending on the specific disorder. For example, cognitive and behavioural techniques, such as role playing and logical argument, may help alter a person's irrational perceptions and assumptions about himself or herself. Certain psychoactive drugs may help control feelings of anxiety, depression, or severe distortions of thought. Psychotherapy may help people to understand the impact of experiences and relationships during childhood.

Psychotherapy is usually ineffective for people with antisocial personality disorder because these individuals tend to be manipulative, unreliable, and dishonest with the therapist. Therefore, most mental health professionals favour removing people with this disorder from their current living situation and placing them in a residential treatment centre. Such residential programs strictly supervise patients' behaviour and impose rigid, consistent rules and responsibilities. These programs appear to help some people, but it is unclear how long their beneficial effects last.

Therapists treating people with borderline personality disorder sometimes use a technique called dialectical behaviour therapy. In this type of therapy, the therapist initially focuses on reducing suicidal tendencies and other behaviours that disrupt treatment. The therapist then helps the person develop skills to cope with anger and self-destructive impulses. In addition, the person learns to achieve personal strength through an acceptance of the many disappointments and interpersonal conflicts that are a natural part of life.

Anxiety, is the emotional state in which people feel uneasy, apprehensive, or fearful. People usually experience anxiety about events they cannot control or predict, or about events that seem threatening or dangerous. For example, students taking an important test may feel anxious because they cannot predict the test questions or feel certain of a good grade. People often use the word's fear and anxiety to describe the same thing. Fear also describes a reaction to immediate danger characterized by a strong desire to escape the situation.

The physical symptoms of anxiety reflect upon the chronic 'readiness' to deal with some future threat. These symptoms may include fidgeting, muscle tension, sleeping problems, and headaches. Higher levels of anxiety may produce such symptoms as rapid heartbeat, sweating, increased blood pressure, nausea, and dizziness.

All people experience anxiety to some degree. Most people feel anxious when faced with a new situation, such as a first date, or when trying to do something well, such as give a public speech. A mild to moderate amount of anxiety in these situations is normal and even beneficial. Anxiety can motivate people to prepare for an upcoming event and can help keep them focussed on the task at hand.

However, too little anxiety or too much anxiety can cause problems. Individuals wheel no anxiety when faced with. An important situation may lack alertness and focus. On the other hand, individuals who experience an abnormally high amount of anxiety often feel overwhelmed, immobilized, and unable to accomplish the task at hand. People with too much anxiety often suffer from one of the anxiety disorders, a group of mental illnesses. In fact, more people experience anxiety disorders than any other type of mental illness, from which a survey of people aged 15 to 54 in the United States found that about 17 percent of this population suffers from an anxiety disorder during any given year.

People with generalized anxiety disorder feel anxious most of the time. They worry excessively about routine events or circumstances in their lives. Their worries fall within the realm of relatedness, family, personal health, and relationships with others. Although they recognize their anxiety as irrational or out of proportion to actual events, they feel unable to control their worrying. For example, they may worry uncontrollably and intensely about money despite evidence that their financial situation is stable. Children with this disorder typically worry about their performance at school or about catastrophic events, such as tornadoes, earthquakes, and nuclear war.

People with generalized anxiety disorder often find that their worries interfere with their ability function at work or concentrate on tasks. Physical symptoms, such as disturbed sleep, irritability, muscle aches, and tension, may accompany the anxiety. To receive a diagnosis of this disorder, individuals must have experienced its symptoms for at least six months.

Generalized anxiety disorder affects about 3 percent of people in the general population in any given year. From 55 to 66 percent of people with this disorder are female.

A phobia is an excessive, enduring fear of clearly defined objects or situations that interferes with a person's normal functioning. Although they know their fear is irrational, people with phobias always try to avoid the source of their fear. Common phobias include fear of heights (acrophobia), fear of enclosed places (claustrophobia), fear of insects, snakes, or other animals, and fear of air travel. Social phobias involve a fear of performing, of critical evaluation, or of being embarrassed in front of other people.

Panic is an intense, overpowering surge of fear. People with panic disorder experience panic attacks—periods of quickly escalating, intense fear and discomfort accompanied by such physical symptoms as rapid heartbeat, trembling, shortness of breath, dizziness, and nausea. Because people with this disorder cannot predict when these attacks will strike, they develop anxiety about having additional panic attacks and may limit their activities outside the home.

In obsessive-compulsive disorder, people persistently experience certain intrusive thoughts or images (obsessions) or feel compelled to perform certain behaviours (compulsions). Obsessions may include unwanted thoughts about inadvertently poisoning others or injuring a pedestrian while driving. Common compulsions include repetitive hand washing or such mental acts as repeated counting. People with this disorder often perform compulsions to reduce the anxiety produced by their obsessions. The obsessions and compulsions significantly interfere with their ability function and may consume a great deal of time.

Post-traumatic stress disorder sometimes occurs after people experience traumatic or catastrophic events, such as physical or sexual assaults, natural disasters, accidents, and wars. People with this disorder relive the traumatic event through recurrent dreams or intrusive memories called flashbacks. They avoid things or places associated with the trauma and may feel emotionally detached or estranged from others. Other symptoms may include difficulty sleeping, irritability, and trouble concentrating.

Most anxiety disorders do not have an obvious cause. They result from a combination of biological, psychological, and social factors.

Studies suggest that anxiety disorders run in families. That is, children and close relatives of people with disorders are more likely than most to develop anxiety disorders. Some people may inherit genes that make them particularly vulnerable to anxiety. These genes do not necessarily cause people to be anxious, but the genes may increase the risk of anxiety disorders when certain psychological and social factors are also present.

Anxiety also appears to be related to certain brain functions. Chemicals in the brain called neurotransmitters enable neurons, or brain cells, to communicate with each other. One neurotransmitter, gamma-amino butyric acid (GABA), appears to play a role in regulating one's level of anxiety. Lower levels of GABA are associated with higher levels of anxiety. Some studies suggest that the neurotransmitter's norepinephrine and serotonin play a role in panic disorder.

Psychologists have proposed a variety of models to explain anxiety. Austrian psychoanalyst Sigmund Freud suggested that anxiety result from internal, unconscious conflicts. He believed that a person's mind represses wishes and fantasies about which the person feels uncomfortable. This repression, Freud believed, results in anxiety disorders, which he called neuroses.

More recently, behavioural researchers have challenged Freud's model of anxiety. They believe one's anxiety level relates to how much a person believes events can be predicted or controlled. Children who have little control over events, perhaps because of overprotective parents, may have little confidence in their ability to handle problems as adults. This lack of confidence can lead to increased anxiety.

Behavioural theorists also believe that children may learn anxiety from a role model, such as a parent. By observing their parent's anxious response to difficult situations, the child may learn a similar anxious response. A child may also learn anxiety as a conditioned response. For example, an infant often startled by a loud noise while playing with a toy may become anxious just at the sight of the toy. Some experts suggest that people with a high level of anxiety misinterpret normal events as threatening. For instance, they may believe their rapid heartbeat indicates they are experiencing a panic attack when in reality it may be the result of exercise.

While some people may be biologically and psychologically predisposed feel anxious, most anxiety is triggered by social factors. Many people feel anxious in response to stress, such as a divorce, starting a new job, or moving. Also, how a person expresses anxiety appears to be shaped by social factors. For example, many cultures accept the expression of anxiety and emotion in women, but expect more reserved emotional displays from men.

Mental health professionals use a variety of methods to help people overcome anxiety disorders. These include psychoactive drugs and psychotherapy, particularly behaviour therapy. Other techniques, such as exercise, hypnosis, meditation, and biofeedback, may also prove helpful.

Psychiatrists often prescribe benzodiazepines, a group of tranquillizing drugs, to reduce anxiety in people with high levels of anxiety. Benzodiazepines help to reduce anxiety by stimulating the GABA neurotransmitter system. Common benzodiazepines include alprazolam (Xanax), clonazepam (Klonopin), and diazepam (Valium). Two classes of antidepressant drugs—tricyclics and selective serotonin reuptake inhibitors (SSRIs)—also have proven effective in treating certain anxiety disorders.

Benzodiazepines can work quickly with few unpleasant side effects, but they can also be addictive. In addition, benzodiazepines can slow down or impair motor behaviour or thinking and must be used with caution, particularly in elderly persons. SSRIs take longer to work than the benzodiazepines but are not addictive. Some people experience anxiety symptoms again when they stop taking the medications.

Therapists who attribute the cause of anxiety to unconscious, internal conflicts may use psychoanalysis to better help in the understanding and resolution of conflicts. Other types of psychotherapy, such as cognitive-behavioural therapy, have proven effective in treating anxiety disorders. In cognitive-behavioural therapy, the therapist often educates the person about the nature of his or her particular anxiety disorder. Then, the therapist may help the person challenge, and irrational thoughts that lead to anxiety. For example, to treat a person with a snake phobia, a therapist might gradually expose the person to snakes, beginning with pictures of snakes and progressing to rubber snakes and real snakes. The patient can use relaxation techniques acquired in therapy to overcome the fear of snakes.

Research has shown psychotherapy to be as effective or more effective than medications in treating many anxiety disorders. Psychotherapy may also provide more lasting benefits than medications when patients discontinue treatment.

Developments in the interactional description of schizophrenia have not been parallelled in the area of depression. As yet, concepts such as pseudomutuality, double-bind, schism, and skew have found no counterparts. Kubler and Stotland (1964) have argued, that, emotional disturbance, even the most severe, cannot be understood unless the field in which it develops and exists is examined. The manifestation of the difficulty in the disturbed individually has dependently given as a meaning to the aspects of the field. The significant aspects of the field are usually interpersonal. Yet the study of depression has focussed on the individual and his behaviour out of his interactional context. To a large degree, the depressed person's monotonously reiterate complaints and self accusations, and his provocative and often annoying behaviour has distracted investigators from considerations of his environment and the role it may play in the maintenance of his behaviour. The possibility that the characteristic pattern of depressed behaviour might be interwoven has seldom been explored.

For the most part, it has been assumed that the depressed person is relatively impervious to the influence of others. Ruesch (1962) stated that to talk to the depressed person makes little sense: To listen, little more. Grinker (1964) conceptualized depressive symptomatology as communication to others, but argued that the depressed person is not responsive to communication for the purpose of action, as he cannot perceive the cues of reality, he makes statements but does not care if he is understood.

In the phrasing terminological comprehending of systems theory (von Bertalanffy, 1950; Allport, 1960 and Miller, 1971), usually conceptualize upon the depressed person for one of a closed system. Grinker (1964) was explicit in stating that the depressed person repeats his message and behaviour without receptive satisfactions or acceptance to the resulting exposures. Beck (1964, 1967) described the cognitive distortions that dominate the information processing of the depressed person so that experiences are rightly interpreted to maintain existing schema of personal deficiency, self-blame and negative expectations.

The implicit assumption of these and other writers has been that the support and information available to the repressed person are incongruent with his depression, and the persistence of his symptomatology is evidence of a failure to receive or accept this information. Withdrawal, isolated intrapsychic processes, or as Beck directly describes (1967), interactions of degressive schema and affective structures, produce a downward depressive spiral. If a depressive spiral develops, it is mutually causative, deviation-amplifying process (Maruyama, 1963) in the interaction of the depressed person with his environment. Thus, what is customarily viewed as some internal process is. That is, in part, a characteristic of interaction with the environment and much of what his customarily viewed as cognitive distortion or misperception is characteristic of information flow from the environment.

It should be noted that while the depressed person's different interpretations of his predicament are traditionally attributed to his distortion or misperception, general disorders of thought and perception are defining neither criteria nor common among depressed patients (McPartland and Hornstra, 1964). An observer wills to take into account for the intricacies of someone's relationship to his environment. Frequently attributed to his characteristic approach for being or revealing a quality specific or identifying to an individual or group that he does not propose, or leave significant aspects of his unexplained experience (Watzlawick, 1967). Feedback introduces phenomena that cannot be adequately explained by reference to the isolated individual alone (Ashby, 1960, 1062). As for the study of depression, identification as a pattern of depressive feedback surfaces from the environmental demands, however, to a greater extent then complexity as conceptualized as the deranging plexuity, than one explaining its phenomena with reference to the isolated depressed person.

Lemert (1962) in his study of the interpersonal dynamics of paranoia, argued that the net effect of the developing interaction pattern between the paranoid person and others is that (1) the flow of information to the person is stopped, (2) a real discrepancy between expressed ideas and affect among those who he earnestly acts upon to increase in measure or degree as to intensify the emphasis placed upon the study of the causes that he created, and (3) the situation or group image as to commence to be as ambiguous for him as he is for others., In this context of attenuated relationships, exclusion, and disrupted communication, the paranoid person cannot get the feedback on his behaviour that is essential in order for him to correct his interpretation of social relationships. Lemert concluded that the paranoid person may be delusional, but that it is also true that in a real sense he is able to elicit covertly organized action and conspiratorial behaviour.

It should be made clear that such an interpretation concerning those in consideration for depression, might that be to deny the existence of important intrapersonal factors involved within depression. As many writers have pointed out that the depressed person's feelings of worthlessness and helplessness do not arise of an immediate stimulus situation (Chodoff, 1972). McCranie (1971) has argued that there is a 'depressed-core' in the personality of the individual's depressive complaints, for within the consisting of a tendency feel worthless and helpless and oversensitive to stimulus that impinge upon these feelings together, these are aroused from dormancy by specific situations such as loss and that to self-esteem. Even so, the emphasis placed by which of the environment comes into congruence with these feedings. The depressive's most of all, are vague but generalized feelings that there is something wrong with him, and his search for this among his minor depressive substances of his personality, is, nonetheless, the confusing responses from his surrounding environment which servers to validate these feelings. Likewise, conflicts about the reception of support and approval from others are deeply rooted in the depressive's intrapersonal style, but these conflicts can only be aggravated by the mixed messages of approval and rejection received from significant others, and by their withdrawal from him despite reassurances to the contrary.

Since Freud, the accredited categorical priorities were to clarify the bewildering number of interrelated observations uncovered by psychoanalytic exploration led to the development of a model of the structure of the psychic system. Three functional systems are distinguished that are conveniently designated as the id, ego, and Superego.

The first system refers to the sexual and aggressive tendencies that arise from the body, as distinguished from the mind. Freud called these tendencies Triebe, which literally means 'drives,' but which is often inaccurately translated as 'instincts' to indicate their innate character. These inherent drives claim immediate satisfaction, which is experienced as pleasurable; the id thus is dominated by the pleasure principle. In his later writings, Freud tended more toward psychological rather than biological conceptualization of the drives.

How the conditions for satisfaction are to be brought about is the task of the second system, the ego, which is the domain of such functions as perception, thinking, and motor control that can accurately assess environmental conditions. In order to fulfil its function of adaptation, or reality testing, the ego must be capable of enforcing the postponement of satisfaction of the instinctual impulses originating in the id. To defend itself against unacceptable impulses, the ego develops specific psychic means, known as defence mechanisms. These include repression, the exclusion of impulses from conscious awareness; projection, the process of ascribing to others one's own unacknowledged desires; and reaction formation, the establishing for a pattern of behaviour, directly opposed to a strong unconscious opportunity or requirement to employ a pressing absence of something essential, as the obligation to need. Such defence mechanisms are put into operation whenever anxiety signals a danger that the original unacceptable impulses may reemerge.

An id impulse becomes unacceptable, not only as a result of a temporary need for postponing its satisfaction until suitable reality conditions can be found, but more often because of a prohibition imposed on the individual by others, originally the parents. The totality of these demands and prohibitions constitutes the major content of the third system, the Superego, the function of which is to control the ego in accordance with the internalized standards of parental figures. If the demands of the Superego are not fulfilled, the person may feel shame or guilt. Because the Superego, in Freudian theory, originates in the struggle to overcome the Oedipal conflict, it has a power akin to an instinctual drive, is in part unconscious, and can give rise feelings of guilt not justified by any conscious transgression. The ego, having to mediate among the demands of the id, the Superego, and the outside world, may not be strong enough to reconcile these conflicting forces. The more the ego is impeded in its development because of being enmeshed in its earlier conflicts, called fixations or complexes, or the more it reverts to earlier satisfactions and archaic modes of functioning, known as regression, the greater is the likelihood of succumbing to these pressures. Unable function normally, it can maintain its limited control and integrity only at the price of symptom formation, in which the tensions are expressed in neurotic symptoms.

The Freudian terminological phrasing ordered by the linguistic representations as imposed upon the id, whereby, the finding located in the literalised translations inside the psychoanalytic theory. The id, is one of the three basic elements of personality, that being of the other two are the ego and the Superego? The id can be equated with the unconscious as settled to some common usage, which is the reservoir of the instinctual drives of the individual, including biological urges, wishes, and affective motives. The id is dominated by the pleasure principle, through which the individual is pressed for immediate gratification of his or her desires. In strict Freudian theory the energy behind the instinctual drives of the id is known as the libido, a generalized force, basically sexual in nature, through which the sexual and psychosexual nature of the individual finds expression.

Ego, in psychoanalysis, is the term denoting the central part of the personality structure that deals with reality and is influenced by social forces. According to the psychoanalytic theories developed by Sigmund Freud, the ego constitutes one of the three basic provinces of the mind, two for being id, and the other two are sustained of the ego and Superego. The id, is first to encounter with the external world of people and things. The ego learns to modify behaviour by controlling those impulses that are socially unacceptable. Its role is that of mediator between unconscious impulses and acquired social and personal standards.

In philosophy, ego means the conscious self or 'I.' It was viewed by some philosophers, notably the 17th-century Frenchman René Descartes and the 18th-century German Johann Gottlieb Fichte, as the sole basis of reality; they saw the universe as existing only in the individual's knowledge and experience of it. Other philosophers, such as the 18th-century German Immanuel Kant, proposed two as the ego, of one perceiving and the other thinking.

Superego, in psychoanalytic theory is one of the three basic constituents of the mind, the others being the id and the ego. As postulated by Sigmund Freud, the term designates the element of the mind that, in normal personalities, automatically modifies and inhibits those instinctual impulses or drives of the id that tend to produce antisocial actions and thoughts. An id impulse becomes unacceptable, not only as a result of a temporary need for postponing its satisfaction until suitable reality conditions can be found, but more often because of a prohibition imposed on the individual by others, originally the parents. The totality of these demands and prohibitions constitutes the major content of the third system, the Superego, the function of which is to control the ego in accordance with the internalized standards of parental figures. If the demands of the Superego are not fulfilled, the person may feel shame or guilt. Because the Superego, in Freudian theory, originates in the struggle to overcome the Oedipal conflict, it has a power akin to an instinctual drive, is in part unconscious, and can give rise feelings of guilt not justified by any conscious transgression. The ego, having to mediate among the demands of the id, the Superego, and the outside world, may not be strong enough to reconcile these conflicting forces. The more the ego is impeded in its development because of being enmeshed in its earlier conflicts, called fixations or complexes, or the more it reverts to earlier satisfactions and archaic modes of functioning, known as regression, the greater is the likelihood of succumbing to these pressures. Unable function normally, it can maintain its limited control and integrity only at the price of symptom formation, in which the tensions are expressed in neurotic symptoms.

According to psychoanalytic theory, the Superego develops as the child gradually and unconsciously adopts the values and standards, first of his or her parents, and later of the social environment. According to modern Freudian psychoanalysts, the Superego includes the positive ego, or conscious self-image, or ego ideal, that each individual develops.

Nevertheless, through such things as the precariousness for concerning about some circumstance of an episodic action, displaced across the length of some transversely directed effect of operations, from which actions are dependent. The dynamic function of a kindly action as something already done or effected. The operational reaction precedes the activity for which a reactional procedure vigorously actified as one who takes of an exhibit for stimulating happenings in real life.

In psychoanalysis, is the emotional relation between subject and objects which, through a process of identification, are believed to constitute the developing ego. In this context, the word object refers to any person or thing, or representational aspect of them, with which the subject forms an intense emotional relationship.

Object relations were first described by German psychoanalyst Karl Abraham in an influential paper, published in 1924. In the paper he developed the ideas of the founder of psychoanalysis, Sigmund Freud, on infantile sexuality and the development of the libido. Object-relations theory has become one of the central themes of post-Freudian psychoanalysis, particularly through the writings of British psychoanalysts Melanie Klein, Ronald Fairbairn, and Donald Winnicott, all deeply influenced by Abraham. They have each developed distinctly, though complementary, approaches to analysis, evolving theories of personal development based on early parental attachments.

People with depression often experience feelings of worthlessness, helplessness, guilt, and self-blame. They may interpret a minor failing on their part as a sign of incompetence or interpret minor criticism as condemnation. Some depressed people complain of being spiritually or morally dead. The mirror seems to reflect someone ugly and repulsive. Even a competent and decent person may feel deficient, cruel, stupid, phony, or guilty of having deceived others. People with major depression may experience such extreme emotional pain that they consider or attempt suicide. At least 15 percent of seriously depressed people commit suicide, and many more attempt it.

Bipolar disorder is much less common than depression. In North America and Europe, about 1 percent of people experience bipolar disorder during their lives. Rates of bipolar disorder are similar throughout the world. In comparison, at least 8 percent of people experience serious depression during their lives. Bipolar disorder affects men and women about equally and is somewhat more common in higher socioeconomic classes. At least 15 percent of people with bipolar disorder commit suicide. This rate roughly equals the rate for people with major depression, the most severe form of depression.

The psychological worries of depression, is the mental illness in which a person experiences deep, unshakable sadness and diminished interest in nearly all activities. People also use the term depression to describe the temporary sadness, loneliness, or blues that everyone feels from time to time. In contrast to normal sadness, severe depression, also called major depression, can dramatically impair a person's ability function in social situations and at work. People with major depression often have feelings of despair, hopelessness, and worthlessness, as well as thoughts of committing suicide.

Depression can take several other forms. In bipolar disorder, sometimes called manic-depressive illness, a person's mood swings back and forth between depression and mania. People with seasonal affective disorder typically suffer from depression only during autumn and winter, when there are fewer hours of daylight. In dysthymia (pronounced dis-THI-mee-uh), people feel depressed, have low self-esteem, and concentrate poorly most of the time—often for a period of years—but their symptoms are milder than in major depression. Some people with dysthymia experience occasional episodes of major depression. Mental health professionals use the term clinical depression to refer to any of the above forms of depression.

Surveys indicate that people commonly view depression as a sign of personal weakness, but psychiatrists and psychologists view it as a real illness. In the United States, the National Institute of Mental Health has estimated that depression cost's society many billions of dollars each year, mostly in lost work time.

Depression is one of the most common mental illnesses. At least 8 percent of adults in the United States experience serious depression at some point during their lives, and estimates range as high as 17 percent. The illness affects all people, regardless of sex, race, ethnicity, or socioeconomic standing. However, women are two to three times more likely than men to suffer from depression. Experts disagree on the reason for this difference. Some cite differences in hormones, and others point to the stress caused by society's expectations of women.

Depression occurs in all parts of the world, although the pattern of symptoms can vary. The prevalence of depression in other countries varies widely, from 1.5 percent of people in Taiwan to 19 percent of people in Lebanon. Some researchers believe methods of gathering data on depression account for different rates.

A number of large-scale studies indicate that depression rates have increased worldwide over the past several decades. Furthermore, younger generations are experiencing depression at an earlier age than did previous generations. Social scientists have proposed many explanations, including changes in family structure, urbanization, and reduced cultural and religious influences.

Although it may appear anytime from childhood to old age, depression usually begins during a person's 20s or 30s. The illness may come on slowly, then deepen gradually over months or years. On the other hand, it may erupt suddenly in a few weeks or days. A person who develops severe depression may appear so confuse, frightened, and unbalance that observers speak of a 'nervous breakdown.' However it begins, and depression causes serious changes in a person's feelings and outlook. A person with major depression feels sad nearly every day and may cry often. People, work, and activities that used to bring them pleasure no longer do.

Symptoms of depression can vary by age. In younger children, depression may include physical complaints, such as stomachaches and headaches, as well as irritability, 'moping around,' social withdrawal, and changes in eating habits. They may feel unenthusiastic about school and other activities. In adolescents, common symptoms include sad mood, sleep disturbances, and lack of energy. Elderly people with depression usually complain of physical rather than emotional problems, which sometimes leads doctors to misdiagnose the illness.

Symptoms of depression can also vary by culture. In some cultures, depressed people may not experience sadness or guilt but may complain of physical problems. In Mediterranean cultures, for example, depressed people may complain of headaches or nerves. In Asian cultures they may complain of weakness, fatigue, or imbalance.

If left untreated, an episode of major depression typically lasts eight or nine months. About 85 percent of people who experience one bout of depression will experience future episodes.

Depression usually alters a person's appetite, sometimes increasing it, but usually reducing it. Sleep habits are given to change as well. People with depression may oversleep or, more commonly, sleep for fewer hours. A depressed person might go to sleep at midnight, sleep restlessly, then wake up at 5:00 a.m. feeling tired and blue. For many depressed people, early morning is the saddest time of the day.

Depression also changes one's energy level. Some depressed people may be restless and agitated, engaging in fidgety movements and pacing. Others may feel sluggish and inactive, experiencing great fatigue, lack of energy, and a feeling of being worn out or carrying a heavy burden. Depressed people may also have difficulty thinking, poor concentration, and problems with memory.

People with depression often experience feelings of worthlessness, helplessness, guilt, and self-blame. They may interpret a minor failing on their part as a sign of incompetence or interpret minor criticism as condemnation. Some depressed people complain of being spiritually or morally dead. The mirror seems to reflect someone ugly and repulsive. Even a competent and decent person may feel deficient, cruel, stupid, phony, or guilty of having deceived others. People with major depression may experience such extreme emotional pain that they consider or attempt suicide. At least 15 percent of seriously depressed people commit suicide, and many more attempt it.

In some cases, people with depression may experience psychotic symptoms, such as delusions (false beliefs) and hallucinations (false sensory perceptions). Psychotic symptoms indicate an especially severe illness. Compared to other depressed people, those with psychotic symptoms have longer hospital stays, and after leaving, they are more likely to be moody and unhappy. They are also more likely to commit suicide.

Some depressions seem to come out of the blue, even when things are going well. Others seem to have an obvious cause: a marital conflict, financial difficulty, or some personal failure. Yet many people with these problems do not become deeply depressed. Most psychologists believe depression results from an interaction between stressful life events and a person's biological and psychological vulnerabilities.

Clinical depression is one of the most common forms of mental illness. Although depression can be treated with psychotherapy, many scientists believe there are biological causes for the disease. In this June 1998 Scientific American article, Neurobiologist Charles B. Nemeroff discusses the connection between biochemical changes in the brain and depression.

Depression runs in families. By studying twins, researchers have found evidence of a strong genetic influence in depression. Genetically identical twins raised in the same environment are three times more likely to have depression in common than fraternal twins, who have only about half of their genes in common. In addition, identical twins are five times more likely to have bipolar disorder in common. These findings suggest that vulnerability to depression and bipolar disorder can be inherited. Adoption studies have provided more evidence of a genetic role in depression. These studies show that children of depressed people are vulnerable to depression even when raised by adoptive parents.

Genes may influence depression by causing abnormal activity in the brain. Studies have shown that certain brain chemicals called neurotransmitters play an important role in regulating moods and emotions. Neurotransmitters involved in depression include norepinephrine, dopamine, and serotonin. Research in the 1960s suggested that depression result from lower than normal levels of these neurotransmitters in parts of the brain. Support for this theory came from the effects of antidepressant drugs, which work by increasing the levels of neurotransmitters involved in depression. However, later studies have discredited this simple explanation and have suggested a more complex relationship between neurotransmitter levels and depression.

An imbalance of hormones may also play a role in depression. Many depressed people have higher than normal levels of hydrocortisone (cortisol), a hormone secreted by the adrenal gland in response to stress. In addition, an underactive or overactive thyroid gland can lead to depression.

Psychological theories of depression focus on the way people think and behave. In a 1917 essay, Austrian psychoanalyst Sigmund Freud explained melancholia, or major depression, as a response to loss—either real loss, such as the death of a spouse, or symbolic loss, such as the failure to achieve an important goal. Freud believed that a person's unconscious anger over loss weakens the ego, resulting in self-hate and self-destructive behaviour.

Cognitive theories of depression emphasize the role of irrational thought processes. American psychiatrist Aaron Beck proposed that depressed people tend to view themselves, their environment, and the future in a negative light because of errors in thinking. These errors include focussing on the negative aspects of any situation, misinterpreting facts in negative ways, and blaming themselves for any misfortune. In Beck's view, people learn these self-defeating ways of looking at the world during early childhood. This negative thinking makes situations seem much worse than they really are and increases the risk of depression, especially in stressful situations.

Meir Steiner and his co-workers at McMaster University suggest that if serotonin mediates between an organism and its environment and if the neurotransmitter is regulated differently in men and women, it might explain gender patterns not only in depression but also in a range of psychiatric illnesses. Specifically, whereas depression and anxiety are more common among women, alcoholism and severe aggression are more common among men. And just as low serotonin levels have been implicated in depression and anxiety disorders in women, they have also been found in the brains of men with severe forms of alcoholism and aggression.

Such gender differences in the serotonergic system might ensure that females respond to stress with psychiatric disturbances that involve behavioural inhibition, whereas men respond to stress with a loss of behavioural control. Steiner suggests that such gender differences in the serotonergic system evolved because child rearing is more successful (in the narrow sense of more children surviving to adulthood) in species in which aggressive impulses are cu

A researcher espousing either the sociological or psychological explanation of depression's gender bias might counter Steiner's theory by arguing that men are socialized to respond to stress with 'acting out' behaviours, such as alcoholism or aggression. In contrast, society teaches women to respond to stress with 'acting in' behaviours, such as depression. To support this idea, they might point to epidemiological studies done in Amish and Jewish populations. In these communities, alcoholism is less common than in the population at large, and, interestingly, the rates of depression are as high in men as in women.

These contradictory data leave no doubt that the explanations behind depression and other psychiatric diseases are not straightforward. Biological and social influences not only coexist but also probably reinforce one of the others. After all, we would expect gender socialization patterns to evolve so that they complement biological differences between the sexes. In other words, we would expect to 'nurture' in the reinforcements, than oppose of the hidden nature. And because nurture involves learning—and learning occurs when certain neural connections in the brain are strengthened—it is clear that both nurture and nature involves biological processes.

Scientists have made tremendous strides in treating depression. With the advent of such antidepressants as Prozac (which acts on the serotonergic system), more than 80 percent of depressed patients now respond to medication or psychotherapy, or a combination of the two. But much more work remains to be done. Because depression is so common, its cost to society is high. The National Institute of Mental Health estimates that depression claims $30.4 billion in treatment and in lost productivity from the US economy every year.

And these costs are on the rise: depression is becoming more common in successive generations (the so-called cohort effect). No one knows what is causing the cohort effect—but it is moving much too quickly to have a genetic basis. Theories about what is causing the cohort effect range from increased drug abuse and familial disarray to the suggestion that perhaps older people are simply more likely to forget past depressive episodes when asked. The cohort effect and depression in general remain very much a mystery. And for the men and women who suffer from it, it is a mystery that cannot be solved soon enough.

When the electrical signal reaches the tip of an axon, it stimulates small presynaptic vesicles in the cell. These vesicles contain chemicals called neurotransmitters, which are released into the microscopic space between neurons (the synaptic cleft). The neurotransmitters attach to specific receptors on the surface of the adjacent neuron. This stimulus causes the adjacent cell to depolarize and propagate an action potential of its own. The duration of a stimulus from a neurotransmitter is limited by the breakdown of the chemicals in the synaptic cleft and the reuptake by the neuron that produced them. Formerly, each neuron was thought to make only one transmitter, but recent studies have shown that some cells make to or more.

Serotonin neurotransmitters, or the chemical compositions that component parts of chemical transmissions were messages transmitted across the synapses, or gaps between adjacent cells, for which as among its many functions, that serotonin is released from blood cells called platelets to activate blood vessel constriction and blood clotting. In the gastrointestinal tract, serotonin inhibits gastric acid production and stimulates muscle contraction in the intestinal wall. Its functions in the central nervous system and effects on human behaviour—including mood, memory, and appetite control has been the subject of a great deal of—research. This intensive study of serotonin has revealed important knowledge about the serotonin-related cause and treatment of many illnesses

Serotonin is produced in the brain from the amino acid tryptophan, which is derived from foods high in protein, such as meat and dairy products. Tryptophan is transported to the brain, where it is broken down by enzymes to produce serotonin. In the process of neurotransmission, serotonin is transferred from one nerve cell, or neuron, to another, triggering an electrical impulse that stimulates or inhibits cell activity as needed. Serotonin is then reabsorbed by the first attachable neuron, in a process known as reuptake, where it is recycled and used again or converted into an inactive chemical form and excreted.

While the complete picture of serotonin's function in the body is still being investigated, many disorders are known to be associated with an imbalance of serotonin in the brain. Drugs that manipulate serotonin levels have been used to alleviate the symptoms of serotonin imbalances. Some of these drugs, known as selective serotonin reuptake inhibitors (SSRIs), block or inhibit the reuptake of serotonin into neurons, enabling serotonin to remain active in the synapses for a longer period of time. These medications are used to treat such psychiatric disorders as depression; obsessive-compulsive disorder, in which repetitive and disturbing thoughts trigger bizarre, ritualistic behaviours; and impulsive aggressive behaviours. Fluoxetine (more commonly known by the brand name Prozac), is a widely prescribed SSRI used to treat depression, and more recently, obsessive-compulsive disorder.

Drugs that affect serotonin levels may prove beneficial in the treatment of nonpsychiatric disorders as well, including diabetic neuropathy (degeneration of nerves outside the central nervous system in diabetics) and premenstrual syndrome. Recently the serotonin-releasing agent dexfenfluramine has been approved for patients who are 30 percent or more over their ideal body weight. By preventing serotonin reuptake, dexfenfluramine promotes satiety, or fullness, after eating less food

Drugs known as antagonists bind with neurons to prevent serotonin neurotransmission. Some antagonists have been found effective in treating the nausea that typically accompanies radiation and chemotherapy in cancer treatment. Antagonists are also being tested to treat high blood pressure and other cardiovascular disorders by blocking serotonin's ability to constrict blood vessels. Other antagonists may produce an effect on learning and memory in age-associated memory impairment.

Neurotransmitters are released into a microscopic gap, called a synapse, that separates the transmitting neuron from the cell receiving the chemical signal. The cell that generates the signal is called the presynaptic cell, while the receiving cell is termed the postsynaptic cell.

Neurotransmitter, are chemically made by neurons, or nerve cells. Neurons send out neurotransmitters as chemical signals to activate or inhibit the function of neighbouring cells

Within the central nervous system, which consists of the brain and the spinal cord, neurotransmitters pass from neuron to neuron. In the peripheral nervous system, which is made up of the nerves that run from the central nervous system to the rest of the body, the chemical signals pass between a neuron and an adjacent muscle or gland cell.

Nine chemical compounds—belonging to three chemical families—are widely recognized as neurotransmitters. In addition, certain other body chemicals, including adenosine, histamine, enkephalins, endorphins, and epinephrine, have neurotransmitter like properties. Experts believe that there are many more neurotransmitters as yet undiscovered.

The first of the three families is composed of amines, a group of compounds containing molecules of carbon, hydrogen, and nitrogen. Among the amines neurotransmitters are acetylcholine, norepinephrine, dopamine, and serotonin. Acetylcholine is the most widely used neurotransmitter in the body, and neurons that leave the central nervous system (for example, those running to skeletal muscle) use acetylcholine as their neurotransmitter; Neurons that run to the heart, blood vessels, and other organs may use acetylcholine or norepinephrine. Dopamine is involved in the movement of muscles, and it controls the secretion of the pituitary hormone prolactin, which triggers milk production in nursing mothers.

The second neurotransmitter family is composed of amino acids, organic compounds containing both an amino group (NH2) and a carboxylic acid group (COOH). Amino acids that serve as neurotransmitters include glycine, glutamic and aspartic acids, and gamma-amino butyric acid (GABA). Glutamic acid and GABA are the most abundant neurotransmitters within the central nervous system, and especially in the cerebral cortex, which is largely responsible for such higher brain functions as thought and interpreting sensations.

The third neurotransmitter family is composed of peptides, which are compounds that contain at least 2, and sometimes as many as 100 amino acids. Peptide neurotransmitters are poorly understood, but scientists know that the peptide neurotransmitter called substance P influences the sensation of pain.

Neurotransmitters are manufactured from precursor compounds like amino acids, glucose, and the dietary amine-called choline. Neurons modify the structure of these precursor compounds in a series of reactions enzymes. Neurotransmitters that comes from amino acids include serotonin, which is derived from tryptophan, dopamine and norepinephrine, which are derived from tyrosine, and glycine, in turn is derived from threonine. Surrounding the neurotransmitters composite characteristics made up from glucose are glutamate, aspartate, and GABA. Choline serves as the precursor for acetylcholine

Neurotransmitters are released into a microscopic gap, called a synapse, that separates the transmitting neuron from the cell receiving the chemical signal. The cell that generates the signal is called the presynaptic cell, while the receiving cell is termed the postsynaptic cell.

After their release into the synapse, neurotransmitters combine chemically with highly specific protein molecules, termed receptors, that are embedded in the surface membranes of the postsynaptic cell. When this combination occurs, the voltage, or electrical force, of the postsynaptic cell is either increased (excited) or decreased (inhibited).

If the postsynaptic cell is a muscle cell rather than a neuron, an excitatory neurotransmitter will cause the muscle to contract. If the postsynaptic cell is a gland cell, an excitatory neurotransmitter will cause the cell to secrete its contents.

While most neurotransmitters interact with their receptors to create new electrical nerve impulses that energize or inhibit the adjoining cell, some neurotransmitter interactions do not generate or suppress nerve impulses. Instead, they interact with a second type of receptor that changes the internal chemistry of the postsynaptic cell by either causing or blocking the formation of chemicals called second messenger molecules. These second messengers regulate the postsynaptic cell's biochemical processes and enable it to conduct the maintenance necessary to continue synthesizing neurotransmitters and conducting nerve impulses. Examples of second messengers, which are formed and entirely contained within the postsynaptic cell, include cyclic adenosine monophosphate, diacylglycerol, and inositol phosphates.

Once neurotransmitters have been secreted into synapses and have passed on their chemical signals, the presynaptic neuron clears the synapse of neurotransmitter molecules. For example, acetylcholine is broken down by the enzyme acetylcholinesterase into choline and acetate. Neurotransmitters like dopamine, serotonin, and GABA is removed by a physical process called reuptake. In reuptake, a protein in the presynaptic membrane acts as a sort of sponge, causing the neurotransmitters to reenter the presynaptic neuron, where they can be broken down by enzymes or repackaged for reuse.

Neurotransmitters also play a role in Parkinson disease, which slowly attacks the nervous system, causing symptoms that worsen over time. Fatigue, mental confusion, a mastlike facial expression, stooping posture, shuffling gait, and problems with and speaking is among the difficulties suffered by Parkinson victims. These symptoms have been partly linked to the deterioration and eventual death of neurons that run from the base of the brain to the basal ganglia, a collection of nerve cells that manufacture the neurotransmitter dopamine. The reasons why such neurons die are yet to be understood, but the related symptoms can be alleviated. L-dopa, or levodopa, widely used to treat Parkinson disease, acts as a supplementary precursor for dopamine. It causes the surviving neurons in the basal ganglia to increase their production of dopamine, thereby compensating to some extent for the disabled neurons.

Dopamine, chemical known as a neurotransmitter essential to the functioning of the central nervous system. In the process of neurotransmission, dopamine is transferred from one nerve cell, or neuron, to another, playing a key role in brain function and human behaviour.

Dopamine forms from a precursor molecule called Dopa, which is manufactured in the liver from the amino acid tyrosine. Dopa is then transported by the circulatory system to neurons in the brain, where the conversion to dopamine takes place.

Dopamine is a versatile neurotransmitter. Among its many functions, it plays a major role in two activities of the central nervous system: one that helps control movement, and a second that are strongly associated emotional-based behaviours.

The pathway involved in movement control is called the nigrostriatal pathway. Dopamine is released by neurons that originate from an area of the brain called the substantia nigra and connect to the part of the brain known as the corpora striata, an area known to be important in controlling the musculoskeletal system.

The second brain pathway in which dopamine plays a major characteristic role is called the mesocorticolimbic pathway. Neurons in an area of the brain called the ventral tegmentalarea transmits the diamine to other neurons connected to various parts of the limbic system, which is responsible for regulating emotion, motivation, behaviour, the sense of smell, and variously autonomic, or involuntary, functions like heartbeat and breathing.

A growing body of evidence suggests that dopamine is involved in several major brain disorders. Narcolepsy, a disorder characterized by brief, recurring episodes of sudden, deep sleep, is associated with abnormally high levels of both dopamine and a second neurotransmitter, acetylcholine. Huntington's chorea, an inherited, fatal illness in which neurons in the base of the brain are progressively destroyed, is also linked to an excess of dopamine.

Commonly known as shaking palsy, Parkinson disease is another brain disorder in which dopamine is involved. Besides tremors of the limbs, Parkinson patients suffer from muscular rigidity, which leads to difficulties in walking, writing, and speaking. This disorder results from the degeneration and death of neurons in the nigrostriatal pathway, resulting in low levels of dopamine. The symptoms of Parkinson disease can be minimized by treatment with a drug called levodopa, or L-dopa, which converts to dopamine in the brain.

Schizophrenia is a psychiatric disorder characterized by loss of contact with reality and major changes in personality. Schizophrenics have normal levels of dopamine in the brain, but because they are highly sensitive to this neurotransmitter, these normal levels of dopamine trigger unusual behaviours. Drugs such as thorazine that blocks the action of dopamine have been found to decrease the symptoms of schizophrenia.

Studies indicate that people who are addicted to alcohol and other drugs similar to cocaine and nicotine have less dopamine in the mesocorticolimbic pathway. These drugs appear to increase dopamine levels, resulting in the pleasurable feelings associated with the drugs.

Another group of antidepressants, known as selective serotonin reuptake inhibitors (SSRI), became available in 1987. SSRIs block the reuptake of the neurotransmitter serotonin into presynaptic neurons, thereby prolonging its activity. There are currently four SSRIs available for use in the United States: Fluoxetine, sertraline, paroxetine, and fluvoxamine. Of this group, the best known is Fluoxetine, commonly known by its brand name, Prozac.

Another antidepressant is venlafaxine, which works like TCAs but does not share their chemical structure, and it also causes different side effects. The antidepressant nefazodone prevents serotonin from binding to neighbouring neurons at one specific binding site (serotonin can bind to neurons on many sites), as weakly blocks the reuptake of serotonin.

All antidepressants decrease symptoms of depression in about 70 percent of depressed people who take them. Most antidepressants take about two to three weeks of treatment before beneficial effects occur. Because no antidepressant is more effective than the others, doctors determine which antidepressant to prescribe according to the type of side effects an individual can tolerate. For instance, a person who takes TCAs and MAO inhibitors may notice dizziness and fainting when standing up, mouth dryness, difficulty urinating, constipation, and drowsiness. If people who take MAO inhibitors eat certain foods, such as aged cheese or some aged meats, they can experience severe headaches and raised blood pressure. SSRIs can cause side effects such as restlessness, difficulty sleeping, and interference with sexual function.

The theory Edward Bibring presents in 'The Mechanism of Depression' (1953) is deliberately limited to the ego of psychology depression. He wrote: ' . . . the conception of depression presents is not invalidated for which of an accepted theory of the role which orality and aggression play in the various types of depression'. Yet his theory points up the inadequacy of the theory, Bibring stated his view as follows ' . . . the oral and aggressive strivings are not as universal in depression as is generally assumed and . . . consequently the theories built on them do not offer sufficient explanation, but requiring . . ., modification.'

The basic proposition of Bibring's theory is akin to the proposition which Freud built as the structural theory of anxiety. Freud wrote: ' . . . the ego is the real seat of anxiety . . ., Anxiety is an affective state which can, of course, be experienced only by the ego'. Bibring wrote' 'Depression is . . . primarily an ego phenomenon' [it] represents an effective state. '[Anxiety and depression are] both . . . frequent . . . ego reactions . . . [and since] they cannot be reduced any further, it may be justified to call them basic ego reactions'.

Bibring thus set out to explore the structural footing as warranted in the underpinning of depression as an ego state. He used Freud's theory of anxiety, and Fenichel's theory of boredom and some general observations of depersonalization for his directional departure.

We have here a structural theory which treats depression as the reactivation of a structural state. The universal experiences of grief and sadness, ranging from passing sadness to profound depression, indicate differences in the relative ease of and intensities of the reactivation of this state are determined by: (1) Both of a constitutional tolerance for continued frustrations. (2) The severity and extent of the situation of helplessness in early life. (3) The developmental factors which increase or decrease the relative ease with which this state is reactivated and modulate its intensity. (4) The kind and severity of the precipitating condition. As for the dynamic aspect of this theory, the depressive ego state is reactivated by an intra-ego conflict. The factors involved in this conflict, however, are not yet precisely defined. As for the genetic aspect of the theory the depressive ego state is reactivated by an intra-ego conflict. As for the genetic aspect of the theory, in which the origin of the depressive ego state is clear and so is the epigenesis of the 'narcissistic aspirations' involved.

The economic and adaptive aspects of the theory, however, are directly treated by Bibring, but Freud made several attempts to account for various aspects of the economics of depression.

For instance, he wrote: ' . . . the ego's inhibited condition and loss of interest were fully accounted for by the absorbing work of mourning', or, for instance: The conflict in the ego, and its meaning at that time the conflicts between the ego and the Superego, which in melancholia is substituted for the struggle surging round the object, must act like a painful wound which calls out unusually strong anticathexis.

But Freud also indicated that these assumptions are insufficient and we need 'some insight into the economic condition. First, of bodily pain, and then of the mental pain' before we can understand the economics of depression and that:

> . . . we do not know by what economic measures the work of mourning is carried through, possibly, however, a conjecture may help us here. Reality passes its verdict—that the object no longer exists—upon each single one of the memories and hopes through which the libido was attached to the lost object, and the ego, confronted as it were with the decision whether it will share this fate, is persuaded by the sum of narcissistic satisfactions in being alive to sever its attachment to the nonexistent object.

And that:

> This character of withdrawing the libido it is . . . to be ascribed alike to mourning and to melancholia, it is probably sustained by the same economic arrangements and serves the same purpose in both.

And finally:

> Why this process of carrying out the behest of reality bit by bit . . . should be extraordinarily painful is not at all easy to explain in terms of mental economics.

Though it is clear that the phenomenon from which the economic explanation must start is the inhibition of the ego, the economics of depression is still not understood. Bibring quotes Fenichel's formulation: ' . . . the greater percentage of the available mental energy is used up in un conflicts, [and] not enough is left to provide the normal enjoyment of life and vitality' (Bibring,

1953). But he finds this statement insufficient to explain depressive inhibition, and proceeds to reconsider the nature of inhibition. He writes:

> Freud (1926) defines inhibition as a 'restriction of functions of the ego' and mentions two major causes for such restrictions, either they have been imposed upon the person as a measure of precaution, e.g., to present the development of anxiety or feeling of guilt, or brought about as a result of exhaustion of energy of the ego engaged in intense defensive activities.

Bibring concludes:

> The inhibition in depression . . . does not fall under either category it is rather due to the fact that certain strivings of the person become meaningless—since the ego appears incapable ever to gratify them.

Bibring implies:

> Anxiety as a reaction to (external or internal) danger indicates the ego's desire to survive. The ego, challenged by the danger, mobiles the signal of anxiety and prepares for fight or flight. In depression, the [opposite takes place, the ego is paralysed because it finds itself incapable to meet the 'danger' [in certain instances] . . . depression may follow anxiety, [and then] the mobilization of energy . . . [is] replaced by a decrease of self-reliance.

Thus Bibring's search for an economic explanation of degressive inhibition ends in the undefined term 'decrease of self-reliance' which, as it stands, is not an economic concept.

The effort to clarify the bewildering number of interrelated observations uncovered by psychoanalytic exploration led to the development of a model of the structure of the psychic system. Three functional systems are distinguished that are conveniently designated as the id, ego, and Superego.

The first system refers to the sexual and aggressive tendencies that arise from the body, as distinguished from the mind. Freud called these tendencies Triebe, which literally means 'drives,' but which is often inaccurately translated as 'instincts' to indicate their innate character. These inherent drives claim immediate satisfaction, which is experienced as pleasurable; the id thus is dominated by the pleasure principle. In his later writings, Freud tended more toward psychological rather than biological conceptualization of the drives.

How the conditions for satisfaction are to be brought about is the task of the second system, the ego, which is the domain of such functions as perception, thinking, and motor control that can accurately assess environmental conditions. In order to fulfill its function of adaptation, or reality testing, the ego must be capable of enforcing the postponement of satisfaction of the instinctual impulses originating in the id. To defend itself against unacceptable impulses, the ego develops specific psychic means, known as defence mechanisms. These include repression, the exclusion of impulses from conscious awareness; projection, the process of ascribing to others one's own unacknowledged desires; and reaction formation, the establishment of a pattern of behaviour directly opposed two strong unconscious needs. Such defence mechanisms are put into operation whenever anxiety signals a danger that the original unacceptable impulses may reemerge.

An id impulse becomes unacceptable, not only as a result of a temporary need for postponing its satisfaction until suitable reality conditions can be found, but more often because of a prohibition imposed on the individual by others, originally the parents. The totality of these demands and prohibitions constitutes the major content of the third system, the Superego, the function of which is to control the ego in accordance with the internalized standards of parental figures. If the demands of the Superego are not fulfilled, the person may feel shame or guilt. Because the Superego, in Freudian theory, originates in the struggle to overcome the Oedipal conflict, it has a power akin to an instinctual drive, is in part unconscious, and can give rise feelings of guilt not justified by any conscious transgression. The ego, having to mediate among the demands of the id, the Superego, and the outside world, may not be strong enough to reconcile these conflicting forces. The more the ego is impeded in its development because of being enmeshed in its

185

earlier conflicts, called fixations or complexes, or the more it reverts to earlier satisfactions and archaic modes of functioning, known as regression, the greater is the likelihood of succumbing to these pressures. Unable function normally, it can maintain its limited control and integrity only at the price of symptom formation, in which the tensions are expressed in neurotic symptoms.

The Freudian terminological standardization expresses of three representations which are imposed as the id, and used in psychoanalytic theory, one of the three basic elements of personality, the others being the ego and the Superego. The id can be equated with the unconscious of common usage, which is the reservoir of the instinctual drives of the individual, including biological urges, wishes, and affective motives. The id is dominated by the pleasure principle, through which the individual is pressed for immediate gratification of his or her desires. In strict Freudian theory the energy behind the instinctual drives of the id is known as the libido, a generalized force, basically sexual in nature, through which the sexual and psychosexual nature of the individual finds expression.

Once, again, in Ego analysis, is the term denoting the central part of the personality structure that deals with reality and is influenced by social forces. According to the psychoanalytic theories developed by Sigmund Freud, the ego constitutes one of the three basic provinces of the mind, the others being the id and the Superego. The formation of the ego begins at birth in the first encounters with the external world of people and things. The ego learns to modify behaviour by controlling those impulses that are socially unacceptable. Its role is that of mediator between unconscious impulses and acquired social and personal standards.

In philosophy, ego means the conscious self or 'I.' It was viewed by some philosophers, notably the 17th-century Frenchman René Descartes and the 18th-century German Johann Gottlieb Fichte, as the sole basis of reality; they saw the universe as existing only in the individual's knowledge and experience of it. Other philosophers, such as the 18th-century German Immanuel Kant, proposed two of the ego function, one perceiving and the other thinking.

Superego, in psychoanalytic theory is one of the three basic constituents of the mind, the others being the id and the ego. As postulated by Sigmund Freud, the term designates the element of the mind that, in normal personalities, automatically modifies and inhibits those instinctual impulses or drives of the id that tend to produce antisocial actions and thoughts.

According to psychoanalytic theory, the Superego develops as the child gradually and unconsciously adopts the values and standards, first of his or her parents, and later of the social environment. According to modern Freudian psychoanalysts, the Superego includes the positive ego, or conscious self-image, or ego ideal, that each individual develops.

The effort to clarify the bewildering number of interrelated observations uncovered by psychoanalytic exploration led to the development of a model of the structure of the psychic system. Three functional systems are distinguished that are conveniently designated as the id, ego, and Superego.

The first system refers to the sexual and aggressive tendencies that arise from the body, as distinguished from the mind. Freud called these tendencies Triebe, which literally means 'drives,' but which is often inaccurately translated as 'instincts' to indicate their innate character. These inherent drives claim immediate satisfaction, which is experienced as pleasurable; the id thus is dominated by the pleasure principle. In his later writings, Freud tended more toward psychological rather than biological conceptualization of the drives.

How the conditions for satisfaction are to be brought about is the task of the second system, the ego, which is the domain of such functions as perception, thinking, and motor control that can accurately assess environmental conditions. In order to fulfill its function of adaptation, or reality testing, the ego must be capable of enforcing the postponement of satisfaction of the instinctual impulses originating in the id. To defend itself against unacceptable impulses, the ego develops specific psychic means, known as defence mechanisms. These include repression, the exclusion of impulses from conscious awareness; projection, the process of ascribing to others one's own unacknowledged desires; and reaction formation, the establishments of a pattern of behaviour directly opposed to one's interests as an adverse balance of acting against or in a contrary direction of which requires an unconscious lack of need. Such as provided with everything needful, as in the defence mechanisms are put into operation, form wherever anxiety signals a danger that the original unacceptable impulses may reemerge.

An id impulse becomes unacceptable, not only as a result of a temporary need for postponing its satisfaction until suitable reality conditions can be found, but more often because of a prohibition imposed on the individual by others, originally the parents. The totality of these demands and prohibitions constitutes the major content of the third system, the Superego, the function of which is to control the ego in accordance with the internalized standards of parental figures. If the demands of the Superego are not fulfilled, the person may feel shame or guilt. Because the Superego, in Freudian theory, originates in the struggle to overcome the Oedipal conflict, it has a power akin to an instinctual drive, is in part unconscious, and can give rise feelings of guilt not justified by any conscious transgression. The ego, having to mediate among the demands of the id, the Superego, and the outside world, may not be strong enough to reconcile these conflicting forces. The more the ego is impeded in its development because of being enmeshed in its earlier conflicts, called fixations or complexes, or the more it reverts to earlier satisfactions and archaic modes of functioning, known as regression, the greater is the likelihood of succumbing to these pressures. Unable function normally, it can maintain its limited control and integrity only at the price of symptom formation, in which the tensions are expressed in neurotic symptoms.

The Freudians terminological of three representations are imposed as the id, as used in psychoanalytic theory, one of the three basic elements of personality, the others being the ego and the Superego. The id can be equated with the unconscious of common usage, which is the reservoir of the instinctual drives of the individual, including biological urges, wishes, and affective motives. The id is dominated by the pleasure principle, through which the individual is pressed for immediate gratification of his or her desires. In strict Freudian theory the energy behind the instinctual drives of the id is known as the libido, a generalized force, basically sexual in nature, through which the sexual and psychosexual nature of the individual finds expression.

Ego, in psychoanalysis, is the term denoting the central part of the personality structure that deals with reality and is influenced by social forces. According to the psychoanalytic theories developed by Sigmund Freud.

A Superego, in psychoanalytic theory is one of the three basic constituents of the mind, the others being the id and the ego. As postulated by Sigmund Freud, the term designates the element of the mind that, in normal personalities, automatically modifies and inhibits those instinctual impulses or drives of the id that tend to produce antisocial actions and thoughts.

According to psychoanalytic theory, the Superego develops as the child gradually and unconsciously adopts the values and standards, first of his or her parents, and later of the social environment. According to modern Freudian psychoanalysts, the Superego includes the positive ego, or conscious self-image, or ego ideal, that each individual develops.

Object Relations in the psychoanalysis, is the emotional relation between subject and object, which through a process of identification are believed to constitute the developing ego. In this context, the word object refers to any person or thing, or representational aspect of them, with which the subject forms an intense emotional relationship.

Object relations were first described by German psychoanalyst Karl Abraham in an influential paper, published in 1924. In the paper he developed the ideas of the founder of psychoanalysis, Sigmund Freud, on infantile sexuality and the development of the libido. Object-relations theory has become one of the central themes of post-Freudian psychoanalysis, particularly through the writings of British psychoanalysts Melanie Klein, Ronald Fairbairn, and Donald Winnicott, all deeply influenced by Abraham. They have each developed distinctly, though complementary, approaches to analysis, evolving theories of personal development based on early parental attachments.

There are many kinds of psychotherapy. Cognitive-behavioural therapy assumes that depression stem from negative, often irrational thinking about oneself and one's future. In this type of therapy, a person learns to understand and eventually eliminate those habits of negative thinking. In interpersonal therapy, the therapist helps a person resolve problems in relationships with others that may have caused the depression. The subsequent improvement in social relationships and support helps alleviate the depression. Psychodynamic therapy views depression as the result of internal, unconscious conflicts. Psychodynamic therapists focus on a person's past experiences and the resolution of childhood conflicts. Psychoanalysis is an example of this type of therapy. Critics of long-term Psychodynamic therapy argue that its effectiveness is scientifically unproven

There are almost no pure cognitive or behavioural therapists. Usually therapists combine cognitive and behavioural techniques in an approach known as cognitive-behavioural therapy. For example, to treat a woman with depression, a therapist may help her identify irrational thinking patterns that cause the distressing feelings and to replace these irrational thoughts with new ways of thinking. The therapist may also train her in relaxation techniques and have her try new behaviours that help her become more active and less depressed. The client then reports the results conversely, as in the direction to the therapist.

Therapists who attribute the cause of anxiety to unconscious, internal conflicts may use psychoanalysis to help in the understanding and resolve their conflicts. Other types of psychotherapy, such as cognitive-behavioural therapy, have proven effective in treating anxiety disorders. In cognitive-behavioural therapy, the therapist often educates the person about the nature of his or her particular anxiety disorder. Then, the therapist may help the person challenge. Irrational thoughts that lead to anxiety. For example, to treat a person with a snake phobia, a therapist might gradually expose the person to snakes, beginning with pictures of snakes and progressing to rubber snakes and real snakes. The patient can use relaxation techniques acquired in therapy to overcome the fear of snakes.

Research has shown psychotherapy to be as effective or more effective than medications in treating many anxiety disorders. Psychotherapy may also provide more lasting benefits than medications when patients discontinue treatment.

The goal of cognitive therapy is to identify patterns of irrational thinking that cause a person to behave abnormally. The therapist teaches skills that enable the person to recognize the irrationality of the thoughts. The person eventually learns to perceive people, situations, and himself or herself in a more realistic way and develops improved problem-solving and coping skills. Psychotherapists use cognitive therapy to treat depression, panic disorder, and some personality disorders.

Cognition, act or process of knowing. Cognition includes attention, perception, memory, reasoning, judgment, imagining, thinking, and speech. Attempts to explain the way in which cognition works are as old as itself; the term, in fact, comes from the writings of Plato and Aristotle. With the advent of psychology as a discipline separate from cognizance has been investigated from several viewpoints.

An entire field—cognitive psychology—has arisen since the 1950s. It studies cognition mainly from the standpoint of information handling. Parallels are stressed between the functions of the human brain and the computer concepts such as the coding, storing, retrieving, and buffering of information. The actual physiology of cognition is of little interest to cognitive psychologists, but their theoretical models of cognition have deepened understanding of memory, psycholinguistics, and the development of intelligence.

Social psychologists since the mid-1960s have written extensively on the topic of cognitive consistency—that is, the tendency of a person's beliefs and actions to be logically consistent with one and the other. When cognitive dissonance, or the lack of such consistency, arises, the person unconsciously seeks to restore consistency by changing his or her behaviour, beliefs, or perceptions. The manner in which a particular individual classifies cognition in order to impose order has been termed cognitive style

Research is a central activity of clinical psychologists who work in academic or clinical settings. Primarily, these clinical psychologists study the causes of mental disorders and try to determine the most effective methods of diagnosis and treatment. They also try to improve methods of testing and measuring personality, intelligence, and other personal characteristics.

There are two dominant views on what cause's psychological disorders and how they should be treated: the biological perspective and the psychological perspective. The biological perspective, also called the medical model, views mental illnesses as having a biological cause, just as physical illnesses do. Over the years, this perspective has gained support from the fact that certain medical interventions—such as Antipsychotic drugs, antianxiety drugs, antidepressants, mood stabilizers, and electroconvulsive therapy—have helped enormously in the treatment of certain psychological disorders. Biologically oriented researchers' study genetic predispositions to mental illness, damage to the brain and nervous system, biochemical imbalances, and other physiological underpinnings of mental disorders.

In contrast to the medical model is the psychological perspective, which holds that psychological disorders are caused and maintained by past and present life experiences. This perspective asserts that mental disorders result from negative life events such as prolonged illness, stress, physical and sexual abuse, divorce, poverty, war, the death of a loved one, peer rejection, and chronic failure. Today, most psychologists and psychiatrists believe that mental disorders are caused by a combination of biological and psychological factors.

Another important area of research in clinical psychology concerns the effectiveness of psychotherapy. Most studies have found that no one method of psychotherapy is superior to another. Rather, the different types of psychotherapy are about equally effective, in part because they all share certain qualities. For example, all psychotherapies provide people in distress with hope for recovery, personal support and encouragement, and an opportunity to open up and talk freely about their problems of research in clinical psychology concerns the effectiveness of psychotherapy. Most studies have found that no one method of psychotherapy is superior to another. Rather, the different types of psychotherapy are about equally effective, in part because they all share certain qualities. For example, all psychotherapies provide people in distress with hope for recovery, personal support and encouragement, and an opportunity to open up and talk freely about their problems.

Cognitive Psychology, the scientific study of cognition. Cognition refers to the process of knowing, and cognitive psychology is the study of all mental activities related to acquiring, storing, and using knowledge. The domain of cognitive psychology spans the entire spectrum of conscious and unconscious mental activities: sensation and perception, learning and memory, thinking and reasoning, attention and consciousness, imagining and dreaming, decision making, and problem solving. Other topics that fascinate cognitive psychologists include creativity, intelligence, and how people learn, understand, and use language.

Over the years, cognitive psychologists have discovered that mental activities that seem simple and natural are, in fact, extraordinarily complex. For example, most children have no trouble learning language from their parents. But how do young children decode the meanings of sounds and grasp the basic rules of grammar? Why do children learn language more easily and rapidly than adults? Explaining these puzzles has proven very difficult, and attempts to duplicate true language ability in machines have failed.

Even the most advanced computers have trouble understanding the meaning of a simple story or conversation. Cognitive psychologists have found similar complexity in other mental processes.

Cognitive Psychology, the scientific study of cognition. Cognition refers to the process of knowing, and cognitive psychology is the study of all mental activities related to acquiring, storing, and using knowledge. The domain of cognitive psychology spans the entire spectrum of conscious and unconscious mental activities: sensation and perception, learning and memory, thinking and reasoning, attention and consciousness, imagining and dreaming, decision making, and problem solving. Other topics that fascinate cognitive psychologists include creativity, intelligence, and how people learn, understand, and use language.

Cognitive therapies are similar to behavioural therapies in that they focus on specific problems. However, they emphasize changing beliefs and thoughts, rather than observable behaviours. Cognitive therapists believe that irrational beliefs or distorted thinking patterns can cause a variety of serious problems, including depression and chronic anxiety. They try to teach people to think in more rational, constructive ways.

An important school of thought is based on the teachings of the British psychoanalyst Melanie Klein. Because most of Klein's followers worked with her in England, this has come to be known as the English school. Its influence, nevertheless, is very strong throughout the European continent and in South America. Its principal theories were derived from observations made in the psychoanalysis of children. Klein posited the existence of complex unconscious fantasies in children under the age of six months. The principal source of anxiety arises from the threat to existence posed by the death instinct. Depending on how concrete representations of the destructive forces are dealt within the unconscious fantasy life of the child, two basic early mental attitudes result that Klein characterized as a 'depressive position' and a 'paranoid position.' In the paranoid position, the ego's defence consists of projecting the dangerous internal object onto some external representative, which is treated as a genuine threat emanating from the external world. In the depressive position, the threatening object is introjected and treated in fantasy as concretely retained within the person. Depressive and hypochondriacal symptoms result. Although considerable doubt exists that such complex unconscious fantasies operate in the minds of infants, these observations have been of the utmost importance to the psychology of unconscious fantasies, paranoid delusions, and theory concerning early object relations.

Psychotherapy is an important form of treatment for many kinds of psychological problems. Two of the most common problems for which people seek help from a therapist are depression and persistent anxiety. People with depression may have low self-esteem, and a sense of hopelessness about the future, and a lack of interest in people and activities once found pleasurable. People with anxiety disorders may feel anxious all the time or suffer from phobias, a fear of specific objects or situations. Psychotherapy, by itself or in combination with drug treatment, can often help people overcome or manage these problems.

People with depression often experience feelings of worthlessness, helplessness, guilt, and self-blame. They may interpret a minor failing on their part as a sign of incompetence or interpret minor criticism as condemnation. Some depressed people complain of being spiritually or morally dead. The mirror seems to reflect someone ugly and repulsive. Even a competent and decent person may feel deficient, cruel, stupid, phony, or guilty of having deceived others. People with major depression may experience such extreme emotional pain that they consider or attempt suicide. At least 15 percent of seriously depressed people commit suicide, and many more attempt it.

The pervasive and chronic nature of personality disorders makes them difficult to treat. People with these disorders often fail to recognize that their personality has contributed to their social, occupational, and personal problems. They may not think they have any real problems despite a history of drug abuse, failed relationships, and irregular employment. Thus, therapists must first focus on helping the person understand and become aware of the significance of their personality traits.

People with personality disorders sometimes feel that they can never change their dysfunctional behaviour because they have always acted the same way. Although personality change is exceedingly difficult, sometimes people can change the most dysfunctional aspects of their feelings and behaviour.

Therapists use a variety of methods to treat personality disorders, depending on the specific disorder. For example, cognitive and behavioural techniques, such as role playing and logical argument, may help alter a person's irrational perceptions and assumptions about himself or herself. Certain psychoactive drugs may help control feelings of anxiety, depression, or severe distortions of thought. Psychotherapy may help people to understand the impact of experiences and relationships during childhood.

Psychotherapy is usually ineffective for people with antisocial personality disorder because these individuals tend to be manipulative, unreliable, and dishonest with the therapist. Therefore, most mental health professionals favour removing people with this disorder from their current living situation and placing them in a residential treatment centre. Such residential programs strictly supervise patients' behaviour and impose rigid, consistent rules and responsibilities. These programs appear to help some people, but it is unclear how long their beneficial effects last.

Therapists treating people with borderline personality disorder sometimes use a technique called dialectical behaviour therapy. In this type of therapy, the therapist initially focuses on reducing suicidal tendencies and other behaviours that disrupt treatment. The therapist then helps the person develop skills to cope with anger and self-destructive impulses. In addition, the person learns to achieve personal strength through an acceptance of the many disappointments and interpersonal conflicts that are a natural part of life.

The Psychodynamic perspective was developed earlier that the others, and this is reflected in the style of the article that resented it. They were written in a period chiefly characterize d by bolder speculative theoretical formulations and by insightful clinical studies. It was a richly productive era in which sensitive and intuitive observers mapped out whole continents of the mind that had previously been unexplored. It was a rea of large scale conceptualizations and generalization (Mendelson, 1960). The Mendelson's words, those papers are a partial section as sectioned on the basis of ability and a distinct segment of a 'Great Debate' regarding the development of vulnerability to depression, what roles are to be assigned to aggression and dependence, and what significance is to be attached to depressed persons' self-reproach. In the absence of anybody of independent research data to which appeals could be made, the debate was often rhetorical and even polemical.

The Psychodynamic approach path begins with the lost object as becoming an ego loss, as it is incorporated into the ego. The ego identifies with the lost object, and the conflict between the ego and the lost object becomes a conflict within the ego. Hostility that cannot be expressed directly to the lost object is heaped upon the portion of the ego that is identified with it, and this is reflected in a loss of loss of self-esteem and punishing self-criticism. Freud argued that this process did not happen in just anyone facing a loss. It requires a predisposition that underlies in the basic ambivalence to the love object and an underlying tendency toward narcissistic object choices. The vulnerable person choses love objects that are similar enough to the self that they can be easily abandoned and confused with it.

However, Bibring was careful to state that he did not reject outright the formulations offered by Freud and Abraham, but he suggested that they needed modification because oral and aggressive striving may not be as universal in depression as these formulations supposed. Yet, the adjusting modifications that he presents prove to be quite radical. For Bibring, what was most fundamental about depression is a fall in self-esteem due to 'the ego's shocking awareness of its helpfulness in regard to its aspiration'. Depression occurs when the person both feels powerless to achieve some narcissistically important goal and the goal is not relinquished.

Personality is deeply ingrained and relatively enduring patterns of thought, feeling, and behaviour. Personalities usually reorientate or reconstruct to that which is unique about a person, the characteristics that distinguish him or her from other people. Though, emotion, and behaviour as such do not constitute a personality, which is, rather, the dispositions that underlie these elements. Personality implies predictability about how a person will act or react under different circumstances.

We have avoided using the term Superego, thus far, and have not involved the cruel, punishing Superego in our attempted explanation of the depression. It is our opinion that utilization of the term Superego in this way merely conceals the problem rather than explain it. There are several basic questions regarding the problems of conscience and guilt in the manic depressive. First, what influences account for the severe and hypermoral standards of these people.' And second, what is the dynamic function of the self-punishing acts and attitudes which are engaged in during the periods of illness?

196

The overcritical standards of manic depressives are not explicable as direct taking-over of the standards of the parents, since these patients in childhood have usually been treated with rather exceptional overindulgence. However, the peculiar combination of lack of conviction of worth and a standard of behaviour in the family coupled with an intense devotion to conventional morality and what other people say. It is logical that a child risen by an inconsistent mother who is, at times grossly overindulgent and at others severely rejecting would be unable to build up a reasonable code of conduct for himself. Therefore, his code is focussed around what an impersonal authority is supposed to expect of him and based on no concept of parental reliability or strength. Whereupon, both over severe and frightening in its impersonality, that in all probability, much of his moral code is based on the struggle to acquire those qualities of strength and virtue which he finds missing in his parents. That it to say, that in dealing with authority this type of patient shows a rigid preconception of what authority expects of him as well as a persistent conviction that he must fit in with these expectations which are beyond the reach of reason or experience. The authority appears, that, at times as an incorporated Superego and at other times as a projection, impersonal but tyrannical force. Or, rather, every significant person in the patient's social field is invested with the quality of authority.

In this relationship with authority, the self-punitive acts and experiencing of guilt can be expressed as devices for placating the impersonal tyrant. The guilt expresses by the depressive, and, do not put into effect upon any of the genuine feeling of regret or effort to change behaviour. It is, rather, a means to an end. Merely suffering feelings of guilt is expected to suffice for regaining approval. Nonetheless, it may also be seen that achieving a permanent, secure, human relationship with authority is regarded as hopeless. Therefore, no effort to change relationships or to integrate on a better level of behaviour is undertaken, and the patient merely resorts to the magic of uttering guilty cries to placate authority.

The behavioural perspective emphasizes the analysis of psychopathology in terms of observable behaviour in relation to preceding and consequential events in the environment—controlling stimuli and reinforcement consequences. Yet, a behavioural definition of depression has remained rather elusive. Depression does not refer to a single response class, at least, as it has traditionally been defined, its primary symptom is a state of subjective distress. It is often the case that depressed persons do not exhibit any marked changes in overt behaviour despite their considerable distress and sense of personal inadequacy. As a group, depressed persons do not share much in common in terms of specific behavioural excesses or deficiencies. Furthermore, depression often seems to involve change in behaviours without any apparent change in the conditions that have previously maintained them (Costello, 1972). For instance, upon leaning that his former girl friend back home has become engaged to someone else, a college student might stop eating regularly, withdraw from his friends on campus, and neglect his studying.

Of necessity, the two most influential behavioural formulations of depression involved the introduction of some concepts that go substantially beyond the usual analysis of reinforcement contingencies. Consistent with more general trends is psychology, such that they both were later modified to include an emphasis on cognition.

Lewinsohn developed a model of depression that was an extension of an earlier model presented by Ferster (1973, 1974), in which the central feature of the disorder was identified as a reduction in the emission of positively reinforces behaviour. A major innovation in the Lewinsohn formulation was its emphasis on the concept of total amount of response-contingent positive reinforcement 'reconposre'. The emission of some given adaptive behaviour is seen as not being merely a function of specific rewards available for it. Rather, it is also a function of the overall amount of positive reinforcement that is available as consequences for any available response. It is not a matter of this reinforcement for any available response. Rather, it is also a function of the overall amount of positive reinforcement that is available as consequences for any available response. It is not as matter of this reinforcement being available but often being contingent upon the person making a response. Thus, according to Lewinsohn, a retired person who receives a paycheck without having to work may emit less adaptive behaviours and become depressed.

The Lewinsohn model has been the basis for the development of an extensive research program and a behavioural approach to therapy for depression that includes a self-treatment course (Lewinsohn, 1978) Lewinsohn subsequently posited as relationship between the total number of aversive events in a patient's life and depression, and development and instrument assessing unpleasant events that parallelled the earlier Pleasant Events Schedule (Lewinsohn and Takington, 1970). In his most recent work. Lewinsohn has become more eclectic in both his model of therapy and his research program (Lewinsohn and Hoberman, 1982) and has given attention to the role of cognition in depression. However, he had assumed that the complaints of depressed persons are not necessarily distortions and that most instead reflect the depressed person's inability to obtain valued rewards. His research has even been interpreted as suggesting that depressed persons are more accurate in their self-perceptions than nondepressed persons are (Lewinsohn, 1980).

The universal experience of grief and sadness, ranging from passing sadness to profound depression, indicates that such an ego state exits in all men. We may infer that individual differences in the relative case of and interest of the reactivation of this state are determinants by: (1) the constitution tolerance of continued frustration (2) the severity and extent of the situation of helplessness in early life (3) the development factors which increase and decrease the relative ease with which this state is reactivated and modulate its intent, and (4) their kind and severity of the precipitating conditions. As for dynamic aspects of this theory. The depressive state is reactivated by an intra-ego conflict. The factors involved in this conflict, however, are not yet precisely defined. As for the genetic aspect of the theory: The origin of the depressive ego state is clar and some as the epigenesis of the 'narcissistic aspirations' involved.

The economic and adaptive aspects of the theory, are, nonetheless, not directly by Bibring. It is in regard to these aspects that much work is still in need of attention

Freud made several attempts to account for various aspects of the economy of depression.

For instance, he wrote' ' . . . the ego's inhibited condition and loss of interest was fully accounted for by the absorbing work of mourning (1917), for instance: That the conflict the ego [meaning at that time the conflict between the ego and the Superego which in melancholia is substituted for the struggle round the object, must act like a painful new wound which calls unusually strong cathexes.

But Freud also indicated that these assumptions are insufficient and we need 'some insight into other economic conditions, First, of bodily pain, and then of the mental pain, and then the mental pain, before we can understand the economics of depression; and that, . . . We do not even know by what economic measure the work of mourning is carried through, possibly, however, a conjecture my help in the reality passing its verdict—that the object no longer exists—upon each single of the memories and hopes through which the libido was attached to the lost object, and the ego, confronted, such as it was with the decision whether it will share this falsification is persuaded by the sum of narcissistic satisfactions in being alive to sever its attachment within the nonexistent object, . . . and that . . . this character of withdrawing the libido bit by bit is . . . to be ascribed alike to mourning and to melancholia; it is probably sustained by the same economic arrangements and serves the same purpose in both; finally, why this process of carrying out the behest of reality bit by bit . . . should be so extraordinarily painful is not at all easy to explain in terms of mental economics. Though it is clear that the phenomenon from which the economic explanation must start is the inhibition of the ego, the economic of depression are still not understood. Bibring quoters Fenichel's formulation ' . . . the greater percentage of the available mental energy is used up in unconscious conflicts, [and] not enough is left to provide the normal enjoyment of life and vitality' (Bibring, 1953). But he finds this statement insufficient to explain depressive inhibitions, and proceeds to reconsider the nature of inhibitions. He writes:

> Freud (1926) defines inhibition as a 'restriction of functions of the0 ego, and mention s two major causes for such restrictions; either have imposed upon the person as a measurable precaution, e.g., to prevent the development t of anxiety of feelings of guilt, or brought about as a result in the exhaustion of energy of the ego engaged in intense defensive activities.

. . . . Such that the inhibition in depression . . . does not fall under either category . . . It is rather due to the fact that certain striving of the person becomes meaning less—since the ego appears incapable ever to gratify them.

As a comparison of depression to anxiety, as a reaction to (external or internal) danger indicates the ego's desire to survive. The ego, challenges by the danger, mobilizes the signal of anxiety and prepares for fight or flight. In depression to meet the 'danger' [In certain instances] . . . Depression may follow anxiety, [and then] the mobilization of energy . . . [is] replaced by a decease of self-reliance. Thus, for an economic explanation of depression inhibition ends in the undefined term 'decrease of 'self-reliance' which, as it stands, is not an economic concept.

What does it mean that 'the ego is paralysed because it finds itself incapable to meet the 'danger'?' clearly 'paralysed' refers to the state of helplessness, one of the corollaries of which is the 'loss of self-esteem'. The danger is the potential loss of object; the traumatic situation is that of the loss of object, 'helplessness' as Bibring defines it is the persisting state of loss of object. The anxiety signal anticipates the loss in order to prevent the reactivation of the traumatic situation, that is, of panic-anxiety. Fluctuations of self-esteem anticipate, and initiate measures to prevent, the reactivation of the state of persisting loss of object, that is of the state of helplessness of self-esteem and 'helplessness' which are accompanied by loss of self-esteem in similar to the reaction between anxiety signal and panic-anxiety. Fluctuations of self-esteem are the structured, tamed forms of and signals to anticipate and to preclude reactivation of the state of helplessness. Yet, according to the accepted theory, fluctuations of self-esteem, are the functions of the Superego's relation to the ego, just as anxiety was considered, prior to 1926, as an operative function of repression that is enforced by the Superego. In 1926, however, Superego anxiety was recognized as merely one kind of anxiety and the repression, and hence anxiety relationship was reversed into anxiety signal hence repression. Bibring achieves an analogous reversal when he formulated, . . . our contention, as based on clinical observation, that it is the ego's awareness of its helplessness which in certain cases forces it to turn the aggression from the object against the self, thus, aggravating and complicating the structure of depression.' While in the accepted theory it is assumed that the aggression 'turned round upon the subject', resulting in passivity and helplessness, in Bibring's conception it is the helplessness which is the cause of this 'turning round'.

Like Freud's structural theory of anxiety and Fenichel's of guilt (1945), leads to a broadening of our conception of the ego's apparatuses and functions, even more of a problem of aggression, we know that 'turn round upon the subject' was the basic mechanism Freud used before the 'death-instinctual theory' to explain major forms in which aggression manifests itself, that Freud wrote, . . . sadism . . . seems to press toward a quite special aim:—the infliction of pain, in addition to subjection and mastery of the object. Now psychoanalysis would seem to show that infliction of pain plays no part in the original aims sought by [sadism] . . . : The sadistic child takes no notice of whether or not it inflicts pain, nor is it part of its purpose to do so. But when once the transformation into masochism has taken place, the experience of the pain is very well adapted to serve as a passive masochistic aim . . . Where once the suffering of pain has been experienced as a masochistic aim, it can be carried back into the sadistic situation and result in a sadistic aim of inflicting pain (1955).

Thus, Bibring's view that 'turning round upon the subject' is brought about by helplessness calls attention to some of Freud's early formulations, and prompts to re-evaluate the conception of aggression. Nonetheless, it may lead to a theory of aggression which is an alterative to those which have been proposed, namely Freud's death-instinct theory, Fenichel's frustration-aggression theory, and the Hartmann-Kris-Loewenstein theory of an independent aggressive instinctual drive.

Briefly, the relationship between helplessness (involving loss of self-esteem) and simultaneously maintains the narcissistic aspirations, to take note, would in itself sustain of an intra-ego conflict, if we are to assume, however, that of Bibring, may have been implied by Freud when he wrote in 'Mourning and Melancholia,' "That a good, capable, conscientious [person] . . . is more likely to all that are ill. disease than [one] . . . of whom we too should have nothing good to say" (1917).

In the study of the examining the manic-depressive character by means of the intense psychoanalytic psychotherapy, this is potentially useful, since, the newer understanding of interpersonal processes and the problematic issue belonging to anxiety has not been brought to bar. However, the older psychoanalytic studies of the psychopathology of the manic depressive. Thus, to use a simple example, the manic depressive is said to have an oral character. Nonetheless, the question of how or why he developed an oral character is left unconsidered except t that such factors as a constitutional overintensity of oral drives, or overindulgence or frustration during the oral phase are proven significant. By studying the transference, we can make inferences about earlier experiences; conversely, by understanding the patient historically, we can make inferences about the transference relationship and grasp of the patient's part of the pattern of interaction with his therapist improves, as we can gain some concept of what goals of satisfaction he is pursuing, as well as to what sort of anxieties he is striving to cope with. We may then intervene through our part in the interaction to assist him more successfully to achieve his goals of satisfaction and to resolve some of the conflicts which are at the source of his anxiety.

At the end of the last century, Kraepelin (1904) attempted to classify the psychiatric syndromes, including the manic-depressive or circular psychosis, as nosological entities. While his classifications in general brought some order into the existing confusion, he was unable to establish a pathological substratum or a specific etiological factor for either dementia praecox or manic-degressive psychosis, and this situation still exists.

Abraham, in 1911, was first to systematically apply the psychoanalytic method to the treatment of the circular psychosis. He concluded that manically and depressive phases are dominated by the same complexities, the depressive being defeated by them, the manic ignoring and denying them. Some of his ideas on depression might be summarized as follows: The regression to the oral level of libidinal development brought out the characterological factures of impatience and envy, increased egocentricity, and intense ambivalence, the capacity to love is paralysed by hate, sands this inability to love leads' feelings of impoverishment. The depressive stupor represents a form of dying. Abraham thought that the indecision of ambivalence is close to the doubts of the compulsive e neurotic, and that in the free interval, the manic depressive is an obsessional neurotic. He recommended psychoanalysis in the first interval, since, in the acute phases of the psychosis, it is very difficult to establish rapport.

Dooley, like Abraham found considerable resistance in her patient's extraverted egocentricity, fort which she accepted White's concert of 'flight into reality'. According to White, this tendency toward extraversion of the libido makes the prognosis of manic-depressive psychosis more favourable, in terms of spontaneous recovery, than that of schizophrenia. He felt that because of the dominance of his egocentric wishes, the manic-depressive patient can make 'use of every object in range of his sense'. However, Dooley found that the resistance of the manic degressive against analysis is even stronger than those of schizophrenics. Dooley suggested that the manic attack is a defence against the realization of failure. The patient cannot look at himself in the mirror of psychoanalysis; he cannot hear the truth. Patient's who manifest frequent manic attacks are likely to be headstrong, self-sufficient, know-it-all types of person, who will get the upper hand of the analyst.,.. The analyst is really only an appendage for the greater inflated ego. Since the life conditions of the manic depressive are often no more unsatisfactory than those of many a normal person, there must be a lack of integration which keeps the manic depressive from achieving the sublimation which he is potentially capable of. Dooley came to the conclusion that the manic and depressive episodes are due to deep regressions to the sadomasochistic level of the child. 'Autoerotic wishes were satisfied by hypochondriacal complaints'. In a much later paper on 'The Relation of Humour to Masochism' Dooley mentioned a manic-depressive patient who began to develop humour in the analysis as she became aware that she 'could neither hurt me, nor wrangle me into living him'. Dooley considered this kind of insightful humour to be a milestone in the healing process of the excessive mood swings; it indicates that the Superego is losing its tragically condemning cruelty and is permitting laughter at the overweening, pestering child-ego.

In 1916-1917, Freud compared melancholia to normal mourning, as, the loss of a love object elicits the labour of mourning, which is as struggle between libido attachment and detachment—love and hate. In normal mourning this struggle of ambivalence under pressure of confrontation with reality leads to gradual rechannelization of the libido toward new objects. In the case of melancholia, or frustration, remains unconscious, and the reorientation exacted reality elicits strong resistance, since the narcissistic characters of the disturbed relations do not permit detachment. In this way, an intensified identification with the frustrating love object in the unconscious results. The shadows of the object have fallen on the Ego.' The whole struggle of ambivalence is internalized in a battle with the conscience. The exaggerated self-accusations are reproaches against the internalized object of love and hate: The self-torture is a form of revenge, and simultaneously, attempts at reconciliation with the internalized partner. The narcissistic, ambivalent character of the elation to the lost love object either is the result of transitory regression or is constitutionally conditioned. Thus, the loss of self-esteem and the intense self-hate in the melancholia become understandable.

In 1921, Freud added some statements about mania to his earlier interpretations of depression. He suggested that the mood swings of normal and neurotic persons are caused by the tensions between ego and ego ideal. These mood swings are excessive in the case of manic-depressive illness because after the frustrating of lost object has been reestablished by identifications in the ego, it is then tormented by the cruel severity of the ego ideal, against which, in turn, the ego rebels. According to Freud, the manic represent a triumphant reunion between ego and ego ideal, in the sense of expansive self-inflation, but not in the sense of stability as the continuum for being dimensionalized through something connoting the equilibrium.

Abraham, in 1924, pursued his interest in biological development and tried to finding the specific fixation points for mental illness in different phases of libido development. He interpreted character traits for being highly symbolized derivatives of pregenital instinctual impulses that were, in the case of the mentally ill person, hampered in their normal development by frustration or overindulgence. Because of Abraham's influence, psychoanalytic research in ego development has for a long time been dependent on highly schematized concepts, to which the manic depressive periodically regresses for being at the end of the second biting oral phase and the beginning of the first expelling anal phase. This assumption could explain the frequent preoccupation of the manic depressive with cannibalistic phantasies as well. His character trends of impatience, envy and exploitativeness, dominating possessiveness, and exaggerated optimism or pessimism: His intense ambivalence, and his explosive riddance reactions. The object loss that precedes the onset of a depression is mostly not conscious but, according to Abraham, repeats a primal depression, a frustration at the time of transition from the oral to the anal phase, when the child was disappointed in the mother. The oral dependence may be constitutionally overemphasized in the manic depressive.

In 1927 Râdo went a step further in the theory of identification. Freud and Abraham's theories imply an incorporation of the lost or flustrating object, in both the tormented ego and the punishing ego-ideal or Superego. This double incorporation, Râdo postulated, corresponds to an ambivalent splitting into a 'good'—that is, of a gratifying—object, and a 'badly' or frustrating object; at an early stage of development, when the synthetic function of the ego is still weak, both of these are the mother. The good parent by whom the child wants to be loved is incorporated in the Superego, endowed with the privilege of punishing the bad parent who is incorporated in the ego. This bad object in the ego may be punished to the point of total destruction (suicide). But the ultimate goal of this raging orgy of self-torture is expiation, reconciliation, synthesis. Râdo describes the manic phase as an unstable reconciliation reached on the basis of denial of guilt. The automatized cycle of guilt, expiation, and reconciliation is patterned after the sequence of infantile oral experience, as, rages, hunger, drinking. The drinking, which resembles the state of reunion of reconciliation, culminates in a satiated pleasure experience, which Râdo called the 'alimentary orgasm'. In a paper published in 1933 Râdo described the way in which the drug addict, in the artificially produced intoxication, expresses the same yearning for reconciliation and blissful reunion with the gratifying mother.

In the same year, 1933, Deutsch illustrated the theory of manic depressive psychoses, as developed up to that time, by several abbreviated case presentations. She agreed with Râdo that the melancholic phase is sometimes introduced by a phase of rebellion of the ego against the cruel Superego. After the ego succumbs to the Superego's punishment with the unconscious intention of bribing the Superego and of gaining forgiveness by such submission, the ego may rescue itself from the dangerous introjection by projecting the threatening enemy onto the outside world; aggression can then be directed against the projected Superego, which has become an external persecutor. Another form of escape from the melancholic predicament is the denial of any narcissistic deprivation—be it the loss of mother's breast or the absence of a penis—in a glorious triumph of manic or hypomanic excitement. Deutsch regarded mania and paranoia as alternative defences against the intense danger to survival to an ego oppressed by melancholia. In the hypomanic patient, the underling depression has to be lifted into consciousness if therapy is to be successful. In 1938, Jacob's made similar observations on a periodically manic patient.

Gero illustrated 'The Construction of Depression' (1936) by two case presentations. One was of a woman patient with an obsessional character structure built up as a defence against the painful ambivalence in her family relations. Only after these character defences yielded to analysis could this patient see avenues of realistic satisfactions and therewith surmount the depressions. The other case was a male patient, who had identified with an overambitious, over exacting father, and a rejecting mother, and had repressed the rage against both frustrating parents by withdrawal into repressed regression, punishing therewith the internalized objects of his hate and rage. After his father's death, he had himself changed into a sick old man. The liberation of rage and hate in the transference freed the genital aggressiveness from the odium and guilt of sadomasochistic distortions. In both cases the analyst succeeded in winning the patients from a hopeless negativism to a hopeful confirmation of life.

Jacobson described in 1943 a severely depressed patient, with strongly suicidal argues, intense experiences of depersonalization and 'Weltuntergang' phantasies—a case on the borderlines between manic degressive psychosis and schizophrenia. Jacobson was able to uncover a primal depression in this patient at the age of three and a half, when the birth of a brother coincided with a disruption of the parental marital elation. Turning from mother father and back to mother left the patient empty. Threatened by complete loss of objects, she maintained a masochistic dependence on her mother. As substitutes for the disappointing parents, she built up phantasies of idealism, perfect parents who endowed her Superego with cruel severity, so that she lived in constant danger of complete desertion and in horror of punishment.

Weiss in 1944 pursued a slightly different approach. He postulated that melancholic episodes are a reaction to the realization of antisocial, dishonest, or egotistical aspects of the personality. The inability of the patient to reach an integration between his antisocial wishes and his moral standards causes a tension in his 'agreeing' so that the patient hastes himself. The exaggerated guilt reaction maintains the split between persecuting and persecuted 'introjects'. Identifications with hated objects may make the task of ego integration very difficult. Such that the manic phase, the passive objectionable introjective projection, and the ego, by something assertively assumed, are that the active role of the persecuting Superego against objects of condemnation in the outside world. Weiss points out that in paranoia, the ego does not cling strongly to the Superego, and the persecuting introjects, the Superego, is projected' in mania, however, the persecuted introject is projected. The paranoiac, by this projection, succeeds in preserving his narcissistic position, while the melancholic fails, the result of his inner persecuting may be self-destruction.

Recently, Bibring has summed up all the features that different kinds of depression have in common, including not only the depressions of circular psychosis, but also the reactive depressions and depressions in the course of physical illness and in states of fatigue or exhaustion. A common factor is the lowering of self-esteem, the loss of self-love, which, in melancholia, is intensified into self-hate. Bibring compares depression with states of depersonalization and boredom. In the mildly depressed person, there is not so much haste turned against the self as there is an exhaustion of the narcissistic supply of self-love. The mildly depressed person is less inclined to kill himself than to let of himself and others to die.

Frank in a lecture on 'The Defensive Aspects of Depression' follows a line of thought similar to Bibring's. He compares unspecific depressions of the hibernation of animals. A defensive response frustrating life conditions. Depression as a defence tine down the desires and expectations to a lower key, so that of a defence line of unavoidable frustration is reduced to a minimum.

The manic aspect of the manic-depressive psychosis has on the whole, elicited less attention on the part of psychoanalysis than has the depressed aspect, probably because the manic patient does not frequently seek therapeutic help. B., Lewin, in a monograph on 'The Psychoanalysis of Elation' regards elation as a decence of denial against depression. During the analytic process, Lewin suggests, normal mourning increases insight into the self and terminate in a sense of heightening well-being, increased sexual potency, and capacity for work and sublimation. But elation or depression resist the testing of reality; they produce negative therapeutic reactions in the face of insight that cannot at the time be emotionally assimilated. The depressed and the elation ego are not trying to separate the 'true' from the 'false' but the 'good' from the 'bad' as well. Reality-testing is replaced by morality-testing. Lewin compares mania to sleep, in sleep the ego disappears; in mania the Superego vanishes. Sleep stems from oral satisfaction—the infant drops asleep when he is satiated with nursing at the mother's breast. But the manic patient is notoriously poor sleeper, and he is haunted by 'the triad of oral wishes'—to devour, into be devoured, and to sleep. The wish-fear to be devoured transforms the wish to sleep into a fear of dying. The yearning for the gratifying maternal breast—the wish to sleep—may be transmuted into a desire for union with the Superego. In the artist this union is accomplished, as a result of the inspiration and actualization of this inspiration in the creative process, which satisfies both the Superego and the world of the artist's contemporaries.

While psychosocial research has identified the etiologic role of stressful events and several promising psychological treatments have been formulated, a number of important research and clinical; issues have been identified. For instance, why do stressful life circumstances lead to depression among some persons but not others? How can one explain the finding that different psychosocial intervention's appar to have similar effects on depression? To what distinguishable extent of a surface, and especially of the earth's surfaces should preventive efforts be targeted?

Adler very early saw the importance of self-esteem in depression. More recently, Bibring (1953) signalled a truly radical break with the older theory in psychoanalysis, by postulating that an undermining of self-esteem was the primary focus in depression, that it was principally to be understood as an ego-phenomenon, and only secondarily as a consequence of self-directed aggression.

It would be impossible to overestimate the significance of this shift in emphasis. In spite of Bibring's own protestations to the contrary, theories about the role of orality and aggression, is that, if self-esteem is the primary focus of depressions than does physiology. An ego-based theory of depression broadens the area of explanation from a purely 'intrapsychic battlefield' to the entire range of social phenomena. Since the ego is rooted in social reality, since self-esteem is composed of social symbols and social motives, depression is to become distinctively functional, as that of a cognitively apprehended symbolic world. Nothing less than a full sweep of cultural activity is bought into consideration in the single case of depression.

Hardly at all, ever, that more recently a crucial sociological dimension was added to the theory of depression—again from within psychoanalysis (Szasz, 1961). In the classical formulation of depression, mourning and melancholic states, Freud had presented the psychoanalysis with a model (1917). He postulated that since the ego grows by developing responses to an identification with objects. The loss of an object was a threat to the ego. This, Freud reasoned, was the basic dynamic of mourning and melancholic states. The loss of an object in the real world meant a corresponding depletion in the ego: To relinquish a loved object was to subject oneself to a sometimes massive trauma. Freud theorized on the rather elaborate procedures that society sets up to ease this relinquishing of objects: The funeral rites, mourning rituals, and so on. There is nothing fundamentally wrong with Freud's view of depression. It explains a good deal. Its principal drawback is that it is used to explain too much.

Szasz's objection to the traditional view of depression is precisely its insistence on the predominant importance of object-loss in unleashing dependency cravings and hostility. He proposes to emend this by stressing that the loss of a 'game' is fully as significant in depression as is the loss of object. 'Game' in this context, is a series of norms of rules for significant action. And for the symbolic animal, there is nothing 'playful' about significance. Szasz said that . . . persons need not only human objects but also norms or rules—or, more generally—game that are worth playing. It is a matter of everyday observation that their object world might remain more or less intact. To account for this and similar events, it is necessary to consider the relationship of the ego or self to games. Otherwise, one is forced to reduce all manners of personal suffering to consideration of object relationships . . . Conversely, since loss of a real or external object implies the loss of a player from the game—unless an exact substitute can be found—such loss inevitably results in at least some changes in the game. It is thus, evident that the words 'player' and 'game' describe interdependent variables making dynamic steady states (1961).

With this broadening out of traditional object-loss theory, there is no longer any valid pretense for keeping the phenomenon of depression within the realm of medicine. Psychoanalysis is fully linked as, with social science, since, as Szasz insists, objects and games are inseparably joined, self and society must be seen as a single phenomenon. People 'create' objects by acting according to social rules. They 'create' themselves as they create objects. Social rules are objects provide man with a staged drama of significance which is the theatre of his action. Man discovers himself by making appeal for his identity to the society in which he performs. To lose an object, then, is to lose someone to whom one has made appeal for self-validation. To lose a game is to lose a performance part in which identity is fabricated and sustained.

For the most part, this model represents the advanced theoretical cogitations of the psychiatric profession on a perplexing human phenomenon. This much must be said, as it is not easy to comprehend why anyone would opt out of life. It is understandable that we would be quick to look for some basic genetic taint, some stunted early development, that would mark such an individual off from others. But the matter is not quite simple: The fact is that a good proposition of depressed patient's has led mature and responsible lives; some have achieved notable success, financial and personal. We distort our vision if we use the theoretical proponents as to explain why these people become abysmally depressed.

It is amazing that human action could have been so consistently and thoroughly conceived in instinctual and compartmentalized terms. It is to the credit of some psychoanalysts that they themselves have begun to breakout of their own inherited theories, and to range more broadly for an explanation of depression. This is part of the natural development of ego psychology. As the view of man as a cultural animal shaped by learning takes over from the older instinctual explanations, the way in clear for a full theoretical understanding, that if the ego is the basis for action, and if a warm feeling of self-value must pervade one's acts, then it is only a step focussing on the really crucial dynamic of a breakdown in action, in the undermining of the individual's sense of self-value.

We take to note, that the answering to one common human problem is given by one thing in answering the need for sentiment: That as the object of primary value in the world of meaning (Hallowell, 1955). Data from anthropology support that nowhere on this once-vast globe had man been able to act unless he had a basic sentiment of self-value. Unless the individual feels worthwhile, and unless his actions are considered worthwhile and life grinds to a halt. Whole cultures have begun to expire in this way.

Behaviour models of depression are relatively new, compared to the Psychodynamic formulations that have just been presented. The behavioural perspective on psychopathology development later, but it is also true that behaviourists at first neglected the subject of depression. A few papers appeared in the late sixties (Burgess, 1968 and Lazarus, 1968), but they were highly speculative and lacked rigorous definition or analysis of depressive behaviour.

The behavioural perspective emphasizes the analysis of psychopathology in term s of observable behaviour in relation to preceding and consequential events in the environment—controlling stimuli and reinforcement consequences. Yet a behavioural definition of depression has remained rather elusive. Depression does not refer to a single response class, at least, as it has traditionally been defined, its primary symptom is a state of subjective distress. It is often the case that depressed persons do not exhibit any marked changes in overt behaviour despite their considerable distress and sense of personal inadequacy. As a group, depressed do not share of personal inadequacy, of specific behavioural excessive or deficiencies. Furthermore, depression often seems to involve a change in behaviour without any apparent change in the conditions that have previously maintained them (Costello, 1972). For instance, upon leaning that his former girl friend back home has become engaged to someone else, a college student might stop eating regularly, withdraw from his friends on campus, and neglect his studying.

Of necessity, the two most influential behavioural formulations of depression (Lewinsohn, Miller, Roselling and Seligman) involved the introduction of some concepts that go substantially beyond the usual analysis of reinforcement contingencies. Consistent with more general trends in psychology, they both also were later modified to include an emphasis on cognition.

Lewinsohn developed a model of depression that was an extension of an earlier model presented by Ferster (1973, 1974), in which the central features of the disorder were identified as a reduction in the emission of positively reenforced behaviour. A major innovation in the Lewinsohn formulation was its emphasis on the concept of total amount of response-contingently positive reinforcement 'reconposre'. The emission of some given adaptation is seen as not being merely a function of specific rewards available for it. Rather, it is also a function of the overall amount of positive reenforcement that is available as consequences for any available response. It is not a matter of this reinforcement being available but of its being contingent upon the person making a response. Thus, according to Lewinsohn, a retired person who receives a paycheck without having to work may emit less adaptive behaviour and become depressed.

Depression is conceptualized a low rate of behaviour and a state of dysphoria that occur when there is a low rate of reconposre. There is a potential for a vicious cycle to develop, with a lower rate of positive reinforcement leading to a lower rate of adaptive behaviour, leading to a further reduction in reinforcement, and worth. Expression of distress may be met with reassurance, and in this way depressive behaviour can become the primary way of obtaining reinforcement.

The rate of response-contingent reinforcement available is dependent upon three sets of factors: The events that is potentially reinforcing to a person, of these, those that are available in the immediate environment, and the extent to which the person possesses the necessary skills to receive this reinforcement. Events that precipitate depression may do so by affecting one or more of these factors. For instance: For a man who has just become divorced, the availability to reinforcing events has been changed, and if he may become depressed.

The Lewinsohn model has been the basis for the development of an extensive research program, and a behavioural approach to therapy for depression that includes a self-treatment course (Lewinsohn, 1978). However, the given attention to the role of cognition in depression, that he has assumed that the complaints of depressed persons are not necessarily distortions and that they may instead reflect depressed persons' inability to obtain valued rewards. His research has been interpreted as suggesting that depressed persons are more accurate in their self-perceptions than nondepressed persons are (Lewinsohn, 1980).

Lewinsohn cites one study in particular as a major reason for his shift to move eclectically and a more cognitive model. Leiss, Lewinsohn and Munoz (1979) compared social skills training, the scheduling of pleasant activities, and cognitive therapy as treatments for depression. The result of the study indicated that not only were this treatment equally effective in reducing depression, but that they were not specific, i.e., cognitive therapy had as much effect on pleasant activities as did the scheduling of these activities.

By now it should have become apparent that the phenomenon of depression is vague, delineate and poorly understood. Seligman and his colleagues have provided a fine example of the strategy for dealing with this problem: The construction can be achieved.

The term 'learned helplessness' was first used in connection with laboratory experiments in which dogs were exposed to shock from which they could not escape (Overmier and Seligmam, 1967). After repeated trials, the dogs tended to sit passively when the shock came on. Expose d to a new situation from which they could escape a hock by jumping over a barrier, but they failed to initiate the appropriate response. Some would occasionally jump over the barrier and escape, but they would generally revert to taking the shock passively. Fo r the purpose of constructing an analogue of clinical depression, the behaviour of the dogs, is significant in suggesting that exposure to uncontrollable aversive situations and an inability to learn that responding is effective.

One cayuse of laboratory produced helplessness seems to be learning that one cannot control important events. Learning that responses and reinforcement are independent results in a cognitive set that has two effects—fewer responses to control reinforcement are initiated, and associating successful responses with reinforcement becomes more difficult.

The anchoring grounds of the analogy to depression are the view of the disorder for being fundamentally a matter of depressed persons being passive, e.g., as failing to initiate appropriate responses to cope with their predicaments—and unable to perceive that their responses make a difference. Thus, Lewinsohn invoked the concept of the total amount of response-contingent reinforcement to explain the rather generalized problems of depressed persons. Selgman and his colleagues introduce the notion of a generalized inhibition of response and an acquired perception of response-reinforcement independence.

The analogy to depression was bolstered by initial fi8ndings that in a variety of tasks situations, depressed human subjects resembled nondepressed subjects who had received repeated failure experiences. For instance, compared to non-depressed subjects who had not received repeated, failure experiences, the two groups of subjects took longer to solve anagrams and apparently failed to perceive the pattern underlying their successful solution (Klein and Seligman, 12976). While other researches by Miller, Rosellin and Seligman, 1976, were to suggest that the parallel between other groups that leaned helplessness and depression were not limited with regard to etiology, treatment, and prevention.

The original learned helplessness model stimulated a large body of research and considerable controversy (Buchward, Coyne and Cole, 1978, as well as, Costello, 1978). Ultimately, the accumulated research led to questions about both the adequacies of the learned-helplessness explanation for the behaviour of nondepressed subjects who had been exposed failure as well as the appropriateness of learned helplessness as an analogue of depression. For instance, it was shown that the performance deficits of subjects who had been given a typical learned helplessness induction were very much situation-specific (Cole and Coyne, 1977) and that these deficits might better be explained as the result of anxious self-preoccupation, rather than the perception of responses-reinforcement independence (Coyne, Metalsky, and Lavelle, 1980). Furthermore, the characterization of depressed persons as passive and lacking in aggression was challenged. Difficulties with the original leaned helplessness model led to a major reformulation.

Rehm`s self-control model of depression is less developed than either of the preceding two models, bu t it adds an additional dimension in the literature or the role played of cognition in depression. Rehm draws on the work of Kanfer (1070) and others suggesting that depression is a matter of some interrelated problems in self-control. Briefly, the self-control model assumes that people may regulate their own behaviour in a way that allows them to be somewhat independent of their immediate environment and the controlling stimuli and reinforcement contingencies that it offers. Self-monitoring involves attending to ones own behaviour and its antecedent and consequence. Self-evaluation is a matter of interpreting ones behaviour and comparing it to internal standards.

Nevertheless, Rehm is explicit in his indebtedness to other cognitive and behavioural models of depression. However, this model can go beyond the more behavioural models in providing an alternative in the way of explaining depression. Moreover, the identification of deficiencies in self-control processes suggests specific therapeutic intervention. To alter them would not be suggested by the other interventions. To alter them would not be suggested by the other approaches. In addition, as number of studies have produced results consistent with hypotheses derived from the model (Kanfer and Zeiss, 1983) although questions have been raised as to whether deficits in self-monitoring, self-evaluation and self-reward are specific to depression (Gotlib, 1981).

Beck noted that there was a lack of systematic psychological research on depression, least of mention, the cognitive model he presented did much to change that situation. A recent review (Coyne and Gotlib, 1983), cited 100 studies generated by the prevailing of the cognitive model.

Cognitive models of depression have a strong intuitive appeal. The self-deprecating and pessimistic talk of depressed persons and their apparent failure to take obvious steps to remedy their situations readily invites the suggestion that they suffer from distorted cognitive processes.

In the model presented by Kovacs and Beck, three sets of interrelated cognitive concepts are used to explain the psychological phenomenon of depression: The cognitive triad, schemata, and cognitive distortion or faculty information processing. These cognitive factors are seen as having a causal primacy over the affective, motivational, and behavioural features of depression.

The cognitive triad consists of thinking patterns that lead depressed persons to construe themselves, their current situation, and their future possibilities in negative terms. The concept of schematises are used to explain why depressed persons persist in these negative and self-defeating attitudes, even in the face of contradictory evidence. Cognitive schematises are stable, organized representations of past experiences that provide for the screening, differentiations, and encoding of information from the environment. In depression, prepotent dysfunctional schemata dominate information processing so that depressed persons may not even be able to consider processing so that depressed persons may not even be able to consider alternative interpretations of their experience that are more positive or optimistic. They overgeneralized from negative experiences, selectively abstract negative details out of context, and negatively characterized themselves in absolutist terms—always, never, nothing by, etc.

These cognitive processes are activated in the depressed person by stressful experiences, but they exist before a depressive episode in a latent state. In explaining how a vulnerability of these thinking processes comes about, Beck (1974) has offered an account that bears a strong resemblance to Psychodynamic formulations: It is said, that, in the course of his development, the depression-prone person may become sensitized by certain unfavourable types of life situations such as the loss of a parent or chronic rejection by peers. Other unfavourable conditions of a more insidious nature may similarly produce vulnerability to depression. These traumatic experiences predispose the individual to overact to analogous situations later in life. He has a tendency to make extreme, absolute judgements when such situations occur.

Although the original learned-helplessness model could also be said to be cognitive in the sense that it invoked the concept of a perception of response-reinforcement independence, it defines this perception in terms of its environment antecedents and behavioural consequences. Overall, the model gave little attention to higher cognitive processes. In the reformulation model, such that Abramson, Seligman and Teasdale have emphasized, to those of a learned helplessness in which people inappropriately generalize the expectation of contingency to a new, controllable situation. It is important to point out that the old hypothesis does not require an inappropriate generalization for helplessness. Helplessness exists when a person shows motivational and cognitive deficits as a consequence of an expectation of situations over which it occurs are irrelevantly to demonstrating helplessness. But the old hypothesis does not specify where and when a person who expects outcomes to be uncontrollable will show deficits.

Nonetheless, the additional requirement was that the person must come to expect that future outcomes would also be uncontrollable, and higher cognitive processes were assumed to mediate the development of his expectation. 'When a person finds that he is helpless, he asks 'why' he is helpless. The causal attributions that determine the generality and chronicity of his helplessness deficits as well as his later self-esteem.

According to the helplessness view, the central theme in successful therapy should be having the patient discover and come to accept that his responses produce the gratification that he desires—that he is, in short, an effective human being. Some therapists that reportedly alleviate depression are consonant with a learned helplessness model. However, it is important to note that the success of a therapy often has little to do with its theoretical underpinning. So, with the exception of Klein and Seligman (1976), the following 'evidence' should not be regarded as a test of the model, but merely as a set of examples that seem to have exposure to response-produced success as a cure for depression.

Consonant with their helplessness-centred views of the etiology depression. Bibring (1953), Beck (1967) and Melges and Bowlby (1969) all stressed that revering helplessness alleviates depression. For example, Bibring has stated, in that, the same conditions which bring about depression (helplessness) in reverse serve frequently the restitution from depression. Generally one can say that depression subsides either (1) when the narcissistically important goals and objects appear to be again within reach (which is frequently followed by temporary elation) or (2) when they become sufficiently modified or reduced to become realizable, or (3) when they are altogether relinquished, or (4) when they together relinquished, or (5) when the ego recovers from the narcissistic shock by regaining its self-esteem with the help of various recovery mechanisms (with or without any change of objective or goal).

In their review of therapies for depression, Seligman, Klein and Miller (1976) indicated that most of the therapies have strong elements of inducing the patient to discover that responses produce the reinforcement he desires. In antidepression milieu therapy (Taulbee and Wright, 1971)m for example, the patient is forced to emit one of the most powerful response people have for controlling others—anger—and when this response is dragged out of his depleted behaviour repertoire, he is powerfully reinforced. Beck's (1770) cognitive therapy is aimed at similar goals. He sees success manipulations as changing the negative cognitive set ('I'm an effective person') of the depressive to a more positive set, and argues that the primary task of the therapist is to change the negative expectations of the depressed patient to more optimistic ones. In both Burgess's (1968) therapy and the graded task assignment (Beck, Seligman, Binik, and Brill), the patient makes instrumental responses of gradually increasing therapy for depression (Hersen, Eislere, Alford and Agras, 1973; Reisinger, 1972), by definition, arranges the contingencies so that responses control the occurrence of reinforcement; the patient's recognition of this relationship should alleviate depression. Lewinsohn's therapy also has this element: Participation in activity and other nondepressed behaviour controls therapy time (Lewinsohn, Weinsyein and Shaw, 1969). In assertive training (Wolpe, 1968), the patient must emit social responses to bring about a desired change in his environment.

As in learned helplessness, the passage of time has been found to alleviate depression. Electroconvulsive therapy, which alleviates helplessness. Probably alleviates endogenous depression (Carney, Roth and Garside, 1965), but it s effect s on reactive depression are unclear. The role of atropine is largely unknown (Janowsky, 1972).

Dramatic success in medicine has come more frequently from prevention than from treatment, and we would hazard a guess that inoculation and immunization have saved many more lives than any cure. Psychotherapy is almost exclusively limited to use as a cure, and preventive procedures rarely play an explicit role. In our studies of animals we found that behavioural immunization provided an easy and effective means of preventing learned helplessness.

One can also look at successful therapy as prevention. After all, therapy is usually not focussed just on undoing past problems. It also should arm the patient against future depressions. Would therapy for depression be more successful if it were explicitly aimed at providing the patient with a wide repertoire of coping responses that he could use in future situations where he found he could not control reinforcement by his responses?

Finally, we can speculate about child rearing. What kinds of experience can best protect our children against the debilitating effect of helplessness and depression? A tentative answer follows from the learned helplessness view of depression: A childhood of experiences in which one's own actions are instrumental in bringing about gratification and removing annoyances. Seeing oneself as an effective human being mat require a childhood filled with powerfully synchronous, between responding and its consequences.

Testing the learned helplessness model of depression requires the demonstration of similarities in symptoms, etiology, cure and prevention of learned helplessness. The current evidence, reviewed in this model, indicates that in many respects the major symptoms of helplessness parallel those of depression. In addition, it has been suggested that the cure of both reactive depression and learned helplessness is the belief that responses do not control important reinforcers. Finally, we have speculated that the methods that succeed in curing and preventing learned helplessness has their parallels in the cure and prevention of depression. Much remains to be tested, however, we can believe that a common theme has emerged as both depression and learned helplessness have at their core the belief in the futility of responding.

Psychosis, is a mental illness in which a person loses contact with reality and has difficulty functioning in daily life. Psychotic symptoms can indicate severe mental illnesses, such as schizophrenia and bipolar disorder (manic-depressive illness). Unlike people with less severe psychological problems, psychotic individuals do not usually recognize that their mental functioning is disturbed.

Mental health professionals generally divide psychotic symptoms into three broad types: hallucinations, delusions, and bizarre behaviour. Hallucinations refer to hearing, seeing, smelling, feeling, or tasting something when nothing in the environment actually caused that sensation. For example, a person experiencing an auditory hallucination might hear a voice calling her or his name even though no one else is actually present. A delusion is a false belief held by a person that appears obviously untrue to other people in that person's culture. For example, a man may believe that Martians have implanted a microchip in his brain that controls his thoughts. Bizarre behaviour refers to behaviour in a person that is strange or incomprehensible to others who know the person. For example, hoarding unused scraps of tin because of their 'magical properties' would be a type of bizarre behaviour.

Psychosis can occur in a number of mental illnesses. These include schizophrenia and schizophrenia-related disorders, bipolar disorder, paranoid personality disorder, and delusional disorder. Less commonly, psychotic symptoms occur in major depression (severe depression), Dissociative disorders, and post-traumatic stress disorder.

Psychotic symptoms can also result from substance abuse. Stimulants, such as cocaine and amphetamines, can cause psychotic symptoms, especially if taken in high doses or over long periods of time. Hallucinogenic substances, such as lysergic acid diethylamide (LSD), mescaline, and phencyclidine (PCP), can cause psychosis. Alcohol and marijuana can occasionally cause psychotic symptoms as well. Individuals with alcoholism may experience psychotic symptoms, especially hallucinations, as they withdraw from alcohol use. Alcohol dependence over a long period of time can result in Korsakoff's psychosis, a syndrome that may include psychotic symptoms and an inability form new memories. Certain medical conditions can also cause psychosis. Syphilis, especially if untreated for many years, can lead to psychosis. Brain tumours can also lead to psychotic symptoms.

Treatment of psychotic symptoms usually involved taking antipsychoticdrugs, and called neuroleptics. Common Antipsychotic drugs include chlorpromazine (Thorazine), fluphenazine (Prolixin), thioridazine (Mellaril), trifluoperazine (Stelazine), clozapine (Clozaril), haloperidol (Haldol), olanzapine (Zyprexa), and risperidone (Risperdal). These medications can help reduce psychotic symptoms and prevent symptoms from returning. However, they can also cause severe side effects, such as muscle spasms, tremors, and tardive dyskinesia, a permanent condition marked by uncontrollable lip smacking, grimacing, and tongue movements. Psychotic symptoms in individuals with bipolar disorder may respond to other types of medication, including lithium, carbamazepine (Tegretol), and valproate (Depakene).

Psychotic symptoms that occur as a result of substance abuse usually disappear gradually after the person stops using the substances. Physicians sometimes use Antipsychotic medications temporarily to treat these individuals. Physicians have not discovered any effective treatments for Korsakoff's psychosis. Psychotic symptoms resulting from medical conditions often disappear after treatment of the underlying medical problem

Neurosis, in psychoanalysis, a mental illness characterized by anxiety and disturbances in one's personality. Generally, only psychologists who adhere to a psychoanalytic or Psychodynamic model of abnormal behaviour use the term neurosis. Psychiatrists and psychologists no longer accept the term as a formal diagnosis. Layperson sometimes uses the word neurotic to describe an emotionally unstable person.

Scottish physician William Cullen coined the term neurosis near the end of the 18th century to describe a wide variety of nervous behaviours with no apparent physical cause. Austrian psychoanalyst Sigmund Freud and his followers popularized the word in the late 19th and early 20th centuries. Freud defined neurosis as one class of mental illnesses. In his view, people became neurotic when their conscious mind repressed inappropriate fantasies of the unconscious mind.

Until 1980 neurosis appeared as a specific diagnostic category in the Diagnostic and Statistical Manual of Mental Disorders, a handbook for mental health professionals. Neurosis encompassed a variety of mental illnesses, including Dissociative disorders, anxiety disorders, and phobias.

In the psychoanalytic model, neurosis differs from psychosis, another general term used to describe mental illnesses. Individuals with neuroses can function at work and in social situations, whereas people with psychoses find it quite difficult function adequately. People with neuroses do not grossly distort or misinterpret reality as those with psychoses do. In addition, neurotic individuals recognize that their mental functioning is disturbed while psychotic individuals usually do not. Most mental health professionals now use the term psychosis to refer to symptoms such as hallucinations, delusions, and bizarre behaviour.

Dissociative Identity Disorder, often called multiple personality disorder, mental illness in which a person has two or more distinct identities or personality states, which recurrently take control of the person's consciousness and behaviour. The person often gives the alternate identities their own personal names, and these identities may have characteristics that differ sharply from the person's primary identity. In addition, person with this disorder experience some degree of amnesia, in that one personality usually will not recall what occurred when another personality controlled the person.

People often act and feel differently in various settings. For example, teenagers may act differently at a party than they do at school. However, people in good mental health maintain continuous awareness of themselves no matter what the situation. Individuals with Dissociative identity disorder do not. They experience sudden shifts in consciousness, identity, and memory. They may find themselves in a strange apartment and not remember how they got there, or discover new clothing in their closet without knowing how it was purchased. Their identity is fragmented into pieces with different emotions, memories, and styles of interacting with people. They may shift from being passive and accepting of advice from others to being hostile and uncooperative. They are often at war with themselves, with certain personalities being quite critical of other personalities. At times one personality may go as inflicting physical harm on one of the other personalities. In one case, a woman with Dissociative identity disorder carved the words 'I hate Joan' on her forearm while in a different personality state.

In 1994 the American Psychiatric Association (APA) changed the name of the disorder from multiple personality disorder to Dissociative identity disorder. Psychiatrists wanted to emphasize the fact that the disorder does not really consist of many personalities living in one body, but rather of a failure to integrate various aspects of identity into a unified personality. In a sense, people with this disorder suffer not from having more than one personality but rather from having less than one personality.

Typically the disorder begins in childhood or adolescence, although the symptoms may not become evident to others for many years. In childhood, individuals with Dissociative identity disorder often appear moody or irresponsible because they may switch personalities suddenly or deny having done something them no longer remember. Doctors often misdiagnose people with this disorder as having other mental illnesses. Although critics claim the disorder is an invention of therapists, most experts agree it is a real but rare condition.

Most individuals with Dissociative identity disorder report histories of severe and repeated physical, sexual, or emotional abuse in childhood. This does not mean that everyone with the disorder was necessarily mistreated. However, most psychiatrists now understand the disorder as a reaction to chronic trauma and stress. People frequently enter altered states of consciousness during traumatic events such as physical or sexual assault, natural disasters, motor vehicle accidents, or combat. They detach or dissociate themselves from their immediate circumstances as a means of protecting themselves from overwhelming mental or physical pain. In Dissociative identity disorder this useful ability may become conditioned by repeated trauma, leading to separate personality states that may be triggered by any anxiety or stress.

The best treatment for the disorder is long-term psychotherapy aimed at helping patients to gain insight into each of their personality states, work through the aftermath of traumatic memories, achieve greater self-acceptance, and reduce self-damaging behaviour. Hypnosis may help a person control spontaneous switching of personality states. Many people with this disorder suffer from depression and may benefit from antidepressant medication as well.

Some evidence suggests that schizophrenia may result from an imbalance of chemicals in the brain called neurotransmitters. These chemicals enable neurons (brain cells) to communicate with other. Some scientists suggest that schizophrenia results from excess activity of the neurotransmitter dopamine in certain parts of the brain or from an abnormal sensitivity to dopamine. Support for this hypothesis comes from Antipsychotic drugs, which reduce psychotic symptoms in schizophrenia by blocking brain receptors for dopamine. In addition, amphetamines, which increase dopamine activity, intensify psychotic symptoms in people with schizophrenia. Despite these findings, many experts believe that excess dopamine activity alone cannot account for schizophrenia. Other neurotransmitters, such as serotonin and norepinephrine, may play important roles as well.

Brain imaging techniques, such as magnetic resonance imaging and positron-emission tomography, have led researchers to discover specific structural abnormalities in the brains of people with schizophrenia. For example, people with chronic schizophrenia tend to have enlarged brain ventricles (cavities in the brain that contains cerebrospinal fluid). They also have a smaller overall volume of brain tissue compared to mentally healthy people. Other people with schizophrenia show abnormally low activity in the frontal lobe of the brain, which governs abstract thought, planning, and judgment. Research has identified possible abnormalities in many other parts of the brain, including the temporal lobes, basal ganglia, thalamus, hippocampus, and superior temporal gyrus. These defects may partially explain the abnormal thoughts, perceptions, and behaviours that characterize schizophrenia.

Evidence suggests that factors in the prenatal environment and during birth can increase the risk of a person later developing schizophrenia. These events are believed to affect the brain development of the fetus during a critical period. For example, pregnant women who have been exposed to the influenza virus or who have poor nutrition have a slightly increased chance of giving birth to a child who later develops schizophrenia. In addition, obstetric complications during the birth of a child—for example, delivery with forceps—can slightly increase the chances of the child later developing schizophrenia.

Although scientists favour a biological cause of schizophrenia, stress in the environment may affect the onset and course of the illness. Stressful life circumstances—such as growing up and living in poverty, the death of a loved one, an important change in jobs or relationships, or chronic tension and hostility at home—can increase the chances of schizophrenia in a person biologically predisposed to the disease. In addition, stressful events can trigger a relapse of symptoms in a person who already has the illness. Individuals who have effective skills for managing stress may be less susceptible to its negative effects. Psychological and social rehabilitation can help patients develop more effective skills for dealing with stress.

Although there is no cure for schizophrenia, effective treatment exists that can improve the long-term course of the illness. With many years of treatment and rehabilitation, significant numbers of people with schizophrenia experience partial or full remission of their symptoms.

Treatment of schizophrenia usually involves a combination of medication, rehabilitation, and treatment of other problems the person may have. Antipsychotic drugs (also called neuroleptics) are the most frequently used medications for treatment of schizophrenia. Psychological and social rehabilitation programs may help people with schizophrenia function in the community and reduce stress related to their symptoms. Treatment of secondary problems, such as substance abuse and infectious diseases, is also an important part of an overall treatment program.

Common psychotherapeutic drugs as Antipsychotic medications, developed in the mid-1950s, can dramatically improve the quality of life for people with schizophrenia. The drugs reduce or eliminate psychotic symptoms such as hallucinations and delusions. The medications can also help prevent these symptoms from returning. Common Antipsychotic drugs include risperidone (Risperdal), olanzapine (Zyprexa), clozapine (Clozaril), quetiapine (Seroquel), haloperidol (Haldol), thioridazine (Mellaril), chlorpromazine (Thorazine), fluphenazine (Prolixin), and trifluoperazine (Stelazine). People with schizophrenia usually must take medication for the rest of their lives to control psychotic symptoms. Antipsychotic medications appear to be less effective at treating other symptoms of schizophrenia, such as social withdrawal and apathy.

Antipsychotic drugs help reduce symptoms in 80 to 90 percent of people with schizophrenia. However, those who benefit often stop taking medication because they do not understand that they are ill or because of unpleasant side effects. Minor side effects include weight gain, dry mouth, blurred vision, restlessness, constipation, dizziness, and drowsiness. Other side effects are more serious and debilitating. These may include muscle spasms or cramps, tremors, and tardive dyskinesia, an irreversible condition marked by uncontrollable movements of the lips, mouth, and tongue. Newer drugs, such as clozapine, olanzapine, risperidone, and quetiapine, tend to produce fewer of these side effects. However, clozapine can cause agranulocytosis, a significant reduction in white blood cells necessary tight infections. This condition can be fatal if not detected early enough. For this reason, people taking clozapine must have weekly tests to monitor their blood.

Because many patients with schizophrenia continue to experience difficulties despite taking medication, psychological and social rehabilitation is often necessary. A variety of methods can be effective. Social skills training help people with schizophrenia learn specific behaviours for functioning in society, such as making friends, purchasing items at a store, or initiating conversations. Behavioural training methods can also help them learn self-care skills such as personal hygiene, money management, and proper nutrition. In addition, cognitive-Behavioural therapy, a type of psychotherapy, can help reduce persistent symptoms such as hallucinations, delusions, and social withdrawal.

Family intervention programs can also benefit people with schizophrenia. These programs focus on helping family members understand the nature and treatment of schizophrenia, how to monitor the illness, and how to help the patient make progress toward personal goals and greater independence. They can also lower the stress experienced by everyone in the family and help prevent the patient from relapsing or being rehospitalized.

Because many patients have difficulty obtaining or keeping jobs, supported employment programs that help patients find and maintain jobs are a helpful part of rehabilitation. In these programs, the patient works alongside people without disabilities and earns competitive wages. An employment specialist (or vocational specialist) helps the person maintain their job by, for example, training the person in specific skills, helping the employer accommodate the person, arranging transportation, and monitoring performance. These programs are most effective when the supported employment is closely integrated with other aspects of treatment, such as medication and monitoring of symptoms.

Some people with schizophrenia are vulnerable frequent crises because they do not regularly go to mental health centres to receive the treatment they need. These individuals often relapse and face rehospitalization. To ensure that such patients take their medication and receive appropriate psychological and social rehabilitation, assertive community treatment (ACT) programs have been developed that deliver treatment to patients in natural settings, such as in their homes, in restaurants, or on the street.

People with schizophrenia often have other medical problems, so an effective treatment program must attend to these as well. One of the most common associated problems is substance abuse. Successful treatment of substance abuse in patients with schizophrenia requires careful coordination with their mental health care, so that the same clinicians are treating both disorders at the same time.

The high rate of substance abuse in patients with schizophrenia contributes to a high prevalence of infectious diseases, including hepatitis B and C and the human immunodeficiency virus (HIV). Assessment, education, and treatment or management of these illnesses is critical for the long-term health of patients.

Other problems frequently associated with schizophrenia include housing instability and homelessness, legal problems, violence, trauma and post-traumatic stress disorder, anxiety, depression, and suicide attempts. Close monitoring and psychotherapeutic interventions are often helpful in addressing these problems.

Several other psychiatric disorders are closely related to schizophrenia. In schizoaffective disorder, a person shows symptoms of schizophrenia combined with mania or severe depression. Schizophreniform disorder refers to an illness in which a person experiences schizophrenic symptoms for more than one month but fewer than six months. In schizotypal personality disorder, a person engages in odd thinking, speech, and behaviour, but usually does not lose contact with reality. Sometimes mental health professionals refer to these disorders together as schizophrenia-spectrum disorders

Schizophrenia, is a severe mental illness characterized by a variety of symptoms, including loss of contact with reality, bizarre behaviour, disorganized thinking and speech, decreased emotional expressiveness, and social withdrawal. Usually only some of these symptoms occur in any one person. The term schizophrenia comes from Greek words meaning 'split mind.' However, contrary to common belief, schizophrenia does not refer to a person with a split personality or multiple personality. (For a description of a mental illness in which a person has multiple personalities, To observers, schizophrenia may seem like madness or insanity.

Perhaps more than any other mental illness, schizophrenia has a debilitating effect on the lives of the people who suffer from it. A person with schizophrenia may have difficulty telling the difference between real and unreal experiences, logical and illogical thoughts, or appropriate and inappropriate behaviour. Schizophrenia seriously impairs a person's ability to work, go to school, enjoy relationships with others, or take care of oneself. In addition, people with schizophrenia frequently require hospitalization because they pose a danger to themselves. About 10 percent of people with schizophrenia commit suicide, and many others attempt suicide. Once people develop schizophrenia, they usually suffer from the illness for the rest of their lives. Although there is no cure, treatment can help many people with schizophrenia lead productive lives.

Schizophrenia also carries an enormous cost to society. People with schizophrenia occupy about one-third of all beds in psychiatric hospitals in the United States. In addition, people with schizophrenia account for at least 10 percent of the homeless population in the United States. The National Institute of Mental Health has estimated that schizophrenia costs the United States tens of billions of dollars each year in direct treatment, social services, and lost productivity.

Approximately 1 percent of people develop schizophrenia at some time during their lives. Experts estimate that about 1.8 million people in the United States have schizophrenia. The prevalence of schizophrenia is the same regardless of sex, race, and culture. Although women are just as likely as men to develop schizophrenia, women tend to experience the illness less severely, with fewer hospitalizations and better social functioning in the community.

Schizophrenia usually develops in late adolescence or early adulthood, between the ages of 15 and 30. Much less commonly, schizophrenia develops later in life. The illness may begin abruptly, but it usually develops slowly over months or years. Mental health professionals diagnose schizophrenia based on an interview with the patient in which they determine whether the person has experienced specific symptoms of the illness.

Symptoms and functioning in people with schizophrenia tend to vary over time, sometimes worsening and other times improving. For many patients the symptoms gradually become less severe as they grow older. About 25 percent of people with schizophrenia become symptom-free later in their lives.

A variety of symptoms characterize schizophrenia. The most prominent include symptoms of psychosis—such as delusions and hallucinations—as well as bizarre behaviour, strange movements, and disorganized thinking and speech. Many people with schizophrenia do not recognize that their mental functioning is disturbed.

Some people with schizophrenia experience delusions of persecution—false beliefs that other people are plotting against them. This interview between a patient with schizophrenia and his therapist illustrates the paranoia that can affect people with this illness.

`Delusions are false beliefs that appear obviously untrue to other people. For example, a person with schizophrenia may believe that he is the king of England when he is not. People with schizophrenia may have delusions that others, such as the police or the FBI, are plotting against them or spying on them. They may believe that aliens are controlling their thoughts or that their own thoughts are being broadcast to the world so that other people can hear them.

Personality Disorders, are mentally apprehended disorders in which one's personality results in personal distress or significantly impairs social or work functioning. Every person has a personality—that is, a characteristic way of thinking, feeling, behaving, and relating to others. Most people experience at least some difficulties and problems that result from their personality. The specific point at which those problems justify the diagnosis of a personality disorder is controversial. To some extent the definition of a personality disorder is arbitrary, reflecting subjectively as well as professional judgments about the person's degree of dysfunction, needs for change, and motivation for change.

Personality disorders involve behaviour that deviates from the norms or expectations of one's culture. However, people who digress from a course or procedure or even from the cultural norms, of such, are not necessarily dysfunctional nor are people who conform to cultural norms necessarily healthy. Many personality disorders represent extreme variants of behaviour patterns that people usually value and encourage. For example, most people value confidence but not arrogance, agreeableness but not submissiveness, and conscientiousness but not perfectionism.

Because no clear line exists between healthy and unhealthy functioning, critics question the reliability of personality disorder diagnoses. A behaviour that seems deviant to one person may seem normal to another depending on one's gender, ethnicity, and cultural background. The personal and cultural biases of mental health professionals may influence their diagnoses of personality disorders.

An estimated 20 percent of people in the general population have one or more personality disorders. Some people with personality disorders have other mental illnesses as well. About 50 percent of people who are treated for any psychiatric disorder have a personality disorder.

Mental health professionals rarely diagnose personality disorders in children because their manner of thinking, feeling, and relating to others does not usually stabilize until young adulthood. Thereafter, personality traits usually remain stable. Personality disorders often decrease in severity as a person ages.

The foundation of the Diagnostic and Statistical Manual of Mental Disorders (DSM-IV), published by the American Psychiatric Association, describes ten personality disorders. This article describes in detail two of the most common personality disorders, antisocial personality disorder and borderline personality disorder. It also provides brief descriptions of other types of personality disorders.

People with antisocial personality disorder act in a way that disregards the feelings and rights of other people. Antisocial personalities often break the law, and they may use or exploit other people for their own gain. They may lie repeatedly, act impulsively, and get into physical fights. They may mistreat their spouses, neglect or abuse their children, and exploit their employees. They may even kill other people. People with this disorder are also sometimes called sociopaths or psychopaths. Antisocial behaviour in people less than 18 years old is called conduct disorder.

Antisocial personalities usually fail to understand that their behaviour is dysfunctional because their abilities feel guilty, remorseful, and anxious is impaired. Guilt, remorse, shame, and anxiety are unpleasant feelings, but they are also necessary for social functioning and even physical survival. For example, people that seem as absent, especially into the ability for feeling anxious and will often fail to anticipate actual dangers and risks. They may take chances that other people would not take.

Antisocial personality disorder affects about 3 percent of males and 1 percent of females. This is the most heavily researched personality disorder, in part because it costs society the most. People with this disorder are at high risk for premature and violent death, injury, imprisonment, loss of employment, bankruptcy, alcoholism, drug dependence, and failed personal relationships.

People with borderline personality disorder experience intense emotional instability, particularly in relationships with others. They may make frantic efforts to avoid real or imagined abandonment by others. They may experience minor problems as major crises. They may also express their anger, frustration, and dismay through suicidal gestures, self-mutilation, and other self-destructive acts. They tend to have an unstable self-image or sense of self.

As children, most people with this disorder were emotionally unstable, impulsive, and often bitter or angry, although their chaotic impulsiveness and intense emotions may have made them popular at school. At first they may impress people as stimulating and exciting, but their relationships tend to be unstable and explosive.

About 2 percent of all people have borderline personality disorder. About 75 percent of people with this disorder are female. Borderline personalities are at high risk for developing depression, alcoholism, drug dependence, bulimia, Dissociative disorders, and post-traumatic stress disorder. As many as 10 percent of people with this disorder commit suicide by the age of 30. People with borderline personality disorder are among the most difficult to treat with psychotherapy, in part because their relationship with their therapist may become as intense and unstable as their other personal relationships.

Avoidant personality disorder is social withdrawal due to intense, anxious shyness. People with Avoidant personalities are reluctant to interact with others unless they feel certain in being liked. They fear being criticized and rejected and often view themselves as socially inept and inferior to others.

Dependent personality disorder involves severe and disabling emotional dependency on others. People with this disorder have difficulty making decisions without a great deal of advice and reassurance from others. They urgently seek out another relationship when a close relationship ends. They feel uncomfortable by themselves.

People with histrionic personality disorder constantly strive to be the centre of attention. They may act overly flirtatious or dress in ways that draw attention. They may also talk in a dramatic or theatrical style and display exaggerated emotional reactions.

People with narcissistic personality disorder have a grandiose sense of self-importance. They seek excessive admiration from others and fantasize about unlimited success or power. They believe they are special, unique, or superior to others. However, they often have very fragile self-esteem.

Obsessive-compulsive personality disorder is characterized by a preoccupation with details, orderliness, perfection, and control. People with this disorder often devote excessive amounts of time to work and productivity and fail to take time for leisure activities and friendships. They tend to be rigid, formal, stubborn, and serious. This disorder differs from obsessive-compulsive disorder, which often includes more bizarre behaviour and rituals.

People with paranoid personality disorder feel constant suspicion and distrust toward other people. They believe that others are against them and constantly look for evidence to support their suspicions. They are hostile toward others and react angrily to perceived insults. Schizoid personality disorder involves social isolation and a lack of desire for close personal relationships. People with this disorder prefer to be alone and seem withdrawn and emotionally detached. They seem indifferent to praise or criticism from other people.

People with schizotypal personality disorder engage in odd thinking, speech, and behaviour. They may ramble or use words and phrases in unusual ways, and they may believe they have magical control over others. They feel very uncomfortable with close personal relationships and tend to be suspicious of others. Some research suggests this disorder is a less severe form of schizophrenia.

Many psychiatrists and psychologists use two additional diagnoses. Depressive personality disorder is characterized by chronic pessimism, gloominess, and cheerlessness. In passive-aggressive personality disorder, a person passively resists completing tasks and chores, criticizes and scorns authority figures, and seems negative and sullen.

Personality disorders result from a complex interaction of inherited traits and life experience, not from a single cause. For example, some cases of antisocial personality disorder may result from a combination of a genetic predisposition to impulsiveness and violence, very inconsistent or erratic parenting, and a harsh environment that discourage feelings of empathy and warmth but rewards exploitation and aggressiveness. Borderline personality disorder may result from a genetic predisposition to impulsiveness and emotional instability combined with parental neglect, intense marital conflicts between parents, and repeated episodes of severe emotional or sexual abuse. Dependent personality disorder may result from genetically based anxiety, an inhibited temperament, and overly protective, clinging, or neglectful parenting.

The pervasive and chronic nature of personality disorders makes them difficult to treat. People with these disorders often fail to recognize that their personality has contributed to their social, occupational, and personal problems. They may not think they have any real problems despite a history of drug abuse, failed relationships, and irregular employment. Thus, therapists must first focus on helping the person understand and become aware of the significance of their personality traits.

People with personality disorders sometimes feel that they can never change their dysfunctional behaviour because they have always acted the same way. Although personality change is exceedingly difficult, sometimes people can change the most dysfunctional aspects of their feelings and behaviour.

Therapists use a variety of methods to treat personality disorders, depending on the specific disorder. For example, cognitive and behavioural techniques, such as role playing and logical argument, may help alter a person's irrational perceptions and assumptions about himself or herself. Certain psychoactive drugs may help control feelings of anxiety, depression, or severe distortions of thought. Psychotherapy may help people to understand the impact of experiences and relationships during childhood.

Psychotherapy is usually ineffective for people with antisocial personality disorder because these individuals tend to be manipulative, unreliable, and dishonest with the therapist. Therefore, most mental health professionals favour removing people with this

233

disorder from their current living situation and placing them in a residential treatment centre. Such residential programs strictly supervise patients' behaviour and impose rigid, consistent rules and responsibilities. These programs appear to help some people, but it is unclear how long their beneficial effects last.

Therapists treating people with borderline personality disorder sometimes use a technique called dialectical behaviour therapy. In this type of therapy, the therapist initially focuses on reducing suicidal tendencies and other behaviours that disrupt treatment. The therapist then helps the person develop skills to cope with anger and self-destructive impulses. In addition, the person learns to achieve personal strength through an acceptance of the many disappointments and interpersonal conflicts that are a natural part of life.

Anxiety, an emotional state in which people feel uneasy, apprehensive, or fearful. People usually experience anxiety about events they cannot control or predict, or about events that seem threatening or dangerous. For example, students taking an important test may feel anxious because they cannot predict the test questions or feel certain of a good grade. People often use the word's fear and anxiety to describe the same thing. Fear also describes a reaction to immediate danger characterized by a strong desire to escape the situation.

The physical symptoms of anxiety reflect a chronic 'readiness' to deal with some future threat. These symptoms may include fidgeting, muscle tension, sleeping problems, and headaches. Higher levels of anxiety may produce such symptoms as rapid heartbeat, sweating, increased blood pressure, nausea, and dizziness.

All people experience anxiety to some degree. Most people feel anxious when faced with a new situation, such as a first date, or when trying to do something well, such as give a public speech. A mild to moderate amount of anxiety in these situations is normal and even beneficial. Anxiety can motivate people to prepare for an upcoming event and can help keep them focussed on the task at hand.

However, too little anxiety or too much anxiety can cause problems. Individuals wheel no anxiety when faced with. An important situation may lack alertness and focus. On the other hand, individuals who experience an abnormally high amount of anxiety often feel overwhelmed, immobilized, and unable to accomplish the task at hand. People with too much anxiety often suffer from one of the anxiety disorders, a group of mental illnesses. In fact, more people experience anxiety disorders than any other type of mental illness. A survey of people aged 15 to 54 in the United States found that about 17 percent of this population suffers from an anxiety disorder during any given year.

People with generalized anxiety disorder feel anxious most of the time. They worry excessively about routine events or circumstances in their lives. Their worries often relate to nuances in family, personal health, and relationships with others. Although they recognize their anxiety as irrational or out of proportion to actual events, they feel unable to control their worrying. For example, they may worry uncontrollably and intensely about money despite evidence that their financial situation is stable. Children with this disorder typically worry about their performance at school or about catastrophic events, such as tornadoes, earthquakes, and nuclear war.

People with generalized anxiety disorder often find that their worries interfere with their ability to function at work or concentrate on tasks. Physical symptoms, such as disturbed sleep, irritability, muscle aches, and tension, may accompany the anxiety. To receive a diagnosis of this disorder, individuals must have experienced its symptoms for at least six months.

Generalized anxiety disorder affects about 3 percent of people in the general population in any given year. From 55 to 66 percent of people with this disorder are female.

A phobia is an excessive, enduring fear of clearly defined objects or situations that interferes with a person's normal functioning. Although they know their fear is irrational, people with phobias always try to avoid the source of their fear. Common phobias include fear of heights (acrophobia), fear of enclosed places (claustrophobia), fear of insects, snakes, or other animals, and fear of air travel. Social phobias involve a fear of performing, of critical evaluation, or of being embarrassed in front of other people.

Panic is an intense, overpowering surge of fear. People with panic disorder experience panic attacks—periods of quickly escalating, intense fear and discomfort accompanied by such physical symptoms as rapid heartbeat, trembling, shortness of breath, dizziness, and nausea. Because people with this disorder cannot predict when these attacks will strike, they develop anxiety about having additional panic attacks and may limit their activities outside the home.

In obsessive-compulsive disorder, people persistently experience certain intrusive thoughts or images (obsessions) or feel compelled to perform certain behaviours (compulsions). Obsessions may include unwanted thoughts about inadvertently poisoning others or injuring a pedestrian while driving. Common compulsions include repetitive hand washing or such mental acts as repeated counting. People with this disorder often perform compulsions to reduce the anxiety produced by their obsessions. The obsessions and compulsions significantly interfere with their ability ti function and may consume a great deal of time.

Post-traumatic stress disorder sometimes occurs after people experience traumatic or catastrophic events, such as physical or sexual assaults, natural disasters, accidents, and wars. People with this disorder relive the traumatic event through recurrent dreams or intrusive memories called flashbacks. They avoid things or places associated with the trauma and may feel emotionally detached or estranged from others. Other symptoms may include difficulty sleeping, irritability, and trouble concentrating.

Most anxiety disorders do not have an obvious cause. They result from a combination of biological, psychological, and social factors.

Studies suggest that anxiety disorders run in families. That is, children and close relatives of people with disorders are more likely than most to develop anxiety disorders. Some people may inherit genes that make them particularly vulnerable to anxiety. These genes do not necessarily cause people to be anxious, but the genes may increase the risk of anxiety disorders when certain psychological and social factors are also present.

Anxiety also appears to be related to certain brain functions. Chemicals in the brain called neurotransmitters enable neurons, or brain cells, to communicate with each other. One neurotransmitter, gamma-amino butyric acid (GABA), appears to play a role in regulating one's level of anxiety. Lower levels of GABA are associated with higher levels of anxiety. Some studies suggest that the neurotransmitter's norepinephrine and serotonin play a role in panic disorder.

Psychologists have proposed a variety of models to explain anxiety. Austrian psychoanalyst Sigmund Freud suggested that anxiety results from internal, unconscious conflicts. He believed that a person's mind represses wishes and fantasies about which the person feels uncomfortable. This repression, Freud believed, results in anxiety disorders, which he called neuroses.

More recently, behavioural researchers have challenged Freud's model of anxiety. They believe one's anxiety level relates to how much a person believes events can be predicted or controlled. Children who have little control over events, perhaps because of overprotective parents, may have little confidence in their ability to handle problems as adults. This lack of confidence can lead to increased anxiety.

Behavioural theorists also believe that children may learn anxiety from a role model, such as a parent. By observing their parent's anxious response to difficult situations, the child may learn a similar anxious response. A child may also learn anxiety as a conditioned response. For example, an infant often startled by a loud noise while playing with a toy may become anxious just at the sight of the toy. Some experts suggest that people with a high level of anxiety misinterpret normal events as threatening. For instance, they may believe their rapid heartbeat indicates they are experiencing a panic attack when in reality it may be the result of exercise.

While some people may be biologically and psychologically predisposed anxiousness, most anxiety is triggered by social factors. Many people feel anxious in response to stress, such as a divorce, starting a new job, or moving. Also, how a person expresses anxiety appears to be shaped by social factors. For example, many cultures accept the expression of anxiety and emotion in women, but expect more reserved emotional displays from men.

Mental health professionals use a variety of methods to help people overcome anxiety disorders. These include psychoactive drugs and psychotherapy, particularly behaviour therapy. Other techniques, such as exercise, hypnosis, meditation, and biofeedback, may also prove helpful.

Psychiatrists often prescribe benzodiazepines, a group of tranquillizing drugs, to reduce anxiety in people with high levels of anxiety. Benzodiazepines help to reduce anxiety by stimulating the GABA neurotransmitter system. Common benzodiazepines include alprazolam (Xanax), clonazepam (Klonopin), and diazepam (Valium). Two classes of antidepressant drugs—tricyclics and selective serotonin reuptake inhibitors (SSRIs)—also have proven effective in treating certain anxiety disorders.

Benzodiazepines can work quickly with few unpleasant side effects, but they can also be addictive. In addition, benzodiazepines can slow down or impair motor behaviour or thinking and must be used with caution, particularly in elderly persons. SSRIs take longer to work than the benzodiazepines but are not addictive. Some people experience anxiety symptoms again when they stop taking the medications.

Therapists who attribute the cause of anxiety to unconscious, internal conflicts may use psychoanalysis to help patient's to understand and so, resolve their conflicts. Other types of psychotherapy, such as cognitive-behavioural therapy, have proven effective in treating anxiety disorders. In cognitive-behavioural therapy, the therapist often educates the person about the nature of his or her particular anxiety disorder. Then, the therapist may help the person challenge, and irrational thoughts that lead to anxiety. For example, to treat a person with a snake phobia, a therapist might gradually expose the person to snakes, beginning with pictures of snakes and progressing to rubber snakes and real snakes. The patient can use relaxation techniques acquired in therapy to overcome the fear of snakes.

Research has shown psychotherapy to be as effective or more effective than medications in treating many anxiety disorders. Psychotherapy may also provide more lasting benefits than medications when patients discontinue treatment.

Developments in the interactional description of schizophrenia have not been parallelled in the area of depression. As yet, concepts such as pseudomutuality, double-bind, schism, and skew have found no counterparts. Kubler and Stotland (1964) have argued, that, emotional disturbance, even the most severe, cannot be understood unless the field in which it develops and exists is examined. The manifestations of differentiated difficulty that in the disturbed individually has himself a meaning, even so, this depends upon the appearing aspects that face the field of significance. These ascribing to the general aspects of the field, especially to a supposed cause, source, or the connected attachment upon the usual inter-personality. Yet, the study of depression has focussed on the individual and his behaviour out of his interactional context. That to a large degree, the depressed person's monotonously reiterates complaints and self accusations, for which is his provocative, but often annoying behaviour has distracted investigators from considerations of his environment and the role it may restrain in the maintenance of his behaviour. The possibility that the characteristic pattern of depressed behaviour might be interwoven has seldom been explored.

For the most part, it has been assumed that the depressed person is relatively impervious to the influence of others. Ruesch (1962) stated that to talk to the depressed person makes little sense: To listen, little more. Grinker (1964) conceptualized depressive symptomatology as communication to others, but argued that the depressed person is not responsive to communication for the purpose of action, as he cannot perceive the cues of reality, he makes statements but does not care if he is understood.

In terms of systems theory (von Bertalanffy, 1950; Allport, 1960 and Miller, 1971), the usual conceptualization of the depressed person is one of a closed system. Grinker (1964) was explicit in stating that the depressed person repeats his message and behaviour without reception or acceptance of resulting feedback. Beck (1964, 1967) described the cognitive distortions that dominate the information processing of the depressed person so that experiences are rightly interpreted to maintain existing schema of personal deficiency, self-blame and negative expectations.

The implicit assumption of these and other writers has been that the support and information available to the repressed person are incongruent with his depression, and the persistence of his symptomatology is evidence of a failure to receive or accept this information. Withdrawal, isolated intrapsychic processes, or as Beck describes (1967), interactions of degressive schema and affective structures, produce a downward depressive spiral. If a depressive spiral develops, it is mutually causative, deviation-amplifying process (Maruyama, 1963) in the interaction of the depressed person with his environment. Thus, what is customarily viewed as some internal process is. That is, in part, a characteristic of interaction with the environment and much of what his customarily viewed as cognitive distortion or misperception is characteristic of information flow from the environment.

It should be noted that while the depressed person's different interpretations of his predicament are traditionally attributed to his distortion or misperception, general disorders of thought and perception are defining neither criteria nor common among depressed patients (McPartland and Hornstra, 1964). An observer takes into account the intricacies of someone's relationship to his environment frequently attribute to his characteristics that he does not posses, or leaves significant aspects of his unexplained experience (Watzlawick, 1967). Feedback introduces phenomena that cannot be adequately explained by reference to the isolated individual alone (Ashby, 1960, 1062). For the study of depression, identifications of a pattern of depressive feedback from the environment demands a more complex conceptualization of the disorder than one explaining its phenomena with reference to the isolated depressed person.

Lemert (1962) in his study of the interpersonal dynamics of paranoia, argued that the net effect of the developing interaction pattern between the paranoid person and others is that (1) the flow of information to the person is stopped, (2) a real discrepancy between expressed ideas and affect among those who he interacts is created, and (3) the situation or group image becomes as ambiguous for him as he is for others. In this context of attenuated relationships, exclusion, and disrupted communication, the paranoid person cannot get the feedback on his behaviour that is essential in order for him to correct his interpretation of social relationships. Lemert concluded that the paranoid person may be delusional, but that it is also true that in a real sense he is able to elicit covertly organized action and conspiratorial behaviour.

It should be made clear that some localized perceptive's do not deny the existence of important intrapersonal factors in depression. Numerous writers have pointed out that the depressed person's feelings of worthlessness and helplessness do not arise of an immediate stimulus situation (Chodoff, 1972). McCranie (1971) has argued that there is a 'depressed-core' in the personality of the depression-prone person, consisting of a tendency to feel worthless and helpless and over-sensitivity to the stimuli that impinge on these feelings, together, these are aroused from dormancy by specific situations such as loss and that to self-esteem. However, the emphasis, by which the environment comes into congruence with these feedings. The depressive's vague, generalized feeling that there is something wrong with him, and his search for this among his minor depressive centres of his personality, is, nonetheless, the confusing response from the environment servers to validate these feelings. Likewise, conflicts about the reception of support and approval from others are deeply rooted in the depressive's intrapersonal style, but these conflicts can only be aggravated by the mixed messages of approval and rejection received from significant others, and by their withdrawal from him despite reassurances to the contrary.

It should be made clear that such a perspective does not deny the existence of important interpersonal factors in depression. Numerous writers have pointed out that the depressed person's stimulus situation (Chodoff, 1972) McCraine (1971) have argued that there is a 'depressive-core' in the personality of the depression-prone person consisting of a tendency to feel worthless and helpless and an over-sensitivity to stimuli that impinge on these feelings. Together, these are aroused from dormancy by specific situations such as loss and threat to self-esteem. However, the emphasis as such, comes into congruence with these feelings. The depressives vaguely feel that there is something wrong with him, and his search for this among his minor-effects, imperfection, and personal attributes, may arise from a depressive-core of his personality, but at the same time, the confusing response from the environment serves to validate these feelings. Likewise, deeply rooted in the depressive's intrapersonal style. But these conflicts can only be aggravated by mixed messages of approval and rejection received from significant others, and by their withdrawal from him, despite reassurances to the contrary.

Furthermore, the present exposition does not deny the importance of possible biochemical or genetic factors in the etiology of depression. Price (1974) has argued that even in disorders in which the importance of such factors has been clearly established, there may be a large number of links in the causal chain between specific etiogical factors and the symptoms displayed by the individual. Social and interpersonal variables may determine to a large degree whether disorder occurs and the form its symptoms will take. It is assumed that to initiate the process a person need only begin to display depressive behaviour.

Three functional systems are distinguished that are conveniently designed as the id, ego, and Superego. The first system refers to the sexual and aggressive tendencies that arise from the body, as distinguished from the mind. Freud called these tendencies Triebe, which literally means 'drives,' but which is often inaccurately

241

translated as 'instincts' to indicate their innate character. These inherent drives claim immediate satisfaction, which is experienced as pleasurable; the id thus is dominated by the pleasure principle. In his later writings, Freud tended more toward psychological rather than biological conceptualization of the drives.

How the conditions for satisfaction are to be brought about is the task of the second system, the ego, which is the domain of such functions as perception, thinking, and motor control that can accurately assess environmental conditions. In order to fulfill its function of adaptation, or reality testing, the ego must be capable of enforcing the postponement of satisfaction of the instinctual impulses originating in the id. To defend itself against unacceptable impulses, the ego develops specific psychic means, known as defence mechanisms. These include repression, the exclusion of impulses from conscious awareness; projection, the process of ascribing to others one's own unacknowledged desires; and reaction formation, the establishments of a pattern of behaviour directly opposed to a strong unconscious need. Such defence mechanisms are put into operation whenever anxiety signals a danger that the original unacceptable impulses may reemerge.

An id impulse becomes unacceptable, not only as a result of a temporary need for postponing its satisfaction until suitable reality conditions can be found, but more often because of a prohibition imposed on the individual by others, originally the parents. The totality of these demands and prohibitions constitutes the major content of the third system, the Superego, the function of which is to control the ego in accordance with the internalized standards of parental figures. If the demands of the Superego are not fulfilled, the person may feel shame or guilt. Because the Superego, in Freudian theory, originates in the struggle to overcome the Oedipal conflict, it has a power akin to an instinctual drive, is in part unconscious, and can give rise feelings of guilt not justified by any conscious transgression. The ego, having to mediate among the demands of the id, the Superego, and the outside world, may not be strong enough to reconcile these conflicting forces. The more the ego is impeded in its development because of being enmeshed in its earlier conflicts, called fixations or complexes, or the more it reverts to earlier satisfactions and archaic modes of functioning, known as regression, the greater is the likelihood of succumbing to these pressures. Unable to function normally, it can maintain its limited control and integrity only at the price of symptom formation, in which the tensions are expressed in neurotic symptoms.

The Freudian terminological representations as imposed upon the id; Is spoken of in psychoanalytic theory, one of the three basic elements of personality, the others being the ego and the Superego? The id can be equated with the unconscious of common usage, which is the reservoir of the instinctual drives of the individual, including biological urges, wishes, and affective motives. The id is dominated by the pleasure principle, through which the individual is pressed for immediate gratification of his or her desires. In strict Freudian theory the energy behind the instinctual drives of the id is known as the libido, a generalized force, basically sexual in nature, through which the sexual and psychosexual nature of the individual finds expression.

Ego, in psychoanalysis, is the term denoting the central part of the personality structure that deals with reality and is influenced by social forces. According to the psychoanalytic theories developed by Sigmund Freud, the ego constitutes one of the three basic provinces of the mind, the other two being the id and the Superego. Formation of the ego begins at birth in the first encounters with the external world of people and things. The ego learns to modify behaviour by controlling those impulses that are socially unacceptable. Its role is that of mediator between unconscious impulses and acquired social and personal standards.

Superego, in psychoanalytic theory is one of the three basic constituents of the mind, the others being the id and the ego. As postulated by Sigmund Freud, the term designates the element of the mind that, in normal personalities, automatically modifies and inhibits those instinctual impulses or drives of the id that tend to produce antisocial actions and thoughts. An id impulse becomes unacceptable, not only as a result of a temporary need for postponing its satisfaction until suitable reality conditions can be found, but more often because of a prohibition imposed on the individual by others, originally the parents. The totality of these demands and prohibitions constitutes the major content of the third system, the Superego, the function of which is to control the ego in accordance with the internalized standards of parental figures. If the demands of the Superego are not fulfilled, the person may feel shame or guilt. Because the Superego, in Freudian theory, originates in the struggle to overcome the Oedipal conflict, it has a power akin to an instinctual drive, is in part unconscious, and can give rise feelings of guilt not justified by any conscious transgression. The ego, having to mediate among the demands of the id, the Superego, and the outside world, may not be strong enough to reconcile these conflicting forces. The more the ego is impeded in its development because of being enmeshed in its earlier conflicts, called fixations or complexes, or the more it reverts to earlier satisfactions and archaic modes of functioning, known as regression, the greater is the likelihood of succumbing to these pressures. It can maintain its limited control and integrity only at the price of symptom formation, in which the tensions are expressed in neurotic symptoms.

It is, nonetheless, that according to psychoanalytic theory, the Superego develops as the child gradually and unconsciously adopts the values and standards, first of his or her parents, and later of the social environment. According to modern Freudian psychoanalysts, the Superego includes the positive ego, or conscious self-image, or ego ideal, that each individual develops.

It is, nevertheless, that object relations, in psychoanalysis, is the emotional relations between subject and objects which, through a process of identification, are believed to constitute the developing ego. In this context, the word object refers to any person or thing, or representational aspect of them, with which the subject forms an intense emotional relationship.

Object relations were first described by German psychoanalyst Karl Abraham in an influential paper, published in 1924. In the paper he developed the ideas of the founder of psychoanalysis, Sigmund Freud, on infantile sexuality and the development of the libido. Object-relations theory has become one of the central themes of post-Freudian psychoanalysis, particularly through the writings of British psychoanalysts Melanie Klein, Ronald Fairbairn, and Donald Winnicott, all deeply influenced by Abraham. They have each developed distinctly, though complementary, approaches to analysis, evolving theories of personal development based on early parental attachments.

People with depression often experience feelings of worthlessness, helplessness, guilt, and self-blame. They may interpret a minor failing on their part as a sign of incompetence or interpret minor criticism as condemnation. Some depressed people complain of being spiritually or morally dead. The mirror seems to reflect someone ugly and repulsive. Even a competent and decent person may feel deficient, cruel, stupid, phony, or guilty of having deceived others. People with major depression may experience such extreme emotional pain that they consider or attempt suicide. At least 15 percent of seriously depressed people commit suicide, and many more attempt it.

Bipolar disorder is much less common than depression. In North America and Europe, about 1 percent of people experience bipolar disorder during their lives. Rates of bipolar disorder are similar throughout the world. In comparison, at least 8 percent of people experience serious depression during their lives. Bipolar disorder affects men and women about equally and is somewhat more common in higher socioeconomic classes. At least 15 percent of people with bipolar disorder commit suicide. This rate roughly equals the rate for people with major depression, the most severe form of depression.

Depression (psychology), mental illness in which a person experiences deep, unshakable sadness and diminished interest in nearly all activities. People also use the term depression to describe the temporary sadness, loneliness, or blues that everyone feels from time to time. In contrast to normal sadness, severe depression, also called major depression, can dramatically impair a person's ability to function in social situations and at work. People with major depression often have feelings of despair, hopelessness, and worthlessness, as well as thoughts of committing suicide.

Depression can take several other forms. In bipolar disorder, sometimes called manic-depressive illness, a person's mood swings back and forth between depression and mania. People with seasonal affective disorder typically suffer from depression only during autumn and winter, when there are fewer hours of daylight. In dysthymia, person's feel depressed, had low self-esteem, and concentrate poorly most of the time—often for a period of years—but their symptoms are milder than in major depression. Some people with dysthymia experience occasional episodes of major depression. Mental health professionals use the term clinical depression to refer to any of the above forms of depression.

Surveys indicate that people commonly view depression as a sign of personal weakness, but psychiatrists and psychologists view it as a real illness. In the United States, the National Institute of

Mental Health has estimated that depression cost's society many billions of dollars each year, mostly in lost work time.

Depression is one of the most common mental illnesses. At least 8 percent of adults in the United States experience serious depression at some point during their lives, and estimates range as high as 17 percent. The illness affects all people, regardless of sex, race, ethnicity, or socioeconomic standing. However, women are two to three times more likely than men to suffer from depression. Experts disagree on the reason for this difference. Some cite differences in hormones, and others point to the stress caused by society's expectations of women.

Depression occurs in all parts of the world, although the pattern of symptoms can vary. The prevalence of depression in other countries varies widely, from 1.5 percent of people in Taiwan to 19 percent of people in Lebanon. Some researchers believe methods of gathering data on depression account for different rates.

A number of large-scale studies indicate that depression rates have increased worldwide over the past several decades. Furthermore, younger generations are experiencing depression at an earlier age than did previous generations. Social scientists have proposed many explanations, including changes in family structure, urbanization, and reduced cultural and religious influences.

Although it may appear anytime from childhood to old age, depression usually begins during a person's 20s or 30s. The illness may come on slowly, then deepen gradually over months or years. On the other hand, it may erupt suddenly in a few weeks or days. A person who develops severe depression may appear so confuse, frightened, and unbalance that observers speak of a 'nervous breakdown.' However, it begins. Depression causes serious changes in a person's feelings and outlook. A person with major depression feels sad nearly every day and may cry often. People, work, and activities that used to bring them pleasure no longer do.

Symptoms of depression can vary by age. In younger children, depression may include physical complaints, such as stomachaches and headaches, as well as irritability, 'moping around,' social withdrawal, and changes in eating habits. They may feel unenthusiastic about school and other activities. In adolescents, common symptoms include sad mood, sleep disturbances, and lack of energy. Elderly people with depression usually complain of physically rather than emotional problems, which sometimes leads doctors to misdiagnose the illness.

Symptoms of depression can also vary by culture. In some cultures, depressed people may not experience sadness or guilt but may complain of physical problems. In Mediterranean cultures, for example, depressed people may complain of headaches or nerves. In Asian cultures they may complain of weakness, fatigue, or imbalance.

If left untreated, an episode of major depression typically lasts eight or nine months. About 85 percent of people who experience one bout of depression will experience future episodes.

Depression usually alters a person's appetite, sometimes increasing it, but usually reducing it. Sleep habits frequently become foreign to the differences, as our needs change as we make for or among its times to change of such an aberration to modificational divergencies, in that among the changes of such mutational permutations as well. People with depression may oversleep or, more commonly, sleep for fewer hours. A depressed person might go to sleep at midnight, sleep restlessly, then wake up at 5:00 a.m. feeling tired and blue. For many depressed people, early morning is the saddest time of the day.

Depression also changes one's energy level. Some depressed people may be restless and agitated, engaging in fidgety movements and pacing. Others may feel sluggish and inactive, experiencing great fatigue, lack of energy, and a feeling of being worn out or carrying a heavy burden. Depressed people may also have difficulty thinking, poor concentration, and problems with memory.

People with depression often experience feelings of worthlessness, helplessness, guilt, and self-blame. They may interpret a minor failing on their part as a sign of incompetence or interpret minor criticism as condemnation. Some depressed people complain of being spiritually or morally dead. The mirror seems to reflect someone ugly and repulsive. Even a competent and decent person may feel deficient, cruel, stupid, phony, or guilty of having deceived others. People with major depression may experience such extreme emotional pain that they consider or attempt suicide. At least 15 percent of seriously depressed people commit suicide, and many more attempt it.

In some cases, people with depression may experience psychotic symptoms, such as delusions (false beliefs) and hallucinations (false sensory perceptions). Psychotic symptoms indicate an especially severe illness. Compared to other depressed people, those with psychotic symptoms have longer hospital stays, and after leaving, they are more likely to be moody and unhappy. They are also more likely to commit suicide.

Some depressions seem to come out of the blue, even when things are going well. Others seem to have an obvious cause: a marital conflict, financial difficulty, or some personal failure. Yet many people with these problems do not become deeply depressed. Most psychologists believe depression results from an interaction between stressful life events and a person's biological and psychological vulnerabilities.

Clinical depression is one of the most common forms of mental illness. Although depression can be treated with psychotherapy, many scientists believe there are biological causes for the disease. In this June 1998 Scientific American article, Neurobiologist Charles B. Nemeroff discusses the connection between biochemical changes in the brain and depression.

Depression runs in families. By studying twins, researchers have found evidence of a strong genetic influence in depression. Genetically identical twins raised in the same environment are three times more likely to have depression in common than fraternal twins, who have only about half of their genes in common. In addition, identical twins are five times more likely to have bipolar disorder in common. These findings suggest that vulnerability to depression and bipolar disorder can be inherited. Adoption studies have provided more evidence of a genetic role in depression. These studies show that children of depressed people are vulnerable to depression even when raised by adoptive parents.

Genes may influence depression by causing abnormal activity in the brain. Studies have shown that certain brain chemicals called neurotransmitters play an important role in regulating moods and emotions. Neurotransmitters involved in depression include norepinephrine, dopamine, and serotonin. Research in the 1960s suggested that depression results from lower than normal levels of these neurotransmitters in parts of the brain. Support for this theory came from the effects of antidepressant drugs, which work by increasing the levels of neurotransmitters involved in depression. However, later studies have discredited this simple explanation and have suggested a more complex relationship between neurotransmitter levels and depression.

An imbalance of hormones may also play a role in depression. Many depressed people have higher than normal levels of hydrocortisone (cortisol), a hormone secreted by the adrenal gland in response to stress. In addition, an underactive or overactive thyroid gland can lead to depression.

Psychological theories of depression focus on the way people think and behave. In a 1917 essay, Austrian psychoanalyst Sigmund Freud explained melancholia, or major depression, as a response to loss—either real loss, such as the death of a spouse, or symbolic loss, such as the failure to achieve an important goal. Freud believed that a person's unconscious anger over loss weakens the ego, resulting in self-hate and self-destructive behaviour.

Cognitive theories of depression emphasize the role of irrational thought processes. American psychiatrist Aaron Beck proposed that depressed people tend to view themselves, their environment, and the future in a negative light because of errors in thinking. These errors include focussing on the negative aspects of any situation, misinterpreting facts in negative ways, and blaming themselves for any misfortune. In Beck's view, people learn these self-defeating ways of looking at the world during early childhood. This negative thinking makes situations seem much worse than they really are and increases the risk of depression, especially in stressful situations.

In support of this cognitive view, people with 'depressive' personality traits appear to be more vulnerable than others to actual depression. Examples of depressive personality traits include gloominess, pessimism, introversion, self-criticism, excessive skepticism and criticism of others, deep feelings of inadequacy, and excessive brooding and worrying. In addition, people who regularly behave in dependent, hostile, and impulsive ways appear at greater risk for depression.

American psychologist Martin Seligman proposed that depression stems from 'learned helplessness,' an acquired belief that one cannot control the outcome of events. In this view, prolonged exposure to uncontrollable and inescapable events leads to apathy, pessimism, and loss of motivation. An adaptation of this theory by American psychologist Lynn Abramson and her colleagues argues that depression results not only from helplessness, but also hopelessness. The hopelessness theory attributes depression to a pattern of negative thinking in which people blame themselves for negative life events, view the causes of those events as permanent, and overgeneralize specific weaknesses as applying to many areas of their life.

Psychologists agree that stressful experiences can trigger depression in people who are predisposed to the illness. For example, the death of a loved one may trigger depression. Psychologists usually distinguish true depression from grief, a normal process of mourning a loved one who has died. Other stressful experiences may include divorce, pregnancy, the loss of a job, and even childbirth. About 20 percent of women experience an episode of depression, known as postpartum depression, after having a baby. In addition, people with serious physical illnesses or disabilities often develop depression.

Depression typically cannot be shaken or willed away. An episode must therefore run its course until it weakens either on its own or with treatment. Depression can be treated effectively with antidepressant drugs, psychotherapy, or a combination of both.

Despite the availability of effective treatment, most depressive disorders go untreated and undiagnosed. Studies indicate that general physicians fail to recognize depression in their patients at least half of the time. In addition, many doctors and patients view depression in elderly people as a normal part of aging, even though treatment for depression in older people is usually very effective.

Up to 70 percent of people with depression respond to antidepressant drugs. These medications appear to work by altering the levels of serotonin, norepinephrine, and other neurotransmitters in the brain. They generally take at least two to three weeks to become effective. Doctors cannot predict which type of antidepressant drug will work best for any particular person, so depressed people may need to try several types. Antidepressant drugs are not addictive, but they may produce unwanted side effects. To avoid relapse, people usually must continue taking the medication for several months after their symptoms improve.

Commonly used antidepressant drugs fall into three major classes: tricyclics, Monoamine oxidase inhibitors (MAO inhibitors), and selective serotonin reuptake inhibitors (SSRIs). Tricyclics, named for their three-ring chemical structure, include amitriptyline (Elavil), imipramine (Tofanil), desipramine (Norpramin), doxepin (Sinequan), and nortriptyline (Pamelor). Side effects of tricyclics may include drowsiness, dizziness upon standing, blurred vision, nausea, insomnia, constipation, and dry mouth.

MAO inhibitors include isocarboxazid (Marplan), phenelzine (Nardil), and tranylcypromine (Parnate). People who take MAO inhibitors must follow a diet that excludes tyramine—a substance found in wine, beer, some cheeses, and many fermented foods—to refrain from a dangerous rise in blood pressure. In addition, MAO inhibitors have many of the same side effects as tricyclics.

Selective serotonin reuptake inhibitors include Fluoxetine (Prozac), sertraline (Zoloft), and paroxetine (Paxil). These drugs generally produce fewer and milder side effects than do other types of antidepressants, although SSRIs may cause anxiety, insomnia, drowsiness, headaches, and sexual dysfunction. Some patients have alleged that Prozac causes violent or suicidal behaviour in a small number of cases, but the US Food and Drug Administration has failed to substantiate this claim.

Prozac became the most widely used antidepressant in the world soon after its introduction in the late 1980s by drug manufacturer Eli Lilly and Company. Many people find Prozac extremely effective in lifting depression. In addition, some people have reported that Prozac actually transforms their personality by increasing their self-confidence, optimism, and energy level. However, mental health professionals have expressed serious ethical concerns over Prozac's use as a 'personality enhancer,' especially among people without clinical depression.

Doctors often prescribe lithium carbonate, a natural mineral salt, to treat people with bipolar disorder. People often take lithium during periods of relatively normal mood to delay or even prevent subsequent mood swings. Side effects of lithium include nausea, stomach upset, vertigo, and frequent urination.

Studies have shown that short-term psychotherapy can relieve mild to moderate depression as effectively as antidepressant drugs. Unlike medication, psychotherapy produces no physiological side effects. In addition, depressed people treated with psychotherapy appear less likely to experience a relapse than those treated only with antidepressant medication. However, psychotherapy usually takes longer to produce benefits.

There are many kinds of psychotherapy. Cognitive-behavioural therapy assumes that depression stems from negative, often irrational thinking about oneself and one's future. In this type of therapy, a person learns to understand and eventually eliminate those habits of negative thinking. In interpersonal therapy, the therapist helps a person resolve problems in relationships with others that may have caused the depression. The subsequent improvement in social relationships and support helps alleviate the depression. Psychodynamic therapy views depression as the result of internal, unconscious conflicts. Psychodynamic therapists focus on a person's past experiences and the resolution of childhood conflicts. Psychoanalysis is an example of this type of therapy. Critics of long-term Psychodynamic therapy argue that its effectiveness is scientifically unproven.

Electroconvulsive therapy (ECT) can often relieve severe depression in people who respond to antidepressant medication and psychotherapy. In this type of therapy, a low-voltage electric current is passed through the brain for one to two seconds to produce a controlled seizure. Patients usually receive six to ten ECT treatments over several weeks. ECT remains controversial because it can cause disorientation and memory loss. Nevertheless, research has found it highly effective in alleviating severe depression.

For milder cases of depression, regular aerobic exercise may improve mood as effectively as psychotherapy or medication. In addition, some research indicates that dietary modifications can influence one's mood by changing the level of serotonin in the brain.

An imbalance of hormones may also play a role in depression. Many depressed people have higher than normal levels of hydrocortisone (cortisol), a hormone secreted by the adrenal gland in response to stress. In addition, an underactive or overactive thyroid gland can lead to depression.

A variety of medical conditions can cause depression. These include dietary deficiencies in vitamin B6, vitamin B12, and folic acid, degenerative neurological disorders, such as Alzheimer's disease and Huntington's disease; strokes in the frontal part of the brain; and certain viral infections, such as hepatitis and mononucleosis. Certain medications, such as steroids, may also cause depression.

Psychological theories of depression focus on the way people think and behave. In a 1917 essay, Austrian psychoanalyst Sigmund Freud explained melancholia, or major depression, as a response to loss—either real loss, such as the death of a spouse, or symbolic loss, such as the failure to achieve an important goal. Freud

believed that a person's unconscious anger over loss weakens the ego, resulting in self-hate and self-destructive behaviour.

Cognitive theories of depression emphasize the role of irrational thought processes. American psychiatrist Aaron Beck proposed that depressed people tend to view themselves, their environment, and the future in a negative light because of errors in thinking. These errors include focussing on the negative aspects of any situation, misinterpreting facts in negative ways, and blaming themselves for any misfortune. In Beck's view, people learn these self-defeating ways of looking at the world during early childhood. This negative thinking makes situations seem much worse than they really are and increases the risk of depression, especially in stressful situations.

In support of this cognitive view, people with 'depressive' personality traits appear to be more vulnerable than others to actual depression. Examples of depressive personality traits include gloominess, pessimism, introversion, self-criticism, excessive skepticism and criticism of others, deep feelings of inadequacy, and excessive brooding and worrying. In addition, people who regularly behave in dependent, hostile, and impulsive ways appear at greater risk for depression.

American psychologist Martin Seligman proposed that depression stems from 'learned helplessness,' an acquired belief that one cannot control the outcome of events. In this view, prolonged exposure to uncontrollable and inescapable events leads to apathy, pessimism, and loss of motivation. An adaptation of this theory by American psychologist Lynn Abramson and her colleagues argues that depression results not only from helplessness, but also hopelessness. The hopelessness theory attributes depression to a pattern of negative thinking in which people blame themselves for negative life events, view the causes of those events as permanent, and overgeneralize specific weaknesses as applying to many areas of their life.

Psychologists agree that stressful experiences can trigger depression in people who are predisposed to the illness. For example, the death of a loved one may trigger depression. Psychologists usually distinguish true depression from grief, a normal process of mourning a loved one who has died. Other stressful experiences may include divorce, pregnancy, the loss of a job, and even childbirth. About 20 percent of women experience an episode of depression, known as postpartum depression, after having a baby. In addition, people with serious physical illnesses or disabilities often develop depression.

Death and Dying are the irreversible cessation of life and the imminent approach of death. Death involves a complete change in the status of a living entity—the loss of its essential characteristics.

Many patients in the last stages of a terminal disease elect to forgo medical treatments aimed at curing their disease in favour of hospice care. Usually provided in a patient's home by health professionals and trained volunteers, hospice care seeks to relieve pain and symptoms and provide emotional support for patients and their families.

Should, by obligation or pure necessity that someone is to do or forbear and do service as a courtesy assist by contributory measured as foresee that the suffering and dying patients are allowed to end their own lives, with the aid of a physician? Easing the suffering of terminally ill patients is one way to avoid this difficult problem, but supporters of physician-assisted suicide argue that this is not always possible and that patients should have the option of assisted suicide. Opponents charge that assisted suicide will lead to the active killing of patients. In this Point/Counterpoint Sidebar, attorney Wesley J. Smith of the International Anti-Euthanasia Task Force presents his case against physician-assisted suicide. Margaret P. Battin, professor of at the University of Utah in Salt Lake City, counters with arguments for allowing physician-assisted suicide.

Death occurs at several levels. Somatic death is the death of the organism as a whole; it usually precedes the death of the individual organs, cells, and parts of cells. Somatic death is marked by cessation of heartbeat, respiration, movement, reflexes, and brain activity. The precise time of somatic death is sometimes difficult to determine, however, because the symptoms of such transient states as coma, faint, and trance closely resembles the signs of death.

After somatic death, several changes occur that are used to determine the time and circumstances of death. Algor mortis, the cooling of the body after death, is primarily influenced by the temperature of the immediate environment. Rigormortis, the stiffening of the skeletal muscles begins from five to ten hours after death and disappears after three or four days. Livor mortis, the reddish-blue discolouration that occurs on the underside of the body, results from the settling of the blood. Clotting of the blood begins shortly after death, as does autolysis, the death of the cells. Putrefaction, the decomposition that follows, is caused by the action of enzymes and bacteria.

Organs of the body die at different rates. Although brain cells may survive for no more than 5 minutes after somatic death, those of the hearts can survive for about 15 minutes and those of the kidney for about 30 minutes. For this reason, organs can be removed from a recently dead body and transplanted into a living person.

Ideas about what constitutes death are variously different between cultures and varying in distinct dissimilitude. In Western societies, death has traditionally been seen as the departure of the soul from the body. In this tradition, the essence of being human is independent of physical properties. Because the soul has no corporeal manifestation, its departure cannot be seen or otherwise objectively determined; hence, in this tradition, the cessation of breathing has been taken as the sign of death.

In modern times, death has been thought to occur when the vital functions cease—breathing and circulation (as evidenced by the beating of the heart). This view has been challenged, however, as medical advances have made it possible to sustain respiration and cardiac functioning through mechanical means. Thus, more recently, the concept of brain death has gained acceptance. In this view, the irreversible loss of brain activity is the sign that death has occurred. A majority of the states in the United States had accepted brain death as an essential sign of death by the late 1980s.

Even the concept of brain death has been challenged in recent years, because a person can lose all capacity for higher mental functioning while lower-brain functions, such as spontaneous respiration, continue. For this reason, some authorities now argue that death should be considered the loss of the capacity for consciousness or social interaction. The sign of death, according to this view, is the absence of activity in the higher centres of the brain, principally the neocortex.

Society's conception of death is of more than academic interest. Rapidly advancing medical technology has raised moral questions and introduced new problems in defining death legally. Among the issues being debated are the following: Who shall decide the criteria for death—physicians, legislatures, or each person for him or herself? Is advancement of the moment of death by cutting off artificial support morally and legally permissible? Do people, irrespectively have the rights to demand that extraordinary measures be stopped so that they may die in peace? Can the next of kin or a legal guardian act for the comatose dying person under such circumstances? All these questions have acquired new urgency with the advent of human tissue transplantation. The need for organs must be weighed against the rights of the dying donor.

As a result of such questions, a number of groups have sought to establish an individual's 'right to die,' particularly through the legal means of 'living wills' in which an individual confers the right to withdrawal of life-sustaining treatment upon family members or legal figures. By 1991, 40 states in the United States had recognized the validity of some form of living-will arrangement, although complex questions remain to be settled in all these instances.

The needs of dying patients and their families have also received renewed attention since the 1960s. Thanatologists (those who study the surroundings and inner experiences of persons near death) have identified several stages through which dying persons go: denial and isolation (No, not me!); anger, rage, envy, and resentment (Why me?); bargaining (If I am good, then can I live?); depression (What's the use?); and acceptance. Most authorities believe that these stages do not occur in any predictable order and may be intermingled with feelings of hope, anguish, and terror.

Like dying patients, bereaved families and friends go through stages of denial and acceptance. Bereavement, however, more typically does follow a regular sequence, often beginning before a loved one dies. Such anticipatory grief can help to defuse later distress. The next stage of bereavement, after the death has occurred, is likely to be longer and more severe if the death was unexpected. During this phase, mourners typically cry, have difficulty sleeping, and lose their appetites. Some may feel alarmed, angry, or aggrieved at being deserted. Later, the grief may turn to depression, which sometimes occurs when conventional forms of social support have ceased and outsiders are no longer offering help and solace; loneliness may ensue. Finally, the survivor begins to feel less troubled, regains energy, and restores ties to others.

Care of terminally ill patients may take place in the home but more commonly occurs in hospitals or more specialized institutions called hospices. Such care demands special qualities on the part of physicians and thanatologists, who must deal with their own fear of death before they can adequately comfort the dying. Although physicians commonly disagree, the tenet that most patients should be told that they are dying is now widely accepted. This must, of course, be done with tact and caring. Many persons, even children, know they are dying anyway; helping them to bring it out into the open avoids pretense and encourages the expression of honest feelings. Given safety and security, the informed dying patient can achieve an appropriate death, one marked by dignity and serenity. Concerned therapists or clergy can assist in this achievement simply by allowing the patient to talk about feelings, thoughts, and memories, or by acting as a substitute for family and friends who may grow anxious when the dying patient speaks of death

People who experienced child abuse seem to become visible, as to appear more vulnerable to depression than others. So, too, do people living under chronically stressful conditions, such as single mothers with many children and little or no support from friends or relatives.

Depression typically cannot be shaken or willed away. An episode must therefore run its course until it weakens either on its own or with treatment. Depression can be treated effectively with antidepressant drugs, psychotherapy, or a combination of both.

Despite the availability of effective treatment, most depressive disorders go untreated and undiagnosed. Studies indicate that general physicians fail to recognize depression in their patients at least half of the time. In addition, many doctors and patients view depression in elderly people as a normal part of aging, even though treatment for depression in older people is usually very effective.

Again, Bipolar Disorder is a mental illness in which a person's mood alternates between extreme mania and depression. Bipolar disorder is also called manic-depressive illness. When manic, people with bipolar disorder feel intensely elated, self-important, energetic, and irritable. When depressed, they experience painful sadness, negative thinking, and indifference to things that used to bring them happiness.

Bipolar disorder is much less common than depression. In North America and Europe, about 1 percent of people experience bipolar disorder during their lives. Rates of bipolar disorder are similar throughout the world. In comparison, at least 8 percent of people experience serious depression during their lives. Bipolar disorder affects men and women about equally and is somewhat more common in higher socioeconomic classes. At least 15 percent of people with bipolar disorder commit suicide. This rate roughly equals the rate for people with major depression, the most severe form of depression.

Bipolar disorder usually begins in a person's late teens or 20s. Men usually experience mania as the first mood episode, whereas women typically experience depression first. Episodes of mania and depression usually last from several weeks to several months. On average, people with untreated bipolar disorder experience four episodes of mania or depression over any ten-year period. Many people with bipolar disorder function normally between episodes. In 'rapid-cycling' bipolar disorder, however, which represents 5 to 15 percent of all cases, a person experiences four or more mood episodes within a year and may have little or no normal functioning in between episodes. In rare cases, swings between mania and depression occur over a period of days.

In another type of bipolar disorder, a person experiences major depression and hypomanic episodes, or episodes of milder mania. In a related disorder called cyclothymic disorder, a person's mood alternates between mild depression and mild mania. Some people with cyclothymic disorder later develop full-blown bipolar disorder. Bipolar disorder may allow a seasonal pattern, with a person typically experiencing depression in the fall and winter and mania in the spring or summer.

People in the depressive phase of bipolar disorder feel intensely sad or profoundly foreign and indifferent to work, activities, and people that once brought them pleasure. They think slowly, concentrate poorly, feel tired, and experience changes—usually an increase—in their appetite and sleep. They often feel a sense of worthlessness or helplessness. In addition, they may feel pessimistic or hopeless about the future and may think about or attempt suicide. In some cases of severe depression, people may experience psychotic symptoms, such as delusions (false beliefs) or hallucinations (false sensory perceptions).

In the manic phase of bipolar disorder, people feel intensely and inappropriately happy, self-important, and irritable. In this highly energized state they sleep less, have racing thoughts, and talk in rapid-fire speech that goes off in many directions. They have inflated self-esteem and confidence and may even have delusions of grandeur. Mania may make people impatient and abrasive, and when frustrated, physically abusive. They often behave in socially inappropriate ways, think irrationally, and show impaired judgment. For example, they may take aeroplane trips all over the country, make indecent sexual advances, and formulate grandiose plans involving indiscriminate investments of money. The self-destructive behaviour of mania includes excessive gambling, buying outrageously expensive gifts, abusing alcohol or other drugs, and provoking confrontations with obnoxious or combative behaviour.

Clinical depression is one of the most common forms of mental illness. Although depression can be treated with psychotherapy, many scientists believe there are biological causes for the disease. In this June 1998 Scientific American article, Neurobiologist Charles B. Nemeroff discusses the connection between biochemical changes in the brain and depression.

The genes that a person inherits seem to have a strong influence on whether the person will develop bipolar disorder. Studies of twins provide evidence for this genetic influence. Among genetically identical twins where one twin has bipolar disorder, the other twin has the disorder in more than 70 percent of cases. But among pairs of fraternal twins, who have about half their genes in common, both twins have bipolar disorder in less than 15 percent of cases in which one twin has the disorder. The degree of genetic similarity seems to account for the difference between identical and fraternal twins. Further evidence for a genetic influence comes from studies of adopted children with bipolar disorder. These studies show that biological relatives of the children have a higher incidence of bipolar disorder than do people in the general population. Thus, bipolar disorder seems to run in families for genetic reasons.

Personal or work-related stress can trigger a manic episode, but this usually occurs in people with a genetic vulnerability. Other factors—such as prenatal development, childhood experiences, and social conditions—seem to have relatively little influence in causing bipolar disorder. One study examined the children of identical twins in which only one member of each pair of twins had bipolar disorder. The study found that regardless of whether the parent had bipolar disorder or not, all of the children had the same high 10-percent rate of bipolar disorder. This observation clearly suggests that risk for bipolar illness comes from genetic

259

influence, not from exposure to a parent's bipolar illness or from family problems caused by that illness.

Different therapies may shorten, delay, or even prevent the extreme moods caused by bipolar disorder. Lithium carbonate, a natural mineral salt, can help control both mania and depression in bipolar disorder. The drug generally takes two to three weeks to become effective. People with bipolar disorder may take lithium during periods of relatively normal mood to delay or prevent subsequent episodes of mania or depression. Common side effects of lithium include nausea, increased thirst and urination, vertigo, loss of appetite, and muscle weakness. In addition, long-term use can impair functioning of the kidneys. For this reason, doctors do not prescribe lithium to bipolar patients with kidney disease. Many people find the side effects so unpleasant that they stop taking the medication, which often results in relapse.

From 20 to 40 percent of people do not respond to lithium therapy. For these people, two anticonvulsant drugs may help dampen severe manic episodes: carbamazepine (Tegretol) and valproate (Depakene). The use of traditional antidepressants to treat bipolar disorder carries risks of triggering a manic episode or a rapid-cycling pattern.

Object Relations in psychoanalysis, are the emotional relations between subject and object which, through a process of identification, are believed to constitute the developing ego. In this context, the word object refers to any person or thing, or representational aspect of them, with which the subject forms an intense emotional relationship

In psychoanalytic theory, the energy of the id or major portion of the unconscious mind, responsible for acts of creation. According to the theories of Sigmund Freud, the libido is the sex instinct, and artistic creation is an expression of the sex instinct that has been rechannelled. The Swiss psychiatrist Carl Jung rejected the sexual basis of the libido, believing that the force behind drives to act and create is merely an expression of the general will to live. Object Relations, in psychoanalysis, the emotional relations between subject and object which, through a process of identification, are believed to constitute the developing ego. In this context, the word object refers to any person or thing, or representational aspect of them, with which the subject forms an intense emotional relationship. Object relations were first described by German psychoanalyst Karl

Abraham in an influential paper, published in 1924. In the paper he developed ideas from the founder of psychoanalysis, Sigmund Freud, on infantile sexuality and the development of the libido. The libido (Latin libido, 'pleasure' or 'lust'), in psychoanalytic theory, the energy of the id or major portion of the unconscious mind, responsible for acts of creation. According to the theories of Sigmund Freud, the libido is the sex instinct, and artistic creation is an expression of the sex instinct that has been rechannelled. The Swiss psychiatrist Carl Jung rejected the sexual basis of the libido, believing that the force behind drives to act and create is merely an expression of the general will to live. I believe that the struggle against death, the unconditional and self-willed determination to life, is the motive power behind the lives and activities of all outstanding men.

Personality disorders, are disorders in which one's personality results in personal distress or significantly impair social or work functioning. Every person has, but a personality—that is, a characteristic way of thinking, feeling, behaving, and relating to others. Most people experience at least some difficulties and problems that result from their personality. The specific point at which those problems justify the diagnosis of a personality disorder is controversial. To some extent the definition of a personality disorder is arbitrary, reflecting subjectively as well as professional judgments about the person's degree of dysfunction, needs for change, and motivation for change.

Personality disorders involve behaviour that deviates from the norms or expectations of one's culture. Nonetheless, people who abstractively languish of not accept or receive but decline the invitation from cultural norms yet, not necessarily dysfunctional, nor are people who conform to cultural norms necessarily healthy. Many personality disorders represent extreme variants of behaviour patterns that people usually value and encourage. For example, most people value confidence but not arrogance, agreeableness but not submissiveness, and conscientiousness but not perfectionism.

Because no clear line exists between healthy and unhealthy functioning, critics question the reliability of personality disorder diagnoses. A behaviour that seems deviant to one person may seem normal to another depending on one's gender, ethnicity, and cultural background. The personal and cultural biases of mental health professionals may influence their diagnoses of personality disorders.

RICHARD J. KOSCIEJEW

An estimated 20 percent of people in the general population have one or more personality disorders. Some people with personality disorders have other mental illnesses as well. About 50 percent of people who are treated for any psychiatric disorder have a personality disorder.

Mental health professionals rarely diagnose personality disorders in children because their manner of thinking, feeling, and relating to others does not usually stabilize until young adulthood. Thereafter, personality traits usually remain stable. Personality disorders often decrease in severity as a person ages.

People with antisocial personality disorder act in a way that disregards the feelings and rights of other people. Antisocial personalities often break the law, and they may use or exploit other people for their own gain. They may lie repeatedly, act impulsively, and get into physical fights. They may mistreat their spouses, neglect or abuse their children, and exploit their employees. They may even kill other people. People with this disorder are also sometimes called sociopaths or psychopaths. Antisocial behaviour in people less than 18 years old is called conduct disorder.

Antisocial personality disorder affects about 3 percent of males and 1 percent of females. This is the most heavily researched personality disorder, in part because it costs society the most. People with this disorder are at high risk for premature and violent death, injury, imprisonment, loss of employment, bankruptcy, alcoholism, drug dependence, and failed personal relationships.

People with borderline personality disorder experience intense emotional instability, particularly in relationships with others. They may make frantic efforts to avoid real or imagined abandonment by others. They may experience minor problems as major crises. They may also express their anger, frustration, and dismay through suicidal gestures, self-mutilation, and other self-destructive acts. They tend to have an unstable self-image or sense of self.

As children, most people with this disorder were emotionally unstable, impulsive, and often bitter or angry, although their chaotic impulsiveness and intense emotions may have made them popular at school. At first they may impress people as stimulating and exciting, but their relationships tend to be unstable and explosive.

About 2 percent of all people have borderline personality disorder. About 75 percent of people with this disorder are female. Borderline personalities are at high risk for developing depression, alcoholism, drug dependence, bulimia, Dissociative disorders, and post-traumatic stress disorder. As many as 10 percent of people with this disorder commit suicide by the age of 30. People with borderline personality disorder are among the most difficult to treat with psychotherapy, in part because their relationship with their therapist may become as intense and unstable as their other personal relationships.

Avoidant personality disorder is social withdrawal due to intense, anxious shyness. People with Avoidant personalities are reluctant to interact with others unless they feel certain for being liked. They fear being criticized and rejected. Often they view themselves as socially inept and inferior to others.

Dependent personality disorder involves severe and disabling emotional dependency on others. People with this disorder have difficulty making decisions without a great deal of advice and reassurance from others. They urgently seek out another relationship when a close relationship ends. They feel uncomfortable by themselves.

People with histrionic personality disorder constantly strive to be the centre of attention. They may act overly flirtatious or dress in ways that draw attention. They may also talk in a dramatic or theatrical style and display exaggerated emotional reactions.

People with narcissistic personality disorder have a grandiose sense of self-importance. They seek excessive admiration from others and fantasize about unlimited success or power. They believe they are special, unique, or superior to others. However, they often have very fragile self-esteem.

Obsessive-compulsive personality disorder is characterized by a preoccupation with details, orderliness, perfection, and control. People with this disorder often devote excessive amounts of time to work and productivity and fail to take time for leisure activities and friendships. They tend to be rigid, formal, stubborn, and serious. This disorder differs from obsessive-compulsive disorder, which often includes more bizarre behaviour and rituals.

People with paranoid personality disorder feel constant suspicion and distrust toward other people. They believe that others are against them and constantly look for evidence to support their suspicions. They are hostile toward others and react angrily to perceived insults.

Schizoid personality disorder involves social isolation and a lack of desire for close personal relationships. People with this disorder prefer to be alone and seem withdrawn and emotionally detached. They seem indifferent to praise or criticism from other people.

People with schizotypal personality disorder engage in odd thinking, speech, and behaviour. They may ramble or use words and phrases in unusual ways, and they may believe they have magical control over others. They feel very uncomfortable with close personal relationships and tend to be suspicious of others. Some research suggests this disorder is a less severe form of schizophrenia.

Many psychiatrists and psychologists use two additional diagnoses. Depressive personality disorder is characterized by chronic pessimism, gloominess, and cheerlessness. In passive-aggressive personality disorder, a person passively resists completing tasks and chores, criticizes and scorns authority figures, and seems negative and sullen.

Personality disorders result from a complex interaction of inherited traits and life experience, not from a single cause. For example, some cases of antisocial personality disorder may result from a combination of a genetic predisposition to impulsiveness and violence, very inconsistent or erratic parenting, and a harsh environment that verbal discourse feels as empathy and warmth but rewards exploitation and aggressiveness. Borderline personality disorder may result from a genetic predisposition to impulsiveness and emotional instability combined with parental neglect, intense marital conflicts between parents, and repeated episodes of severe emotional or sexual abuse. Dependent personality disorder may result from genetically based anxiety, an inhibited temperament, and overly protective, clinging, or neglectful parenting.

The pervasive and chronic nature of personality disorders makes them difficult to treat. People with these disorders often fail to recognize that their personality has contributed to their social, occupational, and personal problems. They may not think they have any real problems despite a history of drug abuse, failed relationships, and irregular employment. Thus, therapists must first focus on helping the person understand and become aware of the significance of their personality traits.

People with personality disorders sometimes feel that they can never change their dysfunctional behaviour because they have always acted the same way. Although personality change is exceedingly difficult, sometimes people can change the most dysfunctional aspects of their feelings and behaviour.

Therapists use a variety of methods to treat personality disorders, depending on the specific disorder. For example, cognitive and behavioural techniques, such as role playing and logical argument, may help alter a person's irrational perceptions and assumptions about himself or herself. Certain psychoactive drugs may help control feelings of anxiety, depression, or severe distortions of thought. Psychotherapy may help people to understand the impact of experiences and relationships during childhood.

Psychotherapy is usually ineffective for people with antisocial personality disorder because these individuals tend to be manipulative, unreliable, and dishonest with the therapist. Therefore, most mental health professionals favour removing people with this disorder from their current living situation and placing them in a residential treatment centre. Such residential programs strictly supervise patients' behaviour and impose rigid, consistent rules and responsibilities. These programs appear to help some people, but it is unclear how long their beneficial effects last.

Therapists treating people with borderline personality disorder sometimes use a technique called dialectical behaviour therapy. In this type of therapy, the therapist initially focuses on reducing suicidal tendencies and other behaviours that disrupt treatment. The therapist then helps the person develop skills to cope with anger and self-destructive impulses. In addition, the person learns to achieve personal strength through an acceptance of the many disappointments and interpersonal conflicts that are a natural part of life.

People with depression often experience feelings of worthlessness, helplessness, guilt, and self-blame. They may interpret a minor failing on their part as a sign of incompetence or interpret minor criticism as condemnation. Some depressed people complain of being spiritually or morally dead. The mirror seems to reflect someone ugly and repulsive. Even a competent and decent person may feel deficient, cruel, stupid, phony, or guilty of having deceived others. People with major depression may experience such extreme emotional pain that they consider or attempt suicide. At least 15 percent of seriously depressed people commit suicide, and many more attempt it.

In some cases, people with depression may experience psychotic symptoms, such as delusions (false beliefs) and hallucinations (false sensory perceptions). Psychotic symptoms indicate an especially severe illness. Compared to other depressed people, those with psychotic symptoms have longer hospital stays, and after leaving, they are more likely to be moody and unhappy. They are also more likely to commit suicide.

Some depressions seem to come out of the blue, even when things are going well. Others seem to have an obvious cause: a marital conflict, financial difficulty, or some personal failure. Yet many people with these problems do not become deeply depressed. Most psychologists believe depression results from an interaction between stressful life events and a person's biological and psychological vulnerabilities.

Implications as to the reason for this difference. Some cite differences in hormones, and others point to the stress caused by society's expectations of women.

Depression occurs in all parts of the world, although the pattern of symptoms can vary. The prevalence of depression in other countries varies widely, from 1.5 percent of people in Taiwan to 19 percent of people in Lebanon. Some researchers believe methods of gathering data on depression account for different rates.

A number of large-scale studies indicate that depression rates have increased worldwide over the past several decades. Furthermore, younger generations are experiencing depression at an earlier age than did previous generations. Social scientists have proposed many explanations, including changes in family structure, urbanization, and reduced cultural and religious influences.

Symptoms of depression can vary by age. In younger children, depression may include physical complaints, such as stomachaches and headaches, as well as irritability, 'moping around,' social withdrawal, and changes in eating habits. They may feel unenthusiastic about school and other activities. In adolescents, common symptoms include sad mood, sleep disturbances, and lack of energy. Elderly people with depression usually complain of physically rather than emotional problems, which sometimes leads doctors to misdiagnose the illness.

Symptoms of depression can also vary by culture. In some cultures, depressed people may not experience sadness or guilt but may complain of physical problems. In Mediterranean cultures, for example, depressed people may complain of headaches or nerves. In Asian cultures they may complain of weakness, fatigue, or imbalance.

Depression also changes one's energy level. Some depressed people may be restless and agitated, engaging in fidgety movements and pacing. Others may feel sluggish and inactive, experiencing great fatigue, lack of energy, and a feeling of being worn out or carrying a heavy burden. Depressed people may also have difficulty thinking, poor concentration, and problems with memory.

People with depression often experience feelings of worthlessness, helplessness, guilt, and self-blame. They may interpret a minor failing on their part as a sign of incompetence or interpret minor criticism as condemnation. Some depressed people complain of being spiritually or morally dead. The mirror seems to reflect someone ugly and repulsive. Even a competent and decent person may feel deficient, cruel, stupid, phony, or guilty of having deceived others. People with major depression may experience such extreme emotional pain that they consider or attempt suicide. At least 15 percent of seriously depressed people commit suicide, and many more attempt it.

In some cases, people with depression may experience psychotic symptoms, such as delusions (false beliefs) and hallucinations (false sensory perceptions). Psychotic symptoms indicate an especially severe illness. Compared to other depressed people, those with psychotic symptoms have longer hospital stays, and after leaving, they are more likely to be moody and unhappy. They are also more likely to commit suicide.

Some depressions seem to come out of the blue, even when things are going well. Others seem to have an obvious cause: a marital conflict, financial difficulty, or some personal failure. Yet many people with these problems do not become deeply depressed. Most psychologists believe depression results from an interaction between stressful life events and a person's biological and psychological vulnerabilities.

Clinical depression is one of the most common forms of mental illness. Although depression can be treated with psychotherapy, many scientists believe there are biological causes for the disease. In this June 1998 Scientific American article, Neurobiologist Charles B. Nemeroff discusses the connection between biochemical changes in the brain and depression.

Depression runs in families. By studying twins, researchers have found evidence of a strong genetic influence in depression. Genetically identical twins raised in the same environment are three times more likely to have depression in common than fraternal twins, who have only about half of their genes in common. In addition, identical twins are five times more likely to have bipolar disorder in common. These findings suggest that vulnerability to depression and bipolar disorder can be inherited. Adoption studies have provided more evidence of a genetic role in depression. These studies show that children of depressed people are vulnerable to depression even when raised by adoptive parents.

Genes may influence depression by causing abnormal activity in the brain. Studies have shown that certain brain chemicals called neurotransmitters play an important role in regulating moods and emotions. Neurotransmitters involved in depression include norepinephrine, dopamine, and serotonin. Research in the 1960s suggested that depression results from lower than normal levels of these neurotransmitters in parts of the brain. Support for this theory came from the effects of antidepressant drugs, which work by increasing the levels of neurotransmitters involved in depression. However, later studies have discredited this simple explanation and have suggested a more complex relationship between neurotransmitter levels and depression.

An imbalance of hormones may also play a role in depression. Many depressed people have higher than normal levels of hydrocortisone (cortisol), a hormone secreted by the adrenal gland in response to stress. In addition, an underactive or overactive thyroid gland can lead to depression.

A variety of medical conditions can cause depression. These include dietary deficiencies in vitamin B6, vitamin B12, and folic acid; degenerative neurological disorders, such as Alzheimer's disease and Huntington's disease, strokes in the frontal part of the brain; and certain viral infections, such as hepatitis and mononucleosis. Certain medications, such as steroids, may also cause depression.

Psychological theories of depression focus on the way people think and behave. In a 1917 essay, Austrian psychoanalyst Sigmund Freud explained melancholia, or major depression, as a response to loss—either real loss, such as the death of a spouse, or symbolic loss, such as the failure to achieve an important goal. Freud

believed that a person's unconscious anger over loss weakens the ego, resulting in self-hate and self-destructive behaviour.

Mania, maintains an abnormal mental state and is characterized by an elevated or irritable mood, exaggerated self-importance, racing thoughts, and hyperactivity. People with mania typically feel intoxicated with themselves and with life. They may display an indiscriminate enthusiasm for manipulating people, spending money, and pursuing sexual adventure. Manic people may also display impatience or hostility toward other people. If frustrated, they may physically abuse their friends, children, or spouse.

Mania has many other characteristics. People with mania often have inflated self-esteem and self-confidence, and assume they have more wit, courage, imagination, and artistry than everyone else. Severe mania may include delusions of grandeur, such as the belief that one is chosen by God for a special mission. Mania typically involves a decreased need for sleep, so manic people often wake up early in a highly energized state. Mania makes people extremely talkative. Their loud, rapid-fire speech sometimes continues unabated without regard for others. Mania also involves a flight of ideas, racing thoughts that cause speech to go off in many different directions. People in a manic state become easily distracted by irrelevant sights, sounds or ideas, which further disrupts thinking and speech.

Most people who experience episodes of mania also experience spells of severe depression. This pattern of mood swings between mania and depression defined a mental illness known as bipolar disorder is also called manic-depressive illness. In bipolar disorder, episodes of mania usually begin abruptly and last from several weeks to several months. Mild manic episodes can last a year or more. Depression may follow immediately or begin after a period of relatively normal functioning. Manic episodes may require hospitalization because of impaired social behaviour or the presence of psychotic symptoms.

Personality Disorders, are disorders in which one's personality results in personal distress or significantly impairs social or work functioning. Every person has a personality—that is, a characteristic way of thinking, feeling, behaving, and relating to others. Most people experience at least some difficulties and problems that result from their personality. The specific point at which those problems justify the diagnosis of a personality disorder is controversial. To some extent the definition of a personality disorder is arbitrary, reflecting subjectively as well as professional judgments about the person's degree of dysfunction, needs for change, and motivation for change.

Because no clear line exists between healthy and unhealthy functioning, critics question the reliability of personality disorder diagnoses. A behaviour that seems deviant to one person may seem normal to another depending on one's gender, ethnicity, and cultural background. The personal and cultural biases of mental health professionals may influence their diagnoses of personality disorders.

An estimated 20 percent of people in the general population have one or more personality disorders. Some people with personality disorders have other mental illnesses as well. About 50 percent of people who are treated for any psychiatric disorder have a personality disorder.

Mental health professionals rarely diagnose personality disorders in children because their manner of thinking, feeling, and relating to others does not usually stabilize until young adulthood. Thereafter, personality traits usually remain stable. Personality disorders often decrease in severity as a person ages.

People with antisocial personality disorder act in a way that disregards the feelings and rights of other people. Antisocial personalities often break the law, and they may use or exploit other people for their own gain. They may lie repeatedly, act impulsively, and get into physical fights. They may mistreat their spouses, neglect or abuse their children, and exploit their employees. They may even kill other people. People with this disorder are also sometimes called sociopaths or psychopaths. Antisocial behaviour in people less than 18 years old is called conduct disorder.

Antisocial personalities usually to understand that their behaviour is dysfunctional because their ability to feel guilty, remorseful, and anxious is impaired. Guilt, remorse, shame, and anxiety are unpleasant feelings, but they are also necessary for social functioning and even physical survival. For example, people who lack or to be without something and especially something essential or greatly needed as in the absence of ability to feel anxious will often fail to anticipate actual dangers and risks. They may take chances that other people would not take.

Antisocial personality disorder affects about 3 percent of males and 1 percent of females. This is the most heavily researched personality disorder, in part because it costs society the most. People with this disorder are at high risk for premature and violent death, injury, imprisonment, loss of employment, bankruptcy, alcoholism, drug dependence, and failed personal relationships.

People with borderline personality disorder experience intense emotional instability, particularly in relationships with others. They may make frantic efforts to avoid real or imagined abandonment by others. They may experience minor problems as major crises. They may also express their anger, frustration, and dismay through suicidal gestures, self-mutilation, and other self-destructive acts. They tend to have an unstable self-image or sense of self.

As children, most people with this disorder were emotionally unstable, impulsive, and often bitter or angry, although their chaotic impulsiveness and intense emotions may have made them popular at school. At first they may impress people as stimulating and exciting, but their relationships tend to be unstable and explosive.

About 2 percent of all people have borderline personality disorder. About 75 percent of people with this disorder are female. Borderline personalities are at high risk for developing depression, alcoholism, drug dependence, bulimia, Dissociative disorders, and post-traumatic stress disorder. As many as 10 percent of people with this disorder commit suicide by the age of 30. People with borderline personality disorder are among the most difficult to treat with psychotherapy, in part because their relationship with their therapist may become as intense and unstable as their other personal relationships.

People with histrionic personality disorder constantly strive to be the centre of attention. They may act overly flirtatious or dress in ways that draw attention. They may also talk in a dramatic or theatrical style and display exaggerated emotional reactions.

People with narcissistic personality disorder have a grandiose sense of self-importance. They seek excessive admiration from others and fantasize about unlimited success or power. They believe they are special, unique, or superior to others. However, they often have very fragile self-esteem.

Obsessive-compulsive personality disorder is characterized by a preoccupation with details, orderliness, perfection, and control. People with this disorder often devote excessive amounts of time to work and productivity and fail to take time for leisure activities and friendships. They tend to be rigid, formal, stubborn, and serious. This disorder differs from obsessive-compulsive disorder, which often includes more bizarre behaviour and rituals.

People with paranoid personality disorder feel constant suspicion and distrust toward other people. They believe that others are against them and constantly look for evidence to support their suspicions. They are hostile toward others and react angrily to perceived insults.

Schizoid personality disorder involves social isolation and a lack of desire for close personal relationships. People with this disorder prefer to be alone and seem withdrawn and emotionally detached. They seem indifferent to praise or criticism from other people.

People with schizotypal personality disorder engage in odd thinking, speech, and behaviour. They may ramble or use words and phrases in unusual ways, and they may believe they have magical control over others. They feel very uncomfortable with close personal relationships and tend to be suspicious of others. Some research suggests this disorder is a less severe form of schizophrenia.

Many psychiatrists and psychologists use two additional diagnoses. Depressive personality disorder is characterized by chronic pessimism, gloominess, and cheerlessness. In passive-aggressive personality disorder, a person passively resists completing tasks and chores, criticizes and scorns authority figures, and seems negative and sullen.

Personality disorders result from a complex interaction of inherited traits and life experience, not from a single cause. For example, some cases of antisocial personality disorder may result from a combination of a genetic predisposition to impulsiveness and violence, very inconsistent or erratic parenting, and a harsh environment that discourage feelings of empathy and warmth but rewards exploitation and aggressiveness. Borderline personality disorder may result from a genetic predisposition to impulsiveness and emotional instability combined with parental neglect, intense marital conflicts between parents, and repeated episodes of severe emotional or sexual abuse. Dependent personality disorder may result from genetically based anxiety, an inhibited temperament, and overly protective, clinging, or neglectful parenting.

The pervasive and chronic nature of personality disorders makes them difficult to treat. People with these disorders often fail to recognize that their personality has contributed to their social, occupational, and personal problems. They may not think they have any real problems despite a history of drug abuse, failed relationships, and irregular employment. Thus, therapists must first focus on helping the person understand and become aware of the significance of their personality traits.

People with personality disorders sometimes feel that they can never change their dysfunctional behaviour because they have always acted the same way. Although personality change is exceedingly difficult, sometimes people can change the most dysfunctional aspects of their feelings and behaviour.

Therapists treating people with borderline personality disorder sometimes use a technique called dialectical behaviour therapy. In this type of therapy, the therapist initially focuses on reducing suicidal tendencies and other behaviours that disrupt treatment. The therapist then helps the person develop skills to cope with anger and self-destructive impulses. In addition, the person learns to achieve personal strength through an acceptance of the many disappointments and interpersonal conflicts that are a natural part of life.

Depression is categorized as a mental illness in which a person experiences deep, unshakable sadness and diminished interest in nearly all activities. People also use the term depression to describe the temporary sadness, loneliness, or blues that everyone feels from time to time. In contrast to normal sadness, severe depression, also called major depression, can dramatically impair a person's ability to function in social situations and at work. People with major depression often have feelings of despair, hopelessness, and worthlessness, as well as thoughts of committing suicide.

Depression can take several other forms. In bipolar disorder, sometimes called manic-depressive illness, a person's mood swings back and forth between depression and mania. Some people with dysthymia experience occasional episodes of major depression. Mental health professionals use the term clinical depression to refer to any of the above forms of depression

Depression is one of the most common mental illnesses. At least 8 percent of adults in the United States experience serious depression at some point during their lives, and estimates range as high as 17 percent. The illness affects all people, regardless of sex, race, ethnicity, or socioeconomic standing. However, women are two to three times more likely than men to suffer from depression. Experts disagree on the reason for this difference. Some cite differences in hormones, and others point to the stress caused by society's expectations of women.

Studies indicate that depression is more prevalent among women than it is among men. Genetics and environment seem to be the keys to unlocking this gender-gap mystery, although the complexity of the puzzle makes progress slow. In this article for Scientific American Presents, physician Ellen Leibenluft explores the physiology of depression and explains how scientific research may make it possible to develop better treatments for both sexes.

Depression occurs in all parts of the world, although the pattern of symptoms can vary. The prevalence of depression in other countries varies widely, from 1.5 percent of people in Taiwan to 19 percent of people in Lebanon. Some researchers believe methods of gathering data on depression account for different rates.

A number of large-scale studies indicate that depression rates have increased worldwide over the past several decades. Furthermore, younger generations are experiencing depression at an earlier age than did previous generations. Social scientists have proposed many explanations, including changes in family structure, urbanization, and reduced cultural and religious influences.

Although it may appear anytime from childhood to old age, depression usually begins during a person's 20s or 30s. The illness may come on slowly, then deepen gradually over months or years. On the other hand, it may erupt suddenly in a few weeks or days. A person who develops severe depression may appear so confuse, frightened, and unbalance that observers speak of a 'nervous breakdown.' However, it begins. Depression causes serious changes in a person's feelings and outlook. A person with major depression feels sad nearly every day and may cry often. People, work, and activities that used to bring them pleasure no longer do.

Symptoms of depression can vary by age. In younger children, depression may include physical complaints, such as stomachaches and headaches, as well as irritability, 'moping around,' social withdrawal, and changes in eating habits. They may feel unenthusiastic about school and other activities. In adolescents, common symptoms include sad mood, sleep disturbances, and lack of energy. Elderly people with depression usually complain of physical rather than emotional problems, which sometimes leads doctors to misdiagnose the illness.

Symptoms of depression can also vary by culture. In some cultures, depressed people may not experience sadness or guilt but may complain of physical problems. In Mediterranean cultures, for example, depressed people may complain of headaches or nerves. In Asian cultures they may complain of weakness, fatigue, or imbalance.

People with depression often experience feelings of worthlessness, helplessness, guilt, and self-blame. They may interpret a minor failing on their part as a sign of incompetence or interpret minor criticism as condemnation. Some depressed people complain of being spiritually or morally dead. The mirror seems to reflect someone ugly and repulsive. Even a competent and decent person may feel deficient, cruel, stupid, phony, or guilty of having deceived others. People with major depression may experience such extreme emotional pain that they consider or attempt suicide. At least 15 percent of seriously depressed people commit suicide, and many more attempt it.

Some depressions seem to come out of the blue, even when things are going well. Others seem to have an obvious cause: a marital conflict, financial difficulty, or some personal failure. Yet many people with these problems do not become deeply depressed. Most psychologists believe depression results from an interaction between stressful life events and a person's biological and psychological vulnerabilities.

Genes may influence depression by causing abnormal activity in the brain. Studies have shown that certain brain chemicals called neurotransmitters play an important role in regulating moods and emotions. Neurotransmitters involved in depression include norepinephrine, dopamine, and serotonin. Research in the 1960s suggested that depression results from lower than normal levels of these neurotransmitters in parts of the brain. Support for this theory came from the effects of antidepressant drugs, which work by increasing the levels of neurotransmitters involved in depression. However, later studies have discredited this simple explanation and have suggested a more complex relationship between neurotransmitter levels and depression.

An imbalance of hormones may also play a role in depression. Many depressed people have higher than normal levels of hydrocortisone (cortisol), a hormone secreted by the adrenal gland in response to stress. In addition, an underactive or overactive thyroid gland can lead to depression.

A variety of medical conditions can cause depression. These include dietary deficiencies in vitamin B6, vitamin B12, and folic acid, degenerative neurological disorders, such as Alzheimer's disease and Huntington's disease; strokes in the frontal part of the brain; and certain viral infections, such as hepatitis and mononucleosis. Certain medications, such as steroids, may also cause depression.

Cognitive theories of depression emphasize the role of irrational thought processes. American psychiatrist Aaron Beck proposed that depressed people tend to view themselves, their environment, and the future in a negative light because of errors in thinking. These errors include focussing on the negative aspects of any situation, misinterpreting facts in negative ways, and blaming themselves for any misfortune. In Beck's view, people learn these self-defeating ways of looking at the world during early childhood. This negative thinking makes situations seem much worse than they really are and increases the risk of depression, especially in stressful situations.

In support of this cognitive view, people with 'depressive' personality traits appear to be more vulnerable than others to actual depression. Examples of depressive personality traits include gloominess, pessimism, introversion, self-criticism, excessive skepticism and criticism of others, deep feelings of inadequacy, and excessive brooding and worrying. In addition, people who regularly behave in dependent, hostile, and impulsive ways appear at greater risk for depression.

People who experience child abuse appear more vulnerable to depression than others. So, too, do people living under chronically stressful conditions, such as single mothers with many children and little or no support from friends or relatives.

Depression typically cannot be shaken or willed away. An episode must therefore run its course until it weakens either on its own or with treatment. Depression can be treated effectively with antidepressant drugs, psychotherapy, or a combination of both.

Despite the availability of effective treatment, most depressive disorders go untreated and undiagnosed. Studies indicate that general physicians fail to recognize depression in their patients at least half of the time. In addition, many doctors and patients view depression in elderly people as a normal part of aging, even though treatment for depression in older people is usually very effective.

Studies have shown that short-term psychotherapy can relieve mild to moderate depression as effectively as antidepressant drugs. Unlike medication, psychotherapy produces no physiological side effects. In addition, depressed people treated with psychotherapy appear less likely to experience a relapse than those treated only with antidepressant medication. However, psychotherapy usually takes longer to produce benefits.

There are many kinds of psychotherapy. Cognitive-behavioural therapy assumes that depression stems from negative, often irrational thinking about oneself and one's future. In this type of therapy, a person learns to understand and eventually eliminate those habits of negative thinking. In interpersonal therapy, the therapist helps a person resolve problems in relationships with others that may have caused the depression. The subsequent improvement in social relationships and support helps alleviate the depression. Psychodynamic therapy views depression as the result of internal, unconscious conflicts. Psychodynamic therapists focus on a person's past experiences and the resolution of childhood conflicts. Psychoanalysis is an example of this type of therapy. Critics of long-term Psychodynamic therapy argue that its effectiveness is scientifically unproven.

Mood disorders, also called affective disorders, create disturbances in a person's emotional life. Depression, mania, and bipolar disorder are examples of mood disorders. Symptoms of depression may include feelings of sadness, hopelessness, and worthlessness, as well as complaints of physical pain and changes in appetite, sleep patterns, and energy level. In mania, on the other hand, an individual experiences an abnormally elevated mood, often marked by exaggerated self-importance, irritability, agitation, and a decreased need for sleep. In bipolar disorder, also called manic-depressive illness, a person's mood alternates between extremes of mania and depression.

Personality disorders are mental illnesses in which one's personality results in personal distress or a significant impairment in social or work functioning. In general, people with personality disorders have poor perceptions of themselves or others. They may have low self-esteem or overwhelming narcissism, poor impulse control, troubled social relationships, and inappropriate emotional responses. Considerable controversy exists over where to draw the distinction between a normal personality and a personality disorder.

Cognitive disorders, such as delirium and dementia, involve a significant loss of mental functioning. Dementia, for example, is characterized by impaired memory and difficulties in such functions as speaking, abstract thinking, and the ability to identify familiar objects. The conditions in this category usually result from a medical condition, substance abuse, or verse.

Depression is one of the most common mental illnesses. At least 8 percent of adults in the United States experience serious depression at some point during their lives, and estimates range as high as 17 percent. The illness affects all people, regardless of sex, race, ethnicity, or socioeconomic standing. However, women are two to three times more likely than men to suffer from depression. Experts disagree on the reason for this difference. Some cite differences in hormones, and others point to the stress caused by society's expectations of women.

Depression occurs in all parts of the world, although the pattern of symptoms can vary. The prevalence of depression in other countries varies widely, from 1.5 percent of people in Taiwan to 19 percent of people in Lebanon. Some researchers believe methods of gathering data on depression account for different rates.

A number of large-scale studies indicate that depression rates have increased worldwide over the past several decades. Furthermore, younger generations are experiencing depression at an earlier age than did previous generations. Social scientists have proposed many explanations, including changes in family structure, urbanization, and reduced cultural and religious influences.

Although it may appear anytime from childhood to old age, depression usually begins during a person's 20s or 30s. The illness may come on slowly, then deepen gradually over months or years. On the other hand, it may erupt suddenly in a few weeks or days. A person who develops severe depression may appear for being confused, frightened, and unbalance, in that observers speak of a 'nervous breakdown.' However, it begins. Depression causes serious changes in a person's feelings and outlook. A person with major depression feels sad nearly every day and may cry often.

People, work, and activities that used to bring them pleasure no longer do.

Symptoms of depression can vary by age. In younger children, depression may include physical complaints, such as stomachaches and headaches, as well as irritability, 'moping around,' social withdrawal, and changes in eating habits. They may feel unenthusiastic about school and other activities. In adolescents, common symptoms include sad mood, sleep disturbances, and lack of energy. Elderly people with depression usually complain of physical rather than emotional problems, which sometimes leads doctors to misdiagnose the illness.

Symptoms of depression can also vary by culture. In some cultures, depressed people may not experience sadness or guilt but may complain of physical problems. In Mediterranean cultures, for example, depressed people may complain of headaches or nerves. In Asian cultures they may complain of weakness, fatigue, or imbalance.

If left untreated, an episode of major depression typically lasts eight or nine months. About 85 percent of people who experience one bout of depression will experience future episodes.

Depression usually alters a person's appetite, sometimes increasing it, but usually reducing it. Sleep change frequently as well. People with depression may oversleep or, more commonly, sleep for fewer hours. A depressed person might go to sleep at midnight, sleep restlessly, then wake up at 5:00 a.m. feeling tired and blue. For many depressed people, early morning is the saddest time of the day.

Depression also changes one's energy level. Some depressed people may be restless and agitated, engaging in fidgety movements and pacing. Other energy, and a feeling of being worn out or carrying a heavy burden. Depressed people may also have difficulty thinking, poor concentration, and problems with memory.

Some depressions seem to come out of the blue, even when things are going well. Others seem to have an obvious cause: a marital conflict, financial difficulty, or some personal failure. Yet many people with these problems do not become deeply depressed. Most psychologists believe depression results from an interaction between stressful life events and a person's biological and psychological vulnerabilities.

279

Genes may influence depression by causing abnormal activity in the brain. Studies have shown that certain brain chemicals called neurotransmitters play an important role in regulating moods and emotions. Neurotransmitters involved in depression include norepinephrine, dopamine, and serotonin. Research in the 1960s suggested that depression results from lower than normal levels of these neurotransmitters in parts of the brain. Support for this theory came from the effects of antidepressant drugs, which work by increasing the levels of neurotransmitters involved in depression. However, later studies have discredited this simple explanation and have suggested a more complex relationship between neurotransmitter levels and depression.

An imbalance of hormones may also play a role in depression. Many depressed people have higher than normal levels of hydrocortisone (cortisol), a hormone secreted by the adrenal gland in response to stress. In addition, an underactive or overactive thyroid gland can lead to depression.

A variety of medical conditions can cause depression. These include dietary deficiencies in vitamin B12, vitamin B12, and folic acid; degenerative neurological disorders, such as Alzheimer's disease and Huntington's disease, strokes in the frontal part of the brain; and certain viral infections, such as hepatitis and mononucleosis. Certain medications,

Cognitive theories of depression emphasize the role of irrational thought processes. American psychiatrist Aaron Beck proposed that depressed people tend to view themselves, their environment, and the future in a negative light because of errors in thinking. These errors include focussing on the negative aspects of any situation, misinterpreting facts in negative ways, and blaming themselves for any misfortune. In Beck's view, people learn these self-defeating ways of looking at the world during early childhood. This negative thinking makes situations seem much worse than they really are and increases the risk of depression, especially in stressful situations.

American psychologist Martin Seligman proposed that depression stems from 'learned helplessness,' an acquired belief that one cannot control the outcome of events. In this view, prolonged exposure to uncontrollable and inescapable events leads to apathy, pessimism, and loss of motivation. An adaptation of this theory by American psychologist Lynn Abramson and her colleagues argues that depression results not only from helplessness, but also hopelessness. The hopelessness theory attributes depression to a pattern of negative thinking in which people blame themselves for negative life events, view the causes of those events as permanent, and overgeneralize specific weaknesses as applying to many areas of their life.

People who experience child abuse appear more vulnerable to depression than others. So, too, do people living under chronically stressful conditions, such as single mothers with many children and little or no support from friends or relatives.

Depression typically cannot be shaken or willed away. An episode must therefore run its course until it weakens either on its own or with treatment. Depression can be treated effectively with antidepressant drugs, psychotherapy, or a combination of both.

Despite the availability of effective treatment, most depressive disorders go untreated and undiagnosed. Studies indicate that general physicians fail to recognize depression in their patients at least half of the time. In addition, many doctors and patients view depression in elderly people as a normal part of aging, even though treatment for depression in older people is usually very effective.

Up to 70 percent of people with depression respond to antidepressant drugs. These medications appear to work by altering the levels of serotonin, norepinephrine, and other neurotransmitters in the brain. They generally take at least two to three weeks to become effective. Doctors cannot predict which type of antidepressant drug will work best for any particular person, so depressed people may need to try several types. Antidepressant drugs are not addictive, but they may produce unwanted side effects. To avoid relapse, people usually must continue taking the medication for several months after their symptoms improve.

Commonly used antidepressant drugs fall into three major classes: tricyclics, Monoamine oxidase inhibitors (MAO inhibitors), and selective serotonin reuptake inhibitors (SSRIs). Tricyclics, named for their three-ring chemical structure, include amitriptyline (Elavil), imipramine (Tofanil), desipramine (Norpramin), doxepin (Sinequan), and nortriptyline (Pamelor). Side effects of tricyclics may include drowsiness, dizziness upon standing, blurred vision, nausea, insomnia, constipation, and dry mouth.

MAO inhibitors include isocarboxazid (Marplan), phenelzine (Nardil), and tranylcypromine (Parnate). People who take MAO inhibitors must follow a diet that excludes tyramine—a substance found in wine, beer, some cheeses, and many fermented foods—to avoid a dangerous rise in blood pressure. In addition, MAO inhibitors have many of the same side effects as tricyclics.

Selective serotonin reuptake inhibitors include Fluoxetine (Prozac), sertraline (Zoloft), and paroxetine (Paxil). These drugs generally produce fewer and milder side effects than do other types of antidepressants, although SSRIs may cause anxiety, insomnia, drowsiness, headaches, and sexual dysfunction. Some patients have alleged that Prozac causes violent or suicidal behaviour in a small number of cases, but the US Food and Drug Administration has failed to substantiate this claim.

Prozac became the most widely used antidepressant in the world soon after its introduction in the late 1980s by drug manufacturer Eli Lilly and Company. Many people find Prozac extremely effective in lifting depression. In addition, some people have reported that Prozac actually transforms their personality by increasing their self-confidence, optimism, and energy level. However, mental health professionals have expressed serious ethical concerns over Prozac's use as a 'personality enchanters,' especially among people without clinical depression.

Fluoxetine, the drug known as an antidepressant and is prescribed for the treatment of depression, particularly depression lasting longer than two weeks and interfering with daily functioning. Fluoxetine works by regulating serotonin levels in the brain. Serotonin is a neurotransmitter, a chemical in the body's nervous system associated with maintaining a general sense of well-being. An insufficient amount of serotonin in the brain may contribute to depression. Fluoxetine may also be prescribed for treatment of other conditions related to insufficient levels of serotonin including eating disorders (obesity and bulimia), obsessive-compulsive disorder, and premenstrual syndrome.

Fluoxetine, available by prescription only, is taken orally in tablet form. The effectiveness of Fluoxetine is not altered by food, so the medication can be taken on an empty or full stomach. When Fluoxetine is prescribed to treat depression, the usual dose ranges from 20 to 60 mg per day. It usually requires three tour weeks for the patient feel the effects. After the medication begins to take effect, the dose may be lowered. A lower dose may be sufficient for treatment of conditions other than depression.

Fluoxetine should not be taken in combination with other types of antidepressants known as Monoamine oxidase (MAO) inhibitors. Taking these medications at the same time or even within a month of one another has serious, sometimes fatal results. At least five weeks must be allowed between the last dose of Fluoxetine and the first dose of a MAO inhibitor. Fluoxetine is not recommended for people recovering from heart attack, or for those with kidney or liver disease, diabetes, or a history of seizures. Women who are pregnant or breast-feeding is advised not to take Fluoxetine, and people taking it should not consume alcohol.

Common adverse side effects of Fluoxetine include anxiety, insomnia, headaches, dizziness, changes in appetite, weight loss, nausea, and diarrhea

MAO Inhibitor, any of a group of drugs used to treat depression, anxiety, or phobias. Properly known as Monoamine oxidase (MAO) inhibitors, these drugs work by inhibiting or preventing the enzyme Monoamine oxidase, found in the nervous system, from breaking down neurotransmitters, chemicals in the brain that control nerve impulse transmission and affect mood. MAO inhibitors produce a more balanced emotional state.

MAO inhibitors must be prescribed by a physician. Available in tablet form, these drugs are taken with or without food in one or more doses ranging from 30 to 90 mg per day, depending on the particular drug and the condition being treated. Effectiveness is usually apparent after three tour weeks of treatment, and long-term use for months or even years may be prescribed. MAO inhibitors should not be taken by pregnant women. Their safety for breast-feeding mothers or children under the age of 16 is not known.

These drugs should be used with caution by patients with heart or liver problems, diabetes, or epilepsy. MAO inhibitors can cause serious reactions, including death, if combined with certain foods that contain the chemical substance tyramine. Such foods include beer, wine, cheese, chocolate, sausage, liver, smoked meats or fish, sauerkraut, yogurt, and beverages containing caffeine.

Drugs to avoid while using MAO inhibitors include cold and cough remedies, sinus and hay fever medications, nasal decongestants, appetite suppressant, sleep aids, bronchodilators inhalants, amphetamines, and other antidepressants. Serious interactions can occur up to two weeks after drug treatment ends.

MAO Inhibitor, are those of any of a group of drugs used to treat depression, anxiety, or phobias. Properly known as Monoamine oxidase (MAO) inhibitors, these drugs work by inhibiting or preventing the enzyme Monoamine oxidase, found in the nervous system, from breaking down neurotransmitters, chemicals in the brain that control nerve impulse transmission and affect mood. MAO inhibitors produce a more balanced emotional state.

MAO inhibitors must be prescribed by a physician. Available in tablet form, these drugs are taken with or without food in one or more doses ranging from 30 to 90 mg per day, depending on the particular drug and the condition being treated. Effectiveness is usually apparent after three tour weeks of treatment, and long-term use for months or even years may be prescribed. MAO inhibitors should not be taken by pregnant women. Their safety for breast-feeding mothers or children under the age of 16 is not known.

These drugs should be used with caution by patients with heart or liver problems, diabetes, or epilepsy. MAO inhibitors can cause serious reactions, including death, if combined with certain foods that contain the chemical substance tyramine. Such foods include beer, wine, cheese, chocolate, sausage, liver, smoked meats or fish, sauerkraut, yogurt, and beverages containing caffeine.

Drugs to avoid while using MAO inhibitors include cold and cough remedies, sinus and hay fever medications, nasal decongestants, appetite suppressants, sleep aids, bronchodilator inhalants, amphetamines, and other antidepressants. Serious interactions can occur up to two weeks after drug treatment ends.

One significant side effect of MAO inhibitor drug use is high blood pressure, which may cause frequent headaches, heart palpitations, and vomiting. Other side effects include constipation, dizziness, fatigue, weakness, sleep disorders, digestive disorders, muscle spasms, problems with male sexual performance, and tremors or twitching. Because of the potential for serious side effects, patients taking MAO inhibitors are usually advised to carry a card or wear a bracelet that alerts medical personnel to their use of a MAO inhibitor in case of emergency.

Scientists actively explore the links between genes and behaviour to determine both the patterns and the limits of genetic influence. Such studies continue to be controversial because behaviour or mental processes can be difficult to measure objectively. Furthermore, many behavioural traits, both normal and abnormal, are complex, influenced by many genes as well as by personal experiences.

Studies of the possible genetic components of psychiatric disorders have yielded mixed results. Geneticists have identified at least two genes linked to schizophrenia, a condition characterized by hallucinations, delusion, paranoia, and other symptoms. Other studies that reported the discovery of genes that influence bipolar disorder (also known as manic-depressive illness) and alcoholism has been reversed or questioned. Though attempts to identify genes linked to these disorders have been flawed, scientists have little doubt that the conditions do have a genetic component.

Like physical disorders, mental illnesses may be treated with drugs, particularly antidepressants. However, while drugs help relieve the patient's symptoms, they seldom cure the underlying problems. More useful therapies include techniques that rely heavily on verbal and emotional communication. Collectively referred to as psychotherapy, these techniques help the patient to express, understand, and cope with underlying problems that are not due to physical disease. Emotionally disturbed children who cannot express their problems verbally may be treated by play therapy. The children are encouraged to engage in certain forms of recreation or to act out scenes on the theory that this process will reveal their feelings. Similar treatment, sometimes called psychodrama, may be used to help adults.

The final stage in treatment of physical and mental illnesses is often rehabilitation. This may include physical therapy, which involves exercise, massage, and the application of heat and water (hydrotherapy) to improve or restore functioning to damaged and weakened parts of the body. People with disabilities also benefit from recreational and occupational therapy, which helps people master their personal and work-related activities, such as buttoning clothes or cooking while seated in a wheelchair. Speech therapy is given to people who have speech problems of physical or psychological origin. In addition, people with disabilities may require psychotherapy to help them overcome the emotional and psychological problems that are sometimes associated with disability.

Cohn (1954) again, described the depressed person as seeing others as objects to be manipulated for the purposes of receiving sympathy and reassurances, but also as seeing them for being critical, rejecting, and ungenuine in their support. Further, in the achievement for reassurance, the depressed person finds concealed disapproval and rejection. According to the Cohn formulation, what the depressed person seeks is a dependent relationship in which all his needs are satisfied, and in his failure to obtain this, he resorts to the degressive this resorts to the depressive techniques of complaining and whining. If this, nonetheless, may lose hope, and enter into the psychotic state, where the patterns of emptiness and need continues in the, absence of specific objects.

Grinker (1964) interpreted the factor patterns obtained in an earlier study of depression (Grinker, 1961) as representing relatively constant patterns of communication. 'What is requested seemingly needed by the depressed patient expressed verbally, by gestures or in behaviour, varies and characterizes the pattern syndrome' (1964?).

Binime (1960, 1966) described how the depressed person can dominate his environment with his demands for emotionally comforting responses from others. He considered depression to be a practice, an active way of relating to people in order to achieve pathological satisfactions, and dismissed any suffering the depressed person may incur as secondary to the satisfaction of manipulative needs.

Aggression played a central role in early psychoanalytic formulations of depression (Abraham, 1911; Freud, 1917), but later writers have increasingly disputed its role. (Bibring, 1953) went on to declare that depression was an ego phenomenon. 'Essentially independent of vicissitudes of aggression as well as oral drives.'

Fromm-Reichmann (1959) argued that aggression had been considerably overstressed as a dynamic factor in depression, and that if hostile feelings were found in the depressed person, they were the result of the frustration of his manipulative and exploitative needs. Cohen (1954) attributed the hostility of the depressed person of his 'annoying impact on others, rather than to a primary motivation to do injury to them'. On the other hand,

Bonime found that hurting or defying of others to be essential to depressed behaviour.

Renewed interest in the relationship between hostility and depression—particularly in the psychoanalytic view that depressed persons turn hostility that had originally been directed at others (hostility-out-outward), against themselves (hostility-inward)—has generated a number of empirical studies. Wessmam (1960) suggested that relatively normal persons became hostile toward when depressed, whereas persons tending to become severely depressed were more likely to internalize or suppressed this hostility. The data of Zuckerman (1967) supported this view, indicating that only in the relatively normal was hostility correlated with depression on mood questionnaires or as rated by interviews. Friedman (1964) found depressives to have more 'readily expressed resentment' as shown by their endorsement of adjectives such as 'bitter', 'frustrated', and 'sulky', yet found no greater overt hostility. In a later study, Friedman (1970) showed that feelings of depression and worthlessness were consonant with hostile and resentful feelings, even though depressed persons were not more likely to directly express these feelings to persons in the environment. Schless (1974) inward and outward, with both types of hostility increasing as depression became more severe. However, because these patients' have also seen other people's anger as more readily expressed and more potent, such that they fear retaliation, and therefore expressed hostility only in the form of resentment. In summary, recent studies have been interpreted so as to call into question classical psychoanalytic formulations of the relationship of depression, hostility-inward and hostility-outward. On the other hand, the view that hostility may serve a defensive function increases in hostility that is directed out, but cannot be expressed directly to appropriate objects in the environment is taken as a failure of this defensive function (Friedman, 1970; McCranie, 1971;' Schless, (1974)).

Most writers who comment on the complaints and self-accusations of the depressed person have rejected the idea that they should be taken literally. Lichtenberg (1957) found that attempts to answer them directly with assurance, granting of dependency, and even punishment all increased depression and feelings of personal defect. Freud (1917) suggested that the self-accusations are actually aimed at someone else, a lost love object, and further notes,' . . . it must strike us that after all the melancholic does not behave in quite the same way as a person who is crushed by remorse and self-reproach in a normal fashion. Feelings of shame in front of other people, which would more than anything characterizes this condition, are lacking in the melancholic, or at least, they are not prominent in him. One might emphasize the presence in him of an almost opposite trait of insistent communicativeness which finds satisfaction in self-exposure.'

In an attempt to modify depressive behaviour in a family situation (Liberman and Raskin, 1971), the baseline data indicated that other family members rejected opportunities to interact with the depressed person, and that all initiations of interaction between him hand his family in the baseline period were undertaken by him.

Paykel and Weissman (1973) reported extensive social dysfunction in women during depressive episodes. Interpersonal friction, inhibited communication, and submissive dependency occurred in both the initial episodes and in subsequent relapses. Onset of social difficulties was related to symptoms, but these difficulties continued months after symptoms remitted, a fact that Paykel and Weissman argue must be taken into account in any treatment plan.

Still, the provocative and often annoying behaviour of the depressive has distracted investigators from consideration of the role of the response of others. An exception, Jacobson (1954) noted that 'however exaggerated the patients' hurt', disappointment and hostile derogation of their partner may be, their complaints are usually more justified than may appear on the surface'. According to her, the depressed person often makes his whole environment feel guilty and depressed, and this provokes defensive aggression and even cruelty precisely when he is most vulnerable. Depressives also have a tendency to develop an 'oral interplay' with those around them, so that mutual demands and expectations are built up to inevitable disappointment and depression for everyone concerned.

Lewinsohn and his associate (Lewinsohn and Shaw, 1969; Lewinsohn, 1969, Libet and Lewinsohn, 1973) have undertaken an ambitious clinical research program focussing on a social interaction of the assistants, from a behavioural point of view. In attempting to develop hypotheses about the reinforcement contingencies available to the depressed person. They have attempted a precise specifications of the social behaviour of the depressed person. Libet and Lewinsohn found depressed persons in group therapy to be lower than controls on a number of measures of social skill: Activity level, interpersonal range, rat e of positive reactions emitted and action latency. Their data are subject to alternative interpretations, however, particularly since they wade of positive reactions emitted was higher correlated with rates of positive reactions elicited. While depressed persons may well be deficient in social skills, some of the observed differences in group interaction situations may be due to the fact that fewer people are willing to interact with depressed persons (which results in a narrower interpersonal range and less opportunity for activity), and in this interaction emitted fewer positive responses (thereby, also reducing the positive responses elicited from the depressed). The most useful behavioural conceptualization of social interaction involving depressed persons would specify the lack of social skills of all participants, as evidenced by their inability to alter the contingencies offered or received. Behavioural interventions in the depressed person's marital and family relationships would therefore involve training all participants in these social skills, and beyond simply altering the contingencies available to the depressed person. Behavioural observations and self-reports of a couple in the Lewinsohn study (Lewisohn and Shaw, 1969) seem to support such a view.

Studies of suicide attempts and their effects on interpersonal relationships also provide data as relevantly, while suicide attempts do not have invariable relationship to depression, there is a definite association. McPartland and Hornstra (1964) examine the effects of suicide attempts on subsequent level of depression. They conceptualized depressive symptomatology as 'a set of demanding action by others to alter messages or restore the social space', and examined the relationships between suicide attempts and the ambiguity of the depressive message and the diffuseness of its intended audience. They were able to reliably place depressed patients at definite points along a dimension of interactive stalemate on the basis of the range of intended audience and the stridency of message in depressive communisations. Patients who were farthest along this continuum, whose communication was most diffuse, nonspecific, strident, and unanswerable, were most likely to have long hospital stays and diagnoses of psychosis. Suicide attempts tended to reduce the level of depression, apparently by shifting the interactive burden onto others. Other studies (Rubenstein, 1958; Moss and Hamilton, 1956; Kublere and Stotland, 1964) have indicated that suicide patients who improve following their attempts on their lives consistently have effected changes in their social fields, and those who improve generally have failed to change the their situation fundamentally.

Depression is viewed, in this context as a response to the disruption of the social space in which the person obtains support and validation for his experience, this view, and a view of depressive symptomatology in terms of message value and intended audience, is similar to that of McPartland and Hornstra (1964), but the present analysis will place a greater emphasis on the contribution of the social environment to depressive drift. The interpersonal process described will be a general one, and it is assumed that the course of a specific depressive episode will be highly dependent on the structure of the person's social space. One of the implications of the approach taken as currently by an understanding of the social context is vital to an understanding of depression, although traditionally it has been largely ignored.

Social stresses leading to depression include loss of significant relationships, but collapses of anticipated relationships, demotion (and in some cases, promotion), retirement, mislead chances, or any of a variety of other changes in a person's social structure. Depressive symptomatology is seen as a set of messages demanding reassurance of the person's place in the interactions he is still able to maintain, and further, action by others to alter or restore his loss.

Initial communications—verbal expressions of helplessness and hopelessness—tend to engage others immediately and to shift the interactive burden to others. The receivers of these messages usually attempt to answer the depressed person's request directly. However, as previously noted by Grinker (1964) and Lichtenberg (1957), their literal responses present him with a dilemma. Much of the depressive's communication is aimed at ascertaining the nature of relationship or context in which the interaction is taking place; Grinker (1964) has compared this to the various 'how' and 'why' questions that young children direct to their parents, and suggested that both children and depressives will be left feeling rejected, ignored, or brushed aside if provided with a literal response.

If communication took place at only one level, depression would probably be a less ubiquitous problem. However, the problem is that human beings not only communicate, but communicate about this communication, qualifying or labelling what they say by (1) the context or relationship in which the communication takes place, (2) other verbal messages (3) uttering linguistic patterns, and (4) bodily movement (Haley, 1963). A person may offer support and reassurance with a rejecting tone or he may offer criticism ion a supportive and reassuring tone. Such that, when messages qualify each other incongruently, then incongruent statements are made about the relationship. If probably always qualified what they said in a congruent way, relationships would be defined clearly and simply even though many levels of communications were functioning. However, when a statement is made which by its existence indicates one type of relationship and qualified by a statement denying this, then difficulties in interpersonal relations become inevitable (Haley, 1963).

It is enough that vocal and linguistic patterns and body movements are ambiguous and subject to alternative interpretations. However, a further problem for the depressed person is that the context, the nature of the relationship between the depressed person and the persons communicating to him, may require time and further messages to be clearly defined.

The depressed person's problem is to decide whether others are assuring him that he is worthy and acceptable because they do in fact maintain this attitude toward him, or rather only because he has attempted to elicit such responses. Unwilling or unable to endure the time necessary to answer this question, the depressive used his symptoms to seek repeated feedback in his testing of the nature of his acceptance and the security of his relationships.

While providing continual feedback, these efforts are at the same time profoundly and negatively affecting these relationships. The persistence and repetition of the symptoms are both incomprehensible and aversive to members of the social environment. However, the accompanying indication of distress and suffering is powerful in its ability to arouse guilt in others and to inhibit and direct expression of annoyance and hostility from them, as observed in both the family difficulties of depressed persons

(Jacobson, 1954) and the problem's therapists report in their effort to relate to depressed parents (Cohen, 1954).

Irritated, yet, inhibited and increasingly guilt-ridden, members of the social environment continue to give verbal assurance of support and acceptance. However, a growing discrepancy between the verbal content and the affective quality of these responses provides validation for the depressive's suspicions that he is not really being accepted and that further interaction cannot be assured. To maintain his increasingly uncertain security, the depressives display more symptoms.

At this point, the first of a number of interactive stalemates may be reached. Members of the depressed person's environment who can find a suitable rationalization for their behaviour may leave the field, or, at least, in efforts to indicate that this is not in fact rejection, but given the context, these efforts do little more than reduce credibility and increase the depressive's insecurity, with those members of the social environment who remain, a self-maintaining pattern to mutual manipulation is established. Perhaps in the environment find that they can reduce the aversive behaviour of the depressed person and alleviate the guilt that this depressed behaviour has an uncanny ability to elicit, if they manipulate him with reassurance, support, and denial of the process that is taking place. The depressed person. On the other hand, finds that by displaying symptoms he can manipulate his environment so that it will provide sympathy and reassurance, but he is aware by now that this response from others is not genuine and that they have become critical and rejecting. While this situation is attractive for neither the depressed person nor members of his social environment, it provides a stabilization of what has been a deteriorating situation.

One alternative facing the depressed person is for him to accept the precipitating disruption of his social space and the resulting loss of support and validation. However, now that he has begun showing symptoms, he has invested portions of his remaining relationship in his recovery effort., That is, he has tested these relationships, made demands, and has been frustrated in ways that seriously call into question his conception of these relationships. If he abandons these efforts, he may have to relinquish the support and validation derived from these relationships while accepting the precipitating loss. At this point, he may be too dependent on the remaining relationships to give them up. Furthermore, as a result if the mixed messages he has been receiving from others, he now has an increasing confused and deteriorated self-concept, which must be clarified, with new desperation more symptoms may be displayed.

Various possible efforts by the depressed person to discover what is wrong with him, i.e., why he is being rejected and manipulated one the less, to reestablish a more normal interactive pattern is in this context indistinguishable from the manipulations has used to control the repressed onset of others. Therefore, they are met with the usual manipulation requesting information as to how people really view him is indistinguishable from symptomatic efforts. If the depressed person attempts to discuss the interpersonal process that is taking place, he touches on a sensitive issue, and is likely only to elicit denial by the others or a angry defensive responses. On the other hand, efforts by others to assure the depressed person that he is really accepted and that they are not rejecting him are in this context indistinguishable from previous manipulations that they have employed, and therefore. Serve to strengthen the developing system. Thus, interpersonal manoeuvres directed at changing the emerging pattern become system-maintaining, and any genuine feedback to the repressed person is also indistinguishable from manipulation. Persons leaving the social field increase both the depressed person's feeling s of rejection and his impetus to continue his behaviour patten. Persons just entering the social field can quickly recruit the existing roles. Since their efforts to deal with the depressive people—even if genuine—is likely to be quite similar to those now being employed manipulatively. They therefore, become subject to the compelling manipulations. That the people, come to the compelling lure of manipulations of the depressed person, come to respond manipulatively themselves, and are inducted into the system.

Descriptions of the depressed person at this point in his career focus on the distortions and misperceptions that serve to maintain his depression. What is generally ignored is that these 'distortions' and 'misperceptions' are congruent with the social system in which the depressed person now finds himself. The specific content of the depressive's complaints and accusations may not be accurate, but his environment is a recognition of the attenuation relationships, disrupted comments are a recognition of the attenuated relationships, disrupted communication and lack of genuineness that he faces. These conditions serve to prevent him from receiving the feedback necessary to correct any misperception or distortion. He has played a major role in the creation of this social system, but the emergency of the system has also required the cooperation of others, and established, it tends to be largely beyond the control of its participants.

Depending on characteristics of both the depressed person and his environment, a number of punishing variations on the above pattern may develop. Members of the social environment who have been repeated provoked and made feel guilty may retaliate by withholding the responses for which the depressed person depends on them. The depressed person may become aware of the inhibiting influence his symptoms have on the direct expression of negative feelings, and may use these symptoms aggressively, while limiting the forms that counteraggression can take. He may also discover and exploit the interdependence of others and the frustrations it entails, he may also become aware of the extent to which others are dependent on him, in that their own maintenance of mood and their ability. Because either of an outright hostility, or as a self-defeating effort to convince others of their need be the renegotiated relationship with him, the depressed person may become sympathetic in his withholding of these minimal cooperative behaviour. While hostility may not necessary be a major etiological factor in depression, the frustration, provocations, and manipulations occurring in interactions between depressed persons and others would seem to encourage it.

As efforts to end the interactive stalemate fail, there may be a shift in the depressive's self-presentation to one indicating greater distress and implying that the environment has more responsibility for bringing about the necessary changes. McPartland and Hornstra (1964) found that they could unambiguously differentiate themes of hopelessness and helplessness from more disturbed themes of low energy and physical complaints in communications of depressed patients. The latter themes were associated with longer hospitalization when hospitalized depressed patients were sampled McPartland and Hornstra give the examples of 'I can't sleep and I can't stand it any longer', 'I am too tired to move', My head and my stomach feel funny all the time'. Unable to restore his life space, the depressive now implicitly demands 'a suspension of the rules; a moratorium on the web of obligation; (McPartlant and Hornstra, 1964). With immediate relationships deteriorating, the depressive addresses his plea to a more general audience, but in more confusing and unanswerable terms, literal responses to his communications may involve medial intervention for his specific complaints, but this generally fails to alleviate the problem. Any efforts to move the interactional theme back to the depressive's sense of hopelessness and helplessness threaten to reopen the earlier unfruitful and even punishing patterns of relations, and tend to be resisted. Unable to answer, or in many cases, even to comprehend the depressive's pleas, members of the social environment may withdraw further from him, increasing his desperation, and quickening the depressive's drift.

With a second interactive stalemate now reached, the depressed person may attempt to resolve it by increasing his level of symptomatology and shifting the theme of his self-presentation to one of the worthlessness and evil, 'I am a failure; it's all my fault; I am sinful and worthless.' Unable, either to restore his social space or to reduce his obligations sufficiently for him to continue to cope, the depressive now communicates his bafflement and resignation. The intended audience is now more diffuse. Relationships are even more attenuated, and the new message is more obscure and perplexing. The social environment and the depressive soon arrive at another stalemate, otherwise helpless to alleviate the situation, remaining members of the environment may further withdraw or, alternatively, have the depressives withdrawn through hospitalization. In the absence on any relatedness to others, the depressive may drift into delusions and frankly psychotic behaviour.

Self-value, then, and objects, are inseparable form as drama of life significance. To lose self-esteem, to lose a 'game', and to lose an object, are inseparable aspects of the loss of meaning. Meaning, is not something that springs up from within man, something born into life that unfolds like a lotus. Meaning is not embedded in some obscure 'inner human nature', not something that is destined to be developed by successively 'highly forms of life'. There is, in short, nothing vitalistic or mysteriously implied in the idea of meaning. Meaning is the elaboration of an increasingly intricate ground plan of broad relationships and ramifications, it is the establishment of dependable cause-and-effect sequences which permit ego-mastery and action. Meaning is at the heart of life because it is inseparable from undependable, satisfying actions. Man embroiders his cause-and-effect action sequences with an intricate symbolism that flags, commandment, lace underwear, and secret-codes. The result is that particular kinds and sequences of action take on a life-and-death flavour. The dependable become the indispensable satisfying becomes the necessary. Man's symbolic life is an imbibing of meaning and a relentless creation of this symbolic elaboration of meaning is the Homo sapient's sapient.

Initially, meaning does not need language. We stress that it exists in behaviour. For energy-converting organisms, action is primary. Forward-momentum is enough to build meaning, and possibilities for forward-momentum exist in nature, in his perception and attention. Instinctive action gives experience which, in turn, provides meaning simply because it commands attention and leads to further action. But for the symbolic animal a complication enters: Language replaces instinctive readiness. Language makes action broader and richer for the symbolic animal. But something curious occurs in this process. Language comes to be learned as a means of acting without anxiety. Each of the infant's acts comes to be dressed in words that are provided by his loved objects. As a child, lacking a word, he lacks a safe action. Action and word-prescriptions become inseparable, because they join in permitting anxiety-free conduct. Growing into adulthood, the individual has built his habits into a self-consistent scheme. To lack word is then to lack a meaningful action; the simplest act has to take on meaning, has to point to something beyond itself, exist in a wider referential context. We become paralysed to act unless there is a verbal prescription for the new situation. Even our perceptions come to be built inti a rigid framework. Men lose progressively the capacity to 'act in nature' as he verbally creates his own action world. Words give man the motivation to act, and words justify the act. Life-meaning for man comes to be predominantly an edifice of words and word-sounds.

If the individual can keep verbal referents going in a self-consistent scheme, action remains possible and life retains its meaning. If he cannot, if the integrity of the symbolic meaning-framework is undermined, external action grinds to a halt.

The meanings of words can also change. In Middle English, the word 'nice' usually had the meaning 'foolish' and sometimes 'shy,' but never the modern meaning 'pleasant.' Changes in the meanings of words are known as semantic change and can be viewed as part of the more general phenomenon of lexical change, with language vocabularies words not only can change their meaning but also can become obsolete. For example, modern readers require a note to explain Shakespeare's word 'hent' (take hold of), which is no longer in use. In addition, new words can be created, such as feedback.

Symptoms of depression can vary by age. In younger children, depression may include physical complaints, such as stomachaches and headaches, as well as irritability, "moping around," social withdrawal, and changes in eating habits. They may feel unenthusiastic about school and other activities. In adolescents, common symptoms include sad mood, sleep disturbances, and lack of energy. Elderly people with depression usually complain of physical rather than emotional problems, which sometimes leads doctors to misdiagnose the illness.

Symptoms of depression can also vary by culture. In some cultures, depressed people may not experience sadness or guilt but may complain of physical problems. In Mediterranean cultures, for example, depressed people may complain of headaches or nerves. In Asian cultures they may complain of weakness, fatigue, or imbalance.

If left untreated, an episode of major depression typically lasts eight or nine months. About 85 percent of people who experience one bout of depression will experience future episodes.

Depression usually alters a person's appetite, sometimes increasing it, but usually reducing it. Sleep habits change as well, as people with depression may oversleep or, more commonly, sleep for fewer hours. A depressed person might go to sleep at midnight, sleep restlessly, then wake up at 5:00 a.m. feeling tired and blue. For many depressed people, early morning is the saddest time of the day.

Depression also changes one's energy level. Some depressed people may be restless and agitated, engaging in fidgety movements and pacing. Others may feel sluggish and inactive, experiencing great fatigue, lack of energy, and a feeling of being worn out or carrying a heavy burden. Depressed people may also have difficulty thinking, poor concentration, and problems with memory.

People with depression often experience feelings of worthlessness, helplessness, guilt, and self-blame. They may interpret a minor failing on their part as a sign of incompetence or interpret minor criticism as condemnation. Some depressed people complain of being spiritually or morally dead. The mirror seems to reflect someone ugly and repulsive. Even a competent and decent person may feel deficient, cruel, stupid, phony, or guilty of having deceived others. People with major depression may experience such extreme emotional pain that they consider or attempt suicide. At least 15 percent of seriously depressed people commit suicide, and many more attempt it.

In some cases, people with depression may experience psychotic symptoms, such as delusions (false beliefs) and hallucinations (false sensory perceptions). Psychotic symptoms indicate an especially severe illness. Compared to other depressed people, those with psychotic symptoms have longer hospital stays, and after leaving, they are more likely to be moody and unhappy. They are also more likely to commit suicide.

Some depressions seem to come out of the blue, even when things are going well. Others seem to have an obvious cause: a marital conflict, financial difficulty, or some personal failure. Yet many people with these problems do not become deeply depressed. Most psychologists believe depression results from an interaction between stressful life events and a person's biological and psychological vulnerabilities.

Genes may influence depression by causing abnormal activity in the brain. Studies have shown that certain brain chemicals called neurotransmitters play an important role in regulating moods and emotions. Neurotransmitters involved in depression include norepinephrine, dopamine, and serotonin. Research in the 1960s suggested that depression results from lower than normal levels of these neurotransmitters in parts of the brain. Support for this theory came from the effects of antidepressant drugs, which work by increasing the levels of neurotransmitters involved in depression. However, later studies have discredited this simple explanation and have suggested a more complex relationship between neurotransmitter levels and depression.

An imbalance of hormones may also play a role in depression. Many depressed people have higher than normal levels of hydrocortisone (cortisol), a hormone secreted by the adrenal gland in response to stress. In addition, an underactive or overactive thyroid gland can lead to depression.

A variety of medical conditions can cause depression. These include dietary deficiencies in vitamin B6, vitamin B12, and folic acid; degenerative neurological disorders, such as Alzheimer's disease and Huntington's disease; strokes in the frontal part of the brain; and certain viral infections, such as hepatitis and mononucleosis. Certain medications, such as steroids, may also cause depression.

Psychological theories of depression focus on the way people think and behave. In a 1917 essay, Austrian psychoanalyst Sigmund Freud explained melancholia, or major depression, as a response to loss—either real loss, such as the death of a spouse, or symbolic loss, such as the failure to achieve an important goal. Freud believed that a person's unconscious anger over loss weakens the ego, resulting in self-hate and self-destructive behaviour.

Cognitive theories of depression emphasize the role of irrational thought processes. American psychiatrist Aaron Beck proposed that depressed people tend to view themselves, their environment, and the future in a negative light because of errors in thinking. These errors include focussing on the negative aspects of any situation, misinterpreting facts in negative ways, and blaming themselves for any misfortune. In Beck's view, people learn these self-defeating ways of looking at the world during early childhood. This negative thinking makes situations seem much worse than they really are and increases the risk of depression, especially in stressful situations.

In support of this cognitive view, people with "depressive" personality traits appear to be more vulnerable than others to actual depression. Examples of depressive personality traits include gloominess, pessimism, introversion, self-criticism, excessive skepticism and criticism of others, deep feelings of inadequacy, and excessive brooding and worrying. In addition, people who regularly behave in dependent, hostile, and impulsive ways appear at greater risk for depression.

Mood disorders, also called affective disorders, create disturbances in a person's emotional life. Depression, mania, and bipolar disorder are examples of mood disorders. Symptoms of depression may include feelings of sadness, hopelessness, and worthlessness, as well as complaints of physical pain and changes in appetite, sleep patterns, and energy level. In mania, on the other hand, an individual experiences an abnormally elevated mood, often marked by exaggerated self-importance, irritability, agitation, and a decreased need for sleep. In bipolar disorder, also called manic-depressive illness, a person's mood alternates between extremes of mania and depression.

Some people with schizophrenia experience delusions of persecution—false beliefs that other people are plotting against them. This interview between a patient with schizophrenia and his therapist illustrates the paranoia that can affect people with this illness.

People with schizophrenia and other psychotic disorders lose contact with reality. Symptoms may include delusions and hallucinations, disorganized thinking and speech, bizarre behaviour, a diminished range of emotional responsiveness, and social withdrawal. In addition, people who suffer from these illnesses experience and inability to function in one or more important areas of life, such as social relations, work, or school.

Several other psychiatric disorders are closely related to schizophrenia. In schizoaffective disorder, a person shows symptoms of schizophrenia combined with either mania or severe depression. Schizophreniform disorder refers to an illness in which a person experiences schizophrenic symptoms for more than one month but fewer than six months. In schizotypal personality disorder, a person engages in odd thinking, speech, and behaviour, but usually does not lose contact with reality. Sometimes mental health professionals refer to these disorders together as schizophrenia-spectrum disorders.

Schizophrenia sums up man's coming of age in society. In order to understand it we have had to trace a lengthy picture of the process of becoming human. Depression is much more simple, unlike the schizophrenic, the person has not failed to learn secure answers to a combinality of common problems. His dilemma, in anything, is some what of a paradox: He has learned these answers only too well. He has built himself so firmly into his cultural world that he is imprisoned in his own narrow behavioural mold.

For the most part, this model represents the advanced theoretical cogitations of the psychiatric profession of a perplexing human phenomenon. This much must be said: It is not easy to comprehend why anyone would opt out of life. It is understandable that he would be quick to look for some basic genetic taint, some stunted early development, that would mark such an individual off from others. But the matter is not quite so simple. The fact is that a good proportion of depressed patients have led mature and responsible lives, and some have achieved notable success, financial and personal. We distort our vision if we use of such a punctuated theory to explain why these people become abysmally depressed.

Depression may be seen as a reflection of deficiencies in one or more of such self-control processes. Self-monitoring involves attending to one's own behaviour as self-evaluation is a matter of interpreting one's behaviour and comparing it to internal standards, as self-reinforcement involves administering reinforcement to oneself. These self-control processes may selectively tend to negative aspects of their own behaviour and ignore positive accomplishments. And may involve an attriutional bias so that they are excessively blamed for failures and take insufficient credit for successes. They may employ overly harsh or stringent standards in evaluating themselves. Finally, they may be in rewarding themselves or overly self-punishing.

Self-control has recently become an important focus of behaviour research (Goldfried and Merbaum, 1973; Mahoney and Thoresen, 1974; Thoresen and Mahoney, 1974). Models of self-control have been used to analyse various forms of normal and deviant behaviour and have generates self-administered behaviour change programs applicable to various target behaviours. With slight modifications Kanfer (1970, 1971; Kanfer and Karoly, 1972). Kanger sees self-control as those processes by which an individual alters the probability of a response in the relative absence of immediate external supports. Three processes are postulated in a feedback loop model: Self-monitoring, self-evaluation, and self-reinforcement.

Self-monitoring involves observations of one's own behaviour along with its situational antecedents and its consequences. For instance, in self-control therapy procedures, smokers may note the places in which they smoke, socially anxious males may record the number of contacts they have with females, and overweight person may count calorie. Internal events in the form of proprioceptive, sensory, and affective responses may also be self-monitored. For example, smoker's might be asked to rate their anxiety level at the time of smoking caseation to cigarette. Self-monitoring involve s not only a passive perception awareness of events but a selective attention to certain classes of events and the ability to make accurate discriminations. Deficits in self-control may therefore exist in the manner in which individuals customarily self-monitor. Specific deficits in sel-monitoring behaviour represent on potential of maladaptive self-control.

Self-evaluation refers to a comparison between an estimate of performance, which derives from delf-monitoring, and an internal criterion of standard. For example, the dieter compares the day's calorie count to a goal and judges whether or not the criterion has been met. Standards may be derived from a variety of sources (cf, Kanfer, 1970; Bandura, 1971). Individuals may set their internal criteria by adopting externally imposed standards, e.g., not just an A but 100 per cent correct on every test. Criteria may or may or may not be realistic and, thus, inappropriately selected internal criteria may represent another specific type of deficit in self-control behaviour.

Self-attribution and self-evaluation attriutional processes play a role in self-evaluation and can be incorporated into Kanfer's model. Bandura (1971) notes that in self-evaluation research, judgement that a response is accurate or successful is often confounded with judgement that the response is commendable. In fact, these judgements are not always equivalent. Adults might perceive themselves as accurate and successful on a child's task and not evaluate their performance as commendable in any way. Similarly, people might perceive themselves as inaccurate and failing on a task outside their own area of expertise and not condemn themselves for it. Bandura suggests selecting tasks which minimize these confounding effects, but there are further implications of the problem.

The larger issue is that the positive or negative self-evaluation implies more than a comparison of performance to criteria of success or failure. Such comparisons are modified by the manner in which people perceive themselves as capable and responsible for the behaviour. That is, the cause of the behaviour must be internally attributed. In that Kanfer (1970, 1971) refers to self-control as occurring in the relative absence of external control, efforts to control one's behaviour are premised on, at least, the perception of mental control.

Thus, self-evaluations should be considered to be the comparison of internally attributed performances to a standard or criterion. Performance is commendable only if it visible attributed internally and judged to exceed a criterion of success. Performance is condemnable only of it is both attributed internally and judged to fall below a criterion for failure. Degree of internal attribution interacts with perceived success or failure to determine the value of self-evaluation. Weiner, Heckhausen, Meyer, and Cook (1972) demonstrated this relationship a Correlational study of the tendency to make internal attribution and magnitude of self-reward and self-punishing in normal subjects. Because individual differences in making internal attributions exist, self-attributional deficits are another potential type of maladaptive self-control behaviour.

A basic assumption in behavioural conception of self-control, is that individuals control their own behaviour by the same means that one organism might control a second organism and that the same principles apply. Thus, the administration of covert or covert contingent reward to punishment to oneself is postulated as a mechanism of self-control. The self-control model suggests that self-reinforcement supplements external reinforcement in controlling behaviour. As Bandura (1976) has argued, self-reinforcement must be conceptualized in a context of external reinforcement, that is, while behaviour must generally be seen as directed by and toward gaining external reinforcement, self-reinforcement (overt or covert) functions to maintain consistency and bridge delay when external reinforcers are delayed and immediate reinforcement for alternative behaviour is available.

Self-reinforcement has been a major focus of self-control research and many clinical uses of self-administered reward and punishment programs have been described (Thoresen and Mahoney, 1974). Rates of self-reward and self-punishment yield relatively stable individual differences (Kanfer, Duerfeldt, LePage, 1969; Marston, 1969) and do not necessarily correlate with one another (Kanfer, 1969). Self-control may be maladaptive in terms of either self-reward or self punishment patterns.

The model of self-control which can serve as a heuristic models for studying depression in regard to its symptoms, etiology and therapy. Specific deficits at different stages of self-control may be seen as the basis for specific manifestations of depression.

There are, at least, two ways in which the self-monitoring of depressed persons can be characterized. First, depressed persons tend to attend selectively to negative events, and second, depressed persons tend to attend selectively to immediate versus delayed outcomes of their behaviour. The term 'negative event' is intended to include stimuli which are aversive and other stimuli which are perceived as cues for aversive stimuli. The term has a converse correspondence to Lewinsohn's (1974) 'pleasant event'. From complex experience including both positive and negative events, depressed persons selectively attend to negative (unpleasant) events as the exclusion of positive (pleasurable) events. Ferster (1973) had argued that depressed persons devote disproportionate time to avoidance of or escape from adversive events. This behaviour precludes positive reinforced behaviour. Beck (1972) includes in his discussion of cognitive distortions, but the concepts of 'selective abstraction' and 'arbitrary inference', both of which describe similar processes of attention to negative events. Selective abstraction involves focussing on a detail taken out of a more salient context and using it as a basis for conceptualization for the entire experience. In depression, the detail attended to is usually a negative event embedded in an array of more positive or negative events. Arbitrary inference involves a personal interpretation of an ambiguous or personally irrelevant event. In depression, a negative quality of the event is selectively attended to. An inappropriate attribution may also be involved.

Although no research has been aimed at this specific formulation as yet, there are studies which are interpretable in these terms. The negative perceptions which occur in response to projective stimuli, e.g., Weintraub, Segal, and Beck, 1974) could easily be seen as due to selective attention. Wener and Rehm (1974) found that depressed persons underestimated the percentage of positive feedback they received. A relative inattention to these positive events could be inferred.

Selective attention to immediate versus delayed outcomes is related to Lewinsohn's (1974) concept that depressed behaviour functions to elicit immediate reinforcement from the social environment at the expense of the more important forms of delayed reinforcement. Also related is Lazarus (1968, 1974) suggestions that depressed persons lose their future perspective. They may be seen as attending to immediate outcomes instead.

Correlational evidence consistent with this deficit was obtained by Rehm and Plakosh (1975) who found a greater expressed preference for immediate as opposed to delayed rewards among depressed as compared to nondepressed undergraduates and by Wener and Rehm (1975) who found that depressed persons were influenced to a greater extent by both high and low rates of immediate reinforcements.

The self-control of depressed persons can be characterized as maladaptive in two ways within the self-evaluation phase. First, depressed persons frequently fail to make accurate internal attributions of causality. Second, depressed persons tend to set stringent criteria for self-evaluation.

From an attrbutional point of view, a depressed person an be 'helpless' in either of two ways. In the first, the person make excessive external attributions of causality and thus generally believes that there is a high degree of independence between performance and consequences. Such a person as helpless in Seligman's sense of the word and would seldom engage in self-control behaviour even in an aversive environment. Such a person would be passive and apathetic but would not necessarily be self-derogating. Since aversive consequences are seen as uncontrollable, performance is neither commendable nor condemnable. In the second form of helplessness, the person makes accurate or even excessively internal attributions of causality but perceive himself or herself to be lacking in ability to obtain positive consequences. Thus, the person believes that the world does contain lawful performance-consequence relationships but that she or he is incompetent and ineffective. This person would be self-derogatory and would express inappropriate guilt, e.g., excessive internal attribution of causality for past aversive consequences. The use of the term of 'helplessness' for this latter instance, that is somewhat different from Seligman's use of the term.

The work on learned helplessness in depression can be interpreted as support for either type of inaccurate attribution. For example, Miller and Seligman (1973) found that following success on a skill-defined task, depressed students did not raise their expectations of success as the nondepressed students did. No differences in expectancy change were found after failure of in chance defined tasks. As it is to interpret, that this finding in terms of a generalized perception by depressed persons that reinforcement is response independent. From an attributional framework subjects either perceived the task outcome to have been due to external causes, i.e., chance, not skill, or perceived sustaining their success, i.e., lacking skill. The data admit equally to either interpretation.

Stringent self-evaluative criteria as a characteristic of depression has been previously suggested by Marston (1965) and Bandura (1971). Self-evaluative standards may be stringent in the sense of a high threshold requiring great quantitative or quantitative excellence for self-approval. Golin and Terrel found that depressed college students tend to set higher goal levels for themselves. This deficits together with selective monitoring of negative events result in very few perceived successes. Depressed persons may also have low thresholds for negative self-evaluation. Although these criteria may be relatively independent, clinical observation, (e.g., Beck, 1972) suggests that for some depressed persons they may be almost reciprocals, depressed persons may have 'all or none' self-evaluative criteria, i.e., an effort is either a smashing success or a dismal failure.

Self-evaluative criteria may also be stringent in the sense of excessive dread, or failure, such as for one instance is taken as failure in the entire class of behaviour? For example, failure on one exam is taken as evidence for failure as a student and, perhaps, as a person. Beck (1972) describes overgeneralization as one of the primary mechanisms of cognitive distortion in depression.

The self-reinforcement phase of self-control is particularly importance in accounting for depressive behaviour. Depression can be characterized by the self-administration of relatively low rates of self-reward and of which rates of self-punishment. Low rates of self-reward can be associated with the slowed rates of overt behaviour which typify depression. Lower general activity level, few responses' initiations, lower latencies, and less persistence may be interpreted as resulting from low rates of self-reward.

Self-punishment in normals serves to control behaviour reward, e.g., 'kicking oneself' for going off a diet. Self-punishment may also serve as a cue initiating alternative behaviour for approaching a goal (Kanfer and Karolly, 1972), Because and set stringent self-evaluation criteria, potentially effective behaviour may also be supposed by excessive self-punishing. Vacillation between responding strategies may also result because each alternative is self-punished early in the response chain, e.g., indecisiveness.

Correlational evidence for self-reinforcement deficits in depression was obtained by Rozensky, Rehm, Pry and Roth. Their study demonstrated differences in rates of self-reward and self-punishment between depressed and nondepressed hospital patients. Nevertheless, the former did not differ in correct responses, so that a replicated procedure with college students varying in degrees of depression. Depressed students gave themselves more self-punishment and less self-reward than n nondepressed students although only the former difference obtained statistical significance. The failure to replicate the self-reward finding maybe due to the fact that the latter population was by definition a relatively active group of normals capable of working for long term rewards.

Depression can be accounted for in terms of six deficits in self-control behaviour: (1), selective monitoring of negative events; (2) selective monitoring of immediate as opposed to delayed consequences; (3) stringent self-evaluation criteria; (4) inaccurate attributions of responsibility(5) insignificant self-reward;' and (6) expressive self-punishment.

The self-control model as applied to depression serves as a framework for analysis and integration and provides a framework for distinguishing various depression symptoms, each of which can be logically associated with a particular aspect of self-control. The model encompasses and integrates a range of behaviours on which available models focus exclusively. The model also suggests interrelationships among these behaviours, which have an empirical basis in self-control research, e.g., Kirshenbaum, cited in Kanfer and Weiner, 1972). The model specifies relationships between covert, cognitive behaviour and overt-motor behaviour in depression,

As a heuristic framework, some parts of the model are only suggested in outline and require further refinement and validation. Although the model is consistent with certain empirical findings, the evidence is largely Correlational and further research is clearly needed. The products of research specifically directed by the model will determine its ultimate value.

The self-control model is applied as in semblance to a particular form of psychopathology, namely depression. The deficits postulated may not be exclusive to depression. For instance, Clark and Arkowitz (1975) found stringent self-evaluation criteria among socially anxious college students who rated their own behaviour in an interaction with a confederate. On the other hand, self-control deficits of other kinds may be more characteristic of other forms of psychopathology. Sociopaths may show some of the deficits of depression in reverse: Lenient self-evaluative criteria, excessive self-reward, and insufficient self-punishment. The self-control model may have wider applicability as a model of psychopathology.

Finally, the model may have some limitations as to causes and types of depression. Recent evidence in genetic and biochemical research on depression strongly points to a biological components in some forms of depression. Biological factors and self-control deficits may represent separate sources of variance in accounting for the occurrence of depression or they may interact. Akiskal and McKinney (1973, 1975) have argued for a broad interaction model. In any case, the relative contribution of biological and psychological factors to the etiology, symptomatology, and therapy of depression is an extremely complex set of questions, the answers to which will depend upon a great deal of additional basic research on the separate factors. It is hoped that the self-control model may direct inquiries toward these final solutions.

Developments in the interactional description of schizophrenia have not been parallelled in the area of depression. As yet, concepts such as pseudomutuality, double-bind, schism, and skew have found no counterpart. Kubler and Stotland (1964) have argued, 'emotional disturbance, even the most severe, cannot be understood unless the field in which it develops and exists in examined. The manifestations of the difficulty in the disturbed individual have meaning depending on aspects of the field. The significant aspects of the field are usually interpersonal'. Yet the studies of depression are focussed on the individual and his behaviour out of his interactional context. To a large degree, the depressed person's monotonously reiterated complaints and self-accusations, and his provocative and often annoying behaviour has distracted investigations from consideration of his environment and the role it may play in the maintenance of his behaviour. The possibility that the characteristic pattern of depressed behaviour might be interwoven and concatenated with a corresponding pattern in the response of others has seldom been explored. For the most part, it has been assumed that the depressed person is relatively impervious to the influence of others. Ruesch (1962) stated that to talk to the depressed person makes little sense, if only to listen and listen a little more. Grinker (1964) conceptualized depressive symptomatology as communication to others, but argued that the depressed person is not responsive to commination from others. The depressed person . . . cannot use information for the purpose of action; he cannot perceive the cues of reality' he makes statements but does not care if he is understood'.

It is, nevertheless, in classifying depressed patients into bipolar and unipolar subtypes were proposed in 1962 by Leonhard et al., based on the clinical differentiation of depressed patients with and without mania. In that, family history studies noted that patients with bipolar illness had more psychosis a nd suicide among their relatives than patients with unipolar illness. Since 1962, several studies in Europe and the United Stares have refined and extended this original observation. What is more important, a model for investigation in psychiatry has been developed to the point that genetic data are important for validating clinical diagnosis in psychiatry, particularly among the affective disorders?

The data supporting evidence for genetic factors in the etiological affective disorders, account for the development of methodology for genetic studies, and the resalting classification systems are to suggest that some forms of depression may have an etiology on a genetic bases. In order for a genetic etiology to be proven, several factors should be evident. First of all, the disorder should cluster within families, patients with the illness should have relatives who also demonstrate the illness. Second, studies of twins should show that the illness is more prevalent among monozygotic than dizygotic twins. And the third line of evidence would come from adoption studies. Adoption studies are assigned to differentiate environmental from genetic factors. Data from such studies should oppose by arguing against those that have a biological parent with illness, but who were raised in a foster home developing the illness nevertheless, subjects with biological parents do not have the illness but who were raised in a home where there is affective disorder. Fourth, the illness could be shown to be linked to a gene of known Mendelians transmission.

Affective disorders, particularly manic-depressive illness, are familial. The evidence that bipolar illness clusters in families was reported by Leonhard et al. Perris and Angust both suggested that effectively ill relatives of bipolar patients tended to have bipolar and not unipolar disorders, whereas effectively ill relatives of unipolar patients tended to have unipolar illness and not bipolar illness. In the 1960s the Washington University group published a series of familial studies in manic-degressive illness, particularly bipolar disorders. These studies showed a high familial risk for affective disorder in relatives of manic patients. Second, a very comprehensive family study of affective disorder suggested that manic-depressive illness may be linked to a gene transmitted on the X-chromosome, subsequent studies in the later 1960s from the National Institute of Mental Health (NIMH) also showed a differential familial loading for relatives of patients with bipolar compared with unipolar disorder. Relatives of bipolar patients had elevated morbid risks for bipolar illness, unipolar illness, and suicide, compared to relatives with dipolar patients.

Few twin studies of affective disorder appear in the literature of the last 10 years or so. Kallmann's study is still considered the definitive work, showing very high concordance rates for bipolar illness in monozygotic compared to dizygotic twins,

The adoption technique, utilized in the Danish studies of schizophrenia, has been tried in studies of bipolar illness. Data from adoptees in Iowa indicated that primary affective illness may have a familial factor. Another study of adoptees from manic-depressives also supports the concept of a genetic factor in the etiology of affective disorders.

In the search for genetic linkage of affective disorders, the studies of Winokur had pointed toward a genetic factor on the X-chromosome. Attempts to extend and replicate these findings have resulted in considerable controversy. Mendlewicz and coworkers showed linkage of bipolar affective disorder with two markers on the X-chromosa colour blindedness, and XG blood type, Gershon was unable to replicate these findings and subsequently criticized the data from the Mendlewicz studies on methodological grounds.

In summary, the separation of bipolar affective disorder as a distinct subtype has resulted in a clearer definition of the genetic factors that may be involved in the etiology of affective disorders, most studies attempting to assess genetic factors ineffective illnesses that have separately considered bipolar patients have resulted in positive results. Methecrelatives of bipolar patients show a higher genetic loading and particularly more bipolar illness than relatives of other effectively ill patients. Clearly, unipolar illness as presently defined is a much more heterogeneous collection of disorders than bipolar disorder. Attempts to find subtypes of unipolar disorder using a benefic classification have not been particularly successful. However, Winokur`s group separated unipolar patient into women with an early age c of onset (depressive spectrum disease) whose relatives showed depression and alcoholism, and depressed men with a late age of onset (pure depressive disease) whose relatives showed depression only.

It is apparent that family and genetic support both the search for biological explanation of MDI—has been to define biological characteristics of MDI patients that are diagnostically use, which can help to optimize treatment, and which might even point the way toward the recent family subdues that indicate these rate of mood disorder among first-degree relatives of even the causes of these idiopathic condition, such biological characteristics of MDI (a concept that services as a genetic term for severe mood disorders.)—patients and defined as 'state-pendent'. Thus, while such state-dependent biological alterations can be most useful for diagnosis and for guiding therapy, from a therapeutic perspective they may merely be concomitant variations or secondary changes within the MDI syndrome. Nonetheless, these morbid risk rates for bipolar disorders—that the designing designate for being unipolar—. Often, but not always, that other psychiatric or medical illnesses are did not present to the therapies high incidence of similar disorders. Among close family members, these characteristics have supported the use of terms as, endogenoius, ebdogenomorphic, vital, psychotic or melancholic depressions, as for this subgroup of severe idiopathic illnesses that is most likely to respond favourably to modern medical treatments.

In addition, a concept that has arisen from a research needs to define relatively homogeneous groups of depressed patients with 'primary' depression. That is, mood disorders without additional complicating medical or other psychiatric disorders. Clinically, the value of this concept (except as a reminder to consider fresh cases of mood disorders with a medical differential diagnosis approach) is somewhat limited since some cases of 'secondary' depression have striking endogenomorphic or vital characteristics and respond well to antidepressants.

However, it may help orientation to reiterate that a major thrust of psychiatric researching severe mood disorders over the past 30 years has been to define biological characteristics of mood disorders as patients that are diagnostically useful, which the pathophysiology or even the causes of these idiopathic conditions. While there has been considerable progress in understanding some characteristics that can help to propagate the possibility for treatment, and search for primary causes, for which previously had been unsuccessful. Yet, just about all of the biological characteristics of such mood disorders as they disappear with healing discoveries, however, not for something as a stable biological trait or markers of a possible heritable defect. Thus, while such state-dependent biological alternations can be most useful for diagnosis and for guiding therapy, from a theoretical perspective they may merely be concomitant variations or secondary changes with the MDI syndrome.

The depressed patient is specially prone to quality prior positive experiences and to personalized experiences of failure. Is that, they often interpret as indications of his or her blameworthiness? For example, a patient was not pleased when a short story she had written was accepted for publication because she attributed the acceptance to sheer luck. However, she regarded a rejected article as proof of her incompetence and felt distraught. As similar phenomenon was reported by Stuart, who found that depressive tendencies correlate with evaluative rather than classificatory associations, i.e., associating the word 'apple' with 'sweet' (evaluation) rather than 'fruit' (classification). Empirical work has documented the fact that depressed subjects personalize failure, they ascribe in an experimental task to lack of ability, while they do not attribute success to internal factors. The depressed patient's characteristic stereotypical conclusions and assessments reflect a combination of negative cognitive themes and certain systematic errors of thinking. A characteristic error in degressive e thinking is drawing conclusion in the absence of or contrary to evidence. This process of arbitrary inference is illustrated by the following cognition, 'John did call tonight . . . John probably doesn't want to see me any more'. When depression passes they are comforted with a negative event or they typically magnify the importance, however, the implications of a pleasant event or positive attribution are minimized, for instance, a patient evaluated a slight increase in her dysphoria, is to mean that she was 'deteriorating', while she drew attestation to a well-performed task as was quite insignificant. In clinical work we typically find the patient selectively abstracts isolated elements of a situation that is most consistent with his or her negative and pessimistic world view and ignores other salient cues. A depressed patient decided that, for example, her boss's failure to say hello was ominous; she completely ignored the fact that he was under considerable pressure and preoccupied. As Beck and Shaw have noted, the depressed patient's invariant method of information processing results in over generalization and the ignoring of fine discriminations. Hammen, Krantz, Weintraub and colleagues had ociates and Beck has reported empirical data that document the presence and preponderance of erroneous cognitive processes in depressed college students and depressed patients. The depressive tendency to magnify negative experiences is reflected in depressed subjects' hypersensitivity to experimentally manipulated failure, compared with the reactions of nondepressed subjects. Loeb and associative colleagues and Hammen and Krantz have documented the fact that such manipulations lead to increase dysphoria and pessimism, decreased levels of aspiration, and fewer positive predictions of one's performance on subsequent tasks. However, developments in the interactional description of schizophrenia have been parallelled in the area of depression. As yet, concept such as pseudomutality, double-bind, schism and skew have found no counterparts. Kubler and Stotland (1964) have argued, that 'emotionable' sensitivity and detached emotive sensibilities are served though disturbance, even the most severe, cannot be understood unless the field in which it develops and exists is examined. The manifestations of the difficultly in the disturbed individuals have meaning depending on aspects of the field. The significant aspect of the field usually interpersonal', yet the study of depression has focussed on the individual and his behaviour out of his interactional context. To a large degree, the depressed person's monotonously reiterate complaints and self-accusations, and his provocative and often annoying behaviour has distracted investigators from considerations of his environment and the role it may play in the maintenance of his behaviour. The possibility that the characteristic pattern of depressed behaviour might be interwoven and concatenated with a corresponding pattern in the response of others has seldom been explored.

Grinker (1964) conceptualized symptomalogy as communication to others, but argued that the depressed person is not responsive to communication from others: The depressed person . . . cannot use information for the purpose of action, he cannot perceive the cues of reality, he makes statements but does not care if he is understood. In terms of system theory (von Bertalanffy, 1950; Allport, 1960 and Miller, 1971), the usual conceptualization of the depressed person is one of a closed system. Grinker (1964)was explicit in stating that the depressed person repeats his messages and behaviour without reception or acceptance of resulting feedback. Beck (1964) described the cognitive distortions that dominate the information processing of the depressed person so that experiences are rigidly interpreted to maintain existing schema of personal deficiency, self-blame and negative expectations. The implicit assumption of these and other writers has been that the support and information available to the depressed person are incongruent with his depression, and the persistence of his symptomatology is evidence of a failure to receive or accept this information. Withdrawal of depressive schema and affective-structures, produce a downward depressive spiral. Such that an alternative argument that the depressed person is lost and depressive information elicited. However, this in turn increases the level of depression and strengthens the pathogenic pattern of depressed behaviour and response of others. If a depressive spiral develops, it is mutually causative, deviation-amplifying process (Maruyama, 1963) in the interaction of the depressed person with his environment. Thus, what is customarily viewed as some internal process is, that such of what is customarily viewed as cognitive distortion or misperception is characteristic of information flow from the environment. It should be noted that while the depressed person's different interpretation of his predication is traditionally attributed to his distortion or misperception, generally disorders of thought and perceptions are defining neither criteria nor common among depressed patients (McPartland and Hornstra, 1964). An observer who fails to take into account the intricacy of someone's relationship to his environment frequently attributes to him characteristics that he does not posses, or leaves significant aspects of his experience is unexplained (Watzlawick, 1967). Feedback introduces phenomena that cannot be adequately explained by reference to the isolated individual alone (Ashby, 1960, 1962). For the study of depression, identification of a pattern of depressive feedback from the environment demands a more complex conceptualization of the disorder than one explaining its phenomena with reference to the isolated depressed person. Lemert (1962), in his study of the interpersonal dynamics of paranoia, argued that the net effect of the developing interaction pattern between the paranoid person and others is that (1) The flow of information to the person is stopped, (2) A real discrepancy between expressed ideas and affect among those with whom he interacts is created, and (3) The situation or group image becomes as ambiguous for him as he is for others. In this context of attenuated relationships, exclusion, and disrupted communication, the paranoid person cannot get the feedback on his behaviour that is essential in order for him to correct his interpretations, and at, least be delusional, but that it is also true that in a very real sense he is able to elicit covertly organized action and conspiratorial behaviour. The concurrent manners of the interpersonal dynamics of depression, that includes the interaction and information flow pattern congruent with the established phenomena of depression, and at the same time, indications as to why this than alternative patterns. Persist in the apparent absence of external; constants. Existing descriptions of the interpersonal behaviour of the depressed person will be examined as the attempt to make to reconstruct the interactional context in which this behaviour has meaning. It should be made clear that such perspective does not deny the existence of important intrapersonal factors in depression, as Chodoff, (1972) and McCranie (1971) has argued that there is a 'depressive-core' in the personality of the depression-prone person, consisting of a tendency to feel worthless and helpless and an over-sensitivity to stimuli that impinge on or upon these feelings. Together, these are aroused from dormancy by specific situations such as loss of self-esteem. However, the emphasis of this is shown to be on means by which the environment comes into congruence with these feelings. The depressive's vague, generalized feeling that there is something wrong with him, and his search for this among his minor defects, imperfections, and personal attributes, may arise from a depressive core to his personality, but at the same timer, the confusing response from the environment serves to validate these feelings. Likewise, conflicts about the reception of support and approval from others may be deeply rooted in the depressive's intrapersonal style, but these conflicts can only be aggravated by the mixed messages of approval and rejection received from significant others, and by their withdrawal from him despite reassurances to the contrary. Furthermore, the present exposition does not deny the importance of possible biochemical or genetic factors in the etiology of depression. Price (1974) has argued that even in disorders in which the importance of such factors has been clearly established, there may be a large number of links in the causal chain between specific etiological factors and the symptoms displayed by an individual. Social and interpersonal variables may determine to a large degree whether a disorder occurs and the form its symptoms will take. It is assumed that to initiate the process as a person need only begin to display depressive behaviour. Renewed interest in the relationship between hostility and depression—particularly in the psychoanalytic view that depressed persons turn hostility that had originally been directed at others (hostility-out-ward), against themselves (hostility-inward)—has generated a number of empirical studies. Weissman (1960), suggested that relatively normal persons became hostile outward when depressed, whereas persons tending to become severely depressed were more likely to internalise or suppress this hostility. The data of Zuckerman et al., (1967) supported this view, indicating that only in the relatively normal was hostility correlated with depression on mood questionnaires or as rated by interviewers. Friedman (1964) found depressives to have more 'readily expressed resentment' as shown by their endorsement of adjectives such as 'bitter', 'frustrated', and 'sulky', yet found no greater overt hostility. In a later study, Friedman (1970) showed that feelings of depression and worthlessness were consonant with hostile and resentful feelings, even though depressed persons were not more likely to directly express these feelings to persons in the environment. Schless et al, (1974) found equal numbers of depressed patients turning hostility inward and outward, with both types of hostility increasing as depression became more severe. However, because these patients also saw other people's anger as more readily expressed and more potent, that feared retaliation, and therefore expressed hostility in the form of resentment. In recent studies have been interpreted so as to call into question classical psychoanalytic formulations of the relationship of depression, hostility-inward and hostility-outward. On the other hand, the view that hostility may serve a defensive function against depression has been supported. That depression is preceded by increases in hostility that is directed out but cannot be expressed directly to appropriate that is directed out but cannot be expressed directly to appropriated objects in the environment, is taken as a failure of this defensive function

(Friedman, 1970; McCranie, 1971; Schless et al., 1974). Most writers who comment on the complaints and self-accusations of the depressed person have rejected the idea that they should be taken literally. Lichtenberg (1957) found that attempts to answer them directly with assurance, granting of dependency, and even punishment all increase depression and feelings of personal defect. Freud (1917) suggested that the self-accusations are actually aimed at someone else, a lost love object, and further notes, ' . . . it must strike us that after all the melancholic does not behave in quite the same way as a person who is crushed by remorse and self-reproach, which would more than anything characterize this latter condition, are lacking in the melancholic, at least, they are not prominent in him. One might emphasize the presence in him of an almost opposite trait of insistent communicativeness which finds satisfaction in self-exposure. In an attempt to modify depressive behaviour in a family situation (Liberman and Raskin, 1971) the baseline data indicated that other family members rejected opportunities to interact with the depressed person, and that all initiations of interaction between him and his family in the baseline period were undertaken by him. Paykel and Weissman (1973) reported extensive social dysfunction in women during depressive episodes. Interpersonal friction, inhibited communication, and submissive dependency occurred in both the initial episodes and in subsequent relapses. Onset of social difficulties was related to symptoms, but these difficulties continued months after the symptoms remitted, a fact that Paykel and Weissman argue must be taken into account in any treatment plan. The provocative and often annoying behaviour of the depressive has distracted investigators from considerations of the role of the responses of others. An exception, Jacobson (1954) noted that 'however exaggerated the patients' hurt, disappointment, and hostile derogation of their partners may be, their complaints are usually more justified that may appear to the surface'. According to her, the depressed person often makes his whole environment feel guilty and depressed, and this provokes defensive aggression and even cruelty precisely when he is most vulnerable. Depressives also have a tendency to develop an 'oral interplay' with those around them, so that mutual demands and expectations are built up to inevitable disappointment and depression for everyone concerned. Cohen et al., (1954) found therapists generally uncomfortable working with depressed patients. They identified a tendency of therapists to react to depressive manipulations with unrealistic reassurance and 'seductive promises too great to be fulfilled', followed by hostility and rejection. Such that it became aware of a dramatic example of this when a student therapist showed up at a Florida suicide prevention centre with a recent client. The therapist had attempted to meet her client's complaints of worthlessness and rejection with explicit reassurances that she more than understood her and cared for her, she loved her. After weeks of such reassurance and increasingly frequent sessions, the client finally confronted the therapist with the suggestion that if the therapist really cared for her as she said, they should spend the night together. The therapist panicked and terminated the case, suggesting that the client begin applying her newly acquired insights to her daily life. The client continued to appear for previously scheduled appointments and made vague suicidal gestures, at which time her therapist brought her to the suicide prevention centre. When it was suggested that the therapist should honestly confront her client with what had happened in the relationship, the therapist angrily refused to speak to her, stating that she truly loved her client and would do nothing to hurt her. Lewinsohn and his associate (Lewinsohn and Shaw, 1969; Lewinsohn, 1969, Lewinsohn, 1970; Libet and Lewinsohn, 1973) have undertaken an ambitious clinical research program focussing on a social interaction of the depressed person from a behavioural point of view. In attempting to develop hypotheses about the reinforcement contingencies available to the depressed person, they have attempted a precise specification of the social behaviour of the depressed person. Libet and Lewinsohn found depressed persons in group therapy to be lower than controls on a number of measures of social skills: Activity level, interpersonal range, rate of positive reactions emitted and action latency. Their data are subject to alternative interpretations, however, particularly since they also found that rate of positive reactions emitted was highly correlated with rate of positive reaction elicited. While depressed persons may well be deficient in social shills, some of the observed differences in group interaction situations may be due to the fact that fewer people are willing interact with depressed persons (which results in the narrowing interpersonal range and less opportunity for activity), and in this interaction emitted fewer positive responses (thereby also reducing the positive responses elicit from the depressed). The most useful behavioural conceptualization of social interaction involving depressed persons would specify the lack of social skills of all participants, as evidenced by their inability to alter the contingencies offered or received. Behavioural interventions in the depressed person's marital and family relationships would therefore involve training all participants in these social skills, and go beyond simply altering the contingencies available to the depressed person. Behavioural observations and self-reports of a couple in the Lewinsohn study (Lewinsohn and Shaw., 1969) seem to support such a view. Studies of suicide attempts and their effects on interpersonal relationships also provide data relevance, while suicide attempts do not have an invariable relationship on depression, there is a definite association. McPartland and Hornstra (1964) examined the effects of suicide attempts on subsequent level of depression. They conceptualized depressive symptomatology as 'a set of messages demanding action by others to alter or restore the social space'. And examined the relationships between suicide attempts and the ambiguity of the depressive message and the diffuseness of its intended audience. They were able to realizably place depressed patients at definite points along a dimension of interactive stalemate on the basis of the range of intended audience and the stridency of message in depressive communications. Patients who were farthest along this continuum, whose communication was most diffuse, nonspecific, strident and unanswerable. Were most likely to have long hospital stays and diagnoses of psychosis? Suicide attempts tended to reduce the level of depression, apparently by shifting the interactive burden onto others. Other studies (Rubenstein et al., 1958; Moss and Hamilton, 1956' Kubler and Stotland, 1964) have indicated that suicidal patients who improve following their attempt on their lives consistently have effected changes on social fields, and those who fail to improve generally have failed to change their situation fundamentally. Depression is viewed as a response to the disruption of the social space in which the person obtains support and validation for his experience. This view, and a view of depressive symptomatololgy in terms that is similar to that of McPartland and Hornstra (1964). However, one of the implications of the approach taken, is that an understanding of the social context is vital to an understanding of depression, although traditionally it has been largely ignored. Social stresses leading to depression included loss of significant relationships, collapsed of anticipated relationships, demotions (and in some cases, promotions), retirement, missed chances, or any of a variety of other changes in a person's social structure. Depressive symptomatololgy is seen as a set of massages demanding reassurance of the person's place in the interactions he is still able to maintain, and further, action by others to alter or restore his loss. Initial communications—verbal expressions of helplessness and hopelessness—tend to engage others immediately and to shift the interactive burden to others. The receivers of these messages usually attempt to answer the depressed person's request directly, however, as previously noted by Grinker (1964) and Lichtenberg (1957), their literal responses present him with a dilemma. Much of the depressive's communication is aimed at ascertaining the nature of relationships or context in which the interaction is taking place. Grinker (1964) has compared this to the various 'how' and 'why' questions that young children direct to their parents, and has suggested that both children and depressive's will be left feeling rejected, ignored, or brushed aside if provided with a literal response. If communication took place at only one level, depression would probably be a less ubiquitous problem. However, the problem is that human beings not only communicate, but communications about this communicative communication, qualifying or labelling what they say by (1) The context or relationship in which the communication takes place, (2) other verbal messages, (3) vocal and linguistic patterns, and (4) bodily movement (Haley, 1963). A person may offer support and reassurance with a rejecting tone or he may offer criticism in a supportive and reassuring tone. It is enough that vocal and linguistic patterns and body movements are ambiguous and subject to alternative interpretations. However, a further problem for the depressed person is that the context, the nature of the relationship between the depressed person and the persons communicating to him, may require time and further messages to be clearly defined.` The depressed person's problem is to decide whether others are assuring him that he is worthy and acceptable because they do in fact maintain this attitude toward him, or rather only because he has attempted to elicit such responses, unwilling or unable to endure the time necessary to answer this question, the depressive uses his symptoms to seek repeated feedback in his testing of the nature of his acceptance and the security of his relationships. While providing continual feedback, these efforts are at the same time profoundly and negatively affecting these relationships. The persistence and repetition of the symptoms are both incomprehensible and aversive to members of the social environment. However, the accompanying indication of distress and suffering is powerful in its ability to arouse guilt in others and to inhibit and direct expression of annoyance and hostility from them, as observed in both the family difficulties of depressed persons (Jacobson, 1954) and the problem's therapists report in their efforts to relate to depressed patients (Cohn et al., 1954). Irritated, yet inhibited and increasingly guilt-ridden, members of the social environment continue to give verbal assurance of support and acceptance. However, a growing discrepancy between the verbal content and the affective quality of these responses provides validation for the depressive's suspicions that he is not really being accepted and that further interaction cannot be assured, to maintain his increasingly uncertain security, the depressive displays more symptoms. Nonetheless, at this point the first of a number of interactive stalemates may be reached. Members of the depressed person's environment who can find a suitable rationalization for their behaviour may leave the field or at least, reduce their interactions with him. Considerable effort may be involved in efforts to indicate that this is not in fact rejection, but given the context, these efforts do little more than reduce credibility and increase the depressive's insecurity. With those members of the social environment who remain, a self-maintaining pattern of mutual manipulation is established. Persons in the environment find that they can reduce the aversive behaviour of the depressed person and alleviate the guilt that this depressed behaviour has an uncanny ability to elicit, if they manipulate him with reassurance, support, and denial of the process that is taking place. The depressed person, finds that by displaying symptoms he can manipulate his environment so that it will provide sympathy and reassurance, but he is aware by now that this response from others is not genuine and that they have become critical and rejecting. While this situation is attractive for neither the depressed person nor members of social environment, it provides a stabilization of what has been a deteriorating situation. One alternative facing the depressed person is for him to accept the precipitating disruption of his social space and the resulting loss of support and validation.

However, now that he has begun showing symptoms, he has invested portions of his remaining relationship in his recovery effort. That is, he was tested these relationships, made demands, and has been frustrated in ways that seriously call into question his conception of these relationships. If he abandons these efforts, he may have to relinquish the support and validation derived from these relationships while accepting the precipitating loss. At this point he may be too dependent upon the remaining relationships to give them up. Furthermore, as a result of the mixed messages he has been received from others, he now has increasingly confusions and deteriorate self-concepts, which must be clarified. With new desperation more symptoms may be uncovered. Various possible efforts by the depressed person to discover what is wrong with him (i.e., why he is being rejected and manipulated) and to reestablish a more normal interactive patterns are in this context indistinguishable from the manipulation he has used to control the responses of others. Therefore they are met with the usual counter manipulation. Requesting information as to how people really view him is indistinguishable from symptomatic efforts. If the depressed person attempts to discuss the interpersonal process that is taking place, he touches on a sensitive issue, and is likely only to elicit denial by the others or an angry defensive response. Yet, efforts by others to assure the depressed person that he is really accepted and that they are not rejecting him are in this context also indistinguishable from previous manipulations that they have employed, and therefore serve to strengthen the developing system. Thus, interpersonal manoeuvres directed at changing the emerging pattern become system-maintaining and any genuine feedback to the depressed person is also indistinguishable from manipulations. Persons leaving the social field increase both the depressed person's feelings of rejection and his impetus to continue his behaviour pattern. Persons just entering the social field can be quickly recruited into the existing roles, since their efforts to deal with the depressed person—even if genuine are likely to be quite similar to those now being employed manipulatively. They therefore become subject to the compelling counter-manipulations of the depressed person, come to respond manipulatively themselves, and are inducted into the system. Descriptions of the depressed person at this point in his career focus on the distortions and misperceptions that serve to maintain his depression. What is generally ignored is that these 'distortions' and 'misperceptions' are contingent with the social system in which the depressed person now finds himself. The specific content of the depressive's complaints and accusations may not be accurate, but his comments are a recognition of the attenuated relationships, disrupted communication, and lack of genuineness that he faces. These conditions serve to prevent him from receiving the feedback necessary to correct any misperceptions or distortions. He has played a major role in the creation of this social system, but the emergence of the system has also required the cooperation of others, and once established, it tends to be largely beyond th control of its participants. Depending on characteristics of both the depressed person and his environment, a number of punishing variations on the above patterns may develop. Members of the social environment who have been repeatedly provoked and made to feel guilty may retaliate by withholding the responses for which the depressed person depends on them. The depressed person may become aware of the inhibiting influence his symptoms have on the direct expression of negative feelings, and may use these symptoms aggressively, while limiting the forms that counter-aggression can take. He may also discover and exploit the interdependence of others and himself. While he is being made acutely aware of his dependence on others and the frustrations it entails, he may also become aware of the extent to which others are dependent on him. In that their own maintenance of mood and their ability to engage in varieties of activities required in some way his cooperation. Because either of outright hostility, or as a self-defeating effort to convince other of their need to renegotiate their relationship with him, the depressed person may become symptomatic in his withholding of these minimal cooperative behaviours. While hostility may not necessarily be a more etiological factor in depression, the frustrations, provocations, and manipulations occurring in interactions between depressed persons and others would seem to encourage it. As efforts to end the interactive stalemate fail, there may be a shift in the depressive's self-presentation to one indicating greater distress and implying that the environment has more responsibility for bringing about the necessary changes. McPartland and Hornstra (1964) found that they could unambiguously differentiate themes of hopelessness and helplessness from more disturbed themes and how energy and physical complaints in communications of depressed patients. The latter themes were associated with longer hospitalization when hospitalized depressed patients were sampled. McPartland and Hornstra give the examples of, 'I can't sleep and I can't stand it any longer'. 'I am too tired to move': 'My head and my stomach feel funny all the time'. Unable to restore his life space, the depressive now implicitly demands 'a suspension of the rules; a moratorium on the web of obligations under which the person lives, such as admission to the sick role' (McPartland and Hornstra, 1964). With immediate relationships deteriorating, the depressive addresses his plea to a more general audience, but in more confusing and unanswerable terms. Literal responses to his communications may involve medical intervention for his specific complaints, but this generally fails to alleviate the problem. Any efforts to move the interactional theme back to the depressive's sense of hopelessness and helplessness threaten to reopen the earlier unfruitful and even punishing patterns of relations, and tend to be resisted. Unable to answer, or in many cases, even to comprehend the depressive's pleas, members of the social environment may withdraw further from him, increasing his desperation, and quickening the depressive's drift. With a second interactive stalemate now reached, the depressed person may attempt to resolve it by increasing his level of symptomatology and shifting the theme of his self-presentation to one of the worthlessness and evil. 'I am a failure; its all my fault; I am sinful and worthless'. Unable either to restore his social space or to reduce his obligations sufficiently for him to continue to cope, the depressive now communicates his bafflement and resignation. The intended audience is now more diffuse, relationships are even more attenuate, and the new message is more obscure and perplexing. The social environment and the depressive soon arrive at another stalemate. Otherwise helpless to alleviate the situation, remaining members of the environment may further withdraw or, alternatively, have the depressives withdrawn through hospitalization. In the absence on any relatedness to others, the depressive may drift into delusions and frankly psychotic behaviour. Once an individual has suffered a disrupt ion of his social space, his ability to avoid depressive shifts, or to abort the process once it has begun, depends on the structure of his social space and on his interpretational skills. With regard to the latter, it is generally ignored that the person facing this situation is dealing with a changing environment, and that the skills needed to deal with it are likely to be different from those required by a more stable, normal environment. Consequently, persons who previously have had adequate skills to deal with their life situation may lack the skills to cope with a disrupted social space. With regard to the structure of this social space, resistance to depression seems to depend on the availability of alternative sources of support and validation. Particularly of the type that cannot be threatened by depressive symptomatology, further, the availability of direct nonpunitive feedback should the person's behaviour become annoying or incomprehensible, and the ability of the social space to generate new sources of support and meaning that are unambiguously independent of the presence or absence of symptoms. Earlier speculative writings (Abraham, 1911) and later behavioural studies (Lewinsohn, 1969) have suggested that depressive persons tend to be quite limited in their range of interactions, and that this may be a major source of their vulnerability. ADVANCE \d4 Stable relationships may generally provide a buffer against depression, but when they are stable yet low in support and validation, they may encourage a chronic depressive cycle. If, for instance, in a marriage of this type, the depressed people recognize that his spouse is tolerating more than is reasonable from him without protest, he may begin to assume that she is staying with him out of some obligations, rather than because she accepts him and wants a relationship (Haley, 1963). The depressed person may then test whether he is really accepted by driving the other person to the point of separation with his symptoms. Yet if the spouse passes the test by continuing to tolerate the annoying behaviour. The depressed person may not necessarily be reassured about his acceptance, but he may only be convinced that his spouse remains because she is unable to leave. However, if she makes an effort to leave the situation, she may be indicating that their relationship has been voluntary and that he had been accepted. With reconciliation the spouse may again, seem too tolerant and a new series of doubts, testing, and strife may be enacted. While such a cycle may produce chronic difficulties, it may also be an alternative to a downward depressive spiral. Essentially the depressed person finds himself in the awkward situation of wanting to avoid rejection, yet at the same time fearing acceptance. The constraints operating on the person who suffered a disruption in his social space are his need for support and validation, and the investment of his remaining relationships in his efforts to receive such support. The symptoms of the depressed person offer a powerful constraint on the ability of members of the social environment to offer adjustive feedback, and while eliciting verbal messages of sympathy, support, and reassurance, these symptoms disrupt the relationships and cultivate hostility and rejection. Those who resist induction into the system without rejecting the depressed person do so because they are able to resist the pressure to convey discrepant messages. A successful therapist in Cohen et al., study stated, 'I keep in mind that I am talking to the patients not so much verbally as preverbally. I use the verbal communication as a means of carrying inflection and an accompaniment of facial expression and postural components'. Several writers have suggested that the emerging communication context can be disrupted by strong affective expressions such as anger, excitement, and amusement (Lazarus, 1968), which are incompatible with the pattern of mutual manipulation that maintains the context. Although many writers have indicated that a depressive reaction lifts when a patient regains his ability to express anger toward others (Friedman, 1970), some research indicates that the mobilization of anger is not necessary for symptomatic improvement (Weissman, et al., 1971; Klerman and Gershon. 1970). Interpersonally, hostility may be one of a number of means of disrupting or blocking the operation of a depressive interpersonal system. Involvement in this system is difficult to avoid once it has begun. The symptoms of depression have an ability to perpetuate themselves through the involvements of others in a system of manipulation and coanter-manipulations that soon gets beyond the control of its participants. Within the presently engaged research that examines the responses of others to depression and the quality of the communications context that emerges. Preliminary results from a study involving an interpersonal behaviour questionnaire suggest that a person is less likely to respond in an overtly hostile manner to the behaviour of another person when the second person is depressed. This inhibition persists even when it is indicate that the second person is responding hostility. The inhibition of appropriate hostile behaviour may be a characteristic of interactions involving the depressed person, and not just of the depressed person. Another study involves twenty-minute phone conversation between naive subjects and target individuals from three groups: Depressed outpatients, nondepressed outpatients, and normals. Preliminary results suggest that subjects respond with unrealistic reassurance and useless advice to the depressed outpatient. They are more likely to be depressed, anxious, and hostile themselves after conversations with depressed patients, and are more likely to reject opportunities for future interaction. For the most part, changes in the subjects' mood remain concealed during the conversation, and the depressed patients are given little indication of their impact on occasional statements, such as 'You certainty seems to have had a lot a problems, but problems are what allows us to grow, and so you'll have lots of opportunity to grow in the future';. Further research is needed to examine the nature of the depressive's social field so that the specific relationships that resist or perpetuate the depressive interpersonal system can be identified and describe. We use the term 'depression' to refer to the syndrome of behaviour that have been identified in descriptive studies of depressed individuals (e.g., Grinker, et al., 1961). It includes verbal statements of dysphoria, self-depreciating, guilt, material burden, social insolation, somatic complaints, and a reduced rate of much behaviours. We assume depression to be a continuous variable which can be conceptualized as a 'state 'which fluctuates over time as well as a 'trait' (some people are mo e pone to becoming depressed than others). Being depressed does not exclude other psychopathological conditions such as schizophrenia, psychosis, sexual deviation, or alcoholism. For research purposes a patient (subject) is defined as 'depressed' if he meets certain experiential criteria (e.g., Lewinsohn & Libet 1972) based on selected MMPI scales and on the interview factor's identified by Grinker (1961) It would seem important that any study relying on differences between depressed and nondepressed groups for its conclusions have a 'normal control' as well as a 'psychiatric control' group (i.e., patients for whom anxiety or other neurotic symptoms but not depression constitute the major psychopathology (if any observed normal group differences are to be attributed to depression (depressed, psychiatric control normal control). We accumulatively gather of three assumptions regarding the behavioural theory of depression: A schematic representation of the theory is shown by (I) A low rate of response-contingent positive reenforcement (response) acts as an eliciting (unconditioned) stimulus for some depressive behaviours, such as feeling of dysphoria, fatigue, and other somatic symptoms (2) A low rate of response constitutes a sufficient explanation for other part of the depressive syndrome such as the low rate of behaviour. For the latter the depressed person is considered to be on a prolonged extinction schedule. (3) The total amount of reconposre received by an individual is presumed to be a function of three sets of variables: (I) The number of events (including activities) that are potentially reinforced (PotRe) for the individual. PotRe is assumed to be a variable subject of individual differences, uninfluenced by biological (e.g., sex and age) and experiential variables, and (ii) The number off potentially reinforcing events that can be provided by the environment, i.e., the availability of reinforcement in the environment (AvaiRe). (iii) The instrumental behaviour of the individual, i.e., the extent to which he possesses the skill and emits those behaviours that will elicit reinforcement for him from his environment. The behavioural theory requires that (1) the total amount of response received by depressed persons be less than that received by nondepressed persons, and similarly, it will be less when the individual is repressed than when he is not depressed; (2) The onset of depression is accompanied by a reduction ion response, (3) intensity of depression convary with rate of reconposre, and (4) Improvement is accompanied by an increase in reconposre. Even so, the following examinations of relevant empirical studies are several additional clarifications and hypotheses.

First, even where such predictions are affirmed, but further data would be needed to ascertain whether the differences between depressed and non-depressed individuals in regard to response are due to: (x) differences in the number and kinds of activities and events which are potentially reinforcing ({PotRe); (y) and/or the possibility the depressed individuals may be more likely to be in situations which lack reinforcement for them (AvaiRe), (z) and/or differences between depressed and non-depressed individuals in those skills which are necessary to obtain reenforcement from one's environment. Second, the degree to which the individual's behaviour is maintained (followed) by reinforcement is assumed to be the critical antecedent condition for the occurrence of depression, rather than the total amount of reinforcement received. It is a well-known clinical fact that 'giving' (i.e., noncontingently) to depressed individuals does not decrease their depression. We assume that the occurrence of behaviour followed by positive reinforcement is vital if depression is to be avoided. Such that depression when the probability is low that the individual's behaviour will be followed by reinforcement, and also, when the probability is high that the individual will be 'reinforced' when he does not emit the behaviour (e.g., the retired person receiving his paycheck regardless of what he does). Under both conditions the probability of the individual emitting behaviour reduced. The behavioural view of other aspects of depression may include :Low self-esteem, pessimism, feelings of guilt, and other elated phenomena are cognitive changes which are commonly observed in depressed individuals, even though the specific manifestations vary considerably from individual to individual. Thus, there are depressed patient who do not have low self-esteem and there are many who lack feelings of guilt. Theorists such as Aaron T. Beck (1967) assign primary causal significance to these cognitive changes. A behavioural theory assumes these qualify as secondary elaborations of the feeling of dysphoria, which in turn is presumed to be the consequence of a low-rate of reconposre. The first thing that happens when an individual becomes depressed is that he is experiencing an unpleasant feeling state (dysphoria). He is feeling bad. This feeling state is difficult for the individual to label; and a number of alternative 'explanations' are available to him including. 'I am sick' (somatic symptoms). 'I am weak or otherwise inadequate' (low self-esteem), 'I am bad' (feeling of guiltiness), or, 'I am not likeable' (feelings of social isolation). The research of Stanley Schachter (Schachter & Singer 1962) may contain important implications for this aspect of the behaviour of depressed individuals and for treatment as well (cognitive relabelling). If the depressed individual can be helped to relabel his emotion (e.g., 'I am worthless' into 'I am feeling bad because I am lacking something that is important to my welfare'), he may be in a much better position to do something about his predicament. 2. Relationship between hostility and depression, in which the role of hostility is central to psycho dynamically-oriented theories of depression (i.e., depression is caused by internalized hostility) is hypothesized to be secondary to the low rate of reconposre. In a manner analogous to the way in which aggressive behaviour is elicited by an aversive stimulus, in Azrin's (1966) studies, aggressive behaviour may be assumed to be elicited by a low rate of response in the depressed individual. When these aggressive responses are expressed, they serve to alienate other people and therefore contribute even further to the social isolation of the depressed individual. He therefore learns to avoid expressing hostile tendencies by suppressing (or repressing) them. 3. Role or precipitating factors in occurrence of depression that in a substantial number of depressed patients, the depression can be shown to have begun after certain environmental events (e.g., Paykel, 1969). Many of these events involve a serious reduction of positive reenforcement in that the event deprives the individual of an important source of reinforcement (e.g., death of spouse) or of an important set of skills (e.g., spinal cord injuries or brain disease). The relationship between the occurrence of such events and depression is considered with the behavioural theory of depression. There are, however, also instances of depression following 'success' experiences (e.g., promotions or professional success). It is also not at all uncommon for an individual to become depressed following the attainment of some important and long-sought goal (e.g., award of PhD degree). The existence of such precipitating factors would seem at first glance to contradict the notion of a relation between a reduction in positive reinforcement and depression. Two considerations would seem relevant (a) That the individual is judged to be a 'success' by external criteria (e.g., is promoted) events not necessarily mean that the number of potentially reinforcing events available to him has increased. Thus, for example, a promotion may actually involve a serious reduction in the amount of social reinforcements obtained by the individual. The behavioural theory would predict depression for an individuals who attain a goal for which he has worked long and hard if the reward (e.g., aware of degree) turns out to be a weak reinforcement for him. In that case he has worked hard for too little, i.e., his rate of response is low. Developments in the interactional description of schizophrenia have not been parallelled in the area of depression. As yet, concepts such as pseudomutality, double-bind, schism, and skew found no counterparts. Kubler and Stotland (1964)have argued, 'emotional disturbance', even the most severe, cannot be understood unless the field in which it develops and exists is examined. The manifestations of the difficulty in the disturbed individual have meaning depending on aspects of the field. The significant aspects of the field are usually interpersonal. Yet, the study of depression has focussed on the individual and his behaviour out of his interactional context. To a larger extent, the depressed person's monotonously reiterated complaints and self-accusations, and his provocative and often annoying behaviour has distracted investigators from considerations of his environment and the role it may play in the maintenance of his behaviour. The possibility that the characteristic pattern of depressed behaviour might be interwoven and concatenated with a corresponding pattern in the response of others has seldom been explored. For the most part, it has been assumed that the depressed person is relatively impervious to the influence of others. Ruersch (1962) stated that to talk to the depressed person makes little sense, to listen, little more. Grinker (1964) conceptualized depressive symptomatology as communication tom others, but argued that the depressed person is not responsive to communication from others: 'The depressed person . . . cannot use information for the purpose of action, he cannot perceive the cues of reality, he makes statements but does not care if he is understood.Its difficulty of communication is the primary problem in therapy of establishing a communication relationship, which is, of course, a reflection on the patient's basic life difficulties. The most characteristic aspect of the manic depressive's defence in his ability to avoid anxiety by erecting conventional barriers to emotional interchange, we have learned to interpret this as a defence rather than a defect in the patient 's experience, and we have found that when it is interpreted as a defence, he responds by developing a greater ability to communicate his feeling and to establish empathic relationships. Initial communications—verbal expressions of helplessness and hopelessness, withdrawal from interaction, slowing, irritability and agitation tend to engage others immediately and to shift the interactive situation to others, the receivers of these messages usually attempt to answer the depressive person's requires directly. However, as previously noted by Grinker (1964) and Lichtenberg (1957), theory literal responses present him with a dilemma, much of the depressive's communication is aimed at ascertaining the nature of relationship or context in which the interaction is taking place. Grinker (1964) has compared this to the various 'how' and 'why' questions that young children direct to their parents, and has suggested that children and progressives will be left feeling rejected, ignored or brushed aside if provided with a literal response. Depression has been conceptualized as a self-perpetuating interpersonal system. Depressive symptomatology is congruent

331

with the developing interpersonal situation of the depressed person, and the symptoms have a mutually maintaining relationship with the response of the social environment, essentially, the depressed person and others within his social space collude to create a system in which feedback cannot be received, and various efforts to change become system-maintaining. Depressed persons tend to withdraw from social activities, and their close relationships tend to be strained and conflictual. Depressed women have more intensely studied than depressed men, in part because women are approximately twice as likely to be depressed (Radloff). Depressed women are dependent, acquiescent, and inhibited their communication in close relationships, and prone to interpersonal tension, friction and open conflict (Weissman & Paykel, 1974). Interestingly, the interpersonal difficulties of depressed persons are less pronounced when they are interacting with strangers than with intimates (Hinchcliffe, Hooper, and Roberrtys, 1975). About half of all depressed persons report marital turmoil (Rousanville, Weissman, Prusdoff, and Heraey-Baron, 1979) there is considerable hostility between depressed persons and their spouses, but often there is more between depressed persons and their children. Being depressed makes it more difficult to be a warm, affectionate, consistent parent (McLean, 1976). The children of depressed parents are more likely to have a full range of psychological and social difficulties than the children of normal or even schizophrenic parents (Emery, Weintraub, and Neale, 1982), yet one must be cautious in making causal inferences. There is evidence that the child's problems are more related to a conflictual marital relationship and stressful home life than depression of the parent per se (Sameroff,. Barocass, Siefer). Depression thus tends to be indicative of an interpersonal situation fraught with difficulties, and this needs to be given more attention in both theorizing and planning treatment. Although depression is associated with interpersonal problems, within a sample of depressed persons the correlation between severity of depression and the extent of interpersonal problems tend to be modest. This may suggest that these problems are a matter no only of how depressed persons are functioning, but of the response of key people around them as well (Coyne, Kahn, & Gotlib, 1985). One can make a list of the symptoms of depression, and assign any person a depression score on the basis of the number symptoms present. Even if one assumes a continuity between normal depressed mood and clinical depression, it may still prove useful to make a distinction between the presence and absence of significant depression. One may wish to insure that a research study does not include a preponderance of persons whose depression is only mild or transient. Virtually no signs or symptoms are specified to depression, and yet in many context, one may need to distinguish depression from other descriptors or explanations for a person's distress and behaviour. In working with the elderly, for instance, it is important to distinguish between depression and dementia. In medical patients in general, there is a high prevalence of symptoms associated with depression, both because of physical illness and the stress of hospitalization (Cavanaugh, 1984), and, whether for research or practical purposes, one, may wish to establish criteria for who is to be considered depressed and who is not. Finally, persons who are labelled schizophrenic or alcoholic for many purposes to lump them with those persons whose primary problem is depression. Thus, for the purpose of research, treatment, and professional communication, it proves useful to have some means of specifying some boundary conditions for the term 'depression', in terms of some minimal level of severity as well as some coherence and specificity to what is included in the concept—even if one rejects the notion that it is a discrete entity, discontinuous with normal mood. The problem of diagnosis is most critical in biomedical approaches to depression. The assumption is generally made that depression is a matter of one or more disease entities with specific etiologies and treatment. The statement, 'Nosology precedes etiology' conveys the idea that the ability to identify the causes of depression depends upon the existence of an adequate diagnostic and classification system. For instance, to take a simplified hypothetical example, suppose that a particular biological abnormality occurs in 60 percent of all depressed persons and is specified to depression. Suppose also that, with the accepted diagnosis criteria, only 60 percent of the persons identified as such are 'actually depressed'. If these conditions occurred, then research might indicate that only 36 precent of depressed persons possesses the abnormality. An effective treatment for depression may also be misjudged or misapplied in the absence of an adequate diagnostic system. This was made apparent recently after a drug company had undertaken a large study to compare the effectiveness of a new drug to that of both an established drug treatment for depression and a placebo (Carroll, 1984). At five of the six research sites, the new drug proved to be no more effective than a placebo, but interpretation of this was limited by the additional finding that the established treatment proved no better. Patient s identified as depressed by current criteria did not respond to drug treatment that had proven efficacious in a large body of past research. The past research was misleading either, the current diagnosis criteria invalid, or, most likely, they were misapplied by reputable investigators. Contemporary diagnosis systems owe much to the work of Kraepelin at the turn of the century. He divided major psychopathology into two broad syndromes: Dementia praecox (schizophrenia) and manic-depressive illness. The latter category included almost all serious mood disturbance, including depression in the absence of an episode of mania. As retained today, the term generally is a synonym for bipolar disorder. Of all the distinctions that have been proposed, the most widely accepted and least controversial is that between unipolar and bipolar depressive. Classifying depressed patients into bipolar and unipolar subtypes was first proposed in 1962 by Leonhard et al., based on the clinical differentiation of depressed patients with and without mania, family history studies noted that patients with bipolar illness had more psychosis and suicide among their relatives than patients with unipolar illness. Since 1962 several studies in Europe and the United States have refined and extended this original observation. More important, a model for investigation in psychiatry has been developed to the point that genetic data are important for validating clinical diagnosis in psychiatry, particularly among the affective disorders. Several lines of evidence suggest that some forms of depression may have an etiology on a genetic basis. In order for a genetic etiology to be proven, several factors should be evident. First of all, the disorder should cluster within families; patients with the illness should have relatives who also demonstrate studies of twins should show that the illness is more prevalent among monozygotic than dizygotic twins. A third line of evidence would come from adoption studies. Adoption studies are designed to differentiate environmental from genetic factors. Data from such studies should reveal that subjects who have a biological parent with illness but who were raised in foster home develop the illness nevertheless, whereas subjects whose biological parents do not have the illness but who were raised in a home. Where there is affective disorder, do not develop affective disorder in excess of controls. Fourth, the illness could be shown to be linked to a gene known of Mendelian transmission. Affective disorders, particularly manic-depressive illness, are familiar. The evidence that bipolar illness clusters in families was reported by Leonhard et al., Perris and Angst both suggested that effectively ill relatives of bipolar patients tended to have bipolar and not unipolar disorders, whereas affectively ill relatives of unipolar patients tended to have unipolar illness and not bipolar illness. In the 1960s the Washington University group published a series of familiar studies in manic-depressive illness, particularly bipolar disorders. These studies showed a high familiarity risk for affective disorder in relatives of manic patients. Second, a very comprehensive family study of affective disorder suggested that manic-depressive illness may be linked to a gene transmitted on the X-chromosome. Subsequent studies in the late 1960s from the National Institute of Mental Health (NIMH) also show a differential familial loading for relatives of patients with bipolar compared with unipolar disorders. Relatives of bipolar patients had elevated morbid risks for bipolar illness, unipolar illness, and suicide, compared to relatives with unipolar patients. Few twin studies of affective disorder appear in the literature of the last 10 years or so. Kallmasnn's study is still considered the definite work, showing very high concordance rates for bipolar illness in monozygotic compared to dizygotic twins. The adoption technique, utilized in the Danish studies of schizophrenia, has been tried in studies of bipolar illness. Data from adoptees in Iowo indicated that primary affective illness may have a familial factor. Another study of adoptees from manic-depressives also supports the concept of a genetic factor in the etiology of affective disorders. In the search fo r genetic linkage of affective disorder, the studies of Winokur et al., pointed toward a genetic factor on the X-chromosome, colour blindness and XG blood type. Gershon et al., was unable to replicate these findings and subsequently criticized the data from the Mendlewocz studies on methodological grounds. Clearly, unipolar illness as presently defined is a much more heterogeneous collection of disorders than bipolar disorder. Attempts to find subtypes of unipolar disorder using a genetic classification have not been particularly successful. However, Winokur's group separated unipolar patients into women with an early age of onset (depressive spectrum disease) whose relatives showed depression and alcoholism, and depressed men with a late age of onset (pure depressive disease) whose relatives showed depression only. The renewed interest in the genetics of bipolar and unipolar depression in the late 1900s and the interest in defining these disorders led to several family studies in the 1970s. The simplest method, the so-called family history method, was to ask patients about illness in their relatives. This tends to underestimate illness in relatives. An interview (Schedule for Affective Disorder and Schizophrenia-SADS) developed early in the 1970s was used to document illness in relatives. Interviewing relatives directly (the 'family study) led to greater precision regarding the diagnosis of illness in relatives. In a refinement of this technique relatives are interviewed blind to the profound diagnosis in order to decease investigator bias. Most of the recent genetic studies conducted in the United States employed a blind spirited study method; wherein relatives were interviewed with a standardized instrument with the interviewer unaware whether the person being interviewed was the patient, relative, or a control. Nonetheless, it seems that some observers have stated that in the intervals between attacks, the manic depressives have a character structure similar to that of the obsessional neurotic. It has also been asserted that in the psychotic phase the manic-depressive illness is essentially schizophrenic. This latter statement is supported by the fact that many manic-depressives do, in the course of time, evolve into chronic schizophrenic psychoses, usually paranoid in character, and that there are many prosecutory ideas presented both in manic attack and in the depression. In general, there has always been much uncertainty as to who should be diagnosed manic depressive—an uncertainty which is reflected in the widely differing propositions of manic depressives and schizophrenic diagnosed in different mental hospitals. What, then, is the point of singling out a diagnosis category called manic depressive? In our opinion, the manic-depressive syndrome does represent a fairly clear-cut system of defences which are sufficiently unique and of sufficient theoretical interest to deserve special study. We feel that equating the manic-depressive character with the observational character overlooks the distinguishing difference to the manic depressive, use substitutive processes as his chief defence. The manic, uses the previously mentioned lack of interpersonal awareness as his chief defence, together with the defensive processes themselves. The object relations of the obsessional are more stable and well developed than those of the manic depressive. While the obsessional's relations are usually integrations in which there is an intense defence of hostility, control and envy, they do take into consideration the other person as a person. The manic depressive develops an intense dependent, demanding, oral type of relationship which overlooks the particular characteristic and qualities of the other. According to Sullivan's conceptualization of the schizophrenic process, the psychosis is introduced typically by a state of panic, in which there is an acute break with reality resulting from the upsurge of dissociated drives and motivations which are absolutely unacceptable and invest with unbearable anxiety. Following this acute break, a variety of unsuccessful recovery or defensive processes ensue, which we call paranoid, catatonic, or hebephrenic. These represent attempts of the personality to deal with the conflicts which brought about the panic: The paranoid by projection, the catatonic by rigid control; the hebephrenic by focussing on the bodily impulses. According to this conception, the manioc depressive can be differentiated from the schizophrenic by the fact that he does not exhibit the acute break with reality which is seen in the schizophrenic panic. His psychotic processes of depression or, of manic, he can be thought of asserting a depressive function against the still breaker personality disintegration which is represented by the schizophrenic state. This, in persons whose conflicts and anxiety are too severe to be handled by depressive or manic defences, a schizophrenic breakdown may be the end result. Contrasting the schizophrenic and the manic depressive from the point of view of their early relationships, we see that the schizophrenic has accepted the bad mother as his fate, and his relations. He therefore attenuated. He is inclined to withdraw into detachment. He is hypercritical of family and cultural values. He is sensitive and subtle in his criticisms, original but disillusioned. He is disinclined to rely on others and is capable of enduring considerable degrees of loneliness. His reluctance to make demands on the therapist makes the therapist more feel and more sympathetic, and therefore the therapist is frequently in his aggression, he can take the risk of attacking, for he is less afraid of loneliness. He is more sensitively aware of the emotions of the therapist, since the boundaries between ego and environment are more fluid. The schizophrenic is not inclined to pretend, and is not easily fooled by other people's pretenses, Dream and fantasies are nearer to awareness and guilt feelings are also more conscious than unconscious. The typical manic depressive has not accepted the 'bad mother' as his fear. He vacillates between phases in which he fights with the bad mother, and phases in which he feels reunited with the good mother. In there manic phase, his, relationships with reality are more tenuous; he shows a lack of respect for other people, and reality considerations are dismissed for the dark of magic manipulation to make the bad mother over into a good mother. The manic depressive is therefore, mostly a good manipulator, a salesman, a bargaining personality. He is under-critical instead of being hypocritical. He easily sells out his convictions and his originality in esteem. In the depressive phase, he sacrifices himself to gain a good mother or to transform the bad mother into a good mother. In order to do this, he calls himself bad, and suffers to expiate his sins, but these guilt feelings are, in a sense, artificial or expedient, utilized in order to manipulate the bad mother into becoming a good mother. The depressive does not come to terms with realistic guilt feelings. Instead, he uses self-accusations, which frequently sound hypocritical, to convince the mother or a substitute that his need to beloved has absolute urgency. He denies his originality because he is terribly and afraid of aloneness, he is more of a follower than a leader. He is dependent on prestige, and is quite unable to see through the pretense of his own or other people's conventionalities. He shows a high degree of anxiety when his manipulations fail. His lack of subtlety in interpersonal relationships is due to his overruling preoccupation with exploiting the other person in order to fill his emptiness. This operates s as a vicious circle as he has maintained his claims for as good fulfilling mother, but his search for fullness manipulation of another makes him feels helpless and empty. This incorporates of another person for the purpose of filling an inward emptiness, of acquiring a borrow self-esteem, is very different from the lack of ego boundaries in the schizophrenic. The schizophrenic is in danger of losing his ego., And he expresses his danger in fantasies of world catastrophe. The manic depressive is threatened by object loss, since he habitually uses the object to patch up his ego weakness. Object relations in the manic depressive are that clouded by illusions, but even when he waits, demands, and blames the frustrating object, he is—by this very agitated activity in behalf of his own salvation, ineffective as it may be—defended against the loss of the ego. When the manic depressive becomes schizophrenic, this defence breaks down. It should be noted that the infantile dependency and manipulative exploitativeness seen in the manic depressive are not unique to this type of disorder. They occur, in fact, in many forms of severe mental illness. The hysteric, for instance, exemplifies infantile dependency and exploitativeness as dramatically as the manic depressive, and in 'la belle difference' one may see a resemblance to the euphoria of the manic or hypomanic. However, the combination of the dependent and exploitative traits with the other outstanding characteristics of the cyclothymic personality—particularly the communicative defect and the accompanying inability to recognize other persons as anything but good-bad stereotypes and the conventional but hypermoralistic values—does become sufficiently distinct and unique to distinguish these patients characterologically from other types. The diagnosis of manic-depressive character has, in the past, been made largely on the basis of the patient's exhibiting the classic manic and depressive symptomatology. It can, however, be as validly made on the basis of the transference-countertransference pattern, which is set up between the patient and the therapist. The transference pattern is particularly characteristic; the countertransference pattern would, of course, vary considerably according to the personality of the therapist, although it, too, shows a number of quite typical features. The transference pattern shows two outstanding characteristics which could be labelled (1) the exploitative clinging decency, and (2) the stereotyped approach other persons, who are not seen aa personalities in their own right. 1. The dependencies as with other workers in the field of the study of manic depressive illness have apply documented the deep-seated dependency of this type of person (Abraham, Freud, Rado, Klein). The dependency attitudes toward the object are highly ambient. Gratification is demonstrated, but not accepted or experienced as such, and the patient feels that attention, car e, and tenderness must be forced from the other person. The force applied is that of demonstrating to the other person how miserable he is making one, how much the depressed one needs the other, and how responsible and culpable the other is if he fails to meet the depressive's needs. The demands are not directly verbalized but rather consist of a wordless exploitation: The reactive hostility is not experienced as such, but instead is experienced as depression. In the depths of the depression, It seems impossible to satisfy the patient's dependency needs. As one therapist mentions, the patient seems to be saying, 'I am starving, and I won't get what I need.' The amount of time and attention the patient receives, crying out for more. We sense if satisfaction. He remains depressed, but we have not tried the experiment of spending the major portion of each day with a depressive person. Certainly 24-hour-a-day nursing does not suffice to give the patient a sense of gratification. Whether unlimited time from a therapist would have more effect is debatable, in the light of our experience with Mr. Richard, such that when the patient is in a period of relative mental health, these needs are less apparent, this raises the question of what becomes of these needs during such periods: Are they not present and only stirred up again when some unusual deprivation nor treat to security occurs, or are they successfully kept t in repression during the healthy phase? In the manic phase, the demandinngness is much more open but seen by the patient as demanding his rights rather than as asking for favours. Rejection of the demand is met with t hostility rather than with a depressive response. The manic, of course, show, in addition to the demandingness, the tendency to take what he needs by force, if necessary and he will use direct aggression—in contrast to the depressive, who uses reproaches against the other person as a forcing manouevre. 2. The stereotyped response of the manic-depressive personality shows a highly characteristic tendency to look upon others as stereotyped repetitions of parental figures. This has been described elsewhere in reporting as 'a lack of interpersonal sensitivity'. The therapist is regarded, (x) as an object to be manipulated for purposes of getting sympathy and reassurance, (y) as a moral authority who can be manipulated into giving approval, and (z) as, in actuality, a critical and rejecting authority figure who will not give real approval but can be counted on only for token approval which can be achieved by proper behaviour manipulation. This uncritical categorization of the therapist results in the patient's inability to use the therapist to provide himself with a fresh point of view. Everything that the therapist says is reworked into the old pattern of concealed disapproval covered over with the sugar of artificial reassurance. This impenetrability to the reception of new ideas from the therapist represents one of the great obstacles in therapy with this type of patient, who will give lip service to the role of the therapists a noncritical authority without a feeling of conviction that this is do. However, the lip service itself then becomes incorporated into the set of manipulative acts which will receive approval and adds another wall to their defence. Early in the study of these patients, it was felt that the lack of ability to appraise the therapist as a person represented a real learning defect in the patient and that one of the therapeutic tasks therefore was a somewhat educational one of showing the patients how one person could be different from another. On further study we have come to the conclusion that the defect is not an educational one, as evidence for this being that as the anxiety diminishes in an interpretational relation, the sensitivity increases. Mr. Richard is an excellent illustration of this point. His therapist spoke as follows:

> When the patient first entered treatment, I would have described him for being without the ability to emphasize with another. During the subsequent years of treatment, It became apparent that the patient was acutely sensitive to nuances in the attitude of others to him, but that his interpretation of these attitudes was extremely static and stereotyped. Finally, at the end of treatment, he retained much of his sensitivity and had also gained in his ability to respond with accuracy in interpretational situations.

> The therapist, as such, finds to some forwarded attemptive description as the therapist is describing in terms of a maldevelopment of the empathic function. Approaching the problem from the point of view of present-day relationships, we suggest that it is anxiety-arousing fo r the manic depressive to recognize others as persons, as well as to conceive of himself as a person in his own right. The manic depressive's recognition of bad or unacceptable traits in another person would interfere with his dependency on him; but would be necessary for him to abandon the other person for his badness, and this would then leave him alone. In order to avoid this anxiety, the manic depressive avoids the recognition

and identification of the medley of attractive and unpleasant traits in others, and thereby avoid there exchange of a variety of complex feelings. Thus, as is so often true in psychopathology, what begins as developmental defect ends up as an anxiety-avoiding defence.

Whereas, specific states of morbid anxiety have been dealt with more detail, especially in the literature of psychoanalysis, depressive states have hitherto received less attention. Nevertheless the affect of depression is as widely spreading all forms of neurosis and psychoses are that of anxiety. The two affects often present together or successively in one individual; so that a patient suffering from an anxiety-neurosis will be subject to states of mental depression, and a melancholic will complain of having anxiety. One of the earliest results of Freud's investigations of the neurosis was the discovery that neurotic anxiety originated from sexual repression, and this origin served to differentiate it from ordinary fear. In the same was we can distinguish between the affect of sadness or grief and neurotic depression, the latter being unconsciously motivated and a consequence of repression. Anxiety and depression are related to each other in the same way as are fear and grief. We fear a coming evil; we grieve more than one that has occurred. A neurotic will be attacked with anxiety when his instinct strives for a gratification which repression prevents him from attaining; depression sets in when he has to give up his sexual aim without having obtained gratification. He feels himself unloved and incapable of loving, and therefore he despairs of his life and the future. This affect lasts until the cause of it ceases to operate either through an actual change in his situation or through a psychological modification of the displeasurable ideas with which he is faced. Every neurotic state of depression, just like every anxiety-state, to which it is closely related, contains a tendency to deny life. Meaning is not embedded in some obscure 'inner human nature', nor something that is desired to be destined to be developed by successively 'higher forms of life'. There is, in short, nothing vitalistic or mysterious emergent implied in the idea of meaning. Meaning is the elaboration of an increasingly intricate ground plan of broad relationships and ramifications. It is the establishment of dependable cause-and-effect sequences which permit ego-mastery and action. Meaning is at the heart of life because it is inseparable from action sequence with an intricate symbolism, the dependable becoming the indispensable the satisfying become the necessary as Man's symbolic life is an imbibing of meaning and a relentless creation of it. This symbolic elaboration of meaning is The Homo sapient, so to speak, brought by the Neanderthal, into the evolutionary scene and manufactured solely for his use and delight, by means of it, man becomes himself, an illusion that his particular mean-fabric, his culture's concoction of symbols and action, is god-given and timeless. In his imagination, man fuses symbols and action into a cohesion that has atomic tendencies.

But still, it is pardonable for the theorist to make the error of narrowness when he is attempting to understand what is behind stupidly-language or such linguistic uttering as to make the person using them seem childish, whining, and somehow culpable in himself, the person provides a sorry spectacle when he tries to keep his world from caving in upon him with only the limited means at the disposal of his ingenuity. Thus, it is logical to look for selfish motives in those who show themselves cognitively limited and childish. Perhaps, this is another reason why theory has so long been hampered.

But people are not fated to remain childish, they are kept childish by parents and by culture. We train them to live in a certain kind of world, and to accept it dumbly. The culture. In other words, create certain kinds of bondage from which people cannot be released without threatening others. Can a wife be released from a marriage contract when her husband begins neglecting her? Can she begin life anew at 40 when she has not previously provided herself with the withdrawals? Can a factory-operator's wife suddenly join him at 53, untrained as she is, and basically unwanted in a man's world? Anthropology has provided us with the knowledge that there is any number of possible arrangements for human action. And that they all work—for better or for worse. We have discovered that the word 'natural' does not apply to human relationships; these are all learned. When we say that an individual's world 'crumbles' we don't mean that his ;natural' world crumbles but, that his cultural world does. If he had been taught to operate in another kind of world, it would perhaps not have crumbled. The Vows of marriage could have drawn for forbidding the taking of another wife, and that witchcraft depression syndrome would certainly be much reduced

Theorists have considered object-loss to be he principal cause for depression, and had overlooked the importance of 'games' and meaning. One reason for this error of emphasis is that some cultures provide only a narrow range of objects and games. The result is that the object and the limited meaning come to be inseparable, which is to say, the more people to whom one can make appeal for his identity, the easier it is to sustain life-meaning. Object-loss hit hardest when self-justification is limited to a few objects. But object-loss are not crucial—or even necessarily important—when there is the possibility of sustaining one's conduct as before. Action is the basic problem in object-loss, and people devise ingenious ways to sustain it. An excellent illustration is the phenomenon of vengefulness. Harold F. Searles (1956) showed that the revenge process can serve as a way of keeping the object. It cannot be overstressed that an object is never an object in isolation. It is a means of coming in contact with the world. It permits action. By definition, to constitute an object is to create a behaviour pattern. To lose an object is to lose the possibility of undertaking a range of satisfying action. This is foremost, in addition, for man, the object is a private performance audience. It is a locus to which is addressed the continuing identity dialogue of the self and experiencing the continual presence of the object, in other words, its serves as a purchase to the symbolic elaboration of the self. The object need not be present in the outer world; one needed only to have developed behaviour patterns toward it, or modelled on it, and to keep its image in mind. Thus, the object exists on an internal-external continuum. It reflects a process of growth and activity in the actor. Just as the 'external pole' serves as experiential contact with the outer world, so does the 'internal pole' permit a continual fashioning of the identity. Hence we can see that object-loss means not only external performance loss, but inner identity loss as well. This bears repeating, because it enables us to understand the phenomenon of vengefulness. To hate and to seek revenge is to create a continually present object. Searles say that the vindictive person 'has not really give up the other person toward whom his vengefulness is directed, is his preoccupation with vengeful fantasies about that person serves, in effect, as a way of psychological holding onto his,'. Vengefulness is a type of continuous performance, a way of maintaining the object that otherwise would not be there.

Initially, what is called the 'Superego' is the 'internal pole' of our objects. We address our performance to them, by saying ;See how well I am doing, as you would wish me to'. Both action and identity are potentiated. The revenge-object is merely a variation on this. We keep it in order to be able to say, 'See how great I have become, as you did not think I could become' and so forth. It has often been observed that the motif "I`ll show the folks back in my home town' is a primary impetus to success. On the primitive level, revenge murders of the death of a loved one is simply a variation on this. One continues to perform as if the object were still there. The automatic nature of primitive revenge shows how important it is to keep some kind of behaviour pattern, which serves in effect to keep the object. Vilification of the dead in mourning ceremonies is also a way of keeping behaviour patterns toward the object. to remain silent is swamped by the action void.

Finally, 'showing the folks back home' keep the identity rooted in time, gives it the all-important duration and continuity. if one could not keep objects, the identity would have to be continuously recreated in the present. one would be in the position of Jean-Paul Sarte's gambler; the entire past accretion of meaning would be severed. The identity owes its very existence to its rooting in the past.

We have a hard job—in our culture—in realizing how inseparable are object-range and performance-possibilities. But consider the situation in traditional society. There the extended family is the rule, and not the small, tight, nuclear one that is familiar to us, as the consequence of this is that the life-changes and life-meaning of the individual do not depend on a few parental objects. Meaning is generalized to a whole range of kin. The extended family provides a continuing source of esteem and affirmation for the individual actor, even thought significant figures drop out.

In our culture we are familiar with the person who lives his life for the wishes of his parents and becomes depressed when then die and he has reached the ages of forty or fifty. He has lost the only audience for whom the plot in which he was performing was valid. He is left in the hopeless despair in which the actor who knows only one set of lines, and loses the one audience who wants to hear him. The extended family takes care of this problem. Even though it makes rigid prescriptions for the behaviour of each individual. Even though it makes good prescriptions for the behaviour of each individual, still each member can count on an audience for his continuing performance even after his own immediate patent die.

The depths of despondency and dispirited desperation in the loss of or nearly of all hope, despairing in the grief of a discouraging disheartedness, if only to fall into the tyranny as intended within the fate of destiny.

Thus, culture designs the action scene, and outlines the kind of crisis to which the individual will have to adapt. One of the sharpest exposés of the grip in which culture holds the individual, and the breakdown which results from that grip, is Edmund Volkart's study of bereavement (1957). Volkart points out that restriction of the identity-appeal to only a few objects is a type of 'psychological bondage'. We train people to 'love', 'honour;' and 'obey' only a few others. And when death or some other train of events leaves the haplessly loyal person in the sway to and fro, the psychiatry is apt to hold a microscope to his body chemistry, or measure his saliva. Instead of providing for continuing life-designs, instead of training people in critical self-awareness. We actually facilitate the subversion of life-meaning. Volkart does not soft pedal this major personality issue, and can do no more than to quote directly:

> Any culture which, in the name of mental health, entourage's extreme and exclusive emotional investments by one person in a selected few others, but which does not provide suitable outlets and alternatives for the inevitable bereavement, are simply altering the conditions of, and perhaps postponing, severe mental ill health. It may, in the vernacular, be building up for a big led down by exacerbating vulnerabilities (1957).

In other words, in our culture we champion limited horizons—a limited range of objects—and call people 'mentally ill' when they suffer its effects. We make no provision for sustaining meaning when the bottom drops out of someone's life. When a women's children marry, then the mirror begins to reflect the gradual and irrevocable loss of her charm, her performance as a responsible person, culturally desirable, is over. She may find herself left with no part to play, as early as her late 30s—with nothing to justify and sustain her identify. Since this utter subversion of meaning usually coincides with menopause e, psychiatry has labelled the depression that may occur' 'Involutional depression', medical psychiatry has only recently come to focus social role, clinically, it was easier to image that the depression is somehow due to bodily changes or, the psychoanalytic theory might see this as a pampered self-pity over the imagined loss of sexual capacity, over the inevitable diminuation instinctual vigour.

Students of epidemiology first took to studying the social distributions of contributive types of illness in the hope of turning up some answers. Since clinical research did not provide any real understanding of the etiology of depression and schizophrenia, it was hoped that perhaps social research might. Fact does not precede theory, and no amount of counting can ever explain. But statistics on epidemiology did provide some kind of picture. It now seems generally agreed that depression occurs more frequently among persons with cohesive family groupings: Among women, who are more cohesively identified with close in-groups, in higher socioeconomic statuses, in highly tradionalized groups and among professionals.

Schizophrenia, on the other hand, presents a radically different epidemiological picture. It occurs more among men than women; in the lower socioeconomic bracket among dislocated peoples—that is, generally where group membership and identifications are weakest.

Mental illness, as we have been surveying is a form of cultural and individual stupidity, an urge to meaning by those poor in command over vocabularies. If this thesis holds, we should expect some confirmation from the epidemiological picture; action varies according to class, as does awareness; possibilities for self-justification as well as degree of cultural indoctrination vary by class. Nonetheless, the class picture does seem to give some kind of consistent reflection of the views we have detailed.

If depression is a form of meaning-stupidity in an overwhelming frustration situation, we would expect it to be more prevalent in the upper classes, among women, and among people in close identification with others. These are all people who feel that they should find their situation acceptable—but, who somehow does not. The upper classes, having achieved socially approved success,

RICHARD J. KOSCIEJEW

have no reason to be unhappy. Women are given their status in the social structure as a matter of course, and should not question otherwise. People in close and 'loving' identification with others are taught that they should derive all their life satisfactions from the quality of these relations, and from the pattern of rights and obligations which they entail. All the more reason that guilt should present itself as a natural alternative for deep-seated dissatisfaction: One cab will believe himself guilty for not being contentually satisfied where he should not. On the other hand, among the lower classes, dissatisfaction need not necessarily terminate in depressive self-accusation. Any number of scapegoats can be found and other rationalizations used, to justify failure, the rich, the boss, the low status of women in the lower class as compared with the upper 'bad luck', 'hard times' and so on (Prange and Vitols, 1962). In terms of alternative vocabularies of meaning, the lower classes, paradoxically, are less 'stupid' than the upper.

But the situation is quite different with the lower-class schizophrenic. He lacks even that meaning which belongs to his own class—since he has failed to learn to interact effortlessly. He joins a personal 'poverty' to a class poverty; and it has been observed repeatedly that the extreme schizophrenic is more obedient and conservative in accepting ideal formulas for proper behaviour than are his peers. He tends to conform to idealized behaviour standards which deprive him of the possibility of easy scapegoats available to those who flaunt standards.

The upper-class schizophrenic, on the other hand, is in a more fortunate situation. In the first place, he can effect some measure of correspondence between his fantasy world and certain specialized symbolic achievements provided by society. He has more of a chance of having his fantasies, and his identity somewhat validated. Clifford Beers, for example, could assume the identity of mental-hygiene reformer and create some measure of conformity between his omnipotent fantasies and the real action world. Possibilities of symbolic self-justification are more available to upper than to lower-class schizophrenics. Also, it is worthy noting that th upper-class schizophrenic can usually extend his identity back in time, to include family traditions, roots in the Old World, illustrious ancestors, and so on. This socially supported extension of the self in time gives some experiential depth to the personality, and helps buffer present ineptitudes (Strauss, 1959). The lower-class schizophrenic, on the other hand, has no such time depth to his identity, and must rely solely on fantasy and on the unrewarding contemporary situation. Rogler and Hollingshead observed bluntly on the extremely stressful and unrewarding nature of lower-class life. 'The afflicted individual world into an unreal world of fictions. These fictions my be equally unpleasant.

Meaning-poverty then, depends on the type of stupidity: For the schizophrenic. Shallowness of meaning is a result of behavioural poverty; it reflects insufficient participation in interpersonal experiences. The depressed person, suffers instead from a too uncritical participation in a limited range of monopolizing interpersonal experiences. Hitherto, two kinds of failure of the humanization process; the individual who has not been indoctrinated into his culture, and the one who have been only too well imbued with a narrow range of its sentiments. If both of these individuals end up in our mental hospitals, perhaps we cannot blame the psychiatrist for juggling chemical and ignoring culture. The problem one has a narrow medical view of human behaviour. Individual and culture are inseparable. The individual find answers to the four common answers provided for by social institutions—by a whole accumulated tradition of cultural learning. In view of this the psychiatrist may object that it would be much too big a job for the medical practitioner to bring under critical fire the institutions of his society. How can he undertake to determine how people should be' brought up? Quite right, he cannot. This is the task of a broad, unified human science.

Nonetheless, the data of the human sciences are starting to emerge that their relationships are becoming clear. If this revolution, like any other, is to be successful, no vested institution can escape critical review. Nature—in her constitution oh the Homo sapient's sapient—seems to have frames the four common human problems, but man—by his cultural and social world—frames the answers. Anything done by man for man cannot be undone and redone. It suffices to design the problem.

Now, one thing will be immediately obvious about his kind of sharp classification. It can rarely exist in reference to human nature as we have traced its complex development. Schizophrenic and depressive types merge into one another and overlap. They represent different kinds and degrees of adaptation to ranges of object and events which are not mutually exclusive within one behavioural system. Thus, we can see, at the end of this presentation of the two major 'syndromes', that they are not syndromes at all. Rather, they reflect the typical problems that man is prone to, the restrictions, coercions, the lack of control over behaviour, and the confusions in symbolic reconstruction of himself and his experience. All this blends in varying proportions in the individual personality. If we can only rarely see clear 'types' emerging from this, then there is all the more reason to reorient our approach to labelling the human personality.

We use the term 'depression' to refer to the syndrome of behaviours that have been identified in descriptive studies of depressed individuals (e.g., Grinker et al., 1961). It includes verbal statements of dysphoria, self-depreciation, guilt, material burden, social isolation, somatic complaints, and a reduced rate of many behaviours. Is that, we assume depression to be a continuous variable which can be conceptualized as a 'state' which fluctuates over time as well as a 'trait'—(some people are more prone to becoming depressed than others?). Being depressed does not exclude other psychopathological conditions such as schizophrenia, psychosis, sexual deviation, or alcoholism. For purposive reasons, it would seem important that any study relying on differences between depressed and nondepressed groups for its conclusions have a normal control as well as a 'psychiatric control' group (i.e., patients for whom anxiety or other neurotic symptoms but not depression constitute the major psychopathology) if any observed group differences are to be attributed to depression (depression—psychiatric control, normal) and not to the deviation hypothesis (depression, psychiatric control, normal control).

The major assumptions of the behavioural theory of depression follow three laying premises that postulate (1) A low rate of response-contingent positive reenforcement (response) acts as an eliciting (unconditioned) stimulus for some depressive behaviour, such as feeling of dysphoria, fatigue, and other somatic symptoms. (2) A low rate of response constitutes a sufficient explanation for other parts of the depressive syndrome such as the low rate of behaviour. For the latter the depressed person is considered to be on a prolonged extinction schedule. (3) The total amount of response received by an individual is presumed to be a function of three sets of variables: (I) The number of events (including activities) that are potentially reinforces for the individual, influenced by

350

biological (e.g., sex and age) and experiential variables. (ii) The number of potentially reinforcing events that can be provided by the environment, i.e., the availability of reenforcement in the environment. (iii) The instrumental behaviour of the individual, i.e., the extent to which he possesses the skills and emits those behaviours that will elicit reinforcement for him from his environment.

The behaviour theory requires that (1) the total amount of response received by depressed persons be less than that received by nondepressed persons, and similarly, it will be less when the individual is depressed than when he is not depressed; (2) the onset of depression is accompanied by a reduction in response; (3) intensity of depression convary with rate of response, and (4) improvements are accompanied by an increase in response. Before proceeding to an examination of relevant empirical studies several additional clarification and hypotheses are offered.

In terms of system theory (von Bertalanffy, 1950; Allport, 1960; Miller, 1971), the usual conceptualization of the depressed person is one of a relatively closed system. Grinker (1964) was explicitly instating that the depressed person repeats his message and behaviour without reception or acceptance of resulting feedback. Beck (1964, 1967) described the cognitive distortions that dominate the information processing of the depressed person so that experiences are rigidly interpreted to maintain existing schema of personal deficiency, self-blame, and negative expectations.

The implicit assumption of these has been that the support and information available to the depressed person are incongruent with his depression, and the persistence of his symptomatology is evidence of a failure to receive or accept this information. Withdrawal, isolated intrapsychic persecution or as Beck describes (1967), interaction of depressive schema and affective structure, produce a downward depressive spiral. Presently, that is to say, that our adopted alternative is that the depressed person is able to engage others in his environment in such a way that support is lost and depressive information elicited. This in turn increases the level of depression and strengthens the pathogenetic pattern of depressed behaviour rather response of other if a depressive spiral develops, It is mutually causative, deviation-amplifying process (Maruyama, 1963) in the interaction of the depressed person with his environment. Thus, what is customarily viewed as some internal process is, I believe, that, at least in part, a characteristic of interaction with the environment, and much of what is customarily view as cognitive distortions or misperception is characteristic of information flow from the environed, it should be noted that while the depressed person's different interprets his predicament is traditionally attributes to his distortion or misperception, yet disorders of thought and perceptions are nether defining criteria more common among depressed patients (McPartland and Hornstra, 1964). An observer who talks into account the intricacies of someone's relationship to his environment,. Frequently attributes to hin characteristics that he does not possess, or leaves significant aspects of his unexplained experience (Watzlawick, 1967). Feedback introduces phenomena that cannot be adequately explained by reference to the isolated individual alone (Ashby, 1960, 1962), for the study of depression, identification of a pattern of depressive feedback from the environment demands a more complex conceptualization of the disorder that one explaining its phenomena with reference to the isolated depressed person.

Of all the distinctions that have been proposed, the most widely accepted and least controversial is that between unipolar and bipolar disorder. In its simplest form—and as it has been recognized in the DSM-III—the differential diagnosis is based on whether the patient has a personal history of mania. However, recent genetic studies have led to a familial definition of the distinction: Depressed patients who do not have a personal history of mania may still be diagnosed for being bipolar if there has been mania among first-degree relatives.

Valid though the distinction appears to be, it has some important limitations. As yet, no consistent differences in the symptomatology of bipolar and unipolar depression have been identified. Although a bipolar diagnosis predicts a greater likelihood of response to lithium, as many as 40 percent of unipolar patients, nonetheless, respond positively (Depue and Monroe, 1978). By itself, the distinction does not do justice to the heterogeneity among either bipolar or unipolar patients. Currently, persons with bipolar disorder are often subclassified as to whether either manic or depressive symptoms or both have been severe to require hospitalization. Unipolar depressed persons remain a large and tremendously heterogeneous group. Nonetheless, in the continuing controversies as how best to distinguish among depressed persons, the unipolar-bipolar distinction stands out in its usefulness for both clinical and research purposes.

Although little, has been written in the literature of psychoanalysis concerning the psychology of neurotic depression. But the affect of depression in the sphere of the psychosis awaits more precise investigation. This task is complicated by the fact that a good parts of the diseases in question run a ;cyclical' course in which there is an alternation between melancholic and manic states. The few preliminary studies which have hitherto been published have only dealt with one of these two phases at the same time.

The study of the genetics of depression remains in its infancy. Further advances are going to require better ways of subtyping affective disorders and the discovery of biological markers that are not state dependent, that is, tied to whether someone is currently disturbed. Dunner describes some of the distinctions that he and his colleagues have drawn for bipolar disorder, in terms of the severity of manic and depressive phases (e.g., whether one or both require hospitalization). It is probably true that bipolar disorder is more homogeneous and has a stronger genetic component than unipolar depression, and because of this, Dunner suggests that is more likely to yield advances in the near future. Some researchers are attempting to identify subtypes of unipolar depression that 'breeds true' such that the relatives of depressed persons who have a particular pattern of symptoms will themselves show this pattern if they become depressed. There have been some promising findings with concomitant appetite disturbance and excessive guilt (Leckman et al., 1984), but any substantial advances are going to depend ultimately upon the identification of genetic markers that have thus far proven elusive. Riedfer and Gershon (1978) have noted that such markers will need to be stable; heritable, and state independent; capable of differentiating persons with an affective disturbance from persons drawn from the general population, and among the relatives of depressed persons, capable of identifying those who develop affective disturbance from those who do not.

A major source of confusion is due to the fact that the term 'depression' variously refers to a mood state, a set of symptoms, and a clinical syndrome. As a reference to mood, depression identifies a universal human experience, adjectives from a standard measure of mood (The Multiple Affect Adjective Checklist: Zuckerman and Lubin, 1965) point to subjective feelings associated with a depressed mood; sad, unhappy, blue, low, discouraged, bored, hopeless, dejected, and lonely. Similarities between every day-depressed mood and the complaints of depressed patients have encouraged the view that clinical depression is simply an exaggeration of a normal depressed mood, however, patients sometimes indicate that their experience of depression is quite distinct from normal feelings of sadness, even in its extreme form.

Of recent views, that depression is to emphasize that it is primarily a biological disturbance, an illness, the predisposition to which lies in genes and biochemistry, while people may react to their circumstances with happiness and unhappiness, this is of questionable relevance to the clinical phenomena of depression. However, as these definitional problems continue to plague the study of depression, and they are not going to be readily resolved. There remains considerable disagreement as to what extent and for what purpose a depressed mood in relatively normal persons can be seen as one end of a dimensional continuum of mood as taken upon those disturbances as seen of a psychiatric hospital patients, and to what extent the clinical phenomenon is distinct and discontinuous with normal sadness and unhappiness.

One observer may be struck with the frequent complaints about appetite and sleep disturbance by depressed persons and infer that some sort of biological disturbance must be the key to understanding depression. Another might find their self-derogation and pessimism irrational in a way that suggests that these must be some kind of fundamental deficit in self-esteem or cognitive distortion occurring. Still another may listen to the incessant complaining of a depressed person, get annoyed and frustrated, and yet feel guilty in the way that makes it easier to encourage the depressed person to continue to talk in this way than to verbalize these negative feelings. Cognizant of this, the observer might conclude that there is some sort of interpersonal process going on that is critical to any understanding of depression.

Nonetheless, studies have compared the subjective mood of persons who are distressed but seeking help to those who are seeking treatment for depression (Depue and Monroe, 1978). The two groups may be similar in subjective mood, but they differ in other ways. Those persons who are not seeking treatment for depression tend to lack the anxiety and the physical complaints, including loss of appetite, sleep disturbances, and fatigue shown by the group seeking treatment. Still, it could be argued that there is a continuum of dimensional provision, as to the differences between the two groups, with these additional features arising, when a normal depressed mood becomes more prolonged or intensified. The controversy is likely to continue until either questions about the etiology of depression are resolved or unambiguous markers for depression are identified.

Advocates of psychoanalytic, cognitive and behavioural, and interpersonal and social perspective on depression have generally assumed a dimensional quantification between a normal depressed mood and clinical depression. They tend to exclude psychotic and bipolar depressed persons from treatment, but, beyond that, they have tended to disregard classification issues (Gilbert,. 1984) for unipolar depression, at least, they have assumed that whatever discontinuities in the biology of mild and severe moods there might be that are, yet as not excessively necessarily relevant to the psychological and asocial processes, which they are most interested.

Writers since antiquity have noted the core symptoms of depression: Besides a sad or low mood, reduced ability to expression pleasure, pessimism, inhibition and retardation of action, and a variety of physical complaints. As such, that we can distinguish among the emotional, cognitive, motivational, and vegetative symptoms of depression, although these feature s are not alway so neatly divisible. Beyond these symptoms, there are some characteristic interpersonal aspects of depression that are not usually considered as formal symptoms. But they are frequent, distinctive, and troublesome enough tp warrant attention.

Sadness and dejection are not the only emotional manifestations of depression, although about half of all depressed patient report these feelings as their principal complaint. Most depressed persons are also anxious and irritable. Classical descriptions of depression tend to emphasize that depressed persons' feelings of distress, disappointment, and frustration are focussed primarily on themselves, yet a number of studies suggest that their negative feelings, including overt hostility, are also directed at the people around them. Depressed persons are often intensely angry persons (Kahn, Coyne, and Margolin, Weissman, Klerman and Paykel, 1971).

Perhaps, 10 or 15 percent of severely depressed patients deny feelings of sadness, reporting instead that all emotional experience, including sadness, has been blunted or inhibited (Whybrow, Akiskal and Mckinney, 1984). The identification of these persons as depressed depends upon the presence of other symptoms. The inhibition of emotional expression in severely depressed persons may extend to crying. Whereas, mild and moderately depressed persons may readily and frequently cry, as they become more depressed, as they may continually be in lack of emotionally expressive inhibitions.

Mildly and moderately depressed persons may feel that every activity is a burden, yet they still derive some satisfaction from their accomplishment. Despite their low mood, they may still crack a smile at a joke yet, as depression intensifies, a person may report both a loss of any ability to get gratification from activities that had previously been satisfying—family, work, and social life—and a loss of any sense of humour. Life becomes stale, flat, and not at all amusing. The loss of gratification may extend to the depressed persons' involvement in close relationships. Often, a loss of affection for the spouse and children, a feeling of not being able to care anymore, a sense of a wall being erected between the depressed person and others are the major reasons for seeking treatment.

Perhaps one of the most frustrating aspects of depressed persons for those around them is their difficulty in mobilizing themselves to perform even the most simple tasks. Encouragements, expressions of support even threats and coercion seems only to increase their inertia, leading others to make attributions of laziness, stubbornness, and malingering. Despite their obvious distress and discomfort, depressed persons frequently fail to take a minimal initiative to remedy their situations or do so only halfheartedly. To observers, depressed persons may seem to have a callous indifference to what happens to them.

Depressed persons often procrastinate. They are Avoidant and escapist in their longing for a solacing refuge from demands and responsibilities. In severe depression, the person may experience an abulia or paralysis of will, extending even to getting out of bed, washing, and dressing.

In more severe depressions, there may be psychomotor retardation, expressed in slowed body movements, slowed and monotonous speech, or even muteness. Alternatively, psychomotor agitation may be seen in an inability to be still, pacing, and outbursts of shouting.

The presence of physical or vegetative symptoms is sometimes taken as the dividing line between normal sadness and clinical depression. One of the most common and prominent of vegetative symptoms is fatigue that someone is depressed may be first recognized by the family physician who cannot readily trace the person's complaints of tiredness to other causes.

Depressed persons also often suffer sleep disturbance, and it is tempting to link their tiredness to this, but in a sample of depressed patients, the two complaints are only modestly correlated (Beck, 1967). Depressed persons generally have rouble falling asleep, they sleep restlessly, and awaken easily. Yet, some depressed persons actually sleep considerably more than usual, up to 12 hours a night.

When mildly or moderately depressed, some people eat compulsively and gain considerable weight, but depression is more characteristically associated with loss of appetite and a decrease in weight. For many depressed persons, a loss of appetite is the first sign of an incipient depression, and its return marks the beginning of recovery. Some depressed persons maintain their normal eating habits and weight, but complain that food is tasteless and eating an unsatisfying matter of habit. Besides a loss of appetite, depression is often associated with gastrointestinal disturbance, notably nausea and constipation. Mild depression heightens sexual interest in some people, but generally depression is associated with a loss of interest in sex. In severe depression, there may be an aversion to sex. Overall, though, women who are depressed do not have sex less frequently, but they initiate it, like and enjoy it less, and are less responsive (Weissman and Paykel, 1974).

Finally, depressed persons report diffuse aches and pains. They have frequent headache, and they are more sensitive to existing sources of pain, such as dental problems.

A brief interaction with a depressed person can have a narked impact on one's own mood. Uninformed strangers may react to a conversation with a depressed person with depression, anxiety, hostility, and may be rejecting of further contact (Coyne, 1976). Jacobson (1968) has noted that depressed persons often unwittingly succeed in making everyone in their immediate environment feel guilty and responsible and that others react to the depressed person with hostility and even cruelty. Despite this visible impact of depression on others, there is a persistent tendency in the literature to ignore it and to concentrate instead on the symptoms and complaints of depressed persons out of their interpersonal context. Depressed persons can be difficult, but they may also be facing difficult interpersonal situations within which their distress and behaviour make more sense.

Depressed persons tend to withdraw from social activities, and their close relationships tend to be strained and conflictual. Depressed women have been more intensely studied than depressed men, in part, because women are approximately twice as likely to be depressed. Depressed women are dependent, acquiescent, and inhibited in their communication in close relationships, and prone to interpersonal tension, friction and open conflict (Weissman and Paykel, 1974). Interestingly, the interpersonal difficulties of depressed persons are less pronounced when they are interacting with strangers than with intimates (Hinchcliffe, Hooper and Roberts, 1975).

About half of all depressed persons report martial turmoil (Rousanville, Weissman, Prusoff and Heraey-Baron, 1979). There is considerable hostility between depressed persons and their spouses, but often there is more between depressed persons and their children. Being depressed makes it more difficult to be a warm, affectionate, consistent parent (McLean, 1976). The children of depressed parents are more likely to have a full range of psychological and social difficulties than the children of normal or even schizophrenic parents (Emery, Weintraub and Neale, 1982), yet one must be cautious in making causal inferences. There is evidence that the children's problems are more related to a conflictual marital relationship and a stressful home-life than depression of the parent (Sameroff, Barocas and Siefer).

Depression thus tends to be indicative of an interpersonal situation fraught with difficulties, and this needs to be given more attention in both theorizing and planning treatment. Although depression is associated with interpersonal problems, within a sample of depressed persons the correlation between severity of depression and the extent of interpersonal problems tends to be modest. This may suggest that these problems are a matter not only of how depressed persons are functioning, but of the response of key people around them as well (Coyne, Kahn, and Gotlib, 1985).

In that the diagnosis of depression, one can make a list of the symptoms of depression, and assign any person a depression score on the basis of the number of symptoms present. A number of standard self-report inventories such as the Beck Depression Inventory (Beck, et al., 1961), the Centre for Epistemological Studies Depression Scale (Radlof f, 1977) and the Self-Rating Depression Scales (Zung, 1965) have been validated and are widely used as research tools, screening devices, and measures of the change associated with treatment.

Even if one is to assume a continuity between normal depressed mood and clinical depression, it may still prove useful to make a distinction between the presence and absence of significant depression. One may wish to insure that a research study does not include a preponderance of persons whose depression is only mild or transient. Virtually no signs or symptoms are specific to depression, and yet in its contexts, one may need to distinguish depression from other descriptors or explanations for a person's distress and behaviour in working with elderly, for instance, it is important to distinguish between depression and dementia. In medical patients in general, there is a high prevalence of symptoms associated with depression, both because of physical illness and the stress of hospitalization (Cavanaugh, 1984), and, whether for research pr practical purposes, one may wish to establish criteria for who is to be considered depressed and who is not. Finally persons who are labelled schizophrenic or alcoholic may show considerable depression, but it would be undesirable for many purposes to lump them with those persons whose primary problem is depression. Thus, for purposes of communication, treatment and research, it may prove useful to have some means of specifying some boundary conditions for the term 'depression'. In terms of some minimal level of severity as well as some coherence and specificity to what is included in the concept—even if one rejects the notion that it is a discrete entity, discontinuous with normal mood.

The problem of diagnosis is most critical in biomedical approaches to depression are for the assumption that is generally made that depression is a matter of one or more diseased entities with specific etiologies and treatments. The statement, 'Nosology precedes etiology' conveys the idea that the ability to identify the causes of depression depends upon the existence of an adequate diagnostic and classificatory system. For instance, to take a simplified hypothetical example, suppose that a particular biological abnormality occurs in 60 percent of all depressed persons and is specific to depression. Suppose also, with the accepted diagnosis criteria, only 60 percent of the persons identify as such are 'actually depressed'. If these conditions occurred, then research might indicate that only 36 percent of depressed persons' posses the abnormality.

An effective treatment for depression may also be misjudged or misapplied in the absence of an adequate diagnostic system. This was made apparent recently after a drug company had undertaken a large study to compare the effectiveness of a new frug to that of both an established drug treatment for depression and a placebo (Carroll, 1984). At five of the six research sites. The new drug proves to be no more effective than the placebo, but interpretation of this was limited by the additional finding that the established treatment proved no better. Patients identified as depressed by current criteria did not respond to drug treatment that had proven efficacious in a large body of past research. Either the past research was misleading, the current diagnostic criteria are invalid, or most likely, they were misapplied by reputable investigators.

Contemporary diagnostic systems owe much to the work of Kraepelin at the turn of the century. He divided major psychopathology into two broad syndromes: Dementia praecox (schizophrenia) and manic-depressive illness. The latter category included almost all serious mood disturbance, including depression in the absence of an episode of mania. As retained today, the term generally is a synonym for bipolar disorder. It is also still sometimes used as a genetic term for severe depression. Kraepelin considered manic-depressive illness a biological derangement. Although it might in some cases be precipitated by psychological factors, 'the real cause for the malady must be sought in permanent internal changes which are very often, and, perhaps always innate', (Kraepelin, 1921). Once started, the illness runs its course autonomously, independent of changes in the person's situation. Kraepelin also identified a group of psychogenic depression, which were depressive illness and reactive to change in these circumstances.

For more than 30 years, the dominant diagnostic system in the United States has been, the Diagnostic and Statistical Manual of Mental Disorders of the American Psychiatric Association, which is currently in its third edition (DSM-III). In its first edition it integrated the ideas of Kraepelin with those of Adolph Meyer and Sigmund Freud. While accepting Kraepelin's basic distinction between affective disturbance and schizophrenia, it also reflected Meyer's psychobiological view that mental disturbance represented not a simple disease entity, but the reaction of the personality to the matrix of psychological, social, and biological factors. By its second edition, the Meyerian term 'reaction' was no longer used throughout, but Meyer's influence remained. Freud 's ideas about the etiology of psychopathology were built into the criteria for specific disorders. Thus, the defining characteristics of neuroses were anxiety, but for purposed of diagnostic decisions, it could be manifest and observable or inferred to be operating 'unconsciously and automatically' in someone who was not visibly anxious.

The author of DSM-III attempted to avoid past controversies and answer many of the criticisms of its two predecessors. A decision was made to define diagnostic categories as precisely as possible, using descriptive data, rather than inferences about etiology. From a biomedical perspective, the ideal diagnostic and classificatory system would integrate knowledge about etiology with overt symptomatology. However, it was concluded that the present understanding of the causes of most disorders is too limited for this purpose. Furthermore, the sense was that 'the inclusion of etiological theories would be an obstacle to use of the manual by clinicians and varying theoretical orientations, since it would not be possible to present all reasonable etiological theories for each disorder (American Psychiatric Association, 1980).

In considering depression, the author's of DSM-III attempted to sidestep a number of longstanding controversies, including that of whether there is a continuum or a discontinuity between normal mood and clinical depression, as well as that of the role of precipitating life circumstances in distinguishing among types of depression. Depressive neurosis disappeared, along with the other neuroses. Depression is now encompassed in two main categories. The first category, major affective disorder, involves the presence of a full affective syndrome, with the subcategories of bipolar and major depression distinguished by whether there has ever been a manic episode. The second category, other specific affective disorders, includes conditions in which the depression is not severe enough to warrant a diagnosis of major affective disorder, but severe enough to warrant a diagnosis of major affective disorder, but the mood disturbance has been intermittent or chronic for at least two years.

The criterion for major depression is subclassified as to whether it is a single episode or recurrent and also as to whether melancholia is present. Melancholia involves a complaint of a loss of pleasure in all or almost all activities, a lack of reactivity to pleasant events: A quality of depressed mood, that is distinct from grief or sadness; depression worse in the morning; early morning wakening; marked psychomotor agitation or retardation; significant weight loss; and excessive quilt. The designation was intended as an acknowledgement that some more symptoms and might be more responsive to treatment with drugs or electroshock. However, it should be noted that there is considerable consensus that such a distinction should be made, but the exact nature of it remains controversial. There are exclusions

Criteria, including schizophrenia and what is judged to be normal or uncomplicated grief.

In general, these diagnostic systems are viewed as significant improvements over past efforts, but there is widespread dissatisfaction with them. Nonetheless, are those logically oriented researcher how are lamented:

> An astute observer will find little that is intellectually satisfying about the DSM-III diagnostic criteria for major depressive disorder. These criteria amount to catalogue of symptoms, and they are in no way linked by coherent underlying constructs. They also suffer from the problem of being cast as disjunctive criteria. This means that, for example, patients need to satisfy only of the possible symptomatological evaluations or appraising analyzes. Therefore (and this occurs in practice), several patients may be assigned the same categorical diagnosis without having any symptoms in common (Carroll, 1984).

Carroll goes on to note that as the result of an inadequate diagnostic system, research studies are limited by the flaws in the diagnosis used as independent variables, and drug treatment of an individual patient tends to remain a matter of trial and error.

We are far from an adequate diagnostic system for depression. If one is to be achieved, it will have to come to terms with the enormous heterogeneity in the signs and symptoms; level of severity, causal factors to this heterogeneity with a variety of classificatory systems. Kendall (1976) has suggested that almost every classificatory system that is logically possible has been proposed at some point in this period, but he notes that little consensus has been achieved. Winokur reviews some of the current controversies, but it would be useful to identify a few of the distinctions that have been made before we turn to the major theoretical perspectives on the disorder.

Of all the distinctions that have been proposed, the most widely accepted and least controversial is that between unipolar and bipolar disorder. In its simplest form—and as it has been recognized in the DSM-III—the differential diagnosis is based on whether the patient has a personal history of mania. However, recent genetic studies have led to a familial definition of the distinction: Depressed patients who do not have a personal history of mania may still be diagnosed as bipolar if there has been mania among first-degree relatives.

Work by Perris (1966) first established that bipolar disorder starts on the average of 15 years earlier than unipolar depression and recurs more frequently. Individual episodes are shorter, and there is a greater risk of disorder among the first-degree relatives of bipolar patients. Furthermore, there as a tendency for unipolar and bipolar disorders to breed true, with first-degree relatives of bipolar patients tending toward bipolar disorder, and first-degree relatives of unipolar patients tending to have little more risk of mania than the general population. The unipolar-bipolar distinction has proven to be clinically useful; depressed bipolar patients respond significantly better to lithium than unipolar depressed patients.

Valid though the distinction appears to be, it has some important limitations. As yet, no consistent differences in the symptomatolology of bipolar and unipolar depression have been identified. Though a bipolar diagnosis predicts the greater likelihood of response to lithium, as many as 40 percent of unipolar patients, nonetheless, respond positively (Depue and Monroe, 1978). By itself, the distinction does not do justice to the heterogeneity among either bipolar or unipolar patients. Currently, persons with bipolar disorder often subclassified as to whether either manic or depressive symptoms or both have been severe to require hospitalization. Unipolar depressed persons remain a large tremendously heterogeneous group. Nonetheless, in the continuing controversies as how best to distinguish among depressed persons, the unipolar-bipolar distinction stands out in its usefulness for both clinical and research purposes.

Many issues in the study of unipolar depression have coalesced in the concept of endogenous versus nonendogenous depression. The differentiation is most often identified for being between endogenous and reactive depression, although this has been used interchangeably with the endogenous-neurotic and psychotic-neurotic distinction. The hope for the distinction has often been that it would prove to be the boundary between biological versus psychological and social concerns. Traditionally, the term 'endogenous' has been invoked to differentiate depressions that are purportedly biological in etiology, without environmental precipitants, and that is less amenable to psychotherapy. Also, endogenous depressions are expected to be more responsive to somatically oriented interventions, notably electroconvulsive shock therapy and antidepressant medication. 'Reactive' has inferred to depressions that are viewed as understandable reaction to some precipitating stress and that is more suitable for psychotherapy and less responsive to somatic therapies. The distinction was originally based on the supposition that some depressions are related to precipitating events and others seem to appear without them and that would predict response to treatment and clinical course.

People, encompassed within the depressive point of bipolar disorder, experience the intensely sad or profoundly transferring formation showing the indifference to work, activities, and people that once brought them pleasure. They think slowly, concentrate poorly, feel tired, and experience changes—usually an increase—in their appetite and sleep. They often feel a sense of worthlessness or helplessness. In addition, they may feel pessimistic or hopeless about the future and may think about or attempt suicide. In some cases of severe depression, people may experience psychotic symptoms, such as delusions (false beliefs) or hallucinations (false sensory perceptions).

In the manic phase of bipolar disorder, people feel intensely and inappropriately happy, self-important, and irritable. In this highly energized state they sleep less, have racing thoughts, and talk in rapid-fire speech that goes off in many directions. They have inflated self-esteem and confidence and may even have delusions of grandeur. Mania may make people impatient and abrasive, and when frustrated, physically abusive. They often behave in socially inappropriate ways, think irrationally, and show impaired judgment. For example, they may take aeroplane trips all over the country, make indecent sexual advances, and formulate grandiose plans involving indiscriminate investments of money. The self-destructive behaviour of mania includes excessive gambling, buying outrageously expensive gifts, abusing alcohol or other drugs, and provoking confrontations with obnoxious or combative behaviour.

Clinical depression is one of the most common forms of mental illness. Although depression can be treated with psychotherapy, many scientists believe there are biological causes for the disease. The June 1998 publication, of the Scientific American, in the article that Neurobiologist Charles B. Nemeroff exchanges views about something in order to arrive at the truth or to convince others that the connection concerning those of considering that they have differentiated between biochemical changes in the brain and the finding of the depression.

The genes that a person inherits seem to have a strong influence on whether the person will develop bipolar disorder. Studies of twins provide evidence for this genetic influence. Among genetically identical twins where one twin has bipolar disorder, the other twin has the disorder in more than 70 percent of cases. But among pairs of fraternal twins, who have about half their genes in common, both twins have bipolar disorder in less than 15 percent of cases in which one twin has the disorder. The degree of genetic similarity seems to account for the difference between identical and fraternal twins. Further evidence for a genetic influence comes from studies of adopted children with bipolar disorder. These studies show that biological relatives of the children have a higher incidence of bipolar disorder than do people in the general population. Thus, bipolar disorder seems to run in families for genetic reasons.

Owing or relating to, or affecting a particular person, over which a personal allegiance about the concerns and considerations or work-related stress can trigger a manic episode, but this usually occurs in people with genetic vulnerabilities, other factors—such as prenatal development, childhood experiences, and social conditions—seem to have relatively little influence in causing bipolar disorder. One study examined the children of identical twins in which only one member of each pair of twins had bipolar disorder. The study found that regardless of whether the parent had bipolar disorder or not, all of the children had the same high 10-percent rate of bipolar disorder. This observation clearly suggests that risk for bipolar illness comes from genetic influence, not from exposure to a parent's bipolar illness or from family problems caused by that illness.

Different therapies may shorten, delay, or even prevent the extreme moods caused by bipolar disorder. Lithium carbonates, a natural mineral salt, can help control both mania and depression in bipolar disorder. The drug generally takes two to three weeks to become effective. People with bipolar disorder may take lithium during periods of relatively normal moods to delay or prevent subsequent episodes of mania or depression. Common side effects of lithium include nausea, increased thirst and urination, vertigo, loss of appetite, and muscle weakness. In additiona1, long-term use can impair functioning of the kidneys. For this reason, doctors do not prescribe lithium to bipolar patients with kidney disease. Many people find the side effects so unpleasant that they stop taking the medication, which often results in a relapse.

From 20 to 40 percent of people do not respond to lithium therapy. For these people, two anticonvulsant drugs may help dampen severe manic episodes: carbamazepine (Tegretol) and valproate (Depakene). The use of traditional antidepressants to treat bipolar disorder carries risks of triggering a manic episode or a rapid-cycling pattern.

Controlled studies have not found that the endogenous-reactive distinction predicts response to psychotherapy (Blackburn, 1981; Kovacs, 1980; Rush, 1984), the presence or absence of precipitating stress has not proved to be a good predictor of response to treatment (Leff, Roatch and Bunney, 1970) and the endogenous-reactive distinction has been found to be deficient in a number of ways. Yet, it remains considerably utility. Reactivity to changes in life circumstances during a depressive episode have been found to predict response to electroconvulsive shock and antidepressant medication (Fowles and Gerch, 1979). Other symptoms that have been associated with a positive response to somantic treatment include quality of a mood and whether there has been a los of the ability to experience pleasure; psychomotor retardation; feeling worse in the morning after than the evening, such symptoms are now accepted as criteria for endogenous depression than is the absence of precipitating stress.

This consensus about the feature of endogenous depression still leaves questions about its polar opposite, reactive or neurotic depression. In clinical practice, it tends to be defined in terms of milder mood disturbances a preponderance of psychological rather than vegetative symptoms, and the presence of a precipitating stress, although there are particular doubts about the validity of this last feature. Akiskal (1978) found that reactive or neurotic depression is the single most common type of diagnosis of inpatient and outpatient settings, but they raised the issue of whether it was useful to consider it a unified entity or type. In about a quarter of all the cases of such depression studied, it appeared to be truly reactive, in the sense that it developed in the face of overwhelming stress, the persons who had previously seemed reasonably well functioning, but in another quarter of the cases, it seemed to reflect a greater or fewer of chronic tendencies to respond to normative stress with depressed moods and to the experience of social difficulties. Many of these patients were described as dependent, manipulative, hostile and unstable. Follow-up revealed overall that only 40 percent of the total sample was considered to have been suffering primarily from an affective disturbance in the absence of some of other condition. Some of the sub-sample, who had faced a clear precipitating stress developed endogenous features. In 10 percent of the sample, the depression seemed secondary to a medial-surgical illness. In 38 percent of the sample, the depression was secondary to some nonaffective disorder, ranging from an anxiety disorder to schizophrenia. In these patients with medical-surgical or nonaffective psychiatric conditions, intermittent depression seemed to follow the course of the other difficulties. A final 10 percent of the sample remained undiagnosed, but depression was considered the probable diagnosis. The work of Akiskal et al, (1978) is further evidence of the problems in attempting to draw any sharp distinctions in the classification and diagnosis of depression. Beyond this, it suggests both the utility and the

RICHARD J. KOSCIEJEW

difficulty of distinguishing between depression that is primary and that which is secondary to other conditions. Furthermore, the work suggests the usefulness of attempting to understand depression in terms of the presence or absence of characterologic al or lifestyle difficulties.

Thus, the endogenous pole of the endogenous-reactive distinction is more clearly defined than its counterpart. After a long history of debate and controversy, there is a growing consensus that the differentiation of endogenous and reactive depression is useful but that they represent points along a dimensional continuum, rather than two distinct forms of disorder, it is sometimes suggested that endogenous depressions are simply more severe, but this leave s unanswered questions about differences in etiology or the determinants of one depressive episode progressing to an endogenous course and another not. Biomedically oriented researcher looks to the identification of familial patterns of affective disturbance. The development of biological markers, and the refinement of diagnosis laboratory tests is the solution to the ambiguity and confusion. Baldessarini notes the promise of recent developments such as the dexamethasone suppression test, but he cautions that:

> While there has been considerable progress toward a biological and clinically robust diagnosis scheme, and in understanding some characteristics that can help to guide treatment, search for primary causes have been unsuccessful so far. Even so, virtually all of the biological characteristics of severely depressed patients that have been identified are 'state-dependent' (this, they disappear with recovery) and are not stable biological traits or markers of a possible heritable defect.

Even so, and by now it should have become apparent that the phenomena of depression are vaguely delineated and poorly understood. Seligman and his colleagues have provided a fine example of a strategy for dealing with this problem . . . its construction of a laboratory model or analogue with which greater precision can be achieved.

Let us return once more to the relation between helplessness (involving loss of self-esteem) and the simultaneously maintained narcissistic aspirations, noting that their intra-ego conflict assumed by Bibring and Melancholia: such that Bibring's theory opens two new vistas. One leads us to consider self-esteem as a signal, that is, an ego function, rather than as an effectual relation between the ego and the Superego. The other suggests that we recognize the role of the ego, and particularly of its helplessness, in the origin and function of the instinctual vicissitude called turning round upon the subject.

Though it is clear that the phenomenon from which the economic explanation must start is the inhibition of the ego, the economics of depression is still not understood. Bibring quote Fenichel's formulation as to, . . . The greater percentage of the available mental energy is used up in unconscious conflicts, and, not enough is left to provide the normal enjoyment of life and vitality (Bibring, 1953). But he finds this statement insufficient to explain depressive inhibition, and proceeds to reconsider the nature of inhibition such that:

> Freud (1926) prescribes for the sake of order and of a clear understanding for which of two major causes for restrictive impairment that of either having been imposed upon as the person or its measure of precautions, i.e., to prevent the development of anxiety or the feelings of guilt. This having brought about as a result of exhaustion, as to infer upon the energy of the ego, to which is engaged in some intense defensive activities. Bibring implies his own explanation in his comparison of depression to anxiety.

Anxiety as a reaction to external or internal danger indicates that the ego's desire to survive. The ego, challenged by the danger, mobilizes the signal of anxiety and prepares for fight or flight. In depression, the opposite takes place, the ego is paralysed because it finds itself incapable to meet the 'danger'. In certain instances, . . . depression may follow anxiety, then the mobilization of energy . . . is replaced by a decrease of self-reliance.

Thus Bibring's search for an economic explanation of depressive inhibition ends in the undefined term 'deceased of self-reliance', which as it stands, is not an economic concept.

What does that mean, that 'The ego is paralysed because it finds itself incapable to meet the danger'? Clearly 'paralysed' refers to the state of helplessness, one of the corollaries of which is the 'loss of self-esteem'. The danger is the potential loss of the object; The traumatic situation is that of the loss of an object—'helplessness' as Bibring defines, it is the persisting state of loss of an object. The anxiety signal anticipates the loss in order to prevent the reactivation of the traumatic situation, that is, of panic-anxiety. Perturbing fluctuations of self-esteem anticipates the initiation of measures that are preventions, such, are the reactivations in the state of persisting of the loss of its object, from which the state of helplessness would only have to be of its involving in the loss of self-esteem, thus, the relations between perturbing fluctuations of self-esteem and 'helplessness', which is accompanied by its loss of self-esteem, but maintaining the similarity between the relation of its own dose of anxiety and the signalling of the panic-anxiety. Fluctuations of self-esteem are then structurally tamed by forms of and signals to anticipate as to preclude reactivation of the state of helplessness. Yet, according to the accepted theory, fluctuations of self-esteem are the functions of the Superego's relation to the ego, just as anxiety was considered, prior to 1926, as a function of repression enforced by the Superego. In 1926, however, Superego anxiety was recognized as merely one kind of anxiety and the repression, hence anxiety relationship was reversed into anxiety signals and hence, repression. Bibring achieves an analogous observation that is the ego's awareness of its helplessness which in certain cased forces it to turn the aggression from the object against the self, thus aggravating and complicating the structure of depression. While in the accepted theory it is assumed that the aggression 'turned round upon the subject'', results in passivity and helplessness, in Bibring's conception it is the helplessness which is the cause of this 'turn round'.

Thus, Bibring's theory opens upon two new vistas. One leads us to consider self-esteem as a signal, that is, an ego function, rather from an open condition to the enclosing effect of an aggressive relation between the ego and the Superego. The other suggests that we reconsider the role of the ego, and particularly of its helplessness, in the origin and function of the instinctual vicissitude called turning round upon the subject.

The first of these, like Freud's structural theory of anxiety and Fenichel's of quilts (1945), leads to a broadening of our conception of the ego's apparatuses and functions. The second is even more far-reaching, it seems to go to the very core of the problem of aggression. We know that 'turning round upon the subject' was the basic mechanism for which Freud used before the 'death-instinct theory' to explain the major forms in which aggression manifests itself. It was in connection with this 'turning round upon the subject; Freud wrote:

> . . . sadism . . . seems to press toward a quite special aim—the infliction of pain, in addition t subjection and mastery of the object. Now a psychoanalysis would seem to show that infliction of pain plays no part in the original aims sought by sadism . . . the sadistic child takes no notice of whether or not it inflicts pain, nor of its purpose to do so. But when once the transformation into masochism has taken place, the experience of pain is ver y well adapted too severely as a passive masochistic aim . . . Where once the suffering of pain has been experienced as a masochistic aim, it can be carried back into the sadistic situation and result in a sadistic aim of inflicting pain (1915).

Thus Bibring's view that 'turning round upon the subject' is brought about by helplessness calling attention to some of Freud's early formulations. And prompt us to re-evaluate our conception of aggression. As it may lead to a theory of aggression which is an alternative to those which have so far been proposed, namely Freud's death-instinct theory. Fenichel's frustration-aggression theory, and the Hartmann-Kris-Loewenstein theory of an independent aggressive instinctual drive.

Let us return once more to the relation between helplessness, which involves the loss of self-esteem, and the simultaneously maintained narcissistic aspirations, such that their intra-ego conflict assumed by Bibring may have been implied by Freud when he wrote in "Mourning and Melancholia." 'A good, capable, conscientious person, . . . is more likely to fall ill of this . . . disease than one . . . of whom we too should have nothing good to say' (1917).

Fenichel's summary of the accepted view of the fate of self-esteem in depression is:

> . . . A greater or lesser loss of self-esteem is in the foreground. The subjective formula is-I have lost everything; now the world is empty, if the loss of self-esteem is mainly due to a loss of external supplies, or-I have lost everything because I do not deserve anything. If it is mainly due to a loss of internal supplies from the Superego (1945).

Fenichel's implied definition of supplies reads: 'The small child loses self-esteem when he loses love and attains it when he regains love . . . children . . . need . . . narcissistic supplies of affection . . . (1945)

Though the term 'supplies' have never been explicitly defined as a concept, it has become an apparently indispensable terminological acceptance in the psychoanalysis, and particularly in the theory of depression. In Bibring's theory, supplies are the goals of narcissistic aspirations. This gives them a central role in the theory, highlighting the urgent need to define them. Moreover, Bibring's comparison of depression and boredom hints at the direction in which such a definition might be sought by alerting us to the fact that there is a lack of supplies in boredom also. 'Stimulus hunger; is Fenichel's term for the immediate consequence of this lack? 'Boredom is characterized by the coexistence of a need for activity and activity-inhibition, as well as by stimulus-hunger and dissatisfaction with the available stimuli (1934). That an adequate stimulus is the lacking of supplies, which are available of either to be close to the object of the repressed instinctual drive or the resistance, the distant from it and thus of holding to no interests'

Bibring's juxtaposition of depression and boredom suggests that narcissistic supplies may be a special kind of adequate stimuli and narcissistic agitations a special kind of stimulus hunger. The implications of this suggestion become clearer if we note that it is the lack of narcissistic supplies which are responsible for the structuralization of the primitive state of helplessness, the reactivation of which is, according to Bibring's theory, the essencity depression.

The conception which emerges if we pursue these implications of Bibring's theory is this: (1) The development of the ego requires the presence of 'adequate stimuli', in this case love of objects; when such stimuli are consistently absent, a primitive ego state comes into existence, the later reactivation of which is the state of depression. (2) Normal development lowers the intensity of this ego state and its potentiality for reactivation, and limits its reactivation to those reality situations to which grief and sadness are appropriated reactions. (3) Recurrent absence of adequate stimuli in the course of development works against the lowering of the intensity of this ego state and increases the likelihood of its being reactivated, that is to say, established a predisposition of depression.

This conception is consonant with present-day ego psychology and also elucidates the economic and the adaptive aspects of Bibring's theory. The role of stimulation in the development of ego structure is a crucial implication of the concept of adaption. At the same time, since psychoanalytic theory explains the effects of stimulation in terms of changes in the distribution of attention cathexes, the role of stimulation in ego-structure development, to which is referred, and might that well be the starting point for an understanding of the economics of the ego state of depression.

All the same, our present discussion of the structural, genetic, dynamic, economic, and adaptive aspects of Edward Bibring's theory gives us a crystalline glimpse of its fertility. But does not exhaust either its implications or the problems it poses. An attempt to trace more or less of these would require a detailed analysis of those points where Bibring's views shade into other findings and theories of psychoanalytic ego psychology, and is therefore beyond our scope tonight.

However, of completing of the three points from which take root of Edward Bibring's theory which are less obvious than the observations and formulations so far discussed,

The first of its roots in the technique of the psychoanalysis, Bibring wrote:

> From an . . . a therapeutic point of view one
> has to pay attention not only to the dynamic and

RICHARD J. KOSCIEJEW

> genetic basis of the persisting narcissistic aspirations, the frustrations of which the ego cannot tolerate, but also the dynamic and genetic conditions which forced the infantile ego to become fixated to feelings of helplessness . . . the importance of these feelings of helplessness in the therapy of depression is obvious.

This formulation seems to say nothing more than the well-known technical rule that 'Analysis must always go on in the layers accessible to the ego at the moment' (Feniche l, 1938-39). But it does say more, because it specifies that it is the helplessness, the lack of interest, and the lowered self-esteem which are immediately accessible in depression. It is safe to assume that the clinically observed accessibility of this was one of the roots of Bibring's theory.

A second root of the theory is in Bibring's critique of the English school of a psychoanalysis. A study of this critique shows that on the one hand, Bibring found some of this school's observations on depression sound and, like his own observations, incompatible with the accepted theory of depression, and, on the other hand, he found this schools' theory of depression incompatible with psychoanalytic theory proper. It seems that Bibring intended his theory of depression to account for the sound observations of this school within the framework of psychoanalytic theory.

Finally, a third root of Bibring's theory seems to be related to the problems raised by the so-called 'existential analysis'. So far the only evidence for Edward Bibring's interest in the critical attitude toward 'existential analysis' is in the memories of those people who discussed the subject with him. Though his interest in phenomenology is obvious in his paper on depression, his interest in existentialism proper is expressed in only a few passages, like [Depression] is—essentially—'a human way of reacting to frustration and misery' whenever the ego finds itself in a state of real or imaginary helplessness against 'overwhelming odds'. Bibring's intent seems to have been to put the sound observations and psychoanalytically relevant concepts of 'existential analysis' into the framework of psychoanalytic ego psychology.

Briefly, the relevance within a behavioural framework, depression is conceptualized as an extinction phenomenon. On

374

reading the gerontological literature one is struck by the many behavioural similarities between the depressed and the elderly person: (1) One of the most striking features of both old age and depression is a progressive reduction in the rate of behaviour. The concept of 'disengagement' has been advanced to account for this reduction of behaviour. It is assumed to be a natural process which the elderly person accepts and desires, and which is thought to have intrinsic determinants (Cumming and Henry, 1961). From a behavioural framework, the elderly person's reduced rate of behaviour suggests that his behaviour is no longer being reinforced by his environment, i.e., that he, like the depressed person, is on an extinction schedule. (2) Other aspects of the depressive syndrome (feeling rejected, and so forth) are quite common among the elderly (Wolf, 1959). (3) Motivation is a critical problem in the elderly, as it is in the depressed patient. It is hard to find effective reinforcers for either. The number of potentially reinforcing events seems reduced. (4) The elderly person and the depressed person are turned inward, and focus on themselves, their memories, fantasies, and the past. The hypothesis immediately caused to suggest in itself, that a reduction in the response contingent rate of positive reinforcement is a critical antecedent condition for many of the behavioural changes have discussed of exchanging views about something in order to arrive at the truth or to convince others that lounges in and about the geriatric clients.

It is, nonetheless, that depression, that it is for this reason it needs a model. The clinical 'entity' has multifaceted symptoms, but let us look at those that seem central to the diagnosis and that may be related to learned helplessness. The symptoms of learned helplessness that we have discussed all have parallels in depression.

Sustaining the lowered response initiation the word 'depression' is a behavioural description that denotes a reduction or depression in responding. Even so, it is not surprising that a prominent symptom of depression is failure, or slowness of a patient to initiate responses. Such is the systematic study of the symptoms of depression. Grinker, Miller, Sabishin, Nunn, and Nunally (1961) all describe this in a number of ways:

> Isolated and withdrawn, prefers to remain by himself, stays in bed much of the time . . .
> Gait and general behaviour slowed and retarded . . .

> Volume of the voice deceased, sits alone very quietly
> Feels unable to act, feels unable to make
> decisions . . .
> [They] give the appearance of an 'entity' person
> who has 'given up . . .

Mendels (1970) described the slowdown in responding associated with depression as:

> Loss of interest, decrease in energy, inability to
> accomplish tasks, difficulty in concentration and the
> erosion of motivation, as these are ambitions that
> combine to impair efficient functioning. For many
> depressives the first signs of the illness are in the
> area of their increasing inability to cope with their
> work and responsibilities.

Aaron Beck (1967) describes the 'paralysis of the will' as a striking feature of depression:

> In the severity of cases, these are often completed
> in the paralysis of the will. The patient has no desire
> to do anything, even those things which are essential
> to life. Consequently, he may be relatively immobile
> unless prodded or pushed into activity by others. It
> is sometime necessary to put the patient out of bed,
> wash, dress, and feed him.

The characteristic passivity and lowered response initiation of depressives have been demonstrated in a large number of studies, i.e., Miller, 1975. Psychomotor retardation differentiates depressives from normal people and a direct example of reduced voluntary response initiation. In addition, depressives engage in fewer activities and the y show reduced interpersonal responding and reduced nonverbal communication. Finally, the intellectual slowness and learning, memory, and IQ deficits found in depressed patients may be viewed as resulting from reduced motivation to initiate cognitive actions such as memory scanning and mental arithmetic. These deficits all parallel the lowered response initiation in learned helplessness.

Recent laboratory experiments have demonstrated a striking similarity between the lowered response initiation of learned helplessness and depression (Klein, Fencil-Morse and Seligman, 1976; Miller and Seligman, 1975) in each of these studies, depressed and nondepressed students were first-divide into three groups; group (1) experienced inescapable loud noise (or unsolvable concept formation problems) (2) heard the loud noise but could turn it off by pressing a button (or was provided with a solvable problem), group (3) heard no noise (or did not work on any problems). All subjects then worked on a series of patterned anagrams, and half of all subjects were depressed; half were not depressed. As in the earlier study by Hiroto and Seligman (1975), nondepressed subjects in a group (1), who had previously been exposed to inescapable noise or unsolvable problems, showed response initiation deficits on the anagrams, while nondepressed subjects in a group (2) and (3) exhibited no deficit. Moreover, depressed subjects in all groups, including those of the group (3) who had no pretreatment, showed poorer response initiation on the anagrams than the nondepressed subjects in the group (3). Nondepressed subjects given a helplessness pretreatment showed response initiation deficits wholly parallel to those found in naturally occurring depression. Klein and Seligman (1976) showed the same parallel deficits between depressed subjects and nondepressed helpless subjects on tasks involving noise escape.

Also having a negative cognitive set of depressives that not only make fewer responses, but they interpret their few responses as failures or as doomed to failure, this negative cognitive se t directly mirrors the difficulty that helpless subjects have in learning that responding produces relief from an aversive situation.

Beck (1967) considers this negativistic cognition as the set to be primarily characteristic of depression:

> The depressed patient is peculiarly sensitive to any impediments to his goal-directed activity. An obstacle is regarded as an impossible barrier, but difficulty in dealing with a problem is interpreted as a total failure. His cognitive response to a problem or difficulty is likely to be an idea such as 'I'm licked'. 'I'll never be able to do this,' or 'I'm blocked no mater what I do'.

In truth, Beck views the passive and retarded behaviour of depressed patients as stemming from their negative expectations of their own effectiveness:

> The loss of spontaneous motivation, or paralysis of the will, has been considered a symptom of depression in the classical literature. The loss of motivation may be viewed as the result of the patient's hopelessness and pessimism. As long as he expects a negative outcome from any course of action; he is stripped of any internal stimulation to do anything.

This cognitive set crops up repeatedly in experiments with depressives. Friedman (1964) observed that although a patient was performing adequately during a test, the patient would occasionally reiterate this original protest of 'I can't do it,' or 'I don't know how'. This is also our experience in testing depressed patients.

Experimental demonstrations of negative cognitive set in depressed college students were provided by Miller and Seligman (1973) and Miller, Seligman, and Kurlander (1975). These studies showed that depressed students view their skilled actions very much as if they were only chance actions. In other words, depressed subjects, more than nondepressed subjects, tend to perceive reinforcement in a skill task as independent of their behaviour. Miller, Seligman, and Kurlander (1975) found this perception to be specific to depression: anxious and non-anxious students matched for extent of depression did not differ in their perceptions of reinforcement contingencies.

Miller and Seligman (1975, 1976), Klein, Fencil-Morse and Seligman (1976), and Klein and Seligman (1976) more directly demonstrated the parallel between the negative cognitive set in learned helplessness and depression. While replicating the findings of Miller and Seligman (1976) and Klein and Seligman (1976) found that nondepressed subjects who had been exposed to inescapable noise perceived reinforcement as less contingent than nondepressed subjects who had been exposed to either escapable or no noise during a skilful task. Pretreatment had no effect on perception of reinforcement in chance tasks. So, the effects of learned helplessness and depression on perception of reinforcement are parallel.

Cognitive deficits were also found in the previous studies of Miller and Seligman (1975), Klein et al. (1976) and Klein and Seligman (1976). These studies measured the degree to which subjects were able to benefit from successful anagram solutions or escapes from high volume noise. As with response initiation, depressed subjects in the untreated groups showed cognitive deficits relative to nondepressed subjects, and nondepressed subjects who had experienced inescapable noise or unsolvable problems exhibits cognitive deficits relative to nondepressed subjects in the control groups on measures of cognitive functioning.

Some studies indicate that negative cognitive set may also explain poor discrimination learning by depressives (Martin and Rees, 1966), and may be partly responsible for their lowered cognitive abilities (Payne, 1961; and Miller, 1975).

Depression, like learned helplessness, seems to have its time course. In discussing the 'disaster syndrome' Wallace (1957) reported that people experience a day or so of depression following sudden catastrophes, and then they again function normally. It seems possible that multiple traumatic events intervening between the initial disaster recovery might exacerbate depression in human considerably, as they do in dogs. We should also note that endogenously or process depression is characterized by fluctuations of weeks or months between depression and mania. Moreover, it is commonly thought that almost all depressions dissipate in time, although whether they last days, weeks, months, or years are a matter of some dispute (Paskind, 1929, 1930; Lundquist, 1945; Kraines, 1957).

According to psychoanalysts, the lowered aggression of depressives is due to introjected hostility. In fact, psychoanalysts view introjection of hostility as the primary mechanism producing symptoms of depression. We do not believe that the increased self-blame in depression results from hostility turned inward, but it seems undeniable that hostility, even in dreams (Beck and Hurvich, 1959; Beck and Ward, 1961), are reduced among depressive. This symptom corresponds to the lack of aggression in learned helplessness.

Depressives commonly show reduced interest in food, sex, and interpersonal relations. These symptoms correspond to the anorexia, weight loss, and sexual and social deficits in learned helplessness.

According to the catecholamine hypothesis of affective disorders, depression is associated with deficiencies of repinehrine (NE) at receptor sites in the brain, whereas elation may be associated with its excess. This hypothesis is based on evidence that imipramine, a drug that increases the NE available in the central nervous system, causes depression to end. Klerma and Cole (1965) and Cole (1964) experimented with imipramine and placebos on depressed patients and reported positive results of imipramine over placebos. Monoamineoxidase (MAO) inhibitors, which prevent the breakdown of NE, also may be useful in relieving depression (Cole, 1964; Davis, 1965). Reserpine, an antihypertensive medication that depletes NE, often produces depression as a side-effect in man (Beck, 1967). There is also some suggestion of cholinergic medication of depression. Janowsky et al. (1972) reported that physostigmine, a cholinergic stimulators, produced depressive effect in normal people. Atropine, a linergic blocker, reversed these symptoms. So, NE depletion and cholinergic activation are implicated in both depression and learned helplessness (Thomas and DeWald, 1977). However, Mendels and Frazer (1974) reviewed the behavioural effects of drugs that deplete brain catecholamines and they contend that the behavioural changes associated with reserpine are better interpreted as a psychomotor retardation-sedation syndrome than as depression. Moreover, selective depletion of brain catecholamines by alpha-methyl-para-tyrosine (AMPT) fails to produce some of the key features of depression, despite the fact that this drug produces a consistently greater reduction in amine metabolate concentration than occur s in depression. So depletion of catecholamines in itself may not be sufficient to account for depression.

Nonetheless, depressed people say they feel helpless, hopeless, and powerless, and by this they mean that they believe they are unable to control or influence those aspects of their lives that are significant to them. Grinker and coworkers (1961) describe the 'characteristics of hopelessness, helplessness, failure, sadness, unworthiness, guilt and internal suffering' as the 'essence of depression'. Melges and Bowlby (1969) also characterize depressed patients in this way and Bibring (1953) defines depression 'as the emotional expression [indicative] of a state of helplessness and powerlessness of the ego.'

They clearly are considerable parallels between the forms of behaviour that define helplessness and major symptoms of depression.

Differences:—But there are substantial gaps:—

First, there are two symptoms found with uncontrollable shock that may or may not correspond to symptoms of depression. Stomach ulcers occur more frequently and severely in rats receiving uncontrollable shock than in rats receiving controllable shock (Weiss, 1968, 1971). We know of no study examining the relationship of depression to stomach ulcers. Second, uncontrollable shock produces more anxiety, measured subjectively, behaviourally, and physiologically, than controllable shock (Seligman and Binik, 1976). The question of whether depressed people are more anxious than nondepressed people do not have a clear answer. Beck (1967) reported that although both depression and anxiety can be observed in some people, only a small positive correlation was found in a study of 600 people. Yet, Miller et al. (1975) found very few depressed college students who were not also anxious. We can speculate that anxiety and depression are related in the following way: When a man or animal is confronted with a threat or a loss, they initially respond with fear or anxiety. If he learns that the threat is wholly controllable, anxiety, having served its function, disappears. If he remains uncertain about his ability to control the threat, his anxiety remains. If he learns or is convinced that the threat is utterly uncontrollable, depression emerges.

A number of facts out depression have been insufficiently investigated for parallels in learned helplessness. Preeminent among these are the depressive symptoms that cannot be investigated in animals; dejected moods, feelings of self-blame and self-dislike, loss of mirth, suicidal thoughts and crying, but now, that learned helplessness has been reliably produced in man (Hiroto, 1974. Hiroto and Seligman, 1975; Klein, 1976; Klein and Seligman, 1976; Miller and Seligman, 1975, 1976; Racinskas, 1971; Roth and Kubal, 1975; Thornton and Jacobs, 1970; Dweck and Reppucci, 1973), we can now determine whether any of these states occur in helplessness.

Finally, we know of no evidence that disconfirms the correspondence of symptoms in learned helplessness and depression.

The term 'learned helplessness' was first used in connection with laboratory experiments in which dogs were exposed to shock from which they could not escape (Overmier and Seligman, 1967). After repeated trials, the dogs tended to sit passively when the shock came on. Exposed to a new situation from which they could escape a shock by jumping over a barrier, they failed to initiate

RICHARD J. KOSCIEJEW

the appropriate response. Some would occasionally jump over the barrier and escape, but they would generally revert to taking the shock passively. For the purposes of constructing an analogue of clinical depression, the behaviour of the dogs is significant in suggesting that exposure to uncontrollable aversive events may lead to a failure to initiate appropriate responses in new situations and an inability to learn that responding is effective.

The analogy to depression was bolstered by initial findings that in a variety of task situations, depressed human subjects resembled nondepressed subjects who had received repeated failure experiences. For instance, compared to nondepressed subjects who had not received repeated failure experiences, these groups of subjects took longer to solve anagrams and apparently failed to perceive the pattern underlying their successful solution (Klein and Seligman, 1976). Miller, Rosellini, and Seligman, and other research suggested that the parallels between the laboratory learned helplessness and depression were not limited to similarities in behaviour. Promising leads were also established with regard to etiology, treatment, and prevention.

The original learned helplessness model stimulated a large body of research and considerable controversy (Buchwald, Coyne, and Cole, 1978; Costello, 1978). Ultimately, the accumulated research led to questions about both the adequacy of the learned-helplessness explanation for the behaviour of nondepressed subjects who has been exposed to failure as well as the appropriateness of learned helplessness as an analogue of depression. For instance, it was shown that the performance deficits of subjects who had been given a typical learned helplessness induction were very much situation-specific (Cole and Coyne, 1977) and that these deficits might better be explained as the result of anxious self-preoccupation, rather than the perception of response-reinforcement independence (Coyne, Metalsky and Lavelle, 1980). Furthermore, the characterization of depressed persons as passive and lacking in aggression was challenged. Difficulties with the original learned helplessness model led to a major reformulation (Abramson, Seligman and Teasdale).

We used to designate with the term, learned helplessness, to describe the interference with adaptive responses produced by inescapable shock and also as a short hand to describe the process that we believe underlies the behaviour that we cannot control of which the distinction between controllable and uncontrollable reinforcement is central to the phenomenon and the theory of helplessness. Learned helplessness in the dog is defined by two types of behaviour. (1) Dogs that have had shock or are slower to make responses than naive dogs, and (2) if the dog does make a response that turns off shock, it has more trouble than a naive dog learning that responding is effective.

However, if we are to propose a model of depression in man, we must have proof that learned helplessness occurs in man.

Besides passivity and retarded response-relief learning, other characteristics associated with learned helplessness are relevant to depression in man. First, helplessness has a time course. In dogs, inescapable shock produces transient as well as permanent interference with escape (Overmier and Seligman, 1967) and avoidance (Overmier, 1968): 24 hours after one session of inescapable shock, dogs are helpless; but after 48 hours their response is normal. This is also true of goldfish (Padilla, 1970). After multiple sessions of inescapable shock, helplessness is not transient (Seligman and Groves, 1970; Seligman, Maier and Geer, 1968) Weiss (1968) found a parallel time course for weight loss in rats given uncontrollable shock, but other that this no time course has been found in rats or in other species (e.g., Anderson, Cole, and McVaugh, 1968; Seligman, Rosellini, and Kozak, 1975). Nonetheless, uncontrollable trauma produces a number of effects found in depression. The two basic effects are these: animals and humans become passive—they are slower to initiate responses to alleviate trauma and may not respond at all; and animals and humans are retarded in learning that their behaviour may control trauma. If a response is made that does produce relief, they often have trouble realizing that one causes the other. This maladaptive behaviour has been observed in a variety of species over a range of tasks that require voluntary responding. In addition, this phenomenon dissipates in time in the dog, and it causes lowered aggression, loss of appetite, and norepinephrine depletion.

The passivity of dogs, rats and men in the face of trauma and their difficulty on benefiting from response-relief contingencies results in what we believe, from having learned that responding and traumas are independent—that trauma is uncontrollable. This is the heart of the learned helplessness hypothesis. The hypothesis states that when shock is inescapable, the organism learns that responses and shock termination are independent (the probability of shock termination given any response doesn't differ from its probability in the absence of that response). Learning that trauma is uncontrollable has three effects.

(1) A motivational effect—it reduces the probability that the subject will initiate responses to escape, because part of the incentive for making such responses is the expectation that they will bring relief. If the subject has previously learned that its responses have no effect on trauma, this contravenes the expectation, thus, the organism's motivation to respond is undermined by experience with reinforcers it cannot control. Such that this motivational effect undermines passivity in learned helplessness, and, if the model is valid, in depression.

(2) The cognitive effect—learning that responses and shock are independent makes it more difficult to learn that responses do produce relief when the organism makes a response that actually terminates shock. In general, if we have acquired a cognitive set in which A's are irrelevant to B's, it will be harder for us to learn that A's produce B's when they do. By the helplessness hypothesis, this mechanism is responsible for the difficulty that helpless organisms have in learning that responding produces relief, even after they respond and successfully turn off shock. Further, if the model is valid, this mechanism produces the 'negative expectations' of depression.

(3) An emotional effect—although it does not follow directly from the helplessness hypothesis—such that uncontrollable shock produces more conditioned fear, ulcers, weight loss, defecation, and pain than controllable shock.

One cause of laboratory-produced helplessness seems to be learning that one cannot control important events. Learning that responses and reinforcement are independent results in a cognitive set that has two effects: fewer responses to control reinforcement are initiated and associating successful responses with reenforcement becomes more difficult.

Nevertheless, some of the events that typically precipitate depression; failure in work or school; death or loss of loved ones; rejection by or separation from loved ones; physical disease, and growing old. What do all these have in common?

Four recent theories of depression seem to be largely in agreement about the etiology of depression, and what they agree on is the centrality of helplessness and hopelessness. Bibring (1953), arguing from a dynamic viewpoint, sees helplessness as the cause of depression:

> What has been described as the basic mechanism of depression, the ego's shocking awareness of its helplessness in regard to its aspirations, is assumed to represent the core of normal, neurotic and probably also psychotic depression.

Melges and Bowlby (1969) see a similar cause of depression:

> Our thesis is that while a depressed patient's goals remain unchanged, however, his estimate of the likelihood of achieving then and his confidence in the efficacy of his own skilled actions is both diminished . . . the depressed person believes that his plans of action are no longer effective in reaching his continuing and long range goals . . . From this state of mind is derived, we believe, much depressive symptomalogy, including indecisiveness, inability to an act, making increased demands on others, and feelings of worthlessness and guilt about not discharging duties.

Beck (1967, 1970) sees depression as resulting primarily from a patient's negative cognitive set, largely about his abilities to change his life:

> A primary factor appears to be the activation of idiosyncratic cognitive patterns which divert the thinking into specific channels that deviate from reality. As a result, the patient perseverates in making negative judgements and interpretations

of experience, negative evaluations of the self, and negative expectations of the future.

Lichtenberg (1957) sees hopelessness as the defining characteristic of depression:

> Depression is defined as a manifestation of felt hopelessness regarding the attainment of goals when responsibility for the hopelessness is attributed to one's personal defects. In this context hope is conceived to be a function of the perceived probability of success with respect to goal attainment.

Even so, it means that all of a person's efforts have been in vain, his responses have failed to bring about the gratification he desires; he cannot find responses that control reinforcement. When a person is rejected by someone he loves, he can no longer control this significant source of gratification and support. When a parent or lover dies, the bereaved people are powerless to produce or an influence of love from a dead person. Physical disease and growing old are obvious helplessness experiences. In these conditions, the person's own responses are ineffective and he must rely on the care of others. So, we would predict that life events do not produce depression (Alarcon and Cori, 1972) but uncontrollable life events.

However, Ferster (1969, 1973), Kaufman and Rosenblum (1967); Mckinney and Bunney (1969), and Liberman and Raskin (1971) have suggested that depression is caused by extinction procedures or the loss of reinforcers. There is no contradiction between the learned-helplessness and extinction view of depression; helplessness, however, is more general. Briefly, extinction is a special case of independence between responding and reinforcement. Reinforcement, just the same, may also be presented with a probability greater than zero, and still be presented independent of responding. This occurs in the typical helplessness paradigm and cause responses to decrease in probability (Recorta and Skucy, 1969). Therefore, a view talks about independence between responding and reinforcement assumes the extinction view and, in addition, suggests that situations in which reinforcers still occur independent of responding also will cause depression.

Both learned helplessness and depression may be caused by learning that responses and reinforcement are independent. But this view runs into several problems. Can depression actually be caused by situations other than extinction in which reinforcement still occur but are not under the individual's control? To put it another way, 'is a net loss of reinforcement necessary for depression, or can depression occur when there is only loss of control without loss of reinforcement?' Would a Casanova who made love with seven new women every week become depressed if he found out that women wanted him not because of his amatory prowess but because of his wealth or because his fairy god mother wished it? We can only speculate.

It seems appropriate to mention 'success' depression in this context. When people finally reach a goal after years of striving—being promoted or obtaining a PhD—many become depressed. This puzzling phenomenon is clearly a problem for a loss of reinforcement view of depression. From a helplessness view, success depression may occur because reinforcement is no longer contingent on present responding. After years of goal-directed instrumental activity, the reinforcement automatically changes. One now gets his reinforcement because of whom he is rather than what he is doing. The common clinical impression that many beautiful women become depressed and attempt suicide also presents problems for the loss of reinforcement theory: positive reinforcers abound not because of what they do but because of how they look. Would be a generation of children risen with abundant positive reinforcers that they received independently to what, and they did become clinically depressed?

According to the helplessness view, the central theme in successful therapy should be having the patient discover and come to accept that his responses produce the gratification that he desires—that he is, in short, an effective human being. Some therapies that reportedly alleviate depression are consonant with a learned helplessness model, however, it is important to note that the success of a therapy often has little to do with its theoretical underpinning. So, with the exception of Klein and Seligman (1976), as a se t of examples that seem as a test of the model, but merely as a set of examples that seem to have exposure to response-produced success as a cure for depression.

RICHARD J. KOSCIEJEW

Consonant with their helplessness-centred views of the etiology of depression, Bibring (1957), Beck (1967), and Melges and Bowlby (1969) all stressed that reversing helplessness alleviates depression. For example, Bibring (1953) has stated:

> The same conditions which bring about depression (helplessness) in reverse serve frequently the restitution from depression. Generally, one can say that depression subsides either (I) when the narcissistically important goals and objects appear to be again within reach (which is frequently followed by a temporary elation) or (ii) when they become sufficiently modified or reduced to becoming realizable, or (iii) when they are altogether relinquished, or (iv) when the ego recovers from the narcissistic shock by regaining its self-esteem with the help of various recovery mechanisms (with or without any change of objective or goal).

In their review of therapies for depression, Seligan, Klein, and Miller (1976) indicated that most of the therapies have strong elements of inducing the patient to discover that responses produce the reinforcement he desires. In antidepression milieu therapy (Taulbee and Wright, 1971), for example, the patient is forced to emit one of the most powerful responses people have for controlling others—anger—and when this response is dragged out of his depleted behaviour repertoire, he is powerfully reinforced. Becks' (1970) cognitive therapy is aimed at similar goals. He sees success manipulations as changing the negative cognitive set ('I'm an ineffective person) of the depressive to a more positive set, and argues that the primary task of the therapist is to change the negative expectations of the depressed patient to more optimistic ones. Even so, both Burgess (1968), therapy and the categorically hierarchical task assigned (Beck, Seligman, Binik, Schuyler, and Brill, unpublished data), the patient makes instrumental responses of gradually increasing complexity, and each is reinforced. Similarly, all instrumental behaviour therapy for depression (Hersen, Eisler, Alford, and Agras, 1973; Reisinger. 1972), by definition, arrange the contingencies so that responses control the occurrence of reinforcement; the patient's recognition of this relationship should alleviate depression. Lewinsohn's therapy also has this element; participation in activity and other nondepressed behaviour controls therapy time. (Lewinsohn, Weinstein, and Shaw, 1969). In assertive training (Wolpe, 1968), the patient must emit social responses to bring about a desired change in his environment. Such that the study provides a useful method fo r testing the effectiveness of any therapy for depression in the laboratory because we can bring depression into the laboratory, in that, both in its naturally occurring state and in the form of learned helplessness, we can now see what reverses it in the laboratory. Will assertive training, emotive expression or atropine given to helpless and depressed subjects in the laboratory reverse the symptoms of depression and helplessness?

In order to explain depression, Burgess (1968) and others have relied heavily on the reinforcement the patient gets for his depressed behaviour, it is tempting to seek to remove this reinforcement during therapy, but caution is in order, so to explain the persistence or maintenance of some depressive behaviours, but it does not explain how they began. Helplessness suggests that failure to initiate active responses originates in the perception that the patient cannot control reinforcement. Thus, there can be two sources of a depressed patient's passivity: (a) patients are passive for instrumental reasons, because they think staying depressed brings them sympathy, love and attention, and (b) patients are passive because they believe that no response at all will be effective in controlling their environment. In this sense, it means that there is at least some response that believes he can effectively perform. Maier (1970) found that dogs who were reinforced for being passive by shock termination were not nearly as debilitated as dogs for whom all responses were independent of shock termination. Similarly, patients who use their depression in a way of controlling reinforcement are less helpless than those who have given up. Nonetheless, depression may be directly antagonized when patients come to see that their own responses are effective in alleviating their suffering and produced gratifications.

Nonetheless, many therapies, from psychoanalysis to cognitive understandings, claim to be able to cure depression. The evidence presented is selective as only those treatments that seemed compatible with helplessness were such that was possible that when other therapies work it. It is, because they reinstate the patient's sense of efficacy. However, evidence on the effectiveness of therapy in depression that is less anecdotal and selective is sorely needed. The recent study of Klein and Seligman (1976) may provide a laboratory procedure for evaluating the effectiveness of any therapy suggested for learned helplessness and depression.

All the same, a behavioural self-control model for the study of depression is focussed on different subsets of depressive phenomena. Such that the self-control model organizes and relates these phenomena and has its own implications for symptomatology, etiology, and therapy. Depression has certain properties which make the development of a model particularly difficult, however, the term depression refers to a syndrome which encompasses a broad set of symptoms with diverse behavioural referents (Beck, 1972; Levitt and Lubin, 1975; Mendels, 1970; Woodruff, Goodwin and Guze, 1974). Especially notable is the diversity among cognitive symptoms. Aside from manifest subjective sadness, depressed persons show clinical symptoms such as quilt, pessimism, low sel-esteem, self-derogation, and helplessness. Accounting for these distinctive cognitive behaviours and integrating them with the various overt-moto r behaviours characteristic of depression is limited to verbal-cognitive and overt-motor variables are appropriate since no reliable physiological index has been clearly identified as a symptom of depression (Bruder, 1970).

A recent resurgence of interest in psychological aspects of depression has become evident, and, with it, new and innovative models have been advanced. Behavioural and cognitive modes proposed by Lewinsohn (1974), Seligman (1974) and Beck (1974) have been most prominent and influential in behavioural research and clinical application.

Lewinsohn (1974; Lewinsohn, Weinstein, and Shaw, 1969) have to develop a clinical research program which looks at depression as a self-extinctive phenomenon. A loss or lack of response contingent positive reinforcement results in reduced rates of common overt-motor behaviour and also elicits a basic dysphoria. All other cognitive-verbal symptoms of depression are secondary elaborations of these basic dysphoria. Susceptivity to depression and ability to overcome depression is related to social skill, the range of events which are potentially reinforcing to the person, and reinforcement availability. The etiology of depression is therefore, the joint function of external environmental changes and individual differences in reinforcement potential and social skills. Therapy procedures are aimed at identifying potential sources of reinforcement in the person's environment and developing strategies to increase their frequency of occurrence (Lewinsohn, 1976. Lewinsohn and Shaffer, 1971; Robinson and Lewinsohn, 1973) In other instances, therapy consists of isolating deficits in social interaction and training subjects in modifying these socially skilled behaviours (Lewinsohn, Biglan and Zeiss, 1976); Lewinsohn and Shaw, 1969; Lewinsohn, Weinstein and Alper, 1970).

Also, Seligman has proposed a model of depression based on a laboratory paradigm of learned helplessness (Seligman, 1974, 1975). A situation in which the probability of the consequence given a response is equal to the probability of the consequence given no response produces the phenomenon of learned helplessness. Noncontingent punishment has been the situation most studied. Learned helplessness has properties which parallel the symptoms of depression: (1) lowered response initiation (passivity), (2) negative cognitive se t (belief that one's actions are doomed to failure; (3) dissipation over time, (4) lack of aggression, (5) loss of libido and appetite, and (6) norepinephrine depletion and cholinergic activity (Seligman, Klein, and Miller, 1974). Cognition is given a central position in this model in that of the 'depressive retardation is caused by a brief in response-reinforcement independence'; (Seligman. 1974). Other cognitive symptoms are held to be elaborations on this central belief. No therapy studies have been directly generated by this model to date, however, Klein and Seligman (1976) has demonstrated the reversibility of learned helplessness and depression following experience with solvable problems.

From a different perspective, Beck (1970, 1972, 1974) has evolved a cognitive model of depression which holds that depression consists of a primary triad of cognitive patterns or schema (1) a negative view of the world; (2) a negative view of the self, and (3) a negative view of the future. These views are maintained by distorted models of cognition such as selective abstraction, arbitrary inference, and overgeneralization,. The over—behavioural symptoms of depression follow from cognitive distortion. Distorted schemas develop in early childhood and leave individuals susceptible to depression in the face of stress. Therapy involves the identification of distortions and their confrontation with the evidence of objective experience. Case studies employing these modifications have been described by Beck (1972) and Rush,

Khatami, and Beck (1975). Group studies have shown that therapy based on a Beck's cognitive behaviour modification model is superior to a program based on Lewinsohn's model, a nondirective control therapy and a waiting list control and are more effective than treatment with imipramine hydrochloride (Rush, Beck, Kovacs, and Hollon).

The severe disorders of mood or effect are among the most simple of the major psychiatric syndromes. Lifetime expectancy rates for such disorders are between 3 and 8 percent of the general population. Only a minority is treated by psychiatrists or in psychiatric hospitals and about 70 percent of prescriptions for antidepressants are written by nonpsychiatrist physicians. These and other modern medical treatments of severe mood disorders have contributed to a virtual revolution in the theory and practice of modern psychiatry since the introduction of mood-altering drugs three decades ago. These agent s include lithium salts (1949), and Monoamine oxidase (MAO) inhibitors (1952), and the antimanic and Antipsychotic (neuroleptics) agents such as chlorpromazine (1952), and the Tricyclic or heterocyclic (imipramine-like) antidepressants (1957). In addition, electroconvulsive therapy (ECT) continues to have a place in the treatment of very severe and acute mood disorders, especially life-threatening forms of depression.

The development of these modern medical therapies has had several important effects. First. These agents have provided for a simple and specific effect among the safe forms of treatment with a profound impact on current patterns of medical practice, for example, many depressed or hypomanic patients can be managed adequately in outpatient facilities to avoid prolonged, expensive, and disruptive hospitalization which were formerly common. Second, partial understanding of the pharmacology of the psychotropic drugs has led to imaginative hypotheses concerning the pathophysiology or etiology of severe mood disorders. These, in turn, have encouraged a revolution on experimental psychiatry in which the hypotheses have been tested in clinical research. Many of the earlier hypotheses have been found wanting or simplistic, nevertheless, they have led to increased understanding of the diagnosis, biology, and treatment of mood disorders and to newer research that represents a third level of development. This is the focus of the practical clinical benefits of now and in the near future.

In the light of this some characteristics of infant development during this holding phase can be enumerated. It is at this stage that:

(1) primary process, (2) primary identification, (3) auto-erotism, (4) primary narcissism, and (5) living realities.

In this phase the ego changes over from an unintegrated state to a structure integration, and so the infant becomes able to experience anxiety associated with disintegration. The word disintegration begins to have meant which it did not possess before go integration became a fact. In healthy development at this stage the infant retains the capacity for re-experiencing unintegrated states, but this depends on the continuation of reliable maternal care or on the built-up in the infant of memories of material care beginning gradually to be perceived as such. The result of healthy progress in the infant's development during this stage is that he attains to what might be called 'unit status'. The infant becomes a person, an individual in his own right.

Associated with this attainment is the infant 's psychosomatic existence which begins to take on a personal pattern: that is, that the basis for this for this indwelling is a linkage of motor and sensory and functional experience with the infant's new state of being a person. As a further development there comes into existence what might be called a limiting membrane, which to some extent (in health) is equated with the surface of the skin, and has a position between the infant's 'me' and his 'not me'. So the infant comes to have an inside and an outside, and a body-scheme. In this way meaning comes to the function of intake and output, moreover, it gradually become meaningful to postulate a personal or inner psychic reality for the infant.

During the holding phase other processes are initiated; the most important is the dawn of intelligence and the beginning of a mind as something distinct from the psyche, and, from this, the secondary processes and symbolic functioning, and of the organization of a personal psychic content, which forms a basis for dreaming and for living relationships.

At the same time there starts in the infant a joining up of two roots of impulsive behaviours. The term 'fusion' indicates the positive process whereby diffuse elements that belong to movement and to muscle erotism that becomes fused with the orgiastic functioning of the erotogenic zones. This concept is more familiar as the reverse process of defusion, which is a complex and complication defence in which aggression becomes separated out from erotic experience after a period in which a degree of fusion has been achieved. All these developments belong to the environmental condition of 'holding', and without being good enough holding the stages cannot be attained, or once attained cannot become established,

A further development in the capacity for object relationships. In that, the infant changes from relationship to objectively conceived object to a relationship to an object objectively perceived. This change is closely bound up with the infant's change from being merged with the mother to being separate from her, or to relating to her as a separate and 'not-me', This development is not specifically related to the holding, but is related to the phase of 'living with' . . .

In the holding phase the infant is maximally dependent. One can classify dependence thus:

(I) Absolute Dependence: In this state the infant has no means of knowing about the maternal care, which is largely a matter of prophylaxis. He cannot gain control over what is well and what is badly done, but is only a position to gain profit or to suffer disturbances,

(ii) Relative Dependence: The infant can become aware of the need for the details of maternal care, and to a growing extent relate them to personal impulse, and then later, in a psychoanalytic treatment, can reproduce them in the transference,

(iii) The infant develops the means for doing without actual care. This is accomplished through the accumulation of memories of care, the projection of personal needs and the introjection of care details, with the development of confidence on the environment, and must be added that, the element of intellectual understanding with its tremendous implications.

Nonetheless, in borderline cases the analyst does not always wait in vain, that in the course of time the patient becomes able to make use of the psychoanalytic interpretations of the original trauma projection. It may even happen that he is able to accept for what is in the environment as a projection of the simple and stable going-on-being elements that derive from his own inherent potential.

Such that it is necessary to attempt to state briefly what happens to the inherented potential if this is to develop into an infant, and thereafter onto a child reaching toward independent existence, because if the plexuity of the subject such a statement must be made in the assumption of satisfactory material care, which means parental care. Satisfactory parental care can be classified roughly into three overlapping states.

1. Holding.
2. Mother and infant living together, as the father's function (on dealing with the environment for the mother) is not known to the infant
3. Father, mother, and infant, all three living together.

The term 'holding' is used to denote not only the actual physical holding of the infant, but also the total environmental provision prior to the concept of living with. In other words, it refers to a three-dimensional or space relationship (spatiality) with time gradually added. This overlaps with, but initiate prior to, instinctual experiences that in time would determine the object relationships. It includes the management of experiences that are inherent in existence, such as the completion (and therefore, the noncompeting) of processes, such ss the completion and, the noncomcompletion of specific processes which from the outside may seem to be purely physiological but which belong to infant psychology and take place on a complex psychological field, particularly, by determining the awareness and the empathy of the mother.

The term 'living with' implies object relationships, and the emergence of the infant from the state of being merged with the mother, or his perception of objects external to the self.

The paradox is that what is good and bad in the infant's environment is not in fact a projection, but in spite of this it is necessary, if the individual infant is to develop healthily, that everything will seem to him to be a projection. We find omnipotence and the pleasure principle in operation, as they certainly are in earliest infancy; and to this observation we can add that the recognition of a true 'not-me' is a matter of the intellect; it belongs to extreme sophistication and to the maturity of the individual.

In the writings of Freud most of the formulations concerning infancy derive from a study of adults in analysis. At first sight it would seem that a great deal of psychoanalytic theory is about early childhood and infancy, but in one sense Freud can be said to have neglected unfancy as a stare. This is brought out by a footnote in 'Formulations of the Two Principles of Mental Functioning,' of which he shows that he knows he is taking for granted the very things that are under discussion, as in the text he traces the development from the pleasure-principle to the reality-principle, following his usual course of reconstructing the infancy of his adult patients. The note runs as follows:

> It will rightly be objected that an organization which was a slave to the pleasure principle and neglected the reality of the external world could not maintain itself alive for the shortest time, so that it could not have come into existence at all. The employment of a fiction like this is. However, justified when one considers that the infant—provided one includes with it the care it receives from its mother—does almost realize a psychical system of this kind.

Freud paid full tribute to the function of maternal care, and it must be assumed that he left this subject alone only because he was not ready to talk about its implications. The note continues:

> It probably hallucinates the fulfilment of its internal needs; it betrays its unpleasure, when there is an increase of stimulus and absence of satisfaction, by the motor discharge of screaming and beating about with its arms and legs, and it then experiences the satisfaction it has hallucinated. Later, as an older child, it learns to employ these manifestations of discharge intentionally for which of methods for

expressing its feelings. Since the later care of children is modelled in the care of infants, the dominance of the pleasure principle can really come to an end when a child has achieved complete physical detachment from its parents.

The words: 'provide one includes with it the care it receives from its mother' have of a great importance in the immediate contextual presentation. The infant and the maternal care together from a unit. certainly if one is to study the theory of the parent-infant relationship one must come to a decision about these matters, which concern the real meaning of the word dependence or dependency. It is not enough that it is acknowledged that the environment is important if there is to be a discussion of the theory of the parent-infant relationship, then we are divided into two of the same who do not allow that at the earliest stages the infant and the maternal care belong to each other and cannot be disentangled. These two things, the infant and the maternal case, disentangle and dissociate themselves in health, which means as to do many things, to some extent it means a disentanglement of maternal care from something which we then call the infant, or the beginning of a growing child. This idea is covered by Freud's words at the end of the footnote, explaining that: The dominance of the pleasure principle can really come to an end only when a child has achieved complete physical detachment from its parents.

It is axiomatic in these matters of maternal care of holding variety that when things go well the infant has no means of knowing what is being properly provided and what is being prevented. Such, that when things do not go well that the infant becomes aware, not of the failure of maternal care, but of the results, whatever they may be, of that failure: That in saying, as a result of success in maternal care there is built up in th infant a continuity of being which is the basis of ego strength' of being interrupted by reactions to the consequences of that failure, The resultant of ego-weakening. Such interruptions constitute annihilation, and are evidently associated with pain of psychotic quality and intensity. In the extreme case the infant exists only on the basis of a continuity of reactions to impingement and of recoveries from such reactions. This is in great contras t to the continuity for being that which is our conception of ego strength.

The transition stage has been described as a stage of;'Quasi-Independence'; and the reason for the adoption if this description is of sufficient importance to demand special attention. It emerges with the utmost clarity from the study of schizoid cases that the most characteristic feature of the state if infantile dependence is identification with the object. Still, it would not be going too far to say that, psychologically speaking, identification with the object and infantile dependence is really the same phenomenon. In that the mature dependence involves a relationship between two kinds of dependence is identical with Freudian distinctions between the narcissistic and the anaclitic choice of objects. The relationship involved in mature dependence is, if course, only the theoretically possible. Nevertheless, it remains true that the more mature a relationship is, the less it is characterized by identification, for what identification essentially represents is failure to differentiate the object. It is when identification persists at the expense of differentiation that a markedly compulsive element enters into the individual's attitude toward its objects. This is well seen in the infatuation of schizoid individuals. It may also be observed in almost uncontrollable impulse so commonly experienced by schizoid and depressive soldiers to return to their wives or their homes, when separated from them owing to military necessities. The abandonment of infantile dependence involves an abandonment with differentiated objects. In the dreams of schizoids the process of differentiation is frequently represented by the process of differentiations is frequently repressed by the theme of trying to cross a gulf or chasm, albeit the crossing which is attempted may also occur in a regressive direction. The process itself is commonly attended by considerable anxiety, and the anxiety attending it finds characteristic expression on dreams.

The process of differentiation of the object derives particular significance from the fact that infantile dependence is characterized not only by identification, but also by an oral attitude of incorporation. In virtue of this fact the object with which the individual is identified is also an incorporated object or, to put the matter in a more arresting fashion, the object in which the individual is incorporate d may well prove the key to man y metaphysical puzzles. But that it may, however, it is common to find in dreams a complete equivalence between being inside an object and having the object inside.

Such then being the situation, the task of differentiating the object resolves itself into a problem of expelling an incorporated object, i.e., it becomes a problem of expelling contents. Herein lies the rationale of Abraham's 'anal phases,' and it is in this direction that we must look for the significance of the anal techniques which play such an important part during the transition stage. It is important as elsewhere, to insure that the cart is not placed before the horse, and to recognize that it is not a case of individual being occupied with the disposal of contents at this stage because he is anal, but of his being anal because he is preoccupied at this stage with the disposal of content.

The great conflict of the transition stage may now be formulated as a conflict between a progressive urge to surrender the infantile attitude of identification with the object and a regressive urge to maintain that attitude. During this period, accordingly, the behaviour of the individual is characterized both by desperate and endeavours on his part to separate himself from the object and desperate endeavour to achieve reunion with the object—desperate attempts 'to escape from prison' and desperate e attempts 'to return home'. Although one of these attitudes may become to preponderate, there is in the first instance a constant oscillation between the owing and the anxiety attending each. The anxiety attending separation manifests itself as a fear of isolation; and the anxiety attending identification manifests itself as a fear of being shut in, imprisoned or engulfed ('cribbed, cabined and confined'). These anxieties, it will be noticed, are essentially phobic anxieties. In may accordingly be inferred that it is to the conflict between the progressive urge toward separation from the object and the regressive lure of identification with the object that we must look for the explanation of the phobic state.

Owing to the intimate connection existing between identification and oral incorporation, and consequently between separation and excretory expulsion, the conflict of the transition period also presented itself as a conflict between an urge to expel and an urge to retain contents. Just as between separation and reunion, such that either of these oscillation between expulsion and retention, although either of these attitudes may have become dominant. Both attitudes are attended by anxiety—the attitude of expulsion being attended by a fear of bursting (often accompanied or replaced by a fear of some internal disease like cancer). Such anxieties are essentially obsessional anxieties, and it is the conflict between an urge to expel the objet as content and an urge conflict as the object content s that underlies the obsessional state.

The phobic and obsessional techniques are thus seen as to represent two differing methods of dealing with the same basic conflict: In these two differing methods correspond to two differing attitudes toward the object. From the phobic point of view the conflict presents itself as in between flight from and return to the object. From the obsessional point of view, as the conflict presents itself as one between expulsion and retention of the object. It thus becomes obvious that the phobic techniques correspond to an active attitude. The obsessional technique also expresses a much higher degree of aggression toward the object; For, whether the objects are expelled or retained, it is being subject to forcible control. For the phobic individual, the choice lies between escaping from the power of the object and submitting to it. In other words, while the obsessional technique is essentially sadistic in nature, the phobic technique is essentially masochistic.

In the hysterical state we can recognize the operation of another technique for attempting to deal with the basic conflict of the transition period. In this case, the conflict appears to be formulated as simply one between acceptance and rejection of the object. Acceptance of the object is clearly manifested in the intense love-relationships which are so typical of the hysteric; but the very exaggeration of these emotional relationships in itself raises a suspicion that a rejection is being overcompensated. The suspicion is confirmed by th propensity of the hysteric to dissociation phenomena. That these Dissociative phenomena represent a rejection of the genitals need not be stressed, but, as the analysis can always unmask an identification of the rejected genitals with the breast as the original object of the libidinal impulses during the period of infantile dependence. This being so, it is of note, that what is dissociated by the hysteric is an organ function in himself. This can only have meant—that the rejected object is an internalization object, however, the hysteric's over-valuation of his objects leaves no room for doubt that in his case the accepted object and rejection of the internalized object.

If the paranoid and the hysteric states are now compared, we are confronted with a significant contrast. Whereas, the hysteric over-values objects in the outer world, the paranoid individual regards them as persecutors, and, whereas, the hysteric dissociation is a form of self-depreciation, the attitude of the paranoid individual is one of extravagant grandiosity. The paranoid state must, accordingly, be regarded as representing rejection of the externalized object and acceptance of the internalized object.

Having interpreted the hysterical and paranoid technique in terms of the acceptance and rejection of objects, we can now obtain interesting results by applying a similar interpretation to the phobic and obsessional techniques. The conflict underlying the phobic state may be concisely formulated as one between flight and the object and flight from the object. In the former case, is, of course, the object is accepted, whereas, in the latter case the object is rejected. In both cases, the object is treated as external, in the obsessional state, the conflict presents itself as one between the exclusion and the rejection of content. In this case, accordingly, both the accepted and the rejected objects are treated as internal. If in the case of the phobic state both the accepted and the rejected objects are treated as external and in the obsessional state both are treated as internal, the situation as regarding these hysterical and paranoid states is that one of these objects is treated as an externalized object and the other as an internalized object, in the hysterical state. It is the accepted object that is externalized, and the paranoid state, the object which is externalized is the rejected object.

The chief features of the stage of transition between infantile and adult dependence may now be briefly summarized. The transition period is characterized by a process of development, whereby object—relationships based upon identification gradually give place to relationships with differentiated objects. Satisfactory development during this period, therefore, depends upon the success which attends the process of differentiation of the object, and this in turn depends upon the issue of a conflict or separation from the object—situations which are both desired and feared. The conflict in question may call into operation any or all characteristic techniques—the obsessional, the paranoid, the hysterical and the phobic: and, if object-relationships are unsatisfactory, these techniques are liable to form the basis of characteristic psychopathological developments in later life. The various techniques cannot be classified in any order corresponding to presumptive levels of libidinal development. On the contrary, they must be regarded as alternative techniques, all belonging to the same stage in the development of object-relationships. Which of the techniques is employed, or to what extent each is employed would appear to depend on large measure upon the nature of the object-relationships established during the preceding stage of infantile dependence. In particular, it would seem to depend upon the degrees which have been established between the developing ego and its internalized objects.

The infant is completely dependent upon his object not only for his existence and physical well-being, but also for the satisfaction of his psychological needs. It is true, nonetheless, that mature individuals are likewise dependent upon one and the other, for the satisfaction of psychological and, no less, than their physical needs. Nevertheless, on the psychological side, the dependence of mature individuals sufficient to render him dependent in an unconditional sense. We also notice that, whereas in the case of the adult object-relationship has a considerable spread, in the case of the infant it tends to be focussed upon a single object. The loss of an object is thus, much more devastating in the case of the infant. If a mature individual loses an object, least of mention, he still has some objects remaining. His eggs are not all in one basket. Further, he has a choice of objects and can desert one for another. The infant, on the other hand, has no choice. He has no alternative but to accept or to reject his object—an alternative which is liable to present itself to him as a choice between life and death. His psychological dependence is further accentuated by the very nature of his object-relationship, for, as we have seen, this is based essentially upon identification. Dependence is exhibited in its most extreme form, in the intra-uterine state, and we may legitimately infer that on its psychological side this state is characterized by an absolute degree of identification. Identification may thus be regarded as representing the persistence into extra-uterine life of a relationship existing before birth. In so far as, identification persists after birth. The individual's object constitutes not only his world, but also himself. It is this fact has already been pointed out, that we must attribute the compulsive attitude of many schizoids and repressive individuals placed toward their objects.

Normal development is characterized by a process whereby progressive differentiations of the object is accompanied by progressive decreases in identification. So long as infantile dependence is to persist, that identification remains the most characteristic feature of the individual's emotional relationship with his object. Infantile dependence is equivalent to oral dependence—a fact which should be interpreted, not in the sens that the infant is inherently oral, but in the sense that the breast is the original object. During the oral phases, accordingly, identification remains the most characteristic feature of the individual's emotional relationship with his object. The tendency to identification, which is so characteristic of emotional relationships during these phases, also invade s the cognitive sphere, with the result that certain orally fixated individuals have only to hear of someone else suffering from any given disease in order to believe that they are suffering from it themselves. In the conative sphere, that identification has its counterpart in oral incorporation. And it is the merging of emotional identification with oral incorporations that confer s upon the stage of infantile dependence its most distinctive feature. These features are based upon the fundamental equivalence for the infant of being held in his mother's arms and incorporating the contents of her breast.

The phenomenon of narcissism, which is one of the most prominent characteristics of infantile dependence, is an attitude arising out of identification with the object. Such that primary narcissism may be simply defined as just such a state of identification with the object, secondary narcissism being a state of identification with an object which is internalized. While narcissism is a feature common to both the early and the late oral phase, the latter phase differs from the former in virtue of a change in the nature of the object. In the early oral phase the natural object is the breast; but in the later oral phase, the natural object becomes the mother. The transition from one phase to the other is thus marked by the substitution of a whole object (or the person) for a part-object. Nevertheless, the object continues to be treated as a part-object (the breast) with the result that the person of the mother becomes an object for incorporation. The transition from the early to the late oral phases are also characterized by the emergence of the biting tendency. Whereas in the early oral phase the libidinal attitude of incorporation monopolizes the field, in the late oral phase it is in competing with an accompanying attitude of biting. Now biting must be regarded for being essentially of all differentiated aggression. Consequently, the dawn of the late oral phase heralds the emergence of emotional ambivalence. The late oral phase is well described as pre-ambivalent. Nonetheless, one which aggression has not yet been differentiated from the libido. The early urges toward incorporation are essentially a libidinal urge, to which true aggression makes no contribution, even as a component factor. The recognition of this fact is greatly important for an understanding of the essential problems underlying to schizoid states. In the understanding, it is true that the incorporation urge is destructive in its gross effect, in the sense that the object which is eaten disappears. Nevertheless, the urge is not destructive in aim. When, as a child is to say, that he 'loves' cake, as it is certain to imply that the cake will vanish, and then consumingly destroyed. At the same time the destruction of the cake is not the aim of the child's 'love'. On the contrary, the disappearance of the cake is, from the child's point of view. A most regrettable consequence of his 'love' for it. What he really desires, is for himself, is to have his cake and eat it to. If the cake proves to be 'bad,' that if he spits it out or become sick. As this spiting out is specifically characteristic of the early oral phase, in that he rejects the bad cake, least of mention, he does not bite the cake with intentions for its being bad. This type of behaviour is specifically characterized of the early oral phasing, then, what is, so far as the object presents itself as 'good', it is incorporated, and, presents itself as 'bad', it is rejected, but, even when it appears to be bad, no attempt is made to destroy it. Again, it is the good object that is 'destroyed.' Albeit only incidentally and not by intention. In the late oral phase the situation is foreign, in that things are done differently, for in this phase the object may be bitten as well as incorporated. This means that direct aggression, as well as libidinal forces, is such that may be directed toward the object. Hence the appearance of the ambivalence which characterizes the late oral phase.

It soon becomes evident that the emotional oral phase takes the form of the alternative that to incorporate or not to incorporate, i.e., 'to love or not to love.' This is the conflict underlying the depressive state. It will be seen, accordingly, that the problem of the schizoid individual is how to love without destroying by love, whereas, the greater of problems is for the depressive individual, is how to love without destroying completely by hate. These are two very different problems.

The conflict underlying the schizoid state is, of course, much more devastating than the conflict underlying the depressive stat e, and, since the schizoid reaction has its roots in an earlier stage of development than the depressive reaction, the schizoid individual is less capable of dealing with conflict than is the depressive. It is owing to these two facts that the disturbance of the personality found in schizophrenia is so much more profound than found in depression. The devastating nature of the conflict associated with the early oral phase lies in the fact that, if it seems a terrible thing for an individual to destroy his object by love. It is the great tragedy of the schizoid individual that it is his love which seems to destroy; and it is because his love seems so destructive that he experiences such difficulty in directing his libido toward objects outer reality. He becomes afraid to love, and therefore he erects barriers between his objects and himself. He tends both to keep his objects at a distance and to make himself remote from them. He rejects his objects, and at the same time, he withdraws his libido from them. This withdrawal of libidinal energies may be carried to all lengths. It may be carried to a point at which all emotional and physical contacts with other persons are renounced; and it may even go so far that all libidinal links with outer reality are surrendered. All interest in the world around fades and everything becomes meaningless. In proportion as libido is withdrawn from outer objects it is directed toward the internalization with its accompanied objects; and, in proportion as this happens, the individual becomes introverted. And, incidently, it is on the observation that this process of introversion is characteristic on the onset of schizoid states that are themselves based on the conclusion that the introvert is essentially a schizoid. It is essentially in inner reality that the values of the schizoid are to be found. So far as he is concerned, the world of internalized objects is always encroaching upon the world of external objects; and in proportion as this happens his real objects become lost to him.

If loss of the real objects were the only trauma of the schizoid state the position of the schizoid individual would not be so precarious. It is necessary, nonetheless, to bear in mind the vicissitudes of the ego, which accompany loss of the object. Reference has already been made to the narcissism which results from an excessive libidinalization of internalized objects; and such narcissism is specially characteristic of the schizoid. Accompanying it, we invariably find an attitude of superiority which may manifest itself in consciousness to a varying degree as an actual sense of superiority. It should be of note, in that, this attitude of superiority is based upon an orientation toward internalized objects, and that in relation to objects in the world of outer reality the attitude of the schizoid is essentially one of inferiority. It is true, that the externally oriented inferiority may be masked by a façade of superiority, as based upon an identification of external with internalized objects. Nevertheless, it is invariably present, and it is evidence of a weakness in the ego. What chiefly compromises the development of the ego. In the case of the schizoid individual is the apparently insoluble dilemma which attends the direction of the libido toward objects. Failure to direct a libido toward the object is, of course, equivalent to loss of the object: But since, from the point of view of the schizoid, the libido is itself destructive, the object is equally lost when the libido is directed toward it. It can thus readily be understood that, if the dilemma becomes sufficiently pronounced, the result is a complete impasse, which reduces the ego onto a state of utter impotence. The ego becomes quite incapable of expressing itself; and, in so far as this is so, it's very existence become s compromised. This can be exemplified by the following, as: 'I can' t say anything. I have nothing to say. I'm empty. There's nothing of m e, . . . I feel quite useless; I haven' t don e anything. I've gone cold and hard; I don't feel anything . . . I can't express myself' I feel futile.' Such descriptions are well illustrated, not only the state of impotence to which the ego is compromised in the schizoid dilemma. The last quoted remark of this is, perhaps, as drawing attentions to the characteristic affect of the schizoid state: For the characteristic affect of the schizoid state is undoubtedly a sense of futility.

The libido may be withdrawn in varying degrees even from that part of the psyche which is, so to speak, nearest to external objects. It may be withdrawn from the realm of the conscious into the unconscious. When this occasions, the effect is as if the ego itself had withdrawn into the unconscious: But the actual position would seem to be that, when the libido deserts the conscious part of the ego (such as it is), the unconscious part of the ego is all that is left to behave as a functioning ego. In extreme cases the libido would seem to desert even the unconscious part of the ego and relapse into the primal id, leaving both surface only the picture with which Kraepelin has familiarize us in his account of the last phase of dementia præcox. Whether such a mass-withdrawal of the libido can properly be ascribe d to repression is a debatable question, although where the process is restricted to a withdrawal from object-relationships, it may give that impression. At any rate, the effectual withdrawal of the libido 'feels quite different' from that of simple repression. There can be no doubt, nonetheless, that withdrawal of the libido from the conscious part of the ego has the effect of relieving emotional tension and mitigating the danger of violent outbursts of precipitate action. There can be equally little doubt that much of the schizoid individual's anxiety really represents fear of such outbursts occurring. This fear commonly manifests itself as a fear of going insane or as a fear of imminent disaster. It is possible, therefore, that massive withdrawal of the libido has the significance of as desperate effort on the part of an ego threatened with repression of the basic impulse which urge the individual on to make emotional contacts. In the case of the schizoid, of course, these impulses are essentially oral impulses. It is when this effort is within measurable distance of succeeding that the individual begins to tell us that he feels as if there were nothing of him, or as if he had los t his identity, or as if he was dead, or as if he had ceased to exist. The fact is that in renouncing the libido the ego renounces the very form of energy which holds it together—and the ego thus becomes lost. Loss of the ego is the ultimate psychopathological disaster which the schizoid individual is constantly struggling, with more or less success, to avert by exploiting all available techniques (including the transitional techniques) for the control of his libido. In essence, therefore, the schizoid state is not a defence, although evidence of the presence of defences may be detected in it. It represented the major disaster which may befall the individual who has failed to outgrow the early stage of dependence.

If the problem which confronts the individual in the early oral phase is how to love the object without destroying it by love, the problem which confronts the individual in the oral phase is how to love the object without destroying it by hate. Accordingly, since the depressive reaction has its roots in the late oral phase, It is the disposal of his hate, rather than the disposal of his love, that constitutes the difficulty of the depressive individual. The formidable as this difficulty is, the depressive is at any rate spared the devastating experience of feeling that his love is bad. Since his love, at any rate, seems good, he remains inherently capable of a libidinal relationship with outer objects in a sense in which the schizoid is not. His difficulty in maintaining such a relationship arises out of his ambivalence. This ambivalence in turn arises out of the fact that during the late oral phase, he was more successful than the schizoid in substituting direct aggression (biting) for simple rejection of the object. While his aggression has been differentiated, that, nonetheless, he has failed in some degree to achieve that further step in development which is represented by dichotomy of the object. This further step, had been taken, it would have enabled him to dispose of his hate by directing it, predominantly at least, toward the rejected object and he would have been left free to direct toward his accepted object love which was relatively unaccompanied by hate. In so far as he failed to take such a step, the depressive remains in that state which characterized his attitude toward his object during the late oral phase. His external object during that phase, of course, a whole object (his mother); and his libidinal attitude toward it was incorporative. The incorporated object to the depressive thus comes to be an undivided whole object, which he adopts an ambivalent attitude. The presence of such an inner situation is less disabling so far as outer adjustments are concerned than is the corresponding inner situation, in the case of the schizoid, for in the case of the depressive there is no formidable barrier obstructing the outward flow of libido. Consequently, the depressive individual readily establishes libidinal contacts with others; and, if his libidinal contact with others appears satisfactory with others, and if his libidinal contacts are satisfactory to him, his progress through life may appear fairly smooth, as the inner situation is always present, and it is readily reactivated if his libidinal relationship becomes disturbed. Any such disturbance if his libidinal relationships become disturbed, such disturbances immediately calls into operation the hating element in his ambivalent t attitude; and, when his hate becomes directed toward the internalized object, a depressive reaction supervene any frustration in object-relationships is, o f course, functionally equivalent to loss of the object. Whether partial or complete, since severe depression is so common a sequel to actual loss of the object (whether by the death of a loved person or things as severally otherwise). Loss of the object must be regarded as the essential trauma which provokes the depressive state.

Physical injury or illness is obviously represents to himself, whom is to any, that such a loss, e.g., the loss of an eye or a limb, represent the symbolic castration as taken that we no further, for it still remains to be explained why a reaction which is characteristically provoked by loss of the object should also b e provoked by loss of part of the body. The true explanation lies in the fact that the depressive individual still remains to a be a distinctive feature of degrees to an actual state of infantile identification with his object. To him, is, therefore, bodily loss is functionally equivalent to loss of the object, and this equivalence is reinforced by the presence of an internalized object which, so speak, suffuses the individual's bod y and imparts it to narcissistic value.

A brief dispositional representation as the presentation for which of 'narcissism', is to mean, that the cathexis of the own 'self' with libido, is used in the term 'self' because the state of primary narcissism exists only prior to any ego differentiation, a point made by Hartmann. What is called the secondary narcissism is the late return of object cathexis to the own person.

There still remains to be explained is the phenomenon of Involutional melancholia. According to Freud and Abraham, the functional process in melancholia is the loss of the loved objects, the real, or some similar situation having the same significance, result in the object becoming installed within the ego. Owing, however, to an excess of cannibalistic impulses in the object, this introjection miscarries and the consequence is illness.

All the same, are those who tend to regard the etiology of this condition as entirely different from that of 'reactive depression', nonetheless, the two conditions have sufficiencies in common clinical standpoints, to justify, as to invoke the principle of, 'entia non sunt multicanda præter necessitate.' It is not of anything real but melancholia, by definition closely associated with the climacteric; and the climacteric would seem to be in itself evidence of a definite waning of libidinal urges. It cannot be said, nonetheless, that there is any equivalent diminution of aggression. The balance between the libidinal and the aggressive urges is thus disturbed, and, further, It is disturbed in the same direction as when the hate of any ambivalent individual is activated by loss of the object. Accordingly, in an individual of the depressive type the climacteric has the effect of establishing the same situation as does actual loss of the object where object-relationships are concerned; and the result is a depressive reaction. If the prospect of recovery in the case of Involutional melancholia is less hopeful than in cases of reactive depression,

This is not difficult to explain: For, whereas the latter case a libido is still available for a restoration of the balance in the former case, it is not. Involutional melancholia is thus seen to conform to the general configuration of the depressive state, and it imposes upon as holding of no necessity to modify the conclusion already envisaged—that loss of the object is the basic trauma underlying the depressive state. As in the case of the schizoid state, this state is not a defence, on the contrary, it is a state against which the individual seeks to defend himself by means of such techniques (including the transitional techniques) as are available for the control of his aggression. It represents the major disaster which may befall the individual who failed to outgrow the late oral stage of infantile dependance.

Owing or relating to, or affecting a particular person, over which a personal allegiance about the concerns and considerations or work-related stress can trigger a manic episode, but this usually occurs in people with genetic vulnerabilities, other factors—such as prenatal development, childhood experiences, and social conditions—seem to have relatively little influence in causing bipolar disorder. One study examined the children of identical twins in which only one member of each pair of twins had bipolar disorder. The study found that regardless of whether the parent had bipolar disorder or not, all of the children had the same high 10-percent rate of bipolar disorder. This observation clearly suggests that risk for bipolar illness comes from genetic influence, not from exposure to a parent's bipolar illness or from family problems caused by that illness.

Different therapies may shorten, delay, or even prevent the extreme moods caused by bipolar disorder. Lithium carbonates, a natural mineral salt, can help control both mania and depression in bipolar disorder. The drug generally takes two to three weeks to become effective. People with bipolar disorder may take lithium during periods of relatively normal moods to delay or prevent subsequent episodes of mania or depression. Common side effects of lithium include nausea, increased thirst and urination, vertigo, loss of appetite, and muscle weakness. In addition, long-term use can impair functioning of the kidneys. For this reason, doctors do not prescribe lithium to bipolar patients with kidney disease. Many people find the side effects so unpleasant that they stop taking the medication, which often results in a relapse.

From 20 to 40 percent of people do not respond to lithium therapy. For these people, two anticonvulsant drugs may help dampen severe manic episodes: carbamazepine (Tegretol) and valproate (Depakene). The use of traditional antidepressants to treat bipolar disorder carries risks of triggering a manic episode or a rapid-cycling pattern.

Controlled studies have not found that the endogenous-reactive distinction predicts response to psychotherapy (Blackburn, 1981; Kovacs, 1980; Rush, 1984), the presence or absence of precipitating stress has not proved to be a good predictor of response to treatment (Leff, Roatch and Bunney, 1970) and the endogenous-reactive distinction has been found to be deficient in a number of ways. Yet, it remains considerably utility. Reactivity to changes in life circumstances during a depressive episode have been found to predict response to electroconvulsive shock and antidepressant medication (Fowles and Gerch, 1979). Other symptoms that have been associated with a positive response to somantic treatment include quality of a mood and whether there has been a los of the ability to experience pleasure; psychomotor retardation; feeling worse in the morning after than the irregularity for an evening and sleep, on which the appetite is also irregular. Such symptoms are now accepted as criteria for endogenous depression than is the absence of precipitating stress.

This consensus about the feature of endogenous depression still leaves questions about its polar opposite, reactive or neurotic depression. In clinical practice, it tends to be defined in terms of milder mood disturbances a preponderance of psychological rather than vegetative symptoms, and the presence of a precipitating stress, although there are particular doubts about the validity of this last feature. Akiskal (1978) found that reactive or neurotic depressions were the single most customary in the inpatient and outpatients' advance, but they raised the issue of whether it was useful to consider it a unified entity or type. In about a quarter of all the cases of such depression studied, it appeared to be truly reactive, in the sense that it developed a confrontational perspective about the overwhelming stress in persons who had previously seemed reasonably well functioning. In another quarter of the cases, it seemed to reflect a greater or fewer of chronic tendencies to respond to normative stress with depressed moods and to experience social difficulties. Many of these patients were described as dependent, manipulative, hostile and unstable. Follow-up revealed overall that only 40 percent of the total sample was considered to have been suffering primarily from an affective disturbance in the absence of some of other condition. Some of the

411

sub-sample, who had faced a clear precipitating stress developed endogenous features. In 10 percent of the sample, the depression seemed secondary to a medial-surgical illness. In 38 percent of the sample, the depression was secondary to some nonaffective disorder, ranging from an anxiety disorder to schizophrenia. In these patients with medical-surgical or nonaffective psychiatric conditions, intermittent depression seemed to follow the course of the other difficulties. A final 10 percent of the sample remained undiagnosed, but depression was considered the probable diagnosis. The work of Akiskal et al, (1978) is further evidence of the problems in attempting to draw any sharp distinctions in the classification and diagnosis of depression. Beyond this, it suggests both the utility and the difficulty of distinguishing between depression that is primary and that which is secondary to other conditions. Furthermore, the work suggests the usefulness of attempting to understand depression in terms of the presence or absence of characterological or lifestyle difficulties.

Thus, the endogenous pole of the endogenous-reactive distinction is more clearly defined than its counterpart. After a long history of debate and controversy, there is a growing consensus that the differentiation of endogenous and reactive depression is useful but that they represent points along a dimensional continuum, rather than two distinct forms of disorder, it is sometimes suggested that endogenous depressions are simply more severe, but this leave s unanswered questions about differences in etiology or the determinants of one depressive episode progressing to an endogenous course and another not. Biomedically oriented researcher looks to the identification of familial patterns of affective disturbance. The development of biological markers, and the refinement of diagnosis laboratory tests is the solution to the ambiguity and confusion. Baldessarini notes the promise of recent developments such as the dexamethasone suppression test, but he cautions that:

> While there has been considerable progress toward a biological and clinically robust diagnosis scheme, and in understanding some characteristics that can help to guide treatment, search for primary causes have been unsuccessful so far. Even so, virtually all of the biological characteristics of

severely depressed patients that have been identified are 'state-dependent' (this, they disappear with recovery) and are not stable biological traits or markers of a possible heritable defect.

Even so, and by now it should have become apparent that the phenomena of depression are vaguely delineated and poorly understood. Seligman and his colleagues have provided a fine example of a strategy for dealing with this problem . . . its construction of a laboratory model or analogue with which greater precision can be achieved.

Let us return once more to the relation between helplessness (involving loss of self-esteem) and the simultaneously maintained narcissistic aspirations, noting that their intra-ego conflict assumed by Bibring and Melancholia: such that Bibring's theory opens two new vistas. One leads us to consider self-esteem as a signal, that is, an ego function, rather than as an effectual relation between the ego and the Superego. The other suggests that we recognize the role of the ego, and particularly of its helplessness, in the origin and function of the instinctual vicissitude called turning round upon the subject.

Though it is clear that the phenomenon from which the economic explanation must start is the inhibition of the ego, the economics of depression is still not understood. Bibring quote Fenichel's formulation as to, . . . The greater percentage of the available mental energy is used up in unconscious conflicts, and, not enough is left to provide the normal enjoyment of life and vitality (Bibring, 1953). But he finds this statement insufficient to explain depressive inhibition, and proceeds to reconsider the nature of inhibition such that:

> Freud (1926) brings to a definition about the inhibition as felt by the restriction of functions of the ego, and mentions two major causes for such restrictions; Either having been imposed upon as the person or its measure of a precaution, i.e., to prevent the development of anxiety or the feelings of guilt, this having brought about as a result of exhaustion, as to infer upon the energy of the ego, of which it is engaged in some intense defensive

activities. Bibring implies his own explanation in his comparison of depression to anxiety.

Anxiety as a reaction to external or internal danger indicates that the ego's desire to survive. The ego, challenged by the danger, mobilizes the signal of anxiety and prepares for fight or flight. In depression, the opposite takes place, the ego is paralysed because it finds itself incapable to meet the 'danger'. In certain instances, . . . depression may follow anxiety, then the mobilization of energy . . . is replaced by a decrease of self-reliance.

What does that mean, that 'The ego is paralysed because it finds itself incapable to meet the danger'? Clearly 'paralysed' refers to the state of helplessness, one of the corollaries of which is the 'loss of self-esteem'. The danger is the potential loss of the object; The traumatic situation is that of the loss of an object—'helplessness' as Bibring defines, it is the persisting state of loss of an object. The anxiety signal anticipates the loss in order to prevent the reactivation of the traumatic situation, that is, of panic-anxiety. Perturbing fluctuations of self-esteem anticipates the initiation of measures that are preventions, such, are the reactivations in the state of persisting of the loss of its object, from which the state of helplessness would only have to be of its involving in the loss of self-esteem, thus, the relations between perturbing fluctuations of self-esteem and 'helplessness', which is accompanied by its loss of self-esteem, but maintaining the similarity between the relation of its own dose of anxiety and the signalling of the panic-anxiety. Fluctuations of self-esteem are then structurally tamed by forms of and signals to anticipate as to preclude reactivation of the state of helplessness. Yet, according to the accepted theory, fluctuations of self-esteem are the functions of the Superego's relation to the ego, just as anxiety was considered, prior to 1926, as a function of repression enforced by the Superego. In 1926, however, Superego anxiety was recognized as merely one kind of anxiety and the repression, hence anxiety relationship was reversed into anxiety signals and hence, repression. Bibring achieves an analogous observation that is the ego's awareness of its helplessness which in certain cased forces it to turn the aggression from the object against the self, thus aggravating and complicating the structure of depression. While in the accepted theory it is assumed that the aggression 'turned round upon the subject'', results in passivity and helplessness, in Bibring's conception it is the helplessness which is the cause of this 'turn round'.

Thus, Bibring's theory opens upon two new vistas. One leads us to consider self-esteem as a signal, that is, an ego function, rather from an open condition to the enclosing effect of an aggressive relation between the ego and the Superego. The other suggests that we reconsider the role of the ego, and particularly of its helplessness, in the origin and function of the instinctual vicissitude called turning round upon the subject.

The first of these, like Freud's structural theory of anxiety and Fenichel's of quilts (1945), leads to a broadening of our conception of the ego's apparatuses and functions. The second is even more far-reaching, it seems to go to the very core of the problem of aggression. We know that 'turning round upon the subject' was the basic mechanism for which Freud used before the 'death-instinct theory' to explain the major forms in which aggression manifests itself. It was in connection with this 'turning round upon the subject; Freud wrote:

> . . . sadism . . . seems to press toward a quite special aim—the infliction of pain, in addition t subjection and mastery of the object. Now a psychoanalysis would seem to show that infliction of pain plays no part in the original aims sought by sadism . . . the sadistic child takes no notice of whether or not it inflicts pain, nor of its purpose to do so. But when once the transformation into masochism has taken place, the experience of pain is ver y well adapted too severely as a passive masochistic aim . . . Where once the suffering of pain has been experienced as a masochistic aim, it can be carried back into the sadistic situation and result in a sadistic aim of inflicting pain (1915).

Thus Bibring's view that 'turning round upon the subject' is brought about by helplessness calling attention to some of Freud's early formulations. And prompt us to re-evaluate our conception of aggression. As it may lead to a theory of aggression which is an alternative to those which have so far been proposed, namely Freud's death-instinct theory. Fenichel's frustration-aggression theory, and the Hartmann-Kris-Loewenstein theory of an independent aggressive instinctual drive.

Let us return once more to the relation between helplessness, which involves the loss of self-esteem, and the simultaneously maintained narcissistic aspirations, such that their intra-ego conflict assumed by Bibring may have been implied by Freud when he wrote in "Mourning and Melancholia." 'A good, capable, conscientious person, . . . is more likely to fall ill of this . . . disease than one . . . of whom we too should have nothing good to say' (1917).

Fenichel's summary of the accepted view of the fate of self-esteem in depression is:

> . . . A greater or lesser loss of self-esteem is in the foreground. The subjective formula is-I have lost everything; now the world is empty, if the loss of self-esteem is mainly due to a loss of external supplies, or-I have lost everything because I do not deserve anything. If it is mainly due to a loss of internal supplies from the Superego (1945).

Fenichel's implied definition of supplies reads: 'The small child loses self-esteem when he loses love and attains it when he regains love . . . children . . . need . . ., narcissistic supplies of affection . . . (1945)

Though the term 'supplies' has never been explicitly defined as a concept, it has become an apparently indispensable terminological acceptance in the psychoanalysis, and particularly in the theory of depression. In Bibring's theory, supplies are the goals of narcissistic aspirations. This gives them a central role in the theory, highlighting the urgent need to define them. Moreover, Bibring's comparison of depression and boredom hints at the direction in which such a definition might be sought by alerting us to the fact that there is a lack of supplies in boredom also. 'Stimulus hunger; is Fenichel's term for the immediate consequence of this lack? 'Boredom is characterized by the coexistence of a need for activity and activity-inhibition, as well as by stimulus-hunger and dissatisfaction with the available stimuli (1934). That an adequate stimulus is the lacking of supplies, which are available of either to be too close to the object of the repressed instinctual drive or the resistance, the distant from it and thus of holding to no interests'

Bibring's juxtaposition of depression and boredom suggests that narcissistic supplies may be a special kind of adequate stimuli and narcissistic agitations a special kind of stimulus hunger. The implications of this suggestion become clearer if we note that it is the lack of narcissistic supplies which is responsible for the structuralization of the primitive state of helplessness, the reactivation of which is, according to Bibring's theory, the essencity depression.

The conception which emerges if we pursue these implications of Bibring's theory is this: (1) The development of the ego requires the presence of 'adequate stimuli', in this case love of objects; when such stimuli are consistently absent, a primitive ego state comes into existence, the later reactivation of which is the state of depression. (2) Normal development lowers the intensity of this ego state and its potentiality for reactivation, and limits its reactivation to those reality situations to which grief and sadness are appropriated reactions. (3) Recurrent absence of adequate stimuli in the course of development works against the lowering of the intensity of this ego state and increases the likelihood of its being reactivated, that is to say, established a predisposition of depression.

This conception is consonant with present-day ego psychology and also elucidates the economic and the adaptive aspects of Bibring's theory. The role of stimulation in the development of ego structure is a crucial implication of the concept of adaption. At the same time, since psychoanalytic theory explains the effects of stimulation in terms of changes in the distribution of attention cathexes, the role of stimulation in ego-structure development, to which is referred, and might that well be the starting point for an understanding of the economics of the ego state of depression.

All the same, our present discussion of the structural, genetic, dynamic, economic, and adaptive aspects of Edward Bibring's theory gives us a crystalline glimpse of its fertility. But does not exhaust either its implications or the problems it poses. An attempt to trace more or less of these would require a detailed analysis of those points where Bibring's views shade into other findings and theories of psychoanalytic ego psychology, and is therefore beyond our scope tonight.

However, of completing of the three points from which take root of Edward Bibring's theory which are less obvious than the observations and formulations so far discussed,

417

The first of its roots in the technique of the psychoanalysis, Bibring wrote:

> From a . . . therapeutic points of view one has to pay attention not only to the dynamic and genetic basis of the persisting narcissistic aspirations, the frustrations of which the ego cannot tolerate, but also the dynamic and genetic conditions which forced the infantile ego to become fixated to feelings of helplessness . . . the importance of these feelings of helplessness in the therapy of depression is obvious.

This formulation seems to say nothing more than the well-known technical rule that 'Analysis must always go on in the layers accessible to the ego at the moment' (Fenichel, 1938-39). But it does say more, because it specifies that it is the helplessness, the lack of interest, and the lowered self-esteem which are immediately accessible in depression. It is safe to assume that the clinically observed accessibility of this was one of the roots of Bibring's theory.

A second root of the theory is in Bibring's critique of the English school of a psychoanalysis. A study of this critique shows that on the one hand, Bibring found some of this school's observations on depression sound and, like his own observations, incompatible with the accepted theory of depression, and, on the other hand, he found this schools' theory of depression incompatible with psychoanalytic theory proper. It seems that Bibring intended his theory of depression to account for the sound observations of this school within the framework of psychoanalytic theory.

Finally, a third root of Bibring's theory seems to be related to the problems raised by the so-called 'existential analysis'. So far the only evidence for Edward Bibring's interest in the critical attitude toward 'existential analysis' is in the memories of those people who discussed the subject with him. Though his interest in phenomenology is obvious in his paper on depression, his interest in existentialism proper is expressed in only a few passages, like [Depression] is—essentially—'a human way of reacting to frustration and misery' whenever the ego finds itself in a state of real or imaginary helplessness against 'overwhelming odds'. Bibring's intent seems to have been to put the sound observations and psychoanalytically relevant concepts of 'existential analysis' into the framework of psychoanalytic ego psychology.

Briefly, the relevance within a behavioural framework, depression is conceptualized as an extinction phenomenon. On reading the gerontological literature one is struck by the many behavioural similarities between the depressed and the elderly person: (1) One of the most striking features of both old age and depression is a progressive reduction in the rate of behaviour. The concept of 'disengagement' has been advanced to account for this reduction of behaviour. It is assumed to be a natural process which the elderly person accepts and desires, and which is thought to have intrinsic determinants (Cumming and Henry, 1961). From a behavioural framework, the elderly person's reduced rate of behaviour suggests that his behaviour is no longer being reinforced by his environment, i.e., that he, like the depressed person, is on an extinction schedule. (2) Other aspects of the depressive syndrome (feeling rejected, and so forth) are quite common among the elderly (Wolf, 1959). (3) Motivation is a critical problem in the elderly, as it is in the depressed patient. It is hard to find effective reinforcers for either. The number of potentially reinforcing events seems reduced. (4) The elderly person and the depressed person are turned inward, and focus on themselves, their memories, fantasies, and the past. The hypothesis immediately passes, if to suggest of itself that a reduction in the response contingent rate in positive reinforcement is a critical antecedent's condition, but many of the behavioural changes are described in the elderly person.

It is, nonetheless, that depression, that it is for this reason it needs a model. The clinical 'entity' has multifaceted symptoms, but let us look at those that seem central to the diagnosis and that may be related to learned helplessness. The symptoms of learned helplessness that we have discussed all have parallels in depression.

Sustaining the lowered response initiation the word 'depression' is a behavioural description that denotes a reduction o r depression in responding. Even so, it is not surprising that a prominent symptom of depression is failure, or slowness of a patient to initiate responses. Such is the systematic study of the symptoms of depression. Grinker, Miller, Sabishin, Nunn, and Nunally (1961) all describe this in a number of ways: Isolated and withdrawn, prefers to remain by himself, stays in bed much of the time . . . Gait and general behaviour slow and retarded . . . Volume of the voice deceased, sits alone very quietly . . . Feels unable to act, feels unable to make decisions . . . [They] give the appearance of an 'entity' person who has 'given up.'

Mendels (1970) described the slowdown in responding associated with depression as: Loss of interest, decrease in energy, inability to accomplish tasks, difficulty in concentration and the erosion of motivation, as these are ambitions that combine to impair efficient functioning. For many depressives the first signs of the illness are in the area of their increasing inability to cope with their work and reasonability.

Aaron Beck (1967) describes 'paralysis of the will' as a striking feature of depression:

> In the severity of some cases, these are often completed in the paralysis of the will. The patient has no desire to do anything, even those things which are essential to life. Consequently, he may be relatively immobile unless prodded or pushed into activity by others. It is sometime necessary to put the patient out of bed, wash, dress, and feed him.

The characteristic passivity and lowered response initiation of depressives have been demonstrated in a large number of studies, i.e., Miller, 1975. Psychomotor retardation differentiates depressives from normal people and a direct example of reduced voluntary response initiation. In addition, depressives engage in fewer activities and the y show reduced interpersonal responding and reduced nonverbal communication. Finally, the intellectual slowness and learning, memory, and IQ deficits found in depressed patients may be viewed as resulting from reduced motivation to initiate cognitive actions such as memory scanning and mental arithmetic. These deficits all parallel the lowered response initiation in learned helplessness.

Recent laboratory experiments have demonstrated a striking similarity between the lowered response initiation of learned helplessness and depression (Klein, Fencil-Morse and Seligman, 1976; Miller and Seligman, 1975) in each of these studies, depressed and nondepressed students were first-divide into three groups; group (1) experienced inescapable loud noise (or unsolvable concept formation problems), group (2) heard the loud noise but could turn it off by pressing a button (or was provided with a solvable problem), group (3) heard no noise (or did not work on any problems). All subjects then worked on a series of patterned anagrams, and half of all subjects were depressed; half were not depressed. As in the earlier study by Hiroto and Seligman (1975), nondepressed subjects in the group (1), who had previously been exposed to inescapable noise or unsolvable problems, showed response initiation deficits on the anagrams, while nondepressed subjects in the group (2) and (3) exhibited no deficit. Moreover, depressed subjects in all groups, including those of a group (3) who had no pretreatment, showed poorer response initiation on the anagrams than the nondepressed subjects in the group (3). Nondepressed subjects given a helplessness pretreatment showed response initiation deficits wholly parallel to those found in naturally occurring depression. Klein and Seligman (1976) showed the same parallel deficits between depressed subjects and nondepressed helpless subjects on tasks involving noise escape.

Also having a negative cognitive set of depressives that not only make fewer responses, but they interpret their few responses as failures or as doomed to failure, this negative cognitive se t directly mirrors the difficulty that helpless subjects have in learning that responding produces relief from an aversive situation.

Aaron Beck (1967) considers this negativistic cognition as the set to be primarily characteristic of depression:

> The depressed patient is peculiarly sensitive to any impediments to his goal-directed activity. An obstacle is regarded as an impossible barrier, but difficulty in dealing with a problem is interpreted as a total failure. His cognitive response to a problem or difficulty is likely to be an idea such as 'I'm licked'. 'I'll never be able to do this,' or 'I'm blocked no mater what I do'.

In truth, Beck views the passive and retarded behaviour of depressed patients as stemming from their negative expectations of their own effectiveness:

> The loss of spontaneous motivation, or paralysis of the will, has been considered a symptom of depression

in the classical literature. The loss of motivation may be viewed as the result of the patient's hopelessness and pessimism. As long as he expects a negative outcome from any course of action; he is stripped of any internal stimulation to do anything.

This cognitive set crops up repeatedly in experiments with depressives. Friedman (1964) observed that although a patient was performing adequately during a test, the patient would occasionally reiterate this original protest of 'I can't do it,' or 'I don't know how'. This is also our experience in testing depressed patients.

Experimental demonstrations of negative cognitive set in depressed college students were provided by Miller and Seligman (1973) and Miller, Seligman, and Kurlander (1975). These studies showed that depressed students view their skilled actions very much as if they were only chance actions. In other words, depressed subjects, more than nondepressed subjects, tend to perceive reinforcement in a skill task as independent of their behaviour. Miller, Seligman, and Kurlander (1975) found this perception to be specific to depression: anxious and non-anxious students matched for extent of depression did not differ in their perceptions of reinforcement contingencies.

Miller and Seligman (1975, 1976), Klein, Fencil-Morse and Seligman (1976), and Klein and Seligman (1976) more directly demonstrated the parallel between the negative cognitive set in learned helplessness and depression. While replicating the findings of Miller and Seligman (1976) and Klein and Seligman (1976) found that nondepressed subjects who had been exposed to inescapable noise perceived reinforcement as to a lesser extent of a responsive contingence than nondepressed subjects who had been exposed to either escapable or no noise during a skilful task. Pretreatment had no effect on perception of reinforcement in chance tasks. So, the effects of learned helplessness and depression on perception of reinforcement are parallel.

Cognitive deficits were also found in the previous studies of Miller and Seligman (1975), Klein et al. (1976) and Klein and Seligman (1976). These studies measured the degree to which subjects were able to benefit from successful anagram solutions or escapes from high volume noise. As with response initiation, depressed subjects in the untreated groups showed cognitive deficits relative to nondepressed subjects, and nondepressed subjects who had experienced inescapable noise or unsolvable problems exhibits cognitive deficits relative to nondepressed subjects in the control groups on measures of cognitive functioning.

Some studies indicate that negative cognitive set may also explain poor discrimination learning by depressives (Martin and Rees, 1966), and may be partly responsible for their lowered cognitive abilities (Payne, 1961; Miller, 1975).

Depression, like learned helplessness, seems to have its time course. In discussing the 'disaster syndrome' Wallace (1957) reported that people experience a day or so of depression following sudden catastrophes, and then they again function normally. It seems possible that multiple traumatic events intervening between the initial disaster recovery might exacerbate depression in human considerably, as they do in dogs. We should also note that endogenously or process depression is characterized by fluctuations of weeks or months between depression and mania. Moreover, it is commonly thought that almost all depressions dissipate in time, although whether they last days, weeks, months, or years is a matter of some dispute (Paskind, 1929, 1930; Lundquist, 1945; Kraines, 1957).

According to psychoanalysts, the lowered aggression of depressives is due to introjected hostility. In fact, psychoanalysts view introjection of hostility as the primary mechanism producing symptoms of depression. We do not believe that the increased self-blame in depression results from hostility turned inward, but it seems undeniable that hostility, even in dreams (Beck and Hurvich, 1959; Beck and Ward, 1961), is reduced among depressive. This symptom corresponds to the lack of aggression in learned helplessness.

Depressives commonly show reduced interest in food, sex, and interpersonal relations. These symptoms correspond to the anorexia, weight loss, and sexual and social deficits in learned helplessness.

According to the catecholamine hypothesis of affective disorders, depression is associated with the deficiency of norepinehrine (NE) at receptor sites in the brain, whereas elation may be associated with its excess. This hypothesis is based on evidence that imipramine, a drug that increases the NE available in the central nervous system, causes depression to end. Klerma and Cole (1965) and Cole (1964) experimented with imipramine and placebos on depressed patients and reported positive results of imipramine over placebos. Monoamineoxidase (MAO) inhibitors, which prevent the breakdown of NE, also may be useful in relieving depression (Cole, 1964; Davis, 1965). Reserpine, an antihypertensive medication that depletes NE, often produces depression as a side-effect in man (Beck, 1967). There is also some suggestion of cholinergic medication of depression. Janowsky et al. (1972) reported that physostigmine, a cholinergic stimulators, produced depressive affect in normal people. Atropine, a linergic blocker, reversed these symptoms. So, NE depletion and cholinergic activation are implicated in both depression and learned helplessness (Thomas and DeWald, 1977). However, Mendels and Frazer (1974) reviewed the behavioural effects of drugs that deplete brain catecholamines and they contend that the behavioural changes associated with reserpine are better interpreted as a psychomotor retardation-sedation syndrome than as depression. Moreover, selective depletion of brain catecholamines by alpha-methyl-para-tyrosine (AMPT) fails to produce some of the key features of depression, despite the fact that this drug produce a consistently greater reduction in amine metabolate concentration than occur s in depression. So depletion of catecholamines in itself may not be sufficient to account for depression.

Nonetheless, depressed people say they feel helpless, hopeless, and powerless, and by this they mean that they believe they are unable to control or influence those aspects of their lives that are significant to them. Grinker and coworkers (1961) describe the 'characteristics of hopelessness, helplessness, failure, sadness, unworthiness, guilt and internal suffering' as the 'essence of depression'. Melges and Bowlby (1969) also characterize depressed patients in this way and Bibring (1953) defines depression 'as the emotional expression [indicative] of a state of helplessness and powerlessness of the ego.'

They clearly are considerable parallels between the forms of behaviour that define helplessness and major symptoms of depression.

Differences:—But there are substantial gaps:—

First, there are two symptoms found with uncontrollable shock that may or may not correspond to symptoms of depression. Stomach ulcers occur more frequently and severely in rats receiving uncontrollable shock than in rats receiving controllable shock (Weiss, 1968, 1971). We know of no study examining the relationship of depression to stomach ulcers. Second, uncontrollable shock produces more anxiety, measured subjectively, behaviourally, and physiologically, than controllable shock (Seligman and Binik, 1976). The question of whether depressed people are more anxious than nondepressed people does not have a clear answer. Beck (1967) reported that although both depression and anxiety can be observed in some people, only a small positive correlation was found in a study of 600 people. Yet, Miller et al. (1975) found very few depressed college students who were not also anxious. We can speculate that anxiety and depression are related in the following way: When a man or animal is confronted with a threat or a loss, he initially respond with fear or anxiety. If he learns that the threat is wholly controllable, anxiety, having served its function, disappears. If he remains uncertain about his ability to control the threat, his anxiety remains. If he learns or is convinced that the threat is utterly uncontrollable, depression emerges.

A number of facts out depression have been insufficiently investigated for parallels in learned helplessness. Preeminent among these are the depressive symptoms that cannot be investigated in animals; dejected moods, feelings of self-blame and self-dislike, loss of mirth, suicidal thoughts and crying, but now, that learned helplessness has been reliably produced in man (Hiroto, 1974. Hiroto and Seligman, 1975; Klein et al., 1976; Klein and Seligman, 1976' Miller and Seligman, 1975, 1976; Racinskas, 1971; Roth and Kubal, 1975; Thornton and Jacobs, 1970; Dweck and Reppucci, 1973), we can determine whether any of these states occur in helplessness.

Finally, we know of no evidence that disconfirms the correspondence of symptoms in learned helplessness and depression.

The term 'learned helplessness' was first used in connection with laboratory experiments in which dogs were exposed to shock from which they could not escape (Overmier and Seligman, 1967). After repeated trials, the dogs tended to sit passively when the shock came on. Exposed to a new situation from which the y could escape a shock by jumping over a barrier, they failed to initiate the appropriate response. Some would occasionally jump over the barrier and escape, but they would generally revert to taking the shock passively. For the purposes of constructing an analogue of clinical depression, the behaviour of the dogs is significant in suggesting that exposure to uncontrollable aversive events may lead to a failure to initiate appropriate responses in new situations and an inability to learn that responding is effective.

The analogy to depression was bolstered by initial findings that in a variety of task situations, depressed human subjects resembled nondepressed subjects who had received repeated failure experiences. For instance, compared to nondepressed subjects who had not received repeated failure experiences, these groups of subjects took longer to solve anagrams and apparently failed to perceive the pattern underlying their successful solution (Klein and Seligman, 1976). Miller, Rosellini, and Seligman, and other research suggested that the parallels between a laboratory learned helplessness and depression were not limited to similarities in behaviour. Promising leads were also established with regard to etiology, treatment, and prevention.

The original learned helplessness model stimulated a large body of research and considerable controversy (Buchwald, Coyne, and Cole, 1978; Costello, 1978). Ultimately, the accumulated research led to questions about both the adequacy of the learned-helplessness explanation for the behaviour of nondepressed subjects who has been exposed to failure as well as the appropriateness of learned helplessness as an analogue of depression. For instance, it was shown that the performance deficits of subjects who had been given a typical learned helplessness, induction were very much situation-specific (Cole and Coyne, 1977) and that these deficits might better be explained as the result of anxious self-preoccupation, rather than the perception of response-reinforcement independence (Coyne, Metalsky and Lavelle, 1980). Furthermore, the characterization of depressed persons as passive and lacking in aggression was challenged. Difficulties with the original learned helplessness model led to a major reformulation (Abramson, Seligman and Teasdale).

We use the term learned helplessness to describe the interference with adaptive responses produced by inescapable shock and also as a short hand to describe the process that we believe underlies the behaviour that we cannot control of which the distinction between controllable and uncontrollable reinforcement is central to the phenomenon and the theory of helplessness. Learned helplessness in the dog is defined by two types of behaviour. (1) Dogs that have had shock or are slower to make responses than naive dogs, and (2) if the dog does make a response that turns off shock, it has more trouble than a naive dog learning that responding is effective.

However, if we are to propose a model of depression in man, we must have proof that learned helplessness occurs in man.

Besides passivity and retarded response-relief learning, other characteristics associated with learned helplessness are relevant to depression in man. First, helplessness has a time course. In dogs, inescapable shock produces transient as well as permanent interference with escape (Overmier and Seligman, 1967) and avoidance (Overmier, 1968): 24 hours after one session of inescapable shock, dogs are helpless; but after 48 hours their response is normal. This is also true of goldfish (Padilla, 1970). After multiple sessions of inescapable shock, helplessness is not transient (Seligman and Groves, 1970; Seligman, Maier and Geer, 1968) Weiss (1968) found a parallel time course for weight loss in rats given uncontrollable shock, but other that this no time course has been found in rats or in other species (e.g., Anderson, Cole, and McVaugh, 1968; Seligman, Rosellini, and Kozak, 1975). Nonetheless, uncontrollable trauma produces a number of effects found in depression. The two basic effects are these: an animal and humans become passive—they are slower to initiate responses to alleviate trauma and may not respond at all; And animals and humans are retarded in learning that their behaviour may control trauma, if a response is made that is to produce relief, they often have trouble realizing that one causes the other. This maladaptive behaviour has been observed in a variety of species over a range of tasks that require voluntary responding. In addition, this phenomenon dissipates in time in the dog, and it causes lowered aggression, loss of appetite, and norepinephrine depletion.

The passivity of dogs, rats and men in the face of trauma and their difficulty on benefiting from response-relief contingencies result; that we believe, from their having learned that responding and trauma are independent—that trauma is uncontrollable. This is the hear t of the learned helplessness hypothesis. The hypothesis states that when shock is inescapable, the organism learns that responses and shock termination are independent (the probability of shock termination given any response doesn't differ from its probability in the absence of that response). Learning that trauma is uncontrollable has three effects.

(1) A motivational effect—it reduces the probability that the subject will initiate responses to escape, because part of the incentive for making such responses is the expectation that they will bring relief. If the subject has previously learned that its responses have no effect on trauma, this contravenes the expectation, thus, the organism's motivation to respond is undermined by experience with reinforcers it cannot control. Such that this motivational effect undermines passivity in learned helplessness, and, if the model is valid, in depression.

(2) The cognitive effect—learning that responses and shock are independent makes it more difficult to learn that responses do produce relief when the organism makes a response that actually terminates shock. In general, if we have acquired a cognitive set in which A's are irrelevant to B's, it will be harder for us to learn that A's produce B's when they do. By the helplessness hypothesis, this mechanism is responsible for the difficulty that helpless organisms have in learning that responding produces relief, even after they respond and successfully turn off shock. Further, if the model is valid, this mechanism produces the 'negative expectations' of depression.

(3) An emotional effect—although it does not follow directly from the helplessness hypothesis—such that uncontrollable shock produces more conditioned fear, ulcers, weight loss, defecation, and pain than controllable shock.

One cause of laboratory-produced helplessness seems to be learning that one cannot control important events. Learning that responses and reinforcement are independent results in a cognitive set that has two effects: fewer responses to control reinforcement are initiated and associating successful responses with reenforcement becomes more difficult.

Nevertheless, some of the events that typically precipitate depression; failure in work or school; death or loss of loved ones; rejection by or separation from loved ones; physical disease, and growing old. What do all these have in common?

Four recent theories of depression seem to be largely in agreement about the etiology of depression, and what they agree on is the centrality of helplessness and hopelessness. Bibring (1953), arguing from a dynamic viewpoint, sees helplessness as the cause of depression:

> What has been described as the basic mechanism of depression, the ego's shocking awareness of its helplessness in regard to its aspirations, is assumed to represent the core of normal, neurotic and probably also psychotic depression.

Melges and Bowlby (1969) see a similar cause of depression:

> Our thesis is that while a depressed patient's goals remain relatively unchanged his estimate of the likelihood of achieving then and his confidence in the efficacy of his own skilled actions are both diminished . . . the depressed person believes that his plans of action are no longer effective in reaching his continuing and long range goals . . . From this state of mind is derived, we believe, much depressive symptomalogy, including indecisiveness, inability to act, making increased demands on others, and feelings of worthlessness and guilt about not discharging duties.

Beck (1967, 1970) sees depression as resulting primarily from a patient's negative cognitive set, largely about his abilities to change his life:

> A primary factor appears to be the activation of idiosyncratic cognitive patterns which divert the thinking into specific channels that deviate from reality. As a result, the patient perseverates in making negative judgements and interpretations of experience, negative evaluations of the self, and negative expectations of the future.

Lichtenberg (1957) sees hopelessness as the defining characteristic of depression:

> Depression is defined as a manifestation of felt hopelessness regarding the attainment of

goals when responsibility for the hopelessness is attributed to one's personal defects. In this context hope is conceived to be a function of the perceived probability of success with respect to goal attainment.

Even so, it means that all of a person's efforts have been in vain, his responses have failed to bring about the gratification he desires; he cannot find responses that control reinforcement. When a person is rejected by someone he loves, he can no longer control this significant source of gratification and support. When a parent or lover dies, the bereaved person is powerless to produce or influence love from a dead person. Physical disease and growing old are obvious helplessness experiences. In these conditions, the person's own responses are ineffective and he must rely on the care of others. So, we would predict that it is not life events that produce depression (Alarcon and Cori, 1972) but uncontrollable life events.

However, Ferster (1969, 1973), Kaufman and Rosenblum (1967); McKinney and Bunney (1969), and Liberman and Raskin (1971) have suggested that depression is caused by extinction procedures or the loss of reinforcers. There is no contradiction between the learned-helplessness and extinction view of depression; helplessness, however, is more general. Briefly, extinction is a special case of independence between responding and reinforcement. Reinforcement, just the same, may also be presented with a probability greater than zero, and still be presented independent of responding. This occurs in the typical helplessness paradigm and cause responses to decrease in probability (Recorta and Skucy, 1969). Therefore, a view talks about independence between responding and reinforcement assumes the extinction view and, in addition, suggests that situations in which reinforcers still occur independent of responding also will cause depression.

Both learned helplessness and depression may be caused by learning that responses and reinforcement are independent. But this view runs into several problems. Can depression actually be caused by situations other than extinction in which reinforcement still occur but are not under the individual's control? To put it another way, 'is a net loss of reinforcement necessary for depression, or can depression occur when there is only loss of control without loss of reinforcement?' Would a Casanova who made love with seven new women every week become depressed if he found out that women wanted him not because of his amatory prowess but because of his wealth or because his fairy god mother wished it? We can only speculate.

It seems appropriate to mention 'success' depression in this context. When people finally reach a goal after years of striving—being promoted or obtaining a PhD—many become depressed. This puzzling phenomenon is clearly a problem for a loss of reinforcement view of depression. From a helplessness view, success depression may occur because reinforcement are no longer contingent on present responding. After years of goal-directed instrumental activity, the reinforcement automatically changes. One now gets his reinforcement because of whom he is rather than what he is doing. The common clinical impression that many beautiful women become depressed and attempt suicide also presents problems for the loss of reinforcement theory: positive reinforcers abound not because of what they do but because of how they look. Would be a generation of children risen with abundant positive reinforcers that they received independently to what, and they did become clinically depressed?

According to the helplessness view, the central theme in successful therapy should be having the patient discover and come to accept that his responses produce the gratification that he desires—that he is, in short, an effective human being. Some therapies that reportedly alleviate depression are consonant with a learned helplessness model, however, it is important to note that the success of a therapy often has little to do with its theoretical underpinning. So, with the exception of Klein and Seligman (1976), as a se t of examples that seem as a test of the model, but merely as a set of examples that seem to have exposure to response-produced success as a cure for depression.

Consonant with their helplessness-centred views of the etiology of depression, Bibring (1957), Beck (1967), and Melges and Bowlby (1969) all stressed that reversing helplessness alleviates depression. For example, Bibring (1953) has stated:

> The same conditions which bring about depression (helplessness) in reverse serve frequently the restitution from depression. Generally, one can

431

say that depression subsides either (I) when the narcissistically important goals and objects appear to be again within reach (which is frequently followed by a temporary elation) or (ii) when they become sufficiently modified or reduced to becoming realizable, or (iii) when they are altogether relinquished, or (iv) when the ego recovers from the narcissistic shock by regaining its self-esteem with the help of various recovery mechanisms (with or without any change of objective or goal).

In their review of therapies for depression, Seligan, Klein, and Miller (1976) indicated that most of the therapies have strong elements of inducing the patient to discover that responses produce the reinforcement he desires. In antidepression milieu therapy (Taulbee and Wright, 1971), for example, the patient is forced to emit one of the most powerful responses people have for controlling others—anger—and when this response is dragged out of his depleted behaviour repertoire, he is powerfully reinforced. Becks' (1970) cognitive therapy is aimed at similar goals. He sees success manipulations as changing the negative cognitive set ('I'm an ineffective person) of the depressive to a more positive set, and argues that the primary task of the therapist is to change the negative expectations of the depressed patient to more optimistic ones. Even so, both Burgess's (1968), therapy and the graded task assigned (Beck, Seligman, Binik, Schuyler, and Brill, unpublished data), the patient makes instrumental responses of gradually increasing complexity, and each is reinforced. Similarly, all instrumental behaviour therapy for depression (Hersen, Eisler, Alford, and Agras, 1973; Reisinger. 1972), by definition, arrange the contingencies so that responses control the occurrence of reinforcement; the patient's recognition of this relationship should alleviate depression. Lewinsohn's therapy also has this element; participation in activity and other nondepressed behaviour controls therapy time. (Lewinsohn, Weinstein, and Shaw, 1969). In assertive training (Wolpe, 1968), the patient must emit social responses to bring about a desired change in his environment. Such that the study provides a useful method fo r testing the effectiveness of any therapy for depression in the laboratory because we can bring depression into the laboratory, in that, both in its naturally occurring state and in the form of learned helplessness, we can now see what reverses it in the laboratory. Will assertive training, emotive expression or atropine given to helpless and depressed subjects in the laboratory reverse the symptoms of depression and helplessness?

In order to explain depression, Burgess (1968) and others have relied heavily on the reinforcement the patient gets for his depressed behaviour, it is tempting to seek to remove this reinforcement during therapy, but caution is in order, so to explain the persistence or maintenance of some depressive behaviours, but it does not explain how they began. Helplessness suggests that failure to initiate active responses originates in the perception that the patient cannot control reinforcement. Thus, there can be two sources of a depressed patient's passivity: (a) patients are passive for instrumental reasons, because they think staying depressed brings them sympathy, love and attention, and (b) patients are passive because they believe that no response at all will be effective in controlling their environment. In this sense, it means that there is at least some response that believes he can effectively perform. Maier (1970) found that dogs who were reinforced for being passive by shock termination were not nearly as debilitated as dogs for whom all responses were independent of shock termination. Similarly, patients who use their depression in a way of controlling reinforcement are less helpless than those who have given up. Nonetheless, depression may be directly antagonized when patients come to see that their own responses are effective in alleviating their suffering and produced gratifications.

Nonetheless, many therapies, from psychoanalysis to cognitive understandings, claim to be able to cure depression. The evidence presented is selective as only those treatments that seemed compatible with helplessness were such that was possible that when other therapies work it. It is, because they reinstate the patient's sense of efficacy. However, evidence on the effectiveness of therapy in depression that is less anecdotal and selective is sorely needed. The recent study of Klein and Seligman (1976) may provide a laboratory procedure for evaluating the effectiveness of any therapy suggested for learned helplessness and depression.

All the same, a behavioural self-control model for the study of depression is focussed on different subsets of depressive phenomena. Such that the self-control model organizes and relates these phenomena and has its own implications for symptomatology, etiology, and therapy. Depression has certain properties which make the development of a model particularly difficult, however, the term depression refers to a syndrome which encompass a broad set of symptoms with diverse behavioural referents (Beck, 1972; Levitt and Lubin, 1975; Mendels, 1970; Woodruff, Goodwin and Guze, 1974). Especially notable is the diversity among cognitive symptoms. Aside from manifest subjective sadness, depressed persons show clinical symptoms such as quilt, pessimism, low sel-esteem, self-derogation, and helplessness. Accounting for these distinctive cognitive behaviours and integrating them with the various overt-moto r behaviours characteristic of depression are limited to verbal-cognitive and overt-motor variables is appropriate since no reliable physiological index has been clearly identified as a symptom of depression (Bruder, 1970).

A recent resurgence of interest in psychological aspects of depression has become evident, and, with it, new and innovative models have been advanced. Behavioural and cognitive modes proposed by Lewinsohn (1974), Seligman (1974) and Beck (1974) have been most prominent and influential in behavioural research and clinical application.

Lewinsohn (1974; Lewinsohn, Weinstein, and Shaw, 1969) has developed a clinical and research program which looks at depression as an extinction phenomenon. A loss or lack of response contingent positive reinforcement results in reduced rates of common overt-motor behaviour and also elicits a basic dysphoria. All other cognitive-verbal symptoms of depression are secondary elaborations of these basic dysphoria. Susceptivity to depression and ability to overcome depression are related to social skill, the range of events which are potentially reinforcing to the person, and reinforcement availability. The etiology of depression is therefore, the joint function of external environmental changes and individual differences in reinforcement potential and social skills. Therapy procedures are aimed at identifying potential sources of reinforcement in the person's environment and developing strategies to increase their frequency of occurrence (Lewinsohn, 1976. Lewinsohn and Shaffer, 1971; Robinson and Lewinsohn, 1973) In other instances, therapy consists of isolating deficits in social interaction and training subjects in modifying these socially skilled behaviours (Lewinsohn, Biglan and Zeiss, 1976); Lewinsohn and Shaw, 1969; Lewinsohn, Weinstein and Alper, 1970).

Also, Seligman has proposed a model of depression based on a laboratory paradigm of learned helplessness (Seligman, 1974, 1975). A situation in which the probability of the consequence given a response is equal to the probability of the consequence given no response produces the phenomenon of learned helplessness. Noncontingent punishment has been the situation most studied. Learned helplessness has properties which parallel the symptoms of depression: (1) lowered response initiation (passivity), (2) negative cognitive se t (belief that one's actions are doomed to failure; (3) dissipation over time, (4) lack of aggression, (5) loss of libido and appetite, and (6) norepinephrine depletion and cholinergic activity (Seligman, Klein, and Miller, 1974). Cognition is given a central position in this model in that of the 'depressive retardation is caused by a brief in response-reinforcement independence'; (Seligman. 1974). Other cognitive symptoms are held to be elaborations on this central belief. No therapy studies have been directly generated by this model to date, however, Klein and Seligman (1976) have demonstrated the reversibility of learned helplessness and depression following experience with solvable problems.

From a different perspective, Beck (1970, 1972, 1974) has evolved a cognitive model of depression which holds that depression consists of a primary triad of cognitive patterns or schema (1) a negative view of the world; (2) a negative view of the self, and (3) a negative view of the future. These views are maintained by distorted models of cognition such as selective abstraction, arbitrary inference, and overgeneralization,. The over—behavioural symptoms of depression follow from cognitive distortion. Distorted schema develop in early childhood and leave individuals susceptible to depression in the face of stress. Therapy involves the identification of distortions and their confrontation with the evidence of objective experience. Case studies employing these modifications have been described by Beck (1972) and Rush, Khatami, and Beck (1975). Group studies have shown that therapy based on a Beck's cognitive behaviour modification model is superior to a program based on Lewinsohn's model, a nondirective control therapy and a waiting list control and is more effective than treatment with imipramine hydrochloride (Rush, Beck, Kovacs, and Hollon).

435

RICHARD J. KOSCIEJEW

The severe disorders of mood or effect are among the most regulars of the major psychiatric syndromes. Lifetime expectancy rates for such disorders are between 3 and 8 percent of the general population. Only a minority are treated by psychiatrists or in psychiatric hospitals and about 70 percent of prescriptions for antidepressants are written by nonpsychiatrist physicians. These and other modern medical treatments of severe mood disorders have contributed to a virtual revolution in the theory and practice of modern psychiatry since the introduction of mood-altering drugs three decades ago. These agent s include lithium salts (1949), and Monoamine oxidase (MAO) inhibitors (1952), and the antimanic and Antipsychotic (neuroleptics) agents such as chlorpromazine (1952), and the Tricyclic or heterocyclic (imipramine-like) antidepressants (1957). In addition, electroconvulsive therapy (ECT) continues to have a place in the treatment of very severe and acute mood disorders, especially life-threatening forms of depression.

The development of these modern medical therapies has had several important effects. First. These agents have provided of a relatively simple specific effect and safe forms of treatment with a profound impact on current patterns of medical practice, for example, many depressed or hypomanic patients can be managed adequately in outpatient facilities to avoid prolonged, expensive, and disruptive hospitalization which were formerly common. Second, partial understanding of the pharmacology of the psychotropic drugs has led to imaginative hypotheses concerning the pathophysiology or etiology of severe mood disorders. These, in turn, have encouraged a revolution on experimental psychiatry in which the hypotheses have been tested in clinical research. Many of the earlier hypotheses have been found wanting or simplistic, nevertheless, they have led to increased understanding of the diagnosis, biology, and treatment of mood disorders and to newer research that represents a third level of development. This is the focus of the practical clinical benefits of now and in the near future.

In the light of this some characteristics of infant development during this holding phase can be enumerated. It is at this stage that:

(1) primary process, (2) primary identification, (3) autoerotism, (4) primary narcissism, and (5) living realities.

In this phase the ego changes over from an unintegrated state to a structure integration, and so the infant becomes able to experience anxiety associated with disintegration. The word disintegration begins to have been meaning which it did not possess before go integration became a fact. In healthy development at this stage the infant retains the capacity for re-experiencing unintegrated states, but this depends on the continuation of reliable maternal care or on the built-up in the infant of memories of material care beginning gradually to be perceived as such. The result of healthy progress in the infant's development during this stage is that he attains to what might be called "unit status." The infant become a person, an individual in his own right.

Associated with this attainment is the infant's psychosomatic existence which begins to take on a personal pattern: that is, that the basis for this for this indwelling is a linkage of motor and sensory and functional experience with the infant's new state of being a person. As a further development there comes into existence what might be called a limiting membrane, which to some extent (in health) is equated with the surface of the skin, and has a position between the infant's "me" and his "not me." So the infant comes to have an inside and an outside, and a body-scheme. In this way meaning comes to the function of intake and output, moreover, it gradually become meaningful to postulate a personal or inner psychic reality for the infant.

During the holding phase other processes are initiated; the most important is the dawn of intelligence and the beginning of a mind as something distinct from the psyche, and, from this, the secondary processes and symbolic functioning, and of the organization of a personal psychic content, which forms a basis for dreaming and for living relationships.

At the same time there starts in the infant a joining up of two roots of impulsive behaviours. The term "fusion" indicates the positive process whereby diffuse elements that belong to movement and to muscle erotism becomes fused with the orgiastic functioning of the erotogenic zones. This concept is more familiar as the reverse process of defusion, which is a complex and complication defence in which aggression becomes separated out from erotic experience after a period in which a degree of fusion has been achieved. All these developments belong to the environmental condition of "holding," and without "good" so as to be adequately holding the stages cannot be attained, or once attained cannot become established,

A further development in the capacity for object relationships. In that, the infant changes from relationship to objectively conceived object to a relationship to an object objectively perceived. This change is closely bound up with the infant's change from being merged with the mother to being separate from her, or to relating to her as a separate and "not-me," This development is not specifically related to the holding, but is related to the phase of "living with" . . .

In the holding phase the infant is maximally dependent. One can classify dependence thus:

(I) Absolute Dependence: In this state the infant has no means of knowing about the maternal care, which is largely a matter of prophylaxis. He cannot gain control over what is well and what is badly done, but is only a position to gain profit or to suffer disturbances,

(ii) Relative Dependence: The infant can become aware of the need for the details of maternal care, and to a growing extent relate them to personal impulse, and then later, in a psychoanalytic treatment, can reproduce them in the transference,

(iii) The infant develops the means for doing without actual care. This is accomplished through the accumulation of memories of care, the projection of personal needs and the introjection of care details, with the development of confidence on the environment, and must be added that, the element of intellectual understanding with its tremendous implications.

Nonetheless, in borderline cases the analyst does not always wait in vain, that in the course of time the patient becomes able to make use of the psychoanalytic interpretations of the original trauma projection. It may even happen that he is able to accept for what is in the environment as a projection of the simple and stable going-on-being elements that derive from his own inherent potential.

Such that it is necessary to attempt to state briefly what happens to the inherented potential if this is to develop into an infant, and thereafter onto a child reaching toward independent existence, because if the plexuity of the subject such a statement must be made in the assumption of satisfactory material care, which means parental care. Satisfactory parental care can be classified roughly into three overlapping states.

1. Holding.
2. Mother and infant living together, as the father's function (on dealing with the environment for the mother) is not known to the infant
3. Father, mother, and infant, all three living together.

The term "holding" is used to denote not only the actual physical holding of the infant, but also the total environmental provision prior to the concept of living with. In other words, it refers to a three-dimensional or space relationship (spatiality) with time gradually added. This overlaps with, but initiate prior to, instinctual experiences that in time would determine the object relationships. It includes the management of experiences that are inherent in existence, such as the completion (and therefore, the noncompeting) of processes, such ss the completion and, the noncomcompletion of specific processes which from the outside may seem to be purely physiological but which belong to infant psychology and take place on a complex psychological field, particularly, by determining the awareness and the empathy of the mother.

The term "living with" implies object relationships, and the emergence of the infant from the state of being merged with the mother, or his perception of objects external to the self.

The paradox is that what is good and bad in the infant's environment is not in fact a projection, but in spite of this it is necessary, if the individual infant is to develop healthily, that everything will seem to him to be a projection. We find omnipotence and the pleasure principle in operation, as they certainly are in earliest infancy; and to this observation we can add that the recognition of a true "not-me" is a matter of the intellect; it belongs to extreme sophistication and to the maturity of the individual.

In the writings of Freud most of the formulations concerning infancy derive from a study of adults in analysis. At first sight it would seem that a great deal of psychoanalytic theory is about early childhood and infancy, but in one sense Freud can be said to have neglected unfancy as a stare. This is brought out by a footnote in "Formulations of the Two Principles of Mental Functioning," of which he shows that he knows he is taking for granted the very things that are under discussion, as in the text he traces the development from the pleasure-principle to the reality-principle, following his usual course of reconstructing the infancy of his adult patients. The note runs as follows:

> It will rightly be objected that an organization which was a slave to the pleasure principle and neglected the reality of the external world could not maintain itself alive for the shortest time, so that it could not have come into existence at all. The employment of a fiction like this is. However, justified when one considers that the infant—provided one includes with it the care it receives from its mother—does almost realize a psychical system of this kind.

Freud paid full tribute to the function of maternal care, and it must be assumed that he left this subject alone only because he was not ready to talk about its implications. The note continues:

> It probably hallucinates the fulfilment of its internal needs; it betrays its unpleasure, when there is an increase of stimulus and absence of satisfaction, by the motor discharge of screaming and beating about with its arms and legs, and it then experiences the satisfaction it has hallucinated. Later, as an older child, it learns too employ these manifestations of discharge intentionally for which of methods for expressing its feelings. Since the later care of children is modelled in the care of infants, the dominance of the pleasure principle can really come to an end when a child has achieved complete physical detachment from its parents.

The words: "provide one includes with it the care it receives from its mother" have of a great importance in the immediate contextual presentation. The infant and the maternal care together from a unit. certainly if one is to study the theory of the parent-infant relationship one must come to a decision about these matters, which concern the real meaning of the word dependence or dependency. It is not enough that it is acknowledged that the environment is important if there is to be a discussion of the theory of the parent-infant relationship, then we are divided into two of the same who do not allow that at the earliest stages the infant and the maternal care belong to each other and cannot be disentangled. These two things, the infant and the maternal case, disentangle and dissociate themselves in health, which means as to do many things, to some extent it means a disentanglement of maternal care from something which we then call the infant, or the beginning of a growing child. This idea is covered by Freud's words at the end of the footnote, explaining that: The dominance of the pleasure principle can really come to an end only when a child has achieved complete physical detachment from its parents.

It is axiomatic in these matters of maternal care of holding variety that when things go well the infant has no means of knowing what is being properly provided and what is being prevented. Such, that when things do not go well that the infant becomes aware, not of the failure of maternal care, but of the results, whatever they may be, of that failure: That in saying, as a result of success in maternal care there is built up in th infant, a continuity of being which is the basis of ego strength of being interrupted by reactions to the consequences of that failure, The resultant of ego-weakening. Such interruptions constitute annihilation, and are evidently associated with pain of psychotic quality and intensity. In the extreme case the infant exists only on the basis of a continuity of reactions to impingement and of recoveries from such reactions. This is in great contras t to the continuity for being that which is our conception of ego strength.

The transition stage has been described as a stage of Quasi-Independence, as the reason posits for the adoption if this description is of sufficient importance to demand special attention. It emerges with the utmost clarity from the study of schizoid cases that the most characteristic feature of the state if infantile dependence is identification with the object. Still, it would not be going too far to say that, psychologically speaking, identification with the object

441

RICHARD J. KOSCIEJEW

and infantile dependence are really the same phenomenon. In that the mature dependence involves a relationship between two kinds of dependence is identical with Freudian distinctions between the narcissistic and the anaclitic choice of objects. The relationship involved in mature dependence is, if course, only the theoretically possible. Nevertheless, it remains true that the more mature a relationship is, the less it is characterized by identification, for what identification essentially represents is failure to differentiate the object. It is when identification persists at the expense of differentiation that a markedly compulsive element enters into the individual's attitude toward its objects. This is well seen in the infatuation of schizoid individuals. It may also be observed in almost uncontrollable impulse so commonly experienced by schizoid and depressive soldiers to return to their wives or their homes, when separated from them owing to military necessities. The abandonment of infantile dependence involves an abandonment with differentiated objects. In the dreams of schizoids the process of differentiation is frequently represented by the process of differentiations is frequently repressed by the theme of trying to cross a gulf or chasm, albeit the crossing which is attempted may also occur in a regressive direction. The process itself is commonly attended by considerable anxiety, and the anxiety attending it finds characteristic expression on dreams.

The process of differentiation of the object derives particular significance from the fact that infantile dependence is characterized not only by identification, but also by an oral attitude of incorporation. In virtue of this fact the object with which the individual is identified is also an incorporated object or, to put the matter in a more arresting fashion, the object in which the individual is incorporate d may well prove the key to man y metaphysical puzzles. But that it may, however, it is common to find in dreams a complete equivalence between being inside an object and having the object inside.

Such then being the situation, the task of differentiating the object resolves itself into a problem of expelling an incorporated object, i.e., it becomes a problem of expelling contents. Herein lies the rationale of Abraham's "anal phases," and it is in this direction that we must look for the significance of the anal techniques which play such an important part during the transition stage. It is important as elsewhere, too insure that the cart is not placed before the horse, and to recognize that it is not a case of individual being occupied with the disposal of contents at this stage because he is anal, but of his being anal because he is preoccupied at this stage with the disposal of content.

The great conflict of the transition stage may now be formulated as a conflict between a progressive urge to surrender the infantile attitude of identification with the object and a regressive urge to maintain that attitude. During this period, accordingly, the behaviour of the individual is characterized both by desperate and endeavour on his part to separate himself from the object and desperate endeavour to achieve reunion with the object—desperate attempts "to escape from prison" and desperate e attempts "to return home." Although one of these attitudes may become to preponderate, there is in the first instance a constant oscillation between the owing and the anxiety attending each. The anxiety attending separation manifests itself as a fear of isolation; and the anxiety attending identification manifests itself as a fear of being shut in, imprisoned or engulfed ("cribbed, cabined and confined"). These anxieties, it will be noticed, are essentially phobic anxieties. In may accordingly be inferred that it is to the conflict between the progressive urge toward separation from the object and the regressive lure of identification with the object that we must look for the explanation of the phobic state.

Owing to the intimate connection existing between identification and oral incorporation, and consequently between separation and excretory expulsion, the conflict of the transition period also presented itself as a conflict between an urge to expel and an urge to retain contents. Just as between separation and reunion, such that either of these oscillation between expulsion and retention, although either of these attitudes may have become dominant. Both attitudes are attended by anxiety—the attitude of expulsion being attended by a fear of bursting (often accompanied or replaced by a fear of some internal disease like cancer). Such anxieties are essentially obsessional anxieties, and it is the conflict between an urge to expel the objet as content and an urge conflict as the object content s that underlies the obsessional state.

The phobic and obsessional techniques are thus seen as to represent two differing methods of dealing with the same basic conflict: In these two differing methods correspond to two differing attitudes toward the object. From the phobic point of view the conflict presents itself as in between flight from and return to the object. From the obsessional point of view, as the conflict presents itself as one between expulsion and retention of the object. It thus becomes obvious that the phobic technique correspond to an active attitude. The obsessional technique also expresses a much higher degree of aggression toward the object; For, whether the object be expelled or retained, it is being subject to forcible control. For the phobic individual, the choice lies between escaping from the power of the object and submitting to it. In other words, while the obsessional technique is essentially sadistic in nature, the phobic technique is essentially masochistic.

In the hysterical state we can recognize the operation of another technique for attempting to deal with the basic conflict of the transition period. In this case, the conflict appears to be formulated as simply one between acceptance and rejection of the object. Acceptance of the object is clearly manifested in the intense love-relationships which are so typical of the hysteric; but the very exaggeration of these emotional relationships in itself raises a suspicion that a rejection is being overcompensated. The suspicion is confirmed by th propensity of the hysteric to dissociation phenomena. That these Dissociative phenomena represent a rejection of the genitals need not be stressed, but, as the analysis can always unmask an identification of the rejected genitals with the breast as the original object of the libidinal impulses during the period of infantile dependence. This being so, it is of note, that what is dissociated by the hysteric is an organ function in himself. This can only have meant—that the rejected object is an internalization object, however, the hysteric's overvaluation of his objects leaves no room for doubt that in his case the accepted object and rejection of the internalized object.

If the paranoid and the hysteric states are now compared, we are confronted with a significant contrast. Whereas, the hysteric overvalue objects in the outer world, the paranoid individual regards them as persecutors, and, whereas, the hysteric dissociation is a form of self-depreciation, the attitude of the paranoid individual is one of extravagant grandiosity. The paranoid state must, accordingly, be regarded as representing rejection of the externalized object and acceptance of the internalized object.

Having interpreted the hysterical and paranoid technique in terms of the acceptance and rejection of objects, we can now obtain interesting results by applying a similar interpretation to

444

the phobic and obsessional techniques. The conflict underlying the phobic state may be concisely formulated as one between flight to the object and flight from the object. In the former case, is, of course, the object is accepted, whereas, in the latter case the object is rejected. In both cases, the object is treated as external, in the obsessional state, the conflict presents itself as one between the exclusion and the rejection of content. In this case, accordingly, both the accepted and the rejected objects are treated as internal. If in the case of the phobic state both the accepted and the rejected objects are treated as external and in the obsessional state both are treated as internal, the situation as regarding these hysterical and paranoid states is that one of these objects is treated as an externalized object and the other as an internalized object, in the hysterical state. It is the accepted object that is externalized, and the paranoid state, the object which is externalized is the rejected object.

The chief features of the stage of transition between infantile and adult dependence may now be briefly summarized. The transition period is characterized by a process of development, whereby object—relationships based upon identification gradually give place to relationships with differentiated objects. Satisfactory development during this period, therefore, depends upon the success which attends the process of differentiation of the object, and this in turn depends upon the issue of a conflict or separation from the object—a situation which is both desire d and feared. The conflict in question may call into operation any or all characteristic techniques—the obsessional, the paranoid, the hysterical and the phobic: and, if object—relationships are unsatisfactory, these techniques are liable to form the basis of characteristic psychopathological developments in later life. The various techniques cannot be classified in any order corresponding to presumptive levels of libidinal development. On the contrary, they must be regarded as alternative techniques, all belonging to the same stage in the development of object-relationships. Which of the techniques is employed, or to what extent each is employed would appear to depend on large measure upon the nature of the object-relationships established during the preceding stage of infantile dependence. In particular,. It would seem to depend upon the degree which have been established between the developing ego and its internalized objects.

The infant is completely dependent upon his object not only for his existence and physical well-being, but also for the satisfaction of his psychological needs. It is true, nonetheless, that mature individuals are likewise dependent upon one another for the satisfaction of their psychological, and, no less than their physical, needs. Nevertheless, on the psychological side, the dependence of mature individuals sufficient to render him dependent in an unconditional sense. We also notice that, whereas in the case of the adult object-relationship has a considerable spread, in the case of the infant it tends to be focussed upon a single object. The loss of an object is thus, much more devastating in the case of the infant. If a mature individual loses an object, least of mention, he still has some objects remaining. His eggs are not all in one basket. Further, he has a choice of objects and can desert one for another. The infant, on the other hand, has no choice. He has no alternative but to accept or to reject his object—an alternative which is liable to present itself to him as a choice between life and death. His psychological dependence is further accentuated by the very nature of his object-relationship, for, as we have seen, this is based essentially upon identification. Dependence is exhibited in its most extreme form, in the intra-uterine state, and we may legitimately infer that on its psychological side this state is characterized by an absolute degree of identification. Identification may thus be regarded as representing the persistence into extrauterine life of a relationship existing before birth. In so far as, identification persists after birth. The individual's object constitutes not only his world, but also himself; and it is this fact, as has already been pointed out, that we must attribute the compulsive attitude of many schizoids and de repressive individuals toward their objects.

Normal development is characterized by a process whereby progressive differentiations of the object is accompanied by progressive decreases in identification. So long as infantile dependence persists, however, identification remains the most characteristic feature of the individual's emotional relationship with his object. Infantile dependence is equivalent to oral dependence—a fact which should be interpreted, not in the sens that the infant is inherently oral, but in the sense that the breast is the original object. During the oral phases, accordingly, identification remains the most characteristic feature of the individual's emotional relationship with his object. The tendency to identification, which is so characteristic of emotional relationships during these phases, also invade s the cognitive sphere, with the result that certain orally fixated individuals have only to hear of someone else suffering from any given disease in order to believe that they are suffering from it themselves. In the conative sphere, that identification has its counterpart in oral incorporation. And it is the merging of emotional identification with oral incorporation that confer s upon the stage of infantile dependence its most distinctive feature. These features are based upon the fundamental equivalence for the infant of being held in his mother's arms and incorporating the contents of her breast.

The phenomenon of narcissism, which is one of the most prominent characteristics of infantile dependence, is an attitude arising out of identification with the object. Such that primary narcissism may be simply defined as just such a state of identification with the object, secondary narcissism being a state of identification with an object which is internalized. While narcissism is a feature common to both the early and the late oral phase, the latter phase differs from the former in virtue of a change in the nature of the object. In the early oral phase the natural object is the breast; but in the later oral phase, the natural object becomes the mother. The transition from one phase to the other is thus marked by the substitution of a whole object (or person) for a part-object. Nevertheless, the object continues to be treated as a part-object (the breast) with the result that the person of the mother becomes an object for incorporation. The transition from the early to the late oral phases are also characterized by the emergence of the biting tendency. Whereas in the early oral phase the libidinal attitude of incorporation monopolizes the field, in the late oral phase it is in competing with an accompanying attitude of biting. Now biting must be regarded for being essentially of all differentiated aggression. Consequently, the dawn of the late oral phase heralds the emergence of emotional ambivalence. The late oral phase is well described as pre-ambivalent. Nonetheless, one which aggression has not yet been differentiated from the libido. The earl y urge to incorporate is essentially a libidinal urge, to which true aggression makes no contribution, even as a component factor. The recognition of this fact is of the greatest importance for an understanding of the essential problem underlying schizoid states, and it is understanding. It is true that the incorporation urge is destructive in its gross effect, in the sense that the object which is eaten disappears. Nevertheless, the urge is not destructive in aim. When, as a child says that he "loves" cake, it is certain to imply that the cake will vanish, and then consumingly destroyed. At the same time the destruction of the cake is not the aim of the child's "love." On the contrary, the disappearance of the cake is, from the child's point of view. A most regrettable consequence of his "love" for it. What he really desires, is for himself, is to have his cake and eat it to. If the cake proves to be "bad" he either differentiate to its splitting or unhinging of, in that, even he becomes sick. As this spiting out is specifically characteristic of the early oral phase, in that he rejects the bad cake, least of mention, he does not bite the cake with intentions for its being bad. This type of behaviour is specifically characterized of the early oral phasing, then, what is, so far as the object presents itself as "moving apart," it is incorporated, and, presents itself as "bad," it is rejected, but, even when it appears to be bad, no attempt is made to destroy it. Again, it is the good object that is "destroyed." Albeit only incidentally and not by intention. In the late oral phase the situation is foreign, in that things are done differently, for in this phase the object may be bitten as well as incorporated. This mean that a direct aggression, as well as libidinal forces, are such that may be directed toward the object. Hence the appearance of the ambivalence which characterizes the late oral phase.

It soon becomes evident that the emotional oral phase takes the form of the alternative that to incorporate or not to incorporate, i.e., "to love or not to love." This is the conflict underlying the depressive state. It will be seen, accordingly, that the problem of the schizoid individual is how to love without destroying by love, whereas, the greater of problems is for the depressive individual, is how to love without destroying by hate. These are two very different problems.

The conflict underlying the schizoid state is, of course, much more devastating than the conflict underlying the depressive stat e, and, since the schizoid reaction has its roots in an earlier stage of development than the depressive reaction, the schizoid individual is less capable of dealing with conflict than is the depressive. It is owing to these two facts that the disturbance of the personality found in schizophrenia is so much more profound than found in depression. The devastating nature of the conflict associated with the early oral phase lies in the fact that, if it seems a terrible thing

448

for an individual to destroy his object by love. It is the great tragedy of the schizoid individual that it is his love which seems to destroy; and it is because his love seems so destructive that he experiences such difficulty in directing his libido toward objects outer reality. He becomes afraid to love, and therefore he erects barriers between his objects and himself. He tends both to keep his objects at a distance and to make himself remote from them. He rejects his objects, and at the same time, he withdraws his libido from them. This withdrawal of libidinal energies may be carried to all lengths. It may be carried to a point at which all emotional and physical contacts with other persons are renounced; and it may even go so far that all libidinal links with outer reality are surrendered. All interests in the world fades and everything becomes meaningless. In proportion as libido is withdrawn from outer objects it is directed toward the internalization with its accompanied objects; and, in proportion as this happens, the individual becomes introverted. And, incidentally, it is on the observation that this process of introversion is so characteristic on the onset of schizoid states that are themselves based on the conclusion that the introvert is essentially a schizoid. It is essentially in inner reality that the values of the schizoid are to be found. So far as he is concerned, the world of internalized objects is always encroaching upon the world of external objects; and in proportion as this happens his real objects become lost to him.

If loss of the real objects were the only trauma of the schizoid state the position of the schizoid individual would not be so precarious. It is necessary, nonetheless, to bear in mind the vicissitudes of the ego, which accompany loss of the object. Reference has already been made to the narcissism which results from an excessive libidinalization of internalized objects; and such narcissism is specially characteristic of the schizoid. Accompanying it, we invariably find an attitude of superiority which may manifest itself in consciousness to a varying degree as an actual sense of superiority. It should be of note, in that, this attitude of superiority is based upon an orientation toward internalized objects, and that in relation to objects in the world of outer reality the attitude of the schizoid is essentially one of inferiority. It is true, that the externally oriented inferiority may be masked by a façade of superiority, as based upon an identification of external with internalized objects. Nevertheless, it is invariably present, and it is evidence of a weakness in the ego. What chiefly compromises the development of the ego.

In the case of the schizoid individual is the apparently insoluble dilemma which attends the direction of libido toward objects. Failure to direct libido toward the object is, of course, equivalent to loss of the object: But since, from the point of view of the schizoid, the libido is itself destructive, the object is equally lost when libido is directed toward it. It can thus readily be understood that, if the dilemma becomes sufficiently pronounced, the result is a complete impasse, which reduces the ego onto a state of utter impotence. The ego becomes quite incapable of expressing itself; and, in so far as this is so, its very existence becomes compromised. This can be exemplified by the following, as: "I can't say anything. I have nothing to say. I'm empty. There's nothing of me, . . . I feel quite useless; I haven't done anything. I've gone cold and hard: I don't feel anything . . . I can't express myself. And, I feel futile. Such descriptions are well illustrated, not only the state of impotence to which the ego is compromised in the schizoid dilemma. The last quoted remark of this is, perhaps, as drawing attentions to the characteristic affect of the schizoid state: For the characteristic affect of the schizoid state is undoubtedly a sense of futility.

The libido may be withdrawn in varying degrees even from that part of the psyche which is, so to speak, nearest to external objects. It may be withdrawn from the realm of the conscious into the unconscious. When this occasions, the effect is as if the ego itself had withdrawn into the unconscious: But the actual position would seem to be that, when the libido deserts the conscious part of the ego (such as it is), the unconscious part of the ego is all that is left to behave as a functioning ego. In extreme cases the libido would seem to desert even the unconscious part of the ego and relapse into the primal id, leaving both surface only the picture with which Kraepelin has familiarize us in his account of the last phase of dementia præcox. Whether such a mass-withdrawal of the libido can properly be ascribe d to repression is a debatable question, although where the process is restricted to a withdrawal from object-relationships, it may give that impression. At any rate, the effectual withdrawal of the libido "feels quite different" from that of simple repression. There can be no doubt, nonetheless, that withdrawal of the libido from the conscious part of the ego has the effect of relieving emotional tension and mitigating the danger of violent outbursts of precipitate action. There can be equally little doubt that much of the schizoid individual's anxiety really represents fear of such outbursts occurring. This fear commonly manifests itself as a fear of going insane or as a fear of imminent disaster. It is possible, therefore, that massive withdrawal of the libido has the significance of as desperate effort on the part of an ego threatened with repression of the basic impulse which urge the individual on to make emotional contacts. In the case of the schizoid, of course, these impulses are essentially oral impulses. It is when this effort is within measurable distance of succeeding that the individual begins to tell us that he feels as if there were nothing of him, or as if he had los t his identity, or as if he were dead, or as if he had ceased to exist. The fact is that in renouncing the libido the ego renounces the very form of energy which holds it together—and the ego thus becomes lost. Loss of the ego is the ultimate psychopathological disaster which the schizoid individual is constantly struggling, with more or less success, too avert by exploiting all available techniques (including the transitional techniques) for the control of his libido. In essence, therefore, the schizoid state is not a defence, although evidence of the presence of defences may be detected in it. It represented the major disaster which may befall the individual who has failed to outgrow the early stage of dependence.

If the problem which confronts the individual in the early oral phase is how to love the object without destroying it by love, the problem which confronts the individual in the oral phase is how to love the object without destroying it by hate. Accordingly, since the depressive reaction has its roots in the late oral phase, It is the disposal of his hate, rather than the disposal of his love, that constitutes the difficulty of the depressive individual. The formidable as this difficulty is, the depressive is at any rate spared the devastating experience of feeling that his love is bad. Since his love, at any rate, seems good, he remains inherently capable of a libidinal relationship with outer objects in a sense in which the schizoid is not. His difficulty in maintaining such a relationship arises out of his ambivalence. This ambivalence in turn arises out of the fact that during the late oral phase, he was more successful than the schizoid in substituting direct aggression (biting) for simple rejection of the object. While his aggression has been differentiated, that, nonetheless, he has failed in some degree to achieve that further step in development which is represented by dichotomy of the object. This further step, had he taken it, would have enabled him to dispose of his hate by directing it, predominantly at least, toward the rejected object and he would have been left free to direct toward his accepted object love which was relatively unaccompanied by hate. In so far as he failed to take such a step, the depressive remains in that state which characterized his attitude toward his object during the late oral phase. His external object during that phase, of course, a whole object (his mother); and his libidinal attitude toward it was incorporative. The incorporated object to the depressive thus comes to be an undivided whole object, which he adopts an ambivalent attitude. The presence of such an inner situation is less disabling so far as outer adjustments are concerned than is the corresponding inner situation, in the case of the schizoid, for in the case of the depressive there is no formidable barrier obstructing the outward flow of libido. Consequently, the depressive individual readily establishes libidinal contacts with others; and, if his libidinal contact with others appear satisfactory with others, and if his libidinal contacts are satisfactory to him, his progress through life may appear fairly smooth, as the inner situation is always present, and it is readily reactivated if his libidinal relationships becomes disturbed. Any such disturbance if his libidinal relationships become disturbed, such disturbances immediately calls into operation the hating element in his ambivalent t attitude; and, when his hate becomes directed toward the internalized object, a depressive reaction supervene s any frustration in object-relationships is, o f course, functionally equivalent to loss of the object. Whether partial or complete, since severe depression is so common a sequel to actual loss of the object (whether by the death of a loved person or things as severally otherwise). Loss of the object must be regarded as the essential trauma which provokes the depressive state.

Physical injury or illness is obviously represents himself, which is to say, that such a loss, e.g., the loss of an eye or a limb, represent the symbolic castration as taken that we no further, for it still remains to be explained why a reaction which is characteristically provoked by loss of the object should also b e provoked by loss of par t of the body. The true explanation lies in the fact that the depressive individual still remains to a be a distinctive feature of degrees to an actual state of infantile identification with his object. To him, is, therefore, bodily loss is functionally equivalent to loss of the object, and this equivalence is reinforced by the presence of an internalized object which, so speak, suffuses the individual's bod y and imparts it to narcissistic value.

A brief dispositional representation as the presentation for which of "narcissism," is to mean, that the cathexis of the own self with libido, is used in the term self because the state of primary narcissism exists only prior to any ego differentiation, a point made by Hartmann. What is called the secondary narcissism is the late return of object cathexis to the own person.

There still remains to be explained is the phenomenon of Involutional melancholia. According to Freud and Abraham, the functional process in melancholia is the loss of the loved objects, the real, or some similar situation having the same significance, result in the object becoming installed within the ego. Owing, however, to an excess of cannibalistic impulses in the object, this introjection miscarries and the consequence is illness.

All the same, are those who tend to regard the etiology of this condition as entirely different from that of "reactive depression," nonetheless, the two conditions have sufficiencies in common clinical standpoints, to justify, as to invoke the principle of, "entia non sunt multicanda præter necessitate." It is not really, but melancholia is by definition closely associated with the climacteric; and the climacteric would seem to be in itself evidence of a definite waning of libidinal urges. It cannot be said, nonetheless, that there is any equivalent diminution of aggression. The balance between the libidinal and the aggressive urges is thus disturbed, and, further, It is disturbed in the same direction as when the hate of any ambivalent individual is activated by loss of the object. Accordingly, in an individual of the depressive type the climacteric has the effect of establishing the same situation as does actual loss of the object where object-relationships are concerned; and the result is a depressive reaction. If the prospect of recovery in the case of Involutional melancholia is less hopeful than in cases of reactive depression, This is not difficult to explain: For, whereas the latter case a libido is still available for a restoration of the balance in the former case, it is not. Involutional melancholia is thus seen to conform to the general configuration of the depressive state, and it imposes upon as holding of no necessity to modify the conclusion already envisaged—that loss of the object is the basic trauma underlying the depressive state. As in the case of the schizoid state, this state is not a defence, on the contrary, it is a state against which the individual seeks to defend himself by means of such techniques (including the transitional techniques) as are available for the control of his aggression. It represents the major disaster which may befall the individual who failed to outgrow the late oral stage of infantile dependance.

We find ourselves confronted with two basic psychopathological conditions, each arising out of a failure in the past of the individual to establish a satisfactory object-relationship during the period of infantile dependence. The first of these conditions, by which the schizoid state, is associated with an unsatisfactory object-relationships during the early oral phase; and the second of these conditions, stem from or are directed in the depressive state, is associated with an unsatisfactory object-relationship during the early oral phase. It emerges quite clearly, however, from the analysis of both schizoid and depressive individuals that unsatisfactory object-relations hips during the early and late oral phases, only give rise to their characteristic psychopathological effects when object-relationships continue to be unsatisfactory during the succeeding years of early childhood. The schizoid and depressive states must, accordingly, be regarded as dependent upon a regressive reactivation, during early childhood of situations arising, respectively, during the early and late oral phases. The traumatic situation in either case is one in which the child feels that he is not really loved. If the phase in which infantile object-relationships have been pre-eminent, this phase in which infantile object-relationships have been pre-eminently unsatisfactory, is the early oral phase, this trauma provides in the child a reaction conforming t to the idea that he is not loved because his own love is bad and destructive, and this reaction provides the basis for a subsequent schizoid tendency. If, the phase in which infantile object-relationships have been pre-eminently unsatisfied, as to a later idea that he is not loved because he presents of his badness and destructiveness, in that he is not loved because he presents of these distortions. This reaction provide the basis for a subsequent depressive tendency. Whether in any given case a schizoid or depressive state depends, in par t, of course, upon the circumstance which the individual is called upon to face in his later life But the most important determining factor is the degree to which objects have been incorporated during the oral phase. The various defensive techniques which characterize the transition period, i.e., the obsessional, paranoid, hysterical and phobic techniques. All represent attempts to deal with difficulties and conflicts attending object-relationships in consequence of the persistence of corporatised objects. These defensive techniques are accordingly seen to resolve themselves into differing methods of controlling an underlying schizoid or depressive tendency, and thus averting the onset of a schizoid or depressive state, as the case may be. Where a schizoid tendency is present, they represent methods designed to avert the ultimate psychopathological disaster which follows from loss of the ego, and, where a depressive tendency is present, they represent methods designed to avert the ultimate psychopathological disaster, in which follows from loss of the object.

It is so fortunate as to enjoy a perfect object-relationship during the impressionable period of infantile dependence, or for that matter during the transition period of infantile dependence. Consequently, no one ever becomes completely emancipated from the state of infantile dependence, or from some proportionate degree of oral fixation; and there is no one who has completely escaped the necessity of incorporating this early enacting of objects. It may consequently be inferred that there is present in everyone either an underlying schizoid or his underlying depressive tendency, according as it as in the early or in the late oral phase that difficulties chiefly attended infantile object-relationships. We are thus introduced to the conception that every individual may be classified as falling into one or two psychological types—the schizoid and the depressive. It is not necessary to regard these two types as having more than phenomenological significance, nevertheless, it is impossible to ignore the fact that in the determination of these two types some part may be played by a hereditary factor—such that the relative strength of the inborn tendencies of sucking and biting.

Of these, we are reminded of Jung's dualistic theory of psychological types. According to Jung, is, of course, the "introvert" and the "extravert" representation to the fundamental types, into the constitution of which psychopathological factors do not primarily enter. There is, however, another essentially dualistic conception of psychological types, with which a conceptual representation prolonging the conception with which is expounded by Kretschmer in his works entitled "Physique and Character" and "The Psychology of Men of Genius" and according to which the two basic psychological types are the "schizothymic" and the "cyclothymic." As these terms they imply, the reverential inference of cyclothymic individuals, as predisposed to circular or manic-depressive psychoses, and the schizothymic individual to schizophrenia, there is thus, a striking agreement between Kretschmer's conclusions and explanations that are envisaged types—an agreement all the more striking since the envisaged types of alternative operatives. The only significant divergence between the two analytic approaches arises out of the fact that Kretschmer regards the temperamental differences between the types as based essentially upon constitution factors and attributes to the psychopathological propensities to this temperamental differences. Whereas in viewing the psychopathological factors used during the period of infantile dependence making of any rate a considerable contribution to the temperamental difference. The sufficient agreement between Kretschmer's views and those as provided some independent support for autonomously unconfined study, however, Kretschmer's views also provide some independent support or an underlying depressive tendency, as presented at some level in every individual, and that all individuals may be classified upon this basis, so, as far as their psychopathological propensities are concerned.

Every theory of basic types is inevitably confronted with the problem of "mixed types." Kretschmer freely acknowledges the existence of mixed types, and he explains their occasioned occurrence on the grounds that the incidence (and perhaps, hormonic) groups of factors, which it may be usually of some mixed types is to be explained not so much in terms of fixations in developmental phases. Where difficulties over object-relationships assert themselves pre-eminently during the early oral phase, a schizoid tendency is established, and, where difficulties over object-relationships assert themselves pre-eminently during the late oral phase, the establishment of a depressive tendency is the result. In so far, is that, nonetheless, that such difficulties are fairly distributed between the two phases, we may expect to find a fixation in the late oral phase superimposed upon one in the early oral phases, and in that case a deeper schizoid tendency will be found underlying a superimposed depressive tendencies, that such a phenomenon may occur admits of no doubt whatsoever, and even the most "normal" person must be regarded as having persuasions toward schizoid potentialities at the deepest levels. It is open to equally little question that even the most normal person may on certain circumstances become depressed. Similarly, schizoid individuals are not wholly immune to depression, and depressed individuals are sometimes grounded by displaying certain schizoid characteristics. Whether a depressive or a schizoid state will declare itself in any given case doubtless depends in part upon whether the precipitating circumstances take the form of the real object or of difficulties in object-relationships assuming in some other form; and where there is a fairly even balance between fixation in the early and the late phases. This may be the determining factor. Even so, the most important factor must always remain the degrees of regression, which is provoked; and this is determined primarily by the relative strength of fixation. In the last instance the degree of regression must depend upon whether the chief problem of the individualities that lies in the disposal of his love or in the disposal of his hate and there must be few individuals in whom the disposal of love and the disposal of hate are attended by equal difficulty.

When we use as primary source not our own clinical data but the experience and insights of other fields., We betray a sese of our unease. Such behaviour indicates that our understanding of the clinical phenomena or of the analytic theory that we adduce to interpret them is not as firmly based as we would want it to be. Thus, Altman (1977), after an erudite and charming discourse on the vicissitudes of love ends by saying, . . . the vicissitudes of love are so interrelated with every aspect of human development, its ambiguities so numerous and persuasive, that we may still be obliged to ask, "What is this thing called love?"

Altman observed, for instance, that when psychoanalysts are asked about love, they respond as cultured lay people, rather than as professionals. They do no t couch their responses in the language of scientific psychology. This should make us aware that from the very beginning, psychoanalytic discussion of love has been burdened by the analyst's entailment in his own culture, in its values and its social structure. In Western society, love is put forward as the "summum bonun" of human relations. All moral teaching whether founded in faith in the supernatural or not, sanctifies love. Dealing fairly with one's neighbour and curbing one's aggression toward others ultimately involve an essential compassionate attitude toward people, that is, a capacity for positively-tinged affective identification with others. Since love is sanctified and regarded as sacred, it falls within the realm of the taboo. Accordingly, objectivity may be inhibited and curiosity curbed when we attempt to study love scientifically. An analyze love, especially the creative, "nonconflictual" aspects of the phenomenon, may even imply a certain degree of sacrilege, a desecration of what should be revered rather than understood, of what should be cherished rather than analysed.

The high moral value we place on loving strengthens the Superego's influence on how we treat the subject during therapy and how we conceptualize love scientifically. "What's wrong with a good love relationship?" Essentially, it is a rhetorical question. We almost always take a good love relationship for granted. Such a question constitutes a moral rather than an intellectual challenge.

The most recent literature concerning the phenomenology of love has emphasized the importance of early object love. In large measure, this has been occasioned by the stage of interest in narcissistic character disorder, and the so-called borderline condition. The connection between loving and these conditions arising from the fact that identification and narcissistic object choice is common to all of them, investigation of the etiology, therefore, has centered on the vicissitudes of the early mother-child as the matrix out of which identification and individuation are affected. Moreover, these are conditions in which vulnerability of self-esteem is of major significance. Freud (1914) placed variation of self-esteem in the centre of his discussion of falling in love and being in love, explaining the phenomenon in economic terms—in shifts of libidinal investment from the self-representation to the object-representation and back. According to object relations theorists, the nature of the earliest interaction between the child and the mother determines the quality of the child's subsequent love relationships. Bak (1973) states that falling in love is an attempt to undo the original separation from the mother, and Bergmann (1971) says, that love revived if not direct memories, then . . . archaic ego states that were once active in the symbiotic phase. He cites Mahler (1967) to the effect in the symbiosis is to be understood as "hallucinatory of delusional, somatopsychic, omnipotence fusion with the representation of the mother. In other words, the state of being in love reactivates or reflects the state of object relations that prevailed before the distinction between the self and the object developed. During the symbiotic phase, fusion with the mother is supposedly experienced as unalloyed bliss, while separation is tantamount to its annihilation and death."

It was connection with Feud's revolutionary approach to the subject of sex and love that he developed the concept of the object.

Discussing the nature of the energy of the erotic drive, the libido, Freud (1905) distinguished between the zone of origin of the libido, the aim of the libidinal instinct that the libido as the object of the instinct. It is upon the object that the libido is discharged and this process of discharge is experienced as pleasure. He said that the object is the mental representation of something which is the source of intense libidinal gratification, something highly cathected with libido. The mental representation grows out of a mnemic image, a recollected set of sensory impressions accompanied by a pleasurable feeling, in that which, according to the dominant principle, one's wishful attempt to reconstitute as a sensory impression. Accordingly, the object may be the representation of something which is part of one's own person—the lips, skin. Mouth, and so forth, for example—or, it may be the mental representation of something inanimate which at a certain stage of cognitive development is still regarded as par t of one's own person. Fenichel (1945) observed that at particular stages in the child's development, the faecal mass is viewed sometimes as part of the self and sometimes as part of the external world. This is a striking parallel to Winnicott's (1953) concept of the transitional object. at a later stage the object may be an external representation of another person existing independently of the self. In each stag e of this development, it should be emphasized, we are dealing with a technical term, the concept of a mental representation. According to libido theory, it is no t the external thing which is vested with energy, It is the metal representation of the thing or person so cathected. The mental representation bears a special relationship to processes of instinctual discharge.

Emphasizing the representational aspect of the object highlights two kind s of confusion that pertain to the use of the object concept. The first of these confusions is shown by the theories of Wilhelm Reich (1942). Basing his views on Freud's earlier neurophysiological concept of the set or in the body of another person. This approach has perpetuated the confusion between what is internal and what is external. That is, where in the physical world the material libido is to be found. It disregards the fact that at all times we are dealing with a psychological experience, the mental representation of an object, a persistently "internal" experience.

The second confusion is illustrated by the concept of a part object, as opposed to a whole object. Whatever it is that is represented mentally as instinctually cathected constitute an object. Instinctual wishes of an aggressive or libidinal nature may centre on mental representations of parts of one's own body, parts of someone else's body, or on mental representation of one's own or some other person's whole body. Any one of these may be taken as an object. The type of unconscious fantasy involved determines whether or not the person's body is regarded as a penis or whether the person as a whole is regarded as a breast or, as in the case of narcissistic object choice, whether another person is regarded as a representation of one's own self. When we make judgements about psychological experiences, whether for the purpose of clinical interpretation or a theory building, what we try to determine is the nature of the unconscious fantasy which underlies the thought or behaviour of the individual, either in regard to other persons or things or in regard to that individual (Arlow, 1969). In such fantasies of a real external person or, conversely, one's whole body in an unconscious fantasy may be conceived as a representation of one's own or someone else's penis, breast, or faeces. In any event, we are dealing with mental representations of an object in the sense as defined by itself, as whether that mental representation corresponds to the totality of another person's body or to a part of one's own or another person 's body.

A consequence of the confusion, it may be observed in the tendency to use the term's interpersonal relations and object relations interchangeably. They are not identical. In fact, they represent two different realms of discourse. A young man, for example, disappointed in his beloved, does not search for a new object. He is really looking for another woman, who may in time become the source of pleasurable cathected mental representations. Fundamentally, it is the effect of unconscious fantasy wishes, connected with special mental representations of objects, that colour, distorts and affects between the person and the object. This is essentially the core of transference, in which the person in the real world is confused with a mental representation of a childhood object, a mental representation of what once was either a person or a thing. These issues are no t simply semantic ones. They bear directly on any discussions of love and narcissism and the role of object relation s in ego development.

According to Freud (1911), the operation of the pleasure principle is expressed through a tendency to reestablish and experience a se t of sensory perceptions of a pleasurable nature identical with the memory of earlier experience or pleasure. Thus, the first and fundamental categorization of experience is in terms of pleasant or unpleasant. (Brenner [1974], in his study, the development of affects, has demonstrated the fundamental role that this categorization plays in all subsequent affective structure.) This is t e abiding principle by which perceptions are integrated and organized in memory according to the quality of similarity with or differences from earlier memory traces. On the basis of how the memory of earlier perceptions has been organized, subsequent experience in interpreted metaphorically (Arlow, 1979) note once again, Freud (1925) wrote in, "Negation":

. . . The function of judgement is concerned in the main with two sorts of decisions. It affirms or disaffirms the possession by a thing of a particular attribute; and it asserts or disputes that a presentation has an existence in reality. The attribute to be decided about may originally have been good or bad, useful or harmful. Expressed in the language of the oldest—the oral—instinctual impulses, the judgement is: "I should like to eat this," or "I should like to spit it out." That is to say: "I will be inside me;, or, "It will be outside me." The original pleasure-ego want is to introject into itself, such that everything that is good and to eject from itself everything that is bad. What is bad, what is alien to the ego and what is external are, to begin with, identical.

. . . The other sort of decision made by the function of judgement—as to the real existence of something of which there is a presentation (reality-testing)—is a concern of the definitive reality-ego, which develops out of the initial pleasure-ego. It is now no longer a question of whether what has been perceived (a thing) as a presentation can be rediscovered in perception (reality) as well. It is, we see, once more a question of external and internal. What is unreal, merely a presentation and subjective, is only internal; what is real is also there outside. In this stage of development regard for the pleasure has been set outside. experience has shown the subject has it is not only important whether a thing (an object

461

of satisfaction for him) possesses the "good" attribute and so deserves to be taken into his ego, but also whether it is there in the external world, so that he can get hold of it whenever he needs it. In order to understand this step forward we must recollect that all presentations or origin from perceptions are repetitions of them. Thus originally the mere existence of a presentation was a guarantee of the reality of what was presented. The antithesis between subjective and objective does not exist from the first. It only comes into being from the fact that thinking possesses the capacity to bring before the mind once more, something that has once been perceived, by reproducing it as a presentation without the external object having still to be there. The first and immediate aim, therefore, of reality-testing is, not to find an object in real perception which corresponds to the one presented, but to refined such an object, to convince oneself that it is still there.

We can see in this quotation from Freud that there is an all-pervasive series of equivalents which come to serve as the background for all judgements and interpretations of stimuli. What is pleasurable is at first treated as part of the self, and in keeping with the pleasure principle, the psychic apparatus operates toward trying to institute a repetition of these perceptions. It is not hard to understand how reality testing and the interpretations of sensory data, Functions acquire with such effort, and easily and readily set aside in the compulsive wishful strivings of dreams, fantasies, and neurotic symptoms, as well as under the influence of great passion or prejudice, and, of course, in love. The fundamental tendency to seek an identity of pleasurable perceptions goes far in explaining the persistent influence of unconscious childhood fantasies.

What is later organized and conceptualized as the need-gratifying object originates out of the memories of repetitive sensory impressions accompanied by feelings or gratification. Object seeking is predominantly oriented by the needs to try to achieve the identity of pleasurable perceptions remembered but dependently attained by infants. The disparity between infant's wishes and their limited capacity to achieve them in reality is a fundamental fact of human development connected with an external person become organize into a coherent memory structure, a mental representation of a person, which we call "object." The term, object, therefore, represents a concept pertaining to a persistent, that is, a structural experience in parallel fashion a coherent organization of memory traces of representations connected with pain may serve as the basis for the concept of another kind of object representation. Thus, it happens that two sets of memories of sensory impressions may be organized as mental representations, one associated with pain, the other pleasure. The pleasant representation of such memories may be labelled as "good", the unpleasant one's as "bad." It is in this sense that we can understand what the Kleians mean when they talk about "good" objects and "bad" objects in referring to the psychic events in the earliest months of life.

It is only later in the course of development that the seemingly disparate mental representations of objects having identical sensory impressions are fused into the concept of an external person whose mental representations psychologically may be vested or associated with memories of pain as well as pleasure. From a psychological point of view the individual's concept of a person is a conglomerate of many earlier object representations. This coherent, organized concept may be dissolved regressively into its antecedent object representations. It is not necessarily the re-emergence of an earlier structure, but rather the reactivation of memory traces of the good object representation that is distinct from the good object representation, thus, the splitting of the representation of a person does not necessarily occur only in case of severe personality regression. When there is a painful interaction between two people, one can observe in the dreams and fantasies of the patient how the qualities of good and bad become sharply dissociated in the mental representation of the object. The individual, in turn, may respond to the other person as if that person were the repetition of the earlier mental representation of the bad object. At the same time, such an individual may be functioning at an advanced level of mental development: The ease with which the coherent concept of the object may regressively dissolve into earlier separate mental representations is a measure of ego weakness. The tendency to split the object representations int a good and bad antecedent expressions is usually reversible. In severe pathology, however, the process is irreversible and the split of the object representation becomes fixed and persistent.

Mahler's (1975) concepts of separation-individuation and the observational base for these concepts has been well established. Her ideas are frequently invoked to explain certain phenomena observed on the borderline states, the psychosis, falling in love, and the experience of

463

the orgasm. The stages prior to the phases of separation-individuation have been associated with the period of primary identification—the stage during which there is no differentiation between the self and the object. Regression to primary identification is a hypothesis which appeals to those who view a good segment of psycho pathology as reflecting a "loss of boundaries" between the self and the object. According to some, this is the condition which is regressively reactivated in the psychopathological formations. However, it should of note, that feeling at one with something, being completely identified with someone, thinking that someone experiences and feels everything that another person seems to feel, is not necessarily a recapitulation of the vague, undefined state that precedes the distinction between the self and the object world. When poets describe the ecstasy of love or orgasm by saying that they feel completely united and indissolubly fused with the beloved, there is, nonetheless, some concomitant awareness of the existence of the other person as an independent object. This is equally true for descriptions of timelessness and the so-called "oceanic" feeling, two states of mind often associated with being in love as well as with loss of the sense of self or of "ego boundaries." In a study of distortions of the sense of time (Arlow, 1974, in that, the ability to demonstrate, from detailed presentations of the material of the analysis was not that of the fusion of self and object. ; in one instance, the fantasy expressed a woman's wish to have the oedipal love object forever. In the case of a male patient, it represented an overcoming of the fear of castration, a wish for immortality to counteract the pressing awareness off the danger of castration as represented by a fear of death.

Freud (1914), in his work titled "On Narcissism" emphasized that in severe, regressive narcissistic disorders, there is not only a break with reality and withdrawal from objects of the external world, but at the same time, one is unable to find any trace of cathexis of mental representations of objects in fantasy, conscious or unconscious. It should be emphasized that it is not the clinical phenomenon of relations or withdrawal from people which indicates a break of object relations, but rather the evidence if withdrawal of cathexis from mental representations of objects. This is an important distinction to bear in mind: Otherwise one is tempted to make extrapolations from phenomenology without appreciating the characteristic feature of psychoanalysis, namely, the nature of the unconsciously psychological experience. It is possible for certain individuals to have limited or few relations with people, but at the same time to maintain a very high quality of object constancy in fantasy life. One has to avoid judging the significance of an experience by externally observable phenomena alone.

After, at least a beginning attempt at individuation and after the phase of the transitional object, the different constellations of the memories of sensory experiences of pleasure and pain may be organized around the common source of perceptions into the concept of the good or bad mother, the good and bad object. One aspect of the child's growing ability to master ambivalence resides in the capacity too integrate the two contradictory concepts into a specific, unified concept of a person in the external world. Developmental psychologists differ as to exactly when this achievement is attained—probably sometimes in the second year of life. It is an attainment however that is easily and regularly undone by regression. The concept of the object, as well as the concept of the self and even of the Superego, may undergo regressive dissolution into their antecedent identifications. This may be observed and dreams and in psycho pathology, especially in patients suffering from depression, both in the borderline states and the psychoses.

The Superego is not a unified agency, is such, that, if closely observed, it can be seen top constitute an organization of contradictory trends based upon an attempt to integrate various impressions of experiences of judging a nd of having judged, of reward and punishment from objects. This agency of the mind is built up for the most part, by way of identification with objects in very specific contexts. The self-condemning prosecutory hallucinations observed in various forms of severe depression represent memories of fantasies, distorted, it is true, by the process of defence, but memories which have been regressively transformed into visual o r auditory perceptions. Under such circumstances, the delusional material regressively recapitulates, by way of identifications. The process reveals that the identifications in the Superego represent discrete, historic episodes, selective identification in terms of the individual's previous conflicts.

These considerations are important because identification plays a major role in object relations theory, especially as applied to love. Identifications, like object t relations, cannot be separated from drive derivatives. The two concepts are indissolubly of internalized object relations, but such object relations are part of a continuum

465

of drive discharge. An identification is not effected with the totality of another person or object but with some specific aspect of the person's behaviour in a very specific context. The aspects of the individual's behaviour that are selected for purposes of identification are congruent with or correspond to certain specific drive needs of the individual. These may relate to Superego efforts directed toward self-punishment.

With these considerations concerning the development of the object concept and object relations in mind, are turned, once, again, to the psychology of love.

The realization of dealing essentially with the differentiated patterns of object choice, we are struck by the dramatic compulsive quality with which certain, but buy no means all, individuals from other repetitive, seemingly compulsive, uncontrollable, unstable compromise formation effected by the three psychic agencies in other normal and pathological processes—for example, symptom formation, dreams, perverse impulses? The varieties of loving are surely as diverse as the varieties of psychopathological formations, as well as the varieties of normal compromise reaction. From this point of view it is difficult o agree completely with Bak (1973) or Bergmann (1971), who try to trace the psychology of loving to a specific developmental vicissitude, the wish to re-achieve symbiotic fusion with the mother in order to undo the primordial separation. This early vicissitude of object relations must have some bearing on the patterns of loving, but while it is pertinent, it is not necessarily decisive.

The great diversity of patterns of loving can be illustrated from the experience in any analyst's practice. There is a rich literature ranging from Freud's studies in the psychology of love to the more recent discussions of self-object narcissistic choice. Freud (1917) "Taboo of Virginity" is important in one special way, inasmuch as it illustrates the aggression in the choice of the love object and in the pattern of loving. The same principles apply to object choices made in certain of the sexual perversions. But the truly complex nature of the pattern of loving and object choice can best be shown by the study of individual patients.

In any individual it is possible to observe different patterns of loving and varieties of object choice, for example, the typical oedipal evolution of the patient traumatized by the primal scene who develops a persistent unconscious rescue fantasy together with a need for a degraded love object. A concomitant persistent wish may be to wreak vengeance upon surrogates for the betraying, unfaithful mother. Furthermore, in response to the fear of castration generated by the anticipation of retaliation for hostile wishes against the father. The same individual may develop a pattern of passive, submissive, feminine orientation toward men. In such a patient a variety of patterns of loving and object choices toward members of both sexes, characterized by patterns of instinctual gratification that represented both aim-inhibited and aim-fulfilled wishes. In derivatives of several types of unconscious fantasies, representing wishes derived from different moments in his relations to the important objects of, his past, the patient identified himself with different objects—his father, his mother the crucified Christ, certain figures from mythology and fairy tales. Each identification found expression in some form of loving. The identifications were the vehicles for drive derivatives, part of an unconscious fantasy of being either the father, the sexual fathers partner, or some conqueror: His patterns of loving relations with both men and women were determined by the nature of the persistent unconscious fantasies. Loving involves identification, but identification at many levels and at many different times with different objects. It is not necessarily a regressive reactivation of the primitive fusion with a love object or regression to a phase where there is no distinction between the self and the object world.

Within the analytic situation closer examination of the phenomenon of love demonstrates how certain aspects of the real person and of the self are rigorously excluded in the sense of oneness. What is experienced is determined by a fantasy or a se t of wishes centring about specific mental representations deriving from selected memories of experiences with the earlier object or objects—the father, the mother, and in the unusual cases, oneself or parts of one's body.

By way of comparison, one may observe another patient, in whom there were several distinct patterns of love relations. He was, first of all, a very successful Don Juan who typically won. Seduced, and then abruptly dropped his partner. The abruptness with which he terminated these relationships was parallel by the urgent intensity with which he pursued them in the beginning. If one concentrated only on the opening phases of his relationships, he would seem to epitomize the romantic ideal of the love-intoxicated, heartsick young swan. In these affairs, however, the culmination of the relationship was represented not by the successful libidinal gratification, but rather by the gratification of aggression directed toward the women, the promiscuous, disappointing oedipal and post-oedipal mother, but also an abandoning nursemaid who had abruptly left the family's employment when the patient was three and a half years of age.

In contrast, the same patient also had long-lasting devoted sexual attachments to older women, relationships that were regularly stormy, but compulsively maintained, remarkably ambivalent and characterized by vehement mutual recriminations. These relationships recapitulated a clandestine affair he had with a housekeeper-nursemaid, an affair that lasted through the oedipal and latency periods and parallelled in time the disillusioning experiences with his mother. The parallel's love relations with older women were sadomasochistic in quality and articulated specific forms of anal-erotic gratification that could be traced to the character of the housekeeper-nursemaid. Residue of this attachment could be seen in the aim-inhibited love relationship he had with his secretary. A much older women, as well as in the nature of his character structure, which reflected an identification with the clandestine lover through the compulsive and behaviour he pursued in identification with her. The active, phallic nature of this women undoubtedly predisposed the patient to make subsequent oedipal and post-oedipal object choices of women who were active and sensual and whose behaviour corresponded to his fantasy of the women possessing a penis. The Don Juan behaviour was multiple, and determined of a mixture of the fulfilment of erotic and aggressive impulses, an identification with the faithless, promiscuous mother, the abandoning love object, together with elements of defence against castration anxiety. while much more could be said about the determinants of the specific and complex patterns of loving in this case, however, it clearly illustrates the complicated interrelationship of identifications, defence, object relations, and instinctual gratification, all of which play a role in determining the nature of the patient's love. It would be impossible to reduce the plexuity of object-finding and gratification to any of the simple basic formulas proposed by several of the proponents of object relations theory.

The subject of identification quite naturally leads to the topic of the internalization of object relations. This is a concept which is very difficult to differentiate from identification. Does it mean more than the fact that the personality or psychic structure of an individual is transformed as the result of his or her interaction with others? Or do internalized object relations imply the positing of a persistent structure in the psychic apparatus which has a dynamic thrust of its own, a thrust to repeat and reproduce the original experience in a way that is independent of the drive representation? Is there a developmental thrust which asserts itself along predetermined lines through a hierarchical distinction in stages, beginning with the earliest relation and progressing toward an ideal endpoint, commonly known as the mature or genital form of object relationships, which presumably leads to the "highest" stage of love? The discoursing dialogue concerning the internalization as to the object relations theory and love, it seems that this developmental eventuality is considered as the 'sine qua non" of true love.

It would seem that, however surreptitiously, elements of value judgements infiltrate analytic considerations of love. this is a trend which can be traced to the early history of psychoanalysis. It is difficult to avoid a tendency to judge psychological phenomena in terms that essentially mean "good" or "bad". Some such tendency may be discerned in Abraham's (1924) study of the development of the libido. Abraham evaluated the nature of love relationships in terms of biology. The quality of the libidinal tie with any individual, he maintained, is determined by the level of psychosexual development which it reflects the development of sexuality evolved in precise stages and subdivisions by way of a normal, orderly succession of dominance by oral, and phallic instinctual drives. The nature of the object chosen was determined by the drive dominant at that particular stage when the choice was made. The highest stage of development, the mature form of love, was genital love. By way of contrast, choices effected at the pregenital level, Abraham considered the pre-ambivalent or ambivalent, a quality which offered poor prognostic outcome because it conveyed the potentiality for conflict and neurosogenesis. genital love, in it post-ambivalent form, and typified, no t at all surprising, in those qualities which society regards as both desirable and commendable in the relationship between two people of the opposite sex. To be sure, these qualities have unquestioned social utility, in so far as they strengthen the ties which make for a stable marriage and foster the solidarity of the family, the basic unit of society. from society's point of view an ideal post-ambivalent genital relationship is desirable, useful, and therefore "good."

Today, more than half a century later, the terminology and leading conceptualizations may have changed, but the problem remains the same. Formulations are now couched in terms of object relations instead of biology. The distinctions between the self and the object world have become the touchstones. Instead of an orderly, biological predetermined succession of libidinal stages, what is emphasized today is the developmental evolution of an orderly set of stages of object relations.

According to Friedman (1978), this process is considered by many to be equally predetermined as an inexorable developmental thrust, much in the same spirit as Abraham's formulation concerning libidinal phases and the concomitant object choices. While Abraham emphasized the developmental aspects of libidinal drive over the nature and vicissitudes of experience with the object, more recent formulations in terms of object relations theory tended to emphasize the vicissitudes of experience with the object, as well as the resultant cognitive and affective consequences. Thus, certain authors maintain that true love is possible only by culture. In our daily work with patient's, we are constantly passing judgement on whether the patient" s affective response is in keeping with, i.e., appropriate to, of his or her experience. We make such judgements in terms of standards relevant to our culture and to the individual's background. Cultural ambience influences not only how love is expressed, but also how it is experienced. the cultural influence may transcend the specific set of interactions characteristic of the relation s with the infantile love object. The fusion of the tender and the sensuous steams of the libidinal impulse and the idealization of the love object is a notion that was canonized during the romantic period. it is not always the model for the choice of a partner; and even today, it represents a notion as often honoured in the breach as in the observance. Other times and other levels of society had, in fact, institutionalized the distinction between these various components of what we call "being in love." they have done so by distinction of marriage, customs, property arrangements, and sanctioned extramarital liaisons. There have been and still are many polygamous societies. The significance of institutionalisms practice of predominant social patterns for courtship and for choosing a

470

mate can hardly be lost on the younger members of our society. "Love at first sight," "falling head over heels in love," "loving in despair, from afar," "the attraction of the unattainable object." All represent styles of experiencing and expressing love. They are styles that had their ascendancy and decline. in yesteryear, the idealization of the love object and its public expression were encouraged by social norms.

Nonetheless, we face a dilemma. One contributor to the psychology of love from the point of view of object relations that love represents a re-emergence of the earliest, mo t primitive mother-child relationship. While another asserts that love reflects the most developed, most mature form of object relations.

All the same, as analysts, we pass judgement on the phenomenology of love we observe in our patients, we do so in terms of phase-specific anticipations, for example, we accept but hardly ever really analyze reports of impulsive patterns of loving that patients present concerning the adolescent scene. We relate this to the clearly patient psychological transformations of puberty, as we may look disapprovingly at the middle-aged man, and certainly at an elderly man, who falls in love following the adolescent pattern. In the same spirit, one has to note the social bias against older women having liaison with younger men; the reverse pattern is more acceptable. these are subtle, but definitive value judgements as couched in term s of normal, that is, statistical anticipations. Unconsciously, they dictate to us what and how we choose to analyze.

In actual practice we are concerned with what has keep a particular patient to love in her or his particular way; how, among the myriad patterns of love, the patient has come to select the one he or she actually did choose. How well we are able to determine this depends in large measure upon how close the distance is between the choice of object and the pattern of loving, and the central nexus of the patient's unconscious conflicts. the consequence of conflict make it possible for us to analyze the nature of the love relationship, but in those instances in which the pattern of loving is ego-syntonic, but have less of an opportunity to penetrate deeply into the psychology of loving and are therefore, not in a very good position to grasp some understanding of the precursors of the particular patterns of loving. Under such circumstances, the temptation is greatly interpretive, as only to speculate phenomenologically than dynamically. What we do, in effect, is conjecture on the bias of history about what might have been the individuals psychological experience, since we seem unable to trace out the interpretational inferentially from the data in the dynamic context of the analytic situation.

In practice, we deal with how the individual comes to choo s someone to love and how this love is expressed. This is a complex process involving the integration of the individual's total experience. I t is usually organized in terms of a few leading, unconscious fantasies which dominate an individual's inherent perceptions of the world and create the mental set by which she or he perceives and interpret their individual experience.

The existing stage during which there is no differentiation between the self and the object, of which appeals to those who view a good segment of psycho pathology as reflecting a "loss of boundaries", that, between the self and the object. Often associations for being in love as well as with loss of the sense of self of or of "boundaries" the overwhelming sense of time, that from detailed presentations on the material derivatives, is that of the sensations as warranted within the paradigms of the "timelessness" of an unconscious continuum. It should be noted that feeling at one with something, being completely identified with someone, thinking that someone experiences and feels everything that another person seems to feel, is not necessarily a recapitulation of the vague, undefined state that precedes the distinction between the self and the object world.

According to Freud and Abraham, the fundamental process in melancholia is the loss of the loved object. The real loss of a real object, or some similar situation having the same significance, resulting in the object becoming installed within the ego. Owing, however, to an excess of cannibalistic impulses in the subject, this introjection miscarries and the consequence is illness.

Now, why is it that the process of introjection is so specific for melancholia? Perhaps, that the main difference between incorporation in paranoia and in melancholia is connected with changes in the relation of the subject to the object, though it is also a question of a change in the constitution of the introjecting ego. But, according to Edward Glover, the ego, at first but loosely organized, consists of a considerable amount of ego-nuclei, that if existing for the first time, in his view, however, in the first place an oral ego-nucleus and later an oral ego-nucleus predominates over the other. In this ver y early phase, in which oral sadism plays a prominent part and which it seems the basis of schizophrenia, the ego's power of identifying itself with its objects is as yet small, partly because it is itself still uncoordinated and partly because the introjected objects are still mainly partial objects, which it equates with fæces.

In paranoia the characteristic defences are chiefly aimed at annihilating the "persecutor," while anxiety on the ego's account occupies a prominent place in the picture. As the ego becomes more fully organized, the internalized imagos will approximate more closely to reality and the ego will identify itself more fully with "good" objects. The dread of persecution, which was at first felt on the ego's account, now relates to the good object as well and from now on preservation of the good object is regarded as synonymous with the survival of the ego.

The combinality with this development goes a change of the highest importance, namely, from a partial object-relation to the relation to a complete object, through this step the ego arrives at a new position, which forms the foundation of that situation called the "loss of the love object." Not until the object is loved as a whole can it loss be felt as a whole.

With this change in the relation to the object, new anxiety-contents make their appearance and a change takes place in the mechanisms of defence. The development of the libido also is decisively influenced. Paranoid anxiety, lest the objects sadistically destroyed should themselves be a source of poison and danger inside the subject's body, causing him, in that, in spite of the vehemence of his oral-sadistic onslaughts, at the same time to be profoundly mistrustful of them yet, incorporating them.

This leads to a weakening of oral fixations. One manifestation of this may be observed in the difficulties very young children often show in regard to eating, which, in all probability, have a paranoid root. As a child (or an adult) identifies himself more fully with a good object. The libidinal urges increase as he develops a greedy love and desire to devour this object and the mechanism of introjection is reinforced. Besides, he finds himself constantly impelled to repeat the incorporation of a good object partly because he dreads that he has forfeited it by his cannibalism—i.e., the repetition of the

473

act is designed to test the reality of his fears of the internalized persecutors against whom he requires a good object to help him. Nonetheless, the ego is more than ever driven both by love and by the need to introject the object.

Another stimulus for an increase of introjection is the phantasy that the loved object may be preserved in safety inside oneself. In this case the danger of the inside are projected onto the external world.

If, however, consideration for the object increases, and a better acknowledgement of psychic reality sets in, the anxiety least the object should be destroyed in the process of introjecting it leads—as Abraham has described—to various disturbances of the function of introjection.

Furthermore, a deep anxiety as to the dangers which await the object inside the ego. It could not be safely maintained there, as the inside is felt to be a dangerous and poisonous place in which the loved object would perish. Its own obviousness shows one of the situations which can be described as fundamental for "the loss of the loved object," the situation, namely, when the ego becomes fully identified with its good, internalized objects, and at the same time becomes aware of its own incapacity to protect and preserve them against the internalized, persecuting objects and the id. This anxiety is psychologically justified.

For the ego, when it becomes fully identified with the object, it does mot abandon its earlier defence mechanisms. According to Abraham's hypothesis, the annihilation and expulsion of the object—processes characteristic of the earlier anal level—initiate the depressive mechanism. If this be so, it confirms the notion of the genetic connection between paranoia and melancholia. Yet, the paranoiac mechanism of destroying the objects (whether inside the body or in the outside world) by every means which oral, urethral and anal base of sadism can command, persist, but in a lesser degree and with a certain modification due to the dread and least of the good object as it should be expelled along with the causes to the mechanisms of expulsion and projection to lose value. However, the ego makes a greater use of introjection of the good object as a mechanism of defence. This is associated with another important mechanism: That of making reparation to the object.

While, at the same time the existence of this internal world is being depreciated and denied. Both in children an in adults are founded to such infinitive varieties,. Where obsessional neurosis was the most powerful factor in cases, as mounting of such mastery and betoken of a forceful separation of two (or more) objects, to methods more violent, that is to say, the objects were killed but since the subject was omnipotent, it was supposed that he could immediately call them to life again. But the killing corresponded to the defence-mechanism (retained from the earlier phase) of destruction of the object. in this position, the ego effects a similar compromise in its relation to real objects,. the hunger for objects, so characteristic of mania, indicates that the ego has retained one defence-mechanism of the depressive position: The introjection of good objects. The manic subject denies the different forms of anxiety associated with this introjection (anxiety that is to say, least of either, such that he should introject bad objects or else destroy his good objects by the process of introjection); his denial related not merely to the impulses of the id, but to his own concern for the object's safety. Thus, we may suppose that the process by which mania is as follows. The ego incorporates the object in a cannibalistic way (the "feast", as Freud calls it in his account of mania) but denies that it feels any concern for it. 'surely," argues the ego: It is not a matter of such great importance if this particular object is destroyed. there are so many others to be incorporated. This disparagement of the object's importance and the contempt for it is, in that of a specific characteristic of mania and enables the ego to effect that of a partial detachment which we observe side by side with its hunger for objects. Such detachment which the ego cannot achieve in the depressive position, represents an advance, a fortifying of the ego in relation to its objects,. but this advance is counteracted by the regressive mechanisms described which the ego at the same time employs in mania.

Even so, that in this case, when depression came to the fore in full force and the paranoid anxieties diminished, the hypochondriacal anxieties became related to the internalized loved objects and (thus) to the ego, while before they had been experienced in reference to the ego only.

After having attempted to differentiate between the anxiety-contents, feelings and defences at work in paranoia and those in the depressive states, whereby upon viewing the depressive state as based on the paranoid state and genetically derived from it. Wherefore, the depressive state as the result of a mixture of paranoid anxieties and of those anxiety-contents, distressed feelings and defences which are connected with the impending loss of the whole loved object. It seems to me that to introduce a term for those specific anxieties and defences might further the understanding of the structure and nature of paranoia. As well as of the manic-depressive states.

Whenever a state of depression exits, be it in the normal, the neurotic, in manic-depressives or in mixed cases, there is always in this specific grouping of anxieties or in mixed cases, the distressed feelings and different varieties of these defences, but, if this point proves convincing, we should be able to understand those very frequent cases where we are presented with a picture of those of the mixed paranoiac and depressive trend's, since we could then isolate the various elements of which it is composed.

For, in as much as now, it is true, that good and bad objects are more clearly differentiated, the subject's hate is directed rather against the latter, while his love and his attempt at reparation are more focussed on the former; but the excess of his sadism and anxiety acts as a check to this advance in his mental development. Every external or internal stimulus, e.g., every real frustration, is fraught with the utmost danger, not only bad objects but also, the good ones are thus menaced by the id, for every access of hate or anxiety may temporarily abolish the differentiation and thus result in a ";loss of the loved object." And it is not only the vehemence of the subject's uncontrollable hatred but that of his love too, which imperils the object. for at this stage of his development, loving an object and devouring it are very closely connected., a little child which believes her (whether from motives of love or of hate) is tormented by anxiety both her and for the good mother which it has absorbed into itself.

It now becomes plain why, at this phase of development, the ego feels itself constantly menaced in its possession of internalized goo d objects. It is full of anxiety least such objects should be terminated and vanquished, however, both children and adults suffering from depression.

From the very beginning both psychic development there is a constant correlation of real objects with those installed within the ego. It is fo r this reason that the anxiety which is described by their manifestation to itself that, in a child's exaggerated fixation to its mother or whoever looks after it. The absence of the mother in the child's anxiety, least it should be handed over to bad objects, external and internalized, either because of her death or because of her return in the guise of a "bad" mother.

Both cases signify to it that it has lost its loved mother and as the internalize d object becomes a perpetual source of anxiety, least the real mother should perish, though every experience which suggests the loss of the real beloved object, for what stimulates the dread of losing the internalized one too.

That the loss of the loved object takes place during that phase of development in which the ego makes the transition from partial to total incorporation of the object, nonetheless, the processes which subsequently become defined as "loss of the loved object" are determined by the subject's sense of failure (during weaning and in the periods which precede and follow it) to securer his good, internalization for its object, i.e., to posses himself of it. One reason for his failure is that he has been unable to overcome his paranoid dread of internalized persecutor

Deep within this particular station, a point as spatially occupying of space and time. Such that, at this point we are confronted with a question of importance for our whole theory. Simply of the direction as influenced by the early processes of introjection upon both normal and pathological development, in that of the very epoch-making, in some respects other, than has hitherto commonly been accepted in psychoanalytic circles.

According to our views, even the earliest incorporated object's form the basis of the Superego and enter into its structure. The question is by no means a merely theoretical one. As we study the relations of the early infantile ego to its internalized objects and to the id, and come to understand the gradual changes these relations undergo, we obtain a deeper insight into the specific anxiety-situation through which the ego passes and the specific defence-mechanisms which it develops as it becomes more highly organized. Viewed from this standpoint in our experience we find that we arrive at a more complete understanding of the earliest phases of psychic development, especially of the structure of the Superego and of the genesis of psychotic diseases. For which we deal with etiology, it seems essential to regard the libido-disposition not merely as such, but also to consider it in connection with the subject's earliest relations to his internalized and external objects, a consideration which implies an understanding of the defence-mechanisms development by the ego gradually in dealing with its varying anxiety-situations.

If by the greater of chances, we accept this view of the formation of the Superego, its relentless severity in the case of the melancholic becomes more intelligible. The persecutions and demands of bad internalized objects; the attacks of such objects upon one another (especially that are represented by the sadistic coitus of the parents); the urgent necessity to fulfil the very strict demands of the "good objects" and to protect and placate them within the ego, with the resultant hatred of the id; the constant uncertainty as to the "goodness" of a good object, which causes it so readily to become transformed into a bad one—all these factors combine to produce in the ego a sense o f being a prey to contradictory and impossible claims from within, a condition which is felt as a bad conscience. That is to say, the earliest utterances of conscience are associated with persecution by bad objects. The very word "gnawing of conscience" or "biting the stone of conscience-ness" (Gewissensbisse) testifies to the relentless "persecution" of conscience and to the fact that is originally conceived of as devouring its victim.

Among the various internal demands which go to make up the severity of the Superego in the melancholic, least of mention, is the urgent need to comply with the very strict demands of the "good" objects. It is this part of the picture only—namely, the cruelty of the "good", i.e., loved, objects within—which has been recognized hitherto by general analytic opinion, namely, in the relentless severity of the Superego in the melancholic. But in view, it is only by looking at the whole relation of the ego to its fantastically bad objects as well as its good objects, only by looking at the whole picture of the internal situation which of having tried to outline, such that we can understand the slavery to which the ego submits when complying with the extremely cruel demands and admonitions of its loved object which has become installed within the ego, least of mention, the ego endeavours to keep the good apart from the bad, and the real from the unreal objects. The result is a conception of extremely bad and extremely perfect objects that is to say. Its loved objects are in many ways intensely moral and exacting. At the same time, since the ego cannot really keep its good and bad objects apart in its mind, some of the cruelty of the bad objects and of the id becomes related to the good objects and this then again, increase the severity of their demands. These strict demands serve the purpose of supporting the ego in its fight against its uncontrollable hatred and its bad attacking objects, with which the ego is partly identified. The stronger the anxiety is of losing the loved objects, the more the ego strives to save them, and the harder the task of restoration becomes the gruelling labours will grow the demands for which are associated with the Superego.

The anxiety and feeling of suffering are of a much more complex nature, the preservation of the good internalized objects with whom the ego is identified as a whole. The anxiety, least of mention, is the good object and with them the ego should be destroyed, o r that they are in a state of disintegration, is interwoven with continuous and desperate efforts to save the good objects both with internalization and externalization.

Nonetheless, it seems that only when the ego has introjected the object as a whole and has established a better relationship to the external world and to real people is it able fully to realize the disaster created through its sadism and especially through its cannibalism, and to feel distress about it. This distress is related not only to the past but to the present as well, since at this early stage of development the sadism is in full swing. It needs a fuller identification with the loved objects, and a fuller recognition of its value, for the ego to become aware of the state of disintegration to which it has reduced and is continuing to reduce its loved objects. the ego then finds itself confronted with the physical fact that its loved objects are in a state of dissolution—in bits—and the despair. remorse and anxiety deriving from this recognition are at the bottom of numerous anxiety-situations, for examples, that of how to pick out the good bits in the right way and at the right time, also, how to pick out the good bits and do away with the bad ones, and, in addition, how to bring the object to life when it has been away with the bad ones, as well as to say, how to bring the object to life when it has been put together and there is the anxiety for being interfered within this task by bad objects and by one's own hatred, and so on.

Anxiety-situations of this kind are found to be the bottom not only of depression, but of all inhibitions of work. The attempts to save the loved object, to repair and restore it, attempts which in the state of depression are coupled with despair, since the ego doubts its capacity to achieve this restoration, are determining factors for all sublimation and the whole of the ego-development. It appears that the desire for "what is perfection" is rooted in the depressive anxiety of disintegration which is thus of great importance on all sublimations. Nevertheless, the ego comes to a realization of its love for a good object, a whole object and in addition a real object, together with an overwhelming feeling of guilt toward it. Full identification with the object based on the libidinal attachment, first to the breast, then to the whole person, goes hand in hand with anxiety for it (of its disintegration), with guilt and remorse, with a sense of responsibility for preserving it against persecutors and the id, and with sadness relating to expectations of the impending loss of it. These emotions, whether conscious or unconscious, are in view between the essential and fundamental elements of the feeling we call love.

In this connection, brings much similarity with the self-reproaches of the depressive which represent reproachment against the object. But to my mind the ego's hate of the id, which is overbearing in this phase, account is even more for its feelings of unworthiness and despair than do its reproaches against the object. Finding only that these reproaches and the hatred against bad objects are secondarily increases as a defence against the hatred of the id, which is even more unbearable. In the last analysis it is the ego's unconscious knowledge that the hatred, also there as the love, that it may at any time get the upper hand (the ego's anxiety of being carried away by the id and so destroying the loved object), which brings about the sorrow, feelings of guilt and despair which underlie grief. This anxiety is also responsible for the doubt of the goodness of the loved object. As Freud has pointed out, doubt is in reality a doubt of one's own love and "a man who doubts his own love may, or rather must, doubt ever lesser things.

The paranoiac, has also introjected a whole and real object, but has not been able to achieve a full identification with it, or, if he has got as far as this, he has not been able to maintain it. To mention a few of the reasons which are responsible for this failure: The persecution-anxiety is too great; suspicions and anxieties of a fantastic nature stand in the way of a full and stable introjection of good object and a real one. In so far as it has been introjected, there is little capacity to maintain it as a good object, since doubt and suspicion of all kinds will soon turn the loved object again into a persecutor. Thus, his relationship too whole objects and to the real world is still influenced by his early relation to internalized part-objects and fæces as persecutors and may again give way to the latter.

It seems characteristic of the paranoiac that, though, on account of his persecution-anxiety and his suspicions, he develops a very strong and acute power of observation and the external world and of real objects, since his persecution-anxiety makes him look at people mainly from the point of view of whether they are persecutors or not. Where the persecution-anxiety for the ego is in the ascendant, a full and stable identification with another object, in the sense of looking at it and understanding it as it really is, and full capacity for love, are not possible.

Another important reason why the paranoiac cannot maintain his whole-object relation is that while the persecution-anxiety and the anxiety for himself are still so strongly in operation that he cannot endure the endure additional burden of anxieties for a loved object and, besides, the feelings of guilt and remorse which accompany this depressive position. Moreover, in this position he can make far less use of projection, for fear of expelling his goo d objects and so losing them, accountably for reasons for fear of injuring good external objects by expelling what is bad from within himself.

Thus, we see that the suffering connected with the depressive position thrust him back to the paranoiac position. Nevertheless, though he has retreated from it, the depressive position has been reached and, therefore, the liability to depression is always there. This accounts, for the fact that we frequently meet depression along with severe paranoia as well as in milder cases.

If we compare the feelings of the paranoiac with those of the depressive in regard to disintegration, one can see that characteristically the depressive is filled with sorrow and anxiety for the object, which he would strive to unite again into a whole, while to the paranoiac the piece is growing agin into a persecutor. this conception of the dangerous fragments to which the object is reduced seems as to be, in keeping with the introjection of part-objects which equates with fæces (Abraham), and with the anxiety of a multitude of internal persecutors to whom the introjection of many part-objects and the multitude of dangerous fæces gives rise.

Let us now consider the hypochondriacal symptoms in this comparative way, the pains and other manifestations which in phantasy result from the attacks of internally bad object s within against the ego are typically paranoid. The symptoms which derive from the internal warfare in which the ego is identified with the suffering of the good objects, are typically depressive.

For instance, a patient who has been told as a child that he had tapeworm (which he himself never saw) connected the tapeworm within side him with his greediness. In his analysis, however, he had phantasies that a tapeworm was eating its way through his body and a strong anxiety of cancer came to the fore. The patient, who suffered from hypochondriacal and paranoid anxieties, was very suspicious of such things as oriented within his immediate environment, and, among other things, suspected of his surrounding surfaces for being allied with people who were hostile toward him. At this time he dreamed that a detective was arresting a hostile and persecuting person and putting this person in prison. However, when the detective proved unreliable and became the accomplice of the enemy. The detective stood for purposes as gaining in something as externally placed of the whole anxiety for which was internalized, nd was also connected with the tapeworm phantasy. The prison in which the enemy was kept was his own internalization—actually the special part of his inside where the persecutor was to be confined, as the dangerous tapeworm (one of his associations was that the tapeworm is bisexual) represented the two parents in a hostile alliance (actually in intercourse) against him.

At the sam e time the tapeworm phantasies were being analysed the patient developed diarrhea which—as he wrongly thought—was mixed with blood. This frightened him very much; he felt it as a confirmation of dangerous processes going on inside him. This feeling was founded in the phantasies in which he attacked his bad united parents in his insides, with poisonous extracts,. the diarrhea meant to him of poisonous extracts, as well as the bad penis of his father. The blood which he thought was his fæces represented the exteriority of foreign bodies (as, this was shown by association s in which had connected with blood). Thus, the diarrhea was felt to represent dangerous weaponry, with which he was fighting bad internalization, as to the parents, as well as his poisoned and broken-up parents themselves. In his early childhood he had in phantasy attacked his real parents with poisonous excreta and actually disturbed them in having intercourse by defecating. Diarrhea had always been something very frightening to him. Along with these attacks on his real parents this whole war-far became internalized and threatened his ego with destruction. Briefly to note, that this patient remembered during his analysis that at about ten years of age, he had definitely felt that he had a little man inside of his stomach who controlled him and gave him orders, which he, the patient, had to execute, although they were always perverse and wrong (he had, had similar feelings about his real father).

When the analysis progressed and distrust in the analyst had diminished as the patient became very much concerned about the him. He had always worried about his mother's health, but he had not been able to develop real love toward her, though he did his best to please her. Now, together with the concern for therapist, strong feelings of love and gratitude came to the fore, together with feelings of unworthiness, sorrow and depression. The patient had never felt really happy, his depression had been spread out, one might say, over his whole life, but he had not suffered from actual depressive states. In hi s analysis he went through phantasies of deep depression with all the symptoms characteristic of this state of mind. Yet, the feelings and phantasies connected with his hypochondriacal pains changed. For instance, the patient felt anxiety that the cancer would make its way through the lining of his stomach; but now it appeared that, while he feared for his stomach, he really wanted to protect the analyst, who is now inside him—actually the internalized mother—whom he fell t was being attacked by the father's penis and by his own id impulsions. (The cancer). Another time the patient has haemorrhage from which he would die. It became clear that the analyst was identified with the haemorrhage. The good blood represented the analyst. We must remember that, when the paranoid anxieties dominated and the therapist was mainly felt as a persecutor, Wherefore, the identification with bad blood which was mixed with the diarrhoea (with the bad father). Now the precious good blood represented the analyst, as for losing which meant the cancer, which would imply his death. It became clear now, that the cancer which he made responsible for the death of his loved object, as well as for his own, and which stood for the bad father's penis, was even more felt to be his own sadism, especially his greed. That is why he felt so unworthy and so much in despair.

483

While the paranoid anxieties predominantly and the anxiety of his bad united objects prevailed, he felt only hypochondriacal anxieties for his own body. When depression and sorrow had set in, the love and the concern for the good object came to the fore, and the anxiety-contents, as well as the whole feelings of defences altered. In this case, as well as in others it has be found that paranoid fears and suspicions were reinforced as a defence against the depressive position which was overlaid by them.

Wherever a state of depression exists, be it in normal, the neurotic, in manic-depression o in mixed cases, there is always in this specific grouping of anxieties, distressed feelings and different varieties of the defences. If this point of view proves correct, should be able to understand those very frequent cases where we are presented with a picturer of mixed paranoiac and depressive trends, since we could then isolate the various elements of which it is composed.

The consideration about the depressive states may lead us to a better understanding of the still rather enigmatic reaction of suicide. According to the findings of Abraham and James Glover, a suicide is directed against the introjected object. but, while in committing suicide the ego intends to murder its bad objects, that is to say, that it alway aims at saving its loved objects, internal or external. To put it shortly; in some cases the phantasies underlying suicide aim at preserving the internalization of good objects and that part of the ego which is identified with good objects, and also at destroying the other part of the ego which is identified with the bad object and the id. Thus, the ego is enabled to become united with its loved object.

Freud has stated that mania has for its basis the same contents as melancholia and is, in fact, a way of escape from that state. That is to suggest, that in mania and ego seeks refuge not only from melancholia but also from a paranoiac condition which it is unable to master. Its torturing and perilous dependence on its loved objects drives the ego to find freedom. In that, its identification with these objects is too profound to b e renounced. On the other hand, the ego is pursued by its dread of bad objects and the id and, in its effort to escape from all these miseries. It has recourse to many different mechanism as, some of which, since they belong to different phases of develop phases of development, are mutually incompatible.

In the sense of omnipotence, is what, first and foremost characterizes mania and, further (as Helene Deutsch has stated) mania is bases on the mechanism of denial, as Helene Deutsch in the following point. She holds this "denial" is connected with the phallic phase and the castration complex (in girls it is a denial of the lack of the penis)"; which observations have led to conclude that this mechanism of denial originates in that every early phase which the development of denial endeavours to defend itself from the most overpowering and profound anxiety of all its dread of internalized persecutors and the id. That is to say, that which is first of all denied is psychic reality and the ego may then go on to deny a great deal of external reality.

We know that scotomization may lead to the subject's becoming entirely cut off from reality, and to his complete inactivity. In mania, however, denial is associated with an overactivity, although this excess of activity, as Helen e Deutsch points out, often bears no relation to any actual results achieved. Hence is to explain that in this state the source of the conflict is that the ego is unwilling and unable to renounce its goo internal objects and yet endeavour to escape from the perils of dependence on them as well as from its bad objects. its attempt to detach itself from an object as well as from its bad objects. It s attempt to detach itself from bad objects is without the same time of its completion. It is renounced, but it seems to be conditioned by an increase in the ego's own strength it seems in this compromise by denying the importance of its good objects and also the dangers with which it is a menace from its bad object and the id. All and all, it endeavours ceaselessly to master and control of it s objects, and the evidence of this effort is its hyperactivity

Implications that ego identity is the highest level organization of the world of object relations in the broadest sense, and also of the self. This is a very complex development, because while object relations are continuously internalized (as such internalization take place at gradually higher, more differentiated levels). At the same time, the internalized object relations are "depersonified" (Jacobson, 1964) and integrated into higher level ego and Superego structures such as the "ego ideal," character constellations, and autonomous ego functions. Simultaneously, with these processes of internalization and depersonification, internalized object relations are also organized into persistent object images which come to represent internally the external world as experience by the developing ego, which corresponds roughly to what Sandler and Rosenblatt (1962) have called the "representational world." It has to be stressed, however, that this internal world of objects such as seen in conscious., preconscious and unconscious fantasies never reproduced the actual world of real people with whom the individual has established relationships in the past and in the present; it is at most an approximation, always strongly influenced by the very early object images of introjection and identifications. It should be noted, however, it is also, that the "world of inner objects, as used by Klein, which gives the impression of remaining as free floating object images in the psychic apparatus rather than being related to any specific structures, does not do justice to the complexity of integration of object relations, organization of object images takes place both in the object relationships. Organization of object images takes place both in the sector of depersonified ego structures and in the sector of developing identity. Such object images which remain relatively unmodified, the repressed unconscious are less affected by structuralization; in this sense very primitive, distorted object images certainly continue to exist in the unconscious mind. Nevertheless, by far, the greater part of internalized object images is normally integrated into higher level structure, and those which remain as object representations experience modifications over the years were under the influence of ego growth and later object relationships. The normal outcome of identity formation is that identifications are gradually replaced by selective, partial, sublimatory identification, in which only those aspects of object relations are internalized to which are in harmony with the individual identity formation.

Actually, the enrichment of one's personal life by the internal presence of such selective, partial identifications representing people who are loved and admired in a realistic way without indiscriminate internalization, constitutes a major source of emotional depth and well being. The normal process of individualization is marked by the shift from identifications to partial, sublimated identifications under the influence of a well-integrated ego identity. One might say, that depersonification of internalized object relations, reshaping of part of them so that they come to resemble more then the real objects, and individualization are closely relate processes.

The world of inner objects, then, gradually changes and comes closer to the "external" perceptions of the reality of significant objects throughout childhood and later life, without ever becoming an actual copy of the environmental world. "Confirmation," intrapsychically speaking, is the ongoing process of reshaping the world of inner objects under the influence of the reality principle, of ego maturation and development, and through the cycle of projection and introjection. The persistence of "non-metabolized" early introjection is the outcome of a pathological fixation of severely disturbed, early object relationships. A fixation which is intimately related to the pathological development of splitting that which interferes with the integration of self and object images and the depersonification of internalized object relationships in general. Under the pathological circumstances, early, non-integrated object images come to the surface; but even then, as is being stressed throughout, as we never do have "free-floating" internal objects but are always confronted with the specific ego structures which they have crystalized.

Keeping in mind, our reservations about the concept of the "representational world" as a close reproduction of the external world of objects, we might say, that ego identity is the highest level of organizational presentations of the world of object relations in the broadest sense and comprises the concept of the representational world and that of the self on the other.

The concept of instinct, Freud defines as a stimulus; a stimulus not arising in the outer world but "from within the organism," he adds that a better term for an instinctual stimulus is a "need," and says further, that such 'stimuli are the signs of an external world." Freud lays explicit stress on one fundamental implication of his whole consideration of instinct, is, namely that it implies the concept of purpose in the form of what he calls a biological postulate. This postulate runs as follows: The nervous system is an apparatus which has the function of getting rid of the stimuli that reaches it, or of reducing them to the lowest possible level. An instinct is a stimulus from within reaching the nervous system. Since an instinct is a stimulus arising within the organism and acting "always as a constant force," it obliges the nervous system to renounce its ideal intention of keeping off stimuli and compels it "to undertake involved and interconnected activities by which the external world is so changed as to afford satisfaction to the internal source of stimulation.

As instinct brings an inner stimulus reaching the nervous apparatuses, the object of an instinct is "the thing in regard to which or through which the instinct is able to achieve its aim. This aim for being sufficiently satisfactory as convincing properties are adequately satisfied. Nonetheless, the object of an instinct is further described as "what is most variable about an instinct", "not originally connected with it," and as becoming "assigned to it, only in consequence for being peculiarly fitted to make satisfaction possible." It is here that we see instinctual drives being conceived of as "intrapsychic," or originally not related to objects.

In the later of Freud's writings, he gradually moves away from this position. Instincts are no longer define as (inner) stimuli which the nervous apparatuses' deals in accordance with the scheme of the reflex arc, but instinct as found, in, "Beyond the Pleasure Principle," is seen as "an urge inherent in organic life to restore an earlier state of things which the living entity has been obliged to abandon under the pressure of external disturbing forces. He defines instinct in terms equivalent to the terms he used earlier in describing the function of the nervous apparatuses itself. The nervous apparatuses, the "living entity" in its interchange with "external disturbing forces." Instinct is no longer an intrapsychic stimulus but, an expression of the function of the "urge" of the nervous apparatuses to deal with the environment. The intimate and fundamental relationship of instinct s, especially in so far as libido (sexual instinct, Eros) is concerned with objects is more clearly brought out in "The Problem of Anxiety," until originally, in "An Outline of Psychoanalysis," "the aim of the first of these basic instincts [Eros] is to establish ever greater unities and to preserve them thus—in short, to bind together." It is worthy of note, that the relatedness to objects is implicit; the aim of the instinct Eros is no longer formulated in terms of a contentless 'satisfaction," or satisfaction in the sense of abolishing stimuli, but the aim is clearly seen in terms of integration. it is "to bind together." And while Freud feels that it is possible to apply his earlier formula, "to the effect that instinct tended toward a return to an earlier [inanimate] state, to the destructive or death instinct," we are unable to apply the formula to Eros (the love instinct).

The basic concept Instinct has thus changed its contentual representation, since Freud wrote, "Instincts and Their Vicissitudes." In his later writings he does not take as his starting point and model the reflex-arc scheme of a self-contained, closed system, but bases his considerations on a much broader, more modern biological framework. And it should be clear from the last quotation that it is by no means the ego alone to which he assigns the function of no synthesis, of binding together. Eros, one of the two basic instincts, is itself an integrating force. This is in accordance with his concept of primary narcissism as first formulated in "On Narcissism: an Introduction," and further elaborated in his later writings, in, "Civilization and Its Discontents," where objects, reality, are far from being originally not connected with libido, and, are seen as becoming gradually differentiated from a primary narcissistic identity of "inner" and "outer" worlds. Nonetheless, one of Freud's proudest achievements was the transformation of the therapeutic relationship which takes place in psychoanalysis into a tool of scientific investigation. Freud also believed that "the future will probably attribute far greater importance to psychoanalysis as the science of the unconscious than as a therapeutic procedure (Freud, 1926).

You may question whether such a wide variety of differing symptomatic syndromes can be brought together under a single heading. If we consider the issue not in terms of presenting symptoms but in terms of the similar nature of their object relationships, we find many threads united these seemingly disparate disorders.

But, in actual practice we are concerned with what has kept a particular patient to love in her or his particular way; how, among the myriad patterns of love, the patient has come to select the one he or she actually did choose. How well we are able to determine this depends in large measure upon how close the distance is between the choice of an object and the pattern of loving, and the central nexus of the patient's unconscious conflicts. The consequences of conflict make it possible for us to analyze the nature of the love relationship, but in those instances in which the pattern of loving is ego-syntonic, but have less of an opportunity to penetrate deeply into the psychology of loving and are therefore, not in a very good position to grasp some understanding of the precursors of the particular patterns of loving. Under such circumstances, the temptation is greatly interpretive, as only to speculate phenomenologically than dynamically. What we do, in effect, is conjecture on the bias of history about what might have been the individuals psychological experience, since we seem unable to trace out the interpretational inferentially from the data in the dynamic context of the analytic situation.

Developments in the interactional description of schizophrenia have been parallelled in the area of depression. As yet, concepts such as pseudomutuality, double-bind, schism, and skew have found no counterparts. Kubler and Stotland (1964) have argued, that emotional disturbance, even the most severe. But can be understood unless the field in which it develops and exists is examined. The manifestations of the difficulty in the disturbed individual, for having meant of improving to what idea that something conveys to the mind, as to a meaning, is the intendment that significantly sustained by its intention, for which is in the aspects of the field. The substantial aspects of the field are usually interpersonal, yet the study of depression has focussed on the individual and his behaviour, from out of his interactional context. To a large degree, the depressed person's monotonously reiterate complaints and self-accusations, and his provocative and often annoying behaviour has distracted investigators from considerations of his environed and the role it may play in the maintenance of his behaviour. The possibility that the characteristic pattern of depressed behaviour might be interwoven and concatenated with a corresponding pattern in the response of others has seldom been explored.

For the most part, it has been assumed that the depressed person is relatively impervious to the influence of others. Ruesch (1962) states that to talk to the depressed person makes little sense, to listen intently then listen again. Grinker (1964) conceptualized depressive symptomatololgy as communication to others, but argued that the depressed person is not responsive to communication from others. "The depressed persons . . . cannot use information for the purpose of action: he cannot perceive the cues of reality, he makes statements but does not care if he is understood.

In terms sustained by a systems theory are usually conceptualized by things that breath and has life, of which and all, that depressed people seemed that they are of closed but an opened condition. Grinker (1964) was explicit in stating that the depressed person repeats his message and behaviour without reception or acceptance of resulting feedback. Beck (1964, 1967) described the cognitive distortions that dominate the information processing of the depressed person so that experiences are rigidly interpreted to maintain an existing schema of personal deficiency, self-blame and negative expectations.

490

The implicit assumption of these and other writers has been the support and information available to the depressed person are incongruent with his depression, and the persistence of his symptomololgy is evidence of a failure to receive or accept this information. Withdrawal, isolated intrapsychic processes, or as Beck describes, (1967) the interactions of depressive schema and affective structures, produce a downward depressive spiral, this, however, engages of an alterative argument, in that the depressed person is able to adopt in such an argument, that is to say, that the depressed person is able to engage others in his environment, in such a way that support is lost and depressive information elicited. This in turn, increases the level of depression and strengthens the pathogenic pattern of depressed behaviour and responses of others. If a depressive spiral develops, it is a mutually causative deviation-amplifying process (Maruyama, 1963) in the interaction of the depressed person with his environment. Thus, what is customarily viewed as some internal process is, in at least, in part, a characteristic of interaction with the environment t, and much of what is customarily viewed as cognitive distortion or misperception is characteristic of an information flow from the environment. It should be noted that while the depressed person' s different interpretation of this predicament is traditionally attributed to his distortion or interpretation. The general disorders of though t and perception are defining neither criteria nor common among depressed patients (McPartland and Hornstra, 1964). An observer who fails to take onto account the intricacies of someone's relations that he does not posses, or leaves significant aspects of his explaining experience is still unexplained. (Watzlawick, 1967). Feedback introduces phenomena that cannot be adequately explained by reference to the isolated individual alone (Ashby, 1960, 1962). For the study of depression, identification of a pattern of depressive feedback from the environment demands to more complex conceptualizations of the disorder than one explaining its phenomena with reference to the isolated repressive person.

Lemert (1962), in his study of the interpersonal dynamics of paranoia, argued that the net effect of the developing interaction pattern between the paranoid person and others is that (1) the flow of information to the person is stopped, (2) a real discrepancy between expressed ideas and affect among those with whom he interacts is created, and (3) the situation or group image becomes as ambiguous for him as he is for others. In this context of attenuated relationships, exclusion, and disrupted communication, the paranoid person cannot get the feedback on his behaviour, that is essentially in order for him to correct his interpretations of social relationships. Lemert concluded that the paranoid person may be delusional, but that is also true that in very real sense he is able to elicit covertly organized action and conspiratorial behaviouralism.

Nonetheless, it should be made clear that the phenomenon of depression does not deny the existence of important intrapersonal factors in depression, however, that several writers have pointed out that the depressed person's feelings of worthlessness and helplessness, and do not arise in his immediate stimulus situation (Chodoff, 1972). McCranie (1971) has argued that there is a "depressive-core" in the personality of the depression-prone person, consisting of a tendency to feel worthless and helpless and an over-sensitivity to stimuli that impinge upon these feelings. Together, these are aroused from a dormancy by specific situations such as loss and threat to self-esteem. However, the emphasis as of such, will by no means take into account the environmental surfaces, as represented by trait-ful understandings. By which the environment comes into congruence with these feelings, and the depressive's vague, yet, generalized feeling that there is something wrong with him. As his search for this among his minor defects, imperfections, and personal attributions, that may arise from a depressive core to his personality, but at the same time, the confusing response from the environment serves to validate these feelings. Likewise, conflicts about the reception of support and approval from others may be deeply rooted in the depressive's intrapersonal style, but these conflictual situations can only be aggravated by the mixed messages of approval and of rejection for being received from significant others, and by their withdrawal from him, despite reassurances to the contrary.

Also, it does not deny the importance of possible biochemical o r genetic factors in the etiology of depression. Price (1974) has argued that even in disorders in which the importance of such factors has been clearly established there may be a large number of links in the causal chain between specific etiological factors and symptoms displayed by an individual. Social and interpersonal variables may determine to a greater extent of whether a disorder occurs and the form its symptoms will take, that a person need only begin to display depressive behaviour.

Since Freud, real and imagined object losses have been given prominence in the explanation of depression, and depressive process has often been seen as miscarried restitutive work. While most earlier formulations focussed on intrapsychic phenomena, there were implications for interpersonal behaviour. As early as Abraham (1911, 1918), the over-demanding aspects of the depressive's orality were noted. Rado (1928) assigned major etiological importance to an accentuate need for dependency in the depressed person. Fenichel (1945) described the neurotically depressed person's interpersonal manoeuvres that others have brought about the misery, his accusations that others have brought about the misery, and even his blackmailing of others for attention—as desperate attempts to force others to restore damaged self-esteem. Yet, in seeking this gratification, he is at the same time satisfied and to receive it because of the revenge that he expects will accompany it. In the psychotically depressed person, the loss is more complete, the objects have fallen away, and the restitutive effort is aimed exclusively at the Superego.

Cohen (1954) described the depressed as seeing others as objects to be manipulated for the purpose of receiving sympathy and reassurance, bu t also as seeing them as critical, rejecting, and ungenuine in their support. Further, are the achievements o f reassurance, the depressed person finds. Concealed approval and rejection. According to the Cohens' formulation, what the depressed person seeks is a dependent relationship in which all his needs are satisfied, and in his failure to obtain this, he resorts to the depressive techniques of complaining and whinnying, if this too fails, he may loss hope, and enter into the psychotic state, where the pattern of emptiness and continues in the absence of specific objects.

Grinker (1964)interprets the factor patterns obtained in the earlier studies of depression (Grinker, 1961) as representing relatively constant patterns of communication. "What is requested or seemingly needed by the depressed patient expressed verbally, by gestures or in behaviour, varies and characterizes the pattern of the depressed syndrome."

Bonime (1960, 1966) described how the depressed person can dominate his environment with his demands for emotionally comforting responses from others. He considered depression to be a practice, an active way of relating to people in order to achieve pathological satisfactions, and he dismissed any suffering the depressed person may incur as secondary to the satisfaction of manipulative needs.

Aggression played a central role in early psychoanalytic formulations of depression (Abraham, 1911; Freud, 1917), but later writers have increasingly disputed its role. Bibring (1953) went so far as to declare that depression was an ego phenomenon, "essentially independent of the vicissitudes of aggression as well as oral drives."

Fromm-Reichmann (1959) argued that aggression had been considerably over stressed as a dynamic fact or in depression, and that if hostile feelings were found in the depressed person, they were the result of the frustration of his manipulative and exploitative needs. Cohen (1954) attributed the hostility of the depressed person to his "annoying impact on others, rather than to a primary motivation to do injury to them," however, Bonime found the hurting or defying of others to be essential to depressed behaviour.

Renewed interest in the relationship between hostility and depression—particularly in the psychoanalytic view that depressed persons turn hostility that had originally been directed at others (hostility-out-ward), against themselves (hostility-inward)—has generated a number of empirical studies. Weissman (1960) suggested that relatively normal persons became hostile outward when depressed, whereas persons to become severely depressed were more likely to internalize or suppress this hostility. The data of Zuckerman (1967) supported this view, indicating that only in the relatively normal was hostility correlated with depression on mood questionaries or as rated by interviewers. Friedman (1964) found depressives to have more "readily expressed resentment" as shown by their endorsement of adjectives such as "bitter," "frustrated," and "sulky," yet found no greater overt hostility in a later study, Friedman (1970) showed that the feelings of depression and worthlessness were consonant with hostility, and resentful feelings, even though depressed persons were not more likely to directly express these feelings to persons in the environment. Schless (1974) found equal numbers of depressed patients turning hostility inward and outward, with both types of hostility increasing as depression became more severe. However, because these patients also saw other people's anger more readily expressed and more potent, they feared retaliation, and therefore expressed hostility in the form of resentment. In summary, recent studies have been interpreted so as to call into question classical psychoanalytic formulations of the relationship of depression, hostility may serve a defensive function against depression, this has been supported. That depression is preceded by increased hostility that is directed out but cannot be expressed directly to appropriate objects in the environment, as taken for a failing of this defensive function (Freidman, 1970; McCranie, 1971; Schless, 1974).

Most writers who comment on the complaint s and self-accusations of the depressed person have rejected the idea that they should be taken literally. Lichtenberg (1957) found that attempts to answer them directly with assurances, granting dependency, and even punishment all increased depression and feelings of personal defects. Freud (1917) suggested that the self-accusations are actually aimed at someone else, a lot love object and further notes, " . . . It must strike us that after all, the melancholic does not behave in quite the same way as a person who is crushed by remorse and self-reproach in a normal fashion. Feelings of shame in front of other people, which would more than anything characterizes this latter condition. One might emphasize the presence in him of an almost opposite trait of insistent communicativeness which finds, s in fact his self-exposure."

In an attempt to modify depressive behaviour is a family differentiation (Liberman and Raskin, 1971), the baseline data indicated that other family members rejected opportunities to interact with the depressed person, and that all initiations of interaction between him and his family in the baseline period were undertaken by him.

Paykel and Weissman (1973) reported extensive social dysfunctions in women during depressive episodes. Interpersonal friction, inhibits communication, and submissive dependency occurred in both the initial episodes and in subsequent relapses. An onset of social difficulties was related to symptoms, but these difficulties continued months after the symptom's remitted. A fact that Paykel and Weissman argued must have been symptoms remitted in any treatment plan.

The provocation and often annoying behaviour of the depressive has distracted investigators from considerations of both the role the response of others and the given exception Jacobson (1954) noted that "however exaggerated the patient's hurt, disappointment, and hostile derogation of their partners may be, their complaints are usually more justified than may appear on the surface." According to her, the depressed person often makes his whole environment feel guilty and depressed, and this provokes defensive aggression and even cruelty precisely when he is, more vulnerable. Depressives also have a tendency to develop an "oral interplay" with those around him, so that mutual demand and expectations are built up to inevitable disappointment and depression for everyone concerned.

Cohen (1954) found therapists generally uncomfortable working with depressed patients. They identified a tendency of therapists to react to depressed manipulations with unrealistic reassurance and "seductive promises too great to be fulfilled," followed by hostility and rejection.

Lewinsohn and his associate' (Lewinsohn and Shaw, 1969; Lewinsohn, 1969; Lewinsohn, 1970; Libet and Lewinsohn, 1973) have undergone an ambitious clinical research program focussing on a social interaction of the depressed person from a behavioural point of view. In attempting to develop the hypotheses about the reinforcement contingencies as made available to the depressed person, they gainfully attempted a precise specification of the social behaviour of the depressed person. Libet and Lewinsohn found depressed persons in group therapy to be lower than controls on a number of measures of social skill, activity level interpersonal range, rate of positive reactions emitted and action latency. Their data are subject to alternative interpretations, however, particularly since they also found that rate of positive reactions emitted was highly correlated rates of positive reactions elicited. While depressed persons may well be deficient in social skills, some of the observed differences in group interaction situations may be due to the fact that fewer people are willing to interact with depressed persons as (which results in a narrower interpersonal range and less opportunity for activity), and in this interaction emitted fewer positive responses (thereby, reducing the positive responses while elicited from the depressed). The most useful behavioural conceptualization of social interaction involving depressed persons would specify the lack of social skills of all participants, as evidenced by their inability to alter the contingencies offered or received. Behavioural intervention in th depressed people's marital and family relationships would therefore involve training all participants in these social skills, and go beyond simply altering the contingencies available to the depressed persons. Behavioural observations and self-reports of a couple in the Lewinsohn study (Lewinsohn and Shaw, 1969) seem to support such a view.

Studies of suicide attempts and their effects on interpersonal relationships also provide data relevant to this discussion. While suicide attempts do not have an invariable relationship to depression, there is a definite association. McPartland and Hornstra (1964) examined the effects of suicide attempts on subsequent levels of depression. They conceptualized depressive symptomatology as "a set of messages demanding action by others to alter or restore the social space," and examined the relationships between suicide attempts and the ambiguity of the depressive message and the diffuseness of its intended audience. They were able to reliably place depressed patients at definite points along a dimension of interactive stalemate on the basis of the range of intended audience and the stridency of a message in depressive communications. Patients who were farthest along this vector continuum, whose communication was most diffuse, nonspecific, strident, and unanswerable, were most likely to have long hospital stays and diagnoses of the psychosis. Suicide attempts tended to reduce the level of depression, apparently by shifting the interactive burden onto others. Other studies (Rubenstein, 1958; Moss and Hamilton, 1956; Kubler and Stotland, 1964) have indicated that suicide patients who improve following their attempts on their lives fail to improve generally, and have affected changes in their social fields and those who fail to improve generally have failed to change their situation fundamentally.

Depression, as a response to the spatial disruption in which the person obtains support and validation for his experientially viewing of depressive symptomatology, that in terms of message values and intended audience, in similarity to that of McPartland and Hornstra (1964), but the present analysis will take place on the contributions of the social environment of the depressive drift. It is to be assumed that the course of a specific depressive episode will be highly dependent on the structure of the person's social spatiality, such that an understanding of the social context is vital to an understanding of depression, although traditionally, it has been largely ignored.

Nevertheless, it seems, more than enough that vocal and linguistic patterns and body movements are ambiguous and subject to alternative interpretation, however, a further problem for the depressed person is that the "context," the nature of the relationship between the depressed person and the person communicating to him. It may require time and further messages to be clearly defined.

The depressed person's problem is to decide whether others are assuring him that he is worthy and acceptable because they do in fact maintain this attitude toward him, or rather only because he has attempted to elicit such responses. Unwilling or unable to endure the time necessary to answer this question, the depressive uses his symptoms to seek repeated feedback in his testing of the nature of his acceptance and the security of his relationships.

While providing continual feedback, these efforts are at the same time profoundly and negatively affecting these relationships. The persistence and repetition of the symptoms are both incomprehensible and aversive to members of the social environment, however, the accompanying indication of distress and suffering is powerful in its ability to arouse guilt in others and to inhibit and direct expressions of annoyance and hostility from them, as observed in both the family difficulties of depressed persons (Jacobson. 1954), and the problems the therapists report in their efforts to relate to depressed patients (Cohen, 1954).

Irritating, yet inhibited and increasingly guilt-ridden, members of the social environment continue to give verbal assurance of support and acceptance. However, a growing discrepancy between the verbal content and the affective quality of these responses provides validation for the depressive's suspicions that he is not really being accepted and that further interaction cannot be assured. To maintain his increasingly uncertain security, the depressive displays more symptoms.

At this point the first of a number of interactive stalemates may be reached. Members of the depressed person's environment, who can find a suitable rationalization for their behaviour may leave the field or at least, reduce their interactions with him. Considerable effort may be involved in efforts to indicate that this is not in fact rejection, but given the context, these efforts do little more than reduce credibility and increases the depressive's insecurity. With those members of the social environment who remain, a self-maintaining pattern of mutual manipulation is established. Persons in the environment find that they can reduce the aversive behaviour of the depressed person and alleviate the guilt that this depressed behaviour has an uncanny ability to elicit, if they manipulate him with assurance, support, and denial of the process that is taking place. The depressed person, finds that by displaying symptoms he can manipulate his environment, so that it will provide sympathy and reassurance, but he is aware by now that this response from others is not genuine and that they become critical and rejecting. While this situation, is slightly attractive for neither the depressed person nor the members of his social environment, it provides a stabilization of what has been a deteriorating state of affairs.

One alternative facing the depressed person is for him to accept the precipitating disruption of his social space and the resulting loss of support and validation. However, now that he has begun showing symptoms, he has invested portions of his remaining relationship in his recovery effort. That is, he has tested the relationships, made demands, and has been frustrated in ways that seriously call into question his conceptually ascertainment for which are his relationships. If he abandons these efforts he may have to relinquish support and validation derived from these relationships, while accepting the precipitating loss. At this point he may be too descendable on the remaining relationships to give them up. Furthermore, he now has an increasingly confused and deteriorated self-concept, which must be clarified. With new desperation more symptoms may be displayed.

Various possible efforts by the depressed person to discover what is wrong with him (i.e., why he is being rejected and manipulated) and to reestablish a more normal interactive pattern is in his context indistinguishable from the manipulations he has used to control the responses of others. Therefore, they are met with the usual counter-manipulations. Requesting information as to how people really view him is indistinguishable from symptomatic efforts. If the depressed person attempts to discuss the interpersonal process that is taking place, he touches on a sensitive issue, and is likely only to elicit denial by the others or an angry defensive response. Nonetheless, efforts by others to assure the depressed person that he is really accepted and that they are not rejecting him are in this context, also indistinguishable from previous manipulations that they have employed, and, therefore, serve to strengthen the developing system. Thus, interpersonal manoeuvres directed at changing the emerging pattern become system-maintaining, and any genuine feedback to the depressed person is also indistinguishable from manipulations. Persons leaving the social field increase both, depressed person's feelings of rejection and his impetus to continue his behaviour pattern. Persons just entering the social field can be quickly recruited into the existing roles, since their efforts to deal with the depressed person—even if genuine—are likely to be quite similar to those now being employed manipulatively. They therefore, become subject to the compelling counter-manipulations of the depressed person, and come to respond manipulatively themselves, and are inducted into the system.

Descriptions of the depressed person at this point in his career focus on the distortions and misperceptions that serve to maintain his depression. What is generally ignored is that these "distortions" and "misperceptions" are congruent with the social system which the depressed person now finds himself. The specific content of the depressive's complaints and accusations may not be accurate, but his comments are in recognition of the attenuated relationships, are the disrupted communication, and lack of genuineness that he faces. These conditions serve to prevent him from receiving the feedback necessary to correct any misperceptions or distortions. He has played a major role in the creation of this social system, but the emergence of the system has also required the cooperation of others, and once established, it tends to be largely beyond the control of its participants.

Depending on characteristics of both the depressed person and his environment, a number of punishing variations stress of such problematically environmental patterns that may develop. Members of the social environment who have been repeatedly provoked and made to feel guilty may retaliate by withholding their responses or which the depressed person depends on them. The depressed person may become aware of the inhibiting influence his symptoms have on the direct expression of negative feelings, and may use these symptoms aggressively, while limiting the forms that counter-aggression can take. He may also discover and exploit the interdependence of others and the frustrations it entails, he may become aware of the extent to which others are dependent on him, in that their own maintenance of mood and their ability to engage in varieties of activities requiring in some was his cooperation. Because either of outright hostility, or as a self-defeating effort to convince others of their need to renegotiate their relationship with him, the depressed person becomes more symptomatic in his withholding of these minimal cooperative behaviours. While hostility may not necessarily be a major etiogical factor in depression, the frustrations, provocations, and manipulations occurring of the interactions between depressed person's and others would seem to encourage it.

As efforts to end the interactive stalemate fail, there may be a shift in the depressive's self-presentation to on e indicating great distress and implying that the enjoinment has more responsibility for bringing about the necessary changes. McPartland and Hornstra (1964) found that they could unambiguously differentiate themes of hopelessness and helplessness from more disturbed themes of low energy and physical allegement to communications of the depressed patients. The latter theme was associated with longer hospitalization when hospitalized, depressed patients were sampled, McPartlant and Hornstra give these examples of, "I can't sleep and I can't stand in any longer," "I am too tired to mov e," "My head and my stomach feel funny at the time." Unable to restore his life space, the depressive now implicitly demands "a suspension of the rules, a moratorium on the web of obligations under which the person live, such as admission to the sick role" (McPartland and Hornstra, 1964). With immediate relationships deteriorating, the depressive addresses his plea to a more general audience, but in more confusing and unanswerable terms. Literal responses to his communications may involve medical intervention for his specific complaints, but this generally fails to alleviate the problem. Any efforts to move the interaction them e back to the depressive's sense of hopelessness and helplessness threaten to reopen the earlier unfruitful and even punishing patterns of relations, and tend to be resisted, unable to answer or in many cases, even to comprehend the depressive' s pleas, members of the social environment may withdraw further from him, increasing his desperation, and quickening the depressive drift.

With a second interactive stalemate now reached, the depressive person may attempt to resolve it by increasing his level of symptomatology and shifting the theme of his self-presentation to one of the worthlessness and evil, "I am a failure; its all my fault, I am sinful and worthless." Unable either to restore his social space or to reduce his obligations sufficiently for him to continue to cope, the depressive now communicates his bafflement and resignation. The intended audience is now more diffuse, relationships are even more attenuated, and the new message is more obscure and perplexing. The social environment and the depressive soon arrive at another stalemate. Otherwise, helpless to alleviate the situations, remaining members of the environment may further withdraw or, alternatively, have the depressive withdraw through hospitalization. In the absence on any relatedness to others the depressive may drift into delusion and frankly psychotic behaviour.

Once an individual has suffered a disruption of an exiting sociobiological spareness, his abilities to avoid depressively drift, or to abort the process once it has begun, depends on the structure of his sociological space and on his temporal interpretations as regarding to his skills, in with regard to the latter, it is generally ignored that the person facing this situation is dealing with a changing environment, in that, the skills needed to deal with them are likely to be different from those required by a more stable, normative environment. Consequently, persons who previously have had adequate skills to deal with their life situation, but may lack the skills to cope with some disrupted sociological perturbation. With regard to the structure of the existing sociological spaces, resistance too depression seems as to depend on the availability of alternative sources of support and validation, particularly of the type that cannot be threatened by depressive symptomatology, (a) the availability of direct nonpunitive feedback should the person's behaviour become annoying or incompressible, and (b) the ability of sociologically intervening at some imperative to territorial spaces, generating a new source of support and meaning that is unambiguously independent in the presence or absence of symptomatology, earlier speculative writings (Abraham, 1911) and later behavioural studies (Lewinsohn, 1969) in their ranging o f interaction and that this may be a major source of their vulnerability.

Depression has been conceptualized for being a self-perpetuating interpersonal system. Depressive symptomatology is congruent with the developing interpersonal situation of the depressed person, and the symptoms have a mutually maintaining relationship with the response of the social environment

Even so, we use the term 'depression' to refer to the syndrome of behaviours that have been identified in descriptive studies of depressed individuals (e.g., Grinker et al., 1961). It includes verbal statements of dysphoria, self-depreciation, guilt, material burden, social isolation, somatic complaints, and a reduced rate of many behaviours. Is that, we assume depression to be a continuous variable which can be conceptualized as a 'state' which fluctuates over time as well as a 'trait'—(some people are more prone to becoming depressed than others?). Being depressed does not exclude other psychopathological conditions such as schizophrenia, psychosis, sexual deviation, or alcoholism. For purposive reasons, it would seem important that any study relying on differences between depressed and nondepressed groups for its conclusions have a normal control as well as a 'psychiatric control' group (i.e., patients for whom anxiety or other neurotic symptoms but not depression constitute the major psycho pathology) if any observed group differences are to be attributed to depression (depression—psychiatric control, normal) and not to the deviation hypothesis (depression, psychiatric control, normal control).

The major assumptions of the behavioural theory of depression follow three laying premises that postulate (1) A low rate of response-contingent positive reenforcement (response) acts as an eliciting (unconditioned) stimulus for some depressive behaviour, such as feeling of dysphoria, fatigue, and other somatic symptoms. (2) A low rate of response constitutes a sufficient explanation for other parts of the depressive syndrome such as the low rate of behaviour. For the latter the depressed person is considered to be on a prolonged extinction schedule. (3) The total amount of response received by an individual is presumed to be a function of three sets of variables: (I) The number of events (including activities) that are potentially reinforces for the individual, influenced by biological (e.g., sex and age) and experiential variables. (ii) The number of potentially reinforcing events that can be provided by the environment, i.e., the availability of reenforcement in the environment. (iii) The instrumental behaviour of the individual, i.e., the extent to which he possesses the skills and emits those behaviours that will elicit reinforcement for him from his environment.

503

The behaviour theory requires that (1) the total amount of response received by depressed persons be less than that received by nondepressed persons, and similarly, it will be less when the individual is depressed than when he is not depressed; (2) the onset of depression is accompanied by a reduction in response; (3) intensity of depression convary with rate of response, and (4) improvement is accompanied by an increase in response. Before proceeding to an examination of relevant empirical studies several additional clarification and hypotheses are offered.

In terms of system theory (von Bertalanffy, 1950; Allport, 1960; Miller, 1971), the usual conceptualization of the depressed person is one of a relatively closed system. Grinker (1964) was explicitly instating that the depressed person repeats his message and behaviour without reception or acceptance of resulting feedback. Beck (1964, 1967) described the cognitive distortion that dominates the information processing of the depressed person so that experiences are rigidly interpreted to maintain existing schema of personal deficiency, self-blame, and negative expectations.

The implicit assumption of these has been that the support and information available to the depressed person are incongruent with his depression, and the persistence of his symptomatology is evidence of a failure to receive or accept this information. Withdrawal, isolated intrapsychic persecution or as Beck describes (1967), interaction of depressive schema and affective structure, produce a downward depressive spiral. Presently, that is to say, that of enabling to engage others in his environment in such a way that support is lost and depressive information elicited. This in turn increases the level of depression and strengthens the pathogenetic pattern of depressed behaviour rather response of other if a depressive spiral develops, It is mutually causative, deviation-amplifying process (Maruyama, 1963) in the interaction of the depressed person with his environment. Thus, what is customarily viewed as some internal process is, I believe, that, at least in part, a characteristic of interaction with the environment, and much of what is customarily view as cognitive distortions or misperception is characteristic of information flow from the environed, it should be noted that while the depressed person's different interprets his predicament is traditionally attributes to his distortion or misperception, general disorders of thought and perception are nether defining criteria more common among depressed patients (McPartland and Hornstra, 1964). An observer who talks into account the intricacies of someone's relationship to his environment,. Frequently attributes to hin characteristics that he does not possess, or leaves significant aspects of his unexplained experience (Watzlawick, 1967). Feedback introduces phenomena that cannot be adequately explained by reference to the isolated individual alone (Ashby, 1960, 1962), for the stud y of depression, identification of a pattern of depressive feedback from the environment demands a more complex conceptualization of the disorder that one explaining its phenomena with reference to the isolated depressed person.

Of all the distinctions that have been proposed, the most widely accepted and least controversial is that between unipolar and bipolar disorder. In its simplest form—and as it has been recognized in the DSM-III—the differential diagnosis is based on whether the patient has a personal history of mania. However, recent genetic studies have led to a familial definition of the distinction: Depressed patients who do not have a personal history of mania may still be diagnosed for being bipolar if there has been mania among first-degree relatives.

Valid though the distinction appears to be, it has some important limitations. As yet, no consistent differences in the symptomatology of bipolar and unipolar depression have been identified. Although a bipolar diagnosis predicts a greater likelihood of response to lithium, as many as 40 percent of unipolar patients, nonetheless, respond positively (Depue and Monroe, 1978). By itself, the distinction does not do justice to the heterogeneity among either bipolar or unipolar patients. Currently, persons with bipolar disorder are often subclassified as to whether either manic or depressive symptoms or both have been severe to require hospitalization. Unipolar depressed persons stay on a large and tremendously heterogeneous group. Nonetheless, in the continuing controversies as how best to distinguish among depressed persons, the unipolar-bipolar distinctions stand out in its usefulness for both clinical and research purposes.

Although little, has been written in the literature of psychoanalysis concerning the psychology of neurotic depression. But the affect of depression in the sphere of the psychosis awaits more precise investigation. This task is complicated by the fact that a good part of the diseases in question runs a ;cyclical' course in which there is an alternation between melancholic and manic states. The few preliminary studies which have hitherto been published have only dealt with one of these two phases at the same time.

The study of the genetics of depression remains in its infancy. Further advances are going to require better ways of subtyping affective disorders and the discovery of biological markers that are not state dependent, that is, tied to whether someone is currently disturbed. Dunner describes some of the distinctions that he and his colleagues have drawn for bipolar disorder, in terms of the severity of manic and depressive phases (e.g., whether one or both require hospitalization). It is probably true that bipolar disorder is more homogeneous and has a stronger genetic component than unipolar depression, and because of this, Dunner suggests that is more likely to yield advances in the near future. Some researchers are attempting to identify subtypes of unipolar depression that 'breeds true' such that the relatives of depressed persons who have a particular pattern of symptoms will themselves show this pattern if they become depressed. There have been some promising findings with concomitant appetite disturbance and excessive guilt (Leckman et al., 1984), but any substantial advances are going to depend ultimately upon the identification of genetic markers that have thus far proven elusive. Riedfer and Gershon (1978) have noted that such markers will need to be stable; heritable, and state independent; capable of differentiating persons with an affective disturbance from persons drawn from the general population, and among the relatives of depressed persons, capable of identifying those who develop affective disturbance from those who do not.

A major source of confusion is due to the fact that the term 'depression' variously refers to a mood state, a set of symptoms, and a clinical syndrome. As a reference to mood, depression identifies a universal human experience, adjectives from a standard measure of mood (The Multiple Affect Adjective Checklist: Zuckerman and Lubin, 1965) point to subjective feelings associated with a depressed mood; sad, unhappy, blue, low, discouraged, bored, hopeless, dejected, and lonely. Similarities between every day-depressed mood and the complaints of depressed patients have encouraged the view that clinical depression is simply an exaggeration of a normal depressed mood, however, patients sometimes indicate that their experience of depression is quite distinct from normal feelings of sadness, even in its extreme form.

Of recent views, that depression is to emphasize that it is primarily a biological disturbance, an illness, the predisposition to which lies in genes and biochemistry, while people may react to their circumstances with happiness and unhappiness, this is of questionable relevance to the clinical phenomena of depression. However, as these definitional problems continue to plague the study of depression, and they are not going to be readily resolved. There remains considerable disagreement as to what extent and for what purpose a depressed mood in relatively normal persons can be seen as one end of a dimensional continuum of mood as taken upon those disturbances as seen of a psychiatric hospital patients, and to what extent the clinical phenomenon is distinct and discontinuous with normal sadness and unhappiness.

One observer may be struck with the frequent complaints about appetite and sleep disturbance by depressed persons and infer that some sort of biological disturbance must be the key to understanding depression. Another might find their self-derogation and pessimism irrational in a way that suggests that these must be some kind of fundamental deficit in self-esteem or cognitive distortion occurring. Still another may listen to the incessant complaining of a depressed person, get annoyed and frustrated, and yet feel guilty in the way that makes it easier to encourage the depressed person to continue to talk in this way than to verbalize these negative feelings. Cognizant of this, the observer might conclude that there is some sort of interpersonal process going on that is critical to any understanding of depression.

Nonetheless, studies have compared the subjective mood of persons who are distressed but seeking help to those who are seeking treatment for depression (Depue and Monroe, 1978). The two groups may be similar in subjective mood, but they differ in other ways. Those persons who are not seeking treatment for depression tend to lack the anxiety and the physical complaints, including loss of appetite, sleep disturbances, and fatigue shown by the group seeking treatment. Still, it could be argued that there is a continuum of dimensional provision, as to the differences between the two groups, with these additional features arising, when a normal depressed mood becomes more prolonged or intensified. The controversy is likely to continue until either questions about the etiology of depression are resolved or unambiguous markers for depression are identified.

Advocates of psychoanalytic, cognitive and behavioural, and interpersonal and social perspective on depression have generally assumed a dimensional quantification between a normal depressed mood and clinical depression. They tend to exclude psychotic and bipolar depressed persons from treatment, but, beyond that, they have tended to disregard classification issues (Gilbert,. 1984) for unipolar depression, at least, they have assumed that whatever discontinuities in the biology of mild and severe moods there might be that are, yet as not excessively necessarily relevant to the psychological and asocial processes, which they are most interested.

Writers since antiquity have noted the core symptoms of depression: Besides a sad or low mood, reduced ability to expression pleasure, pessimism, inhibition and retardation of action, and a variety of physical complaints. As such, that we can distinguish among the emotional, cognitive, motivational, and vegetative symptoms of depression, although these feature s are not alway so neatly divisible. Beyond these symptoms, there are some characteristic interpersonal aspects of depression that are not usually considered as formal symptoms. But they are frequent, distinctive, and troublesome enough tp warrant attention.

Sadness and dejection are not the only emotional manifestations of depression, although about half of all depressed patient report these feelings as their principal complaint. Most depressed persons are also anxious and irritable. Classical descriptions of depression tend to emphasize that depressed persons' feelings of distress, disappointment, and frustration are focussed primarily on themselves, yet a number of studies suggest that their negative feelings, including overt hostility, are also directed at the people around them. Depressed persons are often intensely angry persons (Kahn, Coyne, and Margolin, Weissman, Klerman and Paykel, 1971).

Perhaps, 10 or 15 percent of severely depressed patients denial in the feelings of sadness, reporting instead that all emotional experience, including sadness, has been blunted or inhibited (Whybrow, Akiskal and McKinney, 1984). The identification of these persons as depressed depends upon the presence of other symptoms. The inhibition of emotional expression in severely depressed persons may extend to crying. Whereas, mild and moderately depressed persons may readily and frequently cry, as they become more depressed, as they may continually be in lack of emotionally expressive inhibitions.

Mildly and moderately depressed persons may feel that every activity is a burden, yet they still derive some satisfaction from their accomplishment. Despite their low mood, they may still crack a smile at a joke yet, as depression intensifies, a person may report both a loss of any ability to get gratification from activities that had previously been satisfying—family, work, and social life—and a loss of any sense of humour. Life becomes stale, flat, and not at all amusing. The loss of gratification may extend to the depressed persons' involvement in close relationships. Often, a loss of affection for the spouse and children, a feeling of not being able to care anymore, a sense of a wall being erected between the depressed person and others are the major reasons for seeking treatment.

Perhaps one of the most frustrating aspects of depressed persons for those around them is their difficulty in mobilizing themselves to perform even the most simple tasks. Encouragements, expressions of support even threats and coercion seems only to increase their inertia, leading others to make attributions of laziness, stubbornness, and malingering. Despite their obvious distress and discomfort, depressed persons frequently fail to take a minimal initiative to remedy their situations or do so only halfheartedly. To observers, depressed persons may seem to have a callous indifference to what happens to them.

Depressed persons often procrastinate. They are avoidant and escapist in their longing for a solacing refuge from demands and responsibilities. In severe depression, the person may experience an abulia or paralysis of will, extending even to getting out of bed, washing, and dressing.

In more severe depressions, there may be psychomotor retardation, expressed in slowed body movements, slowed and monotonous speech, or even muteness. Alternatively, psychomotor agitation may be seen in an inability to be still, pacing, and outbursts of shouting.

The presence of physical or vegetative symptoms is sometimes taken as the dividing line between normal sadness and clinical depression. One of the most common and prominent of vegetative symptoms is fatigue that someone is depressed may be first recognized by the family physician who cannot readily trace the person's complaints of tiredness to other causes.

Depressed persons also often suffer sleep disturbance, and it is tempting to link their tiredness to this, but in a sample of depressed patients, the two complaints are only modestly correlated (Beck, 1967). Depressed persons generally have rouble falling asleep, they sleep restlessly, and awaken easily. Yet, some depressed persons actually sleep considerably more than usual, up to 12 hours a night.

When mildly or moderately depressed, some people eat compulsively and gain considerable weight, but depression is more characteristically associated with loss of appetite and a decrease in weight. For many depressed persons, a loss of appetite is the first sign of an incipient depression, and its return marks the beginning of recovery. Some depressed persons maintain their normal eating habits and weight, but complain that food is tasteless and eating an unsatisfying matter of habit. Besides a loss of appetite, depression is often associated with gastrointestinal disturbance, notably nausea and constipation. Mild depression heightens sexual interest in some people, but generally depression is associated with a loss of interest in sex. In severe depression, there may be an aversion to sex. Overall, though, women who are depressed do not have sex less frequently, but they initiate it, like and enjoy it less, and are less responsive (Weissman and Paykel, 1974).

Finally, depressed persons report diffuse aches and pains. They have frequent headache, and they are more sensitive to existing sources of pain, such as dental problems.

A brief interaction with a depressed person can have a narked impact on one's own mood. Uninformed stranger's may react to a conversation with a depressed person with depression, anxiety, hostility, and may be rejecting of further contact (Coyne, 1976). Jacobson (1968) has noted that depressed persons often unwittingly succeed in making everyone in their immediate environment feel guilty and responsible and that others react to the depressed person with hostility and even cruelty. Despite this visible impact of depression on others, there is a persistent tendency in the literature to ignore it and to concentrate instead on the symptoms and complaints of depressed persons out of their interpersonal context. Depressed persons can be difficult, but they may also be facing difficult interpersonal situations within which their distress and behaviour make more sense.

Depressed persons tend to withdraw from social activities, and their close relationships tend to be strained and conflictual. Depressed women have been more intensely studied than depressed men, in part, because women are approximately twice as likely to be depressed. Depressed women are dependent, acquiescent, and inhibited in their communication in close relationships, and prone to interpersonal tension, friction and open conflict (Weissman and Paykel, 1974). Interestingly, the interpersonal difficulties of depressed persons are less pronounced when they are interacting with strangers than with intimates (Hinchcliffe, Hooper and Roberts, 1975).

About half of all depressed persons report martial turmoil (Rousanville, Weissman, Prusoff and Heraey-Baron, 1979). There is considerable hostility between depressed persons and their spouses, but often there is more between depressed persons and their children. Being depressed makes it more difficult to be a warm, affectionate, consistent parent (McLean, 1976). The children of depressed parents are more likely to have a full range of psychological and social difficulties than the children of normal or even schizophrenic parents (Emery, Weintraub and Neale, 1982), yet one must be cautious in making causal inferences. There is evidence that the child's problems are more related to a conflictual marital relationship and a stressful home-life than depression of the parent (Sameroff, Barocas and Siefer).

Depression thus tends to be indicative of an interpersonal situation fraught with difficulties, and this needs to be given more attention in both theorizing and planning treatment. Although depression is associated with interpersonal problems, within a sample of depressed persons the correlation between severity of depression and the extent of interpersonal problems tends to be modest. This may suggest that these problems are a matter not only of how depressed persons are functioning, but of the response of key people around them as well (Coyne, Kahn, and Gotlib, 1985).

In that the diagnosis of depression, one can make a list of the symptoms of depression, and assign any person a depression score on the basis of the number of symptoms present. A number of standard self-report inventories such as the Beck Depression Inventory (Beck, et al., 1961), the Centre for Epistemological Studies Depression Scale (Radloff, 1977) and the Self-Rating Depression Scales (Zung, 1965) have been validated and are widely used as research tools, screening devices, and measures of the change associated with treatment.

Even if one is to assume a continuity between normal depressed mood and clinical depression, it may still prove useful to make a distinction between the presence and absence of significant depression. One may wish to insure that a research study does not include a preponderance of persons whose depression is only mild or transient. Virtually no signs or symptoms are specific to depression, and yet, in many contexts, one may need to distinguish depression from other descriptors or explanations for a person's distress and behaviour in working with elderly, for instance, it is important to distinguish between depression and dementia. In medical patients in general, there is a high prevalence of symptoms associated with depression, both because of physical illness and the stress of hospitalization (Cavanaugh, 1984), and, whether for research pr practical purposes, one may wish to establish criteria for who is to be considered depressed and who is not. Finally persons who are labelled schizophrenic or alcoholic may show considerable depression, but it would be undesirable for many purposes to lump them with those persons whose primary problem is depression. Thus, for purposes of communication, treatment and research, it may prove useful to have some means of specifying some boundary conditions for the term 'depression'. In terms of some minimal level of severity as well as some coherence and specificity to what is included in the concept—even if one rejects the notion that it is a discrete entity, discontinuous with normal mood.

The problem of diagnosis is most critical in biomedical approaches to depression. The assumption is generally made that depression is a matter of one or more disease entities with specific etiologies and treatments. The statement, 'Nosology precedes etiology' conveys the idea that the abilities of identify the causes of depression depend s upon the existence of an adequate diagnostic and classificatory system. For instance, to take a simplified hypothetical example, suppose that a particular biological abnormality occurs in 60 percent of all depressed persons and is specific to depression. Suppose also, with the accepted diagnosis criteria, only 60 percent of the persons identify as such are 'actually depressed'. If these conditions occurred, then research might indicate that only 36 percent of depressed persons' posses the abnormality.

An effective treatment for depression may also be misjudged or misapplied in the absence of an adequate diagnostic system. This was made apparent recently after a drug company had undertaken a large study to compare the effectiveness of a new frug to that of both an established drug treatment for depression and a placebo (Carroll, 1984). At five of the six research sites. The new drug proves to be no more effective than the placebo, but interpretation of this was limited by the additional finding that the established treatment proved no better. Patients identified as depressed by current criteria did not respond to drug treatment that had proven efficacious in a large body of past research. Either the past research was misleading, the current diagnostic criteria are invalid, or most likely, they were misapplied by reputable investigators.

Contemporary diagnostic systems owe much to the work of Kraepelin at the turn of the century. He divided major psycho pathology into two broad syndromes: Dementia praecox (schizophrenia) and manic-depressive illness. The latter category included almost all serious mood disturbance, including depression in the absence of an episode of mania. As retained today, the term generally is a synonym for bipolar disorder. It is also still sometimes used as a genetic term for severe depression. Kraepelin considered manic-depressive illness a biological derangement. Although it might in some cases be precipitated by psychological factors, 'the real cause for the malady must be sought in permanent internal changes which are very often, and, perhaps always innate', (Kraepelin, 1921). Once started, the illness runs its course autonomously, independent of changes in the person's situation. Kraepelin also identified a group of psychogenic depression, which were depressive illness and reactive to change in these circumstances.

For more than 30 years, the dominant diagnostic system in the United States has been, the Diagnostic and Statistical Manual of Mental Disorders of the American Psychiatric Association, which is currently in its third edition (DSM-III). In its first edition it integrated the ideas of Kraepelin with those of Adolph Meyer and Sigmund Freud. While accepting Kraepelin's basic distinction between affective disturbance and schizophrenia, it also reflected Meyer's psychobiological view that mental disturbance represented not a simple disease entity, but the reaction of the personality to the matrix of psychological, social, and biological factors. By its second edition, the Meyerian term 'reaction' was no longer used throughout, but Meyer's influence remained. Freud 's ideas about the etiology of psycho pathology were built into the criteria for specific disorders. Thus, the defining characteristics of neuroses were anxiety, but for purposed of diagnostic decisions, it could be manifest and observable or inferred to be operating 'unconsciously and automatically' in someone who was not visibly anxious.

The author of DSM-III attempted to avoid past controversies and answer many of the criticisms of its two predecessors. A decision was made to define diagnostic categories as precisely as possible, using descriptive data, rather than inferences about etiology. From a biomedical perspective, the ideal diagnostic and classificatory system would integrate knowledge about etiology with overt symptomatology. However, it was concluded that the present understanding of the causes of most disorders is too limited for this purpose. Furthermore, the sense was that 'the inclusion of etiological theories would be an obstacle to use of the manual by clinicians and varying theoretical orientations, since it would not be possible to present all reasonable etiological theories for each disorder (American Psychiatric Association, 1980).

In considering depression, the author's of DSM-III attempted to sidestep a number of longstanding controversies, including that of whether there is a continuum or a discontinuity between normal mood and clinical depression, as well as that of the role of precipitating life circumstances in distinguishing among types of depression. Depressive neurosis disappeared, along with the other neuroses. Depression is now encompassed in two main categories. The first category, major affective disorder, involves the presence of a full affective syndrome, with the subcategories of bipolar and major depression distinguished by whether there has ever been a manic episode. The second category, other specific affective disorders, includes conditions in which the depression is not severe enough to warrant a diagnosis of major affective disorder, but severe enough to warrant a diagnosis of major affective disorder, but the mood disturbance has been intermittent or chronic for at least two years.

The criteria for major depression are subclassified as to whether it is a single episode or recurrent and also as to whether melancholia is present. Melancholia involves a complaint of a loss of pleasure in all or almost all activities, a lack of reactivity to pleasant events: A quality of depressed mood, that is distinct from grief or sadness; depression worse in the morning; early morning wakening; marked psychomotor agitation or retardation; significant weight loss; and excessive quilt. The designation was intended as an acknowledgement that some more symptoms and might be more responsive to treatment with drugs or electroshock. However, it should be noted that there is considerable consensus that such a distinction should be made, but the exact nature of it remains controversial. There are exclusions.

Criteria, including schizophrenia and what is judged to be normal or uncomplicated grief.

In general, these diagnostic systems are viewed as significant improvements over past effort s, but there is widespread dissatisfaction with them, as a prominent biologically oriented researcher has lamented:

> Anastuteobserverwillfindlittlethatisintellectually satisfying about the DSM-III diagnostic criteria for major depressive disorder. These criteria amount to catalogue of symptoms, and they are in no way linked by coherent underlying constructs. They also suffer from the problem of being cast as disjunctive criteria. This means that, for example, patients need to satisfy only of the possible symptomatological evaluations or appraising analysis. Therefore (and this occurs in practice), several patients may be assigned the same categorical diagnosis without having any symptoms in common (Carroll, 1984).

Carroll goes on to note that as the result of an inadequate diagnostic system, research studies are limited by the flaws in the diagnosis used as independent variables, and drug treatment of an individual patient tends to remain a matter of trial and error.

We are far from an adequate diagnostic system for depression. If one is to be achieved, it will have to come to terms with the enormous heterogeneity in the signs and symptoms; level of severity, causal factors to this heterogeneity with a variety of classificatory systems. Kendall (1976) has suggested that almost every classificatory system that is logically possible has been proposed at some point in this period, but he notes that little consensus has been achieved. Winokur reviews some of the current controversies, but it would be useful to identify a few of the distinctions that have been made before we turn to the major theoretical perspectives on the disorder.

Of all the distinctions that have been proposed, the most widely accepted and least controversial is that between unipolar and bipolar disorder. In its simplest form—and as it has been recognized in the

DSM-III—the differential diagnosis is based on whether the patient has a personal history of mania. However, recent genetic studies have led to a familial definition of the distinction: Depressed patients who do not have a personal history of mania may still be diagnosed as bipolar if there has been mania among first-degree relatives.

Work by Perris (1966) first established that bipolar disorder starts on the average of 15 years earlier than unipolar depression and recurs more frequently. Individual episodes are shorter, and there is a greater risk of disorder among the first-degree relatives of bipolar patients. Furthermore, there as a tendency for unipolar and bipolar disorders to breed true, with first-degree relatives of bipolar patients tending toward bipolar disorder, and first-degree relatives of unipolar patients tending to have little more risk of mania than the general population. The unipolar-bipolar distinction has proven to be clinically useful; depressed bipolar patients respond significantly better to lithium than unipolar depressed patients.

Valid though the distinction appears to be, it has some important limitations. As yet, no consistent differences in the symptomatololgy of bipolar and unipolar depression have been identified. Though a bipolar diagnosis predicts the greater likelihood of response to lithium, as many as 40 percent of unipolar patients, nonetheless, respond positively (Depue and Monroe, 1978). By itself, the distinction does not do justice to the heterogeneity among either bipolar or unipolar patients. Currently, persons with bipolar disorder often subclassified as to whether either manic or depressive symptoms or both have been severe to require hospitalization. Unipolar depressed persons, although remaining to a large heterogeneous group. As the continuing controversies as how best to distinguish among depressed persons, the unipolar-bipolar distinction stands out in its usefulness for both clinical and research purposes.

Many issues in the study of unipolar depression have coalesced in the concept of endogenous versus nonendogenous depression. The differentiation is most often identified for being between endogenous and reactive depression, although this has been used interchangeably with the endogenous-neurotic and psychotic-neurotic distinction. The hope for the distinction has often been that it would prove to be the boundary between biological versus psychological and social concerns. Traditionally, the term 'endogenous' has been invoked to differentiate depressions that are purportedly biological in etiology, without environmental precipitants, and that is less amenable to psychotherapy. Also, endogenous depressions are expected to be more responsive to somatically oriented interventions, notably electroconvulsive shock therapy and antidepressant medication. 'Reactive' has inferred to depressions that are viewed as understandable reaction to some precipitating stress and that is more suitable for psychotherapy and less responsive to somatic therapies. The distinction was originally based on the supposition that some depressions are related to precipitating events and others seem to appear without them and that would predict response to treatment and clinical course.

People, encompassed within the depressive point of bipolar disorder, experience the intensely sad or profoundly transferring formation showing the indifference to work, activities, and people that once brought them pleasure. They think slowly, concentrate poorly, feel tired, and experience changes—usually an increase—in their appetite and sleep. They often feel a sense of worthlessness or helplessness. In addition, they may feel pessimistic or hopeless about the future and may think about or attempt suicide. In some cases of severe depression, people may experience psychotic symptoms, such as delusions (false beliefs) or hallucinations (false sensory perceptions).

In the manic phase of bipolar disorder, people feel intensely and inappropriately happy, self-important, and irritable. In this highly energized state they sleep less, have racing thoughts, and talk in rapid-fire speech that goes off in many directions. They have inflated self-esteem and confidence and may even have delusions of grandeur. Mania may make people impatient and abrasive, and when frustrated, physically abusive. They often behave in socially inappropriate ways, think irrationally, and show impaired judgment. For example, they may take aeroplane trips all over the country, make indecent sexual advances, and formulate grandiose plans involving indiscriminate investments of money. The self-destructive behaviour of mania includes excessive gambling, buying outrageously expensive gifts, abusing alcohol or other drugs, and provoking confrontations with obnoxious or combative behaviour.

Clinical depression is one of the most common forms of mental illness. Although depression can be treated with psychotherapy, many scientists believe there are biological causes for the disease. The June 1998 publication, of the Scientific America, in the article that Neurobiologist Charles B. Nemeroff exchanges views about something in order to arrive at the truth or to convince others that the connection concerning their proper considerations that are differentiated between biochemical changes in the brain and the finding of depression.

The genes that a person inherits seem to have a strong influence on whether the person will develop bipolar disorder. Studies of twins provide evidence for this genetic influence. Among genetically identical twins where one twin has bipolar disorder, the other twin has the disorder in more than 70 percent of cases. But among pairs of fraternal twins, who have about half their genes in common, both twins have bipolar disorder in less than 15 percent of cases in which one twin has the disorder. The degree of genetic similarity seems to account for the difference between identical and fraternal twins. Further evidence for a genetic influence comes from studies of adopted children with bipolar disorder. These studies show that biological relatives of the children have a higher incidence of bipolar disorder than do people in the general population. Thus, bipolar disorder seems to run in families for genetic reasons.

Owing or relating to, or affecting a particular person, over which a personal allegiance about the concerns and considerations or work-related stress can trigger a manic episode, but this usually occurs in people with genetic vulnerabilities, other factors—such as prenatal development, childhood experiences, and social conditions—seem to have relatively little influence in causing bipolar disorder. One study examined the children of identical twins in which only one member of each pair of twins had bipolar disorder. The study found that regardless of whether the parent had bipolar disorder or not, all of the children had the same high 10-percent rate of bipolar disorder. This observation clearly suggests that risk for bipolar illness comes from genetic influence, not from exposure to a parent's bipolar illness or from family problems caused by that illness.

Different therapies may shorten, delay, or even prevent the extreme moods caused by bipolar disorder. Lithium carbonates, a natural mineral salt, can help control both mania and depression in bipolar disorder. The drug generally takes two to three weeks to become effective. People with bipolar disorder may take lithium during periods of relatively normal moods to delay or prevent subsequent episodes of mania or depression. Common side effects of lithium include nausea, increased thirst and urination, vertigo, loss of appetite, and muscle weakness. In addition, long-term use can impair functioning of the kidneys. For this reason, doctors do not prescribe lithium to bipolar patients with kidney disease. Many people find the side effects so unpleasant that they stop taking the medication, which often results in a relapse.

From 20 to 40 percent of people do not respond to lithium therapy. For these people, two anticonvulsant drugs may help dampen severe manic episodes: carbamazepine (Tegretol) and valproate (Depakene). The use of traditional antidepressants to treat bipolar disorder carries risks of triggering a manic episode or a rapid-cycling pattern.

Controlled studies have not found that the endogenous-reactive distinction predicts response to psychotherapy (Blackburn, 1981; Kovacs, 1980; Rush, 1984), the presence or absence of precipitating stress has not proved to be a good predictor of response to treatment (Leff, Roatch and Bunney, 1970) and the endogenous-reactive distinction has been found to be deficient in a number of ways. Yet, it remains considerably utility. Reactivity to changes in life circumstances during a depressive episode have been found to predict response to electroconvulsive shock and antidepressant medication (Fowles and Gerch, 1979). Other symptoms that have been associated with a positive response to somantic treatment include quality of a mood and whether there has been a los of the ability to experience pleasure; psychomotor retardation; feeling worse in the morning rather than the evening; and sleep and appetite become a strong irregularity. Such symptoms are now accepted as criteria for endogenous depression than is the absence of precipitating stress.

This consensus about the feature of endogenous depression still leaves questions about its polar opposite, reactive or neurotic depression. In clinical practice, it tends to be defined in terms of milder mood disturbances a preponderance of psychological rather than vegetative symptoms, and the presence of a precipitating stress, although there are particular doubts about the validity of this last feature. Akiskal (1978) found that reactive or neurotic depression was the single and most common of diagnoses in the inpatient and outpatient's settings, but they raised the issue of whether it was useful to consider it a unified entity or type. In about a quarter of all the cases of such depression studied, it appeared to be truly reactive, in the sense that it developed in the grips of an overwhelming stress, especially, in persons who had previously seemed reasonably well functioning. In another quarter of the cases, it seemed to reflect a greater or fewer of chronic tendencies to respond to normative stress with depressed moods and to experience social difficulties. Many of these patients were described as dependent, manipulative, hostile and unstable. Follow-up revealed overall that only 40 percent of the total sample was considered to have been suffering primarily from an affective disturbance in the absence of some of other condition. Some of the sub-sample, who had faced a clear precipitating stress developed endogenous features. In 10 percent of the sample, the depression seemed secondary to a medial-surgical illness. In 38 percent of the sample, the depression was secondary to some nonaffective disorder, ranging from an anxiety disorder to schizophrenia. In these patients with medical-surgical or nonaffective psychiatric conditions, intermittent depression seemed to follow the course of the other difficulties. A final 10 percent of the sample remained undiagnosed, but depression was considered the probable diagnosis. The work of Akiskal et al, (1978) is further evidence of the problems in attempting to draw any sharp distinctions in the classification and diagnosis of depression. Beyond this, it suggests both the utility and the difficulty of distinguishing between depression that is primary and that which is secondary to other conditions. Furthermore, the work suggests the usefulness of attempting to understand depression in terms of the presence or absence of characterological or lifestyle difficulties.

Thus, the endogenous pole of the endogenous-reactive distinction is more clearly defined than its counterpart. After a long history of debate and controversy, there is a growing consensus that the differentiation of endogenous and reactive depression is useful but that they represent points along a dimensional continuum, rather than two distinct forms of disorder, it is sometimes suggested that endogenous depressions are simply more severe, but this leave s unanswered questions about differences in etiology or the determinants of one depressive episode progressing to an endogenous course and another not. Biomedically oriented researcher looks to the identification of familial patterns of affective disturbance. The development of biological markers, and the refinement of diagnosis laboratory tests is the solution to the ambiguity and confusion. Baldessarini notes the promise of recent developments such as the dexamethasone suppression test, but he cautions that:

While there has been considerable progress toward a biological and clinically robust diagnosis scheme, and in understanding some characteristics that can help to guide treatment, search for primary causes have been unsuccessful so far. Even so, virtually all of the biological characteristics of severely depressed patients that have been identified are 'state-dependent' (this, they disappear with recovery) and are not stable biological traits or markers of a possible heritable defect.

Even so, and by now it should have become apparent that the phenomena of depression are vaguely delineated and poorly understood. Seligman and his colleagues have provided a fine example of a strategy for dealing with this problem . . . its construction of a laboratory model or analogue with which greater precision can be achieved.

Let us return once more to the relation between helplessness (involving loss of self-esteem) and the simultaneously maintained narcissistic aspirations, noting that their intra-ego conflict assumed by Bibring and Melancholia: such that Bibring's theory opens two new vistas. One leads us to consider self-esteem as a signal, that is, an ego function, rather than as an effectual relation between the ego and the Superego. The other suggests that we recognize the role of the ego, and particularly of its helplessness, in the origin and function of the instinctual vicissitude called turning round upon the subject.

Though it is clear that the phenomenon from which the economic explanation must start is the inhibition of the ego, the economics of depression is still not understood. Bibring quote Fenichel's formulation as to, . . . The greater percentage of the available mental energy is used up in unconscious conflicts, and, not enough is left to provide the normal enjoyment of life and vitality (Bibring, 1953). But he finds this statement insufficient to explain depressive inhibition, and proceeds to reconsider the nature of inhibition such that:

Freud (1926) defines inhibition as a 'restriction of functions of the ego, and mentions two major causes for such restrictions; Either having been imposed upon as the person or its measure of a precaution, i.e., to prevent the development of anxiety or the feelings of guilt, this having brought about as a result of exhaustion, as to infer upon the energy of the ego, of which it is engaged in some intense defensive activities. Bibring implies his own explanation in his comparison of depression to anxiety.

Anxiety as a reaction to external or internal danger indicates that the ego's desire to survive. The ego, challenged by the danger, mobilizes the signal of anxiety and prepares for fight or flight. In depression, the opposite takes place, the ego is paralysed because it finds itself incapable to meet the 'danger.' In certain instances, . . . depression may follow anxiety, then the mobilization of energy . . . is replaced by a decrease of self-reliance.

Thus Bibring's search for an economic explanation of depressive inhibition ends in the undefined term 'deceased of self-reliance,' which as it stands, is not an economic concept.

What does that mean, that 'The ego is paralysed because it finds itself incapable to meet the danger?' Clearly 'paralysed' refers to the state of helplessness, one of the corollaries of which is the 'loss of self-esteem.' The danger is the potential loss of the object; The traumatic situation is that of the loss of an object—'helplessness' as Bibring defines, it is the persisting state of loss of an object. The anxiety signal anticipates the loss in order to prevent the reactivation of the traumatic situation, that is, of panic-anxiety. Perturbing fluctuations of self-esteem anticipates the initiation of measures that are preventions, such, are the reactivations in the state of persisting of the loss of its object, from which the state of helplessness would only have to be of its involving in the loss of self-esteem, thus, the relations between perturbing fluctuations of self-esteem and 'helplessness,' which is accompanied by its loss of self-esteem, but maintaining the similarity between the relation of its own dose of anxiety and the signalling of the panic-anxiety. Fluctuations of self-esteem are then structurally tamed by forms of and signals to anticipate as to preclude reactivation of the state of helplessness. Yet, according to the accepted theory, fluctuations of self-esteem are the functions of the Superego's relation to the ego, just as anxiety was considered, prior to 1926, as a function of repression enforced by the Superego. In 1926, however, Superego anxiety was recognized as merely one kind of anxiety and the repression, hence anxiety relationship was reversed into anxiety signals and hence, repression. Bibring achieves an analogous observation that is the ego's awareness of its helplessness which in certain cased forces it to turn the aggression from the object against the self, thus aggravating and complicating the structure of depression. While in the accepted theory it is assumed that the aggression 'turned round upon the subject,' results in passivity and helplessness, in Bibring's conception it is the helplessness which is the cause of this 'turn round.'

Thus, Bibring's theory opens upon two new vistas. One leads us to consider self-esteem as a signal, that is, an ego function, rather from an open condition to the enclosing effect of an aggressive relation between the ego and the Superego. The other suggests that we reconsider the role of the ego, and particularly of its helplessness, in the origin and function of the instinctual vicissitude called turning round upon the subject.

The first of these, like Freud's structural theory of anxiety and Fenichel's of quilts (1945), leads to a broadening of our conception of the ego's apparatuses and functions. The second is even more far-reaching, it seems to go to the very core of the problem of aggression. We know that 'turning round upon the subject' was the basic mechanism for which Freud used before the 'death-instinct theory' to explain the major forms in which aggression manifests itself. It was in connection with this 'turning round upon the subject; Freud wrote:

> . . . sadism . . . seems to press toward a quite special aim—the infliction of pain, in addition t subjection and mastery of the object. Now a psychoanalysis would seem to show that infliction of pain plays no part in the original aims sought by sadism . . . the sadistic child takes no notice of whether or not it inflicts pain, nor of its purpose to do so. But when once the transformation into masochism has taken place, the experience of pain is ver y well adapted too severely as a passive masochistic aim . . . Where once the suffering of pain has been experienced as a masochistic aim, it

can be carried back into the sadistic situation and result in a sadistic aim of inflicting pain (1915).

Thus Bibring's view that 'turning round upon the subject' is brought about by helplessness calling attention to some of Freud's early formulations. And prompt us to re-evaluate our conception of aggression. As it may lead to a theory of aggression which is an alternative to those which have so far been proposed, namely Freud's death-instinct theory. Fenichel's frustration-aggression theory, and the Hartmann-Kris-Loewenstein theory of an independent aggressive instinctual drive.

Let us return once more to the relation between helplessness, which involves the loss of self-esteem, and the simultaneously maintained narcissistic aspirations, such that their intra-ego conflict assumed by Bibring may have been implied by Freud when he wrote in 'Mourning and Melancholia.' 'A good, capable, conscientious person, . . . is more likely to fall ill of this . . . disease than one . . . of whom we too should have nothing good to say' (1917).

Fenichel's summary of the accepted view of the fate of self-esteem in depression is:

. . . A greater or lesser loss of self-esteem is in the foreground. The subjective formula is-I has lost everything; now the world is empty, if the loss of self-esteem is mainly due to a loss of external supplies, or-I has lost everything because I do not deserve anything. If it is mainly due to a loss of internal supplies from the Superego (1945).

Fenichel's implied definition of supplies reads: 'The small child loses self-esteem when he loses love and attains it when he regains love . . . children . . . need . . . narcissistic supplies of affection . . . (1945)

Though the term 'supplies' have never been explicitly defined as a concept, it has become an apparently indispensable terminological acceptance in the psychoanalysis, and particularly in the theory of depression. In Bibring's theory, supplies are the goals of narcissistic aspirations. This gives them a central role in the theory, highlighting the urgent need to define them. Moreover, Bibring's comparison of depression and boredom hints at the direction in which such a definition might be sought by alerting us to the fact that there is a lack of supplies in boredom. Also, stimulus hunger is Fenichel's term for the immediate consequence of this lack? 'Boredom is characterized by the coexistence of a need for activity and activity-inhibition, as well as by stimulus-hunger and dissatisfaction with the available stimuli (1934). That an adequate stimulus is the lacking of supplies, which are available of either to be too, close to the object of the repressed instinctual drive or the resistance, the distant from it and thus of holding to no interests

Bibring's juxtaposition of depression and boredom suggests that narcissistic supplies may be a special kind of adequate stimuli and narcissistic agitations a special kind of stimulus hunger. The implications of this suggestion become clearer if we note that it is the lack of narcissistic supplies which are responsible for the structuralization of the primitive state of helplessness, the reactivation of which is, according to Bibring's theory, and the essencity of depression.

The conception which emerges if we pursue these implications of Bibring's theory is this: (1) The development of the ego requires the presence of 'adequate stimuli,' in this case love of objects; when such stimuli are consistently absent, a primitive ego state comes into existence, the later reactivation of which is the state of depression. (2) Normal development lowers the intensity of this ego state and its potentiality for reactivation, and limits its reactivation to those reality situations to which grief and sadness are appropriated reactions. (3) Recurrent absence of adequate stimuli in the course of development works against the lowering of the intensity of this ego state and increases the likelihood of its being reactivated, that is to say, established a predisposition of depression.

This conception is consonant with present-day ego psychology and also elucidates the economic and the adaptive aspects of Bibring's theory. The role of stimulation in the development of ego structure is a crucial implication of the concept of adaption. At the same time, since psychoanalytic theory explains the effects of stimulation in terms of changes in the distribution of attention cathexes, the role of stimulation in ego-structure development, to which is referred, and might that well be the starting point for an understanding of the economics of the ego state of depression.

All the same, our present discussion of the structural, genetic, dynamic, economic, and adaptive aspects of Edward Bibring's theory gives us a crystalline glimpse of its fertility. But does not exhaust either its implications or the problems it poses. An attempt to trace more or less of these would require a detailed analysis of those points where Bibring's views shade into other findings and theories of psychoanalytic ego psychology, and is therefore beyond our scope tonight.

However, of completing of the three points from which take root of Edward Bibring's theory which are less obvious than the observations and formulations so far discussed,

The first of its roots in the technique of the psychoanalysis, Bibring wrote:

> From an . . . a therapeutic point of view one has to pay attention not only to the dynamic and genetic basis of the persisting narcissistic aspirations, the frustrations of which the ego cannot tolerate, but also the dynamic and genetic conditions which forced the infantile ego to become fixated to feelings of helplessness . . . the importance of these feelings of helplessness in the therapy of depression is obvious.

This formulation seems to say nothing more than the well-known technical rule that 'Analysis must always go on in the layers accessible to the ego at the moment' (Fenichel, 1938-39). But it does say more, because it specifies that it is the helplessness, the lack of interest, and the lowered self-esteem which are immediately accessible in depression. It is safe to assume that the clinically observed accessibility of this was one of the roots of Bibring's theory.

A second root of the theory is in Bibring's critique of the English school of psychoanalysis. A study of this critique shows that on the one hand, Bibring found some of this school's observations on depression sound and, like his own observations, incompatible with the accepted theory of depression, and, on the other hand, he found this schools theory of depression incompatible with psychoanalytic theory proper. It seems that Bibring intended his theory of depression to account for the sound observations of this school within the framework of psychoanalytic theory.

Finally, a third root of Bibring's theory seems to be related to the problems raised by the so-called 'existential analysis.' So far the only evidence for Edward Bibring's interest in the critical attitude toward 'existential analysis' is in the memories of those people who discussed the subject with him. Though his interest in phenomenology is obvious in his paper on depression, his interest in existentialism proper is expressed in only a few passages, like [Depression] is—essentially—'a human way of reacting to frustration and misery' whenever the ego finds itself in a state of real or imaginary helplessness against 'overwhelming odds.' Bibring's intent seems to have been to put the sound observations and psychoanalytically relevant concepts of 'existential analysis' into the framework of psychoanalytic ego psychology.

Briefly, the relevance within a behavioural framework, depression is conceptualized as an extinction phenomenon. On reading the gerontological literature one is struck by the many behavioural similarities between the depressed and the elderly person: (1) One of the most striking features of both old age and depression is a progressive reduction in the rate of behaviour. The concept of 'disengagement' has been advanced to account for this reduction of behaviour. It is assumed to be a natural process which the elderly person accepts and desires, and which is thought to have intrinsic determinants (Cumming and Henry, 1961). From a behavioural framework, the elderly person's reduced rate of behaviour suggests that his behaviour is no longer being reinforced by his environment, i.e., that he, like the depressed person, is on an extinction schedule. (2) Other aspects of the depressive syndrome (feeling rejected, and so forth) are quite common among the elderly (Wolf, 1959). (3) Motivation is a critical problem in the elderly, as it is in the depressed patient. It is hard to find effective reinforcers for either. The number of potentially reinforcing events seems reduced. (4) The elderly person and the depressed person are turned inward, and focus on themselves, their memories, fantasies, and the past. The hypothesis immediately causes to have in making of itself, in that a reduction in the response contingent rate of positive reinforcement is a critical antecedent condition, and for many of the behavioural changes described in the elderly person.

It is, nonetheless, that depression, that it is for this reason it needs a model. The clinical 'entity' has multifaceted symptoms, but let us look at those that seem central to the diagnosis and that may be related to learned helplessness. The symptoms of learned helplessness that we have discussed all have parallels in depression.

Sustaining the lowered response initiation the word 'depression' is a behavioural description that denotes a reduction o r depression in responding. Even so, it is not surprising that a prominent symptom of depression is failure, or slowness of a patient to initiate responses. Such is the systematic study of the symptoms of depression. Grinker, Miller, Sabishin, Nunn, and Nunally (1961) all describe this in a number of ways:

> Isolated and withdrawn, prefers to remain by himself, stays in bed much of the time . . .
> Gait and general behaviour slow and retarded . . .
> Volume of the voice deceased, sits alone very quietly feels unable to act, feels unable to make decisions . . .
> [They] give the appearance of an 'entity' person who has 'given up' . . . .

Mendels (1970) described the slowdown in responding associated with depression as:

> Loss of interest, decrease in energy, inability to accomplish tasks, difficulty in concentration and the erosion of motivation, as these are ambitions that combine to impair efficient functioning. For many depressives the first signs of the illness are in the area of their increasing inability to cope with their work and responsibilities.

Beck (1967) describes 'paralysis of the will' as a striking feature of depression:

> In the severity of cases, these are often completed in the paralysis of the will. The patient has no desire to do anything, even those things which are essential to life. Consequently, he may be relatively immobile unless prodded or pushed into activity by others. It is sometime necessary to put the patient out of bed, wash, dress, and feed him.

The characteristic passivity and lowered response initiation of depressives have been demonstrated in a large number of studies, i.e., Miller, 1975. Psychomotor retardation differentiates depressives from normal people and a direct example of reduced voluntary response initiation. In addition, depressives engage in fewer activities and the y show reduced interpersonal responding and reduced nonverbal communication. Finally, the intellectual slowness and learning, memory, and IQ deficits found in depressed patients may be viewed as resulting from reduced motivation to initiate cognitive actions such as memory scanning and mental arithmetic. These deficits all parallel the lowered response initiation in learned helplessness.

Recent laboratory experiments have demonstrated a striking similarity between the lowered response initiation of learned helplessness and depression (Klein, Fencil-Morse and Seligman, 1976; Miller and Seligman, 1975) in each of these studies, depressed and nondepressed students were first-divide into three groups; group (1) experienced inescapable loud noise (or unsolvable concept formation problems). (2) Heard the loud noise but could turn it off by pressing a button (or was provided with a solvable problem), group (3) heard no noise (or did not work on any problems). All subjects then worked on a series of patterned anagrams, and half of all subjects were depressed; half were not depressed. As in the earlier study by Hiroto and Seligman (1975), nondepressed subjects in the group (1), who had previously been exposed to inescapable noise or unsolvable problems, showed response initiation deficits on the anagrams, while nondepressed subjects in the group (2) and (3) exhibited no deficit. Moreover, depressed subjects in all groups, including those of a group (3) who had no pretreatment, showed poorer response initiation on the anagrams than the nondepressed subjects in a group (3). Nondepressed subjects given a helplessness pretreatment showed response initiation deficits wholly parallel to those found in naturally occurring depression. Klein and Seligman (1976) showed the same parallel deficits between depressed subjects and nondepressed helpless subjects on tasks involving noise escape.

Also having a negative cognitive set of depressives that not only make fewer responses, but they interpret their few responses as failures or as doomed to failure, this negative cognitive se t directly mirrors the difficulty that helpless subjects have in learning that responding produces relief from an aversive situation.

Beck (1967) considers this negativistic cognition as the set to be primarily characteristic of depression:

The depressed patient is peculiarly sensitive to any impediments to his goal-directed activity. An obstacle is regarded as an impossible barrier, but difficulty in dealing with a problem is interpreted as a total failure. His cognitive response to a problem or difficulty is likely to be an idea such as 'I'm licked.' 'I'll never be able to do this,' or 'I'm blocked no mater what I do.'

In truth, Beck views the passive and retarded behaviour of depressed patients as stemming from their negative expectations of their own effectiveness:

The loss of spontaneous motivation, or paralysis of the will, has been considered a symptom of depression in the classical literature. The loss of motivation may be viewed as the result of the patient's hopelessness and pessimism. As long as he expects a negative outcome from any course of action; he is stripped of any internal stimulation to do anything.

This cognitive set crops up repeatedly in experiments with depressives. Friedman (1964) observed that although a patient was performing adequately during a test, the patient would occasionally reiterate this original protest of 'I can't do it,' or 'I don't have a familiarity with how.' This is also our experience in testing depressed patients.

Experimental demonstrations of negative cognitive set in depressed college students were provided by Miller and Seligman (1973) and Miller, Seligman, and Kurlander (1975). These studies showed that depressed students view their skilled actions very much as if they were only chance actions. In other words, depressed subjects, more than nondepressed subjects, tend to perceive reinforcement in a skill task as independent of their behaviour. Miller, Seligman, and Kurlander (1975) found this perception to be specific to depression: anxious and non-anxious students matched for extent of depression did not differ in their perceptions of reinforcement contingencies.

Miller and Seligman (1975, 1976), Klein, Fencil-Morse and Seligman (1976), and Klein and Seligman (1976) more directly demonstrated the parallel between the negative cognitive set in learned helplessness and depression. While replicating the findings of Miller and Seligman (1976) and Klein and Seligman (1976) it has found that nondepressed subjects who had been exposed to inescapable noise had, they perceived reinforcement as of less a response contingent than nondepressed subjects who had been exposed to either escapable or no noise during a skilful task. Pretreatment had no effect on perception of reinforcement in chance tasks. So, the effects of learned helplessness and depression on perception of reinforcement are parallel.

Cognitive deficits were also found in the previous studies of Miller and Seligman (1975), Klein et al. (1976) and Klein and Seligman (1976). These studies measured the degree to which subjects were able to benefit from successful anagram solutions or escapes from high volume noise. As with response initiation, depressed subjects in the untreated groups showed cognitive deficits relative to nondepressed subjects, and nondepressed subjects who had experienced inescapable noise or unsolvable problems exhibit cognitive deficits relative to nondepressed subjects in the control groups on measures of cognitive functioning.

Some studies indicate that negative cognitive set may also explain poor discrimination learning by depressives (Martin and Rees, 1966), and may be partly responsible for their lowered cognitive abilities (Payne, 1961; Miller, 1975).

Depression, like learned helplessness, seems to have its time course. In discussing the 'disaster syndrome' Wallace (1957) reported that people experience a day or so of depression following sudden catastrophes, and then they again function normally. It seems possible that multiple traumatic events intervening between the initial disaster recovery might exacerbate depression in human considerably, as they do in dogs. We should also note that endogenously or process depression is characterized by fluctuations of weeks or months between depression and mania. Moreover, it is commonly thought that almost all depressions dissipate in time, although whether they last days, weeks, months, or years are a matter of some dispute (Paskind, 1929, 1930; Lundquist, 1945; Kraines, 1957).

According to psychoanalysts, the lowered aggression of depressives is due to introjected hostility. In fact, psychoanalysts view introjection of hostility as the primary mechanism producing symptoms of depression. We do not believe that the increased self-blame in depression results from hostility turned inward, but it seems undeniable that hostility, even in dreams (Beck and Hurvich, 1959; Beck and Ward, 1961), is reduced among depressive. This symptom corresponds to the lack of aggression in learned helplessness.

Depressives commonly show reduced interest in food, sex, and interpersonal relations. These symptoms correspond to the anorexia, weight loss, and sexual and social deficits in learned helplessness.

According to the catecholamine hypothesis of affective disorders, depression is associated with a deficiency of norepinehrine (NE) at receptor sites in the brain, whereas elation may be associated with its excess. This hypothesis is based on evidence that imipramine, a drug that increases the NE available in the central nervous system, causes depression to end. Klerma and Cole (1965) and Cole (1964) experimented with imipramine and placebos on depressed patients and reported positive results of imipramine over placebos. Monoamineoxidase (MAO) inhibitors, which prevent the breakdown of NE, also may be useful in relieving depression (Cole, 1964; Davis, 1965). Reserpine, an antihypertensive medication that depletes NE, often produces depression as a side-effect in man (Beck, 1967). There is also some suggestion of cholinergic medication of depression. Janowsky et al. (1972) reported that physostigmine, a cholinergic stimulators, produced depressive effect in normal people. Atropine, a linergic blocker, reversed these symptoms. So, NE depletion and cholinergic activation are implicated in both depression and learned helplessness (Thomas and DeWald, 1977). However, Mendels and Frazer (1974) reviewed the behavioural effects of drugs that deplete brain catecholamines and they contend that the behavioural changes associated with reserpine are better interpreted as a psychomotor retardation-sedation syndrome than as depression. Moreover, selective depletion of brain catecholamines by alpha-methyl-para-tyrosine (AMPT) fails to produce some of the key features of depression, despite the fact that this drug produces a consistently greater reduction in amine metabolate concentration than occur s in depression. So depletion of catecholamines in itself may not be sufficient to account for depression.

Nonetheless, depressed people say they feel helpless, hopeless, and powerless, and by this they mean that they believe they are unable to control or influence those aspects of their lives that are significant to them. Grinker and coworkers (1961) describe the 'characteristics of hopelessness, helplessness, failure, sadness, unworthiness, guilt and internal suffering, as the 'essence of depression.' Melges and Bowlby (1969) also characterize depressed patients in this way and Bibring (1953) defines depression 'as the emotional expression [indicative] of a state of helplessness and powerlessness of the ego.'

They clearly are considerable parallels between the forms of behaviour that define helplessness and major symptoms of depression.

Differences:—But there are substantial gaps:—

First, there are two symptoms found with uncontrollable shock that may or may not correspond to symptoms of depression. Stomach ulcers occur more frequently and severely in rats receiving uncontrollable shock than in rats receiving controllable shock (Weiss, 1968, 1971). We know of no study examining the relationship of depression to stomach ulcers. Second, uncontrollable shock produces more anxiety, measured subjectively, behaviourally, and physiologically, than controllable shock (Seligman and Binik, 1976). The question of whether depressed people are more anxious than nondepressed people do not have a clear answer. Beck (1967) reported that although both depression and anxiety can be observed in some people, only a small positive correlation was found in a study of 600 people. Yet, Miller et al. (1975) found very few depressed college students who were not also anxious. We can speculate that anxiety and depression are related in the following way: When a man or animal is confronted with a threat or a loss, he initially responds with fear or anxiety. If he learns that the threat is wholly controllable, anxiety, having served its function, disappears. If he remains uncertain about his ability to control the threat, his anxiety remains. If he learns or is convinced that the threat is utterly uncontrollable, depression emerges.

A number of facts out depression have been insufficiently investigated for parallels in learned helplessness. Preeminent among these are the depressive symptoms that cannot be investigated in animals; a dejected mood, feelings of self-blame and self-dislike, loss of mirth, suicidal thoughts and crying, but now, that learned helplessness has been reliably produced in man (Hiroto, 1974. Hiroto and Seligman, 1975; Klein et al., 1976; Klein and Seligman, 1976' Miller and Seligman, 1975, 1976; Racinskas, 1971; Roth and Kubal, 1975; Thornton and Jacobs, 1970; Dweck and Reppucci, 1973), we can determine whether any of these states occur in helplessness.

Finally, we know of no evidence that disconfirms the correspondence of symptoms in learned helplessness and depression.

The term 'learned helplessness' was first used in connection with laboratory experiments in which dogs were exposed to shock from which they could not escape (Overmier and Seligman, 1967). After repeated trials, the dogs tended to sit passively when the shock came on. Exposed to a new situation from which the y could escape a shock by jumping over a barrier, they failed to initiate the appropriate response. Some would occasionally jump over the barrier and escape, but they would generally revert to taking the shock passively. For the purposes of constructing an analogue of clinical depression, the behaviour of the dogs is significant in suggesting that exposure to uncontrollable aversive events may lead to a failure to initiate appropriate responses in new situations and an inability to learn that responding is effective.

The analogy to depression was bolstered by initial findings that in a variety of task situations, depressed human subjects resembled nondepressed subjects who had received repeated failure experiences. For instance, compared to nondepressed subjects who had not received repeated failure experiences, these groups of subjects took longer to solve anagrams and apparently failed to perceive the pattern underlying their successful solution (Klein and Seligman, 1976). Miller, Rosellini, and Seligman, and other research suggested that the parallels between the laboratory learned helplessness and depression were not limited to similarities in behaviour. Promising leads were also established with regard to etiology, treatment, and prevention.

The original learned helplessness model stimulated a large body of research and considerable controversy (Buchwald, Coyne, and Cole, 1978; Costello, 1978). Ultimately, the accumulated research led to questions about both the adequacy of the learned-helplessness explanation for the behaviour of nondepressed subjects who has been exposed to failure as well as the appropriateness of learned helplessness as an analogue of depression. For instance, it was shown that the performance deficits of subjects who had been given a typical learned helplessness, inductions were very much situation-specific (Cole and Coyne, 1977) and that these deficits might better be explained as the result of anxious self-preoccupation, rather than the perception of response-reinforcement independence (Coyne, Metalsky and Lavelle, 1980). Furthermore, the characterization of depressed persons as passive and lacking in aggression was challenged. Difficulties with the original learned helplessness model led to a major reformulation (Abramson, Seligman and Teasdale).

We use the term learned helplessness to describe the interference with adaptive responses produced by inescapable shock and also as a short hand to describe the process that we believe underlies the behaviour that we cannot control of which the distinction between controllable and uncontrollable reinforcement is cental to the phenomenon and the theory of helplessness. Learned helplessness in the dog is defined by two types of behaviour. (1) Dogs that have had shock or are slower to make responses than naive dogs, and (2) if the dog does make a response that turns off shock, it has more trouble than a naive dog learning that responding is effective.

However, if we are to propose a model of depression in man, we must have proof that learned helplessness occurs in man.

Besides passivity and retarded response-relief learning, other characteristics associated with learned helplessness are relevant to depression in man. First, helplessness has a time course. In dogs, inescapable shock produces transient as well as permanent interference with escape (Overmier and Seligman, 1967) and avoidance (Overmier, 1968): 24 hours after one session of inescapable shock, dogs are helpless; but after 48 hours their response is normal. This is also true of goldfish (Padilla, 1970). After multiple sessions of inescapable shock, helplessness is not transient (Seligman and Groves, 1970; Seligman, Maier and Geer, 1968) Weiss (1968) found a parallel time course for weight loss in rats given uncontrollable shock, but other that this no time course has been found in rats or in other species (e.g., Anderson, Cole, and McVaugh, 1968; Seligman, Rosellini, and Kozak, 1975). Nonetheless, uncontrollable trauma produces a number of effects found in depression. The two basic effects are these: animal and humans become passive—they are slower to initiate responses to alleviate trauma and may not respond at all; and animals and humans are retarded in learning that their behaviour may control trauma., If a response is made that does produce relief, they often have trouble realizing that one causes the other. This maladaptive behaviour has been observed in a variety of species over a range of tasks that require voluntary responding. In addition, this phenomenon dissipates in time in the dog, and it causes lowered aggression, loss of appetite, and norepinephrine depletion.

The passivity of dogs, rats and men in the face of trauma and their difficulty on benefiting from response-relief contingencies results; that we believe, from their having learned that responding and trauma are independent—that trauma is uncontrollable. This is the hear t of the learned helplessness hypothesis. The hypothesis states that when shock is inescapable, the organism learns that responses and shock termination are independent (the probability of shock termination given any response doesn't differ from its probability in the absence of that response). Learning that trauma is uncontrollable has three effects.

(1) A motivational effect—it reduces the probability that the subject will initiate responses to escape, because part of the incentive for making such responses is the expectation that they will bring relief. If the subject has previously learned that its responses have no effect on trauma, this contravenes the expectation, thus, the organism's motivation to respond is undermined by experience with reinforcers it cannot control. Such that this motivational effect undermines passivity in learned helplessness, and, if the model is valid, in depression.

(2) The cognitive effect—learning that responses and shock are independent makes it more difficult to learn that responses do produce relief when the organism makes a response that actually terminates shock. In general, if we have acquired a cognitive set in which A's are irrelevant to B's, it will be harder for us to learn that A's produce B's when they do. By the helplessness hypothesis, this mechanism is responsible for the difficulty that helpless organisms have in learning

536

that responding produces relief, even after they respond and successfully turn off shock. Further, if the model is valid, this mechanism produces the 'negative expectations' of depression.

(3) An emotional effect—although it does not follow directly from the helplessness hypothesis—such that uncontrollable shock produces more conditioned fear, ulcers, weight loss, defecation, and pain than controllable shock.

One cause of laboratory-produced helplessness seems to be learning that one cannot control important events. Learning that responses and reinforcement are independent results in a cognitive set that has two effects: fewer responses to control reinforcement are initiated and associating successful responses with reenforcement becomes more difficult.

Nevertheless, some of the events that typically precipitate depression; failure in work or school; death or loss of loved ones; rejection by or separation from loved ones; physical disease, and growing old. What do all these have in common?

Four recent theories of depression seem to be largely in agreement about the etiology of depression, and what they agree on is the centrality of helplessness and hopelessness. Bibring (1953), arguing from a dynamic viewpoint, sees helplessness as the cause of depression:

> What has been described as the basic mechanism of depression, the ego's shocking awareness of its helplessness in regard to its aspirations, is assumed to represent the core of normal, neurotic and probably also psychotic depression.

Melges and Bowlby (1969) see a similar cause of depression:

> Our thesis is that while a depressed patient's goals remain relatively unchanged his estimate of the likelihood of achieving then and his confidence in the efficacy of his own skilled actions is both diminished . . . the depressed person believes that his plans of action are no longer effective in

537

reaching his continuing and long range goals . . . From this state of mind is derived, we believe, much depressive symptomalogy, including indecisiveness, inability to act, making increased demands on others, and feelings of worthlessness and guilt about not discharging duties.

Beck (1967, 1970) sees depression as resulting primarily from a patient's negative cognitive set, largely about his abilities to change his life:

A primary factor appears to be the activation of idiosyncratic cognitive patterns which divert the thinking into specific channels that deviate from reality. As a result, the patient perseverates in making negative judgements and interpretations of experience, negative evaluations of the self, and negative expectations of the future.

Lichtenberg (1957) sees hopelessness as the defining characteristic of depression:

Depression is defined as a manifestation of felt hopelessness regarding the attainment of goals when responsibility for the hopelessness is attributed to one's personal defects. In this context hope is conceived to be a function of the perceived probability of success with respect to goal attainment.

Even so, it means that all of a person's efforts have been in vain, his responses have failed to bring about the gratification he desires; he cannot find responses that control reinforcement. When a person is rejected by someone he loves, he can no longer control this significant source of gratification and support. When a parent or lover dies, the bereaved person is powerless to produce or influences love from dead person. Physical disease and growing old are obvious helplessness experiences. In these conditions, the person's own responses are ineffective and he must rely on the care of others. So, we would predict that it is not life events that produce depression (Alarcon and Cori, 1972) but uncontrollable life events.

However, Ferster (1969, 1973), Kaufman and Rosenblum (1967); McKinney and Bunney (1969), and Liberman and Raskin (1971) have suggested that depression is caused by extinction procedures or the loss of reinforcers. There is no contradiction between the learned-helplessness and extinction view of depression; helplessness, however, is more general. Briefly, extinction is a special case of independence between responding and reinforcement. Reinforcement, just the same, may also be presented with a probability greater than zero, and still be presented independent of responding. This occurs in the typical helplessness paradigm and cause responses to decrease in probability (Recorta and Skucy, 1969). Therefore, a view talks about independence between responding and reinforcement assumes the extinction view and, in addition, suggests that situations in which reinforcers still occur independent of responding also will cause depression.

Both learned helplessness and depression may be caused by learning that responses and reinforcement are independent. But this view runs into several problems. Can depression actually be caused by situations other than extinction in which reinforcement still occur but are not under the individual's control? To put it another way, 'is a net loss of reinforcement necessary for depression, or can depression occur when there is only loss of control without loss of reinforcement?' Would a Casanova who made love with seven new women every week become depressed if he found out that women wanted him not because of his amatory prowess but because of his wealth or because his fairy god mother wished it? We can only speculate.

It seems appropriate to mention 'success' depression in this context. When people finally reach a goal after years of striving—being promoted or obtaining a PhD—many become depressed. This puzzling phenomenon is clearly a problem for a loss of reinforcement view of depression. From a helplessness view, success depression may occur because reinforcements are no longer contingent on present responding. After years of goal-directed instrumental activity, the reinforcement automatically changes. One now gets his reinforcement because of whom he is rather than what he is doing. The common clinical impression that many beautiful women become depressed and attempt suicide also presents problems for the loss of reinforcement theory: positive reinforcers abound not because of what they do but because of how they look. Would be a generation of children risen with abundant positive reinforcers that they received independently to what, and they did become clinically depressed?

According to the helplessness view, the central theme in successful therapy should be having the patient discover and come to accept that his responses produce the gratification that he desires—that he is, in short, an effective human being. Some therapies that reportedly alleviate depression are consonant with a learned helplessness model, however, it is important to note that the success of a therapy often has little to do with its theoretical underpinning. So, with the exception of Klein and Seligman (1976), as a se t of examples that seem as a test of the model, but merely as a set of examples that seem to have exposure to response-produced success as a cure for depression.

Consonant with their helplessness-centred views of the etiology of depression, Bibring (1957), Beck (1967), and Melges and Bowlby (1969) all stressed that reversing helplessness alleviates depression. For example, Bibring (1953) has stated:

> The same conditions which bring about depression (helplessness) in reverse serve frequently the restitution from depression. Generally, one can say that depression subsides either (I) when the narcissistically important goals and objects appear to be again within reach (which is frequently followed by a temporary elation) or (ii) when they become sufficiently modified or reduced to becoming realizable, or (iii) when they are altogether relinquished, or (iv) when the ego recovers from the narcissistic shock by regaining its self-esteem with the help of various recovery mechanisms (with or without any change of objective or goal).

In their review of therapies for depression, Seligan, Klein, and Miller (1976) indicated that most of the therapies have strong elements of inducing the patient to discover that responses produce the reinforcement he desires. In antidepression milieu therapy (Taulbee and Wright, 1971), for example, the patient is forced to emit one of the most powerful responses people have for controlling others—anger—and when this response is dragged out of his depleted behaviour repertoire, he is powerfully reinforced. Beck's (1970) cognitive therapy is aimed at similar goals. He sees success manipulations as changing the negative cognitive set ('I'm an ineffective person) of the depressive to a more positive set, and argues that the primary task of the therapist is to change the negative expectations of the depressed patient to more optimistic ones. Even so, both Burgess's (1968), therapy and the graded task assigned (Beck, Seligman, Binik, Schuyler, and Brill, unpublished data), the patient makes instrumental responses of gradually increasing complexity, and each is reinforced. Similarly, all instrumental behaviour therapy for depression (Hersen, Eisler, Alford, and Agras, 1973; Reisinger. 1972), by definition, arrange the contingencies so that responses control the occurrence of reinforcement; the patient's recognition of this relationship should alleviate depression. Lewinsohn's therapy also has this element; participation in activity and other nondepressed behaviour controls therapy time. (Lewinsohn, Weinstein, and Shaw, 1969). In assertive training (Wolpe, 1968), the patient must emit social responses to bring about a desired change in his environment. Such that the study provides a useful method fo r testing the effectiveness of any therapy for depression in the laboratory because we can bring depression into the laboratory, in that, both in its naturally occurring state and in the form of learned helplessness, we can now see what reverses it in the laboratory. Will assertive training, emotive expression or atropine given to helpless and depressed subjects in the laboratory reverse the symptoms of depression and helplessness?

In order to explain depression, Burgess (1968) and others have relied heavily on the reinforcement the patient gets for his depressed behaviour, it is tempting to seek to remove this reinforcement during therapy, but caution is in order, so to explain the persistence or maintenance of some depressive behaviours, but it does not explain how they began. Helplessness suggests that failure to initiate active responses originates in the perception that the patient cannot control reinforcement. Thus, there can be two sources of a depressed patient's passivity: (a) patients are passive for instrumental reasons, because they think staying depressed brings them sympathy, love and attention, and (b) patients are passive because they believe that no response at all will be effective in controlling their environment. In this sense, it means that there is at least some response that believes he can effectively perform. Maier (1970) found that dogs who were reinforced for being passive by shock termination were not nearly as debilitated as dogs for whom all responses were independent of shock termination. Similarly, patients who use their depression in a way of controlling reinforcement are less helpless than those who have given up. Nonetheless, depression may be directly antagonized when patients come to see that their own responses are effective in alleviating their suffering and produced gratifications.

Nonetheless, many therapies, from psychoanalysis to cognitive understandings, claim to be able to cure depression. The evidence presented is selective as only those treatments that seemed compatible with helplessness were such that was possible that when other therapies work it. It is, because they reinstate the patient's sense of efficacy. However, evidence on the effectiveness of therapy in depression that is less anecdotal and selective is sorely needed. The recent study of Klein and Seligman (1976) may provide a laboratory procedure for evaluating the effectiveness of any therapy suggested for learned helplessness and depression.

All the same, a behavioural self-control model for the study of depression is focussed on different subsets of depressive phenomena. Such that the self-control model organizes and relates these phenomena and has its own implications for symptomatology, etiology, and therapy. Depression has certain properties which make the development of a model particularly difficult, however, the term depression refers to a syndromes which encompass a broad set of symptoms with diverse behavioural referents (Beck, 1972; Levitt and Lubin, 1975; Mendels, 1970; Woodruff, Goodwin and Guze, 1974). Especially notable is the diversity among cognitive symptoms. Aside from manifest subjective sadness, depressed persons show clinical symptoms such as quilt, pessimism, low sel-esteem, self-derogation, and helplessness. Accounting for these distinctive cognitive behaviours and integrating them with the various overt-moto r behaviours characteristic of depression is limited to verbal-cognitive and overt-motor variables are appropriate since no reliable physiological index has been clearly identified as a symptom of depression (Bruder, 1970).

A recent resurgence of interest in psychological aspects of depression has become evident, and, with it, new and innovative models have been advanced. Behavioural and cognitive modes proposed by Lewinsohn (1974), Seligman (1974) and Beck (1974) have been most prominent and influential in behavioural research and clinical application.

Lewinsohn (1974; Lewinsohn, Weinstein, and Shaw, 1969) have developed a clinical and research program which looks at depression as an extinction phenomenon. A loss or lack of response contingent positive reinforcement results in reduced rates of common overt-motor behaviour and also elicits a basic dysphoria. All other cognitive-verbal symptoms of depression are secondary elaborations of these basic dysphoria. Susceptivity to depression and ability to overcome depression is related to social skill, the range of events which are potentially reinforcing to the person, and reinforcement availability. The etiology of depression is therefore, the joint function of external environmental changes and individual differences in reinforcement potential and social skills. Therapy procedures are aimed at identifying potential sources of reinforcement in the person's environment and developing strategies to increase their frequency of occurrence (Lewinsohn, 1976. Lewinsohn and Shaffer, 1971; Robinson and Lewinsohn, 1973) In other instances, therapy consists of isolating deficits in social interaction and training subjects in modifying these socially skilled behaviours (Lewinsohn, Biglan and Zeiss, 1976); Lewinsohn and Shaw, 1969; Lewinsohn, Weinstein and Alper, 1970).

Also, Seligman has proposed a model of depression based on a laboratory paradigm of learned helplessness (Seligman, 1974, 1975). A situation in which the probability of the consequence given a response is equal to the probability of the consequence given no response produces the phenomenon of learned helplessness. Noncontingent punishment has been the situation most studied. Learned helplessness has properties which parallel the symptoms of depression: (1) lowered response initiation (passivity), (2) negative cognitive se t (belief that one's actions are doomed to failure; (3) dissipation over time, (4) lack of aggression, (5) loss of libido and appetite, and (6) norepinephrine depletion and cholinergic activity (Seligman, Klein, and Miller, 1974). Cognition is given a central position in this model in that of the 'depressive retardation is caused by a brief in response-reinforcement independence'; (Seligman.

543

1974). Other cognitive symptoms are held to be elaborations on this central belief. No therapy studies have been directly generated by this model to date, however, Klein and Seligman (1976) has demonstrated the reversibility of learned helplessness and depression following experience with solvable problems.

From a different perspective, Beck (1970, 1972, 1974) has evolved a cognitive model of depression which holds that depression consists of a primary triad of cognitive patterns or schema (1) a negative view of the world; (2) a negative view of the self, and (3) a negative view of the future. These views are maintained by distorted models of cognition such as selective abstraction, arbitrary inference, and overgeneralization,. The over—behavioural symptoms of depression follow from cognitive distortion. Distorted schema develops in early childhood and leave individuals susceptible to depression in the face of stress. Therapy involves the identification of distortions and their confrontation with the evidence of objective experience. Case studies employing these modifications have been described by Beck (1972) and Rush, Khatami, and Beck (1975). Group studies have shown that therapy based on a Beck's cognitive behaviour modification model is superior to a program based on Lewinsohn's model, a nondirective control therapy and a waiting list control and are more effective than treatment with imipramine hydrochloride (Rush, Beck, Kovacs, and Hollon).

The severe disorders of mood or effect are among the most regulars of the major psychiatric syndromes. Lifetime expectancy rates for such disorders are between 3 and 8 percent of the general population. Only a minority is treated by psychiatrists or in psychiatric hospitals and about 70 percent of prescriptions for antidepressants are written by nonpsychiatrist physicians. These and other modern medical treatments of severe mood disorders have contributed to a virtual revolution in the theory and practice of modern psychiatry since the introduction of mood-altering drugs three decades ago. These agent s include lithium salts (1949), and Monoamine oxidase (MAO) inhibitors (1952), and the antimanic and antipsychotic (neuroleptics) agents such as chlorpromazine (1952), and the Tricyclic or heterocyclic (imipramine-like) antidepressants (1957). In addition, electroconvulsive therapy (ECT) continues to have a place in the treatment of very severe and acute mood disorders, especially life-threatening forms of depression.

The development of these modern medical therapies has had several important effects. First. These agents have provided of a relatively simple specific effect and safe forms of treatment with a profound impact on current patterns of medical practice, for example, many depressed or hypomanic patients can be managed adequately in outpatient facilities to avoid prolonged, expensive, and disruptive hospitalization which were formerly common. Second, partial understanding of the pharmacology of the psychotropic drugs has led to imaginative hypotheses concerning the pathophysiology or etiology of severe mood disorders. These, in turn, have encouraged a revolution on experimental psychiatry in which the hypotheses have been tested in clinical research. Many of the earlier hypotheses have been found wanting or simplistic, nevertheless, they have led to increased understanding of the diagnosis, biology, and treatment of mood disorders and to newer research that represents a third level of development. This is the focus of the practical clinical benefits of now and in the near future.

In the light of this some characteristics of infant development during this holding phase can be enumerated. It is at this stage that:

(1) primary process, (2) primary identification, (3) autoerotism, (4) primary narcissism, and (5) living realities.

In this phase the ego changes over from an unintegrated state to a structure integration, and so the infant becomes able to experience anxiety associated with disintegration. The word disintegration begins to have been meaning which it did not possess before go integration became a fact. In healthy development at this stage the infant retains the capacity for re-experiencing unintegrated states, but this depends on the continuation of reliable maternal care or on the built-up in the infant of memories of material care beginning gradually to be perceived as such. The result of healthy progress in the infant's development during this stage is that he attains to what might be called 'unit status.' The infant becomes a person, an individual in his own right.

Associated with this attainment is the infant 's psychosomatic existence which begins to take on a personal pattern: that is, that the basis for this for this indwelling is a linkage of motor and sensory and functional experience with the infant's new state of being a person. As a further development there comes into existence what might be called a limiting membrane, which to some extent (in health) is equated with the surface of the skin, and has a position between the infant's 'me' and his 'not me.' So the infant comes to have an inside and an outside, and a body-scheme. In this way meaning comes to the function of intake and output, moreover, it gradually become meaningful to postulate a personal or inner psychic reality for the infant.

During the holding phase other processes are initiated; the most important is the dawn of intelligence and the beginning of a mind as something distinct from the psyche, and, from this, the secondary processes and symbolic functioning, and of the organization of a personal psychic content, which forms a basis for dreaming and for living relationships.

At the same time there starts in the infant a joining up of two roots of impulsive behaviours. The term 'fusion' indicates the positive process whereby diffuse elements that belong to the movement and to muscle erotism for becoming fused with the orgiastic functioning of the erotogenic zones. This concept is more familiar as the reverse process of defusion, which is a complex and complication defence in which aggression becomes separated out from erotic experience after a period in which a degree of fusion has been achieved. All these developments belong to the environmental condition of 'holding,' and without 'good' so as to be adequately holding the stages cannot be attained, or once attained cannot become established,

A further development in the capacity for object relationships. In that, the infant changes from relationship to objectively conceived object to a relationship to an object objectively perceived. This change is closely bound up with the infant's change from being merged with the mother to being separate from her, or to relating to her as a separate and 'not-me,' This development is not specifically related to the holding, but is related to the phase of 'living with' . . .

In the holding phase the infant is maximally dependent. One can classify dependence thus:

(I) Absolute Dependence: In this state the infant has no means of knowing about the maternal care, which is largely a matter of prophylaxis. He cannot gain control over what is well and what is badly done, but is only a position to gain profit or to suffer disturbances,

(ii) Relative Dependence: The infant can become aware of the need for the details of maternal care, and to a growing extent relate them to personal impulse, and then later, in a psychoanalytic treatment, can reproduce them in the transference,

(iii) The infant develops the means for doing without actual care. This is accomplished through the accumulation of memories of care, the projection of personal needs and the introjection of care details, with the development of confidence on the environment, and must be added that, the element of intellectual understanding with its tremendous implications.

Nonetheless, in borderline cases the analyst does not always wait in vain, that in the course of time the patient becomes able to make use of the psychoanalytic interpretations of the original trauma projection. It may even happen that he is able to accept for what is in the environment as a projection of the simple and stable going-on-being elements that derive from his own inherent potential.

Such that it is necessary to attempt to state briefly what happens to the inherented potential if this is to develop into an infant, and thereafter onto a child reaching toward independent existence, because if the plexuity of the subject such a statement must be made in the assumption of satisfactory material care, which means parental care. Satisfactory parental care can be classified roughly into three overlapping states.

1. Holding.
2. Mother and infant living together, as the father's function (on dealing with the environment for the mother) is not known to the infant
3. Father, mother, and infant, all three living together.

RICHARD J. KOSCIEJEW

The term 'holding' is used to denote not only the actual physical holding of the infant, but also the total environmental provision prior to the concept of living with. In other words, it refers to a three-dimensional or space relationship (spatiality) with time gradually added. This overlaps with, but initiate prior to, instinctual experiences that in time would determine the object relationships. It includes the management of experiences that are inherent in existence, such as the completion (and therefore, the noncompeting) of processes, such ss the completion and, the noncomcompletion of specific processes which from the outside may seem to be purely physiological but which belong to infant psychology and take place on a complex psychological field, particularly, by determining the awareness and the empathy of the mother.

The term 'living with' implies object relationships, and the emergence of the infant from the state of being merged with the mother, or his perception of objects external to the self.

The paradox is that what is good and bad in the infant's environment is not in fact a projection, but in spite of this it is necessary, if the individual infant is to develop healthily, that everything will seem to him to be a projection. We find omnipotence and the pleasure principle in operation, as they certainly are in earliest infancy; and to this observation we can add that the recognition of a true 'not-me' is a matter of the intellect; it belongs to extreme sophistication and to the maturity of the individual.

In the writings of Freud most of the formulations concerning infancy derive from a study of adults in analysis. At first sight it would seem that a great deal of psychoanalytic theory is about early childhood and infancy, but in one sense Freud can be said to have neglected unfancy as a stare. This is brought out by a footnote in 'Formulations of the Two Principles of Mental Functioning,' of which he shows that he knows he is taking for granted the very things that are under discussion, as in the text he traces the development from the pleasure-principle to the reality-principle, following his usual course of reconstructing the infancy of his adult patients. The note runs as follows:

It will rightly be objected that an organization which was a slave to the pleasure principle and neglected the reality of the external world could not maintain itself alive for the shortest time, so that

548

it could not have come into existence at all. The employment of a fiction like this is. However, justified when one considers that the infant—provided one includes with it the care it receives from its mother—does almost realize a psychical system of this kind.

Freud paid full tribute to the function of maternal care, and it must be assumed that he left this subject alone only because he was not ready to talk about its implications. The note continues:

It probably hallucinates the fulfilment of its internal needs; it betrays its unpleasure, when there is an increase of stimulus and absence of satisfaction, by the motor discharge of screaming and beating about with its arms and legs, and it then experiences the satisfaction it has hallucinated. Later, as an older child, it learns too employ these manifestations of discharge intentionally for which of methods for expressing its feelings. Since the later care of children is modelled in the care of infants, the dominance of the pleasure principle can really come to an end when a child has achieved complete physical detachment from its parents.

The words: 'provide one includes with it the care it receives from its mother' have of a great importance in the immediate contextual presentation. The infant and the maternal care together from a unit. certainly if one is to study the theory of the parent-infant relationship one must come to a decision about these matters, which concern the real meaning of the word dependence or dependency. It is not enough that it is acknowledged that the environment is important if there is to be a discussion of the theory of the parent-infant relationship, then we are divided into two of the same who do not allow that at the earliest stages the infant and the maternal care belong to each other and cannot be disentangled. These two things, the infant and the maternal case, disentangle and dissociate themselves in health, which means as to do many things, to some extent it means a disentanglement of maternal care from something which we then call the infant, or the beginning of a growing child. This idea is covered by Freud's words at the end of the footnote, explaining that: The dominance of the pleasure principle can really come to an end only when a child has achieved complete physical detachment from its parents.

It is axiomatic in these matters of maternal care of holding variety that when things go well the infant has no means of knowing what is being properly provided and what is being prevented. Such, that when things do not go well that the infant becomes aware, not of the failure of maternal care, but of the results, whatever they may be, of that failure: That in saying, as a result of success in maternal care there is built up in th infant, a continuity of being which is the basis of ego strength of being interrupted by reactions to the consequences of that failure, The resultant of ego-weakening. Such interruptions constitute annihilation, and are evidently associated with pain of psychotic quality and intensity. In the extreme case the infant exists only on the basis of a continuity of reactions to impingement and of recoveries from such reactions. This is in great contras t to the continuity for being that which is our conception of ego strength.

The transition stage has been described as a stage of ;'Quasi-Independence'; and the reason for the adoption if this description is of sufficient importance to demand special attention. It emerges with the utmost clarity from the study of schizoid cases that the most characteristic feature of the state if infantile dependence is identification with the object. Still, it would not be going too far to say that, psychologically speaking, identification with the object and infantile dependence is really the same phenomenon. In that the mature dependence involves a relationship between two kinds of dependence is identical with Freudian distinctions between the narcissistic and the anaclitic choice of objects. The relationship involved in mature dependence is, if course, only the theoretically possible. Nevertheless, it remains true that the more mature a relationship is, the less it is characterized by identification, for what identification essentially represents is failure to differentiate the object. It is when identification persists at the expense of differentiation that a markedly compulsive element enters into the individual's attitude toward its objects. This is well seen in the infatuation of schizoid individuals. It may also be observed in almost uncontrollable impulse so commonly experienced by schizoid and depressive soldiers to return to their wives or their homes, when separated from them owing to military necessities. The abandonment of infantile dependence involves an abandonment with differentiated objects. In the dreams of schizoids the process of differentiation is frequently represented by the process of differentiations is frequently repressed by the theme of trying to cross a gulf or chasm, although the crossing which is attempted may also occur in a regressive direction. The process itself is commonly attended by considerable anxiety, and the anxiety attending it finds characteristic expression on dreams.

The process of differentiation of the object derives particular significance from the fact that infantile dependence is characterized not only by identification, but also by an oral attitude of incorporation. In virtue of this fact the object with which the individual is identified is also an incorporated object or, to put the matter in a more arresting fashion, the object in which the individual is incorporate d may well prove the key to man y metaphysical puzzles. But that it may, however, it is common to find in dreams a complete equivalence between being inside an object and having the object inside.

Such then being the situation, the task of differentiating the object resolves itself into a problem of expelling an incorporated object, i.e., it becomes a problem of expelling contents. Herein lies the rationale of Abraham's 'anal phases,' and it is in this direction that we must look for the significance of the anal techniques which play such an important part during the transition stage. It is important as elsewhere, too insures that the cart is not placed before the horse, and to recognize that it is not a case of individual being occupied with the disposal of contents at this stage because he is anal, but of his being anal because he is preoccupied at this stage with the disposal of content.

The great conflict of the transition stage may now be formulated as a conflict between a progressive urge to surrender the infantile attitude of identification with the object and a regressive urge to maintain that attitude. During this period, accordingly, the behaviour of the individual is characterized both by desperate and endeavours on his part to separate himself from the object and desperate endeavour to achieve reunion with the object—desperate attempts 'to escape from prison' and desperate e attempts 'to return home'. Although one of these attitudes may become to preponderate, there is in the first instance a constant oscillation between the owing and the anxiety attending each. The anxiety attending separation manifests itself as a fear of isolation; and the anxiety attending identification manifests itself as a fear of being shut in, imprisoned or engulfed ('cribbed, cabined and confined'). These anxieties, it will be noticed, are essentially phobic anxieties. In may accordingly be inferred that it is to the conflict between the progressive urge toward separation from the object and the regressive lure of identification with the object that we must look for the explanation of the phobic state.

Owing to the intimate connection existing between identification and oral incorporation, and consequently between separation and excretory expulsion, the conflict of the transition period also presented itself as a conflict between an urge to expel and an urge to retain contents. Just as between separation and reunion, such that either of these oscillation between expulsion and retention, although either of these attitudes may have become dominant. Both attitudes are attended by anxiety—the attitude of expulsion being attended by a fear of bursting (often accompanied or replaced by a fear of some internal disease like cancer). Such anxieties are essentially obsessional anxieties, and it is the conflict between an urge to expel the objet as content and an urge conflict as the object content s that underlies the obsessional state.

The phobic and obsessional techniques are thus seen as to represent two differing methods of dealing with the same basic conflict: In these two differing methods correspond to two differing attitudes toward the object. From the phobic point of view the conflict presents itself as in between flight from and return to the object. From the obsessional point of view, as the conflict presents itself as one between expulsion and retention of the object. It thus becomes obvious that the phobic technique corresponds to an active attitude. The obsessional technique also expresses a much higher degree of aggression toward the object; For, whether the object is expelled or retained, it is being subject to forcible control. For the phobic individual, the choice lies between escaping from the power of the object and submitting to it. In other words, while the obsessional technique is essentially sadistic in nature, the phobic technique is essentially masochistic.

In the hysterical state we can recognize the operation of another technique for attempting to deal with the basic conflict of the transition period. In this case, the conflict appears to be formulated as simply one between acceptance and rejection of the object. Acceptance of the object is clearly manifested in the intense love-relationships which are so typical of the hysteric; but the very exaggeration of these emotional relationships in itself raises a suspicion that a rejection is being overcompensated. The suspicion is confirmed by th propensity of the hysteric to dissociation phenomena. That these Dissociative phenomena represent a rejection of the genitals need not be stressed, but, as the analysis can always unmask an identification of the rejected genitals with the breast as the original object of the libidinal impulses during the period of infantile dependence. This being so, it is of note, that what is dissociated by the hysteric is an organ function in himself. This can only have meant—that the rejected object is an internalization object, however, the hysteric's overvaluation of his objects leaves no room for doubt that in his case the accepted object and rejection of the internalized object.

If the paranoid and the hysteric states are now compared, we are confronted with a significant contrast. Whereas, the hysteric overvalues objects in the outer world, the paranoid individual regards them as persecutors, and, whereas, the hysteric dissociation is a form of self-depreciation, the attitude of the paranoid individual is one of extravagant grandiosity. The paranoid state must, accordingly, be regarded as representing rejection of the externalized object and acceptance of the internalized object.

Having interpreted the hysterical and paranoid technique in terms of the acceptance and rejection of objects, we can now obtain interesting results by applying a similar interpretation to the phobic and obsessional techniques. The conflict underlying the phobic state may be concisely formulated as one between flight to the object and flight from the object. In the former case, is, of course, the object is accepted, whereas, in the latter case the object is rejected. In both cases, the object is treated as external, in the obsessional state, the conflict presents itself as one between the exclusion and the rejection of content. In this case, accordingly, both the accepted and the rejected objects are treated as internal. If in the case of the phobic state both the accepted and the rejected objects are treated as external and in the obsessional state both are treated as internal, the situation as regarding these hysterical and paranoid states is that one of these objects is treated as an externalized object and the other as an internalized object, in the hysterical state. It is the accepted object that is externalized, and the paranoid state, the object which is externalized is the rejected object.

The chief features of the stage of transition between infantile and adult dependence may now be briefly summarized. The transition period is characterized by a process of development, whereby object—relationships based upon identification gradually give place to relationships with differentiated objects. Satisfactory development during this period, therefore, depends upon the success which attends the process of differentiation of the object, and this in turn depends upon the issue of a conflict or separation from the object—a situation which is both desire d and feared. The conflict in question may call into operation any or all characteristic techniques—the obsessional, the paranoid, the hysterical and the phobic: and, if object—relationships are unsatisfactory, these techniques are liable to form the basis of characteristic psychopathological developments in later life. The various techniques cannot be classified in any order corresponding to presumptive levels of libidinal development. On the contrary, they must be regarded as alternative techniques, all belonging to the same stage in the development of object-relationships. Which of the techniques is employed, or to what extent each is employed would appear to depend on large measure upon the nature of the object-relationships established during the preceding stage of infantile dependence. In particular,. It would seem to depend upon the degrees which have been established between the developing ego and its internalized objects.

The infant is completely dependent upon his object not only for his existence and physical well-being, but also for the satisfaction of his psychological needs. It is true, nonetheless, that mature individuals are likewise dependent upon one another for the satisfaction of their psychological, and, no less than their physical, needs. Nevertheless, on the psychological side, the dependence of mature individuals sufficient to render him dependent in an unconditional sense. We also notice that, whereas in the case of the adult object-relationship has a considerable spread, in the case of the infant it tends to be focussed upon a single object. The loss of an object is thus, much more devastating in the case of the infant. If a mature individual loses an object, least of mention, he still has some objects remaining. His eggs are not all in one basket. Further, he has a choice of objects and can desert one for another.

The infant, on the other hand, has no choice. He has no alternative but to accept or to reject his object—an alternative which is liable to present itself to him as a choice between life and death. His psychological dependence is further accentuated by the very nature of his object-relationship, for, as we have seen, this is based essentially upon identification. Dependence is exhibited in its most extreme form, in the intra-uterine state, and we may legitimately infer that on its psychological side this state is characterized by an absolute degree of identification. Identification may thus be regarded as representing the persistence into extrauterine life of a relationship existing before birth. In so far as, identification persists after birth. The individual's object constitutes not only his world, but also himself; and it is this fact, as has already been pointed out, that we must attribute the compulsive attitude of many schizoids and de repressive individuals toward their objects.

Normal development is characterized by a process whereby progressive differentiations of the object is accompanied by progressive decreases in identification. So long as infantile dependence persists, however, identification remains the most characteristic feature of the individual's emotional relationship with his object. Infantile dependence is equivalent to oral dependence—a fact which should be interpreted, not in the sens that the infant is inherently oral, but in the sense that the breast is the original object. During the oral phases, accordingly, identification remains the most characteristic feature of the individual's emotional relationship with his object. The tendency to identification, which is so characteristic of emotional relationships during these phases, also invade s the cognitive sphere, with the result that certain orally fixated individuals have only to hear of someone else suffering from any given disease in order to believe that they are suffering from it themselves. In the conative sphere, that identification has its counterpart in oral incorporation. And it is the merging of emotional identification with oral incorporation that confers upon the stage of infantile dependence its most distinctive feature. These features are based upon the fundamental equivalence for the infant of being held in his mother's arms and incorporating the contents of her breast.

The phenomenon of narcissism, which is one of the most prominent characteristics of infantile dependence, is an attitude arising out of identification with the object. Such that primary narcissism may be simply defined as just such a state of identification with the object, secondary narcissism being a state of identification with an object which is internalized. While narcissism is a feature common to both the early and the late oral phase, the latter phase differs from the former in virtue of a change in the nature of the object. In the early oral phase the natural object is the breast; but in the later oral phase, the natural object becomes the mother. The transition from one phase to the other is thus marked by the substitution of a whole object (or person) for a part-object. Nevertheless, the object continues to be treated as a part-object (the breast) with the result that the person of the mother becomes an object for incorporation. The transition from the early to the late oral phases is also characterized by the emergence of the biting tendency. Whereas in the early oral phase the libidinal attitude of incorporation monopolizes the field, in the late oral phase it is in competing with an accompanying attitude of biting. Now biting must be regarded for being essentially of all differentiated aggression. Consequently, the dawn of the late oral phase heralds the emergence of emotional ambivalence. The late oral phase is well described as pre-ambivalent. Nonetheless, one which aggression has not yet been differentiated from the libido. The early urge to incorporate is essentially a libidinal urge, to which true aggression makes no contribution, even as a component factor. The recognition of this fact is of the greatest importance for an understanding of the essential problem underlying schizoid states, and it is understanding. It is true that the incorporation urge is destructive in its gross effect, in the sense that the object which is eaten disappears. Nevertheless, the urge is not destructive in aim. When, as a child says that he 'loves' cake, it is certain to imply that the cake will vanish, and then consumingly destroyed. At the same time the destruction of the cake is not the aim of the child's 'love'. On the contrary, the disappearance of the cake is, from the child's point of view. A most regrettable consequence of his 'love' for it. What he really desires, is for himself, is to have his cake and eat it to. If the cake proves to be 'bad' he either differentiates to its splitting or unhinging of, in that, even he becomes sick. As this spiting out is specifically characteristic of the early oral phase, in that he rejects the bad cake, least of mention, he does not bite the cake with intentions for its being bad. This type of behaviour is specifically characterized of the early oral phasing, then, what is, so far as the object presents itself as 'moving apart', it is incorporated, and, presents itself as 'bad', it is rejected, but, even when it appears to be bad, no attempt is made to destroy it. Again, it is the good object that is 'destroyed.' Albeit only incidentally and not by intention. In the late oral phase the situation is foreign, in that things are done differently, for in this phase the object may be bitten as well as incorporated. This mean that a direct aggression, as well as libidinal forces, is such that may be directed toward the object. Hence the appearance of the ambivalence which characterizes the late oral phase.

It soon becomes evident that the emotional oral phase takes the form of the alternative that to incorporate or not to incorporate, i.e., 'to love or not to love.' This is the conflict underlying the depressive state. It will be seen, accordingly, that the problem of the schizoid individual is how to love without destroying by love, whereas, the greater of problems is for the depressive individual, is how to love without destroying by hate. These are two very different problems.

The conflict underlying the schizoid state is, of course, much more devastating than the conflict underlying the depressive stat e, and, since the schizoid reaction has its roots in an earlier stage of development than the depressive reaction, the schizoid individual is less capable of dealing with conflict than is the depressive. It is owing to these two facts that the disturbance of the personality found in schizophrenia is so much more profound than found in depression. The devastating nature of the conflict associated with the early oral phase lies in the fact that, if it seems a terrible thing for an individual to destroy his object by love. It is the great tragedy of the schizoid individual that it is his love which seems to destroy; and it is because his love seems so destructive that he experiences such difficulty in directing his libido toward objects outer reality. He becomes afraid to love, and therefore he erects barriers between his objects and himself. He tends both to keep his objects at a distance and to make himself remote from them. He rejects his objects, and at the same time, he withdraws his libido from them. This withdrawal of libidinal energies may be carried to all lengths. It may be carried to a point at which all emotional and physical contacts with other persons are renounced; and it may even go so far that all libidinal links with outer reality are surrendered. All interest in the world around fades and everything becomes meaningless. In proportion as libido is withdrawn from outer objects it is directed toward the internalization with its accompanied objects; and, in proportion as this happens, the individual becomes introverted. And, incidently, it is on the observation that this process of introversion is so characteristic on the onset of schizoid states that are themselves based on the conclusion that the introvert is essentially a schizoid. It is essentially in inner reality that the values of the schizoid are to be found. So far as he is concerned, the world of internalized objects is always encroaching upon the world of external objects; and in proportion as this happens his real objects become lost to him.

If loss of the real objects were the only trauma of the schizoid state the position of the schizoid individual would not be so precarious. It is necessary, nonetheless, to bear in mind the vicissitudes of the ego, which accompany loss of the object. Reference has already been made to the narcissism which results from an excessive libidinalization of internalized objects; and such narcissism is specially characteristic of the schizoid. Accompanying it, we invariably find an attitude of superiority which may manifest itself in consciousness to a varying degree as an actual sense of superiority. It should be of note, in that, this attitude of superiority is based upon an orientation toward internalized objects, and that in relation to objects in the world of outer reality the attitude of the schizoid is essentially one of inferiority. It is true, that the externally oriented inferiority may be masked by a façade of superiority, as based upon an identification of external with internalized objects. Nevertheless, it is invariably present, and it is evidence of a weakness in the ego. What chiefly compromises the development of the ego. In the case of the schizoid individual is the apparently insoluble dilemma which attends the direction of libido toward objects. Failure to direct libido toward the object is, of course, equivalent to loss of the object: But since, from the point of view of the schizoid, the libido is itself destructive, the object is equally lost when libido is directed toward it. It can thus readily be understood that, if the dilemma becomes sufficiently pronounced, the result is a complete impasse, which reduces the ego onto a state of utter impotence. The ego becomes quite incapable of expressing itself; and, in so far as this is so, its very existence become s compromised. This can be exemplified by the following, as: 'I can' t say anything. I have nothing to say. I'm empty. There's nothing of m e, . . . I feel quite useless; I haven' t don e anything. I've gone cold and hard; I don't feel anything . . . I can't express myself' I feel futile.' Such descriptions are well illustrated, not only the state of impotence to which the ego is compromised in the schizoid dilemma. The last quoted remark of this is, perhaps, as drawing attentions to the characteristic affect of the schizoid state: For the characteristic affect of the schizoid state is undoubtedly a sense of futility.

The libido may be withdrawn in varying degrees even from that part of the psyche which is, so to speak, nearest to external objects. It may be withdrawn from the realm of the conscious into the unconscious. When this occasions, the effect is as if the ego itself had withdrawn into the unconscious: But the actual position would seem to be that, when the libido deserts the conscious part of the ego (such as it is), the unconscious part of the ego is all that is left to behave as a functioning ego. In extreme cases the libido would seem to desert even the unconscious part of the ego and relapse into the primal id, leaving both surface only the picture with which Kraepelin has familiarize us in his account of the last phase of dementia præcox. Whether such a mass-withdrawal of the libido can properly be ascribe d to repression is a debatable question, although where the process is restricted to a withdrawal from object-relationships, it may give that impression. At any rate, the effectual withdrawal of the libido 'feels quite different' from that of simple repression. There can be no doubt, nonetheless, that withdrawal of the libido from the conscious part of the ego has the effect of relieving emotional tension and mitigating the danger of violent outbursts of precipitate action. There can be equally little doubt that much of the schizoid individual's anxiety really represents fear of such outbursts occurring. This fear commonly manifests itself as a fear of going insane or as a fear of imminent disaster. It is possible, therefore, that massive withdrawal of the libido has the significance of as desperate effort on the part of an ego threatened with repression of the basic impulse which urge the individual on to make emotional contacts. In the case of the schizoid, of course, these impulses are essentially oral impulses. It is when this effort is within measurable distance of succeeding that the individual begins to tell us that he feels as if there were nothing of him, or as if he had los t his identity, or as if he was dead, or as if he had ceased to exist. The fact is that in renouncing the libido the ego renounces the very form of energy which holds it together—and the ego thus becomes lost. Loss of the ego is the ultimate psychopathological disaster which the schizoid individual

559

is constantly struggling, with more or less success, too avert by exploiting all available techniques (including the transitional techniques) for the control of his libido. In essence, therefore, the schizoid state is not a defence, although evidence of the presence of defences may be detected in it. It represented the major disaster which may befall the individual who has failed to outgrow the early stage of dependence.

If the problem which confronts the individual in the early oral phase is how to love the object without destroying it by love, the problem which confronts the individual in the oral phase is how to love the object without destroying it by hate. Accordingly, since the depressive reaction has its roots in the late oral phase, It is the disposal of his hate, rather than the disposal of his love, that constitutes the difficulty of the depressive individual. The formidable as this difficulty is, the depressive is at any rate spared the devastating experience of feeling that his love is bad. Since his love, at any rate, seems good, he remains inherently capable of a libidinal relationship with outer objects in a sense in which the schizoid is not. His difficulty in maintaining such a relationship arises out of his ambivalence. This ambivalence in turn arises out of the fact that during the late oral phase, he was more successful than the schizoid in substituting direct aggression (biting) for simple rejection of the object. While his aggression has been differentiated, that, nonetheless, he has failed in some degree to achieve that further step in development which is represented by dichotomy of the object. This further step, had he taken it, would have enabled him to dispose of his hate by directing it, predominantly at least, toward the rejected object and he would have been left free to direct toward his accepted object love which was relatively unaccompanied by hate. In so far as he failed to take such a step, the depressive remains in that state which characterized his attitude toward his object during the late oral phase. His external object during that phase, of course, a whole object (his mother); and his libidinal attitude toward it was incorporative. The incorporated object to the depressive thus comes to be an undivided whole object, which he adopts an ambivalent attitude. The presence of such an inner situation is less disabling so far as outer adjustments are concerned than is the corresponding inner situation, in the case of the schizoid, for in the case of the depressive there is no formidable barrier obstructing the outward flow of libido. Consequently, the depressive individual readily establishes libidinal contacts with others; and, if his libidinal contacts with others appear satisfactory with others, and if his libidinal contacts are satisfactory to him, his progress through life may appear fairly smooth, as the inner situation is always present, and it is readily reactivated if his libidinal relationships become disturbed. Any such disturbance if his libidinal relationships become disturbed, such disturbances immediately calls into operation the hating element in his ambivalent t attitude; and, when his hate becomes directed toward the internalized object, a depressive reaction supervenes any frustration in object-relationships is, o f course, functionally equivalent to loss of the object. Whether partial or complete, since severe depression is so common a sequel to actual loss of the object (whether by the death of a loved person or things as severally otherwise). Loss of the object must be regarded as the essential trauma which provokes the depressive state.

Physical injury or illness is obviously represents himself, which is to say, that such a loss, e.g., the loss of an eye or a limb, represents the symbolic castration as taken that we no further, for it still remains to be explained why a reaction which is characteristically provoked by loss of the object should also b e provoked by loss of par t of the body. The true explanation lies in the fact that the depressive individual still remains to a are a distinctive feature of degrees to an actual state of infantile identification with his object. To him, is, therefore, bodily loss is functionally equivalent to loss of the object, and this equivalence is reinforced by the presence of an internalized object which, so speak, suffuses the individual's bod y and imparts it to narcissistic value.

A brief dispositional representation as the presentation for which of 'narcissism', is to mean, that the cathexis of the own 'self' with libido, is used in the term 'self' because the state of primary narcissism exists only prior to any ego differentiation, a point made by Hartmann. What is called the secondary narcissism is the late return of object cathexis to the own person.

There still remains to be explained are the phenomenon of Involutional melancholia. According to Freud and Abraham, the functional process in melancholia is the loss of the loved objects, the real, or some similar situation having the same significance, results in the object becoming installed within the ego. Owing, however, to an excess of cannibalistic impulses in the object, this introjection miscarries and the consequence is illness.

561

All the same, are those who tend to regard the etiology of this condition as entirely different from that of 'reactive depression', nonetheless, the two conditions have sufficiencies in common clinical standpoints, to justify, as to invoke the principle of, 'entia non sunt multicanda præter necessitate.' It is not really, but melancholia is by definition closely associated with the climacteric; and the climacteric would seem to be in itself evidence of a definite waning of libidinal urges. It cannot be said, nonetheless, that there is any equivalent diminution of aggression. The balance between the libidinal and the aggressive urges is thus disturbed, and, further, It is disturbed in the same direction as when the hate of any ambivalent individual is activated by loss of the object. Accordingly, in an individual of the depressive type the climacteric has the effect of establishing the same situation as does actual loss of the object where object-relationships are concerned; and the result is a depressive reaction. If the prospect of recovery in the case of Involutional melancholia is less hopeful than in cases of reactive depression, This is not difficult to explain: For, whereas the latter case a libido is still available for a restoration of the balance in the former case, it is not. Involutional melancholia is thus seen to conform to the general configuration of the depressive state, and it imposes upon as holding of no necessity to modify the conclusion already envisaged—that loss of the object is the basic trauma underlying the depressive state. As in the case of the schizoid state, this state is not a defence, on the contrary, it is a state against which the individual seeks to defend himself by means of such techniques (including the transitional techniques) as are available for the control of his aggression. It represents the major disaster which may befall the individual who failed to outgrow the late oral stage of infantile dependance.

We find ourselves confronted with two basic psychopathological conditions, each arising out of a failure in the past of the individual to establish a satisfactory object-relationship during the period of infantile dependence. The first of these conditions, by which the schizoid state, is associated with an unsatisfactory object-relationships during the early oral phase; and the second of these conditions, stem from or are directed in the depressive state, is associated with an unsatisfactory object-relationship during the early oral phase. It emerges quite clearly, however, from the analysis of both schizoid and depressive individuals that unsatisfactory object-relations hips during the early and late

562

oral phases, only give rise to their characteristic psychopathological effects when object-relationships continue to be unsatisfactory during the succeeding years of early childhood. The schizoid and depressive states must, accordingly, be regarded as dependent upon a regressive reactivation, during early childhood of situations arising, respectively, during the early and late oral phases. The traumatic situation in either case is one in which the child feels that he is not really loved. If the phase in which infantile object-relationships have been pre-eminent, this phase in which infantile object-relationships have been pre-eminently unsatisfactory, is the early oral phase, this trauma provides in the child a reaction conforming t to the idea that he is not loved because his own love is bad and destructive, and this reaction provides the basis for a subsequent schizoid tendency. If, the phase in which infantile object-relationships have been pre-eminently unsatisfied, as to a later idea that he is not loved because he presents of his badness and destructiveness, in that he is not loved because he presents of these distortions. This reaction provides the basis for a subsequent depressive tendency. Whether in any given case a schizoid or depressive state depends, in par t, of course, upon the circumstance which the individual is called upon to face in his later life But the most important determining factor is the degree to which objects have been incorporated during the oral phase. The various defensive techniques which characterize the transition period, i.e., the obsessional, paranoid, hysterical and phobic techniques. All represent attempts to deal with difficulties and conflicts attending object-relationships in consequence of the persistence of corporatised objects. These defensive techniques are accordingly seen to resolve themselves into differing methods of controlling an underlying schizoid or depressive tendency, and thus averting the onset of a schizoid or depressive state, as the case may be. Where a schizoid tendency is present, they represent methods designed to avert the ultimate psychopathological disaster which follows from loss of the ego, and, where a depressive tendency is present, they represent methods designed to avert the ultimate psychopathological disaster, in which follows from loss of the object.

It is so fortunate as to enjoy a perfect object-relationship during the impressionable period of infantile dependence, or for that matter during the transition period of infantile dependence. Consequently, no one ever becomes completely emancipated from the state of infantile dependence, or from some proportionate degree of oral fixation; and there is no one who has completely escaped the necessity of incorporating this early enacting of objects. It may consequently be inferred that there is present in everyone either an underlying schizoid or his underlying depressive tendency, according as it as in the early or in the late oral phase that difficulties chiefly attended infantile object-relationships. We are thus introduced to the conception that every individual may be classified as falling into one or two psychological types—the schizoid and the depressive. It is not necessary to regard these two types as having more than phenomenological significance, nevertheless, it is impossible to ignore the fact that in the determination of these two types some part may be played by a hereditary factor—such that the relative strength of the inborn tendencies of sucking and biting.

Of these, we are reminded of Jung's dualistic theory of psychological types. According to Jung, is, of course, the 'introvert' and the 'extravert' representation to the fundamental types, into the constitution of which psychopathological factors do not primarily enter. There is, however, another essentially dualistic conception of psychological types, with which a conceptual representation prolonging the conception with which is expounded by Kretschmer in his works entitled 'Physique and Character' and 'The Psychology of Men of Genius' and according to which the two basic psychological types are the 'schizothymic' and the 'cyclothymic'. As these terms they imply, the reverential inference of cyclothymic individuals, as predisposed to circular or manic-depressive psychoses, and the schizothymic individual to schizophrenia, there is thus, a striking agreement between Kretschmer's conclusions and explanations that are envisaged types—an agreement all the more striking since the envisaged types of alternative operatives. The only significant divergence between the two analytic approaches arises out of the fact that Kretschmer regards the temperamental differences between the types as based essentially upon constitution factors and attributes to the psychopathological propensities to this temperamental differences. Whereas in viewing the psychopathological factors used during the period of infantile dependence making of any rate a considerable contribution to the temperamental difference. The sufficient agreement between Kretschmer's views and those as provided some independent support for autonomously unconfined study, however, Kretschmer's views also provide some independent support or an underlying depressive tendency, as presented at some level in every individual, and that all individuals may be classified upon this basis, so, as far as their psychopathological propensities are concerned.

Every theory of basic types is inevitably confronted with the problem of 'mixed types'. Kretschmer freely acknowledges the existence of mixed types, and he explains their occasioned occurrence on the grounds that the incidence (and perhaps, hormonic) groups of factors, which it may be usually of some mixed types is to be explained not so much in terms of fixations in developmental phases. Where difficulties over object-relationships assert themselves pre-eminently during the early oral phase, a schizoid tendency is established, and, where difficulties over object-relationships assert themselves pre-eminently during the late oral phase, the establishment of a depressive tendency is the result. In so far, is that, nonetheless, that such difficulties are fairly distributed between the two phases, we may expect to find a fixation in the late oral phase superimposed upon one in the early oral phases, and in that case a deeper schizoid tendency will be found underlying a superimposed depressive tendencies, that such a phenomenon may occur admits of no doubt whatsoever, and even the most 'normal' person must be regarded as having persuasions toward schizoid potentialities at the deepest levels. It is open to equally little questions that even the most normal person may on certain circumstances become depressed. Similarly, schizoid individuals are not wholly immune to depression, and depressed individuals are sometimes grounded by displaying certain schizoid characteristics. Whether a depressive or a schizoid state will declare itself in any given case doubtless depends in part upon whether the precipitating circumstances take the form of the real object or of difficulties in object-relationships assuming in some other form; and where there is a fairly even balance between fixation in the early and the late phases. This may be the determining factor. Even so, the most important factor must always remain the degrees of regression, which is provoked; and this is determined primarily by the relative strength of fixation. In the last instance the degree of regression must depend upon whether the chief problem of the individualities that lies in the disposal of his love or in the disposal of his hate and there must be few individuals in whom the disposal of love and the disposal of hate are attended by equal difficulty.

When we use as primary source not our own clinical data but the experience and insights of other fields., We betray a sese of

RICHARD J. KOSCIEJEW

our unease. Such behaviour indicates that our understanding of the clinical phenomena or of the analytic theory that we adduce to interpret them is not as firmly based as we would want it to be. Thus, Altman (1977), after an erudite and charming discourse on the vicissitudes of love ends by saying, . . . the vicissitudes of love are so interrelated with every aspect of human development, its ambiguities so numerous and persuasive, that we may still be obliged to ask, 'What is this thing called love?'

Altman observed, for instance, that when psychoanalysts are asked about love, they respond as cultured lay people, rather than as professionals. They do no t couch their responses in the language of scientific psychology. This should make us aware that from the very beginning, psychoanalytic discussion of love has been burdened by the analyst's entailment in his own culture, in its values and its social structure. In Western society, love is put forward as the 'summum bonun' of human relations. All moral teaching whether founded in faith in the supernatural or not, sanctifies love. Dealing fairly with one's neighbour and curbing one's aggression toward others ultimately involve an essential compassionate attitude toward people, that is, a capacity for positively-tinged affective identification with others. Since love is sanctified and regarded as sacred, it falls within the realm of the taboo. Accordingly, objectivity may be inhibited and curiosity curbed when we attempt to study love scientifically. An analyze love, especially the creative, 'nonconflictual' aspects of the phenomenon, may even imply a certain degree of sacrilege, a desecration of what should be revered rather than understood, of what should e cherished rather than analysed.

The high moral value we place on loving strengthens the Superego's influence on how we treat the subject during therapy and how we conceptualize love scientifically. 'What's wrong with a good love relationship?' Essentially, it is a rhetorical question. We almost always take a good love relationship for granted. Such a question constitutes a moral rather than an intellectual challenge.

The most recent literature concerning the phenomenology of love has emphasized the importance of early object love. In large measure, this has been occasioned by the stage of interest in narcissistic character disorder, and the so-called borderline condition. The connection between loving and these conditions arising from the fact that identification and narcissistic object choice are common to all of them, investigation of the etiology,

566

therefore, has centered on the vicissitudes of the early mother-child as the matrix out of which identification and individuation are affected. Moreover, these are conditions in which vulnerability of self-esteem is of major significance. Freud (1914) placed variation of self-esteem in the centre of his discussion of falling in love and being in love, explaining the phenomenon in economic terms—in shifts of libidinal investment from the self-representation to the object-representation and back. According to object relations theorists, the nature of the earliest interaction between the child and the mother determines the quality of the child's subsequent love relationships. Bak (1973) states that falling in love is an attempt to undo the original separation from the mother, and Bergmann (1971) says, that love revived if not direct memories, then . . . archaic ego states that were once active in the symbiotic phase. He cites Mahler (1967) to the effect in the symbiosis is to be understood as 'hallucinatory of delusional, somatopsychic, omnipotence fusion with the representation of the mother. In other words, the state of being in love reactivates or reflects the state of object relations that prevailed before the distinction between the self and the object developed. During the symbiotic phase, fusion with the mother is supposedly experienced as unalloyed bliss, while separation is tantamount to its annihilation and death.'

It was connection with Feud's revolutionary approach to the subject of sex and love that he developed the concept of the object. Discussing the nature of the energy of the erotic drive, the libido, Freud (1905) distinguished between the zone of origin of the libido, the aim of the libidinal instinct that the libido as the object of the instinct. It is upon the object that the libido is discharged and this process of discharge is experienced as pleasure. He said that the object is the mental representation of something which is the source of intense libidinal gratification, something highly cathected with libido. The mental representation grows out of a mnemic image, a recollected set of sensory impressions accompanied by a pleasurable feeling, in that which, according to the dominant principle, one's wishful attempt to reconstitute as a sensory impression. Accordingly, the object may be the representation of something which is part of one's own person—the lips, skin. mouth, and so forth, for example—or, it may be the mental representation of something inanimate which at a certain stage of cognitive development is still regarded as par t of one's own person.

Fenichel (1945) observed that at particular stages in the child's development, the faecal mass is viewed sometimes as part of the self and sometimes as part of the external world. This is a striking parallel to Winnicott's (1953) concept of the transitional object. at a later stage the object may be an external representation of another person existing independently of the self. In each stag e of this development, it should be emphasized, we are dealing with a technical term, the concept of a mental representation. According to libido theory, it is no t the external thing which is vested with energy, It is the metal representation of the thing or person so cathected. The mental representation bears a special relationship to processes of instinctual discharge.

Emphasizing the representational aspect of the object highlights two kinds of confusion that pertains to the use of the object concept. The first of these confusions is shown by the theories of Wilhelm Reich (1942). Basing his views on Freud's earlier neurophysiological concept of the set or in the body of another person. This approach has perpetuated the confusion between what is internal and what is external. that is, where in the physical world the material libido is to be found. It disregards the fact that at all times we are dealing with a psychological experience, the mental representation of an object, a persistently 'internal' experience.

The second confusion is illustrated by the concept of a part object, as opposed to a whole object. Whatever it is that is represented mentally as instinctually cathected constitute an object. Instinctual wishes of an aggressive or libidinal nature may centre on mental representations of parts of one's own body, parts of someone else's body, or on mental representation of one's own or some other person's whole body. Any one of these may be taken as an object. The type of unconscious fantasy involved determines whether or not the person's body is regarded as a penis or whether the person as a whole is regarded as a breast or, as in the case of narcissistic object choice, whether another person is regarded as a representation of one's own self. When we make judgements about psychological experiences, whether for the purpose of clinical interpretation or a theory building, what we try to determine is the nature of the unconscious fantasy which underlies the thought or behaviour of the individual, either in regard to other persons or things or in regard to that individual (Arlow, 1969). In such fantasies of a real external person or, conversely, one's whole body in an unconscious fantasy may be conceived as a representation of one's own or someone else's penis, breast, or faeces. In any event, we are dealing with mental representations of an object in the sense as defined by itself, as whether that mental representation corresponds to the totality of another person' s body or to a part of one's own or another person 's body.

A consequence of the confusion, it may be observed in the tendency to use the term's interpersonal relations and object relations interchangeably. They are not identical. In fact, they represent two different realms of discourse. A young man, for example, disappointed in his beloved, does not search for a new object. he is really looking for another woman, who may in time become the source of pleasurable cathected mental representations. Fundamentally, it is the effect of unconscious fantasy wishes, connected with special mental representations of objects, that colour, distorts and affects between the person and the object. this is essentially the core of transference, in which the person in the real world is confused with a mental representation of a childhood object, a mental representation of what once was either a person or a thing. These issues are no t simply semantic ones. They bear directly on any discussions of love and narcissism and the role of object relation s in ego development.

According to Freud (1911), the operation of the pleasure principle is expressed through a tendency to reestablish and experience a se t of sensory perceptions of a pleasurable nature identical with the memory of earlier experience or pleasure. Thus, the first and fundamental categorization of experience is in terms of pleasant or unpleasant. (Brenner [1974], in his study, the development of affects, has demonstrated the fundamental role that this categorization plays in all subsequent affective structure.) This is t e abiding principle by which perceptions are integrated and organized in memory according to the quality of similarity with or differences from earlier memory traces. On the basis of how the memory of earlier perceptions has been organized, subsequent experience in interpreted metaphorically (Arlow, 1979) note once again, Freud (1925) wrote in, 'Negation':

. . . The function of judgement is concerned in the main with two sorts of decisions. It affirms or disaffirms the possession by a thing of a particular attribute; and it asserts or disputes that a presentation has an existence in reality. The attribute to be decided about may originally have been good or bad, useful or harmful. Expressed in the language of the oldest—the oral—instinctual impulses, the judgement is: 'I should like to eat this', or 'I should like to spit it out.' that is to say: 'I will be inside me;, or, 'It will be outside me.' The original pleasure-ego want is to introject into itself, such that everything that is good and to eject from itself everything that is bad. What is bad, what is alien to the ego and what is external are, to begin with, identical.

. . . The other sort of decision made by the function of judgement—as to the real existence of something of which there is a presentation (reality-testing)—is a concern of the definitive reality-ego, which develops out of the initial pleasure-ego. It is now no longer a question of whether what has been perceived (a thing) as a presentation can be rediscovered in perception (reality) as well. It is, we see, once more a question of external and internal. What is unreal, merely a presentation and subjective, is only internal; what is real is also there outside. In this stage of development regard for the pleasure has been set outside. experience has shown the subject has it is not only important whether a thing (an object of satisfaction for him) possesses the 'good' attribute and so deserves to be taken into his ego, but also whether it is there in the external world, so that he can get hold of it whenever he needs it. In order to understand this step forward we must recollect that all presentations or origin from perceptions is repetitions of them. Thus originally the mere existence of a presentation was a guarantee of the reality of what was presented. The antithesis between subjective and objective does not exist from the first. It only comes into being from the fact that thinking possesses the capacity to bring before the mind once more, something that has once been perceived, by reproducing it as a presentation without the external object having still to be there. The first and immediate aim, therefore, of reality-testing is, not to find an object in real perception which corresponds to the one presented, but to refined such an object, to convince oneself that it is still there.

We can see in this quotation from Freud that there is an all-pervasive series of equivalents which come to serve as the background for all judgements and interpretations of stimuli. What is pleasurable is at first treated as part of the self, and in keeping with the pleasure principle, the psychic apparatus operates toward trying to institute a repetition of these perceptions. It is not hard to understand how reality testing and the interpretations of sensory data, Functions acquire with such effort, and easily and readily set aside in the compulsive wishful strivings of dreams, fantasies, and neurotic symptoms, as well as under the influence of great passion or prejudice, and, of course, in love. The fundamental tendency to seek an identity of pleasurable perceptions goes far in explaining the persistent influence of unconscious childhood fantasies.

What is later organized and conceptualized as the need-gratifying object originates out of the memories of repetitive sensory impressions accompanied by feelings or gratification. Object seeking is predominantly oriented by the needs to try to achieve the identity of pleasurable perceptions remembered but dependently attained by infants. The disparity between infant's wishes and their limited capacity to achieve them in reality is a fundamental fact of human development connected with an external person become organize into a coherent memory structure, a mental representation of a person, which we call 'objects.' The term, object, therefore, represents a concept pertaining to a persistent, that is, a structural experience in parallel fashion a coherent organization of memory traces of representations connected with pain may serve as the basis for the concept of another kind of object representation. Thus, it happens that two sets of memories of sensory impressions may be organized as mental representations, one associated with pain, the other pleasure. The pleasant representation of such memories may be labelled as 'good', the unpleasant one's as 'bad.' It is in this sense that we can understand what the Kleians mean when they talk about 'good' objects and 'bad' objects in referring to the psychic events in the earliest months of life.

It is only later in the course of development that the seemingly disparate mental representations of objects having identical sensory impressions are fused into the concept of an external person whose mental representations psychologically may be vested or associated with memories of pain as well as pleasure. From a psychological point of view the individual's concept of a person is a conglomerate of many earlier object representations. This coherent, organized concept may be dissolved regressively into its antecedent object representations. It is not necessarily the re-emergence of an earlier structure, but rather the reactivation of memory traces of the good object representation that is distinct from the good object representation, thus, the splitting of the representation of a person does not necessarily occur only in case of severe personality regression. When there is a painful interaction between two people, one can observe in the dreams and fantasies of the patient how the qualities of good and bad become sharply dissociated in the mental representation of the object. the individual, in turn, may respond to the other person as if that person were the repetition of the earlier mental representation of the bad object. At the same time, such an individual may be functioning at an advanced level of mental development: The ease with which the coherent concept of the object may regressively dissolve into earlier separate mental representations is a measure of ego weakness. The tendency to split the object representations int a good and bad antecedent expressions are usually reversible. In severe pathology, however, the process is irreversible and the split of the object representation becomes fixed and persistent.

Mahler's (1975) concepts of separation-individuation and the observational base for these concepts have been well established. Her ideas are frequently invoked to explain certain phenomena observed on the borderline states, the psychosis, falling in love, and the experience of the orgasm. The stages prior to the phases of separation-individuation have been associated with the period of primary identification—the stage during which there is no differentiation between the self and the object. Regression to primary identification is a hypothesis which appeals to those who view a good segment of psycho pathology as reflecting a 'loss of boundaries' between the self and the object. According to some, this is the condition which is regressively reactivated in the psychopathological formations. However, it should of note, that feeling at one with something, being completely identified with someone, thinking that someone experiences and feels everything that another person seems to feel, is not necessarily a recapitulation of the vague, undefined state that precedes the distinction between the self and the object world. When poets describe the ecstasy of love or orgasm by saying that they feel completely united and indissolubly fused with the beloved, there is, nonetheless, some concomitant awareness of the existence of the other person as an independent object. This is equally true for descriptions of timelessness and the so-called 'oceanic' feeling, two states of mind often associated with being in love as well as with loss of the sens e of self or of 'ego boundaries.' In a study of distortions of the sense of time (Arlow, 1974, in that, the ability to demonstrate, from detailed presentations of the material of the analysis was not that of the fusion of self and object. ; in one instance, the fantasy expressed a woman's wish to have the oedipal love object forever. In the case of a male patient, it represented an overcoming of the fear of castration, a wish for immortality to counteract the pressing awareness off the danger of castration as represented by a fear of death.

Freud (1914), in his work titled 'On Narcissism' emphasized that in severe, regressive narcissistic disorders, there is not only a break with reality and withdrawal from objects of the external world, but at the same time, one is unable to find any trace of cathexis of mental representations of objects in fantasy, conscious or unconscious. It should be emphasized that it is not the clinical phenomenon of relations or withdrawal from people which indicate a break of object relations, but rather the evidence if withdrawal of cathexis from mental representations of objects. This is an important distinction to bear in mind: Otherwise one is tempted to make extrapolations from phenomenology without appreciating the characteristic feature of psychoanalysis, namely, the nature of the unconsciously psychological experience. It is possible for certain individuals to have very poor or few relations with people, but at the same time to maintain a very high quality of object constancy in fantasy life. One has to avoid judging the significance of an experience by externally observable phenomena alone.

After, at least a beginning attempt at individuation and after the phase of the transitional object, the different constellations of the memories of sensory experiences of pleasure and pain may be organized around the common source of perceptions into the concept of the good or bad mother, the good and bad object. One aspect of the child's growing ability to master ambivalence resides in the capacity too integrate the two contradictory concepts into a specific, unified concept of a person in the external world. Developmental psychologists differ as to exactly when this achievement is attained—probably sometimes in the second year of life. It is an attainment however that is easily and regularly undone by regression. The concept of the object, as well as the concept of the self and even of the Superego, may undergo regressive dissolution into their antecedent identifications. This may be observed and dreams and in psycho pathology, especially in patients suffering from depression, both in the borderline states and the psychoses.

The Superego is not a unified agency, is such, that, if closely observed, it can be seen top constitute an organization of contradictory trends based upon an attempt to integrate various impressions of experiences of judging a nd of having judged, of reward and punishment from objects. This agency of the mind is built up for the most part, by way of identification with objects in very specific contexts. The self-condemning prosecutory hallucinations observed in various forms of severe depression represent memories of fantasies, distorted, it is true, by the process of defence, but memories which have been regressively transformed into visual o r auditory perceptions. Under such circumstances, the delusional material regressively recapitulates, by way of identifications. The process reveals that the identifications in the Superego represent discrete, historic episodes, selective identification in terms of the individual's previous conflicts.

These considerations are important because identification plays a major role in object relations theory, especially as applied to love. Identifications, like object t relations, cannot be separated from drive derivatives. The two concepts are indissolubly of internalized object relations, but such object relations are part of a continuum of drive discharge. An identification is not effected with the totality of another person or object but with some specific aspect of the person's behaviour in a very specific context. The aspects of the individual's behaviour that are selected for purposes of identification are congruent with or correspond to certain specific drive needs of the individual. These may relate to Superego efforts directed toward self-punishment.

With these considerations concerning the development of the object concept and object relations in mind, are turned, once, again, to the psychology of love.

The realization of dealing essentially with the differentiated patterns of object choice, we are struck by the dramatic compulsive quality with which certain, but buy no means all, individuals from other repetitive, seemingly compulsive, uncontrollable, unstable compromise formation effected by the three psychic agencies in other normal and pathological processes—for example, symptom formation., dreams, perverse impulses? The varieties of loving is surely as diverse as the varieties of psychopathological formations, as well as the varieties of normal compromise reaction. From this point of view it is difficult to agree completely with Bak (1973) or Bergmann (1971), who try to trace the psychology of loving to a specific developmental vicissitude, the wish to re-achieve symbiotic fusion with the mother in order to undo the primordial separation. This early vicissitude of object relations must have some bearing on the patterns of loving, but while it is pertinent, it is not necessarily decisive.

The great diversity of patterns of loving can be illustrated from the experience in any analyst's practice. There is a rich literature ranging from Freud's studies in the psychology of love to the more recent discussions of self-object narcissistic choice. Freud (1917) 'Taboo of Virginity' is important in one special way, inasmuch as it illustrates the aggression in the choice of the love object and in the pattern of loving. The same principles apply to object choices made in certain of the sexual perversions. But the truly complex nature of the pattern of loving and object choice can best be shown by the study of individual patients.

In any individual it is possible to observe different patterns of loving and varieties of object choice, for example, the typical oedipal evolution of the patient traumatized by the primal scene who develops a persistent unconscious rescue fantasy together with a need for a degraded love object. A concomitant persistent wish may be to wreak vengeance upon surrogates for the betraying, unfaithful mother. Furthermore, in response to the fear of castration generated by the anticipation of retaliation for hostile wishes against the father. The same individual may develop a pattern of passive, submissive, feminine orientation toward men. In such a patient a variety of patterns of loving and object choices toward members of both sexes, characterized by patterns of instinctual gratification that represented both aim-inhibited and aim-fulfilled wishes. In derivatives of several types of unconscious fantasies, representing wishes derived from different moments in his relations to the important objects of, his past, the patient identified himself with different objects—his father, his mother the crucified Christ, certain figures from mythology and fairy tales.

Each identification found expression in some form of loving. The identifications were the vehicles for drive derivatives, part of an unconscious fantasy of being either the father, the sexual partner of the father, or some conqueror: His patterns of loving relations with both men and women were determined by the nature of the persistent unconscious fantasies. Loving involves identification, but identification at many levels and at many different times with different objects. It is not necessarily a regressive reactivation of the primitive fusion with a love object or regression to a phase where there is no distinction between the self and the object world.

Within the analytic situation closer examination of the phenomenon of love demonstrates how certain aspects of the real person and of the self are rigorously excluded in the sense of oneness. What is experienced is determined by a fantasy or a se t of wishes centring about specific mental representations deriving from selected memories of experiences with the earlier object or objects—the father, the mother, and in the unusual cases, oneself or parts of one's body.

By way of comparison, one may observe another patient, in whom there were several distinct patterns of love relations. He was, first of all, a very successful Don Juan who typically won. Seduced, and then abruptly dropped his partner. The abruptness with which he terminated these relationships was parallel by the urgent intensity with which he pursued them in the beginning. If one concentrated only on the opening phases of his relationships, he would seem to epitomize the romantic ideal of the love-intoxicated, heartsick young swan. In these affairs, however, the culmination of the relationship was represented not by the successful libidinal gratification, but rather by the gratification of aggression directed toward the women, the promiscuous, disappointing oedipal and post-oedipal mother, but also an abandoning nursemaid who had abruptly left the family's employment when the patient was three and a half years of age.

In contrast, the same patient also had long-lasting devoted sexual attachments to older women, relationships that were regularly stormy, but compulsively maintained, remarkably ambivalent and characterized by vehement mutual recriminations. These relationships recapitulated a clandestine affair he had with a housekeeper-nursemaid., an affair that lasted through the oedipal and latency periods and parallelled in time the disillusioning experiences with his mother. The parallel's love relations with older women were sadomasochistic in quality and articulated specific forms of anal-erotic gratification that could be traced to the character of the housekeeper-nursemaid. Residue of this attachment could be seen in the aim-inhibited love relationship he had with his secretary. A much older women, as well as in the nature of his character structure, which reflected an identification with the clandestine lover through the compulsive and behaviour he pursued in identification with her. The active, phallic nature of this women undoubtedly predisposed the patient to make subsequent oedipal and post-oedipal object choices of women who were active and sensual and whose behaviour corresponded to his fantasy of the women possessing a penis. The Don Juan behaviour was multiple, and determined of a mixture of the fulfilment of erotic and aggressive impulses, an identification with the faithless, promiscuous mother, the abandoning love object, together with elements of defence against castration anxiety. while much more could be said about the determinants of the specific and complex patterns of loving in this case, however, it clearly illustrates the complicated interrelationship of identifications, defence, object relations, and instinctual gratification, all of which play a role in determining the nature of the patient's love. It would be impossible to reduce the plexuity of object-finding and gratification to any of the simple basic formulas proposed by several of the proponents of object relations theory.

The subject of identification quite naturally leads to the topic of the internalization of object relations. This is a concept which is very difficult to differentiate from identification. Does it mean more than the fact that the personality or psychic structure of an individual is transformed as the result of his or her interaction with others? Or do internalized object relations imply the positing of a persistent structure in the psychic apparatus which has a dynamic thrust of its own, a thrust to repeat and reproduce the original experience in a way that is independent of the drive representation? Is there a developmental thrust which asserts itself along predetermined lines through a hierarchical distinction in stages, beginning with the earliest relation and progressing toward an ideal endpoint, commonly known as the mature or genital form of object relationships, which presumably leads to the 'highest' stage of love? The discoursing dialogue concerning the internalization as to the object relations theory and love, it seems that this developmental eventuality is considered as the 'crucial element' of true love.

It would seem that, however surreptitiously, elements of value judgements infiltrate analytic considerations of love. this is a trend which can be traced to the early history of psychoanalysis. It is difficult to avoid a tendency to judge psychological phenomena in terms that essentially mean 'good' or 'bad'. Some such tendency may be discerned in Abraham's (1924) study of the development of the libido. Abraham evaluated the nature of love relationships in terms of biology. The quality of the libidinal tie with any individual, he maintained, is determined by the level of psychosexual development which it reflects the development of sexuality evolved in precise stages and subdivisions by way of a normal, orderly succession of dominance by oral, and phallic instinctual drives. The nature of the object chosen was determined by the drive dominant at that particular stage when the choice was made. The highest stage of development, the mature form of love, was genital love. By way of contrast, choices effected at the pregenital level, Abraham considered the pre-ambivalent or ambivalent, a quality which offered poor prognostic outcome because it conveyed the potentiality for conflict and neurosogenesis. genital love, in it post-ambivalent form, and typified, no t at all surprising, in those qualities which society regards as both desirable and commendable in the relationship between two people of the opposite sex. To be sure, these qualities have unquestioned social utility, in so far as they strengthen the ties which make for a stable marriage and foster the solidarity of the family, the basic unit of society. from society's point of view an ideal post-ambivalent genital relationship is desirable, useful, and therefore 'good.'

Today, more than half a century later, the terminology and leading conceptualizations may have changed, but the problem remains the same. Formulations are now couched in terms of object relations instead of biology. The distinctions between the self and the object world have become the touchstones. Instead of an orderly, biological predetermined succession of libidinal stages, what is emphasized today is the developmental evolution of an orderly set of stages of object relations.

According to Friedman (1978), this process is considered by many to be equally predetermined as an inexorable developmental thrust, much in the same spirit as Abraham's formulation concerning libidinal phases and the concomitant object choices. While Abraham emphasized the developmental aspects of libidinal drive over the nature and vicissitudes of experience with the object, more recent formulations in terms of object relations theory tended to emphasize the vicissitudes of experience with the object, as well as the resultant cognitive and affective consequences. Thus, certain authors maintain that true love is possible only by culture. In our daily work with patient's, we are constantly passing judgement on whether the patient' s affective response is in keeping with, i.e., appropriate to, of his or her experience. We make such judgements in terms of standards relevant to our culture and to the individual's background. Cultural ambience influences not only how love is expressed, but also how it is experienced. the cultural influence may transcend the specific set of interactions characteristic of the relation s with the infantile love object. The fusion of the tender and the sensuous steams of the libidinal impulse and the idealization of the love object

Nonetheless, we face a dilemma. One contributor to the psychology of love from the point of view of object relations that love represents a re-emergence of the earliest, mo t primitive mother-child relationship. While another asserts that love reflects the most developed, most mature form of object relations.

All the same, as analysts, we pass judgement on the phenomenology of love we observe in our patients, we do so in terms of phase-specific anticipations, for example, we accept but hardly ever really analyze reports of impulsive patterns of loving that patients present concerning the adolescent scene. We relate this to the clearly patient psychological transformations of puberty, as we may look disapprovingly at the middle-aged man, and certainly at an elderly man, who falls in love following the adolescent pattern. In the same spirit, one has to note the social bias against older women having liaison with younger men; the reverse pattern is more acceptable. these are subtle, but definitive value judgements as couched in term s of normal, that is, statistical anticipations. Unconsciously, they dictate to us what and how we choose to analyze.

In actual practice we are concerned with what has keep a particular patient to love in her or his particular way; how, among the myriad patterns of love, the patient has come to select the one he or she actually did choose. How well we are able to determine this depends in large measure upon how close the distance is between the choice of object and the pattern of loving, and the central nexus of the patient's unconscious conflicts. the consequences of conflict make it possible for us to analyze the nature of the love relationship, but in those instances in which the pattern of loving is ego-syntonic, but have less of an opportunity to penetrate deeply into the psychology of loving and are therefore, not in a very good position to grasp some understanding of the precursors of the particular patterns of loving. Under such circumstances, the temptation is greatly interpretive, as only to speculate phenomenologically than dynamically. What we do, in effect, is conjecture on the bias of history about what might have been the individuals psychological experience, since we seem unable to trace out the interpretational inferentially from the data in the dynamic context of the analytic situation.

In practice, we deal with how the individual comes to choo s someone to love and how this love is expressed. This is a complex process involving the integration of the individual's total experience. I t is usually organized in terms of a few leading, unconscious fantasies which dominate an individual's inherent perceptions of the world and create the mental set by which she or he perceives and interpret their individual experience.

The existing stage during which there is no differentiation between the self and the object, of which appeals to those who view a good segment of psycho pathology as reflecting a 'loss of boundaries', that, between the self and the object. Often associations for being in love as well as with loss of the sense of self of or of 'boundaries' the overwhelming sense of time, that form detailed presentations on the material derivatives, is that of the sensations as warranted within the paradigms of the 'timelessness' of an unconscious continuum. It should be noted that feeling at one with something, being completely identified with someone, thinking that someone experiences and feels everything that another person seems to feel, is not necessarily a recapitulation of the vague, undefined state that precedes the distinction between the self and the object world.

According to Freud and Abraham, the fundamental process in melancholia is the loss of the loved object. The real loss of a real object, or some similar situation having the same significance, resulting in the object becoming installed within the ego. Owing, however, to an excess of cannibalistic impulses in the subject, this introjection miscarries and the consequence is illness.

Now, why is it that the process of introjection is so specific for melancholia? Perhaps, that the main difference between incorporation in paranoia and in melancholia is connected with changes in the relation of the subject to the object, though it is also a question of a change in the constitution of the introjecting ego. But, according to Edward Glover, the ego, at first but loosely organized, consists of a considerable number of ego-nuclei. In his view, in the first place an oral ego-nucleus and later an oral ego-nucleus predominate over the other. In this ver y early phase, in which oral sadism plays a prominent part and which it seems the basis of schizophrenia, the ego's power of identifying itself with its objects is as yet small, partly because it is itself still uncoordinated and partly because the introjected objects are still mainly partial objects, which it equates with fæces.

In paranoia the characteristic defences are chiefly aimed at annihilating the 'persecutor,' while anxiety on the ego's account occupies a prominent place in the picture. As the ego becomes more fully organized, the internalized imagos will approximate more closely to reality and the ego will identify itself more fully with 'good' objects. The dread of persecution, which was at first felt on the ego's account, now relates to the good object as well and from now on preservation of the good object is regarded as synonymous with the survival of the ego.

The combinality with this development goes a change of the highest importance, namely, from a partial object-relation to the relation to a complete object, through this step the ego arrives at a new position, which forms the foundation of that situation called the 'loss of the love object.' Not until the object is loved as a whole can it loss is felt as a whole.

With this change in the relation to the object, new anxiety-contents make their appearance and a change takes place in the mechanisms of defence. The development of the libido also is decisively influenced. Paranoid anxiety, lest the objects sadistically destroyed should themselves be a source of poison and danger inside the subject's body, causing him, in that, in spite of the vehemence of his oral-sadistic onslaughts, at the same time to be profoundly mistrustful of them yet, incorporating them.

This leads to a weakening of oral fixations. One manifestation of this may be observed in the difficulties very young children often show in regard to eating, which, in all probability, have a paranoid root. As a child (or an adult) identifies himself more fully with a good object. The libidinal urges increase as he develops a greedy love and desire to devour this object and the mechanism of introjection is reinforced. Besides, he finds himself constantly impelled to repeat the incorporation of a good object partly because he dreads that he has forfeited it by his cannibalism—i.e., the repetition of the act is designed to test the reality of his fears of the internalized persecutors against whom he requires a good object to help him. Nonetheless, the ego is more than ever driven both by love and by the need to introject the object.

Another stimulus for an increase of introjection is the phantasy that the loved object may be preserved in safety inside oneself. In this case the dangers of the inside are projected onto the external world.

If, however, consideration for the object increases, and a better acknowledgement of psychic reality sets in, the anxiety least the object should be destroyed in the process of introjecting it leads—as Abraham has described—to various disturbances of the function of introjection.

Furthermore, a deep anxiety as to the dangers which await the object inside the ego. It could not be safely maintained there, as the inside is felt to be a dangerous and poisonous place in which the loved object would perish. Its own obviousness shows one of the situations which can be described as fundamental for 'the loss of the loved object,' the situation, namely, when the ego becomes fully identified with its good, internalized objects, and at the same time becomes aware of its own incapacity to protect and preserve them against the internalized, persecuting objects and the id. This anxiety is psychologically justified.

For the ego, when it becomes fully identified with the object, it does mot abandon its earlier defence mechanisms. According to Abraham's hypothesis, the annihilation and expulsion of the object—processes characteristic of the earlier anal level—initiate the depressive mechanism. If this is so, it confirms the notion of the genetic connection between paranoia and melancholia. Yet, the paranoiac mechanism of destroying the objects (whether inside the body or in the outside world) by every means which oral, urethral and anal base of sadism can command, persist, but in a lesser degree and with a certain modification due to the dread and least of the good object as it should be expelled along with the causes to the mechanisms of expulsion and projection to lose value. However, the ego makes a greater use of introjection of the good object as a mechanism of defence. This is associated with another important mechanism: That of making reparation to the object.

While, at the same time the existence of this internal world is being depreciated and denied. Both in children an in adults are founded to such infinitive varieties,. Where obsessional neurosis was the most powerful factor in cases, as mounting of such mastery and betokens of a forceful separation of two (or more) objects, to methods more violent, that is to say, the objects were killed but since the subject was omnipotent, it was supposed that he could immediately call them to life again. But the killing corresponded to the defence-mechanism (retained from the earlier phase) of destruction of the object. in this position, the ego effects a similar compromise in its relation to real objects,. the hunger for objects, so characteristic of mania, indicates that the ego has retained one defence-mechanism of the depressive position: The introjection of good objects. The manic subject denies the different forms of anxiety associated with this introjection (anxiety that is to say, least of either, such that he should introject bad objects or else destroy his good objects by the process of introjection); his denial related not merely to the impulses of the id, but to his own concern for the object's safety. Thus, we may suppose that the process by which mania is as follows. The ego incorporates the object in a cannibalistic way (the 'feast', as Freud calls it in his account of mania) but denies that it feels any concern for it. 'surely,' argues the ego: It is not a matter of such great importance if this particular object is destroyed. there are so many others to be incorporated. This disparagement of the object's importance and the contempt for it is, in that of a specific characteristic of mania and enables the ego to effect that of a partial detachment which we observe side by side with its hunger for objects. Such detachment which the ego cannot achieve in the depressive position, represents an advance, a fortifying of the ego in relation to its objects,. but this advance is counteracted by the regressive mechanisms described which the ego at the same time employs in mania.

583

Even so, that in this case, when depression came to the fore in full force and the paranoid anxieties diminished, the hypochondriacal anxieties became related to the internalized loved objects and (thus) to the ego, while before they had been experienced in reference to the ego only.

After having attempted to differentiate between the anxiety-contents, feelings and defences at work in paranoia and those in the depressive states, whereby upon viewing the depressive state as based on the paranoid state and genetically derived from it. Wherefore, the depressives state as the result of a mixture of paranoid anxieties and of those anxiety-contents, distressed feelings and defences which are connected with the impending loss of the whole loved object. It seems to me that to introduce a term for those specific anxieties and defences might further the understanding of the structure and nature of paranoia. As well as of the manic-depressive states.

Whenever a state of depression exits, is it in the normal, the neurotic, in manic-depressives or in mixed cases, there is always in this specific grouping of anxieties or in mixed cases, the distressed feelings and different varieties of these defences, but, if this point proves convincing, we should be able to understand those very frequent cases where we are presented with a picture of those of the mixed paranoiac and depressive trend's, since we could then isolate the various elements of which it is composed.

For, in as much as now, it is true, that good and bad objects are more clearly differentiated, the subject's hate is directed rather against the latter, while his love and his attempt at reparation are more focussed on the former; but the excess of his sadism and anxiety acts as a check to this advance in his mental development. Every external or internal stimulus, e.g., every real frustration, is fraught with the utmost danger, not only bad objects but also, the good ones are thus menaced by the id, for every access of hate or anxiety may temporarily abolish the differentiation and thus result in a ';loss of the loved object.' And it is not only the vehemence of the subject's uncontrollable hatred but that of his love too, which imperils the object. for at this stage of his development, loving an object and devouring it is very closely connected., a little child which believes her (whether from motives of love or of hate) is tormented by anxiety both her and for the good mother which it has absorbed into itself.

It now becomes plain why, at this phase of development, the ego feels itself constantly menaced in its possession of internalized goo d objects. It is full of anxiety least such objects should be terminated and vanquished, however, both children and adults suffering from depression.

From the very beginning both psychic development there is a constant correlation of real objects with those installed within the ego. It is fo r this reason that the anxiety which is described by their manifestation to itself that, in a child's exaggerated fixation to its mother or whoever looks after it. The absence of the mother in the child's anxiety, least it should be handed over to bad objects, external and internalized, either because of her death or because of her return in the guise of a 'bad' mother.

Both cases signify to it that it has lost its loved mother and as the internalize d object becomes a perpetual source of anxiety, least the real mother should perish, though every experience which suggests the loss of the real beloved object, for what stimulates the dread of losing the internalized one too.

That the loss of the loved object takes place during that phase of development in which the ego makes the transition from partial to total incorporation of the object, nonetheless, the processes which subsequently become defined as 'loss of the loved object' are determined by the subject's sense of failure (during weaning and in the periods which precede and follow it) to securer his good, internalization for its object, i.e., to posses himself of it. One reason for his failure is that he has been unable to overcome his paranoid dread of internalized persecutor

Deep within this particular station, a point as spatially occupying of space and time. Such that, at this point we are confronted with a question of importance for our whole theory. Simply of the direction as influenced by the early processes of introjection upon both normal and pathological development, in that of the very epoch-making, in some respects other, than has hitherto commonly been accepted in psychoanalytic circles.

According to our views, even the earliest incorporated object's from the basis of the Superego and enter into its structure. The question is by no means a merely theoretical one. As we study the relations of the early infantile ego to its internalized objects and to the id, and come to understand the gradual changes these relations undergo, we obtain a deeper insight into the specific anxiety-situation through which the ego passes and the specific defence-mechanisms which it develops as it becomes more highly organized. Viewed from this standpoint in our experience we find that we arrive at a more complete understanding of the earliest phases of psychic development, especially of the structure of the Superego and of the genesis of psychotic diseases. For which we deal with etiology, it seems essential to regard the libido-disposition not merely as such, but also to consider it in connection with the subject's earliest relations to his internalized and external objects, a consideration which implies an understanding of the defence-mechanisms development by the ego gradually in dealing with its varying anxiety-situations.

If by the greater of chances, we accept this view of the formation of the Superego, its relentless severity in the case of the melancholic becomes more intelligible. The persecutions and demands of bad internalized objects; the attacks of such objects upon one another (especially that is represented by the sadistic coitus of the parents); the urgent necessity to fulfil the very strict demands of the 'good objects' and to protect and placate them within the ego, with the resultant hatred of the id; the constant uncertainty as to the 'goodness' of a good object, which causes it so readily to become transformed into a bad one—all these factors combine to produce in the ego a sense o f being a prey to contradictory and impossible claims from within, a condition which is felt as a bad conscience. That is to say, the earliest utterances of conscience are associated with persecution by bad objects. The very word 'gnawing of conscience' or 'biting the stone of conscience-ness' (Gewissensbisse) testifies to the relentless 'persecution' of conscience and to the fact that is originally conceived of as devouring its victim.

Among the various internal demands which go to make up the severity of the Superego in the melancholic, least of mention, is the urgent need to comply with the very strict demands of the 'good' objects. It is this part of the picture only—namely, the cruelty of the 'good', i.e., loved, objects within—which has been recognized hitherto by general analytic opinion, namely, in the relentless severity of the Superego in the melancholic. But in view, it is only by looking at the whole relation of the ego to its fantastically bad objects as well as its good objects, only by looking at the whole picture of the internal situation which of having tried to outline, such that we can understand the slavery to which the ego submits when complying with the extremely cruel demands and admonitions of its loved object which has become installed within the ego, least of mention, the ego endeavours to keep the good apart from the bad, and the real from the unreal objects. The result is a conception of extremely bad and extremely perfect objects that is to say. Its loved objects are in many ways intensely moral and exacting. At the same time, since the ego cannot really keep its good and bad objects apart in its mind, some of the cruelty of the bad objects and of the id becomes related to the good objects and this then again, increase the severity of their demands. These strict demands serve the purpose of supporting the ego in its fight against its uncontrollable hatred and its bad attacking objects, with which the ego is partly identified. The stronger the anxiety is of losing the loved objects, the more the ego strives to save them, and the harder the task of restoration becomes the gruelling labours will grow the demands for which are associated with the Superego.

The anxiety and feeling of suffering are of a much more complex nature, the preservation of the good internalized objects with whom the ego is identified as a whole. The anxiety, least of mention, is the good object and with them the ego should be destroyed, o r that they are in a state of disintegration, is interwoven with continuous and desperate efforts to save the good objects both with internalization and externalization.

Nonetheless, it seems that only when the ego has introjected the object as a whole and has established a better relationship to the external world and to real people is it able fully to realize the disaster created through its sadism and especially through its cannibalism, and to feel distress about it. This distress is related not only to the past but to the present as well, since at this early stage of development the sadism is in full swing. It needs a fuller identification with the loved objects, and a fuller recognition of its value, for the ego to become aware of the state of disintegration to which it has reduced and is continuing to reduce its loved objects. the ego then finds itself confronted with the physical fact that its loved objects are in a state of dissolution—in bits—and the despair. remorse and anxiety deriving from this recognition are at the bottom of numerous anxiety-situations, for examples, that of how to pick out the good bits in the right way and at the right time, also, how to pick out the good bits and do away with the bad ones, and, in addition, how to bring the object to life when it has been away with the bad ones, as well as to say, how to bring the object to life when it has been put together and there is the anxiety for being interfered within this task by bad objects and by one's own hatred, and so on.

Anxiety-situations of this kind are found to be the bottom not only of depression, but of all inhibitions of work. The attempts to save the loved object, to repair and restore it, attempts which in the state of depression are coupled with despair, since the ego doubts its capacity to achieve this restoration, are determining factors for all sublimation and the whole of the ego-development. It appears that the desire for 'what is perfection' is rooted in the depressive anxiety of disintegration which is thus of great importance on all sublimations. Nevertheless, the ego comes to a realization of its love for a good object, a whole object and in addition a real object, together with an overwhelming feeling of guilt toward it. Full identification with the object based on libidinal attachment, first to the breast, then to the whole person, goes hand in hand with anxiety for it (of its disintegration), with guilt and remorse, with a sense of responsibility for preserving it against persecutors and the id, and with sadness relating to expectations of the impending loss of it. These emotions, whether conscious or unconscious, are in view between the essential and fundamental elements of the feeling we call love.

In this connection, brings much similarity with the self-reproaches of the depressive which represent reproachment against the object. But to my mind the ego's hate of the id, which is overbearing in this phase, account is even more for its feelings of unworthiness and despair than do its reproaches against the object. Finding only that these reproaches and the hatred against bad objects are secondarily increases as a defence against the hatred of the id, which is even more unbearable. In the last analysis it is the ego's unconscious knowledge that the hatred, also there as the love, that it may at any time get the upper hand (the ego's anxiety of being carried away by the id and so destroying the loved object), which brings about the sorrow, feelings of guilt and despair which underlies grief. This anxiety is also responsible for the doubt of the goodness of the loved object. As Freud has pointed out, doubt is in reality a doubt of one's own love and 'a man who doubts his own love may, or rather must, doubt ever lesser things.'

The paranoiac, has also introjected a whole and real object, but has not been able to achieve a full identification with it, or, if he has got as far as this, he has not been able to maintain it. To mention a few of the reasons which are responsible for this failure: The persecution-anxiety is too great; suspicions and anxieties of a fantastic nature stand in the way of a full and stable introjection of good object and a real one. In so far as it has been introjected, there is little capacity to maintain it as a good object, since doubt and suspicion of all kinds will soon turn the loved object again into a persecutor. Thus, his relationship too whole objects and to the real world is still influenced by his early relation to internalized part-objects and fæces as persecutors and may again give way to the latter.

It seems characteristic of the paranoiac that, though, on account of his persecution-anxiety and his suspicions, he develops a very strong and acute power of observation and the external world and of real objects, since his persecution-anxiety makes him look at people mainly from the point of view of whether they are persecutors or not. Where the persecution-anxiety for the ego is in the ascendant, a full and stable identification with another object, in the sense of looking at it and understanding it as it really is, and full capacity for love, are not possible.

Another important reason why the paranoiac cannot maintain his whole-object relation is that while the persecution-anxiety and the anxiety for himself are still so strongly in operation that he cannot endure the endure additional burden of anxieties for a loved object and, besides, the feelings of guilt and remorse which accompany this depressive position. Moreover, in this position he can make far less use of projection, for fear of expelling his goo d objects and so losing them, accountably for reasons for fear of injuring good external objects by expelling what is bad from within himself.

Thus, we see that the suffering connected with the depressive position thrust him back to the paranoiac position. Nevertheless, though he has retreated from it, the depressive position has been reached and, therefore, the liability to depression is always there. This accounts, for the fact that we frequently meet depression along with severe paranoia as well as in milder cases.

If we compare the feelings of the paranoiac with those of the depressive in regard to disintegration, one can see that characteristically the depressive is filled with sorrow and anxiety for the object, which he would strive to unite again into a whole, while to the paranoiac the piece is growing agin into a persecutor. this conception of the dangerous fragments to which the object is reduced seems as to be, in keeping with the introjection of part-objects which equates with fæces (Abraham), and with the anxiety of a multitude of internal persecutors to whom the introjection of many part-objects and the multitude of dangerous fæces gives rise.

Let us now consider the hypochondriacal symptoms in this comparative way, the pains and other manifestations which in phantasy result from the attacks of internally bad object s within against the ego are typically paranoid. The symptoms which derive from the internal warfare in which the ego is identified with the suffering of the good objects, are typically depressive.

For instance, a patient who has been told as a child that he had tapeworm (which he himself never saw) connected the tapeworm within side him with his greediness. In his analysis, however, he had phantasies that a tapeworm was eating its way through his body and a strong anxiety of cancer came to the fore. The patient, who suffered from hypochondriacal and paranoid anxieties, was very suspicious of such things as oriented within his immediate environment, and, among other things, suspected of his surrounding surfaces for being allied with people who were hostile toward him. At this time he dreamed that a detective was arresting a hostile and persecuting person and putting this person in prison. However, when the detective proved unreliable and became the accomplice of the enemy. The detective stood for purposes as gaining in something as externally placed of the whole anxiety for which was internalized, nd was also connected with the tapeworm phantasy. The prison in which the enemy was kept was his own internalization—actually the special part of his inside where the persecutor was to be confined, as the dangerous tapeworm (one of his associations was that the tapeworm is bisexual) represented the two parents in a hostile alliance (actually in intercourse) against him.

At the sam e time the tapeworm phantasies were being analysed the patient developed diarrhea which—as he wrongly thought—was mixed with blood. This frightened him very much; he felt it as a confirmation of dangerous processes going on inside him. This feeling was founded in the phantasies in which he attacked his bad united parents in his insides, with poisonous extracts,. the diarrhea meant to him of poisonous extracts, as well as the bad penis of his father. The blood which he thought was his fæces represented the exteriority of foreign bodies (as, this was shown by association s in which had connected with blood). Thus, the diarrhea was felt to represent dangerous weaponry, with which he was fighting bad internalization, as to the parents, as well as his poisoned and broken-up parents themselves. In his early childhood he had in phantasy attacked his real parents with poisonous excreta and actually disturbed them in having intercourse by defecating. Diarrhea had always been something very frightening to him. Along with these attacks on his real parents this whole war-far became internalized and threatened his ego with destruction. Briefly to note, that this patient remembered during his analysis that at about ten years of age, he had definitely felt that he had a little man inside of his stomach who controlled him and gave him orders, which he, the patient, had to execute, although they were always perverse and wrong (he had, had similar feelings about his real father).

When the analysis progressed and distrust in the analyst had diminished as the patient became very much concerned about the him. He had always worried about his mother's health, but he had not been able to develop real love toward her, though he did his best to please her. Now, together with the concern for therapist, strong feelings of love and gratitude came to the fore, together with feelings of unworthiness, sorrow and depression. The patient had never felt really happy, his depression had been spread out, one might say, over his whole life, but he had not suffered from actual depressive states. In hi s analysis he went through phantasies of deep depression with all the symptoms characteristic of this state of mind. Yet, the feelings and phantasies connected with his hypochondriacal pains changed. For instance, the patient felt anxiety that the cancer would make its way through the lining of his stomach; but now it appeared that, while he feared for his stomach, he really wanted to protect the analyst, who is now inside him—actually the internalized mother—whom he fell t was being attacked by the father's penis and by his own id impulses. (The cancer). Another time the patient has haemorrhage from which he would die. It became clear that the analyst was identified with the haemorrhage. The good blood represented the analyst. We must remember that, when the paranoid anxieties dominated

591

and the therapist was mainly felt as a persecutor, Wherefore, the identification with bad blood which was mixed with the diarrhoea (with the bad father). Now the precious good blood represented the analyst, as for losing which meant the cancer, which would imply his death. It became clear now, that the cancer which he made responsible for the death of his loved object, as well as for his own, and which stood for the bad father's penis, was even more felt to be his own sadism, especially his greed. That is why he felt so unworthy and so much in despair.

While the paranoid anxieties predominantly and the anxiety of his bad united objects prevailed, he felt only hypochondriacal anxieties for his own body. When depression and sorrow had set in, the love and the concern for the good object came to the fore, and the anxiety-contents, as well as the whole feelings of defences altered. In this case, as well as in others it has be found that paranoid fears and suspicions were reinforced as a defence against the depressive position which was overlaid by them.

Wherever a state of depression exists, be it in normal, the neurotic, in manic-depression o in mixed cases, there is always in this specific grouping of anxieties, distressed feelings and different varieties of the defences. If this point of view proves correct, should be able to understand those very frequent cases where we are presented with a picturer of mixed paranoiac and depressive trends, since we could then isolate the various elements of which it is composed.

The consideration about the depressive states may lead us to a better understanding of the still rather enigmatic reaction of suicide. According to the findings of Abraham and James Glover, a suicide is directed against the introjected object. but, while in committing suicide the ego intends to murder its bad objects, that is to say, that it alway aims at saving its loved objects, internal or external. To put it shortly; in some cases the phantasies underlying suicide aim at preserving the internalization of good objects and that part of the ego which is identified with good objects, and also at destroying the other part of the ego which is identified with the bad object and the id. Thus, the ego is enabled to become united with its loved object.

Freud had stated that mania has for its basis the same contents as melancholia and is, in fact, a way of escape from that state. That is to suggest, that in mania and ego seeks refuge not only from melancholia but also from a paranoiac condition which it is unable to master. Its torturing and perilous dependence on its loved objects drive the ego to find freedom. In that, its identification with these objects is too profound to b e renounced. On the other hand, the ego is pursued by its dread of bad objects and the id and, in its effort to escape from all these miseries. It has recourse to many different mechanism as, some of which, since they belong to different phases of develop phases of development, are mutually incompatible.

In the sense of omnipotence, is what, first and foremost characterizes mania and, further (as Helene Deutsch has stated) mania is bases on the mechanism of denial, as Helene Deutsch in the following point. She holds this 'denial' is connected with the phallic phase and the castration complex (in girls it is a denial of the lack of the penis) which observations have led to conclude that this mechanism of denial originates in that every early phase which the development of denial endeavours to defend itself from the most overpowering and profound anxiety of all its dread of internalized persecutors and the id. That is to say, that which is first of all denied is psychic reality and the ego may then go on to deny a great deal of external reality.

We know that scotomization may lead to the subject's becoming entirely cut off from reality, and to his complete inactivity. In mania, however, denial is associated with an overactivity, although this excess of activity, as Helen e Deutsch points out, often bears no relation to any actual results achieved. Hence is to explain that in this state the source of the conflict is that the ego is unwilling and unable to renounce its goo internal objects and yet endeavour to escape from the perils of dependence on them as well as from its bad objects. its attempt to detach itself from an object as well as from its bad objects. It s attempt to detach itself from bad objects is without the same time of its completion. It is renounced, but it seems to be conditioned by an increase in the ego's own strength it seems in this compromise by denying the importance of its good objects and also the dangers with which it is a menace from its bad object and the id. All and all, it endeavours ceaselessly to master and control of it s objects, and the evidence of this effort are its hyperactivity

Implications that ego identity is the highest level organization of the world of object relations in the broadest sense, and also of the self. This is a very complex development, because while object relations are continuously internalized (as such internalization takes place at gradually higher, more differentiated levels). At the same time, the internalized object relations are 'depersonified' (Jacobson, 1964) and integrated into higher level ego and Superego structures such as the 'ego ideal,' character constellations, and autonomous ego functions. Simultaneously, these processes of internalization and depersonification, internalized object relations are also organized into persistent object images which come to represent internally the external world as experience by the developing ego, which corresponds roughly to what Sandler and Rosenblatt (1962) have called the 'representational world.' It has to be stressed, however, that this internal world of objects such as seen in conscious, preconscious, and unconscious fantasies never reproduced the actual world of real people with whom the individual has established relationships in the past and in the present; it is at most an approximation, always strongly influenced by the very early object images of introjection and identifications. It should be noted, however, it is also, that the 'world of inner objects, as used by Klein, which gives the impression of remaining as free floating object images in the psychic apparatus rather than being related to any specific structures, does not do justice to the complexity of integration of object relations, organization of object images takes place both in the object relationships. Organization of object images takes place both in the sector of depersonified ego structures and in the sector of developing identity. Such object images which remain relatively unmodified, the repressed unconscious is less affected by structuralization; in this sense very primitive, distorted object images certainly continue to exist in the unconscious mind. Nevertheless, by far, the greater part of internalized object images is normally integrated into higher level structure, and those which remain as object representations experiences important modifications over the years, for being under the influence of ego growth and later object relationships. The normal outcome of identity formation is that identifications are gradually replaced by selective, partial, sublimatory identification, in which only those aspects of object relations are internalized to which are in harmony with the individual identity formation.

Actually, the enrichment of one's personal life by the internal presence of such selective, partial identifications representing people who are loved and admired in a realistic way without indiscriminate internalization, constitutes a major source of emotional depth and well being. The normal process of individualization is marked by the shift from identifications to partial, sublimated identifications under the influence of a well-integrated ego identity. One might say, that depersonification of internalized object relations, reshaping of part of them so that they come to resemble more then the real objects, and individualization is closely relate processes.

The world of inner objects, then, gradually changes and comes closer to the 'external' perceptions of the reality of significant objects throughout childhood and later life, without ever becoming an actual copy of the environmental world. 'Confirmation,' intrapsychically speaking, is the ongoing process of reshaping the world of inner objects under the influence of the reality principle, of ego maturation and development, and through the cycle of projection and introjection. The persistence of 'non-metabolized' early introjection is the outcome of a pathological fixation of severely disturbed, early object relationships. A fixation which is intimately related to the pathological development of splitting that which interferes with the integration of self and object images and the depersonification of internalized object relationships in general. Under the pathological circumstances, early, non-integrated object images come to the surface; but even then, as is being stressed throughout, as we never do have 'free-floating' internal objects but are always confronted with the specific ego structures which they have crystalized.

Keeping in mind, our reservations about the concept of the 'representational world' as a close reproduction of the external world of objects, we might say, that ego identity is the highest level of organizational presentations of the world of object relations in the broadest sense and comprises the concept of the representational world and that of the self on the other.

The concept of instinct, Freud defines as a stimulus; a stimulus not arising in the outer world but 'from within the organism,' he adds that a better term for an instinctual stimulus is a 'need,' and says further, that such 'stimuli are the signs of an external world.' Freud lays explicit stress on one fundamental implication of his whole consideration of instinct, is, namely that it implies the concept of purpose in the form of what he calls a biological postulate. This postulate runs as follows: The nervous system is an apparatus which has the function of getting rid of the stimuli that reach it, or of reducing them to the lowest possible level. An instinct is a stimulus from within reaching the nervous system. Since an instinct is a stimulus arising within the organism and acting 'always as a constant force,' it obliges the nervous system to renounce its ideal intention of keeping off stimuli and compels it 'to undertake involved and interconnected activities by which the external world is so changed as to afford satisfaction to the internal source of stimulation.

As instinct brings an inner stimulus reaching the nervous apparatuses, the object of an instinct is 'the thing in regard to which or through which the instinct is able to achieve its aim. This aim for being sufficiently satisfactory as convincing properties are adequately satisfied. Nonetheless, the object of an instinct is further described as 'what is most variable about an instinct', 'not originally connected with it,' and as becoming 'assigned to it, only in consequence for being peculiarly fitted to make satisfaction possible.' It is here that we see instinctual drives being conceived of as 'intrapsychic,' or originally not related to objects.

In the later of Freud's writings, he gradually moves away from this position. Instincts are no longer define as (inner) stimuli which the nervous apparatuses' deals in accordance with the scheme of the reflex arc, but instinct as found, in, 'Beyond the Pleasure Principle,' are seen as 'an urge inherent in organic life to restore an earlier state of things which the living entity has been obliged to abandon under the pressure of external disturbing forces. He defines instinct in terms equivalent to the terms he used earlier in describing the function of the nervous apparatuses itself. The nervous apparatuses, the 'living entity' in its interchange with 'external disturbing forces.' Instinct is no longer an intrapsychic stimulus but, an expression of the function of the 'urge' of the nervous apparatuses to deal with the environment. The intimate and fundamental relationship of instinct s, especially in so far as libido (sexual instinct, Eros) is concerned with objects is more clearly brought out in 'The Problem of Anxiety,' until originally, in 'An Outline of Psychoanalysis,' 'the aim of the first of these basic instincts [Eros] is to establish ever greater unities and to preserve them thus—in short, to bind together.' It is worthy of note, that the relatedness to objects is implicit; the aim of the instinct Eros is no longer formulated in terms of a contentless 'satisfaction,' or satisfaction in the sense of abolishing stimuli, but the aim is clearly seen in terms of integration. it is 'to bind together.' And while Freud feels that it is possible to apply his earlier formula, 'to the effect that instinct tended toward a return to an earlier [inanimate] state, to the destructive or death instinct, 'we are unable to apply the formula to Eros (the love instinct).

The basic concept Instinct has thus changed its contentual representation, since Freud wrote, 'Instincts and Their Vicissitudes.' In his later writings he does not take as his starting point and model the reflex-arc scheme of a self-contained, closed system, but bases his considerations on a much broader, more modern biological framework. And it should be clear from the last quotation that it is by no means the ego alone to which he assigns the function of no synthesis, of binding together. Eros, one of the two basic instincts, is itself an integrating force. This is in accordance with his concept of primary narcissism as first formulated in 'On Narcissism: an Introduction,' and further elaborated in his later writings, in, 'Civilization and Its Discontents,' where objects, reality, are far from being originally not connected with libido, and, are seen as becoming gradually differentiated from a primary narcissistic identity of 'inner' and 'outer' worlds. Nonetheless, one of Freud's proudest achievements was the transformation of the therapeutic relationship which takes place in psychoanalysis into a tool of scientific investigation. Freud also believed that 'the future will probably attribute far greater importance to psychoanalysis as the science of the unconscious than as a therapeutic procedure (Freud, 1926).

You may question whether such a wide variety of differing symptomatic syndromes can be brought together under a single heading. If we consider the issue not in terms of presenting symptoms but in terms of the similar nature of their object relationships, we find many threads united these seemingly disparate disorders.

But, in actual practice we are concerned with what has kept a particular patient to love in her or his particular way; how, among the myriad patterns of love, the patient has come to select the one he or she actually did choose. How well we are able to determine this depends in large measure upon how close the distance is between the choice of an object and the pattern of loving, and the central nexus of the patient's unconscious conflicts. the consequences of conflict make it possible for us to analyze the nature of the love relationship, but in those instances in which the pattern of loving is ego-syntonic, but have less of an opportunity to penetrate deeply into the psychology of loving and are therefore, not in a very good position to grasp some understanding of the precursors of the particular patterns of loving. Under such circumstances, the temptation is greatly interpretive, as only to speculate phenomenologically than dynamically. What we do, in effect, is conjecture on the bias of history about what might have been the individuals psychological experience, since we seem unable to trace out the interpretational inferentially from the data in the dynamic context of the analytic situation.

Developments in the interactional description of schizophrenia have been parallelled in the area of depression. As yet, concepts such as pseudomutuality, double-bind, schism, and skew have found no counterparts. Kubler and Stotland (1964) have argued, 'emotional disturbance, even the most annoying or maddening cannot be understood, unless the field in which it develops and exists is examined. The manifestations of the difficulty in the disturbed individual have meaning depending in the aspects of the field. The significant aspects of the field are usually interpersonal.' Yet the study of depression has focussed on the individual and his behaviour out of his interactional context. To a large degree, the depressed person's monotonously reiterate complaints and self-accusations, and his provocative and often annoying behaviour has distracted investigators from considerations of his environed and the role it may play in the maintenance of his behaviour. The possibility that the characteristic pattern of depressed behaviour might be interwoven and concatenated with a corresponding pattern in the response of others has seldom been explored.

For the most part, it has been assumed that the depressed person is relatively impervious to the influence of others. Ruesch (1962) states that to talk to the depressed person makes little sense, to listen more intently, Grinker (1964) conceptualized depressive symptomatololgy as communication to others, but argued that the depressed person is not responsive to communication from others. 'The depressed persons . . . cannot use information for the purpose of action: he cannot perceive the cues of reality, he makes statements but does not care if he is understood.

In terms of systems theory (von Bertalanffy, 1950' Allport, 1960 and Miller, 1971), as the usually conceptually depressed person is one of a relatively closed systems, for which of Grinker (1964)was explicitly to state that the depressed person repeats his message and behaviour without reception or acceptance of resulting feedback. Beck (1964, 1967) described the cognitive distortions that dominate the information processing of the depressed person so that experiences are rigidly interpreted to maintain an existing schema of personal deficiency, self-blame and negative expectations.

The implicit assumption of these and other writers has been the support and information available to the depressed person are incongruent with his depression, and the persistence of his symptomatololgy is evidence of a failure to receive or accept this information. Withdrawal, isolated intrapsychic processes, or as Beck describes, (1967) the interactions of depressive schema and affective structures, produce a downward depressive spiral, this, however, engages of an alterative argument, in that the depressed person is able to adopt in such an argument, that is to say, that the depressed person is able to engage others in his environment, in such a way that support is lost and depressive information elicited. This in turn, increases the level of depression and strengthens the pathogenic pattern of depressed behaviour and responses of others. If a depressive spiral develops, it is a mutually causative deviation-amplifying process (Maruyama, 1963) in the interaction of the depressed person with his environment. Thus, what is customarily viewed as some internal process is, in at least, in part, a characteristic of interaction with the environment t, and much of what is customarily viewed as cognitive distortion or misperception is characteristic of an information flow from the environment. It should be noted that while the depressed person' s different interpretation of this predicament is traditionally attributed to his distortion or interpretation. The general disorders of though t and perception are defining neither criteria nor common among depressed patients (McPartland and Hornstra, 1964). An observer who fails to take onto account the intricacies of someone's relations that he does not posses, or leaves significant aspects of his unexplained experience (Watzlawick, 1967). Feedback introduces phenomena that cannot be adequately explained by reference to the isolated individual alone (Ashby, 1960, 1962). For the study of depression, identification of a pattern of depressive feedback from the environment of its demanding plexuity as held to the conceptual existence or dealing with what exists only in the mind as the disorder is for one to explain its phenomena with reference to the isolated repressive person.

Lemert (1962), in his study of the interpersonal dynamics of paranoia, argued that the net effect of the developing an interaction pattern between the paranoid person and others is that (1) the flow of information to the person is stopped, (2) a real discrepancy between expressed ideas and persuasively influence among those with whom he interacts is created, and (3) the situation or group image becomes as ambiguous for him as he is for others. In this context of attenuated relationships, exclusion, and disrupted communication, the paranoid person cannot get the feedback on his behaviour, that is essentially in order for him to correct his interpretations of social relationships. Lemert concluded that the paranoid person may be delusional, but that is also true that in very real sense he is able to elicit covertly organized action and conspiratorial behaviouralism.

Nonetheless, it should be made clear that the phenomenon of depression does not deny the existence of important intrapersonal factors in depression, however, that several writers have pointed out that the depressed person's feelings of worthlessness and helplessness, and do not arise in his immediate stimulus situation (Chodoff, 1972). McCranie (1971) has argued that there is a 'depressive-core' in the personality of the depression-prone person, consisting of a tendency to feel worthless and helpless and an over-sensitivity to stimuli that impinge upon these feelings. Together, these are aroused from a dormancy by specific situations such as loss and threat to self-esteem. However, the emphasis as of such, will by no means take into account the environmental surfaces, as represented by trait-ful understandings. By which the environment comes into congruence with these feelings, and the depressive's vague, yet, generalized feeling that there is something wrong with him. As his search for this among his minor defects, imperfections, and personal attributions, that may arise from a depressive core to his personality, but at the same time, the confusing response from the environment serves to validate these feelings. Likewise, conflicts about the reception of support and approval from others may be deeply rooted in the depressive's intrapersonal style, but these conflictual situations can only be aggravated by the mixed messages of approval and of rejection as received from significant others, and by their withdrawal from him, despite reassurances to the contrary.

Also, it does not deny the importance of possible biochemical o r genetic factors in the etiology of depression. Price (1974) has argued that even in disorders in which the importance of such factors has been clearly established there may be a large number of links in the causal chain between specific etiological factors and symptoms displayed by an individual. Social and interpersonal variables may determine to a greater extent of whether a disorder occurs and the form its symptoms will take, that a person need only begin to display depressive behaviour.

Since Freud, real and imagined object losses have been given prominence in the explanation of depression, and depressive process has often been seen as miscarried restitutive work. While most earlier formulations focussed on intrapsychic phenomena, there were implications for interpersonal behaviour. As early as Abraham (1911, 1918), the over-demanding aspects of the depressive's orality were noted. Rado (1928) assigned major etiological importance to accentuate the need for dependency in the depressed person. Fenichel (1945) described the neurotically depressed person's interpersonal manoeuvres that others have brought about the misery, his accusations that others have brought about the misery, and even his blackmailing of others for attention—as desperate attempts to force others to restore damaged self-esteem. Yet, in seeking this gratification, he is at the same time satisfied and to receive it because of the revenge that he expects will accompany it. In the psychotically depressed person, the loss is more complete, the objects have fallen away, and the restitutive effort is aimed exclusively at the Superego.

Cohen (1954) described the depressed as seeing others as objects to be manipulated for the purpose of receiving sympathy and reassurance, bu t also as seeing them as critical, rejecting, and ungenuine in their support. Further, are the achievements of reassurance, for the depressed person is to finding the concealed approval and rejection. According to the Cohen's formulation, what the depressed person seeks is a dependent relationship in which all his needs are satisfied, and in his failure to obtain this, he resorts to the depressive techniques of complaining and whinnying, if this too fails, he may loss hope, and enter into the psychotic state, where the pattern of emptiness and continues in the absence of specific objects.

Grinker (1964)interprets the factor patterns obtained in the earlier studies of depression (Grinker, 1961) as representing relatively constant patterns of communication. 'What is requested or seemingly needed by the depressed patient expressed verbally, by gestures or in behaviour, varies and characterizes the pattern of the depressed syndrome.'

Bonime (1960, 1966) described how the depressed person can dominate his environment with his demands for emotionally comforting responses from others. He considered depression to be a practice, an active way of relating to people in order to achieve pathological satisfactions, and he dismissed any suffering the depressed person may incur as secondary to the satisfaction of manipulative needs.

Aggression played a central role in early psychoanalytic formulations of depression (Abraham, 1911; Freud, 1917), but later writers have increasingly disputed its role. Bibring (1953) went so far as to declare that depression was an ego phenomenon, 'essentially independent of the vicissitudes of aggression as well as oral drives.'

Fromm-Reichmann (1959) argued that aggression had been considerably over stressed as a dynamic fact or in depression, and that if hostile feelings were found in the depressed person, they were the result of the frustration of his manipulative and exploitative needs. Cohen (1954) attributed the hostility of the depressed person to his 'annoying impact on others, rather than to a primary motivation to do injury to them,' however, Bonime found the hurting or defying of others to be essential to depressed behaviour.

Renewed interest in the relationship between hostility and depression—particularly in the psychoanalytic view that depressed persons turn hostility that had originally been directed at others (hostility-out-ward), against themselves (hostility-inward)—has generated a number of empirical studies. Weissman (1960) suggested that relatively normal persons became hostile outward when depressed, whereas persons to become severely depressed were more likely to internalize or suppress this hostility. The data of Zuckerman (1967) supported this view, indicating that only in the relatively normal was hostility correlated with depression on mood questionaries or as rated by interviewers. Friedman (1964) found depressives to have more 'readily expressed resentment' as shown by their endorsement of adjectives such as 'bitter,' 'frustrated,' and 'sulky,' yet found no greater overt hostility in a later study, Friedman (1970) showed that the feelings of depression and worthlessness were consonant with hostility, and resentful feelings, even though depressed persons were not more likely to directly express these feelings to persons in the environment. Schless (1974) found equal numbers of depressed patients turning hostility inward and outward, with both types of hostility increasing as depression became more severe. However, because these patients also saw other people's anger more readily expressed and more potent, they feared retaliation, and therefore expressed hostility in the form of resentment. In summary, recent studies have been interpreted so as to call into question classical psychoanalytic formulations of the relationship of depression, hostility may serve a defensive function against depression, this has been supported. That depression is preceded by increased hostility that is directed out but cannot be expressed directly to appropriate objects in the environment, as taken for a failing of this defensive function (Freidman, 1970; McCranie, 1971; Schless, 1974).

Most writers who comment on the complaint s and self-accusations of the depressed person have rejected the idea that they should be taken literally. Lichtenberg (1957) found that attempts to answer them directly with assurances, granting dependency, and even punishment all increased depression and feelings of personal defects. Freud (1917) suggested that the self-accusations are actually aimed at someone else, a lot love object and further notes . . . It must strike us that after all, the melancholic does not behave in quite the same way as a person who is crushed by remorse and self-reproach in a normal fashion. Feelings of shame in front of other people, which would more than anything characterizes this latter condition. One might emphasize the presence in him of an almost opposite trait of insistent communicativeness which finds, s in fact his self-exposure.'

In an attempt to modify depressive behaviour is a family differentiation (Liberman and Raskin, 1971), the baseline data indicated that other family members rejected opportunities to interact with the depressed person, and that all initiations of interaction between him and his family in the baseline period were undertaken by him.

Paykel and Weissman (1973) reported extensive social dysfunctions in women during depressive episodes. Interpersonal friction, inhibit communication, and submissive dependency occurred in both the initial episodes and in subsequent relapses. An onset of social difficulties was related to symptoms, but these difficulties continued months after the symptom's remitted. A fact that Paykel and Weissman argued must have been symptoms remitted in any treatment plan.

The provocation and often annoying behaviour of the depressive has distracted investigators from considerations of both the role the response of others and the given exception Jacobson (1954) noted that 'however exaggerated the patient's hurt, disappointment, and hostile derogation of their partners may be, their complaints are usually more justified than may appear on the surface.' According to her, the depressed person often makes his whole environment feel guilty and depressed, and this provokes defensive aggression and even cruelty precisely when he is, more vulnerable. Depressives also have a tendency to develop an 'oral interplay' with those around them, so to mutual demands and expectations that are built up to inevitable disappointment and depression for everyone concerned.

Cohen (1954) found therapists generally uncomfortable working with depressed patients. They identified a tendency of therapists to react to depressed manipulations with unrealistic reassurance and 'seductive promises too great to be fulfilled,' followed by hostility and rejection.

Lewinsohn and his associate' (Lewinsohn and Shaw, 1969; Lewinsohn, 1969; Lewinsohn, 1970; Libet and Lewinsohn, 1973) have undergone an ambitious clinical research program focussing on a social interaction of the depressed person from a behavioural point of view. In attempting to develop as a hypotheses about the reinforcement contingencies available to the depressed person, they have attempted of a precise specification for social behaviour especially for the depressed person. Libet and Lewinsohn found depressed persons in group therapy to be lower than controls on a number of measures of social skill, activity level interpersonal range, rate of positive reactions emitted and action latency. Their data are subject to alternative interpretations, however, particularly since they also found that rate of positive reactions emitted was highly correlated with the rate of positive interactions, as having been derived by reason. While depressed persons may well be deficient in social skills, some of the observed differences in group interaction situations may be due to the fact that fewer people are willing to interact with depressed persons as (which results in a narrower interpersonal range and less opportunity for activity), and in this interaction emitted fewer positive responses (thereby, reducing the positive responses while elicited from the depressed). The most useful behavioural conceptualization of social interaction involving depressed persons would specify the lack of social skills of all participants, as evidenced by their inability to alter the contingencies offered or received. Behavioural intervention in the depressed person's marital and family relationships would therefore, involve training among all participants that have these social skills, and go beyond simple alterations, whereas the contingencies available to the depressed persons, might that be, of a behavioural observation and self-reports as to the Lewinsohn study (Lewinsohn and Shaw, 1969) seem to support such a view.

Studies of suicide attempts and their effects on interpersonal relationships also provide data relevant to this discussion. While suicide attempts do not have an invariable relationship to depression, there is a definite association. McPartland and Hornstra (1964) examined the effects of suicide attempts on subsequent levels of depression. They conceptualized depressive symptomatology as 'a set of messages demanding action by others to alter or restore the social space,' and examined the relationships between suicide attempts and the ambiguity of the depressive message and the diffuseness of its intended audience. They were able to reliably place depressed patients at definite points along a dimension of interactive stalemate on the basis of the range of intended audience and the stridency of a message in depressive communications. Patients who were farthest along this vector continuum, whose communication was most diffuse, nonspecific, strident, and unanswerable, were most likely to have long hospital stays and diagnoses of the psychosis. Suicide attempts tended to reduce the level of depression, apparently by shifting the interactive burden onto others. Other studies (Rubenstein, 1958; Moss and Hamilton, 1956; Kubler and Stotland, 1964) have indicated that suicide patients who improve following their attempts on their lives fail to improve generally, and have affected changes in their social fields and those who fail to improve generally have failed to change their situation fundamentally.

Depression, as a response to the spatial disruption in which the person obtains support and validation for his experientially viewing of depressive symptomatology, that in terms of message values and intended audience, in similarity to that of McPartland and Hornstra (1964), but the present analysis will take place on the contributions of the social environment of the depressive drift. It is to be assumed that the course of a specific depressive episode will be highly dependent on the structure of the person's social spatiality, such that an understanding of the social context is vital to an understanding of depression, although traditionally, it has been largely ignored.

Nevertheless, it seems, more than enough that vocal and linguistic patterns and body movements are ambiguous and subject to alternative interpretation, however, a further problem for the depressed person is that the 'context,' the nature of the relationship between the depressed person and the person communicating to him. It may require time and further messages to be clearly defined.

The depressed person's problem is to decide whether others are assuring him that he is worthy and acceptable because they do in fact maintain this attitude toward him, or rather only because he has attempted to elicit such responses. Unwilling or unable to endure the time necessary to answer this question, the depressive uses his symptoms to seek repeated feedback in his testing of the nature of his acceptance and the security of his relationships.

While providing continual feedback, these efforts are at the same time profoundly and negatively affecting these relationships. The persistence and repetition of the symptoms are both incomprehensible and aversive to members of the social environment, however, the accompanying indication of distress and suffering is powerful in its ability to arouse guilt in others and to inhibit and direct expressions of annoyance and hostility from them, as observed in both the family difficulties of depressed persons (Jacobson. 1954), and the problems the therapists report in their efforts to relate to depressed patients (Cohen, 1954).

Irritating, yet inhibited and increasingly guilt-ridden, members of the social environment continue to give verbal assurance of support and acceptance. However, a growing discrepancy between the verbal content and the affective quality of these responses provides validation for the depressive's suspicions that he is not really being accepted and that further interaction cannot be assured. To maintain his increasingly uncertain security, the depressive displays more symptoms.

At this point the first of a number of interactive stalemates may be b e reached. Members of the depressed person's environment, who can find a suitable rationalization for their behaviour may leave the field or at least, reduce their interactions with him. Considerable effort may be involved in efforts to indicate that this is not in fact rejection, but given the context, these efforts do little more than reduce credibility and increases the depressive's insecurity. With those members of the social environment who remain, a self-maintaining pattern of mutual manipulation is established. Persons in the environment find that they can reduce the aversive behaviour of the depressed person and alleviate the guilt that this depressed behaviour has an uncanny ability to elicit, if they manipulate him with assurance, support, and denial of the process that is taking place. The depressed person, finds that by displaying symptoms he can manipulate his environment, so that it will provide sympathy and reassurance, but he is aware by now that this response from others is not genuine and that they become critical and rejecting. While this situation, is slightly attractive for neither the depressed person nor the members of his social environment, it provides a stabilization of what has been a deteriorating state of affairs.

One alternative facing the depressed person is for him to accept the precipitating disruption of his social space and the resulting loss of all supportive validations. However, now that he has begun showing symptoms, he has invested portions of his remaining relationship in his recovery effort. That is, he has tested the relationships, made demands, and has been frustrated in ways that seriously call into question his conceptually ascertainment for which are his relationships. If he abandons these efforts he may have to relinquish support and validation derived from these relationships, while accepting the precipitating loss. At this point he may be too decedents on the remaining relationships to give them up. Furthermore, he now has an increasingly confused and deteriorated self-concept, which must be clarified. With new desperation more symptoms may be displayed.

Various possible efforts by the depressed person to discover what is wrong with him (i.e., why he is being rejected and manipulated) and to reestablish a more normal interactive pattern is in his context indistinguishable from the manipulations he has used to control the responses of others. Therefore, they are met with the usual counter-manipulations. Requesting information as to how people really view him is indistinguishable from symptomatic efforts. If the depressed person attempts to discuss the interpersonal process that is taking place, he touches on a sensitive issue, and is likely only to elicit denial by the others or an angry defensive response. Nonetheless, efforts by others to assure the depressed person that he is really accepted and that they are not rejecting him are in this context, also indistinguishable from previous manipulations that they have employed, and, therefore, serve to strengthen the developing system. Thus, interpersonal manoeuvres directed at changing the emerging pattern become system-maintaining, and any genuine feedback to the depressed person is also indistinguishable from manipulations. Persons leaving the social field increase both, depressed people's feelings of rejection and his impetus to continue his behaviour pattern. Persons just entering the social field can be quickly recruited into the existing roles, since their efforts to deal with the depressed person—even if genuine—are likely to be quite similar to those now being employed manipulatively. They therefore, become subject to the compelling counter-manipulations of the depressed person, and come to respond manipulatively themselves, and are inducted into the system.

Descriptions of the depressed person at this point in his career focus on the distortions and misperceptions that serve to maintain his depression. What is generally ignored is that these 'distortions' and 'misperceptions' are congruent with the social system which the depressed person now finds himself. The specific content of the depressive's complaints and accusations may not be accurate, but his comments are in recognition of the attenuated relationships, are the disrupted communication, and lack of genuineness that he faces. These conditions serve to prevent him from receiving the feedback necessary to correct any misperceptions or distortions. He has played a major role in the creation of this social system, but the emergence of the system has also required the cooperation of others, and once established, it tends to be largely beyond the control of its participants.

Depending on characteristics of both the depressed person and his environment, a number of punishing variations stress of such problematically environmental patterns that may develop. Members of the social environment who have been repeatedly provoked and made to feel guilty may retaliate by withholding their responses or which the depressed person depends on them. The depressed person may become aware of the inhibiting influence his symptoms have on the direct expression of negative feelings, and may use these symptoms aggressively, while limiting the forms that counter-aggression can take. He may also discover and exploit the interdependence of others and the frustrations it entails, he may become aware of the extent to which others are dependent on him, in that their own maintenance of moods and their ability to engage in varieties of activities requiring in some was his cooperation. Because either of outright hostility, or as a self-defeating effort to convince others of their need to renegotiate their relationship with him, the depressed person becomes more symptomatic in his withholding of these minimal cooperative behaviours. While hostility may not necessarily be a major etiogical factor in depression, the frustrations, provocations, and manipulations occurring of the interactions between depressed people's and others would seem to encourage it.

As efforts to end the interactive stalemate fail, there may be a shift in the depressive's self-presentation to on e indicating great distress and implying that the enjoinment has more responsibility for bringing about the necessary changes. McPartland and Hornstra (1964) found that they could unambiguously differentiate themes of hopelessness and helplessness from more disturbed themes of low energy and physical allegement to communications of the depressed patients. The latter theme was associated with longer hospitalization when hospitalized, depressed patients were sampled, McPartlant and Hornstra give these examples of, 'I can't sleep and I can't stand in any longer,' 'I am too tired to mov e,' 'My head and my stomach feel funny at the time.' Unable to restore his life space, the depressive now implicitly demands 'a suspension of the rules, a moratorium on the web of obligations under which the person live, such as admission to the sick role'

(McPartland and Hornstra, 1964). With immediate relationships deteriorating, the depressive addresses his plea to a more general audience, but in more confusing and unanswerable terms. Literal responses to his communications may involve medical intervention for his specific complaints, but this generally fails to alleviate the problem. Any efforts to move the interaction them e back to the depressive's sense of hopelessness and helplessness threaten to reopen the earlier unfruitful and even punishing patterns of relations, and tend to be resisted, unable to answer or in many cases, even to comprehend the depressive' s pleas, members of the social environment may withdraw further from him, increasing his desperation, and quickening the depressive drift.

With a second interactive stalemate now reached, the depressive person may attempt to resolve it by increasing his level of symptomatology and shifting the theme of his self-presentation to one of the worthlessness and evil, 'I am a failure; its all my fault, I am sinful and worthless.' Unable either to restore his social space or to reduce his obligations sufficiently for him to continue to cope, the depressive now communicates his bafflement and resignation. The intended audience is now more diffuse, relationships are even more attenuated, and the new message is more obscure and perplexing. The social environment and the depressive soon arrive at another stalemate. Otherwise, helpless to alleviate the situations, remaining members of the environment may further withdraw or, alternatively, have the depressive withdraw through hospitalization. In the absence on any relatedness to others the depressive may drift into delusion and frankly psychotic behaviour.

Once an individual has suffered a disruption of an exiting sociobiological spareness, his ability to avoid depressive drifts, or to abort the process once it has begun, depends on the structure of his sociological space and on his temporal interpretations as regarding to his skills, in with regard to the latter, it is generally ignored that the person facing this situation is dealing with a changing environment, in that, the skills needed to deal with them are likely to be different from those required by a more stable, normative environment. Consequently, persons who previously have had adequate skills to deal with their life situation, but may lack the skills to cope with some disrupted sociological perturbation. With regard to the structure of the existing sociological spaces, resistance too depression seems as to depend on the availability of alternative sources of support and validation, particularly of the type that cannot be threatened by depressive symptomatology, (a) the availability of direct nonpunitive feedback should the person's behaviour become annoying or incompressible, and (b) the ability of sociologically intervening at some imperative to territorial spaces, generating a new source of support and meaning that is unambiguously independent in the presence or absence of symptomatology, earlier speculative writings (Abraham, 1911) and later behavioural studies (Lewinsohn, 1969) in their ranging of interaction and that this may be a major source of their vulnerability.

Depression has been conceptualized for being a self-perpetuating interpersonal system. Depressive symptomatology is congruent with the developing interpersonal situation of the depressed person, and the symptoms have a mutually maintaining relationship with the response of the social environment. Essentially, the depressed person and others of the sociological spaces, if existing to some imperative gain, as for some territorial position or placing the imparting of information, thus, is given from the spacial environmental traits. In that of knowing of which represented act is in agreement to create a system in which feedback cannot be received, and various efforts to change and become systems for maintaining.

The development of these modern medical therapies has had several important effects. First. These agents have provided of a relatively simple specific effect and safe forms of treatment with a profound impact on current patterns of medical practice, for example, many depressed or hypomanic patients can be managed adequately in outpatient facilities to avoid prolonged, expensive, and disruptive hospitalization which were formerly common. Second, partial understanding of the pharmacology of the psychotropic drugs has led to imaginative hypotheses concerning the pathophysiology or etiology of severe mood disorders. These, in turn, have encouraged a revolution on experimental psychiatry in which the hypotheses have been tested in clinical research. Many of the earlier hypotheses have been found wanting or simplistic, nevertheless, they have led to increased understanding of the diagnosis, biology, and treatment of mood disorders and to newer research that represents a third level of development. this is the focus of the practical clinical benefits of now and in the near future.

In the light of this some characteristics of infant development during this holding phase can be enumerated. It is at this stage that:

(1) primary process, (2) primary identification, (3) auto-erotism, (4) primary narcissism, and (5) living realities.

In this phase the ego changes over from an unintegrated state to a structure integration, and so the infant becomes able to experience anxiety associated with disintegration. The word disintegration begins to have been meaning which it did not possess before go integration became a fact. In healthy development at this stage the infant retains the capacity for re-experiencing unintegrated states, but this depends on the continuation of reliable maternal care or on the built-up in the infant of memories of material care beginning gradually to be perceived as such. The result of healthy progress in the infant's development during this stage is that he attains to what might be called 'unit status'. The infant becomes a person, an individual in his own right.

Associated with this attainment is the infant 's psychosomatic existence which begins to take on a personal pattern: that is, that the basis for this for this indwelling is a linkage of a motor and sensory and functional experience with the infant's new state of being a person. As a further development there comes into existence what might be called a limiting membrane, which to some extent (in health) is equated with the surface of the skin, and has a position between the infant's 'me' and his 'not me'. So the infant comes to have an inside and an outside, and a body-scheme. In this way meaning comes to the function of intake and output, moreover, it gradually become meaningful to postulate a personal or inner psychic reality for the infant.

During the holding phase other processes are initiated; the most important is the dawn of intelligence and the beginning of a mind as something distinct from the psyche, and, from this, the secondary processes and symbolic functioning, and of the organization of a personal psychic content, which forms a basis for dreaming and for living relationships.

At the same time there starts in the infant a joining up of two roots of impulsive behaviours. The term 'fusion' indicates the positive process whereby diffuse elements that belong to movement and to muscle erotism becomes fused with the orgiastic functioning of the erotogenic zones. This concept is more familiar as the reverse process of defusion, which is a complex and complication defence in which aggression becomes separated out from erotic experience after a period in which a degree of fusion has been achieved. All these developments belong to the environmental condition of 'holding', and without a good enough holding the stages cannot be attained, or once attained cannot become established,

A further development in the capacity for object relationships. In that, the infant changes from relationship to objectively conceived objects to a relationship to a object objectively perceived. This change is closely bound up with the infant's change from being merged with the mother to being separate from her, or to relating to her as a separate and 'not-me', This development is not specifically related to the holding, but is related to the phase of 'living with' . . .

In the holding phase the infant is maximally dependent. One can classify dependence thus:

(I) Absolute Dependence: In this state the infant has no means of knowing about the maternal care, which is largely a matter of prophylaxis. He cannot gain control over what is well and what is badly done, but is only a position to gain profit or to suffer disturbances,

(ii) Relative Dependence: The infant can become aware of the need for the details of maternal care, and to a growing extent relate them to personal impulse, and then later, in a psychoanalytic treatment, can reproduce them in the transference,

(iii) The infant develops the means for doing without actual care. This is accomplished through the accumulation of memories of care, the projection of personal needs and the introjection of care details, with the development of confidence on the environment, and must be added that, the element of intellectual understanding with its tremendous implications.

Nonetheless, in borderline cases the analyst does not always wait in vain, that in the course of time the patient becomes able to make use of the psychoanalytic interpretations of the original trauma projection. It may even happen that he is able to accept what is goo in the environment as a projection of the simple and stable going-on-being elements that derive from his own inherent potential.

Such that it is necessary to attempt to state briefly what happens to the inherented potential if this is to develop into an infant, and thereafter onto a child reaching toward independent existence, because if the plexuity of the subject such a statement must be made in the assumption of satisfactory material care, which means parental care. Satisfactory parental care can be classified roughly into three overlapping states.

1. Holding.
2. Mother and infant living together, as the father's function (on dealing with the environment for the mother) is not known to the infant
3. Father, mother, and an infant, all three living together.

The term 'holding' is used to denote not only the actual physical holding of the infant, but also the total environmental provision prior to the concept of living with. In other words, it refers to a three-dimensional or space relationship (spatiality) with time gradually added. This overlaps with, but initiate prior to, instinctual experiences that in time would determine the object relationships. It includes the management of experiences that are inherent in existence, such as the completion (and therefore, the noncompeting) of processes, such ss the completion and, the noncomcompletion of specific processes which from the outside may seem to be purely physiological but which belong to infant psychology and take place on a complex psychological field, particularly, by determining the awareness and the empathy of the mother.

The term 'living with' implies object relationships, and the emergence of the infant from the state of being merged with the mother, or his perception of objects external to the self.

The paradox is that what is good and bad in the infant's environment is not in fact a projection, but in spite of this it is necessary, if the individual infant is to develop healthily, that everything will seem to him to be a projection. We find omnipotence and the pleasure principle in operation, as they certainly are in earliest infancy; and to this observation we can add that the recognition of a true 'not-me' is a matter of the intellect; it belongs to extreme sophistication and to the maturity of the individual.

In the writings of Freud most of the formulations concerning infancy derive from a study of adults in analysis. At first sight it would seem that a great deal of psychoanalytic theory is about early childhood and infancy, but in one sense Freud can be said to have neglected unfancy as a stare. This is brought out by a footnote in 'Formulations of the Two Principles of Mental Functioning,' of which he shows that he knows he is taking for granted the very things that are under discussion, as in the text he traces the development from the pleasure-principle to the reality-principle, following his usual course of reconstructing the infancy of his adult patients. The note runs as follows:

> It will rightly be objected that an organization which was a slave to the pleasure principle and neglected the reality of the external world could not maintain itself alive for the shortest time, so that it could not have come into existence at all. The employment of a fiction like this is. however, justified when one considers that the infant—provided one includes with it the care it receives from its mother—does almost realize a psychical system of this kind.

Freud paid full tribute to the function of maternal care, and it must be assumed that he left this subject alone only because he was not ready to talk about its implications. The note continues:

> It probably hallucinates the fulfilment of its internal needs; it betrays its unpleasure, when there is an increase of stimulus and absence of satisfaction, by the motor discharge of screaming and beating about with its arms and legs, and it then experiences the satisfaction it has hallucinated. Later, as an older child, it learns too employ these

manifestations of discharge intentionally for which of methods for expressing its feelings. Since the later care of children is modelled in the care of infants, the dominance of the pleasure principle can really come to an end when a child has achieved a complete physical detachment from its parents.

The words: 'provide one includes with it the care it receives from its mother' have of a great importance in the immediate contextual presentation. The infant and the maternal care together from a unit. certainly if one is to study the theory of the parent-infant relationship one must come to a decision about these matters, which concern the real meaning of the word dependence or dependency. It is not enough that it is acknowledged that the environment is important if there is to be a discussion of the theory of the parent-infant relationship, then we are divided into two of the same who do not allow that at the earliest stages the infant and the maternal care belong to each other and cannot be disentangled. These two things, the infant and the maternal case, disentangle and dissociate themselves in health, which means as to do many things, to some extent it means a disentanglement of maternal care from something which we then call the infant, or the beginning of a growing child. This idea is covered by Freud's words at the end of the footnote, explaining that: The dominance of the pleasure principle can really come to an end only when a child has achieved a complete physical detachment from its parents.

It is axiomatic in these matters of maternal care of holding variety that when things go well the infant has no means of knowing what is being properly provided and what is being prevented. Such, that when things do not go well that the infant becomes aware, not of the failure of maternal care, but of the results, whatever they may be, of that failure: That in saying, as a result of success in maternal care there is built up in th infant a continuity of being which is the basis of ego strength' of being interrupted by reactions to the consequences of that failure, The resultant of ego-weakening.

Such, that when things do not go well that the infant becomes aware, not of the failure of maternal care, but of the results, whatever they may be, of that failure: That in saying, as a result of success in maternal care there is built up in th infant a continuity of being which is the basis of ego strength' of being interrupted

THE UNUSUAL REALITY OF DEPRESSION

by reactions to the consequences of that failure, The resultant of ego-weakening. Such interruptions constitute annihilation, and are evidently associated with pain of psychotic quality and intensity. In the extreme case the infant exists only on the basis of a continuity of reactions to impingement and of recoveries from such reactions. This is in great contras t to the continuity for being that which is our conception of ego strength.

The transition stage has been described as a stage of ;'Quasi-Independence'; and the reason for the adoption if this description is of sufficient importance to demand special attention. It emerges with the utmost clarity from the study of schizoid cases that the most characteristic feature of the state if infantile dependence is identification with the object. Still, it would not be going too far to say that, psychologically speaking, identification with the object and infantile dependence is really the same phenomenon. In that the mature dependence involves a relationship between two kinds of dependence is identical with Freudian distinctions between the narcissistic and the anaclitic choice of objects. The relationship involved in mature dependence is, of course, only the theoretically possible. Nevertheless, it remains true that the more mature a relationship is, the less it is characterized by identification, for what identification essentially represents is failure to differentiate the object. It is when identification persists at the expense of differentiation that a markedly compulsive element enters into the individual's attitude toward its objects. This is well seen in the infatuation of schizoid individuals. It may also be observed in almost uncontrollable impulse so commonly experienced by schizoid and depressive soldiers to return to their wives or their homes, when separated from them owing to military necessities. The abandonment of infantile dependence involves an abandonment with differentiated objects. In the dreams of schizoids the process of differentiation is frequently represented by the process of differentiations is frequently repressed by the theme of trying to cross a gulf or chasm, albeit the crossing which is attempted may also occur in a regressive direction. The process itself is commonly attended by considerable anxiety, and the anxiety attending it finds characteristic expression on dreams.

The process of differentiation of the object derives particular significance from the fact that infantile dependence is characterized not only by identification, but also by an oral attitude of incorporation. In virtue of this fact the object with which the

617

individual is identified is also an incorporated object or, to put the matter in a more arresting fashion, the object in which the individual is incorporate d may well prove the key to man y metaphysical puzzles. But that it may, however, it is common to find in dreams a complete equivalence between being inside an object and having the object inside.

Such then being the situation, the task of differentiating the object resolves itself into a problem of expelling an incorporated object, i.e., it becomes a problem of expelling contents. Herein lies the rationale of Abraham's 'anal phases,' and it is in this direction that we must look for the significance of the anal techniques which play such an important part during the transition stage. It is important as elsewhere, too insures that the cart is not placed before the horse, and to recognize that it is not a case of individual being occupied with the disposal of contents at this stage because he is anal, but of his being anal because he is preoccupied at this stage with the disposal of content.

The great conflict of the transition stage may now be formulated as a conflict between a progressive urge to surrender the infantile attitude of identification with the object and a regressive urge to maintain that attitude. During this period, accordingly, the behaviour of the individual is characterized both by desperate and endeavours on his part to separate himself from the object and desperate endeavour to achieve reunion with the object—desperate attempts 'to escape from prison' and desperate e attempts 'to return home'. Although one of these attitudes may become to preponderate, there is in the first instance a constant oscillation between the owing to the anxiety attending each. The anxiety attending separation manifests itself as a fear of isolation; and the anxiety attending identification manifests itself as a fear of being shut in, imprisoned or engulfed ('cribbed, cabined and confined'). These anxieties, it will be noticed, are essentially phobic anxieties. In may accordingly be inferred that it is to the conflict between the progressive urge toward separation from the object and the regressive lure of identification with the object that we must look for the explanation of the phobic state.

Owing to the intimate connection existing between identification and oral incorporation, and consequently between separation and excretory expulsion, the conflict of the transition period also presented itself as a conflict between an urge to expel

618

and an urge to retain contents. just as between separation and reunion, such that either of these oscillation between expulsion and retention, although either of these attitudes may have become dominant. Both attitudes are attended by anxiety—the attitude of expulsion being attended by a fear of bursting (often accompanied or replaced by a fear of some internal disease like cancer). Such anxieties are essentially obsessional anxieties, and it is the conflict between an urge to expel the objet as content and an urge conflict as the object content s that underlies the obsessional state.

The phobic and obsessional techniques are thus seen as to represent two differing methods of dealing with the same basic conflict: In these two differing methods correspond to two differing attitudes toward the object. from the phobic point of view the conflict presents itself as in between flight from and return to the object. From the obsessional point of view, as the conflict presents itself as one between expulsion and retention of the object. It thus becomes obvious that the phobic techniques correspond to an active attitude. The obsessional technique also expresses a much higher degree of aggression toward the object; For, whether the object is expelled or retained, it is being subject to forcible control. For the phobic individual, the choice lies between escaping from the power of the object and submitting to it. In other words, while the obsessional technique is essentially sadistic in nature, the phobic technique is essentially masochistic.

In the hysterical state we can recognize the operation of another technique for attempting to deal with the basic conflict of the transition period. In this case, the conflict appears to be formulated as simply one between acceptance and rejection of the object. Acceptance of the object is clearly manifested in the intense love-relationships which are so typical of the hysteric; but the very exaggeration of these emotional relationships in itself raises a suspicion that a rejection is being overcompensated. The suspicion is confirmed by th propensity of the hysteric to dissociation phenomena. That these Dissociative phenomena represent a rejection of the genitals need not be stressed, but, as the analysis can always unmask an identification of the rejected genitals with the breast as the original object of the libidinal impulses during the period of infantile dependence. This being so, it is of note, that what is dissociated by the hysteric is an organ function in himself. This can only have been meaning—that the rejected object is an internalization object, however, the hysteric's over-valuation of his objects leaves no room for doubt that in his case the accepted object and rejection of the internalized object.

If the paranoid and the hysteric states are now compared, we are confronted with a significant contrast. Whereas, the hysteric over-values objects in the outer world, the paranoid individual regards them as persecutors, and, whereas, the hysteric dissociation is a form of self-depreciation, the attitude of the paranoid individual is one of extravagant grandiosity. The paranoid state must, accordingly, be regarded as representing rejection of the externalized object and acceptance of the internalized object.

Having interpreted the hysterical and paranoid technique in terms of the acceptance and rejection of objects, we can now obtain interesting results by applying a similar interpretation to the phobic and obsessional techniques. The conflict underlying the phobic state may be concisely formulated as one between flight to the object and flight from the object. In the former case, is, of course, the object is accepted, whereas, in the latter case the object is rejected. In both cases, the object is treated as external, in the obsessional state, the conflict presents itself as one between the exclusion and the rejection of content. In this case, accordingly, both the accepted and the rejected objects are treated as internal. If in the case of the phobic state both the accepted and the rejected objects are treated as external and in the obsessional state both are treated as internal, the situation as regarding these hysterical and paranoid states is that one of these objects is treated as an externalized object and the other as an internalized object, in the hysterical state. It is the accepted object that is externalized, and the paranoid state, the object which is externalized is the rejected object.

The chief features of the stage of transition between infantile and adult dependence may now be briefly summarized. The transition period is characterized by a process of development, whereby object—relationships based upon identification gradually give place to relationships with differentiated objects. Satisfactory development during this period, therefore, depends upon the success which attends the process of differentiation of the object, and this in turn depends upon the issue of a conflict or separation from the object—a situation which is both desire d and feared. The conflict in question may call into operation any or all characteristic techniques—the obsessional, the paranoid, the hysterical and the phobic: and, if object—relationships are unsatisfactory, these techniques are liable to form the basis of characteristic psychopathological developments in later life. The various techniques cannot be classified in any order corresponding to presumptive levels of libidinal development. On the contrary, they must be regarded as alternative techniques, all belonging to the same stage in the development of object-relationships. Which of the techniques is employed, or to what extent each is employed would appear to depend on large measure upon the nature of the object-relationships established during the preceding stage of infantile dependence. In particular, it would seem to depend upon the degree which has been established between the developing ego and its internalized objects.

The infant is completely dependent upon his object not only for his existence and physical well-being, but also for the satisfaction of his psychological needs. It is true, nonetheless, that mature individuals are likewise dependent upon one another for the satisfaction of their psychological, and, no less than their physical, needs. Nevertheless, on the psychological side, the dependence of mature individuals sufficient to render him dependent in an unconditional sense. We also notice that, whereas in the case of the adult object-relationship has a considerable spread, in the case of the infant it tends to be focussed upon a single object. The loss of an object is thus, much more devastating in the case of the infant. If a mature individual loses an object, least of mention, he still has some objects remaining. His eggs are not all in one basket. Further, he has a choice of objects and can desert one for another. The infant, on the other hand, has no choice. He has no alternative but to accept or to reject his object—an alternative which is liable to present itself to him as a choice between life and death. His psychological dependence is further accentuated by the very nature of his object-relationship, for, as we have seen, this is based essentially upon identification. Dependence is exhibited in its most extreme form, in the intra-uterine state, and we may legitimately infer that on its psychological side this state is characterized by an absolute degree of identification. Identification may thus be regarded as representing the persistence into extra-uterine life of a relationship existing before birth. In so far as, identification persists after birth, and the individual's object constitutes not only his world, but also himself; and it is this fact, as has already been pointed out,

621

that we must attribute the compulsive attitude of many schizoids and de repressive individuals toward their objects.

Normal development is characterized by a process whereby progressive differentiations of the object is accompanied by progressive decreases in identification. So long as infantile dependence persists, however, identification remains the most characteristic feature of the individual's emotional relationship with his object. Infantile dependence is equivalent to oral dependence—a fact which should be interpreted, not in the sens that the infant is inherently oral, but in the sense that the breast is the original object. During the oral phases, accordingly, identification remains the most characteristic feature of the individual's emotional relationship with his object. The tendency to identification, which is so characteristic of emotional relationships during these phases, also invade s the cognitive sphere, with the result that certain orally fixated individuals have only to hear of someone else suffering from any given disease in order to believe that they are suffering from it themselves. In the conative sphere, that identification has its counterpart in oral incorporation. And it is the merging of emotional identification with oral incorporation that confers upon the stage of infantile dependence its most distinctive feature. These features are based upon the fundamental equivalence for the infant of being held in his mother's arms and incorporating the contents of her breast.

The phenomenon of narcissism, which is one of the most prominent characteristics of infantile dependence, is an attitude arising out of identification with the object. Such that primary narcissism may be simply defined as just such a state of identification with the object, secondary narcissism being a state of identification with an object which is internalized. While narcissism is a feature common to both the early and the late oral phase, the latter phase differs from the former in virtue of a change in the nature of the object. In th early oral phase the natural object is the breast; but in the later oral phase, the natural object becomes the mother. The transition from one phase to the other is thus marked by the substitution of a whole object (or person) for a part-object. Nevertheless, the object continues to be treated as a part-object (the breast) with the result that the person of the mother becomes an object for incorporation. The transitions from the early to the late oral phases are also characterized by the emergence of the biting tendency. Whereas in the early oral phase

THE UNUSUAL REALITY OF DEPRESSION

the libidinal attitude of incorporation monopolizes the field, in the late oral phase it is in competing with an accompanying attitude of biting. Now biting must be regarded for being essentially of all differentiated aggression. Consequently, the dawn of the late oral phase heralds the emergence of emotional ambivalence. The late oral phase is well described as pre-ambivalent. Nonetheless, one which aggression has not yet been differentiated from the libido. The early urge to incorporate is essentially a libidinal urge, to which true aggression makes no contribution, even as a component factor. The recognition of this fact is of the greatest importance for an understanding of the essential problem underlying schizoid states. It is understanding. It is true that the incorporation urge is destructive in its gross effect, in the sense that the object which is eaten disappears. Nevertheless, the urge is not destructive in aim. When, as a child says that he 'loves' cake, it is certain to imply that the cake will vanish, and then consumingly destroyed. At the same time the destruction of the cake is not the aim of the child's 'love'. On the contrary, the disappearance of the cake is, from the child's point of view. A most regrettable consequence of his 'love' for it. What he really desires, is for himself, is to have his cake and eat it to. If the cake proves to be 'bad' he either expectorates out or become sick. As this spiting out is specifically characteristic of the early oral phase, in that he rejects the bad cake, least of mention, he does not bite the cake with intentions for its being bad. This type of behaviour is specifically characterized of the early oral phasing, then, what is, so far as the object presents itself as 'good', it is incorporated, and, presents itself as 'bad', it is rejected, but, even when it appears to be bad, no attempt is made to destroy it. Again, it is the good object that is 'destroyed.' Albeit only incidentally and not by intention. In the late oral phase the situation is foreign, in that things are done differently, for in this phase the object may be bitten as well as incorporated. This mean that a direct aggressions, as well as libidinal forces, are such that may be directed toward the object. Hence the appearance of the ambivalence which characterizes the late oral phase.

It soon becomes evident that the emotional oral phase takes the form of the alternative, is that to incorporate or not to incorporate, i.e., 'to love or not to love.' This is the conflict underlying the depressive state. It will be seen, accordingly, that the problem of the schizoid individual is how to love without destroying by love,

623

whereas, the greater of problems is for the depressive individual, is how to love without destroying by hate. These are two very different problems.

The conflict underlying the schizoid state is, of course, much more devastating than the conflict underlying the depressive stat e, and, since the schizoid reaction has its roots in an earlier stage of development than the depressive reaction, the schizoid individual is less capable of dealing with conflict than is the depressive. It is owing to these two facts that the disturbance of the personality found in schizophrenia is so much more profound than found in depression. The devastating nature of the conflict associated with the early oral phase lies in the fact that, if it seems a terrible thing for an individual to destroy his object by love. It is the great tragedy of the schizoid individual that it is his love which seems to destroy; and it is because his love seems so destructive that he experiences such difficulty in directing his libido toward objects outer reality. He becomes afraid to love, and therefore he erects barriers between his objects and himself. He tends both to keep his objects at a distance and to make himself remote from them. He rejects his objects, and at the same time, he withdraws his libido from them. This withdrawal of libidinal energies may be carried to all lengths. It may be carried to a point at which all emotional and physical contacts with other persons are renounced; and it may even go so far that all libidinal links with outer reality are surrendered. All interest in the world around fades and everything becomes meaningless. In proportion as libido is withdrawn from outer objects it is directed toward the internalization with its accompanied objects; and, in proportion as this happens, the individual becomes introverted. And, incidently, it is on the observation that this process of introversion is characteristic on the onset of schizoid states that are themselves based on the conclusion that the introvert is essentially a schizoid. It is essentially in inner reality that the values of the schizoid are to be found. So far as he is concerned, the world of internalized objects is always encroaching upon the world of external objects; and in proportion as this happens his real objects become lost to him.

If loss of the real objects were the only trauma of the schizoid state the position of the schizoid individual would not be so precarious. It is necessary, nonetheless, to bear in mind the vicissitudes of the ego, which accompany loss of the object. Reference has already been made to the narcissism which results from an excessive libidinalization of internalized objects; and such narcissism is specially characteristic of the schizoid. Accompanying it, we invariably find an attitude of superiority which may manifest itself in consciousness to a varying degree as an actual sense of superiority. It should be of note, in that, this attitude of superiority is based upon an orientation toward internalized objects, and that in relation to objects in the world of outer reality the attitude of the schizoid is essentially one of inferiority. It is true, that the externally oriented inferiority may be masked by a façade of superiority, as based upon an identification of external with internalized objects. Nevertheless, it is invariably present, and it is evidence of a weakness in the ego. what chiefly compromises the development of the ego. In the case of the schizoid individual is the apparently insoluble dilemma which attends the direction of libido toward objects. Failure to direct libido toward the object is, of course, equivalent to loss of the object: But since, from the point of view of the schizoid, the libido is itself destructive, the object is equally lost when libido is directed toward it. It can thus readily be understood that, if the dilemma becomes sufficiently pronounced, the result is a complete impasse, which reduces the ego onto a state of utter impotence. The ego becomes quite incapable of expressing itself; and, in so far as this is so, its very existence become s compromised. This can be exemplified by the following, as: 'I can' t say anything. I have nothing to say. I'm empty. There's nothing of m e, . . . I feel quite useless; I haven' t don e anything. I've gone cold and hard; I don't feel anything . . . I can't express myself' I feel futile.' Such descriptions are well illustrated, not only the state of impotence to which the ego is compromised in the schizoid dilemma. The last quoted remark of this is, perhaps, as drawing attentions to the characteristic affect of the schizoid state: For the characteristic affect of the schizoid state is undoubtedly a sense of futility.

The libido may be withdrawn in varying degrees even from that part of the psyche which is, so to speak, nearest to external objects. It may be withdrawn from the realm of the conscious into the unconscious. When this occasions, the effect is as if the ego itself had withdrawn into the unconscious: But the actual position would seem to be that, when the libido deserts the conscious part of the ego (such as it is), the unconscious part of the ego is all that is left to behave as a functioning ego. In extreme cases the libido would seem to desert even the unconscious part of the ego and relapse into the primal id, leaving both surface only the picture with which Kraepelin has familiarize us in his account of the last phase of dementia præcox. Whether such a mass-withdrawal of the libido can properly be ascribe d to repression is a debatable question, although where the process is restricted to a withdrawal from object-relationships, it may give that impression. At any rate, the effectual withdrawal of the libido 'feels quite different' from that of simple repression. There can be no doubt, nonetheless, that withdrawal of the libido from the conscious part of the ego has the effect of relieving emotional tension and mitigating the danger of violent outbursts of precipitate action. There can be equally little doubt that much of the schizoid individual's anxiety really represents fear of such outbursts occurring. This fear commonly manifests itself as a fear of going insane or as a fear of imminent disaster. It is possible, therefore, that massive withdrawal of the libido has the significance of as desperate effort on the part of an ego threatened with repression of the basic impulse which urge the individual on to make emotional contacts. In the case of the schizoid, of course, these impulses are essentially oral impulses. It is when this effort is within measurable distance of succeeding that the individual begins to tell us that he feels as if there were nothing of him, or as if he had los t his identity, or as if he was dead, or as if he had ceased to exist. The fact is that in renouncing the libido the ego renounces the very form of energy which holds it together—and the ego thus becomes lost. Loss of the ego is the ultimate psychopathological disaster which the schizoid individual is constantly struggling, with more or less success, too avert by exploiting all available techniques (including the transitional techniques) for the control of his libido. In essence, therefore, the schizoid state is not a defence, although evidence of the presence of defences may be detected in it. It represented the major disaster which may befall the individual who has failed to outgrow the early stage of dependence.

If the problem which confronts the individual in the early oral phase is how to love the object without destroying it by love, the problem which confronts the individual in the oral phase is how to love the object without destroying it by hate. Accordingly, since the depressive reaction has its roots in the late oral phase, It is the disposal of his hate, rather than the disposal of his love, that constitutes the difficulty of the depressive individual. The formidable as this difficulty is, the depressive is at any rate spared the devastating experience of feeling that his love is bad. Since his love, at any rate, seems good, he remains inherently capable of a libidinal relationship with outer objects in a sense in which the schizoid is not. his difficulty in maintaining such a relationship arises out of his ambivalence. This ambivalence in turn arises out of the fact that during the late oral phase, he was more successful than the schizoid in substituting direct aggression (biting) for simple rejection of the object. While his aggression has been differentiated, that, nonetheless, he has failed in some degree to achieve that further step in development which is represented by dichotomy of the object. This further step, had he taken it, would have enabled him to dispose of his hate by directing it, predominantly at least, toward the rejected object and he would have been left free to direct toward his accepted object love which was relatively unaccompanied by hate. In so far as he failed to take such a step, the depressive remains in that state which characterized his attitude toward his object during the late oral phase. His external object during that phase, of course, a whole object (his mother); and his libidinal attitude toward it was incorporative. The incorporated object to the depressive thus comes to be an undivided whole object, which he adopts an ambivalent attitude. The presence of such an inner situation is less disabling so far as outer adjustments are concerned than is the corresponding inner situation, in the case of the schizoid, for in the case of the depressive there is no formidable barrier obstructing the outward flow of libido. Consequently, the depressive individual readily establishes libidinal contacts with others; and, if his libidinal contact with others appears satisfactory with others, and if his libidinal contacts are satisfactory to him, his progress through life may appear fairly smooth, as the inner situation is always present, and it is readily reactivated if his libidinal relationship becomes disturbed. Any such disturbance if his libidinal relationships become disturbed, such disturbances immediately calls into operation the hating element in his ambivalent t attitude; and, when his hate becomes directed toward the internalized object, a depressive reaction supervenes any frustration in object-relationships is, o f course, functionally equivalent to loss of the object. Whether partial or complete, since severe depression is so common a sequel to actual loss of the object (whether by the death of a loved person or

627

things as severally otherwise). Loss of the object must be regarded as the essential trauma which provokes the depressive state.

Physical injury or illness is obviously represents himself, that is to any, that such a loss, e.g., the loss of an eye or a limb, represent the symbolic castration as taken that we no further, for it still remains to be explained why a reaction which is characteristically provoked by loss of the object should also b e provoked by loss of par t of the body. the true explanation lies in the fact that the depressive individual still remains to a be a distinctive feature of degrees to an actual state of infantile identification with his object. To him, is, therefore, bodily loss is functionally equivalent to loss of the object, and this equivalence is reinforced by the presence of an internalized object which, so speak, suffuses the individual's bod y and imparts it to narcissistic value.

A brief dispositional representation as the presentation for which of 'narcissism', is to mean, that the cathexis of the own 'self' with libido, is used in the term 'self' because the state of primary narcissism exists only prior to any ego differentiation, a point made by Hartmann. What is called the secondary narcissism is the late return of object cathexis to the own person.

There still remains to be explained is the phenomenon of involutional melancholia. According to Freud and Abraham, the functional process in melancholia is the loss of the loved objects, the real, or some similar situation having the same significance, result in the object becoming installed within the ego. Owing, however, to an excess of cannibalistic impulses in the object, this introjection miscarries and the consequence is illness.

All the same, are those who tend to regard the etiology of this condition as entirely different from that of 'reactive depression', nonetheless, the two conditions have sufficiencies in common clinical standpoints, to justify, as to invoke the principle of, 'entia non sunt multicanda præter necessitate.' It is not really melancholia is by definition closely associated with the climacteric; and the climacteric would seem to be in itself evidence of a definite waning of libidinal urges. It cannot be said, nonetheless, that there is any equivalent diminution of aggression. The balance between the libidinal and the aggressive urges is thus disturbed, and, further, It is disturbed in the same direction as when the hate of any ambivalent individual is activated by loss of the object. Accordingly, in an individual of the depressive type the climacteric has the effect of establishing the same situation as does actual loss of the object where object-relationships are concerned; and the result is a depressive reaction. If the prospect of recovery in the case of involutional melancholia is less hopeful than in cases of reactive depression, This is not difficult to explain: For, whereas the latter case a libido is still available for a restoration of the balance in the former case, it is not. Involutional melancholia is thus seen to conform to the general configuration of the depressive state, and it imposes upon as holding of no necessity to modify the conclusion already envisaged—that loss of the object is the basic trauma underlying the depressive state. As in the case of the schizoid state, this state is not a defence, on the contrary, it is a state against which the individual seeks to defend himself by means of such techniques (including the transitional techniques) as are available for the control of his aggression. It represents the major disaster which may befall the individual who failed to outgrow the late oral stage of infantile dependance.

There are many kinds of psychotherapy. Cognitive-behavioural therapy assumes that depression stems from negative, often irrational thinking about oneself and one's future. In this type of therapy, a person learns to understand and eventually eliminate those habits of negative thinking. In interpersonal therapy, the therapist helps a person resolve problems in relationships with others that may have caused the depression. The subsequent improvement in social relationships and support helps alleviate the depression. Psychodynamic therapy views depression as the result of internal, unconscious conflicts. Psychodynamic therapists focus on a person's past experiences and the resolution of childhood conflicts. Psychoanalysis is an example of this type of therapy. Critics of long-term psychodynamic therapy argue that its effectiveness is scientifically unproven.

Electroconvulsive therapy (ECT) can often relieve severe depression in people who respond to antidepressant medication and psychotherapy. In this type of therapy, a low-voltage electric current is passed through the brain for one to two seconds to produce a controlled seizure. Patients usually receive six to ten ECT treatments over several weeks. ECT remains controversial because it can cause disorientation and memory loss. Nevertheless, research has found it highly effective in alleviating severe depression.

For milder cases of depression, regular aerobic exercise may improve mood as effectively as psychotherapy or medication. In addition, some research indicates that dietary modifications can influence one's mood by changing the level of serotonin in the brain.

An imbalance of hormones may also play a role in depression. Many depressed people have higher than normal levels of hydrocortisone (cortisol), a hormone secreted by the adrenal gland in response to stress. In addition, an underactive or overactive thyroid gland can lead to depression.

A variety of medical conditions can cause depression. These include dietary deficiencies in vitamin B6, vitamin B12, and folic acid, degenerative neurological disorders, such as Alzheimer's disease and Huntington's disease; strokes in the frontal part of the brain; and certain viral infections, such as hepatitis and mononucleosis. Certain medications, such as steroids, may also cause depression.

Psychological theories of depression focus on the way people think and behave. In a 1917 essay, Austrian psychoanalyst Sigmund Freud explained melancholia, or major depression, as a response to loss—either real loss, such as the death of a spouse, or symbolic loss, such as the failure to achieve an important goal. Freud believed that a person's unconscious anger over loss weakens the ego, resulting in self-hate and self-destructive behaviour.

Cognitive theories of depression emphasize the role of irrational thought processes. American psychiatrist Aaron Beck proposed that depressed people tend to view themselves, their environment, and the future in a negative light because of errors in thinking. These errors include focussing on the negative aspects of any situation, misinterpreting facts in negative ways, and blaming themselves for any misfortune. In Beck's view, people learn these self-defeating ways of looking at the world during early childhood. This negative thinking makes situations seem much worse than they really are and increases the risk of depression, especially in stressful situations.

In support of this cognitive view, people with 'depressive' personality traits appear to be more vulnerable than others to actual depression. Examples of depressive personality traits include gloominess, pessimism, introversion, self-criticism, excessive skepticism and criticism of others, deep feelings of inadequacy, and excessive brooding and worrying. In addition, people who regularly behave in dependent, hostile, and impulsive ways appear at greater risk for depression.

American psychologist Martin Seligman proposed that depression stems from 'learned helplessness,' an acquired belief that one cannot control the outcome of events. In this view, prolonged exposure to uncontrollable and inescapable events leads to apathy, pessimism, and loss of motivation. An adaptation of this theory by American psychologist Lynn Abramson and her colleagues argues that depression results not only from helplessness, but also hopelessness. The hopelessness theory attributes depression to a pattern of negative thinking in which people blame themselves for negative life events, view the causes of those events as permanent, and overgeneralize specific weaknesses as applying to many areas of their life.

Psychologists agree that stressful experiences can trigger depression in people who are predisposed to the illness. For example, the death of a loved one may trigger depression. Psychologists usually distinguish true depression from grief, a normal process of mourning a loved one who has died. Other stressful experiences may include divorce, pregnancy, the loss of a job, and even childbirth. About 20 percent of women experience an episode of depression, known as postpartum depression, after having a baby. In addition, people with serious physical illnesses or disabilities often develop depression.

Death and Dying are the irreversible cessation of life and the imminent approach of death. Death involves a complete change in the status of a living entity—the loss of its essential characteristics.

Many patients in the last stages of a terminal disease elect to forgo medical treatments aimed at curing their disease in favour of hospice care. Usually provided in a patient's home by health professionals and trained volunteers, hospice care seeks to relieve pain and symptoms and provide emotional support for patients and their families.

Should suffering and dying patients be allowed to end their own lives, with the aid of a physician? Easing the suffering of terminally ill patients is one way to avoid this difficult problem, but supporters of physician-assisted suicide argue that this is not always possible and that patients should have the option of assisted suicide. Opponents charge that assisted suicide will lead to the active killing of patients. In this Point/Counterpoint Sidebar, attorney Wesley J. Smith of the International Anti-Euthanasia Task Force presents his case against physician-assisted suicide. Margaret P. Battin, professor of at the University of Utah in Salt Lake City, counters with arguments for allowing physician-assisted suicide.

Death occurs at several levels. Somatic death is the death of the organism as a whole; it usually precedes the death of the individual organs, cells, and parts of cells. Somatic death is marked by cessation of heartbeat, respiration, movement, reflexes, and brain activity. The precise time of somatic death is sometimes difficult to determine, however, because the symptoms of such transient states as coma, faint, and trance closely resemble the signs of death.

After somatic death, several changes occur that are used to determine the time and circumstances of death. Algor mortis, the cooling of the body after death, is primarily influenced by the temperature of the immediate environment. Rigormortis, the stiffening of the skeletal muscles, begins from five to ten hours after death and disappears after three or four days. Livor mortis, the reddish-blue discolouration that occurs on the underside of the body, results from the settling of the blood. Clotting of the blood begins shortly after death, as does autolysis, the death of the cells. Putrefaction, the decomposition that follows, is caused by the action of enzymes and bacteria.

Organs of the body die at different rates. Although brain cells may survive for no more than 5 minutes after somatic death, those of the heart can survive for about 15 minutes and those of the kidney for about 30 minutes. For this reason, organs can be removed from a recently dead body and transplanted into a living person.

Ideas about what constitutes death vary with different cultures and in different epochs. In Western societies, death has traditionally been seen as the departure of the soul from the body. In this tradition, the essence of being human is independent of physical properties. Because the soul has no corporeal manifestation, its departure cannot be seen or otherwise objectively determined; hence, in this tradition, the cessation of breathing has been taken as the sign of death.

In modern times, death has been thought to occur when the vital functions cease—breathing and circulation (as evidenced by the beating of the heart). This view has been challenged, however, as medical advances have made it possible to sustain respiration and cardiac functioning through mechanical means. Thus, more recently, the concept of brain death has gained acceptance. In this view, the irreversible loss of brain activity is the sign that death has occurred. A majority of the states in the United States had accepted brain death as an essential sign of death by the late 1980s.

Even the concept of brain death has been challenged in recent years, because a person can lose all capacity for higher mental functioning while lower-brain functions, such as spontaneous respiration, continue. For this reason, some authorities now argue that death should be considered the loss of the capacity for consciousness or social interaction. The sign of death, according to this view, is the absence of activity in the higher centres of the brain, principally the neocortex.

Society's conception of death is of more than academic interest. Rapidly advancing medical technology has raised moral questions and introduced new problems in defining death legally. Among the issues being debated are the following: Who shall decide the criteria for death—physicians, legislatures, or each person for him or herself? Is advancement of the moment of death by cutting off artificial support morally and legally permissible? Do people have the right to demand that extraordinary measures be stopped so that they may die in peace? Can the next of kin or a legal guardian act for the comatose dying person under such circumstances? All these questions have acquired new urgency with the advent of human tissue transplantation. The need for organs must be weighed against the rights of the dying donor.

As a result of such questions, a number of groups have sought to establish an individual's 'right to die,' particularly through the legal means of 'living wills' in which an individual confers the right to withdrawal of life-sustaining treatment upon family members or legal figures. By 1991, 40 states in the United States had recognized the validity of some form of living-will arrangement, although complex questions remain to be settled in all these instances.

The needs of dying patients and their families have also received renewed attention since the 1960s. Thanatologists (those who study the surroundings and inner experiences of persons near death) have identified several stages through which dying persons go: denial and isolation (No, not me!); anger, rage, envy, and resentment (Why me?); bargaining (If I am good, then can I live?);

depression (What's the use?); and acceptance. Most authorities believe that these stages do not occur in any predictable order and may be intermingled with feelings of hope, anguish, and terror.

Like dying patients, bereaved families and friends go through stages of denial and acceptance. Bereavement, however, more typically does follow a regular sequence, often beginning before a loved one dies. Such anticipatory grief can help to defuse later distress. The next stage of bereavement, after the death has occurred, is likely to be longer and more severe if the death was unexpected. During this phase, mourners typically cry, have difficulty sleeping, and lose their appetites. Some may feel alarmed, angry, or aggrieved at being deserted. Later, the grief may turn to depression, which sometimes occurs when conventional forms of social support have ceased and outsiders are no longer offering help and solace; loneliness may ensue. Finally, the survivor begins to feel less troubled, regains energy, and restores ties to others.

Care of terminally ill patients may take place in the home but more commonly occurs in hospitals or more specialized institutions called hospices. Such care demands special qualities on the part of physicians and thanatologists, who must deal with their own fear of death before they can adequately comfort the dying. Although physicians commonly disagree, the tenet that most patients should be told that they are dying is now widely accepted. This must, of course, be done with tact and caring. Many persons, even children, know they are dying anyway; helping them to bring it out into the open avoids pretense and encourages the expression of honest feelings. Given safety and security, the informed dying patient can achieve an appropriate death, one marked by dignity and serenity. Concerned therapists or clergy can assist in this achievement simply by allowing the patient to talk about feelings, thoughts, and memories, or by acting as a substitute for family and friends who may grow anxious when the dying patient speaks of death

People who experience child abuse appear more vulnerable to depression than others. So, too, do people living under chronically stressful conditions, such as single mothers with many children and little or no support from friends or relatives.

Depression typically cannot be shaken or willed away. An episode must therefore run its course until it weakens either on its own or with treatment. Depression can be treated effectively with antidepressant drugs, psychotherapy, or a combination of both.

Despite the availability of effective treatment, most depressive disorders go untreated and undiagnosed. Studies indicate that general physicians fail to recognize depression in their patients at least half of the time. In addition, many doctors and patients view depression in elderly people as a normal part of aging, even though treatment for depression in older people is usually very effective.

Again, Bipolar Disorder is a mental illness in which a person's mood alternates between extreme mania and depression. Bipolar disorder is also called manic-depressive illness. When manic, people with bipolar disorder feel intensely elated, self-important, energetic, and irritable. When depressed, they experience painful sadness, negative thinking, and indifference to things that used to bring them happiness.

Bipolar disorder is much less common than depression. In North America and Europe, about 1 percent of people experience bipolar disorder during their lives. Rates of bipolar disorder are similar throughout the world. In comparison, at least 8 percent of people experience serious depression during their lives. Bipolar disorder affects men and women about equally and is somewhat more common in higher socioeconomic classes. At least 15 percent of people with bipolar disorder commit suicide. This rate roughly equals the rate for people with major depression, the most severe form of depression.

Bipolar disorder usually begins in a person's late teens or 20s. Men usually experience mania as the first mood episode, whereas women typically experience depression first. Episodes of mania and depression usually last from several weeks to several months. On average, people with untreated bipolar disorder experience four episodes of mania or depression over any ten-year period. Many people with bipolar disorder function normally between episodes. In 'rapid-cycling' bipolar disorder, however, which represents 5 to 15 percent of all cases, a person experiences four or more mood episodes within a year and may have little or no normal functioning in between episodes. In rare cases, swings between mania and depression occur over a period of days.

In another type of bipolar disorder, a person experiences major depression and hypomanic episodes, or episodes of milder mania. In a related disorder called cyclothymic disorder, a person's mood alternates between mild depression and mild mania. Some people with cyclothymic disorder later develop full-blown bipolar disorder.

Bipolar disorder may allow a seasonal pattern, with a person typically experiencing depression in the fall and winter and mania in the spring or summer.

People in the depressive phase of bipolar disorder feel intensely sad or profoundly foreign and indifferent to work, activities, and people that once brought them pleasure. They think slowly, concentrate poorly, feel tired, and experience changes—usually an increase—in their appetite and sleep. They often feel a sense of worthlessness or helplessness. In addition, they may feel pessimistic or hopeless about the future and may think about or attempt suicide. In some cases of severe depression, people may experience psychotic symptoms, such as delusions (false beliefs) or hallucinations (false sensory perceptions).

In the manic phase of bipolar disorder, people feel intensely and inappropriately happy, self-important, and irritable. In this highly energized state they sleep less, have racing thoughts, and talk in rapid-fire speech that goes off in many directions. They have inflated self-esteem and confidence and may even have delusions of grandeur. Mania may make people impatient and abrasive, and when frustrated, physically abusive. They often behave in socially inappropriate ways, think irrationally, and show impaired judgment. For example, they may take aeroplane trips all over the country, make indecent sexual advances, and formulate grandiose plans involving indiscriminate investments of money. The self-destructive behaviour of mania includes excessive gambling, buying outrageously expensive gifts, abusing alcohol or other drugs, and provoking confrontations with obnoxious or combative behaviour.

Clinical depression is one of the most common forms of mental illness. Although depression can be treated with psychotherapy, many scientists believe there are biological causes for the disease. In this June 1998 Scientific American article, Neurobiologist Charles B. Nemeroff discusses the connection between biochemical changes in the brain and depression.

The genes that a person inherits seem to have a strong influence on whether the person will develop bipolar disorder. Studies of twins provide evidence for this genetic influence. Among genetically identical twins where one twin has bipolar disorder, the other twin has the disorder in more than 70 percent of cases. But among pairs of fraternal twins, who have about half their genes in common, both twins have bipolar disorder in less than 15 percent of cases in which one twin has the disorder. The degree of genetic similarity seems to account for the difference between identical and fraternal twins. Further evidence for a genetic influence comes from studies of adopted children with bipolar disorder. These studies show that biological relatives of the children have a higher incidence of bipolar disorder than do people in the general population. Thus, bipolar disorder seems to run in families for genetic reasons.

Personal or work-related stress can trigger a manic episode, but this usually occurs in people with a genetic vulnerability. Other factors—such as prenatal development, childhood experiences, and social conditions—seem to have relatively little influence in causing bipolar disorder. One study examined the children of identical twins in which only one member of each pair of twins had bipolar disorder. The study found that regardless of whether the parent had bipolar disorder or not, all of the children had the same high 10-percent rate of bipolar disorder. This observation clearly suggests that risk for bipolar illness comes from genetic influence, not from exposure to a parent's bipolar illness or from family problems caused by that illness.

Different therapies may shorten, delay, or even prevent the extreme moods caused by bipolar disorder. Lithium carbonate, a natural mineral salt, can help control both mania and depression in bipolar disorder. The drug generally takes two to three weeks to become effective. People with bipolar disorder may take lithium during periods of relatively normal mood to delay or prevent subsequent episodes of mania or depression. Common side effects of lithium include nausea, increased thirst and urination, vertigo, loss of appetite, and muscle weakness. In addition, long-term use can impair functioning of the kidneys. For this reason, doctors do not prescribe lithium to bipolar patients with kidney disease. Many people find the side effects so unpleasant that they stop taking the medication, which often results in relapse.

From 20 to 40 percent of people do not respond to lithium therapy. For these people, two anticonvulsant drugs may help dampen severe manic episodes: carbamazepine (Tegretol) and valproate (Depakene). The use of traditional antidepressants to treat bipolar disorder carries risks of triggering a manic episode or a rapid-cycling pattern.

Object Relations in psychoanalysis, are the emotional relations between subject and object which, through a process of identification, are believed to constitute the developing ego. In this context, the word object refers to any person or thing, or representational aspect of them, with which the subject forms an intense emotional relationship

In psychoanalytic theory, the energy of the id or major portion of the unconscious mind, responsible for acts of creation. According to the theories of Sigmund Freud, the libido is the sex instinct, and artistic creation is an expression of the sex instinct that has been rechannelled. The Swiss psychiatrist Carl Jung rejected the sexual basis of the libido, believing that the force behind drives to act and create is merely an expression of the general will to live. Object Relations, in psychoanalysis, the emotional relations between subject and object which, through a process of identification, are believed to constitute the developing ego. In this context, the word object refers to any person or thing, or representational aspect of them, with which the subject forms an intense emotional relationship. Object relations were first described by German psychoanalyst Karl Abraham in an influential paper, published in 1924. In the paper he developed ideas from the founder of psychoanalysis, Sigmund Freud, on infantile sexuality and the development of the libido. The libido (Latin libido, 'pleasure' or 'lust'), in psychoanalytic theory, the energy of the id or major portion of the unconscious mind, responsible for acts of creation. According to the theories of Sigmund Freud, the libido is the sex instinct, and artistic creation is an expression of the sex instinct that has been rechannelled. The Swiss psychiatrist Carl Jung rejected the sexual basis of the libido, believing that the force behind drives to act and create is merely an expression of the general will to live. I believe that the struggle against death, the unconditional and self-willed determination to life, is the motive power behind the lives and activities of all outstanding men.

Personality disorders, are disorders in which one's personality results in personal distress or significantly impairs social or work functioning. Every person has a personality—that is, a characteristic way of thinking, feeling, behaving, and relating to others. Most people experience at least some difficulties and problems that result from their personality. The specific point at which those problems justify the diagnosis of a personality disorder is controversial. To some extent the definition of a personality disorder is arbitrary, reflecting subjective as well as professional judgments about the person's degree of dysfunction, need for change, and motivation for change.

Personality disorders involve behaviour that deviates from the norms or expectations of one's culture. However, people who deviate from cultural norms are not necessarily dysfunctional, nor are people who conform to cultural norms necessarily healthy. Many personality disorders represent extreme variants of behaviour patterns that people usually value and encourage. For example, most people value confidence but not arrogance, agreeableness but not submissiveness, and conscientiousness but not perfectionism.

Because no clear line exists between healthy and unhealthy functioning, critics question the reliability of personality disorder diagnoses. A behaviour that seems deviant to one person may seem normal to another depending on one's gender, ethnicity, and cultural background. The personal and cultural biases of mental health professionals may influence their diagnoses of personality disorders.

An estimated 20 percent of people in the general population have one or more personality disorders. Some people with personality disorders have other mental illnesses as well. About 50 percent of people who are treated for any psychiatric disorder have a personality disorder.

Mental health professionals rarely diagnose personality disorders in children because their manner of thinking, feeling, and relating to others does not usually stabilize until young adulthood. Thereafter, personality traits usually remain stable. Personality disorders often decrease in severity as a person ages.

People with antisocial personality disorder act in a way that disregards the feelings and rights of other people. Antisocial personalities often break the law, and they may use or exploit other people for their own gain. They may lie repeatedly, act impulsively, and get into physical fights. They may mistreat their spouses, neglect or abuse their children, and exploit their employees. They may even kill other people. People with this disorder are also sometimes called sociopaths or psychopaths. Antisocial behaviour in people less than 18 years old is called conduct disorder.

Antisocial personality disorder affects about 3 percent of males and 1 percent of females. This is the most heavily researched personality disorder, in part because it costs society the most. People with this disorder are at high risk for premature and violent death, injury, imprisonment, loss of employment, bankruptcy, alcoholism, drug dependence, and failed personal relationships.

People with borderline personality disorder experience intense emotional instability, particularly in relationships with others. They may make frantic efforts to avoid real or imagined abandonment by others. They may experience minor problems as major crises. They may also express their anger, frustration, and dismay through suicidal gestures, self-mutilation, and other self-destructive acts. They tend to have an unstable self-image or sense of self.

As children, most people with this disorder were emotionally unstable, impulsive, and often bitter or angry, although their chaotic impulsiveness and intense emotions may have made them popular at school. At first they may impress people as stimulating and exciting, but their relationships tend to be unstable and explosive.

About 2 percent of all people have borderline personality disorder. About 75 percent of people with this disorder are female. Borderline personalities are at high risk for developing depression, alcoholism, drug dependence, bulimia, dissociative disorders, and post-traumatic stress disorder. As many as 10 percent of people with this disorder commit suicide by the age of 30. People with borderline personality disorder are among the most difficult to treat with psychotherapy, in part because their relationship with their therapist may become as intense and unstable as their other personal relationships.

Avoidant personality disorder is social withdrawal due to intense, anxious shyness. People with Avoidant personalities are reluctant to interact with others unless they feel certain of being liked. They fear being criticized and rejected. Often they view themselves as socially inept and inferior to others.

Dependent personality disorder involves severe and disabling emotional dependency on others. People with this disorder have difficulty making decisions without a great deal of advice and reassurance from others. They urgently seek out another relationship when a close relationship ends. They feel uncomfortable by themselves.

People with histrionic personality disorder constantly strive to be the centre of attention. They may act overly flirtatious or dress in ways that draw attention. They may also talk in a dramatic or theatrical style and display exaggerated emotional reactions.

People with narcissistic personality disorder have a grandiose sense of self-importance. They seek excessive admiration from others and fantasize about unlimited success or power. They believe they are special, unique, or superior to others. However, they often have very fragile self-esteem.

Obsessive-compulsive personality disorder is characterized by a preoccupation with details, orderliness, perfection, and control. People with this disorder often devote excessive amounts of time to work and productivity and fail to take time for leisure activities and friendships. They tend to be rigid, formal, stubborn, and serious. This disorder differs from obsessive-compulsive disorder, which often includes more bizarre behaviour and rituals.

People with paranoid personality disorder feel constant suspicion and distrust toward other people. They believe that others are against them and constantly look for evidence to support their suspicions. They are hostile toward others and react angrily to perceived insults.

Schizoid personality disorder involves social isolation and a lack of desire for close personal relationships. People with this disorder prefer to be alone and seem withdrawn and emotionally detached. They seem indifferent to praise or criticism from other people.

People with schizotypal personality disorder engage in odd thinking, speech, and behaviour. They may ramble or use words and phrases in unusual ways, and they may believe they have magical control over others. They feel very uncomfortable with close personal relationships and tend to be suspicious of others. Some research suggests this disorder is a less severe form of schizophrenia.

Many psychiatrists and psychologists use two additional diagnoses. Depressive personality disorder is characterized by chronic pessimism, gloominess, and cheerlessness. In passive-aggressive personality disorder, a person passively resists completing tasks and chores, criticizes and scorns authority figures, and seems negative and sullen.

Personality disorders result from a complex interaction of inherited traits and life experience, not from a single cause. For example, some cases of antisocial personality disorder may result from a combination of a genetic predisposition to impulsiveness and violence, very inconsistent or erratic parenting, and a harsh environment that discourages feelings of empathy and warmth but rewards exploitation and aggressiveness. Borderline personality disorder may result from a genetic predisposition to impulsiveness and emotional instability combined with parental neglect, intense marital conflicts between parents, and repeated episodes of severe emotional or sexual abuse. Dependent personality disorder may result from genetically based anxiety, an inhibited temperament, and overly protective, clinging, or neglectful parenting.

The pervasive and chronic nature of personality disorders makes them difficult to treat. People with these disorders often fail to recognize that their personality has contributed to their social, occupational, and personal problems. They may not think they have any real problems despite a history of drug abuse, failed relationships, and irregular employment. Thus, therapists must first focus on helping the person understand and become aware of the significance of their personality traits.

People with personality disorders sometimes feel that they can never change their dysfunctional behaviour because they have always acted the same way. Although personality change is exceedingly difficult, sometimes people can change the most dysfunctional aspects of their feelings and behaviour.

Therapists use a variety of methods to treat personality disorders, depending on the specific disorder. For example, cognitive and behavioural techniques, such as role playing and logical argument, may help alter a person's irrational perceptions and assumptions about himself or herself. Certain psychoactive drugs may help control feelings of anxiety, depression, or severe distortions of thought. Psychotherapy may help people to understand the impact of experiences and relationships during childhood.

Psychotherapy is usually ineffective for people with antisocial personality disorder because these individuals tend to be manipulative, unreliable, and dishonest with the therapist. Therefore, most mental health professionals favour removing people with this disorder from their current living situation and placing them in a residential treatment centre. Such residential programs strictly supervise patients' behaviour and impose rigid, consistent rules and responsibilities. These programs appear to help some people, but it is unclear how long their beneficial effects last.

Therapists treating people with borderline personality disorder sometimes use a technique called dialectical behaviour therapy. In this type of therapy, the therapist initially focuses on reducing suicidal tendencies and other behaviours that disrupt treatment. The therapist then helps the person develop skills to cope with anger and self-destructive impulses. In addition, the person learns to achieve personal strength through an acceptance of the many disappointments and interpersonal conflicts that are a natural part of life.

People with depression often experience feelings of worthlessness, helplessness, guilt, and self-blame. They may interpret a minor failing on their part as a sign of incompetence or interpret minor criticism as condemnation. Some depressed people complain of being spiritually or morally dead. The mirror seems to reflect someone ugly and repulsive. Even a competent and decent person may feel deficient, cruel, stupid, phony, or guilty of having deceived others. People with major depression may experience such extreme emotional pain that they consider or attempt suicide. At least 15 percent of seriously depressed people commit suicide, and many more attempt it.

In some cases, people with depression may experience psychotic symptoms, such as delusions (false beliefs) and hallucinations (false sensory perceptions). Psychotic symptoms indicate an especially severe illness. Compared to other depressed people, those with psychotic symptoms have longer hospital stays, and after leaving, they are more likely to be moody and unhappy. They are also more likely to commit suicide.

Some depressions seem to come out of the blue, even when things are going well. Others seem to have an obvious cause: a marital conflict, financial difficulty, or some personal failure. Yet many people with these problems do not become deeply depressed. Most psychologists believe depression results from an interaction between stressful life events and a person's biological and psychological vulnerabilities.

Implications as to the reason for this difference. Some cite differences in hormones, and others point to the stress caused by society's expectations of women.

Depression occurs in all parts of the world, although the pattern of symptoms can vary. The prevalence of depression in other countries varies widely, from 1.5 percent of people in Taiwan to 19 percent of people in Lebanon. Some researchers believe methods of gathering data on depression account for different rates.

A number of large-scale studies indicate that depression rates have increased worldwide over the past several decades. Furthermore, younger generations are experiencing depression at an earlier age than did previous generations. Social scientists have proposed many explanations, including changes in family structure, urbanization, and reduced cultural and religious influences.

Symptoms of depression can vary by age. In younger children, depression may include physical complaints, such as stomachaches and headaches, as well as irritability, 'moping around,' social withdrawal, and changes in eating habits. They may feel unenthusiastic about school and other activities. In adolescents, common symptoms include sad mood, sleep disturbances, and lack of energy. Elderly people with depression usually complain of physically rather than emotional problems, which sometimes leads doctors to misdiagnose the illness.

Symptoms of depression can also vary by culture. In some cultures, depressed people may not experience sadness or guilt but may complain of physical problems. In Mediterranean cultures, for example, depressed people may complain of headaches or nerves. In Asian cultures they may complain of weakness, fatigue, or imbalance.

Depression also changes one's energy level. Some depressed people may be restless and agitated, engaging in fidgety movements and pacing. Others may feel sluggish and inactive, experiencing great fatigue, lack of energy, and a feeling of being worn out or carrying a heavy burden. Depressed people may also have difficulty thinking, poor concentration, and problems with memory.

People with depression often experience feelings of worthlessness, helplessness, guilt, and self-blame. They may interpret a minor failing on their part as a sign of incompetence or interpret minor criticism as condemnation. Some depressed people complain of being spiritually or morally dead. The mirror seems to reflect someone ugly and repulsive. Even a competent and decent person may feel deficient, cruel, stupid, phony, or guilty of having deceived others. People with major depression may experience such extreme emotional pain that they consider or attempt suicide. At least 15 percent of seriously depressed people commit suicide, and many more attempt it.

In some cases, people with depression may experience psychotic symptoms, such as delusions (false beliefs) and hallucinations (false sensory perceptions). Psychotic symptoms indicate an especially severe illness. Compared to other depressed people, those with psychotic symptoms have longer hospital stays, and after leaving, they are more likely to be moody and unhappy. They are also more likely to commit suicide.

Some depressions seem to come out of the blue, even when things are going well. Others seem to have an obvious cause: a marital conflict, financial difficulty, or some personal failure. Yet many people with these problems do not become deeply depressed. Most psychologists believe depression results from an interaction between stressful life events and a person's biological and psychological vulnerabilities.

Clinical depression is one of the most common forms of mental illness. Although depression can be treated with psychotherapy, many scientists believe there are biological causes for the disease. In this June 1998 Scientific American article, Neurobiologist Charles B. Nemeroff discusses the connection between biochemical changes in the brain and depression.

Depression runs in families. By studying twins, researchers have found evidence of a strong genetic influence in depression. Genetically identical twins raised in the same environment are three times more likely to have depression in common than fraternal twins, who have only about half of their genes in common. In addition, identical twins are five times more likely to have bipolar disorder in common. These findings suggest that vulnerability to depression and bipolar disorder can be inherited. Adoption studies have provided more evidence of a genetic role in depression. These studies show that children of depressed people are vulnerable to depression even when raised by adoptive parents.

Genes may influence depression by causing abnormal activity in the brain. Studies have shown that certain brain chemicals called neurotransmitters play an important role in regulating moods and emotions. Neurotransmitters involved in depression include norepinephrine, dopamine, and serotonin. Research in the 1960s suggested that depression results from lower than normal levels of these neurotransmitters in parts of the brain. Support for this theory came from the effects of antidepressant drugs, which work by increasing the levels of neurotransmitters involved in depression. However, later studies have discredited this simple

645

explanation and have suggested a more complex relationship between neurotransmitter levels and depression.

An imbalance of hormones may also play a role in depression. Many depressed people have higher than normal levels of hydrocortisone (cortisol), a hormone secreted by the adrenal gland in response to stress. In addition, an underactive or overactive thyroid gland can lead to depression.

A variety of medical conditions can cause depression. These include dietary deficiencies in vitamin B6, vitamin B12, and folic acid; degenerative neurological disorders, such as Alzheimer's disease and Huntington's disease, strokes in the frontal part of the brain; and certain viral infections, such as hepatitis and mononucleosis. Certain medications, such as steroids, may also cause depression.

Psychological theories of depression focus on the way people think and behave. In a 1917 essay, Austrian psychoanalyst Sigmund Freud explained melancholia, or major depression, as a response to loss—either real loss, such as the death of a spouse, or symbolic loss, such as the failure to achieve an important goal. Freud believed that a person's unconscious anger over loss weakens the ego, resulting in self-hate and self-destructive behaviour.

Mania, maintains an abnormal mental state and is characterized by an elevated or irritable mood, exaggerated self-importance, racing thoughts, and hyperactivity. People with mania typically feel intoxicated with themselves and with life. They may display an indiscriminate enthusiasm for manipulating people, spending money, and pursuing sexual adventure. Manic people may also display impatience or hostility toward other people. If frustrated, they may physically abuse their friends, children, or spouse.

Mania has many other characteristics. People with mania often have inflated self-esteem and self-confidence, and assume they have more wit, courage, imagination, and artistry than everyone else. Severe mania may include delusions of grandeur, such as the belief that one is chosen by God for a special mission. Mania typically involves a decreased need for sleep, so manic people often wake up early in a highly energized state. Mania makes people extremely talkative. Their loud, rapid-fire speech sometimes continues unabated without regard for others. Mania also involves a flight of ideas, racing thoughts that cause speech to go off in many different directions. People in a manic state become easily distracted by irrelevant sights, sounds or ideas, which further disrupts thinking and speech.

Most people who experience episodes of mania also experience spells of severe depression. This pattern of mood swings between mania and depression defined a mental illness known as bipolar disorder, also called manic-depressive illness. In bipolar disorder, episodes of mania usually begin abruptly and last from several weeks to several months. Mild manic episodes can last a year or more. Depression may follow immediately or begin after a period of relatively normal functioning. Manic episodes may require hospitalization because of impaired social behaviour or the presence of psychotic symptoms.

Personality Disorders, are disorders in which one's personality results in personal distress or significantly impairs social or work functioning. Every person has a personality—that is, a characteristic way of thinking, feeling, behaving, and relating to others. Most people experience at least some difficulties and problems that result from their personality. The specific point at which those problems justify the diagnosis of a personality disorder is controversial. To some extent the definition of a personality disorder is arbitrary, reflecting subjective as well as professional judgments about the person's degree of dysfunction, need for change, and motivation for change.

Personality disorders involve behaviour that deviates from the norms or expectations of one's culture. However, people who deviate from cultural norms are not necessarily dysfunctional, nor are people who conform to cultural norms necessarily healthy. Many personality disorders represent extreme variants of behaviour patterns that people usually value and encourage. For example, most people value confidence but not arrogance, agreeableness but not submissiveness, and conscientiousness but not perfectionism.

Because no clear line exists between healthy and unhealthy functioning, critics question the reliability of personality disorder diagnoses. A behaviour that seems deviant to one person may seem normal to another depending on one's gender, ethnicity, and cultural background. The personal and cultural biases of mental health professionals may influence their diagnoses of personality disorders.

An estimated 20 percent of people in the general population have one or more personality disorders. Some people with

647

personality disorders have other mental illnesses as well. About 50 percent of people who are treated for any psychiatric disorder have a personality disorder.

Mental health professionals rarely diagnose personality disorders in children because their manner of thinking, feeling, and relating to others does not usually stabilize until young adulthood. Thereafter, personality traits usually remain stable. Personality disorders often decrease in severity as a person ages.

People with antisocial personality disorder act in a way that disregards the feelings and rights of other people. Antisocial personalities often break the law, and they may use or exploit other people for their own gain. They may lie repeatedly, act impulsively, and get into physical fights. They may mistreat their spouses, neglect or abuse their children, and exploit their employees. They may even kill other people. People with this disorder are also sometimes called sociopaths or psychopaths. Antisocial behaviour in people less than 18 years old is called conduct disorder.

Antisocial personalities usually to understand that their behaviour is dysfunctional because their ability to feel guilty, remorseful, and anxious is impaired. Guilt, remorse, shame, and anxiety are unpleasant feelings, but they are also necessary for social functioning and even physical survival. For example, people who lack the ability to feel anxious will often fail to anticipate actual dangers and risks. They may take chances that other people would not take.

Antisocial personality disorder affects about 3 percent of males and 1 percent of females. This is the most heavily researched personality disorder, in part because it costs society the most. People with this disorder are at high risk for premature and violent death, injury, imprisonment, loss of employment, bankruptcy, alcoholism, drug dependence, and failed personal relationships.

People with borderline personality disorder experience intense emotional instability, particularly in relationships with others. They may make frantic efforts to avoid real or imagined abandonment by others. They may experience minor problems as major crises. They may also express their anger, frustration, and dismay through suicidal gestures, self-mutilation, and other self-destructive acts. They tend to have an unstable self-image or sense of self.

As children, most people with this disorder were emotionally unstable, impulsive, and often bitter or angry, although their chaotic impulsiveness and intense emotions may have made them popular at school. At first they may impress people as stimulating and exciting, but their relationships tend to be unstable and explosive.

About 2 percent of all people have borderline personality disorder. About 75 percent of people with this disorder are female. Borderline personalities are at high risk for developing depression, alcoholism, drug dependence, bulimia, dissociative disorders, and post-traumatic stress disorder. As many as 10 percent of people with this disorder commit suicide by the age of 30. People with borderline personality disorder are among the most difficult to treat with psychotherapy, in part because their relationship with their therapist may become as intense and unstable as their other personal relationships.

Avoidant personality disorder is social withdrawal due to intense, anxious shyness. People with avoidant personalities are reluctant to interact with others unless they feel certain of being liked. They fear being criticized and rejected. Often they view themselves as socially inept and inferior to others.

Dependent personality disorder involves severe and disabling emotional dependency on others. People with this disorder have difficulty making decisions without a great deal of advice and reassurance from others. They urgently seek out another relationship when a close relationship ends. They feel uncomfortable by themselves.

People with histrionic personality disorder constantly strive to be the centre of attention. They may act overly flirtatious or dress in ways that draw attention. They may also talk in a dramatic or theatrical style and display exaggerated emotional reactions.

People with narcissistic personality disorder have a grandiose sense of self-importance. They seek excessive admiration from others and fantasize about unlimited success or power. They believe they are special, unique, or superior to others. However, they often have very fragile self-esteem.

Obsessive-compulsive personality disorder is characterized by a preoccupation with details, orderliness, perfection, and control. People with this disorder often devote excessive amounts of time to work and productivity and fail to take time for leisure activities and friendships. They tend to be rigid, formal, stubborn, and serious. This disorder differs from obsessive-compulsive disorder, which often includes more bizarre behaviour and rituals.

People with paranoid personality disorder feel constant suspicion and distrust toward other people. They believe that others are against them and constantly look for evidence to support their suspicions. They are hostile toward others and react angrily to perceived insults.

Schizoid personality disorder involves social isolation and a lack of desire for close personal relationships. People with this disorder prefer to be alone and seem withdrawn and emotionally detached. They seem indifferent to praise or criticism from other people.

People with schizotypal personality disorder engage in odd thinking, speech, and behaviour. They may ramble or use words and phrases in unusual ways, and they may believe they have magical control over others. They feel very uncomfortable with close personal relationships and tend to be suspicious of others. Some research suggests this disorder is a less severe form of schizophrenia.

Many psychiatrists and psychologists use two additional diagnoses. Depressive personality disorder is characterized by chronic pessimism, gloominess, and cheerlessness. In passive-aggressive personality disorder, a person passively resists completing tasks and chores, criticizes and scorns authority figures, and seems negative and sullen.

Personality disorders result from a complex interaction of inherited traits and life experience, not from a single cause. For example, some cases of antisocial personality disorder may result from a combination of a genetic predisposition to impulsiveness and violence, very inconsistent or erratic parenting, and a harsh environment that discourages feelings of empathy and warmth but rewards exploitation and aggressiveness. Borderline personality disorder may result from a genetic predisposition to impulsiveness and emotional instability combined with parental neglect, intense marital conflicts between parents, and repeated episodes of severe emotional or sexual abuse. Dependent personality disorder may result from genetically based anxiety, an inhibited temperament, and overly protective, clinging, or neglectful parenting.

The pervasive and chronic nature of personality disorders makes them difficult to treat. People with these disorders often fail to recognize that their personality has contributed to their social, occupational, and personal problems. They may not think they have any real problems despite a history of drug abuse, failed relationships, and irregular employment. Thus, therapists must first focus on helping the person understand and become aware of the significance of their personality traits.

People with personality disorders sometimes feel that they can never change their dysfunctional behaviour because they have always acted the same way. Although personality change is exceedingly difficult, sometimes people can change the most dysfunctional aspects of their feelings and behaviour.

Therapists treating people with borderline personality disorder sometimes use a technique called dialectical behaviour therapy. In this type of therapy, the therapist initially focuses on reducing suicidal tendencies and other behaviours that disrupt treatment. The therapist then helps the person develop skills to cope with anger and self-destructive impulses. In addition, the person learns to achieve personal strength through an acceptance of the many disappointments and interpersonal conflicts that are a natural part of life.

Depression is categorized as a mental illness in which a person experiences deep, unshakable sadness and diminished interest in nearly all activities. People also use the term depression to describe the temporary sadness, loneliness, or blues that everyone feels from time to time. In contrast to normal sadness, severe depression, also called major depression, can dramatically impair a person's ability to function in social situations and at work. People with major depression often have feelings of despair, hopelessness, and worthlessness, as well as thoughts of committing suicide.

Depression can take several other forms. In bipolar disorder, sometimes called manic-depressive illness, a person's mood swings back and forth between depression and mania. Some people with dysthymia experience occasional episodes of major depression. Mental health professionals use the term clinical depression to refer to any of the above forms of depression

Depression is one of the most common mental illnesses. At least 8 percent of adults in the United States experience serious depression at some point during their lives, and estimates range as high as 17 percent. The illness affects all people, regardless of sex, race, ethnicity, or socioeconomic standing. However, women are two to three times more likely than men to suffer from depression. Experts disagree on the reason for this difference. Some cite differences in hormones, and others point to the stress caused by society's expectations of women.

Studies indicate that depression is more prevalent among women than it is among men. Genetics and environment seem to be the keys to unlocking this gender-gap mystery, although the complexity of the puzzle makes progress slow. In this article for Scientific American Presents, physician Ellen Leibenluft explores the physiology of depression and explains how scientific research may make it possible to develop better treatments for both sexes.

Depression occurs in all parts of the world, although the pattern of symptoms can vary. The prevalence of depression in other countries varies widely, from 1.5 percent of people in Taiwan to 19 percent of people in Lebanon. Some researchers believe methods of gathering data on depression account for different rates.

A number of large-scale studies indicate that depression rates have increased worldwide over the past several decades. Furthermore, younger generations are experiencing depression at an earlier age than did previous generations. Social scientists have proposed many explanations, including changes in family structure, urbanization, and reduced cultural and religious influences.

Although it may appear anytime from childhood to old age, depression usually begins during a person's 20s or 30s. The illness may come on slowly, then deepen gradually over months or years. On the other hand, it may erupt suddenly in a few weeks or days. A person who develops severe depression may appear so confuse, frightened, and unbalance that observers speak of a 'nervous breakdown.' However it begins, depression causes serious changes in a person's feelings and outlook. A person with major depression feels sad nearly every day and may cry often. People, work, and activities that used to bring them pleasure no longer do.

Symptoms of depression can vary by age. In younger children, depression may include physical complaints, such as stomachaches and headaches, as well as irritability, 'moping around,' social withdrawal, and changes in eating habits. They may feel unenthusiastic about school and other activities. In adolescents, common symptoms include sad mood, sleep disturbances, and lack of energy. Elderly people with depression usually complain of physical rather than emotional problems, which sometimes leads doctors to misdiagnose the illness.

Symptoms of depression can also vary by culture. In some cultures, depressed people may not experience sadness or guilt but may complain of physical problems. In Mediterranean cultures, for example, depressed people may complain of headaches or nerves. In Asian cultures they may complain of weakness, fatigue, or imbalance.

People with depression often experience feelings of worthlessness, helplessness, guilt, and self-blame. They may interpret a minor failing on their part as a sign of incompetence or interpret minor criticism as condemnation. Some depressed people complain of being spiritually or morally dead. The mirror seems to reflect someone ugly and repulsive. Even a competent and decent person may feel deficient, cruel, stupid, phony, or guilty of having deceived others. People with major depression may experience such extreme emotional pain that they consider or attempt suicide. At least 15 percent of seriously depressed people commit suicide, and many more attempt it.

Some depressions seem to come out of the blue, even when things are going well. Others seem to have an obvious cause: a marital conflict, financial difficulty, or some personal failure. Yet many people with these problems do not become deeply depressed. Most psychologists believe depression results from an interaction between stressful life events and a person's biological and psychological vulnerabilities.

Genes may influence depression by causing abnormal activity in the brain. Studies have shown that certain brain chemicals called neurotransmitters play an important role in regulating moods and emotions. Neurotransmitters involved in depression include norepinephrine, dopamine, and serotonin. Research in the 1960s suggested that depression results from lower than normal levels of these neurotransmitters in parts of the brain. Support for this theory came from the effects of antidepressant drugs, which work by increasing the levels of neurotransmitters involved in depression. However, later studies have discredited this simple explanation and have suggested a more complex relationship between neurotransmitter levels and depression.

An imbalance of hormones may also play a role in depression. Many depressed people have higher than normal levels of hydrocortisone (cortisol), a hormone secreted by the adrenal gland in response to stress. In addition, an underactive or overactive thyroid gland can lead to depression.

A variety of medical conditions can cause depression. These include dietary deficiencies in vitamin B6, vitamin B12, and folic acid, degenerative neurological disorders, such as Alzheimer's disease and Huntington's disease; strokes in the frontal part of the brain; and certain viral infections, such as hepatitis and mononucleosis. Certain medications, such as steroids, may also cause depression.

Cognitive theories of depression emphasize the role of irrational thought processes. American psychiatrist Aaron Beck proposed that depressed people tend to view themselves, their environment, and the future in a negative light because of errors in thinking. These errors include focussing on the negative aspects of any situation, misinterpreting facts in negative ways, and blaming themselves for any misfortune. In Beck's view, people learn these self-defeating ways of looking at the world during early childhood. This negative thinking makes situations seem much worse than they really are and increases the risk of depression, especially in stressful situations.

In support of this cognitive view, people with 'depressive' personality traits appear to be more vulnerable than others to actual depression. Examples of depressive personality traits include gloominess, pessimism, introversion, self-criticism, excessive skepticism and criticism of others, deep feelings of inadequacy, and excessive brooding and worrying. In addition, people who regularly behave in dependent, hostile, and impulsive ways appear at greater risk for depression.

People who experience child abuse appear more vulnerable to depression than others. So, too, do people living under chronically stressful conditions, such as single mothers with many children and little or no support from friends or relatives.

Depression typically cannot be shaken or willed away. An episode must therefore run its course until it weakens either on its own or with treatment. Depression can be treated effectively with antidepressant drugs, psychotherapy, or a combination of both.

Despite the availability of effective treatment, most depressive disorders go untreated and undiagnosed. Studies indicate that general physicians fail to recognize depression in their patients at least half of the time. In addition, many doctors and patients view depression in elderly people as a normal part of aging, even though treatment for depression in older people is usually very effective.

Studies have shown that short-term psychotherapy can relieve mild to moderate depression as effectively as antidepressant drugs. Unlike medication, psychotherapy produces no physiological side effects. In addition, depressed people treated with psychotherapy appear less likely to experience a relapse than those treated only with antidepressant medication. However, psychotherapy usually takes longer to produce benefits.

There are many kinds of psychotherapy. Cognitive-behavioural therapy assumes that depression stems from negative, often irrational thinking about oneself and one's future. In this type of therapy, a person learns to understand and eventually eliminate those habits of negative thinking. In interpersonal therapy, the therapist helps a person resolve problems in relationships with others that may have caused the depression. The subsequent improvement in social relationships and support helps alleviate the depression. Psychodynamic therapy views depression as the result of internal, unconscious conflicts. Psychodynamic therapists focus on a person's past experiences and the resolution of childhood conflicts. Psychoanalysis is an example of this type of therapy. Critics of long-term psychodynamic therapy argue that its effectiveness is scientifically unproven.

Mood disorders, also called affective disorders, create disturbances in a person's emotional life. Depression, mania, and bipolar disorder are examples of mood disorders. Symptoms of depression may include feelings of sadness, hopelessness, and worthlessness, as well as complaints of physical pain and changes in appetite, sleep patterns, and energy level. In mania, on the other hand, an individual experiences an abnormally elevated mood, often marked by exaggerated self-importance, irritability, agitation, and a decreased need for sleep. In bipolar disorder, also called manic-depressive illness, a person's mood alternates between extremes of mania and depression.

Personality disorders are mental illnesses in which one's personality results in personal distress or a significant impairment in social or work functioning. In general, people with personality disorders have poor perceptions of themselves or others. They may have low self-esteem or overwhelming narcissism, poor impulse control, troubled social relationships, and inappropriate emotional responses. Considerable controversy exists over where to draw the distinction between a normal personality and a personality disorder.

Cognitive disorders, such as delirium and dementia, involve a significant loss of mental functioning. Dementia, for example, is characterized by impaired memory and difficulties in such functions as speaking, abstract thinking, and the ability to identify familiar objects. The conditions in this category usually result from a medical condition, substance abuse, or verse.

Depression is one of the most common mental illnesses. At least 8 percent of adults in the United States experience serious depression at some point during their lives, and estimates range as high as 17 percent. The illness affects all people, regardless of sex, race, ethnicity, or socioeconomic standing. However, women are two to three times more likely than men to suffer from depression. Experts disagree on the reason for this difference. Some cite differences in hormones, and others point to the stress caused by society's expectations of women.

Depression occurs in all parts of the world, although the pattern of symptoms can vary. The prevalence of depression in other countries varies widely, from 1.5 percent of people in Taiwan to 19 percent of people in Lebanon. Some researchers believe methods of gathering data on depression account for different rates.

A number of large-scale studies indicate that depression rates have increased worldwide over the past several decades. Furthermore, younger generations are experiencing depression at an earlier age than did previous generations. Social scientists have proposed many explanations, including changes in family structure, urbanization, and reduced cultural and religious influences.

Although it may appear anytime from childhood to old age, depression usually begins during a person's 20s or 30s. The illness may come on slowly, then deepen gradually over months or years. On the other hand, it may erupt suddenly in a few weeks or days. A person who develops severe depression may appear so confused, frightened, and unbalanced that observers speak of a 'nervous breakdown.' However it begins, depression causes serious changes in a person's feelings and outlook. A person with major depression feels sad nearly every day and may cry often. People, work, and activities that used to bring them pleasure no longer do.

Symptoms of depression can vary by age. In younger children, depression may include physical complaints, such as stomachaches and headaches, as well as irritability, 'moping around,' social withdrawal, and changes in eating habits. They may feel unenthusiastic about school and other activities. In adolescents, common symptoms include sad mood, sleep disturbances, and lack of energy. Elderly people with depression usually complain of physical rather than emotional problems, which sometimes leads doctors to misdiagnose the illness.

Symptoms of depression can also vary by culture. In some cultures, depressed people may not experience sadness or guilt but may complain of physical problems. In Mediterranean cultures, for example, depressed people may complain of headaches or nerves. In Asian cultures they may complain of weakness, fatigue, or imbalance.

If left untreated, an episode of major depression typically lasts eight or nine months. About 85 percent of people who experience one bout of depression will experience future episodes.

`Depression usually alters a person's appetite, sometimes increasing it, but usually reducing it. Sleep habits often change as well. People with depression may oversleep or, more commonly, sleep for fewer hours. A depressed person might go to sleep at midnight, sleep restlessly, then wake up at 5:00 a.m. feeling tired and blue. For many depressed people, early morning is the saddest time of the day.

Depression also changes one's energy level. Some depressed people may be restless and agitated, engaging in fidgety movements and pacing. Other energy, and a feeling of being worn out or carrying a heavy burden. Depressed people may also have difficulty thinking, poor concentration, and problems with memory.

Some depressions seem to come out of the blue, even when things are going well. Others seem to have an obvious cause: a marital conflict, financial difficulty, or some personal failure. Yet many people with these problems do not become deeply depressed. Most psychologists believe depression results from an interaction between stressful life events and a person's biological and psychological vulnerabilities.

Genes may influence depression by causing abnormal activity in the brain. Studies have shown that certain brain chemicals called neurotransmitters play an important role in regulating moods and emotions. Neurotransmitters involved in depression include norepinephrine, dopamine, and serotonin. Research in the

1960s suggested that depression results from lower than normal levels of these neurotransmitters in parts of the brain. Support for this theory came from the effects of antidepressant drugs, which work by increasing the levels of neurotransmitters involved in depression. However, later studies have discredited this simple explanation and have suggested a more complex relationship between neurotransmitter levels and depression.

An imbalance of hormones may also play a role in depression. Many depressed people have higher than normal levels of hydrocortisone (cortisol), a hormone secreted by the adrenal gland in response to stress. In addition, an underactive or overactive thyroid gland can lead to depression.

A variety of medical conditions can cause depression. These include dietary deficiencies in vitamin B6, vitamin B12, and folic acid; degenerative neurological disorders, such as Alzheimer's disease and Huntington's disease, strokes in the frontal part of the brain; and certain viral infections, such as hepatitis and mononucleosis. Certain medications,

Cognitive theories of depression emphasize the role of irrational thought processes. American psychiatrist Aaron Beck proposed that depressed people tend to view themselves, their environment, and the future in a negative light because of errors in thinking. These errors include focussing on the negative aspects of any situation, misinterpreting facts in negative ways, and blaming themselves for any misfortune. In Beck's view, people learn these self-defeating ways of looking at the world during early childhood. This negative thinking makes situations seem much worse than they really are and increases the risk of depression, especially in stressful situations.

American psychologist Martin Seligman proposed that depression stems from 'learned helplessness,' an acquired belief that one cannot control the outcome of events. In this view, prolonged exposure to uncontrollable and inescapable events leads to apathy, pessimism, and loss of motivation. An adaptation of this theory by American psychologist Lynn Abramson and her colleagues argues that depression results not only from helplessness, but also hopelessness. The hopelessness theory attributes depression to a pattern of negative thinking in which people blame themselves for negative life events, view the causes of those events as permanent, and overgeneralize specific weaknesses as applying to many areas of their life.

People who experience child abuse appear more vulnerable to depression than others. So, too, do people living under chronically stressful conditions, such as single mothers with many children and little or no support from friends or relatives.

Depression typically cannot be shaken or willed away. An episode must therefore run its course until it weakens either on its own or with treatment. Depression can be treated effectively with antidepressant drugs, psychotherapy, or a combination of both.

Despite the availability of effective treatment, most depressive disorders go untreated and undiagnosed. Studies indicate that general physicians fail to recognize depression in their patients at least half of the time. In addition, many doctors and patients view depression in elderly people as a normal part of aging, even though treatment for depression in older people is usually very effective.

Up to 70 percent of people with depression respond to antidepressant drugs. These medications appear to work by altering the levels of serotonin, norepinephrine, and other neurotransmitters in the brain. They generally take at least two to three weeks to become effective. Doctors cannot predict which type of antidepressant drug will work best for any particular person, so depressed people may need to try several types. Antidepressant drugs are not addictive, but they may produce unwanted side effects. To avoid relapse, people usually must continue taking the medication for several months after their symptoms improve.

Commonly used antidepressant drugs fall into three major classes: tricyclics, monoamine oxidase inhibitors (MAO inhibitors), and selective serotonin reuptake inhibitors (SSRIs). Tricyclics, named for their three-ring chemical structure, include amitriptyline (Elavil), imipramine (Tofanil), desipramine (Norpramin), doxepin (Sinequan), and nortriptyline (Pamelor). Side effects of tricyclics may include drowsiness, dizziness upon standing, blurred vision, nausea, insomnia, constipation, and dry mouth.

MAO inhibitors include isocarboxazid (Marplan), phenelzine (Nardil), and tranylcypromine (Parnate). People who take MAO inhibitors must follow a diet that excludes tyramine—a substance found in wine, beer, some cheeses, and many fermented foods—to avoid a dangerous rise in blood pressure. In addition, MAO inhibitors have many of the same side effects as tricyclics.

Selective serotonin reuptake inhibitors include fluoxetine (Prozac), sertraline (Zoloft), and paroxetine (Paxil). These drugs

659

generally produce fewer and milder side effects than do other types of antidepressants, although SSRIs may cause anxiety, insomnia, drowsiness, headaches, and sexual dysfunction. Some patients have alleged that Prozac causes violent or suicidal behaviour in a small number of cases, but the US Food and Drug Administration has failed to substantiate this claim.

Prozac became the most widely used antidepressant in the world soon after its introduction in the late 1980s by drug manufacturer Eli Lilly and Company. Many people find Prozac extremely effective in lifting depression. In addition, some people have reported that Prozac actually transforms their personality by increasing their self-confidence, optimism, and energy level. However, mental health professionals have expressed serious ethical concerns over Prozac's use as a 'personality enchanters,' especially among people without clinical depression.

Fluoxetine, the drug known as an antidepressant and is prescribed for the treatment of depression, particularly depression lasting longer than two weeks and interfering with daily functioning. Fluoxetine works by regulating serotonin levels in the brain. Serotonin is a neurotransmitter, a chemical in the body's nervous system associated with maintaining a general sense of well-being. An insufficient amount of serotonin in the brain may contribute to depression. Fluoxetine may also be prescribed for treatment of other conditions related to insufficient levels of serotonin including eating disorders (obesity and bulimia), obsessive-compulsive disorder, and premenstrual syndrome.

Fluoxetine, available by prescription only, is taken orally in tablet form. The effectiveness of fluoxetine is not altered by food, so the medication can be taken on an empty or full stomach. When fluoxetine is prescribed to treat depression, the usual dose ranges from 20 to 60 mg per day. It usually requires three tour weeks for the patient feel the effects. After the medication begins to take effect, the dose may be lowered. A lower dose may be sufficient for treatment of conditions other than depression.

Fluoxetine should not be taken in combination with other types of antidepressants known as monoamine oxidase (MAO) inhibitors. Taking these medications at the same time or even within a month of one another has serious, sometimes fatal results. At least five weeks must be allowed between the last dose of fluoxetine and the first dose of a MAO inhibitor. Fluoxetine is not recommended for people recovering from heart attack, or for those with kidney or liver disease, diabetes, or a history of seizures. Women who are pregnant or breast-feeding are advised not to take fluoxetine, and people taking it should not consume alcohol.

Common adverse side effects of fluoxetine include anxiety, insomnia, headaches, dizziness, changes in appetite, weight loss, nausea, and diarrhea

MAO Inhibitor, any of a group of drugs used to treat depression, anxiety, or phobias. Properly known as monoamine oxidase (MAO) inhibitors, these drugs work by inhibiting or preventing the enzyme monoamine oxidase, found in the nervous system, from breaking down neurotransmitters, chemicals in the brain that control nerve impulse transmission and affect mood. MAO inhibitors produce a more balanced emotional state.

MAO inhibitors must be prescribed by a physician. Available in tablet form, these drugs are taken with or without food in one or more doses ranging from 30 to 90 mg per day, depending on the particular drug and the condition being treated. Effectiveness is usually apparent after three tour weeks of treatment, and long-term use for months or even years may be prescribed. MAO inhibitors should not be taken by pregnant women. Their safety for breast-feeding mothers or children under the age of 16 is not known.

These drugs should be used with caution by patients with heart or liver problems, diabetes, or epilepsy. MAO inhibitors can cause serious reactions, including death, if combined with certain foods that contain the chemical substance tyramine. Such foods include beer, wine, cheese, chocolate, sausage, liver, smoked meats or fish, sauerkraut, yogurt, and beverages containing caffeine.

Drugs to avoid while using MAO inhibitors include cold and cough remedies, sinus and hay fever medications, nasal decongestants, appetite suppressants, sleep aids, bronchodilators inhalants, amphetamines, and other antidepressants. Serious interactions can occur up to two weeks after drug treatment ends.

MAO Inhibitor, are those of any of a group of drugs used to treat depression, anxiety, or phobias. Properly known as monoamine oxidase (MAO) inhibitors, these drugs work by inhibiting or preventing the enzyme monoamine oxidase, found in the nervous system, from breaking down neurotransmitters, chemicals in the brain that control nerve impulse transmission and affect mood. MAO inhibitors produce a more balanced emotional state.

MAO inhibitors must be prescribed by a physician. Available in tablet form, these drugs are taken with or without food in one or more doses ranging from 30 to 90 mg per day, depending on the particular drug and the condition being treated. Effectiveness is usually apparent after three tour weeks of treatment, and long-term use for months or even years may be prescribed. MAO inhibitors should not be taken by pregnant women. Their safety for breast-feeding mothers or children under the age of 16 is not known.

These drugs should be used with caution by patients with heart or liver problems, diabetes, or epilepsy. MAO inhibitors can cause serious reactions, including death, if combined with certain foods that contain the chemical substance tyramine. Such foods include beer, wine, cheese, chocolate, sausage, liver, smoked meats or fish, sauerkraut, yogurt, and beverages containing caffeine.

Drugs to avoid while using MAO inhibitors include cold and cough remedies, sinus and hay fever medications, nasal decongestants, appetite suppressants, sleep aids, bronchodilator inhalants, amphetamines, and other antidepressants. Serious interactions can occur up to two weeks after drug treatment ends.

One significant side effect of MAO inhibitor drug use is high blood pressure, which may cause frequent headaches, heart palpitations, and vomiting. Other side effects include constipation, dizziness, fatigue, weakness, sleep disorders, digestive disorders, muscle spasms, problems with male sexual performance, and tremors or twitching. Because of the potential for serious side effects, patients taking MAO inhibitors are usually advised to carry a card or wear a bracelet that alerts medical personnel to their use of a MAO inhibitor in case of emergency.

Scientists actively explore the links between genes and behaviour to determine both the patterns and the limits of genetic influence. Such studies continue to be controversial because behaviour or mental processes can be difficult to measure objectively. Furthermore, many behavioural traits, both normal and abnormal, are complex, influenced by many genes as well as by personal experiences.

Studies of the possible genetic components of psychiatric disorders have yielded mixed results. Geneticists have identified at least two genes linked to schizophrenia, a condition characterized by hallucinations, delusion, paranoia, and other symptoms. Other studies that reported the discovery of genes that influence bipolar disorder (also known as manic-depressive illness) and alcoholism have been reversed or questioned. Though attempts to identify genes linked to these disorders have been flawed, scientists have little doubt that the conditions do have a genetic component.

Like physical disorders, mental illnesses may be treated with drugs, particularly antidepressants. However, while drugs help relieve the patient's symptoms, they seldom cure the underlying problems. More useful therapies include techniques that rely heavily on verbal and emotional communication. Collectively referred to as psychotherapy, these techniques help the patient to express, understand, and cope with underlying problems that are not due to physical disease. Emotionally disturbed children who cannot express their problems verbally may be treated by play therapy. The children are encouraged to engage in certain forms of recreation or to act out scenes on the theory that this process will reveal their feelings. Similar treatment, sometimes called psychodrama, may be used to help adults.

The final stage in treatment of physical and mental illnesses is often rehabilitation. This may include physical therapy, which involves exercise, massage, and the application of heat and water (hydrotherapy) to improve or restore functioning to damaged and weakened parts of the body. People with disabilities also benefit from recreational and occupational therapy, which helps people master their personal and work-related activities, such as buttoning clothes or cooking while seated in a wheelchair. Speech therapy is given to people who have speech problems of physical or psychological origin. In addition, people with disabilities may require psychotherapy to help them overcome the emotional and psychological problems that are sometimes associated with disability.

Cohn (1954) again, described the depressed person as seeing others as objects to be manipulated for the purposes of receiving sympathy and reassurances, but also as seeing them for being critical, rejecting, and ungenuine in their support. Further, in the achievement for reassurance, the depressed person finds concealed disapproval and rejection. According to the Cohn formulation, what the depressed person seeks is a dependent relationship in which all his needs are satisfied, and in his failure to obtain this, he resorts to the degressive this resorts to the depressive techniques of complaining and whining. If this, nonetheless, may lose hope, and enter into the psychotic state, where the patterns of emptiness and need continues in the, absence of specific objects.

Grinker (1964) interpreted the factor patterns obtained in an earlier study of depression (Grinker, 1961) as representing relatively constant patterns of communication. 'What is requested seemingly needed by the depressed patient expressed verbally, by gestures or in behaviour, varies and characterizes the pattern syndrome' (1964?).

Binime (1960, 1966) described how the depressed person can dominate his environment with his demands for emotionally comforting responses from others. He considered depression to be a practice, an active way of relating to people in order to achieve pathological satisfactions, and dismissed any suffering the depressed person may incur as secondary to the satisfaction of manipulative needs.

Aggression played a central role in early psychoanalytic formulations of depression (Abraham, 1911; Freud, 1917), but later writers have increasingly disputed its role. (Bibring, 1953) went on to declare that depression was an ego phenomenon. 'Essentially independent of vicissitudes of aggression as well as oral drives.'

Fromm-Reichmann (1959) argued that aggression had been considerably overstressed as a dynamic factor in depression, and that if hostile feelings were found in the depressed person, they were the result of the frustration of his manipulative and exploitative needs. Cohen (1954) attributed the hostility of the depressed person of his 'annoying impact on others, rather than to a primary motivation to do injury to them'. On the other hand, Bonime found that hurting or defying of others to be essential to depressed behaviour.

Renewed interest in the relationship between hostility and depression—particularly in the psychoanalytic view that depressed persons turn hostility that had originally been directed at others (hostility-out-outward), against themselves (hostility-inward)—has generated a number of empirical studies. Wessmam (1960) suggested that relatively normal persons became hostile toward when depressed, whereas persons tending to become severely depressed were more likely to internalize or suppressed this hostility. The data of Zuckerman (1967) supported this view, indicating that only in the relatively normal was hostility correlated with depression on mood questionnaires or as rated by interviews. Friedman (1964) found depressives to have more 'readily expressed resentment' as shown by their endorsement of adjectives such as 'bitter', 'frustrated', and 'sulky', yet found no greater overt hostility. In a later study, Friedman (1970) showed that feelings of depression and worthlessness were consonant with hostile and resentful feelings, even though depressed persons were not more likely to directly express these feelings to persons in the environment. Schless (1974) inward and outward, with both types of hostility increasing as depression became more severe. However, because these patients' also saw other people's anger as more readily expressed and more potent, they feared retaliation, and therefore expressed hostility only in the form of resentment. In summary, recent studies have been interpreted so as to call into question classical psychoanalytic formulations of the relationship of depression, hostility-inward and hostility-outward. On the other hand, the view that hostility may serve a defensive function increases in hostility that is directed out, but cannot be expressed directly to appropriate objects in the environment is taken as a failure of this defensive function (Friedman, 1970; McCranie, 1971;' Schless, (1974)).

Most writers who comment on the complaints and self-accusations of the depressed person have rejected the idea that they should be taken literally. Lichtenberg (1957) found that attempts to answer them directly with assurance, granting of dependency, and even punishment all increased depression and feelings of personal defect. Freud (1917) suggested that the self-accusations are actually aimed at someone else, a lost love object, and further notes,' . . . it must strike us that after all the melancholic does not behave in quite the same way as a person who is crushed by remorse and self-reproach in a normal fashion. Feelings of shame in front of other people, which would more than anything characterize this condition, are lacking in the melancholic, or at least, they are not prominent in him. One might emphasize the presence in him of an almost opposite trait of insistent communicativeness which finds satisfaction in self-exposure.'

In an attempt to modify depressive behaviour in a family situation (Liberman and Raskin, 1971), the baseline data indicated that other family members rejected opportunities to interact with the depressed person, and that all initiations of interaction between him hand his family in the baseline period were undertaken by him.

Paykel and Weissman (1973) reported extensive social dysfunction in women during depressive episodes. Interpersonal friction, inhibited communication, and submissive dependency occurred in both the initial episodes and in subsequent relapses. Onset of social difficulties was related to symptoms, but these difficulties continued months after symptoms remitted, a fact that Paykel and Weissman argue must be taken into account in any treatment plan.

Still, the provocative and often annoying behaviour of the depressive has distracted investigators from consideration of the role of the response of others. An exception, Jacobson (1954) noted that 'however exaggerated the patients' hurt', disappointment and hostile derogation of their partner may be, their complaints are usually more justified than may appear on the surface'. According to her, the depressed person often makes his whole environment feel; guilty and depressed, and this provokes defensive aggression and even cruelty precisely when he is most vulnerable. Depressives also have a tendency to develop an 'oral interplay' with those around them, so that mutual demands and expectations are built up to inevitable disappointment and depression for everyone concerned.

Lewinsohn and his associates (Lewinsohn and Shaw, 1969; Lewinsohn, 1969, Libet and Lewinsohn, 1973) have undertaken an ambitious clinical research program focussing on a social interaction of the depressed person from a behavioural point of view. In attempting to develop hypotheses about the reinforcement contingencies available to the depressed person. They have attempted a precise specifications of the social behaviour of the depressed person. Libet and Lewinsohn found depressed persons in group therapy to be lower than controls on a number of measures of social skill: Activity level, interpersonal range, rat e of positive reactions emitted and action latency. Their data are subject to alternative interpretations, however, particularly since they wade of positive reactions emitted was higher correlated with rates of positive reactions elicited. While depressed persons may well be deficient in social skills, some of the observed differences in group interaction situations may be due to the fact that fewer people are willing to interact with depressed persons (which results in a narrower interpersonal range and less opportunity for activity), and in this interaction emitted fewer positive responses (thereby, also reducing the positive responses elicited from the depressed). The most useful behavioural conceptualization of social interaction involving depressed persons would specify the lack of social skills of all participants, as evidenced by their inability to alter the contingencies offered or received. Behavioural interventions in the depressed person's marital and family relationships would therefore involve training all participants in these social skills, and beyond simply altering the contingencies available to the depressed person. Behavioural observations and self-reports of a couple in the Lewinsohn study (Lewisohn and Shaw, 1969) seem to support such a view.

Studies of suicide attempts and their effects on interpersonal relationships also provide data as relevantly, while suicide attempts do not have invariable relationship to depression, there is a definite association. McPartland and Hornstra (1964) examine the effects of suicide attempts on subsequent level of depression. They conceptualized depressive symptomatology as 'a set of demanding action by others to alter messages or restore the social space', and examined the relationships between suicide attempts and the ambiguity of the depressive message and the diffuseness of its intended audience. They were able to reliably place depressed patients at definite points along a dimension of interactive stalemate on the basis of the range of intended audience and the stridency of message in depressive communisations. Patients who were farthest along this continuum, whose communication was most diffuse, nonspecific, strident, and unanswerable, were most likely to have long hospital stays and diagnoses of psychosis. Suicide attempts tended to reduce the level of depression, apparently by shifting the interactive burden onto others. Other studies (Rubenstein, 1958; Moss and Hamilton, 1956; Kublere and Stotland, 1964) have indicated that suicide patients who improve following their attempts on their lives consistently have effected changes in their social fields, and those who improve generally have failed to change the their situation fundamentally.

RICHARD J. KOSCIEJEW

Depression is viewed, in this context as a response to the disruption of the social space in which the person obtains support and validation for his experience, this view, and a view of depressive symptomatology in terms of message value and intended audience, is similar to that of McPartland and Hornstra (1964), but the present analysis will place a greater emphasis on the contribution of the social environment to depressive drift. The interpersonal process described will be a general one, and it is assumed that the course of a specific depressive episode will be highly dependent on the structure of the person's social space. One of the implications of the approach taken as currently by an understanding of the social context is vital to an understanding of depression, although traditionally it has been largely ignored.

Social stresses leading to depression include loss of significant relationships, collapses of anticipated relationships, demotion (and in some cases, promotion), retirement, mislead chances, or any of a variety of other changes in a person's social structure. Depressive symptomatology is seen as a set of messages demanding reassurance of the person's place in the interactions he is still able to maintain, and further, action by others to alter or restore his loss.

Initial communications—verbal expressions of helplessness and hopelessness—tend to engage others immediately and to shift the interactive burden to others. The receivers of these messages usually attempt to answer the depressed person's request directly. However, as previously noted by Grinker (1964) and Lichtenberg (1957), their literal responses present him with a dilemma. Much of the depressive's communication is aimed at ascertaining the nature of relationship or context in which the interaction is taking place; Grinker (1964) has compared this to the various 'how' and 'why' questions that young children direct to their parents, and suggested that both children and depressives will be left feeling rejected, ignored, or brushed aside if provided with a literal response.

If communication took place at only one level, depression would probably be a less ubiquitous problem. However, the problem is that human beings not only communicate, but communicate about this communication, qualifying or labelling what they say by (1) the context or relationship in which the communication takes place, (2) other verbal messages (3) vocal; and linguistic patterns, and (4) bodily movement (Haley, 1963). A person may offer support and reassurance with a rejecting tone or he may offer criticism ion a supportive and reassuring tone. Such that, when messages qualify each other incongruently, then incongruent statements are made about the relationship. If probably always qualified what they said in a congruent way, relationships would be defined clearly and simply even though many levels of communications were functioning. However, when a statement is made which by its existence indicates one type of relationship and qualified by a statement denying this, then difficulties in interpersonal relations become inevitable (Haley, 1963).

It is enough that vocal and linguistic patterns and body movement are ambiguous and subject to alternative interpretations. However, a further problem for the depressed person is that the context, the nature of the relationship between the depressed person and the persons communicating to him, may require time and further messages to be clearly defined.

The depressed person's problem is to decide whether others are assuring him that he is worthy and acceptable because they do in fact maintain this attitude toward him, or rather only because he has attempted to elicit such responses. Unwilling or unable to endure the time necessary to answer this question, the depressive used his symptoms to seek repeated feedback in his testing of the nature of his acceptance and the security of his relationships.

While providing continual feedback, these efforts are at the same time profoundly and negatively affecting these relationships. The persistence and repetition of the symptoms is both incomprehensible and aversive to members of the social environment. However, the accompanying indication of distress and suffering is powerful in its ability to arouse guilt in others and to inhibit and direct expression of annoyance and hostility from them, as observed in both the family difficulties of depressed persons (Jacobson, 1954) and the problem's therapists report in their effort to relate to depressed parents (Cohen, 1954).

Irritated, yet, inhibited and increasingly guilt-ridden, members of the social environment continue to give verbal assurance of support and acceptance. However, a growing discrepancy between the verbal content and the affective quality of these responses provides validation for the depressive's suspicions that he is not really being accepted and that further interaction cannot be assured. To

669

maintain his increasingly uncertain security, the depressive display more symptoms.

At this point, the first of a number of interactive stalemates may be reached. Members of the depressed person's environment who can find a suitable rationalization for their behaviour may leave the field, or, at least, in efforts to indicate that this is not in fact rejection, but given the context, these efforts do little more than reduce credibility and increase the depressive's insecurity, with those members of the social environment who remain, a self-maintaining pattern to mutual manipulation is established. Perhaps in the environment find that they can reduce the aversive behaviour of the depressed person and alleviate the guilt that this depressed behaviour has an uncanny ability to elicit, if they manipulate him with reassurance, support, and denial of the process that is taking place. The depressed person. On the other hand, finds that by displaying symptoms he can manipulate his environment so that it will provide sympathy and reassurance, but he is aware by now that this response from others is not genuine and that they have become critical and rejecting. While this situation is attractive for neither the depressed person nor members of his social environment, it provides a stabilization of what has been a deteriorating situation.

One alternative facing the depressed person is for him to accept the precipitating disruption of his social space and the resulting loss of support and validation. However, now that he has begun showing symptoms, he has invested portions of his remaining relationships in his recovery effort., That is, he has tested these relationships, made demands, and has been frustrated in ways that seriously call into question his conception of these relationships. If he abandons these efforts, he may have to relinquish the support and validation derived from these relationships while accepting the precipitating loss. At this point, he may be too dependent on the remaining relationships to give them up. Furthermore, as a result if the mixed messages he has been receiving from others, he now has an increasing confused and deteriorated self-concept, which must be clarified, with new desperation more symptoms may be displayed.

Various possible efforts by the depressed person to discover what is wrong with him, i.e., why he is being rejected and manipulated one the less, to reestablish a more normal interactive pattern are in this context indistinguishable from the manipulations has used to control the repressed onset of others. Therefore, they are met with the usual manipulation requesting information as to how people really view him is indistinguishable from symptomatic efforts. If the depressed person attempts to discuss the interpersonal process that is taking place, he touches on a sensitive issue, and is likely only to elicit denial by the others or a angry defensive responses. On the other hand, efforts by others to assure the depressed person that he is really accepted and that they are not rejecting him are in this context indistinguishable from previous manipulations that they have employed, and therefore. Serve to strengthen the developing system. Thus, interpersonal manoeuvres directed at changing the emerging pattern become system-maintaining, and any genuine feedback to the repressed person is also indistinguishable from manipulation. Persons leaving the social field increase both the depressed person's feeling s of rejection and his impetus to continue his behaviour patten. Persons just entering the social field cab be quickly recruited into the existing roles, since their efforts to deal with the depressive person—even if genuine—are likely to be quite similar to those now being employed manipulatively. They therefore, become subject to the compelling manipulations. That the person, come to the compelling lure of manipulations of the depressed person, come to respond manipulatively themselves, and are inducted into the system.

Descriptions of the depressed person at this point in his career focus on the distortions and misperceptions that serve to maintain his depression. What is generally ignored is that these 'distortions' and 'misperceptions' are congruent with the social system in which the depressed person now finds himself. The specific content of the depressive's complaints and accusations may not be accurate, but his environment are a recognition of the attenuation relationships, disrupted comments are a recognition of the attenuated relationships, disrupted communication and lack of genuineness that he faces. These conditions serve to prevent him from receiving the feedback necessary to correct any misperception or distortion. He has played a major role in the creation of this social system, but the emergency of the system has also required the cooperation of others, and established, it tends to be largely beyond the control of its participants.

RICHARD J. KOSCIEJEW

Depending on characteristics of both the depressed person and his environment, a number of punishing variations on the above pattern may develop. Members of the social environment who have been repeated provoked and made feel guilty may retaliate by withholding the responses for which the depressed person depends on them. The depressed person may become aware of the inhibiting influence his symptoms have on the direct expression of negative feelings, and may use these symptoms aggressively, while limiting the forms that counteraggression can take. He may also discover and exploit the interdependence of others and the frustrations it entails, he may also become aware of the extent to which others are dependent on him, in that their own maintenance of mood and their ability. Because either of an outright hostility, or as a self-defeating effort to convince others of their need be the renegotiated relationship with him, the depressed person may become sympathetic in his withholding of these minimal cooperative behaviour. While hostility may not necessary be a major etiological factor in depression, the frustration, provocations, and manipulations occurring in interactions between depressed persons and others would seem to encourage it.

As efforts to end the interactive stalemate fail, there may be a shift in the depressive's self-presentation to one indicating greater distress and implying that the environment has more responsibility for bringing about the necessary changes. McPartland and Hornstra (1964) found that they could unambiguously differentiate themes of hopelessness and helplessness from more disturbed themes of low energy and physical complaints in communications of depressed patients. The latter themes were associated with longer hospitalization when hospitalized depressed patients were sampled McPartland and Hornstra give the examples of 'I can't sleep and I can't stand it any longer', 'I am too tired to move', My head and my stomach feel funny all the time'. Unable to restore his life space, the depressive now implicitly demands 'a suspension of the rules; a moratorium on the web of obligation; (McPartlant and Hornstra, 1964). With immediate relationships deteriorating, the depressive addresses his plea to a more general audience, but in more confusing and unanswerable terms, literal responses to his communications may involve medial intervention for his specific complaints, but this generally fails to alleviate the problem. Any efforts to move the interactional theme back to

672

the depressive's sense of hopelessness and helplessness threaten to reopen the earlier unfruitful and even punishing patterns of relations, and tend to be resisted. Unable to answer, or in many cases, even to comprehend the depressive's pleas, members of the social environment may withdraw further from him, increasing his desperation, and quickening the depressive's drift.

With a second interactive stalemate now reached, the depressed person may attempt to resolve it by increasing his level of symptomatology and shifting the theme of his self-presentation to one of the worthlessness and evil, 'I am a failure; it's all my fault; I am sinful and worthless.' Unable, either to restore his social space or to reduce his obligations sufficiently for him to continue to cope, the depressive now communicates his bafflement and resignation. The intended audience is now more diffuse. Relationships are even more attenuated, and the new message is more obscure and perplexing. The social environment and the depressive soon arrive at another stalemate, otherwise helpless to alleviate the situation, remaining members of the environment may further withdraw or, alternatively, have the depressive withdrawn through hospitalization. In the absence on any relatedness to others, the depressive may drift into delusions and frankly psychotic behaviour.

Self-value, then, and objects, are inseparable form as drama of life significance. To lose self-esteem, to lose a 'game', and to lose an object, are inseparable aspects of the loss of meaning. Meaning, is not something that springs up from within man, something born into life that unfolds like a lotus. Meaning is not embedded in some obscure 'inner human nature', not something that is destined to be developed by successively 'highly forms of life'. There is, in short, nothing vitalistic or mysteriously emergent implied in the idea of meaning. Meaning is the elaboration of an increasingly intricate ground plan of broad relationships and ramifications, it is the establishment of dependable cause-and-effect sequences which permit ego-mastery and action. Meaning is at the heart of life because it is inseparable from undependable, satisfying actions. Man embroiders his cause-and-effect action sequences with an intricate symbolism; flags, commandment, lace underwear, and secret-codes. The result is that particular kinds and sequences of action take on a life-and-death flavour. The dependable becomes the indispensable satisfying becomes the necessary. Man's symbolic life is an imbibing of meaning and a relentless creation of this symbolic elaboration of meaning is the Homo sapient's sapient.

Initially, meaning does not need language. We stress that it exists in behaviour. For energy-converting organisms, action is primary. Forward-momentum is enough to build meaning, and possibilities for forward-momentum exist in nature, in his perception and attention. Instinctive action gives experience which, in turn, provides meaning simply because it commands attention and leads to further action. But for the symbolic animal a complication enters: Language replaces instinctive readiness. Language makes action broader and richer for the symbolic animal. But something curious occurs in this process. Language comes to be learned as a means of acting without anxiety. Each of the infant's acts come to be dressed in words that are provided by his loved objects. As a child, lacking a word, he lacks a safe action. Action and word-prescriptions become inseparable, because they join in permitting anxiety-free conduct. Growing into adulthood, the individual has built his habits into a self-consistent scheme. To lack word is then to lack a meaningful action; the simplest act has to take on meaning, has to point to something beyond itself, exist in a wider referential context. We become paralysed to act unless there is a verbal prescription for the new situation. Even our perceptions come to be built inti a rigid framework. Man lose progressively the capacity to 'act in nature' as he verbally creates his own action world. Words give man the motivation to act, and words justify the act. Life-meaning for man comes to be predominantly an edifice of words and word-sounds.

If the individual can keep verbal referents going in a self-consistent scheme, action remains possible and life retains its meaning. If he cannot, if the integrity of the symbolic meaning-framework is undermined, external action grinds to a halt.

The meanings of words can also change. In Middle English, the word nice usually had the meaning 'foolish,' and sometimes 'shy,' but never the modern meaning 'pleasant.' Change in the meanings of words is known as semantic change and can be viewed as part of the more general phenomenon of lexical change, or change in a language's vocabulary. Words not only can change their meaning but also can become obsolete. For example, modern readers require a note to explain Shakespeare's word hent (take hold of), which is no longer in use. In addition, new words can be created, such as feedback.

Symptoms of depression can vary by age. In younger children, depression may include physical complaints, such as stomachaches and headaches, as well as irritability, "moping around," social withdrawal, and changes in eating habits. They may feel unenthusiastic about school and other activities. In adolescents, common symptoms include sad mood, sleep disturbances, and lack of energy. Elderly people with depression usually complain of physical rather than emotional problems, which sometimes leads doctors to misdiagnose the illness.

Symptoms of depression can also vary by culture. In some cultures, depressed people may not experience sadness or guilt but may complain of physical problems. In Mediterranean cultures, for example, depressed people may complain of headaches or nerves. In Asian cultures they may complain of weakness, fatigue, or imbalance.

If left untreated, an episode of major depression typically lasts eight or nine months. About 85 percent of people who experience one bout of depression will experience future episodes.

Depression usually alters a person's appetite, sometimes increasing it, but usually reducing it. Sleep habits often change as well. People with depression may oversleep or, more commonly, sleep for fewer hours. A depressed person might go to sleep at midnight, sleep restlessly, then wake up at 5:00 a.m. feeling tired and blue. For many depressed people, early morning is the saddest time of the day.

Depression also changes one's energy level. Some depressed people may be restless and agitated, engaging in fidgety movements and pacing. Others may feel sluggish and inactive, experiencing great fatigue, lack of energy, and a feeling of being worn out or carrying a heavy burden. Depressed people may also have difficulty thinking, poor concentration, and problems with memory.

People with depression often experience feelings of worthlessness, helplessness, guilt, and self-blame. They may interpret a minor failing on their part as a sign of incompetence or interpret minor criticism as condemnation. Some depressed people complain of being spiritually or morally dead. The mirror seems to reflect someone ugly and repulsive. Even a competent and decent person may feel deficient, cruel, stupid, phony, or guilty of having deceived others. People with major depression may experience such extreme emotional pain that they consider or attempt suicide.

At least 15 percent of seriously depressed people commit suicide, and many more attempt it.

In some cases, people with depression may experience psychotic symptoms, such as delusions (false beliefs) and hallucinations (false sensory perceptions). Psychotic symptoms indicate an especially severe illness. Compared to other depressed people, those with psychotic symptoms have longer hospital stays, and after leaving, they are more likely to be moody and unhappy. They are also more likely to commit suicide.

Some depressions seem to come out of the blue, even when things are going well. Others seem to have an obvious cause: a marital conflict, financial difficulty, or some personal failure. Yet many people with these problems do not become deeply depressed. Most psychologists believe depression results from an interaction between stressful life events and a person's biological and psychological vulnerabilities.

Genes may influence depression by causing abnormal activity in the brain. Studies have shown that certain brain chemicals called neurotransmitters play an important role in regulating moods and emotions. Neurotransmitters involved in depression include norepinephrine, dopamine, and serotonin. Research in the 1960s suggested that depression results from lower than normal levels of these neurotransmitters in parts of the brain. Support for this theory came from the effects of antidepressant drugs, which work by increasing the levels of neurotransmitters involved in depression. However, later studies have discredited this simple explanation and have suggested a more complex relationship between neurotransmitter levels and depression.

An imbalance of hormones may also play a role in depression. Many depressed people have higher than normal levels of hydrocortisone (cortisol), a hormone secreted by the adrenal gland in response to stress. In addition, an underactive or overactive thyroid gland can lead to depression.

A variety of medical conditions can cause depression. These include dietary deficiencies in vitamin B6, vitamin B12, and folic acid; degenerative neurological disorders, such as Alzheimer's disease and Huntington's disease; strokes in the frontal part of the brain; and certain viral infections, such as hepatitis and mononucleosis. Certain medications, such as steroids, may also cause depression.

Psychological theories of depression focus on the way people think and behave. In a 1917 essay, Austrian psychoanalyst Sigmund Freud explained melancholia, or major depression, as a response to loss—either real loss, such as the death of a spouse, or symbolic loss, such as the failure to achieve an important goal. Freud believed that a person's unconscious anger over loss weakens the ego, resulting in self-hate and self-destructive behaviour.

Cognitive theories of depression emphasize the role of irrational thought processes. American psychiatrist Aaron Beck proposed that depressed people tend to view themselves, their environment, and the future in a negative light because of errors in thinking. These errors include focussing on the negative aspects of any situation, misinterpreting facts in negative ways, and blaming themselves for any misfortune. In Beck's view, people learn these self-defeating ways of looking at the world during early childhood. This negative thinking makes situations seem much worse than they really are and increases the risk of depression, especially in stressful situations.

In support of this cognitive view, people with "depressive" personality traits appear to be more vulnerable than others to actual depression. Examples of depressive personality traits include gloominess, pessimism, introversion, self-criticism, excessive skepticism and criticism of others, deep feelings of inadequacy, and excessive brooding and worrying. In addition, people who regularly behave in dependent, hostile, and impulsive ways appear at greater risk for depression.

Mood disorders, also called affective disorders, create disturbances in a person's emotional life. Depression, mania, and bipolar disorder are examples of mood disorders. Symptoms of depression may include feelings of sadness, hopelessness, and worthlessness, as well as complaints of physical pain and changes in appetite, sleep patterns, and energy level. In mania, on the other hand, an individual experiences an abnormally elevated mood, often marked by exaggerated self-importance, irritability, agitation, and a decreased need for sleep. In bipolar disorder, also called manic-depressive illness, a person's mood alternates between extremes of mania and depression.

Some people with schizophrenia experience delusions of persecution—false beliefs that other people are plotting against them. This interview between a patient with schizophrenia and his

677

therapist illustrates the paranoia that can affect people with this illness.

People with schizophrenia and other psychotic disorders lose contact with reality. Symptoms may include delusions and hallucinations, disorganized thinking and speech, bizarre behaviour, a diminished range of emotional responsiveness, and social withdrawal. In addition, people who suffer from these illnesses experience and inability to function in one or more important areas of life, such as social relations, work, or school.

Several other psychiatric disorders are closely related to schizophrenia. In schizoaffective disorder, a person shows symptoms of schizophrenia combined with either mania or severe depression. Schizophreniform disorder refers to an illness in which a person experiences schizophrenic symptoms for more than one month but fewer than six months. In schizotypal personality disorder, a person engages in odd thinking, speech, and behaviour, but usually does not lose contact with reality. Sometimes mental health professionals refer to these disorders together as schizophrenia-spectrum disorders.

Schizophrenia sums up man's coming of age in society. In order to understand it we have had to trace a lengthy picture of the process of becoming human. Depression is much more simple, unlike the schizophrenic, the person has not failed to learn secure answers to a combinality of common problems. His dilemma, in anything, is some what of a paradox: He has learned these answers only too well. He has built himself so firmly into his cultural world that he is imprisoned in his own narrow behavioural mold.

For the most part, this model represents the advanced theoretical cogitations of the psychiatric profession of a perplexing human phenomenon. This much must be said: It is not easy to comprehend why anyone would opt out of life. It is understandable that he would be quick to look for some basic genetic taint, some stunted early development, that would mark such an individual off from others. But the matter is not quite so simple. The fact is that a good proportion of depressed patients have led mature and responsible lives,; some have achieved notable success, financial and personal. We distort our vision if we use of such a punctuated theory to explain why these people become abysmally depressed.

Depression may be seen as a reflection of deficiencies in one or more of such self-control processes. self-monitoring involves attending to one's own behaviour as self-evaluation is a matter of interpreting one's behaviour and comparing it to internal standards, as self-reinforcement involves administering reinforcement to oneself. These self-control processes may selectively tend to negative aspects of their own behaviour and ignore positive accomplishments. And may involve an attriutional bias so that they are excessively blamed for failures and take insufficient credit for successes. They may employ overly harsh or stringent standards in evaluating themselves. Finally, they may be in rewarding themselves or overly self-punishing.

Self-control has recently become an important focus of behaviour research (Goldfried and Merbaum, 1973; Mahoney and Thoresen, 1974; Thoresen and Mahoney, 1974). Models of self-control have been used to analyse various forms of normal and deviant behaviour and have generates self-administered behaviour change programs applicable to various target behaviours. With slight modifications Kanfer (1970, 1971; Kanfer and Karoly, 1972). Kanger sees self-control as those processes by which an individual alters the probability of a response in the relative absence of immediate external supports,. Three processes are postulated in a feedback loop model : Self-monitoring, self-evaluation, and self-reinforcement.

Self-monitoring involves observations of one's own behaviour along with its situational antecedents and its consequences. For instance, in self-control therapy procedures, smokers may note the places in which they smoke, socially anxious males may record the number of contacts they have with females, and overweight person may count calorie. Internal events in the form of proprioceptive, sensory, and affective responses may also be self-monitored. For example, smoker's mas y be asked to rate their anxiety level at the time of smoking a cigarette. Self-monitoring involve s not only a passive perception awareness of events but a selective attention to certain classes of events and the ability to make accurate discriminations. Deficits in self-control may therefore exist in the manner in which individuals customarily self-monitor. Specific deficits in sel-monitoring behaviour represent on potential of maladaptive self-control.

Self-evaluation refers to a comparison between an estimate of performance, which derives from delf-monitoring, and an internal criterion of standard. For example, the dieter compares the day's calorie count to a goal and judges whether or not the criterion has been met. Standards may be derived from a variety of sources (cf, Kanfer, 1970; Bandura, 1971). Individuals may set their internal criteria by adopting externally imposed standards, e.g., not just an A but 100 per cent correct on every test. Criteria may or may or may not be realistic and, thus, inappropriately selected internal criteria may represent another specific type of deficit in self-control behaviour.

Self-attribution and self-evaluation attriutional processes play a role in self-evaluation and can be incorporated into Kanfer's model. Bandura (1971) notes that in self-evaluation research, judgement that a response is accurate or successful is often confounded with judgement that the response is commendable. In fact, these judgements are not always equivalent. Adults might perceive themselves as accurate and successful on a child's task and not evaluate their performance as commendable in any way. Similarly, people might perceive themselves as inaccurate and failing on a task outside their own area of expertise and not condemn themselves for it. Bandura suggests selecting tasks which minimize these confounding effects, but there are further implications of the problem.

The larger issue is that the positive or negative self-evaluation implies more than a comparison of performance to criteria of success or failure. Such comparisons are modified by the manner in which people perceive themselves as capable and responsible for the behaviour. That is, the cause of the behaviour must be internally attributed. In that Kanfer (1970, 1971) refers to self-control as occurring in the relative absence of external control, efforts to control one's behaviour are premised on, at least, the perception of mental control.

Thus, self-evaluations should be considered to be the comparison of internally attributed performances to a standard or criterion. Performance is commendable only if it visible attributed internally and judged to exceed a criterion of success. Performance is condemnable only of it is both attributed internally and judged to fall below a criterion for failure. Degree of internal attribution interacts with perceived success or failure to determine the value of self-evaluation. Weiner, Heckhausen, Meyer, and Cook (1972) demonstrated this relationship a correlational study of the tendency to make internal attribution and magnitude of self-reward and self-punishing in normal subjects. Because individual differences in making internal attributions exist, self-attributional deficits are another potential type of maladaptive self-control behaviour.

A basic assumption in behavioural conception of self-control, is that individuals control their own behaviour by the same means that one organism might control a second organism and that the same principles apply. Thus, the administration of covert or covert contingent reward to punishment to oneself is postulated as a mechanism of self-control. The self-control model suggests that self-reinforcement supplements external reinforcement in controlling behaviour. As Bandura (1976) has argued, self-reinforcement must be conceptualized in a context of external reinforcement, that is, while behaviour must generally be seen as directed by and toward gaining external reinforcement, self-reinforcement (overt or covert) functions to maintain consistency and bridge delay when external reinforcers are delayed and immediate reinforcement for alternative behaviour is available.

Self-reinforcement has been a major focus of self-control research and many clinical uses of self-administered reward and punishment programs have been described (Thoresen and Mahoney, 1974). Rates of self-reward and self-punishment yield relatively stable individual differences (Kanfer, Duerfeldt, LePage, 1969; Marston, 1969) and do not necessarily correlate with one another (Kanfer, 1969). Self-control may be maladaptive in terms of either self-reward or self punishment patterns.

The model of self-control which can serve as a heuristic model for studying depression in regard to its symptoms, etiology and therapy. Specific deficits at different stages of self-control may be seen as the basis for specific manifestations of depression.

There are, at least, two ways in which the self-monitoring of depressed persons can be characterized. First, depressed persons tend to attend selectively to negative events, and second, depressed persons tend to attend selectively to immediate versus delayed outcomes of their behaviour. The term 'negative event' is intended to include stimuli which are aversive and other stimuli which are perceived as cues for aversive stimuli. The term has a converse correspondence to Lewinsohn's (1974) 'pleasant event'. From complex experience including both positive and negative events, depressed persons selectively attend to negative (unpleasant) events to the relatively exclusion of positive (pleasurable) events.

Ferster (1973) had argued that depressed persons devote disproportionate time to avoidance of or escape from adversive events. This behaviour precludes positive reinforced behaviour. Beck (1972) includes in his discussion of cognitive distortions the concepts of 'selective abstraction' and 'arbitrary inference', both of which describe similar processes of attention to negative events. Selective abstraction involves focussing on a detail taken out of a more salient context and using it as a basis for conceptualization for the entire experience. In depression, the detail attended to is usually a negative event embedded in an array of more positive or negative events. Arbitrary inference involves a personal interpretation of an ambiguous or personally irrelevant event. In depression, a negative quality of the event is selectively attended to. An inappropriate attribution may also be involved.

Although no research has been aimed at this specific formulation as yet, there are studies which are interpretable in these terms. The negative perceptions which occur in response to projective stimuli, e.g., Weintraub, Segal, and Beck, 1974) could easily be seen as due to selective attention. Wener and Rehm (1974) found that depressed persons underestimated the percentage of positive feedback they received. A relative inattention to these positive events could be inferred.

Selective attention to immediate versus delayed outcomes is related to Lewinsohn's (1974) concept that depressed behaviour functions to elicit immediate reinforcement from the social environment at the expense of the more important forms of delayed reinforcement. Also related is Lazarus (1968, 1974) suggestion that depressed persons lose their future perspective. They may be seen as attending to immediate outcomes instead.

Correlational evidence consistent with this deficit was obtained by Rehm and Plakosh (1975) who found a greater expressed preference for immediate as opposed to delayed rewards among depressed as compared to nondepressed undergraduates and by Wener and Rehm (1975) who found that depressed persons were influenced to a greater extent by both high and low rates of immediate reinforcements.

The self-control of depressed persons can be characterized as maladaptive in two ways within the self-evaluation phase. First, depressed persons frequently fail to make accurate internal attributions of causality. Second, depressed persons tend to set stringent criteria for self-evaluation.

From an attrbutional point of view, a depressed person an be 'helpless' in either of two ways. In the first, the person make excessive external attributions of causality and thus generally believes that there is a high degree of independence between performance and consequences. Such a person as helpless in Seligman's sense of the word and would seldom engage in self-control behaviour even in an aversive environment. Such a person would be passive and apathetic but would not necessarily be self-derogating. Since aversive consequences are seen as uncontrollable, performance is neither commendable nor condemnable. In the second form of helplessness, the person makes accurate or even excessively internal attributions of causality but perceives himself or herself to be lacking in ability to obtain positive consequences. Thus, the person believes that the world does contain lawful performance-consequence relationships but that she or he is incompetent and ineffective. This person would be self-derogatory and would express inappropriate guilt, e.g., excessive internal attribution of causality for past aversive consequences. The use of the term helpless is this latter instance is somewhat different from Seligman's use of the term.

The work on learned helplessness in depression can be interpreted as support for either type of inaccurate attribution. For example, Miller and Seligman (1973) found that following success on a skill-defined task, depressed students did not raise their expectations of success as the nondepressed students did. No differences in expectancy change were found after failure of in chance defined tasks. As it is to interpret, that this finding in terms of a generalized perception by depressed persons that reinforcement is response independent. From an attributional framework subjects either perceived the task outcome to have been due to external causes, i.e., chance, not skill, or perceived sustaining their success, i.e., lacking skill. The data admit equally to either interpretation.

Stringent self-evaluative criteria as a characteristic of depression has been previously suggested by Marston (1965) and Bandura (1971). Self-evaluative standards may be stringent in the sense of a high threshold requiring great quantitative or quantitative excellence for self-approval. Golin and Terrel found that depressed college students tend to set higher goal levels for themselves. This deficit together with selective monitoring of negative events result in very few perceived successes. Depressed persons may also have low thresholds for negative self-evaluation. Although these criteria may be relatively independent, clinical observation, (e.g., Beck, 1972) suggests that for some depressed persons they may be almost reciprocals, depressed persons may have 'all or none' self-evaluative criteria, i.e., an effort is either a smashing success or a dismal failure.

Self-evaluative criteria may also be stringent in the sense of excessive breadth, failure in one instance is taken as failure in the entire class of behaviour. for example, failure on one exam is taken as evidence for failure as a student and, perhaps, as a person. Beck (1972) describes overgeneralization as one of the primary mechanisms of cognitive distortion in depression.

The self-reinforcement phase of self-control is particularly importance in accounting for depressive behaviour. Depression can be characterized by the self-administration of relatively low rates of self-reward and of which rates of self-punishment. low rates of self-reward can be associated with the slowed rates of overt behaviour which typify depression. Lower general activity level, few responses' initiations, lower latencies, and less persistence may be interpreted as resulting from low rates of self-reward.

Self-punishment in normals serves to control behaviour reward, e.g., 'kicking oneself' for going off a diet. Self-punishment may also serve as a cue initiating alternative behaviour for approaching a goal (Kanfer and Karolly, 1972), Because and set stringent self-evaluation criteria, potentially effective behaviour may also be supposed by excessive self-punishing. Vacillation between responding strategies may also result because each alternative is self-punished early in the response chain, e.g., indecisiveness.

Correlational evidence for self-reinforcement deficits in depression was obtained by Rozensky, Rehm, Pry and Roth. Their study demonstrated differences in rates of self-reward and self-punishment between depressed and nondepressed hospital patients. Nevertheless,. The former did not differ in correct responses, so that, a replicated procedure with college students varying in degree of depression. Depressed students gave themselves more self-punishment and less self-reward than n nondepressed students although only the former difference obtained statistical significance. The failure to replicate the self-reward finding maybe due to the fact that the latter population was by definition a relatively active group of normals capable of working for long term rewards.

Depression can be accounted for in terms of six deficits in self-control behaviour: (1), selective monitoring of negative events; (2) selective monitoring of immediate as opposed to delayed consequences; (3) stringent self-evaluation criteria; (4) inaccurate attributions of responsibility;(5) insignificant self-reward;' and (6) expressive self-punishment.

The self-control model as applied to depression serves as a framework for analysis and integration and provide a framework for distinguishing various depression symptoms, each of which can be logically associated with a particular aspect of self-control. The model encompasses and integrates a range of behaviours on which available models focus exclusively. The model also suggests interrelationships among these behaviours, which have an empirical basis in self-control research, e.g., Kirshenbaum, cited in Kanfer and Weiner, 1972). The model specifies relationships between covert, cognitive behaviour and overt-motor behaviour in depression,

As a heuristic framework, some parts of the model are only suggested in outline and require further refinement and validation. Although the model is consistent with certain empirical findings, the evidence is largely correlational and further research is clearly needed. The products of research specifically directed by the model will determine its ultimate value.

The self-control model is applied as in semblance to a particular form of psychopathology, namely depression. The deficits postulated may not be exclusive to depression. For instance, Clark and Arkowitz (1975) found stringent self-evaluation criteria among socially anxious college students who rated their own behaviour in an interaction with a confederate. On the other hand, self-control deficits of other kinds may be more characteristic of other forms of psychopathology. Sociopaths may show some of the deficits of depression in reverse: Lenient self-evaluative criteria, excessive self-reward, and insufficient self-punishment. The self-control model may have wider applicability as a model of psychopathology.

Finally, the model may have some limitations as to causes and types of depression. Recent evidence in genetic and biochemical research on depression strongly point to a biological components in some forms of depression. Biological factors and self-control deficits may represent separate sources of variance in accounting for the occurrence of depression or they may interact. Akiskal and McKinney (1973, 1975) have argued for a broad interaction model. In any case, the relative contribution of biological and psychological factors to the etiology, symptomatology, and therapy of depression is an extremely complex set of questions, the answers to which will depend upon a great deal of additional basic research on the separate factors. It is hoped that the self-control model may direct inquiries toward these final solutions.

Developments in the interactional description of schizophrenia have not been parallelled in the area of depression. As yet, concepts such as pseudomutuality, double-bind, schism, and skew have found no counterpart. Kubler and Stotland (1964) have argued, 'emotional disturbance, even the most severe, cannot be understood unless the field in which it develops and exists in examined. The manifestations of the difficulty in the disturbed individual have meaning depending on aspects of the field. The significant aspects of the field are usually interpersonal'. Yet the study of depression are focussed on the individual and his behaviour out of his interactional context. To a large degree, the depressed person's monotonously reiterated complaints and self-accusations, and his provocative and often annoying behaviour have distracted investigations from consideration of his environment and the role it may play in the maintenance of his behaviour. The possibility that the characteristic pattern of depressed behaviour might be interwoven and concatenated with a corresponding pattern in the response of others has seldom been explored. For the most part, it has been assumed that the depressed person is relatively impervious to the influence of others. Ruesch (1962) stated that to talk to the depressed person makes little sense; to listen, little more. Grinker (1964) conceptualized depressive symptomatology as communication to others, but argued that the depressed person is not responsive to commination from others,: The depressed person . . . cannot use information for the purpose of action; he cannot perceive the cues of reality' he makes statements but does not care if he is understood'.

It is, nevertheless, in classifying depressed patients into bipolar and unipolar subtypes was proposed in 1962 by Leonhard et al., based on the clinical differentiation of depressed patients with and without mania. In that, family history studies noted that patients with bipolar illness had more psychosis a nd suicide among their relatives than patients with unipolar illness. Since 1962, several studies in Europe and the United Stares have refined and extended this original observation. What is more important, a model for investigation in psychiatry has been developed to the point that genetic data are important for validating clinical diagnosis in psychiatry, particularly among the affective disorders?

The data supporting evidence for genetic factors in the etiology affective disorders the development of methodology for genetic studies, and the resalting classification systems are to suggest that some forms of depression may have an etiology on a genetic bases. In order for a genetic etiology to be proven, several factors should be evident. First of all, the disorder should cluster within families, patients with the illness should have relatives who also demonstrate the illness. Second, studies of twins should show that the illness is more prevalent among monozygotic than dizygotic twins. And the third line of evidence would come from adoption studies. Adoption studies are assigned to differentiate environmental from genetic factors. Data from such studies should reveal that subject who have a biological parent with illness but who were raised in a foster home develop the illness nevertheless; whereas, subjects whose biological parents do not have the illness but who were raised in a home where there is affective disorder. Fourth, the illness could be shown to be linked to a gene of known Mendelians transmission.

Affective disorders, particularly manic-depressive illness, are familial. The evidence that bipolar illness clusters in families was reported by Leonhard et al. Perris and Angust both suggested that effectively ill relatives of bipolar patients tended to have bipolar and not unipolar disorders, whereas effectively ill relatives of unipolar patients tended to have unipolar illness and not bipolar illness. In the 1960s the Washington University group published a series of familial studies in manic-degressive illness, particularly bipolar disorders. These studies showed a high familial risk for affective disorder in relatives of manic patients. Second, a very comprehensive family study of affective disorder suggested that manic-depressive illness may be linked to a gene transmitted on the X-chromosome, subsequent studies in the later 1960s from the National Institute of Mental Health (NIMH) also showed a differential familial loading for relatives of patients with bipolar compared with unipolar disorder. Relatives of bipolar patients had elevated morbid risks for bipolar illness, unipolar illness, and suicide, compared to relatives with dipolar patients.

Few twin studies of affective disorder appear in the literature of the last 10 years or so. Kallmann's study is still considered the definitive work, showing very high concordance rates for bipolar illness in monozygotic compared to dizygotic twins,

The adoption technique, utilized in the Danish studies of schizophrenia, has been tried in studies of bipolar illness. Data from adoptees in Iowa indicated that primary affective illness may have a familial factor. another study of adoptees from manic-depressives also supports the concept of a genetic factor in the etiology of affective disorders.

In the search for genetic linkage of affective disorders, the studies of Winokur had pointed toward a genetic factor on the X-chromosome. attempts to extend and replicate these findings have resulted in considerable controversy. Mendlewicz and coworkers showed linkage of bipolar affective disorder with two markers on the X-chromosa colour blindedness, and XG blood type, Gershon were unable to replicate these findings and subsequently criticized the data from the Mendlewicz studies on methodological grounds.

In summary, the separation of bipolar affective disorder as a distinct subtype has resulted in a clearer definition of the genetic factors that may be involved in the etiology of affective disorders, most studies attempting to assess genetic factors ineffective illness that have separately considered bipolar patients have resulted in positive results. Methecrelatives of bipolar patients show a higher genetic loading and particularly more bipolar illness than relatives of other effectively ill patients. Clearly, unipolar illness as presently defined is a much more heterogeneous collection of disorders than bipolar disorder. Attempts to find subtypes of unipolar disorder using a benefic classification have not been particularly successful. However, Winokur`s group separated unipolar patient into women with an early age c of onset (depressive spectrum disease) whose relatives showed depression and alcoholism, and depressed men with a late age of onset (pure depressive disease) whose relatives showed depression only.

It is apparent that family and genetic support both the search for biological explanation of MDI—has been to define biological characteristics of MDI patients that are diagnostically use, which can help to optimize treatment, and which might even point the way toward the recent family subdues that indicate these rate of mood disorder among first-degree relatives of even the causes of these idiopathic condition, such biological characteristics of MDI (a concept that services as a genetic term for severe mood disorders.)—patients and defined as 'state-pendent'. Thus, while such state-dependent biological alterations can be most useful for diagnosis and for guiding therapy, from a therapeutic perspective they may merely be concomitant variations or secondary changes within the MDI syndrome. Nonetheless, these morbid risk rates for bipolar disorders—that designate unipolar—. Often, but not always, that other psychiatric or medical illnesses are not present and therapies is a relatively high incidence of similar disorder among close family members, these characteristics have supported the use of terms as ;endogenoius;, 'ebdogenomorphic', 'vital, 'psychotic' or 'melancholic' depressions., it is this subgroup of severe idiopathic illnesses that is most likely to respond favourably to modern medical treatments.

In addition, a concept that has arisen from a research need to define relatively homogeneous groups of depressed patients with 'primary' depression. That is, mood disorders without additional complicating medical or other psychiatric disorders. Clinically, the value of this concept (except as a reminder to consider fresh cases of mood disorders with a medical differential diagnosis approach) is somewhat limited since some cases of 'secondary' depression have striking endogenomorphic or vital characteristics and respond well to antidepressants.

However, it may help orientation to reiterate that a major thrust of psychiatric researching severe mood disorders over the past 30 years has been to define biological characteristics of mood disorders as patients that are diagnostically useful, which the pathophysiology or even the causes of these idiopathic conditions. While there has been considerable progress in understanding some characteristics that can help to guide treatment, search for primary causes has been unsuccessful so far. Yet, virtually, all of the biological characteristics of such mood disorders as they disappear with recovery, and not stable biological traits or markers of a possible heritable defect. Thus, while such state-dependent biological alternations can be most useful for diagnosis and for guiding therapy, from a theoretical perspective they may merely be concomitant variations or secondary changes with the MDI syndrome.

The depressed patient is specially prone to quality prior positive experiences and to personalized experiences of failure. Is that, they often interpret as indications of his or her blameworthiness? For example, a patient was not pleased when a short story she had written was accepted for publication because she attributed the acceptance to sheer luck. However, she regarded a rejected article as proof of her incompetence and felt distraught. As similar phenomenon was reported by Stuart, who found that depressive tendencies correlate with evaluative rather than classificatory associations, i.e., associating the word 'apple' with 'sweet' (evaluation) rather than 'fruit' (classification). Empirical work has documented the fact that depressed subjects personalize failure, they ascribe in an experimental task to lack of ability, while they do not attribute success to internal factors. The depressed patient's characteristic stereotypical conclusions and assessments reflect a combination of negative cognitive themes and certain systematic errors of thinking. A characteristic error in degressive e thinking is drawing conclusion in the absence of or contrary to evidence. This process of arbitrary inference is illustrated by the following cognition, 'John did call tonight . . . He probably doesn't want to see me any more'. When depressed pastiest are comforted with a negative event o r attribute they typically magnify its importance, however, the implications of a pleasant event or positive attribute are minimized. For instance, a patient evaluated a slight increase in her dysphoria to mean that she was 'deteriorating', while she viewed a well-done task as quite insignificant. In clinical work we typically find the patient selectively abstracts isolated elements of a situation that are most consistent with his or her negative and pessimistic world view and ignore other salient cues. A depressed patient decided that, for example, her boss's failure to say hello was ominous; she completely ignored the fact that he was under considerable pressure and preoccupied. As Beck and Shaw have noted, the depressed patient's invariant method of information processing results in over generalization and the ignoring of fine discrimination. Hammen, Krantz, and Weintraub and associates and Beck have reported empirical data that document the presence and preponderance of erroneous cognitive processes in depressed college students and depressed patients. The depressive tendency to magnify negative experiences is reflected in depressed subjects' hypersensitivity to experimentally manipulated failure, compared with the reactions of nondepressed subjects. Loeb and associates and Hammen and Krantz have documented the fact that such manipulations lead to increase dysphoria and pessimism, decreased levels of aspiration, and less positive predictions of one's performance on subsequent tasks. However, developments in the interactional description of schizophrenia has been parallelled in the area of depression. As yet, concept such as pseudomutality, double-bind, schism and skew have found no counterparts. Kubler and Stotland (1964)have argued; 'emotional disturbance, even the most severe, cannot be undershoot unless the field in which it develops and exists is examined. The manifestations of the difficultly in the disturbed individual have meaning depending on aspects of the field. The significant aspect of the field usually interpersonal', yet the study of depression has focussed on the individual and his behaviour out of his interactional context. To a large degree, the depressed person's monotonously reiterate complaints and self-accusations, and his provocative and often annoying behaviour have distracted investigators from considerations of his environment and the role it may play in the maintenance of his behaviour. the possibility that the characteristic pattern of depressed behaviour might be interwoven and concatenated with a corresponding pattern in the response of others has seldom been explored. To address to that possibility, for the most part, it has been assumed that the depressed person is relatively impervious to the influence of others. Ruesch (1962) stated that to talk to the depressed person makes little sense; to listen, little more. Grinker (1964) conceptualized symptomalogy as communication to others, but argued that the depressed person is not responsive to communication from others: The depressed person . . . cannot use information for the purpose of action, he cannot perceive the cues of reality, he makes statements but does not care if he is understood. In terms of system theory (von Bertalanffy, 1950; Allport, 1960 and Miller, 1971), the usual conceptualization of the depressed person is one of a relative ly closed system. Grinker (1964)was explicit in stating that the depressed person repeats his messages and behaviour without reception or acceptance of resulting feedback. Beck (1964) described the cognitive distortions that dominate the information processing of the depressed person so that experiences are rigidly

691

interpreted to maintain existing schema of personal deficiency, self-blame and negative expectations. The implicit assumption of these and other writers has been that the support and information available to the depressed person are incongruent with his depression, and the persistence of his symptomatology is evidence of a failure to receive or accept this information. Withdrawal of depressive schema and affective-structures, produce a downward depressive spiral. Such that an alternative argument that the depressed person is lost and depressive information elicited. However, this in turn increases the level of depression and strengthens the pathogenic pattern of depressed behaviour and response of others. If a depressive spiral develops, it is mutually causative, deviation-amplifying process (Maruyama, 1963) in the interaction of the depressed person with his environment. Thus, what is customarily viewed as some internal process is, that such of what is customarily viewed as cognitive distortion or misperception is characteristic of information flow from the environment. It should be noted that while the depressed person's different interpretation of his predication is traditionally attributed to his distortion or misperception, generally disorders of thought and perceptions are defining neither criteria nor common among depressed patients (McPartland and Hornstra, 1964). An observer who fails to take into account the intricacies of someone's relationship to his environment frequently attributes to him characteristics that he does not posses, or leaves significant aspects of his experience unexplained (Watzlawick et al., 1967). Feedback introduces phenomena that cannot be adequately explained by reference to the isolated individual alone (Ashby, 1960, 1962). For the study of depression, identification of a pattern of depressive feedback from the environment demands a more complex conceptualization of the disorder than one explaining its phenomena with reference to the isolated depressed person. Lemert (1962), in his study of the interpersonal dynamics of paranoia, argued that the net effect of the developing interaction pattern between the paranoid person and others is that (1) The flow of information to the person is stopped, (2) A real discrepancy between expressed ideas and affect among those with whom he interacts is created, and (3) The situation or group image becomes as ambiguous for him as he is for others. In this context of attenuated relationships, exclusion, and disrupted communication, the paranoid person cannot get the feedback on his behaviour that is essential in order for him to correct his interpretations, and at, least be delusional, but that it is also true that in a very real sense he is able to elicit covertly organized action and conspiratorial behaviour. The concurrent manners of the interpersonal dynamics of depression, that includes the interaction and information flow pattern congruent with the established phenomena of depression, and at the same time, indications as to why this than alternative patterns. Persist in the apparent absence of external; constants. Existing descriptions of the interpersonal behaviour of the depressed person will be examined as the attempt to make to reconstruct the interactional context in which this behaviour has meaning. It should be made clear that such perspective does not deny the existence of important intrapersonal factors in depression, as Chodoff, (1972) and McCranie (1971) have argued that there is a 'depressive-core' in the personality of the depression-prone person, consisting of a tendency to feel worthless and helpless and an over-sensitivity to stimuli that impinge on or upon these feelings. Together, these are aroused from dormancy by specific situations such as loss of self-esteem. However, the emphasis of this is shown to be on means by which the environment comes into congruence with these feelings. The depressive's vague, generalized feeling that there is something wrong with him, and his search for this among his minor defects, imperfections, and personal attributes, may arise from a depressive core to his personality, but at the same timer, the confusing response from the environment serves to validate these feelings. Likewise, conflicts about the reception of support and approval from others may be deeply rooted in the depressive's intrapersonal style, but these conflicts can only be aggravated by the mixed messages of approval and rejection received from significant others, and by their withdrawal from him despite reassurances to the contrary. Furthermore, the present exposition does not deny the importance of possible biochemical or genetic factors in the etiology of depression. Price (1974) has argued that even in disorders in which the importance of such factors has been clearly established, there may be a large number of links in the causal chain between specific etiological factors and the symptoms displayed by an individual. Social and interpersonal variables may determine to a large degree whether a disorder occurs and the form its symptoms will take. It is assumed that to initiate the process as a person need only begin to display depressive behaviour. Renewed interest in the relationship between hostility and depression—particularly in the psychoanalytic view that depressed persons turn hostility that had originally been directed at others (hostility-out-ward), against themselves (hostility-inward)—has generated a number of empirical studies. Weissman, (1960) suggested that relatively normal persons became hostile outward when depressed, whereas persons tending to become severely depressed were more likely to internalise or suppress this hostility. The data of Zuckerman et al., (1967) supported this view, indicating that only in the relatively normal was hostility correlated with depression on mood questionnaires or as rated by interviewers. Friedman (1964) found depressives to have more 'readily expressed resentment' as shown by their endorsement of adjectives such as 'bitter', 'frustrated', and 'sulky', yet found no greater overt hostility. In a later study, Friedman (1970) showed that feelings of depression and worthlessness were consonant with hostile and resentful feelings, even though depressed persons were not more likely to directly express these feelings to persons in the environment. Schless et al, (1974) found equal numbers of depressed patients turning hostility inward and outward, with both types of hostility increasing as depression became more severe. However, because these patients also saw other people's anger as more readily expressed and more potent, that feared retaliation, and therefore expressed hostility in the form of resentment. In recent studies have been interpreted so as to call into question classical psychoanalytic formulations of the relationship of depression, hostility-inward and hostility-outward. On the other hand, the view that hostility may serve a defensive function against depression has been supported. That depression is preceded by increases in hostility that is directed out but cannot be expressed directly to appropriate that is directed out but cannot be expressed directly to appropriated objects in the environment, is taken as a failure of this defensive function (Friedman, 1970; McCranie, 1971; Schless et al., 1974). Most writers who comment on the complaints and self-accusations of the depressed person have rejected the idea that they should be taken literally. Lichtenberg (1957) found that attempts to answer them directly with assurance, granting of dependency, and even punishment all increase depression and feelings of personal defect. Freud (1917) suggested that the self-accusations are actually aimed at someone else, a lost love object, and further notes, ' . . . it must strike us that after all the melancholic does not behave in quite the same way as a person who is crushed by remorse and self-reproach, which would more than anything characterize this latter condition, are lacking in the melancholic, at least, they are not prominent in him. One might emphasize the presence in him of an almost opposite trait of insistent communicativeness which finds satisfaction in self-exposure. In an attempt to modify depressive behaviour in a family situation (Liberman and Raskin, 1971) the baseline data indicated that other family members rejected opportunities to interact with the depressed person, and that all initiations of interaction between him and his family in the baseline period were undertaken by him. Paykel and Weissman (1973) reported extensive social dysfunction in women during depressive episodes. Interpersonal friction, inhibited communication, and submissive dependency occurred in both the initial episodes and in subsequent relapses. Onset of social difficulties was related to symptoms, but these difficulties continued months after the symptoms remitted, a fact that Paykel and Weissman argue must be taken into account in any treatment plan. The provocative and often annoying behaviour of the depressive has distracted investigators from considerations of the role of the responses of others. An exception, Jacobson (1954) noted that 'however exaggerated the patients' hurt, disappointment, and hostile derogation of their partners may be, their complaints are usually more justified that may appear to the surface'. According to her, the depressed person often makes his whole environment feel guilty and depressed, and this provokes defensive aggression and even cruelty precisely when he is most vulnerable. Depressives also have a tendency to develop an 'oral interplay' with those around them, so that mutual demands and expectations are built up to inevitable disappointment and depression for everyone concerned. Cohen et al., (1954) found therapists generally uncomfortable working with depressed patients. They identified a tendency of therapists to react to depressive manipulations with unrealistic reassurance and 'seductive promises too great to be fulfilled', followed by hostility and rejection. Such that it became aware of a dramatic example of this when a student therapist showed up at a Florida suicide prevention centre with a recent client. The therapist had attempted to meet her client's complaints of worthlessness and rejection with explicit reassurances that she more than understood her and cared for her, she loved her. After weeks of such reassurance and increasingly frequent sessions, the client finally confronted the therapist with the suggestion that if the therapist really cared for her as she said, they should spend the night together. The therapist panicked and terminated the case, suggesting that the client begin applying her newly acquired insights to her daily life. The client continued to appear for previously scheduled appointments and made vague suicidal gestures, at which time her therapist brought her to the suicide prevention centre. When it was suggested that the therapist should honestly confront her client with what had happened in the relationship, the therapist angrily refused to speak to her, stating that she truly loved her client and would do nothing to hurt her. Lewinsohn and his associates (Lewinsohn and Shaw, 1969; Lewinsohn, 1969, Lewinsohn, 1970; Libet and Lewinsohn, 1973) have undertaken an ambitious clinical research program focussing on a social interaction of the depressed person from a behavioural point of view. In attempting to develop hypotheses about the reinforcement contingencies available to the depressed person, they have attempted a precise specification of the social behaviour of the depressed person. Libet and Lewinsohn found depressed persons in group therapy to be lower than controls on a number of measures of social skills: Activity level, interpersonal range, rate of positive reactions emitted and action latency. Their data are subject to alternative interpretations, however, particularly since they also found that rate of positive reactions emitted was highly correlated with rate of positive reaction elicited. While depressed persons may well be deficient in social shills, some of the observed differences in group interaction situations may be due to the fact that fewer people are willing interact with depressed persons (which results in a narrower interpersonal rang e and less opportunity for activity), and in this interaction emitted fewer positive responses (thereby also reducing the positive responses elicit from the depressed). The most useful behavioural conceptualization of social interaction involving depressed persons would specify the lack of social skills of all participants, as evidenced by their inability to alter the contingencies offered or received. Behavioural interventions in the depressed person's marital and family relationships would therefore involve training all participants in these social skills, and go beyond simply altering the contingencies available to the depressed person. Behavioural observations and self-reports of a couple in the Lewinsohn study (Lewinsohn and Shaw., 1969) seem to support such a view. Studies of suicide attempts and their effects on interpersonal relationships also provide data relevance, while suicide attempts do not have an invariable relationship on depression, there is a definite association. McPartland and Hornstra (1964) examined the effects of suicide attempts on subsequent level of depression. They conceptualized depressive symptomatology as 'a set of messages demanding action by others to alter or restore the social space'. And examined the relationships between suicide attempts and the ambiguity of the depressive message and the diffuseness of its intended audience. They were able to realizably place depressed patients at definite points along a dimension of interactive stalemate on the basis of the range of intended audience and the stridency of message in depressive communications. Patients who were farthest along this continuum, whose communication was most diffuse, nonspecific, strident and unanswerable. Were most likely to have long hospital stays and diagnoses of psychosis? Suicide attempts tended to reduce the level of depression, apparently by shifting the interactive burden onto others. Other studies (Rubenstein et al., 1958; Moss and Hamilton, 1956' Kubler and Stotland, 1964) have indicated that suicidal patients who improve following their attempt on their lives consistently have effected changes on social fields, and those who fail to improve generally have failed to change their situation fundamentally. Depression is viewed as a response to the disruption of the social space in which the person obtains support and validation for his experience. This view, and a view of depressive symptomatolology in terms that is similar to that of McPartland and Hornstra (1964). However, one of the implications of the approach taken, is that an understanding of the social context is vital to an understanding of depression, although traditionally it has been largely ignored. Social stresses leading to depression includes loss of significant relationships, collapse of anticipated relationships, demotions (and in some cases, promotions), retirement, missed chances, or any of a variety of other changes in a person's social structure. Depressive symptomatololgy is seen as a set of massages demanding reassurance of the person's place in the interactions he is still able to maintain, and further, action by others to alter or restore his loss. Initial communications—verbal expressions of helplessness and hopelessness—tend to engage others immediately and to shift the interactive burden to others. The receivers of these messages usually attempt to answer the depressed person's request directly, however, as previously noted by Grinker (1964) and Lichtenberg (1957), their literal responses present him with a dilemma. Much of the depressive's communication is aimed at ascertaining the nature of relationships or context in which the interaction is taking place. Grinker (1964) has compared this to the various 'how' and 'why' questions that young children direct to their parents, and has suggested that both children and depressive's will be left feeling rejected, ignored, or brushed aside if provided with a literal response. If communication took place at only one level, depression would probably be a less ubiquitous problem. However, the problem is that human beings not only communicate, but communications about this communicative communication, qualifying or labelling what they say by (1) The context or relationship in which the communication takes place, (2) other verbal messages, (3) vocal and linguistic patterns, and (4) bodily movement (Haley, 1963). A person may offer support and reassurance with a rejecting tone or he may offer criticism in a supportive and reassuring tone. It is enough that vocal and linguistic patterns and body movement are ambiguous and subject to alternative interpretations. However, a further problem for the depressed person is that the context, the nature of the relationship between the depressed person and the persons communicating to him, may require time and further messages to be clearly defined.` The depressed person's problem is to decide whether others are assuring him that he is worthy and acceptable because they do in fact maintain this attitude toward him, or rather only because he has attempted to elicit such responses, unwilling or unable to endure the time necessary to answer this question, the depressive uses his symptoms to seek repeated feedback in his testing of the nature of his acceptance and the security of his relationships. While providing continual feedback, these efforts are at the same time profoundly and negatively affecting these relationships. The persistence and repetition of the symptoms is both incomprehensible and aversive to members of the social environment. However, the accompanying indication of distress and suffering is powerful in its ability to arouse quilt in others and to inhibit and direct expression of annoyance and hostility from them, as observed in both the family difficulties of depressed persons (Jacobson, 1954) and the problem's therapists report in their efforts to relate to depressed patients (Cohn et al., 1954). Irritated, yet inhibited and increasingly guilt-ridden, members of the social environment continue to give verbal assurance of support and acceptance. However, a growing discrepancy between the verbal content and the affective quality of these responses provides validation for the depressive's suspicions that he is not really being accepted and that further interaction cannot be assured, to maintain his increasingly uncertain security, the depressive displays more symptoms. Nonetheless, at this point the first of a number of interactive stalemates may be reached. Members of the depressed person's environment who can find a suitable rationalization for their behaviour may leave the field or at least, reduce their interactions with him. Considerable effort may be involved in efforts to indicate that this is not in fact rejection, but given the context, these efforts do little more than reduce credibility and increase the depressive's insecurity. With those members of the social environment who remain, a self-maintaining pattern of mutual manipulation is established. Persons in the environment find that they can reduce the aversive behaviour of the depressed person and alleviate the guilt that this depressed behaviour has an uncanny ability to elicit, if they manipulate him with reassurance, support, and denial of the process that is taking place. The depressed person, finds that by displaying symptoms he can manipulate his environment so that it will provide sympathy and reassurance, but he is aware by now that this response from others is not genuine and that they have become critical and rejecting. While this situation is attractive for neither the depressed person nor members of social environment, it provides a stabilization of what has been a deteriorating situation. One alternative facing the depressed person is for him to accept the precipitating disruption of his social space and the resulting loss of support and validation. However, now that he has begun showing symptoms, he has invested portions of his remaining relationships in his recovery effort. That is, he was tested these relationships, made demands, and has been frustrated in ways that seriously call into question his conception of these relationships. If he abandons these efforts, he may have to relinquish the support and validation derived from these relationships while accepting the precipitating loss. At this

699

point he may be too dependent upon the remaining relationships to give them up. Furthermore, as a result of the mixed messages he has been received from others, he now has an increasingly confused and deteriorate self-concept, which must be clarified. With new desperation more symptoms may be displayed. Various possible efforts by the depressed person to discover what is wrong with him (i.e., why he is being rejected and manipulated) and to reestablish amore normal interactive pattern are in this context indistinguishable from the manipulation he has used to control the responses of others. Therefore they are met with the usual counter manipulation. Requesting information as to how people really view him is indistinguishable from symptomatic efforts. If the depressed person attempts to discuss the interpersonal process that is taking place, he touches on a sensitive issue, and is likely only to elicit denial by the others or an angry defensive response. Yet, efforts by others to assure the depressed person that he is really accepted and that they are not rejecting him are in this context also indistinguishable from previous manipulations that they have employed, and therefore serve to strengthen the developing system. Thus, interpersonal manoeuvres directed at changing the emerging pattern become system-maintaining and any genuine feedback to the depressed person is also indistinguishable from manipulations. Persons leaving the social field increase both the depressed person's feelings of rejection and his impetus to continue his behaviour pattern. Persons just entering the social field can be quickly recruited into the existing roles, since their efforts to deal with the depressed person—even if genuine are likely to be quite similar to those now being employed manipulatively. They therefore become subject to the compelling counter-manipulations of the depressed person, come to respond manipulatively themselves, and are inducted into the system. Descriptions of the depressed person at this point in his career focus on the distortions and misperceptions that serve to maintain his depression. What is generally ignored is that these 'distortions' and 'misperceptions' are contingent with the social system in which the depressed person now finds himself. The specific content of the depressive's complaints and accusations may not be accurate, but his comments are a recognition of the attenuated relationships, disrupted communication, and lack of genuineness that he faces. These conditions serve to prevent him from receiving the feedback necessary to correct any misperceptions or distortions. He has played a major role in the creation of this social system, but the emergence of the system has also required the cooperation of others, and once established, it tends to be largely beyond th control of its participants. Depending on characteristics of both the depressed person and his environment, a number of punishing variations on the above patterns may develop. Members of the social environment who have been repeatedly provoked and made to feel guilty may retaliate by withholding the responses for which the depressed person depends on them. The depressed person may become aware of the inhibiting influence his symptoms have on the direct expression of negative feelings, and may use these symptoms aggressively, while limiting the forms that counter-aggression can take. He may also discover and exploit the interdependence of others and himself. While he is being made acutely aware of his dependence on others and the frustrations it entails, he may also become aware of the extent to which others are dependent on him. In that their own maintenance of mood and their ability to engage in varieties of activities required in some way his cooperation. Because either of outright hostility, or as a self-defeating effort to convince other of their need to renegotiate their relationship with him, the depressed person may become symptomatic in his withholding of these minimal cooperative behaviours. While hostility may not necessarily be a more etiological factor in depression, the frustrations, provocations, and manipulations occurring in interactions between depressed persons and others would seem to encourage it. As efforts to end the interactive stalemate fail, there may be a shift in the depressive's self-presentation to one indicating greater distress and implying that the environment has more responsibility for bringing about the necessary changes. McPartland and Hornstra (1964) found that they could unambiguously differentiate themes of hopelessness and helplessness from more disturbed themes and how energy and physical complaints in communications of depressed patients. The latter themes were associated with longer hospitalization when hospitalized depressed patients were sampled. McPartland and Hornstra give the examples of, 'I can't sleep and I can't stand it any longer'. 'I am too tired to move': 'My head and my stomach feel funny all the time'. Unable to restore his life space, the depressive now implicitly demands 'a suspension of the rules; a moratorium on the web of obligations under which the person lives, such as admission to the sick role' (McPartland and Hornstra, 1964). With immediate relationships deteriorating, the depressive addresses his plea to a more general audience, but in more confusing and unanswerable terms. Literal responses to his communications may involve medical intervention for his specific complaints, but this generally fails to alleviate the problem. Any efforts to move the interactional theme back to the depressive's sense of hopelessness and helplessness threaten to reopen the earlier unfruitful and even punishing patterns of relations, and tend to be resisted. Unable to answer, or in many cases, even to comprehend the depressive's pleas, members of the social environment may withdraw further from him, increasing his desperation, and quickening the depressive's drift. With a second interactive stalemate now reached, the depressed person may attempt to resolve it by increasing his level of symptomatology and shifting the theme of his self-presentation to one of the worthlessness and evil. 'I am a failure; its all my fault; I am sinful and worthless'. Unable either to restore his social space or to reduce his obligations sufficiently for him to continue to cope, the depressive now communicates his bafflement and resignation. The intended audience is now more diffuse, relationships are even more attenuate, and the new message is more obscure and perplexing. The social environment and the depressive soon arrive at another stalemate. Otherwise helpless to alleviate the situation, remaining members of the environment may further withdraw or, alternatively, have the depressive withdrawn through hospitalization. In the absence on any relatedness to others, the depressive may drift into delusions and frankly psychotic behaviour. Once an individual has suffered a disrupt ion of his social space, his ability to avoid depressive shift, or to abort the process once it has begun, depends on the structure of his social space and on his interpretational skills. With regard to the latter, it is generally ignored that the person facing this situation is dealing with a changing environment, and that the skills needed to deal with it are likely to be different from those required by a more stable, normal environment. Consequently, persons who previously have had adequate skills to deal with their life situation may lack the skills to cope with a disrupted social space. With regard to the structure of this social space, resistance to depression seems to depend on the availability of alternative sources of support and validation. Particularly of the type that cannot be threatened by depressive symptomatology, further, the availability of direct nonpunitive feedback should the person's behaviour become annoying or incomprehensible, and the ability of the social space to generate new sources of support and meaning that are unambiguously independent of the presence or absence of symptoms. Earlier speculative writings (Abraham, 1911) and later behavioural studies (Lewinsohn, 1969) have suggested that depressive persons tend to be quite limited in their range of interactions, and that this may be a major source of their vulnerability. ADVANCE \d4 Stable relationships may generally provide a buffer against depression, but when they are stable yet low in support and validation, they may encourage a chronic depressive cycle. If, for instance, in a marriage of this type, the depressed person recognize that his spouse is tolerating more than is reasonable from him without protest, he may begin to assume that she is staying with him out of some obligations, rather than because she accepts him and wants a relationship (Haley, 1963). The depressed person may then test whether he is really accepted by driving the other person to the point of separation with his symptoms. Yet if the spouse passes the test by continuing to tolerate the annoying behaviour., the depressed person may not necessarily be reassured about his acceptance. rather he may only be convinced that his spouse remains because she is unable to leave. However, if she makes an effort to leave the situation, she may be indicating that their relationship has been voluntary and that he had been accepted. With reconciliation the spouse may again, seem too tolerant and a new series of doubts, testing, and strife may be enacted. While such a cycle may produce chronic difficulties, it may also be an alternative to a downward depressive spiral. Essentially the depressed person finds himself in the awkward situation of wanting to avoid rejection, yet at the same time fearing acceptance. The constraints operating on the person who suffered a disruption in his social space are his need for support and validation, and the investment of his remaining relationships in his efforts to receive such support. the symptoms of the depressed person offer a powerful constraint on the ability of members of the social environment to offer adjustive feedback, and while eliciting verbal messages of sympathy, support, and reassurance, these symptoms disrupt the relationships and cultivate hostility and rejection. Those who resist induction into the system without rejecting the depressed person do so because they are able to resist the pressure to convey discrepant messages. A successful therapist in Cohen et al., study stated, 'I keep in mind that I am talking to the patients not so much verbally as preverbally. I use the verbal communication as a means of carrying inflection and an accompaniment of facial expression and postural components'. Several writers have suggested that the emerging communication context can be disrupted by strong affective expressions such as anger, excitement, and amusement (Lazarus, 1968), which are incompatible with the pattern of mutual manipulation that maintains the context. Although many writers have indicated that a depressive reaction lifts when a patient regains his ability to express anger toward others (Friedman, 1970), some research indicates that the mobilization of anger is not necessary for symptomatic improvement (Weissman, et al., 1971; Klerman and Gershon. 1970). Interpersonally, hostility may be one of a number of means of disrupting or blocking the operation of a depressive interpersonal system. Involvement in this system is difficult to avoid once it has begun. The symptoms of depression have an ability to perpetuate themselves through the involvements of others in a system of manipulation and counter-manipulations that soon gets beyond the control of its participants. Within the presently engaged research that examines the responses of others to depression and the quality of the communications context that emerges. Preliminary results from a study involving an interpersonal behaviour questionnaire suggest that a person is less likely to respond in an overtly hostile manner to the behaviour of another person when the second person is depressed. This inhibition persists even when it is indicate that the second person is responding hostility. The inhibition of appropriate hostile behaviour may be a characteristic of interactions involving the depressed person, and not just of the depressed person. Another study involves twenty-minute phone conversation between naive subjects and target individuals from three groups: Depressed outpatients, nondepressed outpatients, and normals. Preliminary results suggest that subjects respond with unrealistic reassurance and useless advice to the depressed outpatient. They are more likely to be depressed, anxious, and hostile themselves after conversations with depressed patients, and are more likely to reject opportunities for future interaction. For the most part, changes in the subjects' mood remain concealed during the conversation, and the depressed patients are given little indication of their impact on occasional statements, such as 'You certainty seem to have had a lot a problems, but problems are what allow us to grow, and so you'll have lots of opportunity to grow in the future';. Further research is needed to examine the nature of the depressive's social field so that the specific relationships that resist or perpetuate the depressive interpersonal system can be identified and describe. We use the term 'depression' to refer to the syndrome of behaviour that have been identified in descriptive studies of depressed individuals (e.g., Grinker, et al., 1961). It includes verbal statements of dysphoria, self-depreciating., guilt, material burden, social insolation, somatic complaints, and a reduced rate of much behaviours. we assume depression to be a continuous variable which can be conceptualized as a 'state' which fluctuates over time as well as a 'trait' (some people are mo e pone to becoming depressed than others). Being depressed does not exclude other psychopathological conditions such as schizophrenia, psychosis, sexual deviation, or alcoholism. For research purposes a patient (subject) is defined as 'depressed' if he meets certain experiential criteria (e.g., Lewinsohn & Libet 1972) based on selected MMPI scales and on the interview factor's identified by Grinker (1961). It would seem important that any study relying on differences between depressed and nondepressed groups for its conclusions have a 'normal control' as well as a 'psychiatric control' group (i.e., patients for whom anxiety or other neurotic symptoms but not depression constitute the major psychopathology (if any ordered group differences are to be attributed to depression (depressed, psychiatric control normal control).

We accumulatively gather of three assumptions regarding the behavioural theory of depression: A schematic representation of the theory is shown by (I) A low rate of response-contingent positive reenforcement (response) acts as an eliciting (unconditioned) stimulus for some depressive behaviours, such as feeling of dysphoria, fatigue, and other somatic symptoms (2) A low rate of response constitutes a sufficient explanation for other part of the depressive syndrome such as the low rate of behaviour. For the latter the depressed person is considered to be on a prolonged extinction schedule. (3) The total amount of reconposre received by an individual is presumed to be a function of three sets of variables: (I) The number of events (including activities) that are

705

potentially reinforced (PotRe) for the individual. PotRe is assumed to be a variable subject of individual differences, uninfluenced by biological (e.g., sex and age) and experiential variables, and (ii) The number off potentially reinforcing events that can be provided by the environment, i.e., the availability of reinforcement in the environment (AvaiRe). (iii) The instrumental behaviour of the individual, i.e., the extent to which he possesses the skill and emits those behaviours that will elicit reinforcement for him from his environment. The behavioural theory requires that (1) the total amount of response received by depressed persons be less than that received by nondepressed persons, and similarly, it will be less when the individual is repressed than when he is not depressed; (2) The onset of depression be accompanied by a reduction ion response, (3) intensity of depression convary with rate of reconposre, and (4) Improvement be accompanied by an increase in reconposre. Even so, the following examinations of relevant empirical studies are several additional clarifications and hypotheses. First, even were such predictions affirmed, further data would be needed to ascertain whether the differences between depressed and non-depressed individuals in regard to response are due to: (x) differences in the number and kinds of activities and events which are potentially reinforcing ({PotRe); (y) and/or the possibility the depressed individuals may be more likely to be in situations which lack reinforcement for them (AvaiRe), (z) and/or differences between depressed and non-depressed individuals in those skills which are necessary to obtain reenforcement from one's environment. Second, the degree to which the individual's behaviour is maintained (followed) by reinforcement is assumed to be the critical antecedent condition for the occurrence of depression, rather than the total amount of reinforcement received. It is a well-known clinical fact that 'giving' (i.e., noncontingently) to depressed individuals does not decrease their depression. We assume that the occurrence of behaviour followed by positive reinforcement is vital if depression is to be avoided. Such that depression when the probability is low that the individual's behaviour will be followed by reinforcement, and also, when the probability is high that the individual will be 'reinforced' when he does not emit the behaviour (e.g., the retired person receiving his paycheck regardless of what he does). Under both conditions the probability of the individual emitting behaviour reduced. The behavioural view of other aspects of depression may include :Low self-esteem, pessimism, feelings of guilt, and other elated phenomena are cognitive changes which are commonly observed in depressed individuals, even though the specific manifestations vary considerably from individual to individual. Thus, there are depressed patient who do not have low self-esteem and there are many who lack feelings of guilt. theorists such as Aaron T. Beck (1967) assign primary causal significance to these cognitive changes. A behavioural theory assumes these qualify as secondary elaborations of the feeling of dysphoria, which in turn is presumed to be the consequence of a low-rate of reconposre. The first thing that happens when an individual becomes depressed is that he is experiencing an unpleasant feeling state (dysphoria). He is feeling bad. This feeling state is difficult for the individual to label; and a number of alternative 'explanations' are available to him including. 'I am sick' (somatic symptoms). 'I am weak or otherwise inadequate' (low self-esteem), 'I am bad' (feeling of guilt),. O r 'I am not likeable' (feelings of social isolation). The research of Stanley Schachter (Schachter & Singer 1962) may contain important implications for this aspect of the behaviour of depressed individuals and for treatment as well (cognitive relabelling). If the depressed individual can be helped to relabel his emotion (e.g., 'I am worthless' into 'I am feeling bad because I am lacking something that is important to my welfare'), he may be in a much better position to do something about his predicament. 2. Relationship between hostility and depression, in which the role of hostility is central to psycho dynamically-oriented theories of depression (i.e., depression is caused by internalized hostility) is hypothesized to be secondary to the low rate of reconposre. In a manner analogous to the way in which aggressive behaviour is elicited by an aversive stimulus, in Azrin's (1966) studies, aggressive behaviour may be assumed to be elicited by a low rate of response in the depressed individual. When these aggressive responses are expressed, they serve to alienate other people and therefore contribute even further to the social isolation of the depressed individual. He therefore learns to avoid expressing hostile tendencies by suppressing (or repressing) them. 3. Role or precipitating factors in occurrence of depression that in a substantial number of depressed patients, the depression can be shown to have begun after certain environmental events (e.g., Paykel. et al., 1969). Many of these events involve a serious reduction of positive reenforcement in that the event deprives the individual of an important source of reinforcement (e.g., death of spouse) or of an important set of skills (e.g., spinal cord injuries or brain disease). The relationship between the occurrence of such events and depression is considered with the behavioural theory of depression. There are, however, also instances of depression following 'success' experiences (e.g., promotions or professional success). It is also not at all uncommon for an individual to become depressed following the attainment of some important and long-sought goal (e.g., award of PhD degree). The existence of such precipitating factors would seem at first glance to contradict the notion of a relation between a reduction in positive reinforcement and depression. Two considerations would seem relevant (a) That the individual is judged to be a 'success' by external criteria (e.g., is promoted) events not necessarily mean that the number of potentially reinforcing events available to him has increased. Thus, for example, a promotion may actually involve a serious reduction in the amount of social reinforcements obtained by the individual. The behavioural theory would predict depression for an individual who attain a goal for which he has worked long and hard if the reward (e.g., aware of degree) turns out to be a weak reinforcement for him. In that case he has worked hard for too little, i.e., his rate of response is low. Developments in the interactional description of schizophrenia have not been parallelled in the area of depression. As yet, concepts such as pseudomutality, double-bind, schism, and skew found no counterparts. Kubler and Stotland (1964)have argued, 'emotional disturbance', even the most severe, cannot be understood unless the field in which it develops and exists is examined. The manifestations of the difficulty in the disturbed individual have meaning depending on aspects of the field. The significant aspects of the field are usually interpersonal. Yet, the study of depression has focussed on the individual and his behaviour out of his interactional context. to a larger extent, the depressed person's monotonously reiterated complaints and self-accusations, and his provocative and often annoying behaviour have distracted investigators from considerations of his environment and the role it may play in the maintenance of his behaviour. The possibility that the characteristic pattern of depressed behaviour might be interwoven and concatenated with a corresponding pattern in the response of others has seldom been explored. For the most part, it has been assumed that the depressed person is relatively impervious to the influence of others. Ruersch (1962) stated that to talk to the depressed person makes little sense, to listen, little more. Grinker (1964) conceptualized depressive symptomatology as communication tom others, but argued that the depressed person is not responsive to communication from others: 'The depressed person . . . cannot use information for the purpose of action, he cannot perceive the cues of reality, he makes statements but does not care if he is understood. Its difficulty of communication is the primary problem in therapy of establishing a communication relationship, which is, of course, a reflection on the patient's basic life difficulties. The most characteristic aspect of the manic depressive's defence in his ability to avoid anxiety by erecting conventional barriers to emotional interchange, we have learned to interpret this as a defence rather than a defect in the patient 's experience, and we have found that when it is interpreted as a defence, he responds by developing a greater ability to communicate his feeling and to establish empathic relationships. Initial communications—verbal expressions of helplessness and hopelessness, withdrawal from interaction, slowing, irritability and agitation tend to engage others immediately and to shift the interactive situation to others, the receivers of these messages usually attempt to answer the depressive person's requires directly. However, as previously noted by Grinker (1964) and Lichtenberg (1957), theory literal responses present him with a dilemma, much of the depressive's communication is aimed at ascertaining the nature of relationship or context in which the interaction is taking place. Grinker (1964) has compared this to the various 'how' and 'why' questions that young children direct to their parents, and has suggested that children and progressives will be left feeling rejected, ignored or brushed aside if provided with a literal response. Depression has been conceptualized as a self-perpetuating interpersonal system. Depressive symptomatology is congruent with the developing interpersonal situation of the depressed person, and the symptoms have a mutually maintaining relationship with the response of the social environment, essentially, the depressed person and others within his social space collude to create a system in which feedback cannot be received, and various efforts to change become system-maintaining. Depressed persons tend to withdraw from social activities, and their close relationships tend to be strained and conflictual. Depressed women have more intensely studied than depressed men, in part because women are approximately twice as likely to be depressed (Radloff). Depressed women are dependent, acquiescent, and inhibited their communication in close relationships, and prone to interpersonal tension, friction and open conflict (Weissman & Paykel, 1974). Interestingly, the interpersonal difficulties of depressed persons are less pronounced when they are interacting with strangers than with intimates (Hinchcliffe, Hooper, and Roberrtys, 1975). About half of all depressed persons report marital turmoil (Rousanville, Weissman, Prusdoff, and Heraey-Baron, 1979) there is considerable hostility between depressed persons and their spouses, but often there is more between depressed persons and their children. Being depressed makes it more difficult to be a warm, affectionate, consistent parent (McLean, 1976). The children of depressed parents are more likely to have a full range of psychological and social difficulties than the children of normal or even schizophrenic parents (Emery, Weintraub, and Neale, 1982), yet one must be cautious in making causal inferences. There is evidence that the child's problems are more related to a conflictual marital relationship and stressful home life than depression of the parent per se (Sameroff,. Barocass, Siefer). Depression thus tends to be indicative of an interpersonal situation fraught with difficulties, and this needs to be given more attention in both theorizing and planning treatment. Although depression is associated with interpersonal problems, within a sample of depressed persons the correlation between severity of depression and the extent of interpersonal problems tend to be modest. this may suggest that these problems are a matter no only of how depressed persons are functioning, but of the response of key people around them as well (Coyne, Kahn, & Gotlib, 1985). One can make a list of the symptoms of depression, and assign any person a depression score on the basis of the number symptoms present. Even if one assumes a continuity between normal depressed mood and clinical depression, it may still prove useful to make a distinction between the presence and absence of significant depression. One may wish to insure that a research study does not include a preponderance of persons whose depression is only mild or transient. Virtually no signs or symptoms are specified to depression, and yet in many context, one may need to distinguish depression from other descriptors or explanations for a person's distress and behaviour. In working with the elderly, for instance, it is important to distinguish between depression and dementia. In medical patients in general, there is a high prevalence of symptoms associated with depression, both because of physical illness and the stress of hospitalization (Cavanaugh, 1984), and, whether for research or practical purposes, one, may wish to establish criteria for who is to be considered depressed and who is not. Finally, persons who are labelled schizophrenic or alcoholic for many purposes to lump them with those persons whose primary problem is depression. Thus, for the purpose of research, treatment, and professional communication, it proves useful to have some means of specifying some boundary conditions for the term 'depression', in terms of some minimal level of severity as well as some coherence and specificity to what is included in the concept—even if one rejects the notion that it is a discrete entity, discontinuous with normal mood. The problem of diagnosis is most critical in biomedical approaches to depression. The assumption is generally made that depression is a matter of one or more disease entities with specific etiologies and treatment. The statement, 'Nosology precedes etiology' conveys the idea that the ability to identify the causes of depression depends upon the existence of an adequate diagnostic and classification system. For instance, to take a simplified hypothetical example, suppose that a particular biological abnormality occurs in 60 percent of all depressed persons and is specified to depression. Suppose also that, with the accepted diagnosis criteria, only 60 percent of the persons identified as such are 'actually depressed'. If these conditions occurred, then research might indicate that only 36 precent of depressed persons possess the abnormality. An effective treatment for depression may also be misjudged or misapplied in the absence of an adequate diagnostic system. This was made apparent recently after a drug company had undertaken a large study to compare the effectiveness of a new drug to that of both an established drug treatment for depression and a placebo (Carroll, 1984). At five of the six research sites, the new drug proved to be no more effective than a placebo, but interpretation of this was limited by the additional finding that the established treatment proved no better. Patient s identified as depressed by current criteria did not respond to drug treatment that had proven efficacious in a large body of past research. The past research was misleading

711

either, the current diagnosis criteria invalid, or, most likely, they were misapplied by reputable investigators. Contemporary diagnosis systems owe much to the work of Kraepelin at the turn of the century. He divided major psychopathology into two broad syndromes: Dementia praecox (schizophrenia) and manic-depressive illness. The latter category included almost all serious mood disturbance, including depression in the absence of an episode of mania. As retained today, the term generally is a synonym for bipolar disorder. Of all the distinctions that have been proposed, the most widely accepted and least controversial is that between unipolar and bipolar depressive. Classifying depressed patients into bipolar and unipolar subtypes was first proposed in 1962 by Leonhard et al., based on the clinical differentiation of depressed patients with and without mania, family history studies noted that patients with bipolar illness had more psychosis and suicide among their relatives than patients with unipolar illness. Since 1962 several studies in Europe and the United States have refined and extended this original observation. More important, a model for investigation in psychiatry has been developed to the point that genetic data are important for validating clinical diagnosis in psychiatry, particularly among the affective disorders. Several lines of evidence suggest that some forms of depression may have an etiology on a genetic basis. In order for a genetic etiology to be proven, several factors should be evident. First of all, the disorder should cluster within families; patients with the illness should have relatives who also demonstrate studies of twins should show that the illness is more prevalent among monozygotic than dizygotic twins. A third line of evidence would come from adoption studies. Adoption studies are designed to differentiate environmental from genetic factors. Data from such studies should reveal that subjects who have a biological parent with illness but who were raised in foster home develop the illness nevertheless, whereas subjects whose biological parents do not have the illness but who were raised in a home. Where there is affective disorder, do not develop affective disorder in excess of controls. Fourth, the illness could be shown to be linked to a gene known of Mendelian transmission. Affective disorders, particularly manic-depressive illness, are familiar. the evidence that bipolar illness clusters in families was reported by Leonhard et al., Perris and Angst both suggested that effectively ill relatives of bipolar patients tended to have bipolar and not unipolar disorders, whereas affectively ill relatives of unipolar patients tended to have unipolar illness and not bipolar illness. In the 1960s the Washington University group published a series of familiar studies in manic-depressive illness, particularly bipolar disorders. These studies showed a high familiarity risk for affective disorder in relatives of manic patients. Second, a very comprehensive family study of affective disorder suggested that manic-depressive illness may be linked to a gene transmitted on the X-chromosome. Subsequent studies in the late 1960s from the National Institute of Mental Health (NIMH) also shows a differential familial loading for relatives of patients with bipolar compared with unipolar disorders. Relatives of bipolar patients had elevated morbid risks for bipolar illness, unipolar illness, and suicide, compared to relatives with unipolar patients. Few twin studies of affective disorder appear in the literature of the last 10 years or so. Kallmasnn's study is still considered the definite work, showing very high concordance rates for bipolar illness in monozygotic compared to dizygotic twins. The adoption technique, utilized in the Danish studies of schizophrenia, has been tried in studies of bipolar illness. Data from adoptees in Iowo indicated that primary affective illness may have a familial factor. Another study of adoptees from manic-depressives also supports the concept of a genetic factor in the etiology of affective disorders. In the search fo r genetic linkage of affective disorder, the studies of Winokur et al., pointed toward a genetic factor on the X-chromosome, colour blindness and XG blood type. Gershon et al., were unable to replicate these findings and subsequently criticized the data from the Mendlewocz studies on methodological grounds. Clearly, unipolar illness as presently defined is a much more heterogeneous collection of disorders than bipolar disorder. Attempts to find subtypes of unipolar disorder using a genetic classification have not been particularly successful. However, Winokur's group separated unipolar patients into women with an early age of onset (depressive spectrum disease) whose relatives showed depression and alcoholism, and depressed men with a late age of onset (pure depressive disease) whose relatives showed depression only. The renewed interest in the genetics of bipolar and unipolar depression in the late 1900s and the interest in defining these disorders led to several family studies in the 1970s. The simplest method, the so-called family history method, was to ask patients about illness in their relatives. This tends to underestimate illness in relatives. An interview (Schedule for Affective Disorder and Schizophrenia-SADS) developed early in the 1970s was used to document illness in relatives. Interviewing relatives directly (the 'family study) led to greater precision regarding the diagnosis of illness in relatives. In a refinement of this technique relatives are interviewed blind to the profound diagnosis in order to decease investigator bias. Most of the recent genetic studies conducted in the United States employed a blind gamily study method; wherein relatives were interviewed with a standardized instrument with the interviewer unaware whether the person being interviewed was the patient, relative, or a control. Nonetheless, it seems that some observers have stated that in the intervals between attacks, the manic depressives has a character structure similar to that of the obsessional neurotic. It has also been asserted that in the psychotic phase the manic-depressive illness is essentially schizophrenic. This latter statement is supported by the fact that many manic-depressives do, in the course of time, evolve into chronic schizophrenic psychoses, usually paranoid in character, and that there are many prosecutory ideas presented both in manic attack and in the depression. In general, there has always been much uncertainty as to who should be diagnosed manic depressive—an uncertainty which is reflected in the widely differing propositions of manic depressives and schizophrenic diagnosed in different mental hospitals. What, then, is the point of singling out a diagnosis category called manic depressive? In our opinion, the manic-depressive syndrome does represent a fairly clear-cut system of defences which are sufficiently unique and of sufficient theoretical interest to deserve special study. We feel that equating the manic-depressive character with the observational character overlooks the distinguishing difference to the manic depressive, uses substitutive processes as his chief defence. The manic, uses the previously mentioned lack of interpersonal awareness as his chief defence, together with the defensive processes themselves. The object relations of the obsessional are more stable and well developed than those of the manic depressive. While the obsessional's relations are usually integrations in which there is an intense defence of hostility, control and envy, they do take into consideration the other person as a person. The manic depressive develops an intensely dependent, demanding, oral type of relationship which overlooks the particular characteristic and qualities of the other. According to Sullivan's conceptualization of the schizophrenic process, the psychosis is introduced typically by a state of panic, in which there is an acute break with reality resulting from the upsurge of dissociated drives and motivations which are absolutely unacceptable and invest with unbearable anxiety. Following this acute break, a variety of unsuccessful recovery or defensive processes ensue, which we call paranoid, catatonic, or hebephrenic. These represent attempts of the personality to deal with the conflicts which brought about the panic: The paranoid by projection, the catatonic by rigid control; the hebephrenic by focussing on the bodily impulses. According to this conception, the manioc depressive can be differentiated from the schizophrenic by the fact that he does not exhibit the acute break with reality which is seen in the schizophrenic panic. His psychotic processes of depression or, of manic, he can be thought of asserting a depressive function against the still breaker personality disintegration which is represented by the schizophrenic state. This, in persons whose conflicts and anxiety are too severe to be handled by depressive or manic defences, a schizophrenic breakdown may be the end result. Contrasting the schizophrenic and the manic depressive from the point of view of their early relationships, we see that the schizophrenic has accepted the bad mother as his fate, and his relations. He therefore attenuated. He is inclined to withdraw into detachment. He is hypercritical of family and cultural values. he is sensitive and subtle in his criticisms, original but disillusioned. He is disinclined to rely on others and is capable of enduring considerable degrees of loneliness. His reluctance to make demands on the therapist makes the therapist more feel and more sympathetic, and therefore the therapist is frequently in his aggression, he can take the risk of attacking, for he is less afraid of loneliness. He is more sensitively aware of the emotions of the therapist, since the boundaries between ego and environment are more fluid. The schizophrenic is not inclined to pretend, and is not easily fooled by other people's pretenses, Dream and fantasies are nearer to awareness and guilt feelings are also more conscious than unconscious. The typical manic depressive has not accepted the 'bad mother' as his fear. He vacillates between phases in which he fights with the bad mother, and phases in which he feels reunited with the good mother. In there manic phase, his, relationships with reality is more tenuous; he shows a lack of respect for other people, and reality considerations are dismissed for the dark of magic manipulation to make the bad mother over into a good mother. The manic depressive is therefore, mostly a good manipulator, a salesman, a bargaining personality. He is under-critical instead of being hypocritical. He easily sells out his convictions and his originality in esteem. In the depressive phase, he sacrifices himself to gain a good mother or to transform the bad mother into a good mother. In order to do this, he calls himself bad, and suffers to expiate his sins, but these guilt feelings are, in a sense, artificial or expedient, utilized in order to manipulate the bad mother into becoming a good mother. The depressive does not come to terms with realistic guilt feelings. Instead, he uses self-accusations, which frequently sound hypocritical, to convince the mother or a substitute that his need to beloved has absolute urgency. He denies his originality because he is terribly an afraid of aloneness, he is more of a follower than a leader. He is dependent on prestige, and is quite unable to see through the pretense of his own or other people's conventionalities. He shows a high degree of anxiety when his manipulations fail. His lack of subtlety in interpersonal relationships is due to his overruling preoccupation with exploiting the other person in order to fill his emptiness. This operate s as a vicious circle as he has maintained his claims for as good fulfilling mother, but his search for fullness manipulation of another makes him feel helpless and empty. This incorporates of another person fo r the purpose of filling an inward emptiness, of acquiring a borrow self-esteem, is very different from the lack of ego boundaries in the schizophrenic. The schizophrenic is in danger of losing his ego., and he expresses his danger in fantasies of world catastrophe. The manic depressive is threatened by object loss, since h e habitually uses the object to patch up his ego weakness. Object relations in the manic depressive are, but clouded by illusions, but even when he waits, demands, and blames the frustrating object, he is—by this very agitated activity in behalf of his own salvation, ineffective as it may be—defended against the loss of the ego. When the manic depressive becomes schizophrenic, this defence breaks down. It should be noted that the infantile dependency and manipulative exploitativeness seen in the manic depressive are not unique to this type of disorder. They occur, in fact, in many forms of severe mental illness. The hysteric, for instance, exemplifies infantile dependency and exploitativeness as dramatically as the manic depressive, and in 'la belle difference' one may see a resemblance to the euphoria of the manic or hypomanic. However, the combination of the dependent and exploitative traits with the other outstanding characteristics of the cyclothymic personality—particularly the communicative defect and the accompanying inability to recognize other persons as anything but good-bad stereotypes and the conventional but hypermoralistic values—does become sufficiently distinct and unique to distinguish these patients characterologically from other types. The diagnosis of manic-depressive character has, in the past, been made largely on the basis of the patient's exhibiting the classic manic and depressive symptomatology. It can, however, be as validly made on the basis of the transference-countertransference pattern, which is set up between the patient and the therapist. The transference pattern is particularly characteristic; the countertransference pattern would, of course, vary considerably according to the personality of the therapist, although it, too, shows a number of quite typical features. The transference pattern shows two outstanding characteristics which could be labelled (1) the exploitative clinging decency, and (2) the stereotyped approach other persons, who are not seen aa personalities in their own right. 1. The dependency as with other workers in the field of the study of manic depressive illness has apply documented the deep-seated dependency of this type of person (Abraham, Freud, Rado, Klein). The dependency attitudes toward the object are highly ambient. Gratification is demonstrated, but not accepted or experienced as such, and the patient feels that attention, car e, and tenderness must be forced from the other person. The force applied is that of demonstrating to the other person how miserable he is making one, how much the depressed one needs the other, and how responsible and culpable the other is if he fails to meet the depressive's needs. The demands are not directly verbalized but rather consist of a wordless exploitation: The reactive hostility is not experienced as such, but instead is experienced as depression. In the depths of the depression, It seems impossible to satisfy the patient's dependency needs. As one therapist mentions, the patient seems to be saying, 'I am starving, and I won' t get what I need.' The amount of time and attention the patient receives, crying out for more. We sense if satisfaction. He remains depressed, We have not tried the experiment of spending the major portion of each day with a depressive person. Certainly 24-hour-a-day nursing does not suffice to give the patient a sense of gratification. Whether unlimited time from a therapist would have more effect is debatable, in the light of our experience with Mr. Richard, such that when the patient is in a period of relative mental health, these needs are less apparent, this raises the question of what becomes of these needs during such periods: Are they not present and only stirred up again when some unusual deprivation nor treat to security occurs, or are they successfully kept t in repression during the healthy phase?In the manic phase, the demandinngness is much more open but seen by the patient as demanding his rights rather than as asking for favours. Rejection of the demand is met with t hostility rather than with a depressive response. The manic, of course, show, in addition to the demandingness, the tendency to take what he needs by force, if necessary and he will use direct aggression—in contrast to the depressive, who uses reproaches against the other person as a forcing manouevre. 2. The stereotyped response of the manic-depressive personality shows a highly characteristic tendency to look upon others as stereotyped repetitions of parental figures. This has been described elsewhere in reporting as 'a lack of interpersonal sensitivity'. The therapist is regarded, (x) as an object to be manipulated for purposes of getting sympathy and reassurance, (y) as a moral authority who can be manipulated into giving approval, and (z) as, in actuality, a critical and rejecting authority figure who will not give real approval but can be counted on only for token approval which can be achieved by proper behaviour manipulation. This uncritical categorization of the therapist results in the patient's inability to use the therapist to provide himself with a fresh point of view. Everything that the therapist says is reworked into the old pattern of concealed disapproval covered over with the sugar of artificial reassurance. This impenetrability to the reception of new ideas from the therapist represents one of the great obstacles in therapy with this type of patient, who will give lip service to the role of the therapists a noncritical authority without a feeling of conviction that this is do. However, the lip service itself then becomes incorporated into the set of manipulative acts which will receive approval and adds another wall to their defence. Early in the study of these patients, it was felt that the lack of ability to appraise the therapist as a person represented a real learning defect in the patient and that one of the therapeutic tasks therefore was a somewhat educational one of showing the patient how one person could be different from another. On further study we have come to the conclusion that the defect is not an educational one, as evidence for this being that as the anxiety diminishes in an interpretational relation, the sensitivity increases. Mr. Richard is an excellent illustration of this point. His therapist spoke if him as follows:

> When the patient first entered treatment, I would have described him for being without the ability to emphasize with another. During the subsequent years of treatment, It became apparent that the patient was acutely sensitive to nuances in the attitude of others to him, but that his interpretation of these attitudes was extremely static and stereotyped. Finally, at the end of treatment, he retained much of his sensitivity and had also gained in his ability to respond with accuracy in interpretational situations.

The therapist, as such, finds to some forwarded attemptive description as the therapist is describing in terms of a maldevelopment of the empathic function. Approaching the problem from the point of view of present-day relationships, we suggest that it is anxiety-arousing fo r the manic depressive to recognize others as persons, as well as to conceive of himself as a person in his own right. The manic depressive's recognition of bad or unacceptable traits in another person would interfere with his dependency on him; but would of a necessarily for him to abandon the other person for his badness, and this would then leave him alone. In order to avoid this anxiety, the manic depressive avoids the recognition and identification of the medley of attractive and unpleasant traits in others, and thereby avoid their exchange of a variety of complex feelings. Thus, it is so often true in psychopathology, what begins as developmental defect ends up as an anxiety-avoiding defence. Whereas states of morbid anxiety have been dealt within detail in the literature of psychoanalysis, depressive states have hitherto received less attention. Nevertheless the effect of depression is as widely spreading all forms of neurosis and psychoses are that of anxiety. The two affects often present together or successively in one individual so that a patient suffering from an anxiety-neurosis will be subject to states of mental depression, and melancholic will complain of having anxiety.

One of the earliest results of Freud's investigations of the neurosis was the discovery that neurotic anxiety originated from sexual repression, and this origin served to differentiate it from ordinary fear. In the same was we can distinguish between the affect of sadness or grief and neurotic depression, the latter being unconsciously motivated and a consequence of repression. Anxiety and depression are related to each other in the same way as are fear and grief. We fear a coming evil; we grieve more than one that has occurred. A neurotic will be attacked with anxiety when his instinct strives for a gratification which repression prevents him from attaining; depression sets in when he has to give up his sexual aim without having obtained gratification. He feels himself unloved and incapable of loving, and therefore he despairs of his life and the future. This affect lasts until the cause of it ceases to operate either through an actual change in his situation or through a psychological modification of the displeasurable ideas with which he is faced. Every neurotic state of depression, just like every anxiety-state, to which it is closely related, contains a tendency to deny life.

Meaning is not embedded in some obscure 'inner human nature', nor something that is desired to be destined to be developed by successively 'higher forms of life'. There is, in short, nothing vitalistic or mysteriously emergent implied in the idea of meaning. Meaning is the elaboration of an increasingly intricate ground plan of broad relationships and ramifications. It is the establishment of dependable cause-and-effect sequences which permit ego-mastery and action. Meaning is at the heart of life because it is inseparable from action sequence with an intricate symbolism, the dependable becoming the indispensable the satisfying becomes the necessary as Man's symbolic life is an imbibing of meaning and a relentless creation of it. This symbolic elaboration of meaning is Homo sapiens sapient—home, so to speak—brought by him onto the evolutionary scene and manufactured solely for his use and delight, by means of it, man intoxicate's himself into the illusion that his particular meaning-fabric, his culture's concoction of symbols and action, is god-given and timeless. In his imagination, man fuses symbols and action into a cohesion that has atomic tenacity.

But still, it is pardonable for the theorist to make the error of narrowness when he is attempting to understand what is behind stupidly-language or such linguistic uttering as to make the person using them seem childish, whining, and somehow culpable in himself, the person provides a sorry spectacle when he tries to keep his world from caving in upon him with only the limited means at the disposal of his ingenuity. Thus, it is logical to look for selfish motives in those who show themselves cognitively limited and childish. Perhaps, this is another reason why theory has so long been hampered.

But people are not fated to remain childish, they are kept childish by parents and by culture. We train them to live in a certain kind of world, and to accept it dumbly. The culture. In other words, creates certain kinds of bondage from which people cannot be released without threatening others. Can a wife be released from a marriage contract when her husband begins neglecting her? Can she begin life anew at 40 when she has not previously provided herself with the withdrawals? Can a factory-operator's wife suddenly join him at 53, untrained as she is, and basically unwanted in a man's world? Anthropology has provided us with the knowledge that there are any number of possible arrangements for human action. And that they all work—for better or for worse. We have discovered that the word 'natural' does not apply to human relationships; these are all learned. When we say that an individual's world 'crumbles' we don't mean that his ;natural' world crumbles but, that his cultural world does. If he had been taught to operate in another kind of world, it would perhaps not have crumbled. The Vows of marriage could have drawn for forbidding the taking of another wife, and that witchcraft depression syndrome would certainly be much reduced

Theorists have considered object-loss to be he principal cause for depression, and had overlooked the importance of 'games' and meaning. One reason for this error of emphasis is that some cultures provide only a narrow range of objects and games. The result is that the object and the limited meaning come to be inseparable, which is to say, the more people to whom one can make appeal for his identity, the easier it is to sustain life-meaning. Object-loss hits hardest when self-justification is limited to a few objects. But object-loss is not crucial—or even necessarily important—when there is the possibility of sustaining one's conduct as before. Action is the basic problem in object-loss, and people devise ingenious ways to sustain it. An excellent illustration is the phenomenon of vengefulness. Harold F. Searles (1956) showed that the revenge process can serve as a way of keeping the object. It cannot be overstressed that an object is never an object in isolation. It is a means of coming in contact with the world, it permits action. By definition, to constitute an object is to create a behaviour pattern. To lose an object is to lose the possibility of undertaking a range of satisfying action. This is foremost, in addition, for man, the object is a private performance audience. It is a locus to which is addressed the continuing identity dialogue of the self and experience, the continued presence of the object, in other words, serves as a purchase to the symbolic elaboration of the self. The object need not be present in the outer world; one needs only to have developed behaviour patterns toward it, or modelled on it, and to keep its image in mind. Thus, the object exists on an internal-external continuum, it reflects a process of growth and activity in the actor. Just as the 'external pole' serves as experiential contact with the outer world, so does the 'internal pole' permit a continual fashioning of the identity. Hence we can see that object-loss means not only external performance loss, but inner identity loss as well. This bears repeating, because it enables us to understand the phenomenon of vengefulness. To hate and to seek revenge is to create a continually present object. Searles says that the vindictive person 'has not really give up the other person toward whom his vengefulness is directed, is his preoccupation with vengeful fantasies about that person serves, in effect, as a way of psychological holding onto his,'. Vengefulness is a type of continuous performance, a way of maintaining the object that otherwise would no t be there.

Initially, what is called the 'Superego' is the 'internal pole' of our objects. We address our performance to them, by saying ;See how well I am doing, as you would wish me to'. Both action and identity are potentiated. The revenge-object is merely a variation on this. We keep it in order to be able to say, 'See how great I have become, as you did not think I could become' and so forth. It has often been observed that the motif "I`ll show the folks back in my home town' is a primary impetus to success. On the primitive level, revenge murders of the death of a loved one is simply a variation on this. One continues to perform as if the object were still there. The automatic nature of primitive revenge shows how important it is to keep some kind of behaviour pattern, which serves in effect to keep the object. Vilification of the dead in mourning ceremonies is also a way of keeping behaviour patterns toward the object. to remain silent is swamped by the action void.

Finally, 'showing the folks back home' keep the identity rooted in time, gives it the all-important duration and continuity. if one could not keep objects, the identity would have to be continuously recreated in the present. one would be in the position of Jean-Paul Sarte's gambler; the entire past accretion of meaning would be severed. The identity owes its very existence to its rooting in the past.

We have a hard job—in our culture—in realizing how inseparable are object-range and performance-possibilities. But consider the situation in traditional society. There the extended family is the rule, and not the small, tight, nuclear one that is familiar to us., the consequence of this is that the life-changes and life-meaning of the individual do not depend on a few parental objects. Meaning is generalized to a whole range of kin. The extended family provides a continuing source of esteem and affirmation for the individual actor, even thought significant figures drop out.

In our culture we are familiar with the person who lives his life for the wishes of his parents and becomes depressed when then die and he has reached the ages of forty or fifty. He has lost the only audience for whom the plot in which he was performing was valid. He is left in the hopeless despair in which the actor who knows only one set of lines, and loses the one audience who wants to hear him. The extended family takes care of this problem. Even though it makes rigid prescriptions for the behaviour of each individual. Even though it makes good prescriptions for the behaviour of each individual, still each member can count on an audience for his continuing performance even after his own immediate patent die.

The depths of despondency and dispirited desperation in the loss of or nearly of all hope, despairing in the grief of a discouraging disheartedness, if only to fall into the tyranny as intended within the fate of destiny.

Thus, culture designs the action scene, and outlines the kind of crises to which the individual will have to adapt. One of the sharpest exposés of the grip in which culture holds the individual, and the breakdown which results from that grip, is Edmund Volkart's study of bereavement (1957). Volkart points out that restriction of the identity-appeal to only a few objects is a type of 'psychological bondage'. We train people to 'love', 'honour;' and 'obey' only a few others. and when death or some other train of events leaves the haplessly loyal person in the sway to and fro, the psychiatry is apt to hold a microscope to his body chemistry, or measure his saliva. Instead of providing for continuing life-designs, instead of training people in critical self-awareness. We actually facilitate the subversion of life-meaning. Volkart does not soft pedal this major personality issue, and can do no more than to quote directly:

> Any culture which, in the name of mental health, entourage's extreme and exclusive emotional investments by one person in a selected few others, but which does not provide suitable outlets and alternatives for the inevitable bereavement, is simply altering the conditions of, and perhaps postponing, severe mental ill health. It may, in the vernacular, be building up for a big led down by exacerbating vulnerabilities (1957).

In other words, in our culture we champion limited horizons—a limited range of objects—and call people 'mentally ill' when they suffer its effects. we make no provision for sustaining meaning when the bottom drops out of someone's life. When a women's children marry, then the mirror begins to reflect the gradual and irrevocable loss of her charm, her performance as a responsible person, culturally desirable, is over. She may find herself left with no part to play, as early as her late 30s—with nothing to justify and sustain her identify. Since this utter subversion of meaning usually coincides with menopause e, psychiatry has labelled the depression that may occur' 'involutional depression', medical psychiatry has only recently come to focus social role, clinically, it was easier to image that the depression is somehow due to bodily changes or, the psychoanalytic theory might see this as a pampered self-pity over the imagined loss of sexual capacity, over the inevitable diminuation instinctual vigour.

Students of epidemiology first took to studying the social distributions of contributive types of illness in the hope of turning up some answers. Since clinical research did not provide any real understanding of the etiology of depression and schizophrenia, it was hoped that perhaps social research might. Fact does not precede theory, and no amount of counting can ever explain. But statistics on epidemiology did provide some kind of picture. It now seems generally agreed that depression occurs more frequently among persons with cohesive family groupings: Among women, who are more cohesively identified with close in-groups, in higher socioeconomic statuses, in highly tradionalized groups and among professionals.

Schizophrenia, on the other hand, presents a radically different epidemiological picture. It occurs more among men than women; in the lower socioeconomic bracket among dislocated peoples—that is, generally where group membership and identifications are weakest.

Mental illness, as we have been surveying is a form of cultural and individual stupidity, an urge to meaning by those poor in command over vocabularies. If this thesis holds, we should expect some confirmation from the epidemiological picture; action varies according to class, as does awareness; possibilities for self-justification as well as degree of cultural indoctrination vary by class. Nonetheless, the class picture does seem to give some kind of consistent reflection of the views we have detailed.

If depression is a form of meaning-stupidity in an overwhelming frustration situation, we would expect it to be more prevalent in the upper classes, among women, and among people in close identification with others. These are all people who feel that they should find their situation acceptable—but, who somehow do not. The upper classes, having achieved socially approved success, have no reason to be unhappy. Women are given their status in the social structure as a matter of course, and should not question otherwise. People in close and 'loving' identification with others are taught that they should derive all their life satisfactions from the quality of these relations, and from the pattern of rights and obligations which they entail. All the more reason that guilt should present itself as a natural alternative for deep-seated dissatisfaction: One cab will believe himself guilty for not being contentually satisfied where he should not. On the other hand, among the lower classes, dissatisfaction need not necessarily terminate in depressive self-accusation. Any number of scapegoats can be found and other rationalizations used, to justify failure, the rich, the boss, the low status of women in the lower class as compared with the upper 'bad luck', 'hard times' and so on (Prange and Vitols, 1962). In

725

terms of alternative vocabularies of meaning, the lower classes, paradoxically, are less 'stupid' than the upper.

But the situation is quite different with the lower-class schizophrenic. He lacks even that meaning which belongs to his own class—since he has failed to learn to interact effortlessly. He joins a personal 'poverty' to a class poverty; and it has been observed repeatedly that the extreme schizophrenic is more obedient and conservative in accepting ideal formulas for proper behaviour than are his peers. He tends to conform to idealized behaviour standards which deprive him of the possibility of easy scapegoats available to those who flaunt standards.

The upper-class schizophrenic, on the other hand, is in a more fortunate situation. In the first place, he can effect some measure of correspondence between his fantasy world and certain specialized symbolic achievements provided by society. He has more of a chance of having his fantasies, and his identity somewhat validated. Clifford Beers, for example, could assume the identity of mental-hygiene reformer and create some measure of conformity between his omnipotent fantasies and the real action world. Possibilities of symbolic self-justification are more available to upper than to lower-class schizophrenics. Also, it is worthy noting that th upper-class schizophrenic can usually extend his identity back in time, to include family traditions, roots in the Old World, illustrious ancestors, and so on. This socially supported extension of the self in time gives some experiential depth to the personality, and helps buffer present ineptitudes (Strauss, 1959). The lower-class schizophrenic, on the other hand, has no such time depth to his identity, and must rely solely on fantasy and on the unrewarding contemporary situation. Rogler and Hollingshead observed bluntly on the extremely stressful and unrewarding nature of lower-class life. 'The afflicted individual world into an unreal world of fictions. these fictions my be equally unpleasant.

Meaning-poverty then, depends on the type of stupidity: For the schizophrenic. Shallowness of meaning is a result of behavioural poverty; it reflects insufficient participation in interpersonal experiences. The depressed person, suffers instead from a too uncritical participation in a limited range of monopolizing interpersonal experiences. Hitherto, two kinds of failure of the humanization process; the individual who has not been indoctrinated into his culture, and the one who has been only too well imbued with a narrow range of its sentiments. If both of these individuals end up in our mental hospitals, perhaps we cannot blame the psychiatrist for juggling chemical and ignoring culture. The problem one has a narrow medical view of human behaviour. Individual and culture are inseparable. The individual finds answers to the four common answers provided for by social institutions—by a whole accumulated tradition of cultural learning. In view of this the psychiatrist may object that it would be much too big a job for the medical practitioner to bring under critical fire the institutions of his society. How can he undertake to determine how people should be' brought up? Quite right, he cannot. This is the task of a broad, unified human science.

Nonetheless, the data of the human sciences are starting to emerge, their relationships are becoming clear. If this revolution, like any other, is to be successful, no vested institution can escape critical review. Nature—in her constitution oh the Homo sapient's sapient—seems to have frames the four common human problems, but man—by his cultural and social world—frames the answers. Nothing done by man for man cannot be undone and redone. It suffices to design the problem.

Now, one thing will be immediately obvious about his kind of sharp classification It can rarely exist in reference to human nature as we have traced its complex development. Schizophrenic and depressive types merge into one another and overlap. They represent different kinds and degrees of adaptation to ranges of object and events which are not mutually exclusive within one behavioural system. Thus, we can see, at the end of this presentation of the two major 'syndromes', that they are not syndromes at all. Rather, they reflect the typical problems that man is prone to, the restrictions, coercions, the lack of control over behaviour, and the confusions in symbolic reconstruction of himself and his experience. All this blends in varying proportions in the individual personality. If we can only rarely see clear 'types' emerging from this, then there is all the more reason to reorient our approach to labelling the human personality.

We use the term 'depression' to refer to the syndrome of behaviours that have been identified in descriptive studies of depressed individuals (e.g., Grinker et al., 1961). It includes verbal statements of dysphoria, self-depreciation, guilt, material burden, social isolation, somatic complaints, and a reduced rate of many behaviours. Is that, we assume depression to be a continuous variable which can be conceptualized as a 'state' which fluctuates over time as well as a 'trait'—(some people are more prone to becoming depressed than others?). Being depressed does not exclude other psychopathological conditions such as schizophrenia, psychosis, sexual deviation, or alcoholism. For purposive reasons, it would seem important that any study relying on differences between depressed and nondepressed groups for its conclusions have a normal control as well as a 'psychiatric control' group (i.e., patients for whom anxiety or other neurotic symptoms but not depression constitute the major psychopathology) if any observed group differences are to be attributed to depression (depression—psychiatric control, normal) and not to the deviation hypothesis (depression, psychiatric control, normal control).

The major assumptions of the behavioural theory of depression follows three laying premises that postulate (1) A low rate of response-contingent positive reenforcement (response) acts as an eliciting (unconditioned) stimulus for some depressive behaviour, such as feeling of dysphoria, fatigue, and other somatic symptoms. (2) A low rate of response constitutes a sufficient explanation for other parts of the depressive syndrome such as the low rate of behaviour. For the latter the depressed person is considered to be on a prolonged extinction schedule. (3) The total amount of response received by an individual is presumed to be a function of three sets of variables: (I) The number of events (including activities) that are potentially reinforce for the individual, influenced by biological (e.g., sex and age) and experiential variables. (ii) The number of potentially reinforcing events that can be provided by the environment, i.e., the availability of reenforcement in the environment. (iii) The instrumental behaviour of the individual, i.e., the extent to which he possesses the skills and emits those behaviours that will elicit reinforcement for him from his environment.

The behaviour theory requires that (1) the total amount of response received by depressed persons be less than that received by nondepressed persons, and similarly, it will be less when the individual is depressed than when he is not depressed; (2) the onset of depression be accompanied by a reduction in response; (3) intensity of depression convary with rate of response, and (4) improvement be accompanied by an increase in response. Before proceeding to an examination of relevant empirical studies several additional clarification and hypotheses are offered.

In terms of system theory (von Bertalanffy, 1950; Allport, 1960; Miller, 1971), the usual conceptualization of the depressed person is one of a relatively closed system. Grinker (1964) was explicitly instating that the depressed person repeats his message and behaviour without reception or acceptance of resulting feedback. Beck (1964, 1967) described the cognitive distortion that dominate the information processing of the depressed person so that experiences are rigidly interpreted to maintain existing schema of personal deficiency, self-blame, and negative expectations.

The implicit assumption of these has been that the support and information available to the depressed person are incongruent with his depression, and the persistence of his symptomatology is evidence of a failure to receive or accept this information. Withdrawal, isolated intrapsychic persecution or as Beck describes (1967), interaction of depressive schema and affective structure, produce a downward depressive spiral. Presently, that is to say, that our adopted alternative is that the depressed person is able to engage others in his environment in such a way that support is lost and depressive information elicited. This in turn increases the level of depression and strengthens the pathogenetic pattern of depressed behaviour rather response of other if a depressive spiral develops, It is mutually causative, deviation-amplifying process (Maruyama, 1963) in the interaction of the depressed person with his environment. Thus, what is customarily viewed as some internal process is, I believe, that, at least in part, a characteristic of interaction with the environment, and much of what is customarily view as cognitive distortions or misperception is characteristic of information flow from the environed, it should be noted that while the depressed person's different interprets his predicament is traditionally attributes to his distortion or misperception, genera disorders of thought and perception are nether defining criteria more common among depressed patients (McPartland and Hornstra, 1964). An observer who talks into account the intricacies of someone's relationship to his environment,. Frequently attributes to hin characteristics that he does not possess, or leaves significant aspects of his experience unexplained (Watzlawick, 1967). Feedback introduces phenomena that cannot be adequately explained by reference to the isolated individual alone (Ashby, 1960,

1962), for the stud y of depression, identification of a pattern of depressive feedback from the environment demands a more complex conceptualization of the disorder that one explaining its phenomena with reference to the isolated depressed person.

Of all the distinctions that have been proposed, the most widely accepted and least controversial is that between unipolar and bipolar disorder. In its simplest form—and as it has been recognized in the DSM-III—the differential diagnosis is based on whether the patient has a personal history of mania. However, recent genetic studies have led to a familial definition of the distinction: Depressed patients who do not have a personal history of mania may still be diagnosed for being bipolar if there has been mania among first-degree relatives.

Valid though the distinction appears to be, it has some important limitations. As yet, no consistent differences in the symptomatology of bipolar and unipolar depression have been identified. Although a bipolar diagnosis predicts a greater likelihood of response to lithium, as many as 40 percent of unipolar patients, nonetheless, respond positively (Depue and Monroe, 1978). By itself, the distinction does not do justice to the heterogeneity among either bipolar or unipolar patients. Currently, persons with bipolar disorder are often subclassified as to whether either manic or depressive symptoms or both have been severe to require hospitalization. Unipolar depressed persons remain a large and tremendously heterogeneous group. Nonetheless, in the continuing controversies as how best to distinguish among depressed persons, the unipolar-bipolar distinctions stands out in its usefulness for both clinical and research purposes.

Although little, has been written in the literature of psychoanalysis concerning the psychology of neurotic depression. But the affect of depression in the sphere of the psychosis awaits more precise investigation. This task is complicated by the fact that a good part of the diseases in question run a ;cyclical' course in which there is an alternation between melancholic and manic states. The few preliminary studies which have hitherto been published have only dealt with one of these two phases at the same time.

The study of the genetics of depression remains in its infancy. Further advances are going to require better ways of subtyping affective disorders and the discovery of biological markers that are not state dependent, that is, tied to whether someone is currently disturbed. Dunner describes some of the distinctions that he and his colleagues have drawn for bipolar disorder, in terms of the severity of manic and depressive phases (e.g., whether one or both require hospitalization). It is probably true that bipolar disorder is more homogeneous and has a stronger genetic component than unipolar depression, and because of this, Dunner suggests that is more likely to yield advances in the near future. Some researchers are attempting to identify subtypes of unipolar depression that 'breed true' such that the relatives of depressed persons who have a particular pattern of symptoms will themselves show this pattern if they become depressed. There have been some promising findings with concomitant appetite disturbance and excessive guilt (Leckman et al., 1984), but any substantial advances are going to depend ultimately upon the identification of genetic markers that have thus far proven elusive. Riedfer and Gershon (1978) have noted that such markers will need to be stable; heritable, and state independent; capable of differentiating persons with an affective disturbance from persons drawn from the general population, and among the relatives of depressed persons, capable of identifying those who develop affective disturbance from those who do not.

A major source of confusion is due to the fact that the term 'depression' variously refers to a mood state, a set of symptoms, and a clinical syndrome. As a reference to mood, depression identifies a universal human experience, adjectives from a standard measure of mood (The Multiple Affect Adjective Checklist: Zuckerman and Lubin, 1965) point to subjective feelings associated with a depressed mood; sad, unhappy, blue, low, discouraged, bored, hopeless, dejected, and lonely. Similarities between everyday depressed mood and the complaints of depressed patients have encouraged the view that clinical depression is simply an exaggeration of a normal depressed mood, however, patients sometimes indicate that their experience of depression is quite distinct from normal feelings of sadness, even in its extreme form.

Of recent views, that depression is to emphasize that it is primarily a biological disturbance, an illness, the predisposition to which lies in genes and biochemistry, while people may react to their circumstances with happiness and unhappiness, this is of questionable relevance to the clinical phenomena of depression. However, as these definitional problems continue to plague the study of depression, and they are not going to be readily resolved.

There remains considerable disagreement as to what extent and for what purpose a depressed mood in relatively normal persons can be seen as one end of a dimensional continuum of mood as taken upon those disturbances as seen of a psychiatric hospital patients, and to what extent the clinical phenomena is distinct and discontinuous with normal sadness and unhappiness.

One observer may be struck with the frequent complaints about appetite and sleep disturbance by depressed persons and infer that some sort of biological disturbance mus t be the key to understanding depression. Another might find their self-derogation and pessimism irrational in a way that suggests that these must be some kind of fundamental deficit in self-esteem or cognitive distortion occurring. Still another may listen to the incessant complaining of a depressed person, get annoyed and frustrated, and yet feel guilty in the way that makes it easier to encourage the depressed person to continue to talk in this way than to verbalize these negative feelings. Cognizant of this, the observer might conclude that there is some sort of interpersonal process going on that is critical to any understanding of depression.

Nonetheless, studies have compared the subjective mood of persons who are distressed but seeking help to those who are seeking treatment for depression (Depue and Monroe, 1978). The two groups may be similar in subjective mood, but they differ in other ways. Those persons who are not seeking treatment for depression tend to lack the anxiety and the physical complaints, including loss of appetite, sleep disturbances, and fatigue shown by the group seeking treatment. still, it could be argued that there is a continuum of dimensional provision, as to the differences between the two groups, with these additional features arising, when a normal depressed mood become s more prolonged or intensified. The controversy is likely to continue until either questions about the etiology of depression are resolved or unambiguous markers for depression are identified.

Advocates of psychoanalytic, cognitive and behavioural, and interpersonal and social perspective on depression have generally assumed a dimensional quantification between a normal depressed mood and clinical depression. They tend to exclude psychotic and bipolar depressed persons from treatment, but, beyond that, they have tended to disregard classification issues (Gilbert,. 1984) for unipolar depression, at least, they have assumed that whatever discontinuities in the biology of mild and severe moods there might be that are, yet as not excessively necessarily relevant to the psychological and asocial processes, which they are most interested.

Writers since antiquity have noted the core symptoms of depression: Besides a sad or low mood, reduced ability to expression pleasure, pessimism, inhibition and retardation of action, and a variety of physical complaints. as such, that we can distinguish among the emotional, cognitive, motivational, and vegetative symptoms of depression, although these feature s are not alway so neatly divisible. Beyond these symptoms, there are some characteristic interpersonal aspects of depression that are not usually considered as formal symptoms. But they are frequent, distinctive, and troublesome enough tp warrant attention.

Sadness and dejection are not the only emotional manifestations of depression, although about half of all depressed patient report these feelings as their principal complaint. Most depressed persons are also anxious and irritable. Classical descriptions of depression tend to emphasize that depressed persons' feelings of distress, disappointment, and frustration are focussed primarily on themselves, yet a number of studies suggest that their negative feelings, including overt hostility, are also directed at the people around them. Depressed persons are often intensely angry persons (Kahn, Coyne, and Margolin, Weissman, Klerman and Paykel, 1971).

Perhaps, 10 or 15 percent of severely depressed patients deny feelings of sadness, reporting instead that all emotional experience, including sadness, has been blunted or inhibited (Whybrow, Akiskal and Mckinney, 1984). The identification of these persons as depressed depends upon the presence of other symptoms. The inhibition of emotional expression in severely depressed persons may extend to crying. Whereas, mild and moderately depressed persons may readily and frequently cry, as they become more depressed, as they may continually be in lack of emotionally expressive inhibitions.

Mildly and moderately depressed persons may feel that every activity is a burden, yet they still derive some satisfaction from their accomplishment. Despite their low mood, they may still crack a smile at a joke yet, as depression intensifies, a person may report both a loss of any ability to get gratification from activities that had previously been satisfying—family, work, and social life—and a loss of any sense of humour. Life becomes stale, flat, and not at all amusing. The loss of gratification may extend to the depressed persons' involvement in close relationships. Often, a loss of affection for the spouse and children, a feeling of not being able to care anymore, a sense of a wall being erected between the depressed person and others are the major reasons for seeking treatment.

Perhaps one of the most frustrating aspects of depressed persons for those around them is their difficulty in mobilizing themselves to perform even the most simple tasks. Encouragements, expressions of support even threats and coercion seem only to increase their inertia, leading others to make attributions of laziness, stubbornness, and malingering. Despite their obvious distress and discomfort, depressed persons frequently fail to take a minimal initiative to remedy their situations or do so only halfheartedly. To observers, depressed persons may seem to have a callous indifference to what happens to them.

Depressed persons often procrastinate. They are avoidant and escapist in their longing for a solacing refuge from demands and responsibilities. In severe depression, the person may experience an abulia or paralysis of will, extending even to getting out of bed, washing, and dressing.

In more severe depressions, there may be psychomotor retardation, expressed in slowed body movements, slowed and monotonous speech, or even muteness. Alternatively, psychomotor agitation may be seen in an inability to be still, pacing, and outbursts of shouting.

The presence of physical or vegetative symptoms are sometimes taken as the dividing line between normal sadness and clinical depression. One of the most common and prominent of vegetative symptoms is fatigue that someone is depressed may be first recognized by the family physician who cannot readily trace the person's complaints of tiredness to other causes.

Depressed persons also often suffer sleep disturbance, and it is tempting to link their tiredness to this, but in a sample of depressed patients, the two complaints are only modestly correlated (Beck, 1967). Depressed persons generally have rouble falling asleep, they sleep restlessly, and awaken easily. Yet, some depressed persons actually sleep considerably more than usual, up to 12 hours a night.

When mildly or moderately depressed, some people eat compulsively and gain considerable weight, but depression is more characteristically associated with loss of appetite and a decrease in weight. For many depressed persons, a loss of appetite is the first sign of an incipient depression, and its return marks the beginning of recovery. Some depressed persons maintain their normal eating habits and weight, but complain that food is tasteless and eating an unsatisfying matter of habit. Besides a loss of appetite, depression is often associated with gastrointestinal disturbance, notably nausea and constipation. Mild depression heightens sexual interest in some people, but generally depression is associated with a loss of interest in sex. In severe depression, there may be an aversion to sex. Overall, though, women who are depressed do not have sex less frequently, but they initiate it, like and enjoy it less, and are less responsive (Weissman and Paykel, 1974).

Finally, depressed persons report diffuse aches and pains. They have frequent headache, and they are more sensitive to existing sources of pain, such as dental problems.

A brief interaction with a depressed person can have a narked impact on one's own mood. Uninformed strangers may react to a conversation with a depressed person with depression, anxiety, hostility, and may be rejecting of further contact (Coyne, 1976). Jacobson (1968) has noted that depressed persons often unwittingly succeed in making everyone in their immediate environment feel guilty and responsible and that others react to the depressed person with hostility and even cruelty. Despite this visible impact of depression on others, there is a persistent tendency in the literature to ignore it and to concentrate instead on the symptoms and complaints of depressed persons out of their interpersonal context. Depressed persons can be difficult, but they may also be facing difficult interpersonal situations within which their distress and behaviour makes more sense.

Depressed persons tend to withdraw from social activities, and their close relationships tend to be strained and conflictual. Depressed women have been more intensely studied than depressed men, in part, because women are approximately twice as likely to be depressed. Depressed women are dependent, acquiescent, and inhibited in their communication in close relationships, and prone to interpersonal tension, friction and open conflict (Weissman and Paykel, 1974). Interestingly, the interpersonal difficulties of depressed persons are less pronounced when they are interacting with strangers than with intimates (Hinchcliffe, Hooper and Roberts, 1975).

About half of all depressed persons report martial turmoil (Rousanville, Weissman, Prusoff and Heraey-Baron, 1979). There is considerable hostility between depressed persons and their spouses, but often there is more between depressed persons and their children. Being depressed makes it more difficult to be a warm, affectionate, consistent parent (McLean, 1976). The children of depressed parents are more likely to have a full range of psychological and social difficulties than the children of normal or even schizophrenic parents (Emery, Weintraub and Neale, 1982), yet one must be cautious in making causal inferences. There is evidence that the child problems are more related to a conflictual marital relationship and a stressful home-life than depression of the parent (Sameroff, Barocas and Siefer).

Depression thus tends to be indicative of an interpersonal situation fraught with difficulties, and this needs to be given more attention in both theorizing and planning treatment. Although depression is associated with interpersonal problems, within a sample of depressed persons the correlation between severity of depression and the extent of interpersonal problems tends to be modest. This may suggest that these problems are a matter not only of how depressed persons are functioning, but of the response of key people around them as well (Coyne, Kahn, and Gotlib, 1985).

In that the diagnosis of depression, one can make a list of the symptoms of depression, and assign any person a depression score on the basis of the number of symptoms present. A number of standard self-report inventories such as the Beck Depression Inventory (Beck, et al., 1961), the Centre for Epistemological Studies Depression Scale (Radloff, 1977) and the Self-Rating Depression Scale (Zung, 1965) have been validated and are widely used as research tools, screening devices, and measures of the change associated with treatment.

Even if one is to assume a continuity between normal depressed mood and clinical depression, it may still prove useful to make a distinction between the presence and absence of significant depression. One may wish to insure that a research study does not include a preponderance of persons whose depression is only mild or transient. Virtually no signs or symptoms are specific to depression, and ye t in many contexts, one may need to distinguish depression from other descriptors or explanations for a person's distress and behaviour in working with elderly, for instance, it is important to distinguish between depression and dementia. In medical patients in general, there is a high prevalence of symptoms associated with depression, both because of physical illness and the stress of hospitalization (Cavanaugh, 1984), and, whether for research pr practical purposes, one may wish to establish criteria for who is to be considered depressed and who is not. Finally persons who are labelled schizophrenic or alcoholic may show considerable depression, but it would be undesirable for many purposes to lump them with those persons whose primary problem is depression. Thus, for purposes of communication, treatment and research, it may prove useful to have some means of specifying some boundary conditions for the term 'depression'. In terms of some minimal level of severity as well as some coherence and specificity to what is included in the concept—even if one rejects the notion that it is a discrete entity, discontinuous with normal mood.

The problem of diagnosis is most critical in biomedical approaches to depression, the assumption is generally made that depression is a matter of one or more disease entities with specific etiologies and treatments. The statement, 'Nosology precedes etiology' conveys the idea that the ability of identify the causes of depression depend s upon the existence of an adequate diagnostic and classificatory system. For instance, to take a simplified hypothetical example, suppose that a particular biological abnormality occurs in 60 percent of all depressed persons and is specific to depression. Suppose also, with the accepted diagnosis criteria, only 60 percent of the persons identify as such are 'actually depressed'. If these conditions occurred, then research might indicate that only 36 percent of depressed persons posses the abnormality.

An effective treatment for depression may also be misjudged or misapplied in the absence of an adequate diagnostic system. This was made apparent recently after a drug company had undertaken a large study to compare the effectiveness of a new frug to that of both an established drug treatment for depression and a placebo (Carroll, 1984). At five of the six research sites. The new drug proves to be no more effective than the placebo, but interpretation of this was limited by the additional finding that the established treatment proved no better. Patients identified as depressed by current criteria did not respond to drug treatment that had proven efficacious in a large body of past research. Either the past research was misleading, the current diagnostic criteria are invalid, or most likely, they were misapplied by reputable investigators.

Contemporary diagnostic systems owe much to the work of Kraepelin at the turn of the century. He divided major psychopathology into two broad syndromes: Dementia praecox (schizophrenia) and manic-depressive illness. The latter category included almost all serious mood disturbance, including depression in the absence of an episode of mania. As retained today, the term generally is a synonym for bipolar disorder. It is also still sometimes used as a genetic term for severe depression. Kraepelin considered manic-depressive illness a biological derangement. although it might in some cases be precipitated by psychological factors, 'the real cause for the malady must be sought in permanent internal changes which are very often, and, perhaps always innate', (Kraepelin, 1921). Once started, the illness runs its course autonomously, independent of changes in the person's situation. Kraepelin also identified a group of psychogenic depression, which were depressive illness and reactive to change in these circumstances.

For more than 30 years, the dominant diagnostic system in the United States has been, the Diagnostic and Statistical Manual of Mental Disorders of the American Psychiatric Association, which is currently in its third edition (DSM-III). In its first edition it integrated the ideas of Kraepelin with those of Adolph Meyer and Sigmund Freud. While accepting Kraepelin's basic distinction between affective disturbance and schizophrenia, it also reflected Meyer's psychobiological view that mental disturbance represented not a simple disease entity, but the reaction of the personality to the matrix of psychological, social, and biological factors. By its second edition, the Meyerian term 'reaction' was no longer used throughout, but Meyer's influence remained. Freud 's ideas about the etiology of psychopathology were built into the criteria for specific disorders. Thus, the defining characteristics of neuroses was anxiety, but for purposed of diagnostic decisions, it could be manifest and observable or inferred to be operating 'unconsciously and automatically' in someone who was not visibly anxious.

The author of DSM-III attempted to avoid past controversies and answer many of the criticisms of its two predecessors. A decision was made to define diagnostic categories as precisely as possible, using descriptive data, rather than inferences about etiology. From a biomedical perspective, the ideal diagnostic and classificatory system would integrate knowledge about etiology with overt symptomatology. However, it was concluded that the present understanding of the causes of most disorders is too limited for this purpose. Furthermore, the sense was that 'the inclusion of etiological theories would be an obstacle to use of the manual by clinicians and varying theoretical orientations, since it would not be possible to present all reasonable etiological theories for each disorder (American Psychiatric Association, 1980). in considering depression, the author's of DSM-III attempted to sidestep a number of longstanding controversies, including that of whether there is a continuum or a discontinuity between normal mood and clinical depression, as well as that of the role of precipitating life circumstances in distinguishing among types of depression. Depressive neurosis disappeared, along with the other neuroses. Depression is now encompassed in two main categories. The first category, major affective disorder, involves the presence of a full affective syndrome, with the subcategories of bipolar and major depression distinguished by whether there has ever been a manic episode. The second category, other specific affective disorders, includes conditions in which the depression is not severe enough to warrant a diagnosis of major affective disorder, but severe enough to warrant a diagnosis of major affective disorder, but the mood disturbance has been intermittent or chronic for at least two years.

The criteria for major depression is subclassified as to whether it is a single episode or recurrent and also as to whether melancholia is present. Melancholia involves a complaint of a loss of pleasure in all or almost all activities, a lack of reactivity to pleasant events: A quality of depressed mood, that is distinct from grief or sadness; depression worse in the morning; early morning wakening; marked psychomotor agitation or retardation; significant weight loss; and excessive quilt. The designation was intended as an acknowledgement that some more symptoms and might be more responsive to treatment with drugs or electroshock. However, it should be noted that there is considerable consensus that such a distinction should be made, but the exact nature of it remains controversial. There are exclusion criteria, including schizophrenia and what is judged to be normal or uncomplicated grief.

In general, these diagnostic systems are viewed as significant improvements over past effort s, but there is widespread dissatisfaction with them. A prominent biologically oriented researcher has lamented:

An astute observer will find little that is intellectually satisfying about the DSM-III diagnostic criteria for major depressive disorder. These criteria amount to catalogue of symptoms, and they are in no way linked by coherent underlying constructs. they also suffer from the problem of being cast as disjunctive criteria. This means that, for example, patients need to satisfy only of the possible symptomatological evaluations or appraising analyze. Therefore (and this occurs in practice), several patients may be assigned the same categorical diagnosis without having any symptoms in common (Carroll, 1984).

Carroll goes on to note that as the result of an inadequate diagnostic system, research studies are limited by the flaws in the diagnosis used as independent variables, and drug treatment of an individual patient tends to remain a matter of trial and error.

We are far from an adequate diagnostic system for depression. If one is to be achieved, it will have to come to terms with the enormous heterogeneity in the signs and symptoms; level of severity, causal factors to this heterogeneity with a variety of classificatory systems. Kendall (1976) has suggested that almost every classificatory system that is logically possible has been proposed at some point in this period, but he notes that little consensus has been achieved. Winokur reviews some of the current controversies, but it would be useful to identify a few of the distinctions that have been made before we turn to the major theoretical perspectives on the disorder.

Of all the distinctions that have been proposed, the most widely accepted and least controversial is that between unipolar and bipolar disorder. In its simplest form—and as it has been recognized in the DSM-III—the differential diagnosis is based on whether the patient has a personal history of mania. However, recent genetic studies have led to a familial definition of the distinction: Depressed patients who do not have a personal history of mania may still be diagnosed as bipolar if there has been mania among first-degree relatives.

Work by Perris (1966) firs t established that bipolar disorder starts on the average of 15 years earlier than unipolar depression and recurs more frequently. Individual episodes are shorter, and there is a greater risk of disorder among the first-degree relatives of bipolar patients. Furthermore, there as a tendency for unipolar and bipolar disorders to breed true, with first-degree relatives of bipolar patients tending toward bipolar disorder, and first-degree relatives of unipolar patients tending to have little more risk of mania than the general population. The unipolar-bipolar distinction has proven to be clinically useful; depressed bipolar patients respond significantly better to lithium than unipolar depressed patients.

Valid though the distinction appears to be, it has some important limitations. As yet, no consistent differences in the symptomatololgy of bipolar and unipolar depression have been identified. Though a bipolar . diagnosis predicts the greater likelihood of response to lithium, as many as 40 percent of unipolar patients, nonetheless, respond positively (Depue and Monroe, 1978). By itself, the distinction does not do justice to the heterogeneity among either bipolar or unipolar patients. Currently, persons with bipolar disorder often subclassified as to whether either manic or depressive symptoms or both have been severe to require hospitalization. Unipolar depressed persons remain a large tremendously heterogeneous group. Nonetheless, in the continuing controversies as how best to distinguish among depressed persons, the unipolar-bipolar distinction stands out in its usefulness for both clinical and research purposes.

Many issues in the study of unipolar depression have coalesced in the concept of endogenous versus nonendogenous depression. The differentiation is most often identified for being between endogenous and reactive depression, although this has been used interchangeably with the endogenous-neurotic and psychotic-neurotic distinction. The hope for the distinction has often been that it would prove to be the boundary between biological versus psychological and social concerns. Traditionally, the term 'endogenous' has been invoked to differentiate depressions that are purportedly biological in etiology, without environmental precipitants, and that are less amenable to psychotherapy. Also, endogenous depressions are expected to be more responsive to somatically oriented interventions, notably electroconvulsive shock therapy and antidepressant medication. 'Reactive' has inferred to

741

depressions that are viewed as understandable reaction to some precipitating stress and that are more suitable for psychotherapy and less responsive to somatic therapies. The distinction was originally based on the supposition that some depressions are related to precipitating events and others seem to appear without them and that would predict response to treatment and clinical course.

People, encompassed within the depressive point of bipolar disorder, experience the intensely sad or profoundly transferring formation showing the indifference to work, activities, and people that once brought them pleasure. They think slowly, concentrate poorly, feel tired, and experience changes—usually an increase—in their appetite and sleep. They often feel a sense of worthlessness or helplessness. In addition, they may feel pessimistic or hopeless about the future and may think about or attempt suicide. In some cases of severe depression, people may experience psychotic symptoms, such as delusions (false beliefs) or hallucinations (false sensory perceptions).

In the manic phase of bipolar disorder, people feel intensely and inappropriately happy, self-important, and irritable. In this highly energized state they sleep less, have racing thoughts, and talk in rapid-fire speech that goes off in many directions. They have inflated self-esteem and confidence and may even have delusions of grandeur. Mania may make people impatient and abrasive, and when frustrated, physically abusive. They often behave in socially inappropriate ways, think irrationally, and show impaired judgment. For example, they may take aeroplane trips all over the country, make indecent sexual advances, and formulate grandiose plans involving indiscriminate investments of money. The self-destructive behaviour of mania includes excessive gambling, buying outrageously expensive gifts, abusing alcohol or other drugs, and provoking confrontations with obnoxious or combative behaviour.

Clinical depression is one of the most common forms of mental illness. Although depression can be treated with psychotherapy, many scientists believe there are biological causes for the disease. The June 1998 publication, of the Scientific American, in the article that Neurobiologist Charles B. Nemeroff exchanges views about something in order to arrive at the truth or to convince others that the connection concerning to considerations that are differentiated between biochemical changes in the brain and the finding of depression.

The genes that a person inherits seem to have a strong influence on whether the person will develop bipolar disorder. Studies of twins provide evidence for this genetic influence. Among genetically identical twins where one twin has bipolar disorder, the other twin has the disorder in more than 70 percent of cases. But among pairs of fraternal twins, who have about half their genes in common, both twins have bipolar disorder in less than 15 percent of cases in which one twin has the disorder. The degree of genetic similarity seems to account for the difference between identical and fraternal twins. Further evidence for a genetic influence comes from studies of adopted children with bipolar disorder. These studies show that biological relatives of the children have a higher incidence of bipolar disorder than do people in the general population. Thus, bipolar disorder seems to run in families for genetic reasons.

Owing or relating to, or affecting a particular person, over which a personal allegiance about the concerns and considerations or work-related stress can trigger a manic episode, but this usually occurs in people with genetic vulnerabilities, other factors—such as prenatal development, childhood experiences, and social conditions—seem to have relatively little influence in causing bipolar disorder. One study examined the children of identical twins in which only one member of each pair of twins had bipolar disorder. The study found that regardless of whether the parent had bipolar disorder or not, all of the children had the same high 10-percent rate of bipolar disorder. This observation clearly suggests that risk for bipolar illness comes from genetic influence, not from exposure to a parent's bipolar illness or from family problems caused by that illness.

Different therapies may shorten, delay, or even prevent the extreme moods caused by bipolar disorder. Lithium carbonates, a natural mineral salt, can help control both mania and depression in bipolar disorder. The drug generally takes two to three weeks to become effective. People with bipolar disorder may take lithium during periods of relatively normal moods to delay or prevent subsequent episodes of mania or depression. Common side effects of lithium include nausea, increased thirst and urination, vertigo, loss of appetite, and muscle weakness. In addition, long-term use can impair functioning of the kidneys. For this reason, doctors do not prescribe lithium to bipolar patients with kidney disease. Many people find the side effects so unpleasant that they stop taking the medication, which often results in a relapse.

From 20 to 40 percent of people do not respond to lithium therapy. For these people, two anticonvulsant drugs may help dampen severe manic episodes: carbamazepine (Tegretol) and valproate (Depakene). The use of traditional antidepressants to treat bipolar disorder carries risks of triggering a manic episode or a rapid-cycling pattern.

Controlled studies have not found that the endogenous-reactive distinction predicts response to psychotherapy (Blackburn, 1981; Kovacs, 1980; Rush, 1984), the presence or absence of precipitating stress has not proved to be a good predictor of response to treatment (Leff, Roatch and Bunney, 1970) and the endogenous-reactive distinction has been found to be deficient in a number of ways. Yet, it remains considerably utility. Reactivity to changes in life circumstances during a depressive episode have been found to predict response to electroconvulsive shock and antidepressant medication (Fowles and Gerch, 1979). Other symptoms that have been associated with a positive response to somantic treatment include quality of a mood and whether there has been a los of the ability to experience pleasure; psychomotor retardation; feeling worse in the morning after than the evening; and sleep and appetite irregularity. Such symptoms are now accepted as criteria for endogenous depression than is the absence of precipitating stress.

This consensus about the feature of endogenous depression still leaves questions about its polar opposite, reactive or neurotic depression. In clinical practice, it tends to be defined in terms of milder mood disturbances a preponderance of psychological rather than vegetative symptoms, and the presence of a precipitating stress, although there are particular doubts about the validity of this last feature. Akiskal (1978) found that reactive or neurotic depression was the single most common diagnosis in inpatient and outpatient settings, but they raised the issue of whether it was useful to consider it a unified entity or type. In about a quarter of all the cases of such depression studied, it appeared to be truly reactive, in the sense that it developed in the face of overwhelming stress in persons who had previously seemed reasonably well functioning. In another quarter of the cases, it seemed to reflect a greater or fewer of chronic tendencies to respond to normative stress with depressed moods and to experience social difficulties. Many of these patients were described as dependent, manipulative, hostile and unstable.

Follow-up revealed overall that only 40 percent of the total sample was considered to have been suffering primarily from an affective disturbance in the absence of some of other condition. Some of the sub-sample, who had faced a clear precipitating stress developed endogenous features. In 10 percent of the sample, the depression seemed secondary to a medial-surgical illness. In 38 percent of the sample, the depression was secondary to some nonaffective disorder, ranging from an anxiety disorder to schizophrenia. In these patients with medical-surgical or nonaffective psychiatric conditions, intermittent depression seemed to follow the course of the other difficulties. A final 10 percent of the sample remained undiagnosed, but depression was considered the probable diagnosis. The work of Akiskal et al, (1978) is further evidence of the problems in attempting to draw any sharp distinctions in the classification and diagnosis of depression. Beyond this, it suggests both the utility and the difficulty of distinguishing between depression that is primary and that which is secondary to other conditions. Furthermore, the work suggests the usefulness of attempting to understand depression in terms of the presence or absence of characterological or lifestyle difficulties.

Thus, the endogenous pole of the endogenous-reactive distinction is more clearly defined than its counterpart. After a long history of debate and controversy, there is a growing consensus that the differentiation of endogenous and reactive depression is useful but that they represent points along a dimensional continuum, rather than two distinct forms of disorder, it is sometimes suggested that endogenous depressions are simply more severe, but this leave s unanswered questions about differences in etiology or the determinants of one depressive episode progressing to an endogenous course and another not. Biomedically oriented researcher looks to the identification of familial patterns of affective disturbance. The development of biological markers, and the refinement of diagnosis laboratory tests is the solution to the ambiguity and confusion. Baldessarini notes the promise of recent developments such as the dexamethasone suppression test, but he cautions that:

> While there has been considerable progress toward a biological and clinically robust diagnosis scheme, and in understanding some characteristics

745

that can help to guide treatment, search for primary causes have been unsuccessful so far. Even so, virtually all of the biological characteristics of severely depressed patients that have been identified are 'state-dependent' (this, they disappear with recovery) and are not stable biological traits or markers of a possible heritable defect.

Even so, and by now it should have become apparent that the phenomena of depression are vaguely delineated and poorly understood. Seligman and his colleagues have provided a fine example of a strategy for dealing with this problem . . . its construction of a laboratory model or analogue with which greater precision can be achieved.

Let us return once more to the relation between helplessness (involving loss of self-esteem) and the simultaneously maintained narcissistic aspirations, noting that their intra-ego conflict assumed by Bibring and Melancholia: such that Bibring's theory opens two new vistas. One leads us to consider self-esteem as a signal, that is, an ego function, rather than as an effectual relation between the ego and the Superego. The other suggests that we recognize the role of the ego, and particularly of its helplessness, in the origin and function of the instinctual vicissitude called turning round upon the subject.

Though it is clear that the phenomenon from which the economic explanation must start is the inhibition of the ego, the economics of depression is still not understood. Bibring quote Fenichel's formulation as to, . . . The greater percentage of the available mental energy is used up in unconscious conflicts, and, not enough is left to provide the normal enjoyment of life and vitality (Bibring, 1953). But he finds this statement insufficient to explain depressive inhibition, and proceeds to reconsider the nature of inhibition such that:

Freud (1926) defines inhibition as a 'restriction of functions of the ego, and mentions two major causes for such restrictions; Either having been imposed upon as the person or its measure of a precaution, i.e., to prevent the development of anxiety or the feelings of guilt, this having brought about as a result of exhaustion, as to infer upon the energy of the ego, of which it is engaged in some intense defensive activities. Bibring implies his own explanation in his comparison of depression to anxiety.

Anxiety as a reaction to external or internal danger indicates that the ego's desire to survive. The ego, challenged by the danger, mobilizes the signal of anxiety and prepares for fight or flight. In depression, the opposite takes place, the ego is paralysed because it finds itself incapable to meet the 'danger'. In certain instances, . . . depression may follow anxiety, then the mobilization of energy . . . is replaced by a decrease of self-reliance.

Thus Bibring's search for an economic explanation of depressive inhibition ends in the undefined term 'deceased of self-reliance', which as it stands, is not an economic concept.

What does that mean, that 'The ego is paralysed because it finds itself incapable to meet the danger'? Clearly 'paralysed' refers to the state of helplessness, one of the corollaries of which is the 'loss of self-esteem'. The danger is the potential loss of the object; The traumatic situation is that of the loss of an object—'helplessness' as Bibring defines, it is the persisting state of loss of an object. The anxiety signal anticipates the loss in order to prevent the reactivation of the traumatic situation, that is, of panic-anxiety. Perturbing fluctuations of self-esteem anticipates the initiation of measures that are preventions, such, are the reactivations in the state of persisting of the loss of its object, from which the state of helplessness would only have to be of its involving in the loss of self-esteem, thus, the relation between perturbing fluctuations of self-esteem and 'helplessness', which is accompanied by its loss of self-esteem, but maintaining the similarity between the relation of its own dose of anxiety and the signalling of the panic-anxiety. Fluctuations of self-esteem are then structurally tamed by forms of and signals to anticipate as to preclude reactivation of the state of helplessness. Yet, according to the accepted theory, fluctuations of self-esteem are the functions of the Superego's relation to the ego, just as anxiety was considered, prior to 1926, as a function of repression enforced by the Superego. In 1926, however, Superego anxiety was recognized as merely one kind of anxiety and the repression, hence anxiety relationship was reversed into anxiety signals and hence, repression. Bibring achieves an analogous observation that is the ego's awareness of its helplessness which in certain cased forces it to turn the aggression from the object against the self, thus aggravating and complicating the structure of depression. While in the accepted theory it is assumed that the aggression 'turned round upon the subject'', results in passivity and helplessness, in Bibring's conception it is the helplessness which is the cause of this 'turn round'.

Thus, Bibring's theory opens upon two new vistas. One leads us to consider self-esteem as a signal, that is, an ego function, rather from an open condition to the enclosing effect of an aggressive relation between the ego and the Superego. The other suggests that we reconsider the role of the ego, and particularly of its helplessness, in the origin and function of the instinctual vicissitude called turning round upon the subject.

The first of these, like Freud's structural theory of anxiety and Fenichel's of quilts (1945), leads to a broadening of our conception of the ego's apparatuses and functions. The second is even more far-reaching, it seems to go to the very core of the problem of aggression. We know that 'turning round upon the subject' was the basic mechanism for which Freud used before the 'death-instinct theory' to explain the major forms in which aggression manifests itself. It was in connection with this 'turning round upon the subject; Freud wrote:

> . . . sadism . . . seems to press toward a quite special aim—the infliction of pain, in addition t subjection and mastery of the object. Now a psychoanalysis would seem to show that infliction of pain plays no part in the original aims sought by sadism . . . the sadistic child takes no notice of whether or not it inflicts pain, nor of its purpose to do so. But when once the transformation into masochism has taken place, the experience of pain is ver y well adapted too severely as a passive masochistic aim . . . Where once the suffering of pain has been experienced as a masochistic aim, it can be carried back into the sadistic situation and result in a sadistic aim of inflicting pain (1915).

Thus Bibring's view that 'turning round upon the subject' is brought about by helplessness calling attention to some of Freud's early formulations. And prompt us to re-evaluate our conception of aggression. As it may lead to a theory of aggression which is an alternative to those which have so far been proposed, namely Freud's death-instinct theory. Fenichel's frustration-aggression theory, and the Hartmann-Kris-Loewenstein theory of an independent aggressive instinctual drive.

Let us return once more to the relation between helplessness, which involves the loss of self-esteem, and the simultaneously maintained narcissistic aspirations, such that their intra-ego conflict assumed by Bibring may have been implied by Freud when he wrote in "Mourning and Melancholia." 'A good, capable, conscientious person, . . . is more likely to fall ill of this . . . disease than one . . . of whom we too should have nothing good to say' (1917).

Fenichel's summary of the accepted view of the fate of self-esteem in depression is:

> . . . A greater or lesser loss of self-esteem is in the foreground. The subjective formula is-I have lost everything; now the world is empty, if the loss of self-esteem is mainly due to a loss of external supplies, or-I have lost everything because I do not deserve anything. If it is mainly due to a loss of internal supplies from the Superego (1945).

Fenichel's implied definition of supplies reads: 'The small child loses self-esteem when he loses love and attains it when he regains love . . . children . . . need . . ., narcissistic supplies of affection . . . (1945)

Though the term 'supplies' has never been explicitly defined as a concept, it has become an apparently indispensable terminological acceptance in the psychoanalysis, and particularly in the theory of depression. in Bibring's theory, supplies are the goals of narcissistic aspirations. This gives them a central role in the theory, highlighting the urgent need to define them. Moreover, Bibring's comparison of depression and boredom hints at the direction in which such a definition might be sought by alerting us to the fact that there is a lack of supplies in boredom also. 'Stimulus hunger; is Fenichel's term for the immediate consequence of this lack? 'Boredom is characterized by the coexistence of a need for activity and activity-inhibition, as well as by stimulus-hunger and dissatisfaction with the available stimuli (1934). That an adequate stimuli is the lacking of supplies, which are available of either to be to close to the object of the repressed instinctual drive or the resistance, the distant from it and thus of holding to no interests

Bibring's juxtaposition of depression and boredom suggests that narcissistic supplies may be a special kind of adequate stimuli and narcissistic agitations a special kind of stimulus hunger. The implications of this suggestion become clearer if we note that it is the lack of narcissistic supplies which is responsible for the structuralization of the primitive state of helplessness, the reactivation of which is, according to Bibring's theory, the essencity depression.

The conception which emerges if we pursue these implications of Bibring's theory is this: (1) The development of the ego requires the presence of 'adequate stimuli', in this case love of objects; when such stimuli are consistently absent, a primitive ego state comes into existence, the later reactivation of which is the state of depression. (2) Normal development lowers the intensity of this ego state and its potentiality for reactivation, and limits its reactivation to those reality situations to which grief and sadness are appropriated reactions. (3) Recurrent absence of adequate stimuli in the course of development works against the lowering of the intensity of this ego state and increases the likelihood of its being reactivated, that is to say, established a predisposition of depression.

This conception is consonant with present-day ego psychology and also elucidates the economic and the adaptive aspects of Bibring's theory. the role of stimulation in the development of ego structure is a crucial implication of the concept of adaption. At the same time, since psychoanalytic theory explains the effects of stimulation in terms of changes in the distribution of attention cathexes, the role of stimulation in ego-structure development, to which is referred, and might that well be the starting point for an understanding of the economics of the ego state of depression.

All the same, our present discussion of the structural, genetic, dynamic, economic, and adaptive aspects of Edward Bibring's theory gives us a crystalline glimpse of its fertility. But does not exhaust either its implications or the problems it poses. An attempt to trace more or less of these would require a detailed analysis of those points where Bibring's views shade into other findings and theories of psychoanalytic ego psychology, and is therefore beyond our scope tonight.

However, of completing of the three points from which take root of Edward Bibring's theory which are less obvious than the observations and formulations so far discussed,

The first of its roots in the technique of the psychoanalysis, Bibring wrote:

> From a . . . therapeutic points of view one has to pay attention not only to the dynamic and genetic basis of the persisting narcissistic aspirations, the frustrations of which the ego cannot tolerate, but also the dynamic and genetic conditions which forced the infantile ego to become fixated to feelings of helplessness . . . the importance of these feelings of helplessness in the therapy of depression is obvious.

This formulation seems to say nothing more than the well-known technical rule that 'Analysis must always go on in the layers accessible to the ego at the moment' (Fenichel, 1938-39). But it does say more, because it specifies that it is the helplessness, the lack of interest, and the lowered self-esteem which are immediately accessible in depression. It is safe to assume that the clinically observed accessibility of this was one of the roots of Bibring's theory.

A second root of the theory is in Bibring's critique of the English school of psychoanalysis. A study of this critique shows that on the one hand, Bibring found some of this school's observations on depression sound and, like his own observations, incompatible with the accepted theory of depression, and, on the other hand, he found this schools' theory of depression incompatible with psychoanalytic theory proper. It seems that Bibring intended his theory of depression to account for the sound observations of this school within the framework of psychoanalytic theory.

Finally, a third root of Bibring's theory seems to be related to the problems raised by the so-called 'existential analysis'. So far the only evidence for Edward Bibring's interest in the critical

751

attitude toward 'existential analysis' is in the memories of those people who discussed the subject with him. Though his interest in phenomenology is obvious in his paper on depression, his interest in existentialism proper is expressed in only a few passages, like [Depression] is—essentially—'a human way of reacting to frustration and misery' whenever the ego finds itself in a state of real or imaginary helplessness against 'overwhelming odds'. Bibring's intent seems to have been to put the sound observations and psychoanalytically relevant concepts of 'existential analysis' into the framework of psychoanalytic ego psychology.

Briefly, the relevance within a behavioural framework, depression is conceptualized as an extinction phenomena. On reading the gerontological literature one is struck by the many behavioural similarities between the depressed and the elderly person: (1) One of the most striking features of both old age and depression is a progressive reduction in the rate of behaviour. The concept of 'disengagement' has been advanced to account for this reduction of behaviour. It is assumed to be a natural process which the elderly person accepts and desires, and which is thought to have intrinsic determinants (Cumming and Henry, 1961). From a behavioural framework, the elderly person's reduced rate of behaviour suggests that his behaviour is no longer being reinforced by his environment, i.e., that he, like the depressed person, is on an extinction schedule. (2) Other aspects of the depressive syndrome (feeling rejected, and so forth) are quite common among the elderly (Wolf, 1959). (3) Motivation is a critical problem in the elderly, as it is in the depressed patient. It is hard to find effective reinforcers for either. The number of potentially reinforcing events seems reduced. (4) The elderly person and the depressed person are turned inward, and focus on themselves, their memories, fantasies, and the past. The hypothesis immediately gives to suggest of itself that a reduction in the response contingent rate of positive reinforcement is a critical antecedent condition for many of the behavioural changes described in the elderly person.

It is, nonetheless, that depression, that it is for this reason it needs a model. The clinical 'entity' has multifaceted symptoms, but let us look at those that seem central to the diagnosis and that may be related to learned helplessness. The symptoms of learned helplessness that we have discussed all have parallels in depression.

Sustaining the lowered response initiation the word 'depression' is a behavioural description that denotes a reduction o r depression in responding. Even so, it is not surprising that a prominent symptom of depression is failure, or slowness of a patient to initiate responses. Such is the systematic study of the symptoms of depression. Grinker, Miller, Sabishin, Nunn, and Nunally (1961) all describe this in a number of ways:

Isolated and withdrawn, prefers to remain by himself, stays in bed much of the time . . .
Gait and general behaviour slow and retarded . . .
Volume of the voice deceased, sits alone very quietly . . .
Feels unable to act, feels unable to make decisions . . .
[They] give the appearance of an 'entity' person who has 'given up . . .

Mendels (1970) described the slowdown in responding associated with depression as:

Loss of interest, decrease in energy, inability to accomplish tasks, difficulty in concentration and the erosion of motivation, as these are ambitions that combine to impair efficient functioning. For many depressives the first signs of the illness are in the area of their increasing inability to cope with their work and responsibilities.

Beck (1967) describes 'paralysis of the will' as a striking feature of depression:

In the severity of cases, these are often completed in the paralysis of the will. The patient has no desire to do anything, even those things which are essential to life. Consequently, he may be relatively immobile unless prodded or pushed into activity by others. It is sometime necessary to put the patient out of bed, wash, dress, and feed him.

753

The characteristic passivity and lowered response initiation of depressives have been demonstrated in a large number of studies, i.e., Miller, 1975. Psychomotor retardation differentiates depressives from normal people and a direct example of reduced voluntary response initiation. In addition, depressives engage in fewer activities and the y show reduced interpersonal responding and reduced nonverbal communication. Finally, the intellectual slowness and learning, memory, and IQ deficits found in depressed patients may be viewed as resulting from reduced motivation to initiate cognitive actions such as memory scanning and mental arithmetic. These deficits all parallel the lowered response initiation in learned helplessness.

Recent laboratory experiments have demonstrated a striking similarity between the lowered response initiation of learned helplessness and depression (Klein, Fencil-Morse and Seligman, 1976; Miller and Seligman, 1975) in each of these studies, depressed and nondepressed students were first-divide into three groups; group (1) experienced inescapable loud noise (or unsolvable concept formation problems), group (2) heard the loud noise but could turn it off by pressing a button (or was provided with a solvable problem), group (3) heard no noise (or did not work on any problems). All subjects then worked on a series of patterned anagrams, and half of all subjects were depressed; half were not depressed. As in the earlier study by Hiroto and Seligman (1975), nondepressed subjects in group (1), who had previously been exposed to inescapable noise or unsolvable problem, showed response initiation deficits on the anagrams, while nondepressed subjects in group (2) and (3) exhibited no deficit. moreover, depressed subjects in all groups, including those of group (3) who had no pretreatment, showed poorer response initiation on the anagrams than the nondepressed subjects in group (3). Nondepressed subjects given a helplessness pretreatment showed response initiation deficits wholly parallel to those found in naturally occurring depression. Klein and Seligman (1976) showed the same parallel deficits between depressed subjects and nondepressed helpless subjects on tasks involving noise escape.

Also having a negative cognitive set of depressives that not only make fewer responses, but they interpret their few responses as failures or as doomed to failure, this negative cognitive se t directly mirrors the difficulty that helpless subjects have in learning that responding produces relief from an aversive situation.

Beck (1967) considers this negativistic cognition as the set to be primarily characteristic of depression:

> The depressed patient is peculiarly sensitive to any impediments to his goal-directed activity. An obstacle is regarded as an impossible barrier, but difficulty in dealing with a problem is interpreted as a total failure. His cognitive response to a problem or difficulty is likely to be an idea such as 'I'm licked'. 'I'll never be able to do this,' or 'I'm blocked no mater what I do'.

In truth, Beck views the passive and retarded behaviour of depressed patients as stemming from their negative expectations of their own effectiveness:

> The loss of spontaneous motivation, or paralysis of the will, has been considered a symptom of depression in the classical literature. The loss of motivation may be viewed as the result of the patient's hopelessness and pessimism. As long as he expects a negative outcome from any course of action; he is stripped of any internal stimulation to do anything.

This cognitive set crops up repeatedly in experiments with depressives. Friedman (1964) observed that although a patient was performing adequately during a test, the patient would occasionally reiterate this original protest of 'I can't do it,' or 'I don't know how'. This is also our experience in testing depressed patients.

Experimental demonstrations of negative cognitive set in depressed college students were provided by Miller and Seligman (1973) and Miller, Seligman, and Kurlander (1975). These studies showed that depressed students view their skilled actions very much as if they were only chance actions. In other words, depressed subjects, more than nondepressed subjects, tend to perceive reinforcement in a skill task as independent of their behaviour. Miller, Seligman, and Kurlander (1975) found this perception to be specific to depression: anxious and non-anxious students matched for extent of depression did not differ in their perceptions of reinforcement contingencies.

Miller and Seligman (1975, 1976), Klein, Fencil-Morse and Seligman (1976), and Klein and Seligman (1976) more directly demonstrated the parallel between the negative cognitive set in learned helplessness and depression. While replicating the findings of Miller and Seligman (1976) and Klein and Seligman (1976) found that nondepressed subjects who had been exposed to inescapable noise perceived reinforcement as less response contingent than nondepressed subjects who had been exposed to either escapable or no noise during a skilful task. Pretreatment had no effect on perception of reinforcement in chance tasks. So, the effects of learned helplessness and depression on perception of reinforcement are parallel.

Cognitive deficits were also found in the previous studies of Miller and Seligman (1975), Klein et al. (1976) and Klein and Seligman (1976). These studies measured the degree to which subjects were able to benefit from successful anagram solutions or escapes from high volume noise. As with response initiation, depressed subjects in the untreated groups showed cognitive deficits relative to nondepressed subjects, and nondepressed subjects who had experienced inescapable noise or unsolvable problems exhibits cognitive deficits relative to nondepressed subjects in the control groups on measures of cognitive functioning.

Some studies indicate that negative cognitive set may also explain poor discrimination learning by depressives (Martin and Rees, 1966), and may be partly responsible for their lowered cognitive abilities (Payne, 1961; Miller, 1975).

Depression, like learned helplessness, seems to have its time course. In discussing the 'disaster syndrome' Wallace (1957) reported that people experience a day or so of depression following sudden catastrophes, and then they again function normally. It seems possible that multiple traumatic events intervening between the initial disaster recovery might exacerbate depression in human considerably, as they do in dogs. We should also note that endogenously or process depression is characterized by fluctuations of weeks or months between depression and mania. Moreover, it is commonly thought that almost all depressions dissipate in time, although whether they last days, weeks, months, or years is a matter of some dispute (Paskind, 1929, 1930; Lundquist, 1945; Kraines, 1957).

According to psychoanalysts, the lowered aggression of depressives is due to introjected hostility. In fact, psychoanalysts view introjection of hostility as the primary mechanism producing symptoms of depression. We do not believe that the increased self-blame in depression results from hostility turned inward, but it seems undeniable that hostility, even in dreams (Beck and Hurvich, 1959; Beck and Ward, 1961), is reduced among depressive. This symptom corresponds to the lack of aggression in learned helplessness.

Depressives commonly show reduced interest in food, sex, and interpersonal relations. These symptoms correspond to the anorexia, weight loss, and sexual and social deficits in learned helplessness.

According to the catecholamine hypothesis of affective disorders, depression is associated with a deficient of norepinehrine (NE) at receptor sites in the brain, whereas elation may be associated with its excess. This hypothesis is based on evidence that imipramine, a drug that increases the NE available in the central nervous system, causes depression to end. Klerma and Cole (1965) and Cole (1964) experimented with imipramine and placebos on depressed patients and reported positive results of imipramine over placebos. Monoamineoxidase (MAO) inhibitors, which prevent the breakdown of NE, also may be useful in relieving depression (Cole, 1964; Davis, 1965). Reserpine, an antihypertensive medication that depletes NE, often produces depression as a side-effect in man (Beck, 1967). There is also some suggestion of cholinergic medication of depression. Janowsky et al. (1972) reported that physostigmine, a cholinergic stimulators, produced depressive affect in normal people. Atropine, a linergic blocker, reversed these symptoms. So, NE depletion and cholinergic activation are implicated in both depression and learned helplessness (Thomas and DeWald, 1977). However, Mendels and Frazer (1974) reviewed the behavioural effects of drugs that deplete brain catecholamines and they contend that the behavioural changes associated with reserpine are better interpreted as a psychomotor retardation-sedation syndrome than as depression. Moreover, selective depletion of brain catecholamines by alpha-methyl-para-tyrosine (AMPT) fails to produce some of the key features of depression, despite the fact that this drug produce a consistently greater reduction in amine metabolate concentration than occur s in depression. So depletion of catecholamines in itself may not be sufficient to account for depression.

Nonetheless, depressed people say they feel helpless, hopeless, and powerless, and by this they mean that they believe they are unable to control or influence those aspects of their lives that are significant to them. Grinker and coworkers (1961) describe the 'characteristics of hopelessness, helplessness, failure, sadness, unworthiness, guilt and internal suffering' as the 'essence of depression'. Melges and Bowlby (1969) also characterize depressed patients in this way and Bibring (1953) defines depression 'as the emotional expression [indicative] of a state of helplessness and powerlessness of the ego.'

They clearly are considerable parallels between the forms of behaviour that define helplessness and major symptoms of depression.

Differences:—But there are substantial gaps:—

First, there are two symptoms found with uncontrollable shock that may or may not correspond to symptoms of depression. Stomach ulcers occur more frequently and severely in rats receiving uncontrollable shock than in rats receiving controllable shock (Weiss, 1968, 1971). We know of no study examining the relationship of depression to stomach ulcers. Second, uncontrollable shock produces more anxiety, measured subjectively, behaviourally, and physiologically, than controllable shock (Seligman and Binik, 1976). The question of whether depressed people are more anxious than nondepressed people does not have a clear answer. Beck (1967) reported that although both depression and anxiety can be observed in some people, only a small positive correlation was found in a study of 600 people. Yet, Miller et al. (1975) found very few depressed college students who were not also anxious. We can speculate that anxiety and depression are related in the following way: When a man or animal is confronted with a threat or a loss, he initially respond with fear or anxiety. If he learns that the threat is wholly controllable, anxiety, having served its function, disappears. If he remains uncertain about his ability to control the threat, his anxiety remains. If he learns or is convinced that the threat is utterly uncontrollable, depression emerges.

A number of facts out depression have been insufficiently investigated for parallels in learned helplessness. Preeminent among these are the depressive symptoms that cannot be investigated in animals; dejected mood, feelings of self-blame and self-dislike, loss of mirth, suicidal thoughts and crying, but now, that learned helplessness has been reliably produced in man (Hiroto, 1974. Hiroto and Seligman, 1975; Klein et al., 1976; Klein and Seligman, 1976′ Miller and Seligman, 1975, 1976; Racinskas, 1971; Roth and Kubal, 1975; Thornton and Jacobs, 1970; Dweck and Reppucci, 1973), we can determine whether any of these states occur in helplessness.

Finally, we know of no evidence that disconfirms the correspondence of symptoms in learned helplessness and depression.

The term 'learned helplessness' was first used in connection with laboratory experiments in which dogs were exposed to shock from which they could not escape (Overmier and Seligman, 1967). After repeated trials, the dogs tended to sit passively when the shock came on. Exposed to a new situation from which the y could escape a shock by jumping over a barrier, they failed to initiate the appropriate response. Some would occasionally jump over the barrier and escape, but they would generally revert to taking the shock passively. For the purposes of constructing an analogue of clinical depression, the behaviour of the dogs is significant in suggesting that exposure to uncontrollable aversive events may lead to a failure to initiate appropriate responses in new situations and an inability to learn that responding is effective.

The analogy to depression was bolstered by initial findings that in a variety of task situations, depressed human subjects resembled nondepressed subjects who had received repeated failure experiences. For instance, compared to nondepressed subjects who had not received repeated failure experiences, these groups of subjects took longer to solve anagrams and apparently failed to perceive the pattern underlying their successful solution (Klein and Seligman, 1976). Miller, Rosellini, and Seligman, and other research suggested that the parallels between laboratory learned helplessness and depression were not limited to similarities in behaviour. Promising leads were also established with regard to etiology, treatment, and prevention.

The original learned helplessness model stimulated a large body of research and considerable controversy (Buchwald, Coyne, and Cole, 1978; Costello, 1978). Ultimately, the accumulated research

759

led to questions about both the adequacy of the learned-helplessness explanation for the behaviour of nondepressed subjects who has been exposed to failure as well as the appropriateness of learned helplessness as an analogue of depression. For instance, it was shown that the performance deficits of subjects who had been given a typical learned helplessness, induction were very much situation-specific (Cole and Coyne, 1977) and that these deficits might better be explained as the result of anxious self-preoccupation, rather than the perception of response-reinforcement independence (Coyne, Metalsky and Lavelle, 1980). Furthermore, the characterization of depressed persons as passive and lacking in aggression was challenged. Difficulties with the original learned helplessness model led to a major reformulation (Abramson, Seligman and Teasdale).

We use the term learned helplessness to describe the interference with adaptive responses produced by inescapable shock and also as a short hand to describe the process that we believe underlies the behaviour that we cannot control of which the distinction between controllable and uncontrollable reinforcement is cental to the phenomenon and the theory of helplessness. Learned helplessness in the dog is defined by two types of behaviour. (1) Dogs that have had shock or are slower to make responses than naive dogs, and (2) if the dog does make a response that turns off shock, it has more trouble than a naive dog learning that responding is effective.

However, if we are to propose a model of depression in man, we must have proof that learned helplessness occurs in man.

Besides passivity and retarded response-relief learning, other characteristics associated with learned helplessness are relevant to depression in man. First, helplessness has a time course. In dogs, inescapable shock produces transient as well as permanent interference with escape (Overmier and Seligman, 1967) and avoidance (Overmier, 1968): 24 hours after one session of inescapable shock, dogs are helpless; but after 48 hours their response is normal. This is also true of goldfish (Padilla, 1970). After multiple sessions of inescapable shock, helplessness is not transient (Seligman and Groves, 1970; Seligman, Maier and Geer, 1968) Weiss (1968) found a parallel time course for weight loss in rats given uncontrollable shock, but other that this no time course has been found in rats or in other species (e.g., Anderson, Cole, and McVaugh, 1968; Seligman, Rosellini, and Kozak, 1975). Nonetheless, uncontrollable trauma produces a number of effects found in depression. The two basic effects are these: animal and humans become passive—they are slower to initiate responses to alleviate trauma and may not respond at all; and animals and humans are retarded in learning that their behaviour may control trauma., if a response is made that does produce relief, they often have trouble realizing that one causes the other. This maladaptive behaviour has been observed in a variety of species over a range of tasks that require voluntary responding. In addition, this phenomenon dissipates in time in the dog, and it causes lowered aggression, loss of appetite, and norepinephrine depletion.

The passivity of dogs, rats and men in the face of trauma and their difficulty on benefiting from response-relief contingencies result; that we believe, from their having learned that responding and trauma are independent—that trauma is uncontrollable. This is the hear t of the learned helplessness hypothesis. The hypothesis states that when shock is inescapable, the organism learns that responses and shock termination are independent (the probability of shock termination given any response doesn't differ from its probability in the absence of that response). Learning that trauma is uncontrollable has three effects.

(1) A motivational effect—it reduces the probability that the subject will initiate responses to escape, because part of the incentive for making such responses is the expectation that they will bring relief. If the subject has previously learned that its responses have no effect on trauma, this contravenes the expectation, thus, the organism's motivation to respond is undermined by experience with reinforcers it cannot control. Such that this motivational effect undermines passivity in learned helplessness, and, if the model is valid, in depression.

(2) The cognitive effect—learning that responses and shock are independent makes it more difficult to learn that responses do produce relief when the organism makes a response that actually terminates shock. In general, if we have acquired a cognitive set in which A's are irrelevant to B's, it will be harder for us to learn that A's produce B's when they do. By the helplessness hypothesis, this mechanism is responsible for the difficulty that helpless organisms have in learning that responding produces relief, even after they respond and successfully turn off shock. Further, if the model is valid, this mechanism produces the 'negative expectations' of depression.

(3) An emotional effect—although it does not follow directly from the helplessness hypothesis—such that uncontrollable shock produces more conditioned fear, ulcers, weight loss, defecation, and pain than controllable shock.

One cause of laboratory-produced helplessness seems to be learning that one cannot control important events. Learning that responses and reinforcement are independent results in a cognitive set that has two effects: fewer responses to control reinforcement are initiated and associating successful responses with reenforcement becomes more difficult.

Nevertheless, some of the events that typically precipitate depression; failure in work or school; death or loss of loved ones; rejection by or separation from loved ones; physical disease, and growing old. What do all these have in common?

Four recent theories of depression seem to be largely in agreement about the etiology of depression, and what they agree on is the centrality of helplessness and hopelessness. Bibring (1953), arguing from a dynamic viewpoint, sees helplessness as the cause of depression:

> What has been described as the basic mechanism of depression, the ego's shocking awareness of its helplessness in regard to its aspirations, is assumed to represent the core of normal, neurotic and probably also psychotic depression.

Melges and Bowlby (1969) see a similar cause of depression:

> Our thesis is that while a depressed patient's goals remain relatively unchanged his estimate of the likelihood of achieving then and his confidence in the efficacy of his own skilled actions are both diminished . . . the depressed person believes that his plans of action are no longer effective in reaching his continuing and long range goals . . . From this state of mind is derived, we believe, much depressive symptomalogy, including indecisiveness, inability to act, making increased demands on others, and feelings of worthlessness and guilt about not discharging duties.

Beck (1967, 1970) sees depression as resulting primarily from a patient's negative cognitive set, largely about his abilities to change his life:

A primary factor appears to be the activation of idiosyncratic cognitive patterns which divert the thinking into specific channels that deviate from reality. As a result, the patient perseverates in making negative judgements and interpretations of experience, negative evaluations of the self, and negative expectations of the future.

Lichtenberg (1957) sees hopelessness as the defining characteristic of depression:

Depression is defined as a manifestation of felt hopelessness regarding the attainment of goals when responsibility for the hopelessness is attributed to one's personal defects. In this context hope is conceived to be a function of the perceived probability of success with respect to goal attainment.

Even so, it means that all of a person's efforts have been in vain, his responses have failed to bring about the gratification he desires; he cannot find responses that control reinforcement. When a person is rejected by someone he loves, he can no longer control this significant source of gratification and support. When a parent or lover dies, the bereaved person is powerless to produce or influence love from dead person. Physical disease and growing old are obvious helplessness experiences. In these conditions, the person's own responses are ineffective and he must rely on the care of others. So, we would predict that it is not life events that produce depression (Alarcon and Cori, 1972) but uncontrollable life events.

However, Ferster (1969, 1973), Kaufman and Rosenblum (1967); McKinney and Bunney (1969), and Liberman and Raskin (1971) have suggested that depression is caused by extinction procedures or the loss of reinforcers. There is no contradiction between the learned-helplessness and extinction view of depression;

763

helplessness, however, is more general. Briefly, extinction is a special case of independence between responding and reinforcement. Reinforcement, just the same, may also be presented with a probability greater than zero, and still be presented independent of responding. This occurs in the typical helplessness paradigm and cause responses to decrease in probability (Recorta and Skucy, 1969). Therefore, a view talks about independence between responding and reinforcement assumes the extinction view and, in addition, suggests that situations in which reinforcers still occur independent of responding also will cause depression.

Both learned helplessness and depression may be caused by learning that responses and reinforcement are independent. But this view runs into several problems. Can depression actually be caused by situations other than extinction in which reinforcement still occur but are not under the individual's control? To put it another way, 'is a net loss of reinforcement necessary for depression, or can depression occur when there is only loss of control without loss of reinforcement?' Would a Casanova who made love with seven new women every week become depressed if he found out that women wanted him not because of his amatory prowess but because of his wealth or because his fairy god mother wished it? We can only speculate.

It seems appropriate to mention 'success' depression in this context. When people finally reach a goal after years of striving—being promoted or obtaining a PhD—many become depressed. This puzzling phenomenon is clearly a problem for a loss of reinforcement view of depression. From a helplessness view, success depression may occur because reinforcement are no longer contingent on present responding. After years of goal-directed instrumental activity, the reinforcement automatically changes. One now gets his reinforcement because of whom he is rather than what he is doing. The common clinical impression that many beautiful women become depressed and attempt suicide also presents problems for the loss of reinforcement theory: positive reinforcers abound not because of what they do but because of how they look. Would be a generation of children risen with abundant positive reinforcers that they received independently to what, and they did become clinically depressed?

According to the helplessness view, the central theme in successful therapy should be having the patient discover and come to accept that his responses produce the gratification that he desires—that he is, in short, an effective human being. Some therapies that reportedly alleviate depression are consonant with a learned helplessness model, however, it is important to note that the success of a therapy often has little to do with its theoretical underpinning. So, with the exception of Klein and Seligman (1976), as a se t of examples that seem as a test of the model, but merely as a set of examples that seem to have exposure to response-produced success as a cure for depression.

Consonant with their helplessness-centred views of the etiology of depression, Bibring (1957), Beck (1967), and Melges and Bowlby (1969) all stressed that reversing helplessness alleviates depression. For example, Bibring (1953) has stated:

> The same conditions which bring about depression (helplessness) in reverse serve frequently the restitution from depression. Generally, one can say that depression subsides either (I) when the narcissistically important goals and objects appear to be again within reach (which is frequently followed by a temporary elation) or (ii) when they become sufficiently modified or reduced to becoming realizable, or (iii) when they are altogether relinquished, or (iv) when the ego recovers from the narcissistic shock by regaining its self-esteem with the help of various recovery mechanisms (with or without any change of objective or goal).

In their review of therapies for depression, Seligan, Klein, and Miller (1976) indicated that most of the therapies have strong elements of inducing the patient to discover that responses produce the reinforcement he desires. In antidepression milieu therapy (Taulbee and Wright, 1971), for example, the patient is forced to emit one of the most powerful responses people have for controlling others—anger—and when this response is dragged out of his depleted behaviour repertoire, he is powerfully reinforced. Beck's (1970) cognitive therapy is aimed at similar goals. He sees success manipulations as changing the negative cognitive set ('I'm an ineffective person) of the depressive to a more positive set, and argues that the primary task of the therapist is to change

765

the negative expectations of the depressed patient to more optimistic ones. Even so, both Burgess's (1968), therapy and the graded task assigned (Beck, Seligman, Binik, Schuyler, and Brill, unpublished data), the patient makes instrumental responses of gradually increasing complexity, and each is reinforced. Similarly, all instrumental behaviour therapy for depression (Hersen, Eisler, Alford, and Agras, 1973; Reisinger. 1972), by definition, arrange the contingencies so that responses control the occurrence of reinforcement; the patient's recognition of this relationship should alleviate depression. Lewinsohn's therapy also has this element; participation in activity and other nondepressed behaviour controls therapy time. (Lewinsohn, Weinstein, and Shaw, 1969). In assertive training (Wolpe, 1968), the patient must emit social responses to bring about a desired change in his environment. Such that the study provides a useful method fo r testing the effectiveness of any therapy for depression in the laboratory because we can bring depression into the laboratory, in that, both in its naturally occurring state and in the form of learned helplessness, we can now see what reverses it in the laboratory. Will assertive training, emotive expression or atropine given to helpless and depressed subjects in the laboratory reverse the symptoms of depression and helplessness?

In order to explain depression, Burgess (1968) and others have relied heavily on the reinforcement the patient gets for his depressed behaviour, it is tempting to seek to remove this reinforcement during therapy, but caution is in order, so to explain the persistence or maintenance of some depressive behaviours, but it does not explain how they began. Helplessness suggests that failure to initiate active responses originates in the perception that the patient cannot control reinforcement. Thus, there can be two sources of a depressed patient's passivity: (a) patients are passive for instrumental reasons, because they think staying depressed brings them sympathy, love and attention, and (b) patients are passive because they believe that no response at all will be effective in controlling their environment. In this sense, it means that there is at least some response that believes he can effectively perform. Maier (1970) found that dogs who were reinforced for being passive by shock termination were not nearly as debilitated as dogs for whom all responses were independent of shock termination. Similarly, patients who use their depression in a way of controlling reinforcement are less helpless than those who have given up. Nonetheless, depression may be directly antagonized when patients come to see that their own responses are effective in alleviating their suffering and produced gratifications.

Nonetheless, many therapies, from psychoanalysis to cognitive understandings, claim to be able to cure depression. the evidence presented is selective as only those treatments that seemed compatible with helplessness were such that was possible that when other therapies work it. It is, because they reinstate the patient's sense of efficacy. However, evidence on the effectiveness of therapy in depression that is less anecdotal and selective is sorely needed. The recent study of Klein and Seligman (1976) may provide a laboratory procedure for evaluating the effectiveness of any therapy suggested for learned helplessness and depression.

All the same, a behavioural self-control model for the study of depression is focussed on different subsets of depressive phenomena. Such that the self-control model organizes and relates these phenomena and has its own implications for symptomatology, etiology, and therapy. Depression has certain properties which make the development of a model particularly difficult, however, the term depression refers to a syndrome which encompass a broad set of symptoms with diverse behavioural referents (Beck, 1972; Levitt and Lubin, 1975; Mendels, 1970; Woodruff, Goodwin and Guze, 1974). Especially notable is the diversity among cognitive symptoms. Aside from manifest subjective sadness, depressed persons show clinical symptoms such as quilt, pessimism, low sel-esteem, self-derogation, and helplessness. Accounting for these distinctive cognitive behaviours and integrating them with the various overt-moto r behaviours characteristic of depression are limited to verbal-cognitive and overt-motor variables is appropriate since no reliable physiological index has been clearly identified as a symptom of depression (Bruder, 1970).

A recent resurgence of interest in psychological aspects of depression has become evident, and, with it, new and innovative models have been advanced. Behavioural and cognitive modes proposed by Lewinsohn (1974), Seligman (1974) and Beck (1974) have been most prominent and influential in behavioural research and clinical application.

Lewinsohn (1974; Lewinsohn, Weinstein, and Shaw, 1969) has developed a clinical and research program which looks at depression as an extinction phenomenon. A loss or lack of response contingent positive reinforcement results in reduced rates of common overt-motor behaviour and also elicits a basic dysphoria. All other cognitive-verbal symptoms of depression are secondary elaborations of these basic dysphoria. Susceptivity to depression and ability to overcome depression are related to social skill, the range of events which are potentially reinforcing to the person, and reinforcement availability. The etiology of depression is therefore, the joint function of external environmental changes and individual differences in reinforcement potential and social skills. Therapy procedures are aimed at identifying potential sources of reinforcement in the person's environment and developing strategies to increase their frequency of occurrence (Lewinsohn, 1976. Lewinsohn and Shaffer, 1971; Robinson and Lewinsohn, 1973) In other instances, therapy consists of isolating deficits in social interaction and training subjects in modifying these socially skilled behaviours (Lewinsohn, Biglan and Zeiss, 1976); Lewinsohn and Shaw, 1969; Lewinsohn, Weinstein and Alper, 1970).

Also, Seligman has proposed a model of depression based on a laboratory paradigm of learned helplessness (Seligman, 1974, 1975). A situation in which the probability of the consequence given a response is equal to the probability of the consequence given no response produces the phenomenon of learned helplessness. Noncontingent punishment has been the situation most studied. Learned helplessness has properties which parallel the symptoms of depression: (1) lowered response initiation (passivity), (2) negative cognitive se t (belief that one's actions are doomed to failure; (3) dissipation over time, (4) lack of aggression, (5) loss of libido and appetite, and (6) norepinephrine depletion and cholinergic activity (Seligman, Klein, and Miller, 1974). Cognition is given a central position in this model in that of the 'depressive retardation is caused by a brief in response-reinforcement independence'; (Seligman. 1974). Other cognitive symptoms are held to be elaborations on this central belief. No therapy studies have been directly generated by this model to date, however, Klein and Seligman (1976) have demonstrated the reversibility of learned helplessness and depression following experience with solvable problems.

From a different perspective, Beck (1970, 1972, 1974) has evolved a cognitive model of depression which holds that depression consists of a primary triad of cognitive patterns or schema (1) a negative view of the world; (2) a negative view of the self, and (3) a negative view of the future. These views are maintained by distorted models of cognition such as selective abstraction, arbitrary inference, and overgeneralization,. The over—behavioural symptoms of depression follow from cognitive distortion. Distorted schema develop in early childhood and leave individuals susceptible to depression in the face of stress. Therapy involves the identification of distortions and their confrontation with the evidence of objective experience. Case studies employing these modifications have been described by Beck (1972) and Rush, Khatami, and Beck (1975). Group studies have shown that therapy based on a Beck's cognitive behaviour modification model is superior to a program based on Lewinsohn's model, a nondirective control therapy and a waiting list control and is more effective than treatment with imipramine hydrochloride (Rush, Beck, Kovacs, and Hollon).

The severe disorders of mood or effect are among the most common of the major psychiatric syndromes. Lifetime expectancy rates for such disorders are between 3 and 8 percent of the general population. Only a minority are treated by psychiatrists or in psychiatric hospitals and about 70 percent of prescriptions for antidepressants are written by nonpsychiatrist physicians. These and other modern medical treatments of severe mood disorders have contributed to a virtual revolution in the theory and practice of modern psychiatry since the introduction of mood-altering drugs three decades ago. These agent s include lithium salts (1949), and monoamine oxidase (MAO) inhibitors (1952), and the antimanic and antipsychotic (neuroleptics) agents such as chlorpromazine (1952), and the tricyclic or heterocyclic (imipramine-like) antidepressants (1957). In addition, electroconvulsive therapy (ECT) continues to have a place in the treatment of very severe and acute mood disorders, especially life-threatening forms of depression.

The development of these modern medical therapies has had several important effects. First. These agents have provided of a relatively simple specific effect and safe forms of treatment with a profound impact on current patterns of medical practice, for example, many depressed or hypomanic patients can be managed adequately in outpatient facilities to avoid prolonged, expensive, and disruptive hospitalization which were formerly common. Second, partial understanding of the pharmacology of the psychotropic drugs has led to imaginative hypotheses concerning

769

the pathophysiology or etiology of severe mood disorders. These, in turn, have encouraged a revolution on experimental psychiatry in which the hypotheses have been tested in clinical research. Many of the earlier hypotheses have been found wanting or simplistic, nevertheless, they have led to increased understanding of the diagnosis, biology, and treatment of mood disorders and to newer research that represents a third level of development. this is the focus of the practical clinical benefits of now and in the near future.

In the light of this some characteristics of infant development during this holding phase can be enumerated. It is at this stage that:

(1) primary process, (2) primary identification, (3) auto-erotism, (4) primary narcissism, and (5) living realities.

In this phase the ego changes over from an unintegrated state to a structure integration, and so the infant becomes able to experience anxiety associated with disintegration. The word disintegration begins to have meaning which it did not possess before go integration became a fact. In healthy development at this stage the infant retains the capacity for re-experiencing unintegrated states, but this depends on the continuation of reliable maternal care or on the built-up in the infant of memories of material care beginning gradually to be perceived as such. The result of healthy progress in the infant's development during this stage is that he attains to what might be called 'unit status'. The infant become a person, an individual in his own right.

Associated with this attainment is the infant 's psychosomatic existence which begins to take on a personal pattern: that is, that the basis for this for this indwelling is a linkage of motor and sensory and functional experience with the infant's new state of being a person. As a further development there comes into existence what might be called a limiting membrane, which to some extent (in health) is equated with the surface of the skin, and has a position between the infant's 'me' and his 'not me'. So the infant comes to have an inside and an outside, and a body-scheme. In this way meaning comes to the function of intake and output, moreover, it gradually become meaningful to postulate a personal or inner psychic reality for the infant.

During the holding phase other processes are initiated; the most important is the dawn of intelligence and the beginning of a mind as something distinct from the psyche, and, from this, the secondary processes and symbolic functioning, and of the organization of a personal psychic content, which forms a basis for dreaming and for living relationships.

At the same time there starts in the infant a joining up of two roots of impulsive behaviours. The term 'fusion' indicates the positive process whereby diffuse elements that belong to movement and to muscle erotism become fused with the orgiastic functioning of the erotogenic zones. This concept is more familiar as the reverse process of defusion, which is a complex and complication defence in which aggression becomes separated out from erotic experience after a period in which a degree of fusion has been achieved. All these developments belong to the environmental condition of 'holding', and without a good enough holding the stages cannot be attained, or once attained cannot become established,

A further development in the capacity for object relationships. In that, the infant changes from relationship to objectively conceived object to a relationship to a object objectively perceived. This change is closely bound up with the infant's change from being merged with the mother to being separate from her, or to relating to her as a separate and 'not-me', This development is not specifically related to the holding, but is related to the phase of 'living with' . . .

In the holding phase the infant is maximally dependent. One can classify dependence thus:

(I) Absolute Dependence: In this state the infant has no means of knowing about the maternal care, which is largely a matter of prophylaxis. He cannot gain control over what is well and what is badly done, but is only a position to gain profit or to suffer disturbances,

(ii) Relative Dependence: The infant can become aware of the need for the details of maternal care, and to a growing extent relate them to personal impulse, and then later, in

771

a psychoanalytic treatment, can reproduce them in the transference,

(iii) The infant develops the means for doing without actual care. This is accomplished through the accumulation of memories of care, the projection of personal needs and the introjection of care details, with the development of confidence on the environment, and must be added that, the element of intellectual understanding with its tremendous implications.

Nonetheless, in borderline cases the analyst does not always wait in vain, that in the course of time the patient becomes able to make use of the psychoanalytic interpretations of the original trauma projection. It may even happen that he is able to accept what is in the environment as a projection of the simple and stable going-on-being elements that derive from his own inherent potential.

Such that it is necessary to attempt to state briefly what happens to the inherented potential if this is to develop into an infant, and thereafter onto a child reaching towards independent existence, because if the plexuity of the subject such a statement must be made in the assumption of satisfactory material care, which means parental care. Satisfactory parental care can be classified roughly into three overlapping states.

1. Holding.
2. Mother and infant living together, as the father's function (on dealing with the environment for the mother) is not known to the infant
3. Father, mother, and infant, all three living together.

The term 'holding' is used to denote not only the actual physical holding of the infant, but also the total environmental provision prior to the concept of living with. In other words, it refers to a three-dimensional or space relationship (spatiality) with time gradually added. This overlaps with, but initiate prior to, instinctual experiences that in time would determine the object relationships. It includes the management of experiences that are inherent in existence, such as the completion (and therefore, the noncompeting) of processes, such ss the completion and, the noncomcompletion of specific processes which from the outside may seem to be purely physiological but which belong to infant psychology and take place on a complex psychological field, particularly, by determining the awareness and the empathy of the mother.

The term 'living with' implies object relationships, and the emergence of the infant from the state of being merged with the mother, or his perception of objects external to the self.

The paradox is that what is good and bad in the infant's environment is not in fact a projection, but in spite of this it is necessary, if the individual infant is to develop healthily, that everything will seem to him to be a projection. We find omnipotence and the pleasure principle in operation, as they certainly are in earliest infancy; and to this observation we can add that the recognition of a true 'not-me' is a matter of the intellect; it belongs to extreme sophistication and to the maturity of the individual.

In the writings of Freud most of the formulations concerning infancy derive from a study of adults in analysis. At first sight it would seem that a great deal of psychoanalytic theory is about early childhood and infancy, but in one sense Freud can be said to have neglected unfancy as a stare. This is brought out by a footnote in 'Formulations of the Two Principles of Mental Functioning,' of which he shows that he knows he is taking for granted the very things that are under discussion, as in the text he traces the development from the pleasure-principle to the reality-principle, following his usual course of reconstructing the infancy of his adult patients. The note runs as follows:

> It will rightly be objected that an organization which was a slave to the pleasure principle and neglected the reality of the external world could not maintain itself alive for the shortest time, so that it could not have come into existence at all. The employment of a fiction like this is. however, justified when one considers that the infant—provided one includes with it the care it receives from its mother—does almost realize a psychical system of this kind.

RICHARD J. KOSCIEJEW

Freud paid full tribute to the function of maternal care, and it must be assumed that he left this subject alone only because he was not ready to talk about its implications. The note continues:

It probably hallucinates the fulfilment of its internal needs; it betrays its unpleasure, when there is an increase of stimulus and absence of satisfaction, by the motor discharge of screaming and beating about with its arms and legs, and it then experiences the satisfaction it has hallucinated. Later, as an older child, it learns too employ these manifestations of discharge intentionally for which of methods for expressing its feelings. Since the later care of children is modelled in the care of infants, the dominance of the pleasure principle can really come to an end when a child has achieved complete physical detachment from its parents.

The words: 'provide one includes with it the care it receives from its mother' have of a great importance in the immediate contextual presentation. The infant and the maternal care together from a unit. certainly if one is to study the theory of the parent-infant relationship one must come to a decision about these matters, which concern the real meaning of the word dependence or dependency. It is not enough that it is acknowledged that the environment is important if there is to be a discussion of the theory of the parent-infant relationship, then we are divided into two of the same who do not allow that at the earliest stages the infant and the maternal care belong to each other and cannot be disentangled. These two things, the infant and the maternal case, disentangle and dissociate themselves in health, which means as to do many things, to some extent it means a disentanglement of maternal care from something which we then call the infant, or the beginning of a growing child. This idea is covered by Freud's words at the end of the footnote, explaining that: The dominance of the pleasure principle can really come to an end only when a child has achieved complete physical detachment from its parents.

It is axiomatic in these matters of maternal care of holding variety that when things go well the infant has no means of knowing what is being properly provided and what is being prevented. Such, that

774

when things do not go well that the infant becomes aware, not of the failure of maternal care, but of the results, whatever they may be, of that failure: That in saying, as a result of success in maternal care there is built up in th infant a continuity of being which is the basis of ego strength' of being interrupted by reactions to the consequences of that failure, The resultant of ego-weakening. Such interruptions constitute annihilation, and are evidently associated with pain of psychotic quality and intensity. In the extreme case the infant exists only on the basis of a continuity of reactions to impingement and of recoveries from such reactions. This is in great contras t to the continuity for being that which is our conception of ego strength.

We use the term 'depression' to refer to the syndrome of behaviours that have been identified in descriptive studies of depressed individuals (e.g., Grinker et al., 1961). It includes verbal statements of dysphoria, self-depreciation, guilt, material burden, social isolation, somatic complaints, and a reduced rate of many behaviours. Is that, we assume depression to be a continuous variable which can be conceptualized as a 'state' which fluctuate s over time as well as a 'trait'—(some people are more prone to becoming depressed than others?). Being depressed does not exclude other psychopathological conditions such as schizophrenia, psychosis, sexual deviation, or alcoholism. For purposive reasons, it would seem important that any study relying on differences between depressed and nondepressed groups for its conclusions have a normal control as well as a 'psychiatric control' group (i.e., patients for whom anxiety or other neurotic symptoms but not depression constitute the major psychopathology) if any observed group differences are to be attributed to depression (depression—psychiatric control, normal) and not to the deviation hypothesis (depression, psychiatric control, normal control).

The major assumptions of the behavioural theory of depression follows three laying premises that postulate (1) A low rate of response-contingent positive reenforcement (response) acts as an eliciting (unconditioned) stimulus for some depressive behaviour, such as feeling of dysphoria, fatigue, and other somatic symptoms. (2) A low rate of response constitutes a sufficient explanation for other parts of the depressive syndrome such as the low rate of behaviour. For the latter the depressed person is considered to be on a prolonged extinction schedule. (3) The total amount of response

775

received by an individual is presumed to be a function of three sets of variables: (I) The number of events (including activities) that are potentially reinforce for the individual, influenced by biological (e.g., sex and age) and experiential variables. (ii) The number of potentially reinforcing events that can be provided by the environment, i.e., the availability of reenforcement in the environment. (iii) The instrumental behaviour of the individual, i.e., the extent to which he possesses the skills and emits those behaviours that will elicit reinforcement for him from his environment.

The behaviour theory requires that (1) the total amount of responses received by depressed persons be less than that received by nondepressed persons, and similarly, it will be less when the individual is depressed than when he is not depressed; (2) the onset of depression be accompanied by a reduction in response; (3) intensity of depression convary with rate of response, and (4) improvement be accompanied by an increase in response. Before proceeding to an examination of relevant empirical studies several additional clarification and hypotheses are offered.

In terms of system theory (von Bertalanffy, 1950; Allport, 1960; Miller, 1971), the usual conceptualization of the depressed person is one of a relatively closed system. Grinker (1964) was explicitly instating that the depressed person repeats his message and behaviour without reception or acceptance of resulting feedback. Beck (1964, 1967) described the cognitive distortion that dominate the information processing of the depressed person so that experiences are rigidly interpreted to maintain existing schema of personal deficiency, self-blame, and negative expectations.

The implicit assumption of these has been that the support and information available to the depressed person are incongruent with his depression, and the persistence of his symptomatology is evidence of a failure to receive or accept this information. Withdrawal, isolated intrapsychic persecution or as Beck describes (1967), interaction of depressive schema and affective structure, produce a downward depressive spiral. Presently, that is to say, that our adopted alternative is that the depressed person is able to engage others in his environment in such a way that support is lost and depressive information elicited. This in turn increases the level of depression and strengthens the pathogenetic pattern of depressed behaviour rather response of other if a depressive spiral develops, It is mutually causative, deviation-amplifying process

(Maruyama, 1963) in the interaction of the depressed person with his environment. Thus, what is customarily viewed as some internal process is, I believe, that, at least in part, a characteristic of interaction with the environment, and much of what is customarily view as cognitive distortions or misperception is characteristic of information flow from the environed, it should be noted that while the depressed person's different interprets his predicament is traditionally attributes to his distortion or misperception, genera disorders of thought and perception are nether defining criteria more common among depressed patients (McPartland and Hornstra, 1964). An observer who talks into account the intricacies of someone's relationship to his environment,. Frequently attributes to hin characteristics that he does not possess, or leaves significant aspects of his experience unexplained (Watzlawick, 1967). Feedback introduces phenomena that cannot be adequately explained by reference to the isolated individual alone (Ashby, 1960, 1962), for the stud y of depression, identification of a pattern of depressive feedback from the environment demands a more complex conceptualization of the disorder that one explaining its phenomena with reference to the isolated depressed person.

Of all the distinctions that have been proposed, the most widely accepted and least controversial is that between unipolar and bipolar disorder. In its simplest form—and as it has been recognized in the DSM-III—the differential diagnosis is based on whether the patient has a personal history of mania. However, recent genetic studies have led to a familial definition of the distinction: Depressed patients who do not have a personal history of mania may still be diagnosed for being bipolar if there has been mania among first-degree relatives.

Valid though the distinction appears to be, it has some important limitations. As yet, no consistent differences in the symptomatology of bipolar and unipolar depression have been identified. Although a bipolar diagnosis predicts a greater likelihood of response to lithium, as many as 40 percent of unipolar patients, nonetheless, respond positively (Depue and Monroe, 1978). By itself, the distinction does not do justice to the heterogeneity among either bipolar or unipolar patients. Currently, persons with bipolar disorder are often subclassified as to whether either manic or depressive symptoms or both have been severe to require hospitalization. Unipolar depressed persons remain a large and tremendously heterogeneous group. Nonetheless, in the continuing controversies as how best to distinguish among depressed persons, the unipolar-bipolar distinctions stands out in its usefulness for both clinical and research purposes.

Although little, has been written in the literature of psychoanalysis concerning the psychology of neurotic depression. But the affect of depression in the sphere of the psychosis awaits more precise investigation. This task is complicated by the fact that a good part of the diseases in question run a 'cyclical' course in which there is an alternation between melancholic and manic states. The few preliminary studies which have hitherto been published have only dealt with one of these two phases at the same time.

The study of the genetics of depression remains in its infancy. Further advances are going to require better ways of subtyping affective disorders and the discovery of biological markers that are not state dependent, that is, tied to whether someone is currently disturbed. Dunner describes some of the distinctions that he and his colleagues have drawn for bipolar disorder, in terms of the severity of manic and depressive phases (e.g., whether one or both require hospitalization). It is probably true that bipolar disorder is more homogeneous and has a stronger genetic component than unipolar depression, and because of this, Dunner suggests that is more likely to yield advances in the near future. Some researchers are attempting to identify subtypes of unipolar depression that 'breed true' such that the relatives of depressed persons who have a particular pattern of symptoms will themselves show this pattern if they become depressed. There have been some promising findings with concomitant appetite disturbance and excessive guilt (Leckman et al., 1984), but any substantial advances are going to depend ultimately upon the identification of genetic markers that have thus far proven elusive. Riedfer and Gershon (1978) have noted that such markers will need to be stable; heritable, and state independent; capable of differentiating persons with an affective disturbance from persons drawn from the general population, and among the relatives of depressed persons, capable of identifying those who develop affective disturbance from those who do not.

A major source of confusion is due to the fact that the term 'depression' variously refers to a mood state, a set of symptoms, and a clinical syndrome. As a reference to mood, depression identifies a universal human experience, adjectives from a standard measure of mood (The Multiple Affect Adjective Checklist: Zuckerman and Lubin, 1965) point to subjective feelings associated with a depressed mood; sad, unhappy, blue, low, discouraged, bored, hopeless, dejected, and lonely. Similarities between everyday depressed mood and the complaints of depressed patients have encouraged the view that clinical depression is simply an exaggeration of a normal depressed mood, however, patients sometimes indicate that their experience of depression is quite distinct from normal feelings of sadness, even in its extreme form.

Of recent views, that depression is to emphasize that it is primarily a biological disturbance, an illness, the predisposition to which lies in genes and biochemistry, while people may react to their circumstances with happiness and unhappiness, this is of questionable relevance to the clinical phenomena of depression. However, as these definitional problems continue to plague the study of depression, and they are not going to be readily resolved. There remains considerable disagreement as to what extent and for what purpose a depressed mood in relatively normal persons can be seen as one end of a dimensional continuum of mood as taken upon those disturbances as seen of a psychiatric hospital patients, and to what extent the clinical phenomena is distinct and discontinuous with normal sadness and unhappiness.

One observer may be struck with the frequent complaints about appetite and sleep disturbance by depressed persons and infer that some sort of biological disturbance mus t be the key to understanding depression. Another might find their self-derogation and pessimism irrational in a way that suggests that these must be some kind of fundamental deficit in self-esteem or cognitive distortion occurring. Still another may listen to the incessant complaining of a depressed person, get annoyed and frustrated, and yet feel guilty in the way that makes it easier to encourage the depressed person to continue to talk in this way than to verbalize these negative feelings. Cognizant of this, the observer might conclude that there is some sort of interpersonal process going on that is critical to any understanding of depression.

Nonetheless, studies have compared the subjective mood of persons who are distressed but seeking help to those who are seeking treatment for depression (Depue and Monroe, 1978). The two groups may be similar in subjective mood, but they differ in other ways. Those persons who are not seeking treatment for depression tend to lack the anxiety and the physical complaints, including loss of appetite, sleep disturbances, and fatigue shown by the group seeking treatment. still, it could be argued that there is a continuum of dimensional provision, as to the differences between the two groups, with these additional features arising, when a normal depressed mood become s more prolonged or intensified. The controversy is likely to continue until either questions about the etiology of depression are resolved or unambiguous markers for depression are identified.

Advocates of psychoanalytic, cognitive and behavioural, and interpersonal and social perspective on depression have generally assumed a dimensional quantification between a normal depressed mood and clinical depression. They tend to exclude psychotic and bipolar depressed persons from treatment, but, beyond that, they have tended to disregard classification issues (Gilbert,. 1984) for unipolar depression, at least, they have assumed that whatever discontinuities in the biology of mild and severe moods there might be that are, yet as not excessively necessarily relevant to the psychological and asocial processes, which they are most interested.

Writers since antiquity have noted the core symptoms of depression: Besides a sad or low mood, reduced ability to expression pleasure, pessimism, inhibition and retardation of action, and a variety of physical complaints. as such, that we can distinguish among the emotional, cognitive, motivational, and vegetative symptoms of depression, although these feature s are not alway so neatly divisible. Beyond these symptoms, there are some characteristic interpersonal aspects of depression that are not usually considered as formal symptoms. But they are frequent, distinctive, and troublesome enough tp warrant attention.

Sadness and dejection are not the only emotional manifestations of depression, although about half of all depressed patient report these feelings as their principal complaint. Most depressed persons are also anxious and irritable. Classical descriptions of depression tend to emphasize that depressed persons' feelings of distress, disappointment, and frustration are focussed primarily on themselves, yet a number of studies suggest that their negative feelings, including overt hostility, are also directed at the people around them. Depressed persons are often intensely angry persons (Kahn, Coyne, and Margolin, Weissman, Klerman and Paykel, 1971).

Perhaps, 10 or 15 percent of severely depressed patients deny feelings of sadness, reporting instead that all emotional experience, including sadness, has been blunted or inhibited (Whybrow, Akiskal and Mckinney, 1984). The identification of these persons as depressed depends upon the presence of other symptoms. The inhibition of emotional expression in severely depressed persons may extend to crying. Whereas, mild and moderately depressed persons may readily and frequently cry, as they become more depressed, as they may continually be in lack of emotionally expressive inhibitions.

Mildly and moderately depressed persons may feel that every activity is a burden, yet they still derive some satisfaction from their accomplishment. Despite their low mood, they may still crack a smile at a joke yet, as depression intensifies, a person may report both a loss of any ability to get gratification from activities that had previously been satisfying—family, work, and social life—and a loss of any sense of humour. Life becomes stale, flat, and not at all amusing. The loss of gratification may extend to the depressed persons' involvement in close relationships. Often, a loss of affection for the spouse and children, a feeling of not being able to care anymore, a sense of a wall being erected between the depressed person and others are the major reasons for seeking treatment.

Perhaps one of the most frustrating aspects of depressed persons for those around them is their difficulty in mobilizing themselves to perform even the most simple tasks. Encouragements, expressions of support even threats and coercion seems only to increase their inertia, leading others to make attributions of laziness, stubbornness, and malingering. Despite their obvious distress and discomfort, depressed persons frequently fail to take a minimal initiative to remedy their situations or do so only halfheartedly. To observers, depressed persons may seem to have a callous indifference to what happens to them.

Depressed persons often procrastinate. They are Avoidant and escapist in their longing for a solacing refuge from demands and responsibilities. In severe depression, the person may experience an abulia or paralysis of will, extending even to getting out of bed, washing, and dressing.

In more severe depressions, there may be psychomotor retardation, expressed in slowed body movements, slowed and monotonous speech, or even muteness. Alternatively, psychomotor agitation may be seen in an inability to be still, pacing, and outbursts of shouting.

The presence of physical or vegetative symptoms is sometimes taken as the dividing line between normal sadness and clinical depression. One of the most common and prominent of vegetative symptoms is fatigue that someone is depressed may be first recognized by the family physician who cannot readily trace the person's complaints of tiredness to other causes.

Depressed persons also often suffer sleep disturbance, and it is tempting to link their tiredness to this, but in a sample of depressed patients, the two complaints are only modestly correlated (Beck, 1967). Depressed persons generally have rouble falling asleep, they sleep restlessly, and awaken easily. Yet, some depressed persons actually sleep considerably more than usual, up to 12 hours a night.

When mildly or moderately depressed, some people eat compulsively and gain considerable weight, but depression is more characteristically associated with loss of appetite and a decrease in weight. For many depressed persons, a loss of appetite is the first sign of an incipient depression, and its return marks the beginning of recovery. Some depressed persons maintain their normal eating habits and weight, but complain that food is tasteless and eating an unsatisfying matter of habit. Besides a loss of appetite, depression is often associated with gastrointestinal disturbance, notably nausea and constipation. Mild depression heightens sexual interest in some people, but generally depression is associated with a loss of interest in sex. In severe depression, there may be an aversion to sex. Overall, though, women who are depressed do not have sex less frequently, but they initiate it, like and enjoy it less, and are less responsive (Weissman and Paykel, 1974).

Finally, depressed persons report diffuse aches and pains. They have frequent headache, and they are more sensitive to existing sources of pain, such as dental problems.

A brief interaction with a depressed person can have a narked impact on one's own mood. Uninformed strangers may react to a conversation with a depressed person with depression, anxiety, hostility, and may be rejecting of further contact (Coyne, 1976). Jacobson (1968) has noted that depressed persons often unwittingly succeed in making everyone in their immediate environment feel guilty and responsible and that others react to the depressed person with hostility and even cruelty. Despite this visible impact of depression on others, there is a persistent tendency in the literature to ignore it and to concentrate instead on the symptoms and complaints of depressed persons out of their interpersonal context. Depressed persons can be difficult, but they may also be facing difficult interpersonal situations within which their distress and behaviour make more sense.

Depressed persons tend to withdraw from social activities, and their close relationships tend to be strained and conflictual. Depressed women have been more intensely studied than depressed men, in part, because women are approximately twice as likely to be depressed. Depressed women are dependent, acquiescent, and inhibited in their communication in close relationships, and prone to interpersonal tension, friction and open conflict (Weissman and Paykel, 1974). Interestingly, the interpersonal difficulties of depressed persons are less pronounced when they are interacting with strangers than with intimates (Hinchcliffe, Hooper and Roberts, 1975).

About half of all depressed persons report martial turmoil (Rousanville, Weissman, Prusoff and Heraey-Baron, 1979). There is considerable hostility between depressed persons and their spouses, but often there is more between depressed persons and their children. Being depressed makes it more difficult to be a warm, affectionate, consistent parent (McLean, 1976). The children of depressed parents are more likely to have a full range of psychological and social difficulties than the children of normal or even schizophrenic parents (Emery, Weintraub and Neale, 1982), yet one must be cautious in making causal inferences. There is evidence that the children's problems are more related to a conflictual marital relationship and a stressful home-life than depression of the parent (Sameroff, Barocas and Siefer).

Depression thus tends to be indicative of an interpersonal situation fraught with difficulties, and this needs to be given more attention in both theorizing and planning treatment. Although depression is associated with interpersonal problems, within a sample of depressed persons the correlation between severity of depression and the extent of interpersonal problems tends to be modest. This may suggest that these problems are a matter not only of how depressed persons are functioning, but of the response of key people around them as well (Coyne, Kahn, and Gotlib, 1985).

In that the diagnosis of depression, one can make a list of the symptoms of depression, and assign any person a depression score on the basis of the number of symptoms present. A number of standard self-report inventories such as the Beck Depression Inventory (Beck, et al., 1961), the Centre for Epistemological Studies Depression Scale (Radloff, 1977) and the Self-Rating Depression Scale (Zung, 1965) has been validated and are widely used as research tools, screening devices, and measures of the change associated with treatment.

Even if one is to assume a continuity between normal depressed mood and clinical depression, it may still prove useful to make a distinction between the presence and absence of significant depression. One may wish to insure that a research study does not include a preponderance of persons whose depression is only mild or transient. Virtually no signs or symptoms are specific to depression, and ye t in many contexts, one may need to distinguish depression from other descriptors or explanations for a person's distress and behaviour in working with elderly, for instance, it is important to distinguish between depression and dementia. In medical patients in general, there is a high prevalence of symptoms associated with depression, both because of physical illness and the stress of hospitalization (Cavanaugh, 1984), and, whether for research pr practical purposes, one may wish to establish criteria for who is to be considered depressed and who is not. Finally persons who are labelled schizophrenic or alcoholic may show considerable depression, but it would be undesirable for many purposes to lump them with those persons whose primary problem is depression. Thus, for purposes of communication, treatment and research, it may prove useful to have some means of specifying some boundary conditions for the term 'depression'. In terms of some minimal level of severity as well as some coherence and specificity to what is included in the concept—even if one rejects the notion that it is a discrete entity, discontinuous with normal mood.

The problem of diagnosis is most critical in biomedical approaches to depression, but the assumption is generally made that depression is a matter of one or more disease entities with specific etiologies and treatments. The statement, 'Nosology precedes etiology' conveys the idea that the abilities of identify the causes of depression depend s upon the existence of an adequate diagnostic and classificatory system. For instance, to take a simplified hypothetical example, suppose that a particular biological abnormality occurs in 60 percent of all depressed persons and is specific to depression. Suppose also, with the accepted diagnosis criteria, only 60 percent of the persons identify as such are 'actually depressed'. If these conditions occurred, then research might indicate that only 36 percent of depressed persons' posses the abnormality.

An effective treatment for depression may also be misjudged or misapplied in the absence of an adequate diagnostic system. This was made apparent recently after a drug company had undertaken a large study to compare the effectiveness of a new frug to that of both an established drug treatment for depression and a placebo (Carroll, 1984). At five of the six research sites, the new drug proves to be no more effective than the placebo, but interpretation of this was limited by the additional finding that the established treatment proved no better. Patients identified as depressed by current criteria did not respond to drug treatment that had proven efficacious in a large body of past research. Either the past research was misleading, the current diagnostic criteria are invalid, or most likely, they were misapplied by reputable investigators.

Contemporary diagnostic systems owe much to the work of Kraepelin at the turn of the century. He divided major psychopathology into two broad syndromes: Dementia praecox (schizophrenia) and manic-depressive illness. The latter category included almost all serious mood disturbance, including depression in the absence of an episode of mania. As retained today, the term generally is a synonym for bipolar disorder. It is also still sometimes used as a genetic term for severe depression. Kraepelin considered manic-depressive illness a biological derangement. Although it might in some cases be precipitated by psychological factors, 'the real cause for the malady must be sought in permanent internal changes which are very often, and, perhaps always innate', (Kraepelin, 1921). Once started, the illness runs its course autonomously, independent of changes in the person's situation. Kraepelin also identified a group of psychogenic depression, which were depressive illness and reactive to change in these circumstances.

For more than 30 years, the dominant diagnostic system in the United States has been, the Diagnostic and Statistical Manual of Mental Disorders of the American Psychiatric Association, which is currently in its third edition (DSM-III). In its first edition it integrated the ideas of Kraepelin with those of Adolph Meyer and Sigmund Freud. While accepting Kraepelin's basic distinction between affective disturbance and schizophrenia, it also reflected Meyer's psychobiological view that mental disturbance represented not a simple disease entity, but the reaction of the personality to the matrix of psychological, social, and biological factors. By its second edition, the Meyerian term 'reaction' was no longer used throughout, but Meyer's influence remained. Freud 's ideas about the etiology of psychopathology were built into the criteria for specific disorders. Thus, the defining characteristics of neuroses were anxiety, but for purposed of diagnostic decisions, it could be manifest and observable or inferred to be operating 'unconsciously and automatically' in someone who was not visibly anxious.

The author of DSM-III attempted to avoid past controversies and answer many of the criticisms of its two predecessors. A decision was made to define diagnostic categories as precisely as possible, using descriptive data, rather than inferences about etiology. From a biomedical perspective, the ideal diagnostic and classificatory system would integrate knowledge about etiology with overt symptomatology. However, it was concluded that the present understanding of the causes of most disorders is too limited for this purpose. Furthermore, the sense was that 'the inclusion of etiological theories would be an obstacle to use of the manual by clinicians and varying theoretical orientations, since it would not be possible to present all reasonable etiological theories for each disorder (American Psychiatric Association, 1980).

In considering depression, the author's of DSM-III attempted to sidestep a number of longstanding controversies, including that of whether there is a continuum or a discontinuity between normal mood and clinical depression, as well as that of the role of precipitating life circumstances in distinguishing among types of depression. Depressive neurosis disappeared, along with the other neuroses. Depression is now encompassed in two main categories. The first category, major affective disorder, involves the presence of a full affective syndrome, with the subcategories of bipolar and major depression distinguished by whether there has ever been a manic episode. The second category, other specific affective disorders, includes conditions in which the depression is not severe enough to warrant a diagnosis of major affective disorder, but severe enough to warrant a diagnosis of major affective disorder, but the mood disturbance has been intermittent or chronic for at least two years.

The criterion for major depression is subclassified as to whether it is a single episode or recurrent and also as to whether melancholia is present. Melancholia involves a complaint of a loss of pleasure in all or almost all activities, a lack of reactivity to pleasant events: A quality of depressed mood, that is distinct from grief or sadness; depression worse in the morning; early morning wakening; marked psychomotor agitation or retardation; significant weight loss; and excessive quilt. The designation was intended as an acknowledgement that some more symptoms and might be more responsive to treatment with drugs or electroshock. However, it should be noted that there is considerable consensus that such a distinction should be made, but the exact nature of it remains controversial. There are exclusion criteria, including schizophrenia and what is judged to be normal or uncomplicated grief.

In general, these diagnostic systems are viewed as significant improvements over past effort s, but there is widespread dissatisfaction with them. A prominent biologically oriented researcher has lamented:

> Anastuteobserverwillfindlittlethatisintellectually satisfying about the DSM-III diagnostic criteria for major depressive disorder. These criteria amount to catalogue of symptoms, and they are in no way linked by coherent underlying constructs. they also suffer from the problem of being cast as disjunctive criteria. This means that, for example, patients need to satisfy only of the possible symptomatological evaluations or appraising analyze. Therefore (and this occurs in practice), several patients may be assigned the same categorical diagnosis without having any symptoms in common (Carroll, 1984).

Carroll goes on to note that as the result of an inadequate diagnostic system, research studies are limited by the flaws in the diagnosis used as independent variables, and drug treatment of an individual patient tends to remain a matter of trial and error.

We are far from an adequate diagnostic system for depression. If one is to be achieved, it will have to come to terms with the enormous heterogeneity in the signs and symptoms; level of severity, causal factors to this heterogeneity with a variety of classificatory systems. Kendall (1976) has suggested that almost every classificatory system that is logically possible has been proposed at some point in this period, but he notes that little consensus has been achieved. Winokur reviews some of the current controversies, but it would be useful to identify a few of the distinctions that have been made before we turn to the major theoretical perspectives on the disorder.

Of all the distinctions that have been proposed, the most widely accepted and least controversial is that between unipolar and bipolar disorder. In its simplest form—and as it has been recognized in the DSM-III—the differential diagnosis is based on whether the patient has a personal history of mania. However, recent genetic studies have led to a familial definition of the distinction: Depressed patients who do not have a personal history of mania may still be diagnosed as bipolar if there has been mania among first-degree relatives.

Work by Perris (1966) firs t established that bipolar disorder starts on the average of 15 years earlier than unipolar depression and recurs more frequently. Individual episodes are shorter, and there is a greater risk of disorder among the first-degree relatives of bipolar patients. Furthermore, there as a tendency for unipolar and bipolar disorders to breed true, with first-degree relatives of bipolar patients tending toward bipolar disorder, and first-degree relatives of unipolar patients tending to have little more risk of mania than the general population. The unipolar-bipolar distinction has proven to be clinically useful; depressed bipolar patients respond significantly better to lithium than unipolar depressed patients.

Valid though the distinction appears to be, it has some important limitations. As yet, no consistent differences in the symptomatololgy of bipolar and unipolar depression have been identified. Though a bipolar diagnosis predicts the greater likelihood of response to lithium, as many as 40 percent of unipolar patients, nonetheless, respond positively (Depue and Monroe, 1978). By itself, the distinction does not do justice to the heterogeneity among either bipolar or unipolar patients. Currently, persons with bipolar disorder often subclassified as to whether either manic or depressive symptoms or both have been severe to require hospitalization. Unipolar depressed persons remain a large tremendously heterogeneous group. Nonetheless, in the continuing controversies as how best to distinguish among depressed persons, the unipolar-bipolar distinction stands out in its usefulness for both clinical and research purposes.

Many issues in the study of unipolar depression have coalesced in the concept of endogenous versus nonendogenous depression. The differentiation is most often identified for being between endogenous and reactive depression, although this has been used interchangeably with the endogenous-neurotic and psychotic-neurotic distinction. The hope for the distinction has often been that it would prove to be the boundary between biological versus psychological and social concerns. Traditionally, the term 'endogenous' has been invoked to differentiate depressions that are purportedly biological in etiology, without environmental precipitants, and that are less amenable to psychotherapy. Also, endogenous depressions are expected to be more responsive to somatically oriented interventions, notably electroconvulsive shock therapy and antidepressant medication. 'Reactive' has inferred to depressions that are viewed as understandable reaction to some precipitating stress and that are more suitable for psychotherapy and less responsive to somatic therapies. The distinction was originally based on the supposition that some depressions are related to precipitating events and others seem to appear without them and that would predict response to treatment and clinical course.

People, encompassed within the depressive point of bipolar disorder, experience the intensely sad or profoundly transferring formation showing the indifference to work, activities, and people that once brought them pleasure. They think slowly, concentrate poorly, feel tired, and experience changes—usually an increase—in their appetite and sleep. They often feel a sense of worthlessness or helplessness. In addition, they may feel pessimistic or hopeless about the future and may think about or attempt suicide. In some cases of severe depression, people may experience psychotic symptoms, such as delusions (false beliefs) or hallucinations (false sensory perceptions).

In the manic phase of bipolar disorder, people feel intensely and inappropriately happy, self-important, and irritable. In this highly energized state they sleep less, have racing thoughts, and talk in rapid-fire speech that goes off in many directions. They have

789

RICHARD J. KOSCIEJEW

inflated self-esteem and confidence and may even have delusions of grandeur. Mania may make people impatient and abrasive, and when frustrated, physically abusive. They often behave in socially inappropriate ways, think irrationally, and show impaired judgment. For example, they may take aeroplane trips all over the country, make indecent sexual advances, and formulate grandiose plans involving indiscriminate investments of money. The self-destructive behaviour of mania includes excessive gambling, buying outrageously expensive gifts, abusing alcohol or other drugs, and provoking confrontations with obnoxious or combative behaviour.

Clinical depression is one of the most common forms of mental illness. Although depression can be treated with psychotherapy, many scientists believe there are biological causes for the disease. The June 1998 publication, of the Scientific American, in the article that Neurobiologist Charles B. Nemeroff exchanges views about something in order to arrive at the truth or to convince others that the connection concerning to considerations that are differentiated between biochemical changes in the brain and the finding of depression.

The genes that a person inherits seem to have a strong influence on whether the person will develop bipolar disorder. Studies of twins provide evidence for this genetic influence. Among genetically identical twins where one twin has bipolar disorder, the other twin has the disorder in more than 70 percent of cases. But among pairs of fraternal twins, who have about half their genes in common, both twins have bipolar disorder in less than 15 percent of cases in which one twin has the disorder. The degree of genetic similarity seems to account for the difference between identical and fraternal twins. Further evidence for a genetic influence comes from studies of adopted children with bipolar disorder. These studies show that biological relatives of the children have a higher incidence of bipolar disorder than do people in the general population. Thus, bipolar disorder seems to run in families for genetic reasons.

Owing or relating to, or affecting a particular person, over which a personal allegiance about the concerns and considerations or work-related stress can trigger a manic episode, but this usually occurs in people with genetic vulnerabilities, other factors—such as prenatal development, childhood experiences, and social conditions—seem to have relatively little influence in causing bipolar disorder. One study examined the children of identical twins in which only one member of each pair of twins had bipolar disorder. The study found that regardless of whether the parent had bipolar disorder or not, all of the children had the same high 10-percent rate of bipolar disorder. This observation clearly suggests that risk for bipolar illness comes from genetic influence, not from exposure to a parent's bipolar illness or from family problems caused by that illness.

Different therapies may shorten, delay, or even prevent the extreme moods caused by bipolar disorder. Lithium carbonates, a natural mineral salt, can help control both mania and depression in bipolar disorder. The drug generally takes two to three weeks to become effective. People with bipolar disorder may take lithium during periods of relatively normal moods to delay or prevent subsequent episodes of mania or depression. Common side effects of lithium include nausea, increased thirst and urination, vertigo, loss of appetite, and muscle weakness. In addition, long-term use can impair functioning of the kidneys. For this reason, doctors do not prescribe lithium to bipolar patients with kidney disease. Many people find the side effects so unpleasant that they stop taking the medication, which often results in a relapse.

From 20 to 40 percent of people do not respond to lithium therapy. For these people, two anticonvulsant drugs may help dampen severe manic episodes: carbamazepine (Tegretol) and valproate (Depakene). The use of traditional antidepressants to treat bipolar disorder carries risks of triggering a manic episode or a rapid-cycling pattern.

Controlled studies have not found that the endogenous-reactive distinction predicts response to psychotherapy (Blackburn, 1981; Kovacs, 1980; Rush, 1984), the presence or absence of precipitating stress has not proved to be a good predictor of response to treatment (Leff, Roatch and Bunney, 1970) and the endogenous-reactive distinction has been found to be deficient in a number of ways. Yet, it remains considerably utility. Reactivity to changes in life circumstances during a depressive episode have been found to predict response to electroconvulsive shock and antidepressant medication (Fowles and Gerch, 1979). Other symptoms that have been associated with a positive response to somantic treatment include quality of a mood and whether there has been a los of the ability to experience pleasure; psychomotor retardation; feeling worse in the morning after than the evening; and sleep and appetite irregularity. Such symptoms are now accepted as criteria for endogenous depression than is the absence of precipitating stress.

This consensus about the feature of endogenous depression still leaves questions about its polar opposite, reactive or neurotic depression. In clinical practice, it tends to be defined in terms of milder mood disturbances a preponderance of psychological rather than vegetative symptoms, and the presence of a precipitating stress, although there are particular doubts about the validity of this last feature. Akiskal (1978) found that reactive or neurotic depression was the single most common diagnosis in inpatient and outpatient settings, but they raised the issue of whether it was useful to consider it a unified entity or type. In about a quarter of all the cases of such depression studied, it appeared to be truly reactive, in the sense that it developed in the face of overwhelming stress in persons who had previously seemed reasonably well functioning. In another quarter of the cases, it seemed to reflect a greater or fewer of chronic tendencies to respond to normative stress with depressed moods and to experience social difficulties. Many of these patients were described as dependent, manipulative, hostile and unstable. Follow-up revealed overall that only 40 percent of the total sample was considered to have been suffering primarily from an affective disturbance in the absence of some of other condition. Some of the sub-sample, who had faced a clear precipitating stress developed endogenous features. In 10 percent of the sample, the depression seemed secondary to a medial-surgical illness. In 38 percent of the sample, the depression was secondary to some nonaffective disorder, ranging from an anxiety disorder to schizophrenia. In these patients with medical-surgical or nonaffective psychiatric conditions, intermittent depression seemed to follow the course of the other difficulties. A final 10 percent of the sample remained undiagnosed, but depression was considered the probable diagnosis. The work of Akiskal et al, (1978) is further evidence of the problems in attempting to draw any sharp distinctions in the classification and diagnosis of depression. Beyond this, it suggests both the utility and the difficulty of distinguishing between depression that is primary and that which is secondary to other conditions. Furthermore, the work suggests the usefulness of attempting to understand depression in terms of the presence or absence of characterological or lifestyle difficulties.

Thus, the endogenous pole of the endogenous-reactive distinction is more clearly defined than its counterpart. After a long history of debate and controversy, there is a growing consensus that the differentiation of endogenous and reactive depression is useful but that they represent points along a dimensional continuum, rather than two distinct forms of disorder, it is sometimes suggested that endogenous depressions are simply more severe, but this leave s unanswered questions about differences in etiology or the determinants of one depressive episode progressing to an endogenous course and another not. Biomedically oriented researcher looks to the identification of familial patterns of affective disturbance. The development of biological markers, and the refinement of diagnosis laboratory tests is the solution to the ambiguity and confusion. Baldessarini notes the promise of recent developments such as the dexamethasone suppression test, but he cautions that:

> . . . While there has been considerable progress toward a biological and clinically robust diagnosis scheme, and in understanding some characteristics that can help to guide treatment, search for primary causes have been unsuccessful so far. Even so, virtually all of the biological characteristics of severely depressed patients that have been identified are 'state-dependent' (this, they disappear with recovery) and are not stable biological traits or markers of a possible heritable defect.

Even so, and by now it should have become apparent that the phenomena of depression are vaguely delineated and poorly understood. Seligman and his colleagues have provided a fine example of a strategy for dealing with this problem . . . its construction of a laboratory model or analogue with which greater precision can be achieved.

Let us return once more to the relation between helplessness (involving loss of self-esteem) and the simultaneously maintained narcissistic aspirations, noting that their intra-ego conflict assumed by Bibring and Melancholia: such that Bibring's theory opens two new vistas. One leads us to consider self-esteem as a signal, that is, an ego function, rather than as an effectual relation between the ego and the Superego. The other suggests that we recognize the role of the ego, and particularly of its helplessness, in the origin and function of the instinctual vicissitude called turning round upon the subject.

Though it is clear that the phenomenon from which the economic explanation must start is the inhibition of the ego, the economics of depression is still not understood. Bibring quote Fenichel's formulation as to, . . . The greater percentage of the available mental energy is used up in unconscious conflicts, and, not enough is left to provide the normal enjoyment of life and vitality (Bibring, 1953). But he finds this statement insufficient to explain depressive inhibition, and proceeds to reconsider the nature of inhibition such that:

> Freud (1926) defines inhibition as a 'restriction of functions of the ego, and mentions two major causes for such restrictions; Either having been imposed upon as the person or its measure of a precaution, i.e., to prevent the development of anxiety or the feelings of guilt, this having brought about as a result of exhaustion, as to infer upon the energy of the ego, of which it is engaged in some intense defensive activities. Bibring implies his own explanation in his comparison of depression to anxiety.

Anxiety as a reaction to external or internal danger indicates that the ego's desire to survive. The ego, challenged by the danger, mobilizes the signal of anxiety and prepares for fight or flight. In depression, the opposite takes place, the ego is paralysed because it finds itself incapable to meet the 'danger'. In certain instances, . . . depression may follow anxiety, then the mobilization of energy . . . is replaced by a decrease of self-reliance.

Thus Bibring's search for an economic explanation of depressive inhibition ends in the undefined term 'deceased of self-reliance', which as it stands, is not an economic concept.

What does that mean, that, . . . the ego is paralysed because it finds itself incapable to meet the danger'? Clearly 'paralysed' refers to the state of helplessness, one of the corollaries of which is the 'loss of self-esteem'. The danger is the potential loss of the object; The traumatic situation is that of the loss of an object—'helplessness' as Bibring defines, it is the persisting state of loss of an object.

The anxiety signal anticipates the loss in order to prevent the reactivation of the traumatic situation, that is, of panic-anxiety. Perturbing fluctuations of self-esteem anticipates the initiation of measures that are preventions, such, are the reactivations in the state of persisting of the loss of its object, from which the state of helplessness would only have to be of its involving in the loss of self-esteem, thus, the relation between perturbing fluctuations of self-esteem and 'helplessness', which is accompanied by its loss of self-esteem, but maintaining the similarity between the relation of its own dose of anxiety and the signalling of the panic-anxiety. Fluctuations of self-esteem are then structurally tamed by forms of and signals to anticipate as to preclude reactivation of the state of helplessness. Yet, according to the accepted theory, fluctuations of self-esteem are the functions of the Superego's relation to the ego, just as anxiety was considered, prior to 1926, as a function of repression enforced by the Superego. In 1926, however, Superego anxiety was recognized as merely one kind of anxiety and the repression, hence anxiety relationship was reversed into anxiety signals and hence, repression. Bibring achieves an analogous observation that is the ego's awareness of its helplessness which in certain cased forces it to turn the aggression from the object against the self, thus aggravating and complicating the structure of depression. While in the accepted theory it is assumed that the aggression 'turned round upon the subject", results in passivity and helplessness, in Bibring's conception it is the helplessness which is the cause of this 'turn round'.

Thus, Bibring's theory opens upon two new vistas. One leads us to consider self-esteem as a signal, that is, an ego function, rather from an open condition to the enclosing effect of an aggressive relation between the ego and the Superego. The other suggests that we reconsider the role of the ego, and particularly of its helplessness, in the origin and function of the instinctual vicissitude called turning round upon the subject.

The first of these, like Freud's structural theory of anxiety and Fenichel's of quilts (1945), leads to a broadening of our conception of the ego's apparatuses and functions. The second is even more far-reaching, it seems to go to the very core of the problem of aggression. We know that 'turning round upon the subject' was the basic mechanism for which Freud used before the 'death-instinct theory' to explain the major forms in which aggression manifests itself. It was in connection with this 'turning round upon the subject; Freud wrote:

> . . . sadism . . . seems to press toward a quite special aim—the infliction of pain, in addition t subjection and mastery of the object. Now a psychoanalysis would seem to show that infliction of pain plays no part in the original aims sought by sadism . . . the sadistic child takes no notice of whether or not it inflicts pain, nor of its purpose to do so. But when once the transformation into masochism has taken place, the experience of pain is ver y well adapted too severely as a passive masochistic aim . . . Where once the suffering of pain has been experienced as a masochistic aim, it can be carried back into the sadistic situation and result in a sadistic aim of inflicting pain (1915).

Thus Bibring's view that 'turning round upon the subject' is brought about by helplessness calling attention to some of Freud's early formulations. And prompt us to re-evaluate our conception of aggression. As it may lead to a theory of aggression which is an alternative to those which have so far been proposed, namely Freud's death-instinct theory. Fenichel's frustration-aggression theory, and the Hartmann-Kris-Loewenstein theory of an independent aggressive instinctual drive.

Let us return once more to the relation between helplessness, which involves the loss of self-esteem, and the simultaneously maintained narcissistic aspirations, such that their intra-ego conflict assumed by Bibring may have been implied by Freud when he wrote in "Mourning and Melancholia." 'A good, capable, conscientious person, . . . is more likely to fall ill of this . . . disease than one . . . of whom we too should have nothing good to say' (1917).

Fenichel's summary of the accepted view of the fate of self-esteem in depression is:

> . . . A greater or lesser loss of self-esteem is in the foreground. The subjective formula is-I have lost everything; now the world is empty, if the loss of self-esteem is mainly due to a loss of external

supplies, or-I have lost everything because I do not deserve anything. If it is mainly due to a loss of internal supplies from the Superego (1945).

Fenichel implied definition of supplies reads: 'The small child loses self-esteem when he loses love and attains it when he regains love . . . children need . . ., narcissistic supplies of affection . . . (1945)

Though the term 'supplies' has never been explicitly defined as a concept, it has become an apparently indispensable terminological acceptance in the psychoanalysis, and particularly in the theory of depression. in Bibring's theory, supplies are the goals of narcissistic aspirations. This gives them a central role in the theory, highlighting the urgent need to define them. Moreover, Bibring's comparison of depression and boredom hints at the direction in which such a definition might be sought by alerting us to the fact that there is a lack of supplies in boredom also. 'Stimulus hunger; is Fenichel's term for the immediate consequence of this lack? 'Boredom is characterized by the coexistence of a need for activity and activity-inhibition, as well as by stimulus-hunger and dissatisfaction with the available stimuli (1934). That an adequate stimuli is the lacking of supplies, which are available of either to be to close to the object of the repressed instinctual drive or the resistance, the distant from it and thus of holding to no interests

Bibring's juxtaposition of depression and boredom suggests that narcissistic supplies may be a special kind of adequate stimuli and narcissistic agitations a special kind of stimulus hunger. The implications of this suggestion become clearer if we note that it is the lack of narcissistic supplies which is responsible for the structuralization of the primitive state of helplessness, the reactivation of which is, according to Bibring's theory, the essencity depression.

The conception which emerges if we pursue these implications of Bibring's theory is this: (1) The development of the ego requires the presence of 'adequate stimuli', in this case love of objects; when such stimuli are consistently absent, a primitive ego state comes into existence, the later reactivation of which is the state of depression. (2) Normal development lowers the intensity of this ego state and its potentiality for reactivation, and limits its reactivation to those reality situations to which grief and sadness are appropriated reactions. (3) Recurrent absence of adequate stimuli in the course of development works against the lowering of the intensity of this ego state and increases the likelihood of its being reactivated, that is to say, established a predisposition of depression.

This conception is consonant with present-day ego psychology and also elucidates the economic and the adaptive aspects of Bibring's theory. the role of stimulation in the development of ego structure is a crucial implication of the concept of adaption. At the same time, since psychoanalytic theory explains the effects of stimulation in terms of changes in the distribution of attention cathexes, the role of stimulation in ego-structure development, to which is referred, and might that well be the starting point for an understanding of the economics of the ego state of depression.

All the same, our present discussion of the structural, genetic, dynamic, economic, and adaptive aspects of Edward Bibring's theory gives us a crystalline glimpse of its fertility. But does not exhaust either its implications or the problems it poses. An attempt to trace more or less of these would require a detailed analysis of those points where Bibring's views shade into other findings and theories of psychoanalytic ego psychology, and is therefore beyond our scope tonight.

However, of completing of the three points from which take root of Edward Bibring's theory which are less obvious than the observations and formulations so far discussed,

The first of its roots in the technique of the psychoanalysis, Bibring wrote:

> From a . . . therapeutic points of view one has to pay attention not only to the dynamic and genetic basis of the persisting narcissistic aspirations, the frustrations of which the ego cannot tolerate, but also the dynamic and genetic conditions which forced the infantile ego to become fixated to feelings of helplessness . . . the importance of these feelings of helplessness in the therapy of depression is obvious.

This formulation seems to say nothing more than the well-known technical rule that 'Analysis must always go on in the layers accessible to the ego at the moment' (Fenichel, 1938-39). But it does say more, because it specifies that it is the helplessness, the lack of interest, and the lowered self-esteem which are immediately accessible in depression. It is safe to assume that the clinically observed accessibility of this was one of the roots of Bibring's theory.

A second root of the theory is in Bibring's critique of the English school of psychoanalysis. A study of this critique shows that on the one hand, Bibring found some of this school's observations on depression sound and, like his own observations, incompatible with the accepted theory of depression, and, on the other hand, he found this schools' theory of depression incompatible with psychoanalytic theory proper. It seems that Bibring intended his theory of depression to account for the sound observations of this school within the framework of psychoanalytic theory.

Finally, a third root of Bibring's theory seems to be related to the problems raised by the so-called 'existential analysis'. So far the only evidence for Edward Bibring's interest in the critical attitude toward 'existential analysis' is in the memories of those people who discussed the subject with him. Though his interest in phenomenology is obvious in his paper on depression, his interest in existentialism proper is expressed in only a few passages, like [Depression] is—essentially—'a human way of reacting to frustration and misery' whenever the ego finds itself in a state of real or imaginary helplessness against 'overwhelming odds'. Bibring's intent seems to have been to put the sound observations and psychoanalytically relevant concepts of 'existential analysis' into the framework of psychoanalytic ego psychology.

Briefly, the relevance within a behavioural framework, depression is conceptualized as an extinction phenomena. On reading the gerontological literature one is struck by the many behavioural similarities between the depressed and the elderly person: (1) One of the most striking features of both old age and depression is a progressive reduction in the rate of behaviour. The concept of 'disengagement' has been advanced to account for this reduction of behaviour. It is assumed to be a natural process which the elderly person accepts and desires, and which is thought to have intrinsic determinants (Cumming and Henry, 1961). From a behavioural framework, the elderly person's reduced rate of behaviour suggests that his behaviour is no longer being reinforced by his environment, i.e., that he, like the depressed person, is on an extinction schedule. (2) Other aspects of the depressive syndrome (feeling rejected, and so forth) are quite common among the elderly (Wolf, 1959). (3) Motivation is a critical problem in the elderly, as it is in the depressed patient. It is hard to find effective reinforcers for either. The number of potentially reinforcing events seems reduced. (4) The elderly person and the depressed person are turned inward, and focus on themselves, their memories, fantasies, and the past. The hypothesis immediately gives to suggest of itself that a reduction in the response contingent rate of positive reinforcement is a critical antecedent condition for many of the behavioural changes described in the elderly person.

It is, nonetheless, that depression, that it is for this reason it needs a model. The clinical 'entity' has multifaceted symptoms, but let us look at those that seem central to the diagnosis and that may be related to learned helplessness. The symptoms of learned helplessness that we have discussed all have parallels in depression.

Sustaining the lowered response initiation the word 'depression' is a behavioural description that denotes a reduction o r depression in responding. Even so, it is not surprising that a prominent symptom of depression is failure, or slowness of a patient to initiate responses. Such is the systematic study of the symptoms of depression. Grinker, Miller, Sabishin, Nunn, and Nunally (1961) all describe this in a number of ways:

> Isolated and withdrawn, prefers to remain by himself, stays in bed much of the time . . .
> Gait and general behaviour slow and retarded . . .
> Volume of the voice deceased, sits alone very quietly . . .
> Feels unable to act, feels unable to make decisions . . .
> [They] give the appearance of an 'entity' person who has 'given up . . .

Mendels (1970) described the slowdown in responding associated with depression as:

> Loss of interest, decrease in energy, inability to accomplish tasks, difficulty in concentration and the

800

erosion of motivation, as these are ambitions that combine to impair efficient functioning. For many depressives the first signs of the illness are in the area of their increasing inability to cope with their work and responsibilities.

Beck (1967) describes 'paralysis of the will' as a striking feature of depression:

In the severity of cases, these are often completed in the paralysis of the will. The patient has no desire to do anything, even those things which are essential to life. Consequently, he may be relatively immobile unless prodded or pushed into activity by others. It is sometime necessary to put the patient out of bed, wash, dress, and feed him.

The characteristic passivity and lowered response initiation of depressives have been demonstrated in a large number of studies, i.e., Miller, 1975. Psychomotor retardation differentiates depressives from normal people and a direct example of reduced voluntary response initiation. In addition, depressives engage in fewer activities and the y show reduced interpersonal responding and reduced nonverbal communication. Finally, the intellectual slowness and learning, memory, and IQ deficits found in depressed patients may be viewed as resulting from reduced motivation to initiate cognitive actions such as memory scanning and mental arithmetic. These deficits all parallel the lowered response initiation in learned helplessness.

Recent laboratory experiments have demonstrated a striking similarity between the lowered response initiation of learned helplessness and depression (Klein, Fencil-Morse and Seligman, 1976; Miller and Seligman, 1975) in each of these studies, depressed and nondepressed students were first-divide into three groups; group (1) experienced inescapable loud noise (or unsolvable concept formation problems), group (2) heard the loud noise but could turn it off by pressing a button (or was provided with a solvable problem), group (3) heard no noise (or did not work on any problems). All subjects then worked on a series of patterned anagrams, and half of all subjects were depressed; half were not depressed. As in the earlier study by

Hiroto and Seligman (1975), nondepressed subjects in group (1), who had previously been exposed to inescapable noise or unsolvable problem, showed response initiation deficits on the anagrams, while nondepressed subjects in group (2) and (3) exhibited no deficit. moreover, depressed subjects in all groups, including those of group (3) who had no pretreatment, showed poorer response initiation on the anagrams than the nondepressed subjects in group (3). Nondepressed subjects given a helplessness pretreatment showed response initiation deficits wholly parallel to those found in naturally occurring depression. Klein and Seligman (1976) showed the same parallel deficits between depressed subjects and nondepressed helpless subjects on tasks involving noise escape.

Also having a negative cognitive set of depressives that not only make fewer responses, but they interpret their few responses as failures or as doomed to failure, this negative cognitive se t directly mirrors the difficulty that helpless subjects have in learning that responding produces relief from an aversive situation.

Beck (1967) considers this negativistic cognition as the set to be primarily characteristic of depression:

> The depressed patient is peculiarly sensitive to any impediments to his goal-directed activity. An obstacle is regarded as an impossible barrier, but difficulty in dealing with a problem is interpreted as a total failure. His cognitive response to a problem or difficulty is likely to be an idea such as 'I'm licked'. 'I'll never be able to do this,' or 'I'm blocked no mater what I do'.

In truth, Beck views the passive and retarded behaviour of depressed patients as stemming from their negative expectations of their own effectiveness:

> The loss of spontaneous motivation, or paralysis of the will, has been considered a symptom of depression in the classical literature. The loss of motivation may be viewed as the result of the patient's hopelessness and pessimism. As long as he expects a negative outcome from any course of action; he is stripped of any internal stimulation to do anything.

This cognitive set crops up repeatedly in experiments with depressives. Friedman (1964) observed that although a patient was performing adequately during a test, the patient would occasionally reiterate this original protest of 'I can't do it,' or 'I don't know how'. This is also our experience in testing depressed patients.

Experimental demonstrations of negative cognitive set in depressed college students were provided by Miller and Seligman (1973) and Miller, Seligman, and Kurlander (1975). These studies showed that depressed students view their skilled actions very much as if they were only chance actions. In other words, depressed subjects, more than nondepressed subjects, tend to perceive reinforcement in a skill task as independent of their behaviour. Miller, Seligman, and Kurlander (1975) found this perception to be specific to depression: anxious and non-anxious students matched for extent of depression did not differ in their perceptions of reinforcement contingencies.

Miller and Seligman (1975, 1976), Klein, Fencil-Morse and Seligman (1976), and Klein and Seligman (1976) more directly demonstrated the parallel between the negative cognitive set in learned helplessness and depression. While replicating the findings of Miller and Seligman (1976) and Klein and Seligman (1976) found that nondepressed subjects who had been exposed to inescapable noise perceived reinforcement as less response contingent than nondepressed subjects who had been exposed to either escapable or no noise during a skilful task. Pretreatment had no effect on perception of reinforcement in chance tasks. So, the effects of learned helplessness and depression on perception of reinforcement are parallel.

Cognitive deficits were also found in the previous studies of Miller and Seligman (1975), Klein et al. (1976) and Klein and Seligman (1976). These studies measured the degree to which subjects were able to benefit from successful anagram solutions or escapes from high volume noise. As with response initiation, depressed subjects in the untreated groups showed cognitive deficits relative to nondepressed subjects, and nondepressed subjects who had experienced inescapable noise or unsolvable problems exhibits cognitive deficits relative to nondepressed subjects in the control groups on measures of cognitive functioning.

Some studies indicate that negative cognitive set may also explain poor discrimination learning by depressives (Martin and

Rees, 1966), and may be partly responsible for their lowered cognitive abilities (Payne, 1961; Miller, 1975).

Depression, like learned helplessness, seems to have its time course. In discussing the 'disaster syndrome' Wallace (1957) reported that people experience a day or so of depression following sudden catastrophes, and then they again function normally. It seems possible that multiple traumatic events intervening between the initial disaster recovery might exacerbate depression in human considerably, as they do in dogs. We should also note that endogenously or process depression is characterized by fluctuations of weeks or months between depression and mania. Moreover, it is commonly thought that almost all depressions dissipate in time, although whether they last days, weeks, months, or years is a matter of some dispute (Paskind, 1929, 1930; Lundquist, 1945; Kraines, 1957).

According to psychoanalysts, the lowered aggression of depressives is due to introjected hostility. In fact, psychoanalysts view introjection of hostility as the primary mechanism producing symptoms of depression. We do not believe that the increased self-blame in depression results from hostility turned inward, but it seems undeniable that hostility, even in dreams (Beck and Hurvich, 1959; Beck and Ward, 1961), is reduced among depressive. This symptom corresponds to the lack of aggression in learned helplessness.

Depressives commonly show reduced interest in food, sex, and interpersonal relations. These symptoms correspond to the anorexia, weight loss, and sexual and social deficits in learned helplessness.

According to the catecholamine hypothesis of affective disorders, depression is associated with a deficient of norepinehrine (NE) at receptor sites in the brain, whereas elation may be associated with its excess. This hypothesis is based on evidence that imipramine, a drug that increases the NE available in the central nervous system, causes depression to end. Klerma and Cole (1965) and Cole (1964) experimented with imipramine and placebos on depressed patients and reported positive results of imipramine over placebos. Monoamineoxidase (MAO) inhibitors, which prevent the breakdown of NE, also may be useful in relieving depression (Cole, 1964; Davis, 1965). Reserpine, an antihypertensive medication that depletes NE, often produces depression as a side-effect in man (Beck, 1967). There is also some suggestion of cholinergic medication of depression. Janowsky et al. (1972) reported that physostigmine, a cholinergic stimulators, produced depressive affect in normal people. Atropine, a linergic blocker, reversed these symptoms. So, NE depletion and cholinergic activation are implicated in both depression and learned helplessness (Thomas and DeWald, 1977). However, Mendels and Frazer (1974) reviewed the behavioural effects of drugs that deplete brain catecholamines and they contend that the behavioural changes associated with reserpine are better interpreted as a psychomotor retardation-sedation syndrome than as depression. Moreover, selective depletion of brain catecholamines by alpha-methyl-para-tyrosine (AMPT) fails to produce some of the key features of depression, despite the fact that this drug produce a consistently greater reduction in amine metabolate concentration than occurs in depression. So depletion of catecholamines in itself may not be sufficient to account for depression.

Nonetheless, depressed people say they feel helpless, hopeless, and powerless, and by this they mean that they believe they are unable to control or influence those aspects of their lives that are significant to them. Grinker and coworkers (1961) describe the 'characteristics of hopelessness, helplessness, failure, sadness, unworthiness, guilt and internal suffering' as the 'essence of depression'. Melges and Bowlby (1969) also characterize depressed patients in this way and Bibring (1953) defines depression 'as the emotional expression [indicative] of a state of helplessness and powerlessness of the ego.'

They clearly are considerable parallels between the forms of behaviour that define helplessness and major symptoms of depression.

Differences:—But there are substantial gaps:—

First, there are two symptoms found with uncontrollable shock that may or may not correspond to symptoms of depression. Stomach ulcers occur more frequently and severely in rats receiving uncontrollable shock than in rats receiving controllable shock (Weiss, 1968, 1971). We know of no study examining the relationship of depression to stomach ulcers. Second, uncontrollable shock produces more anxiety, measured subjectively, behaviourally, and physiologically, than controllable shock (Seligman and Binik, 1976). The question of whether depressed people are more anxious than nondepressed people does not have a clear answer. Beck (1967) reported that although both depression and anxiety can be observed in some people, only a small positive correlation was found in a study of 600 people. Yet, Miller et al. (1975) found very few depressed college students who were not also anxious. We can speculate that anxiety and depression are related in the following way: When a man or animal is confronted with a threat or a loss, he initially respond with fear or anxiety. If he learns that the threat is wholly controllable, anxiety, having served its function, disappears. If he remains uncertain about his ability to control the threat, his anxiety remains. If he learns or is convinced that the threat is utterly uncontrollable, depression emerges.

A number of facts out depression have been insufficiently investigated for parallels in learned helplessness. Preeminent among these are the depressive symptoms that cannot be investigated in animals; dejected mood, feelings of self-blame and self-dislike, loss of mirth, suicidal thoughts and crying, but now, that learned helplessness has been reliably produced in man (Hiroto, 1974. Hiroto and Seligman, 1975; Klein et al., 1976; Klein and Seligman, 1976' Miller and Seligman, 1975, 1976; Racinskas, 1971; Roth and Kubal, 1975; Thornton and Jacobs, 1970; Dweck and Reppucci, 1973), we can determine whether any of these states occur in helplessness.

Finally, we know of no evidence that disconfirms the correspondence of symptoms in learned helplessness and depression.

The term 'learned helplessness' was first used in connection with laboratory experiments in which dogs were exposed to shock from which they could not escape (Overmier and Seligman, 1967). After repeated trials, the dogs tended to sit passively when the shock came on. Exposed to a new situation from which the y could escape a shock by jumping over a barrier, they failed to initiate the appropriate response. Some would occasionally jump over the barrier and escape, but they would generally revert to taking the shock passively. For the purposes of constructing an analogue of clinical depression, the behaviour of the dogs is significant in suggesting that exposure to uncontrollable aversive events may lead to a failure to initiate appropriate responses in new situations and an inability to learn that responding is effective.

The analogy to depression was bolstered by initial findings that in a variety of task situations, depressed human subjects resembled nondepressed subjects who had received repeated failure experiences. For instance, compared to nondepressed subjects who had not received repeated failure experiences, these groups of subjects took longer to solve anagrams and apparently failed to perceive the pattern underlying their successful solution (Klein and Seligman, 1976). Miller, Rosellini, and Seligman, and other research suggested that the parallels between laboratory learned helplessness and depression were not limited to similarities in behaviour. Promising leads were also established with regard to etiology, treatment, and prevention.

The original learned helplessness model stimulated a large body of research and considerable controversy (Buchwald, Coyne, and Cole, 1978; Costello, 1978). Ultimately, the accumulated research led to questions about both the adequacy of the learned-helplessness explanation for the behaviour of nondepressed subjects who has been exposed to failure as well as the appropriateness of learned helplessness as an analogue of depression. For instance, it was shown that the performance deficits of subjects who had been given a typical learned helplessness, induction were very much situation-specific (Cole and Coyne, 1977) and that these deficits might better be explained as the result of anxious self-preoccupation, rather than the perception of response-reinforcement independence (Coyne, Metalsky and Lavelle, 1980). Furthermore, the characterization of depressed persons as passive and lacking in aggression was challenged. Difficulties with the original learned helplessness model led to a major reformulation (Abramson, Seligman and Teasdale).

We use the term learned helplessness to describe the interference with adaptive responses produced by inescapable shock and also as a short hand to describe the process that we believe underlies the behaviour that we cannot control of which the distinction between controllable and uncontrollable reinforcement is cental to the phenomenon and the theory of helplessness. Learned helplessness in the dog is defined by two types of behaviour. (1) Dogs that have had shock or are slower to make responses than naive dogs, and (2) if the dog does make a response that turns off shock, it has more trouble than a naive dog learning that responding is effective.

However, if we are to propose a model of depression in man, we must have proof that learned helplessness occurs in man.

Besides passivity and retarded response-relief learning, other characteristics associated with learned helplessness are relevant to depression in man. First, helplessness has a time course. In dogs, inescapable shock produces transient as well as permanent interference with escape (Overmier and Seligman, 1967) and avoidance (Overmier, 1968): 24 hours after one session of inescapable shock, dogs are helpless; but after 48 hours their response is normal. This is also true of goldfish (Padilla, 1970). After multiple sessions of inescapable shock, helplessness is not transient (Seligman and Groves, 1970; Seligman, Maier and Geer, 1968) Weiss (1968) found a parallel time course for weight loss in rats given uncontrollable shock, but other that this no time course has been found in rats or in other species (e.g., Anderson, Cole, and McVaugh, 1968; Seligman, Rosellini, and Kozak, 1975). Nonetheless, uncontrollable trauma produces a number of effects found in depression. The two basic effects are these: animal and humans become passive—they are slower to initiate responses to alleviate trauma and may not respond at all; and animals and humans are retarded in learning that their behaviour may control trauma, if a response is made that does produce relief, they often have trouble realizing that one causes the other. This maladaptive behaviour has been observed in a variety of species over a range of tasks that require voluntary responding. In addition, this phenomenon dissipates in time in the dog, and it causes lowered aggression, loss of appetite, and norepinephrine depletion.

The passivity of dogs, rats and men in the face of trauma and their difficulty on benefiting from response-relief contingencies result; that we believe, from their having learned that responding and trauma are independent—that trauma is uncontrollable. This is the hear t of the learned helplessness hypothesis. The hypothesis states that when shock is inescapable, the organism learns that responses and shock termination are independent (the probability of shock termination given any response doesn't differ from its probability in the absence of that response). Learning that trauma is uncontrollable has three effects.

(1) A motivational effect—it reduces the probability that the subject will initiate responses to escape, because part of the incentive for making such responses is the expectation that they will bring relief. If the subject has previously learned that its responses have no effect on trauma, this contravenes the expectation, thus, the organism's motivation to respond is undermined by experience with reinforcers it cannot control. Such that this motivational effect undermines

passivity in learned helplessness, and, if the model is valid, in depression.

(2) The cognitive effect—learning that responses and shock are independent makes it more difficult to learn that responses do produce relief when the organism makes a response that actually terminates shock. In general, if we have acquired a cognitive set in which A's are irrelevant to B's, it will be harder for us to learn that A's produce B's when they do. By the helplessness hypothesis, this mechanism is responsible for the difficulty that helpless organisms have in learning that responding produces relief, even after they respond and successfully turn off shock. Further, if the model is valid, this mechanism produces the 'negative expectations' of depression.

(3) An emotional effect—although it does not follow directly from the helplessness hypothesis—such that uncontrollable shock produces more conditioned fear, ulcers, weight loss, defecation, and pain than controllable shock.

One cause of laboratory-produced helplessness seems to be learning that one cannot control important events. Learning that responses and reinforcement are independent results in a cognitive set that has two effects: fewer responses to control reinforcement are initiated and associating successful responses with reenforcement becomes more difficult.

Nevertheless, some of the events that typically precipitate depression; failure in work or school; death or loss of loved ones; rejection by or separation from loved ones; physical disease, and growing old. What do all these have in common?

Four recent theories of depression seem to be largely in agreement about the etiology of depression, and what they agree on is the centrality of helplessness and hopelessness. Bibring (1953), arguing from a dynamic viewpoint, sees helplessness as the cause of depression:

> What has been described as the basic mechanism
> of depression, the ego's shocking awareness of its
> helplessness in regard to its aspirations, is assumed

to represent the core of normal, neurotic and probably also psychotic depression.

Melges and Bowlby (1969) see a similar cause of depression:

Our thesis is that while a depressed patient's goals remain relatively unchanged his estimate of the likelihood of achieving then and his confidence in the efficacy of his own skilled actions are both diminished . . . the depressed person believes that his plans of action are no longer effective in reaching his continuing and long range goals . . . From this state of mind is derived, we believe, much depressive symptomalogy, including indecisiveness, inability to act, making increased demands on others, and feelings of worthlessness and guilt about not discharging duties.

Beck (1967, 1970) sees depression as resulting primarily from a patient's negative cognitive set, largely about his abilities to change his life:

A primary factor appears to be the activation of idiosyncratic cognitive patterns which divert the thinking into specific channels that deviate from reality. As a result, the patient perseverates in making negative judgements and interpretations of experience, negative evaluations of the self, and negative expectations of the future.

Lichtenberg (1957) sees hopelessness as the defining characteristic of depression: Depression is defined as a manifestation of felt hopelessness regarding the attainment of goals when responsibility for the hopelessness is attributed to one's personal defects. In this context hope is conceived to be a function of the perceived probability of success with respect to goal attainment.

Even so, it means that all of a person's efforts have been in vain, his responses have failed to bring about the gratification he desires; he cannot find responses that control reinforcement. When a person is rejected by someone he loves, he can no longer control this significant source of gratification and support. When a parent or lover dies, the bereaved person is powerless to produce or influence love from dead person. Physical disease and growing old are obvious helplessness experiences. In these conditions, the person's own responses are ineffective and he must rely on the care of others. So, we would predict that it is not life events that produce depression (Alarcon and Cori, 1972) but uncontrollable life events.

However, Ferster (1969, 1973), Kaufman and Rosenblum (1967); McKinney and Bunney (1969), and Liberman and Raskin (1971) have suggested that depression is caused by extinction procedures or the loss of reinforcers. There is no contradiction between the learned-helplessness and extinction view of depression; helplessness, however, is more general. Briefly, extinction is a special case of independence between responding and reinforcement. Reinforcement, just the same, may also be presented with a probability greater than zero, and still be presented independent of responding. This occurs in the typical helplessness paradigm and cause responses to decrease in probability (Recorta and Skucy, 1969). Therefore, a view talks about independence between responding and reinforcement assumes the extinction view and, in addition, suggests that situations in which reinforcers still occur independent of responding also will cause depression.

Both learned helplessness and depression may be caused by learning that responses and reinforcement are independent. But this view runs into several problems. Can depression actually be caused by situations other than extinction in which reinforcement still occur but are not under the individual's control? To put it another way, 'is a net loss of reinforcement necessary for depression, or can depression occur when there is only loss of control without loss of reinforcement?' Would a Casanova who made love with seven new women every week become depressed if he found out that women wanted him not because of his amatory prowess but because of his wealth or because his fairy god mother wished it? We can only speculate.

It seems appropriate to mention 'success' depression in this context. When people finally reach a goal after years of striving—being promoted or obtaining a PhD—many become depressed. This puzzling phenomenon is clearly a problem for a loss of reinforcement view of depression. From a helplessness view, success depression may occur because reinforcement are no longer contingent on present responding. After years of goal-directed instrumental activity, the reinforcement automatically changes. One now gets his reinforcement because of whom he is rather than what he is doing. The common clinical impression that many beautiful women become depressed and attempt suicide also presents problems for the loss of reinforcement theory: positive reinforcers abound not because of what they do but because of how they look. Would be a generation of children risen with abundant positive reinforcers that they received independently to what, and they did become clinically depressed?

According to the helplessness view, the central theme in successful therapy should be having the patient discover and come to accept that his responses produce the gratification that he desires—that he is, in short, an effective human being. Some therapies that reportedly alleviate depression are consonant with a learned helplessness model, however, it is important to note that the success of a therapy often has little to do with its theoretical underpinning. So, with the exception of Klein and Seligman (1976), as a se t of examples that seem as a test of the model, but merely as a set of examples that seem to have exposure to response-produced success as a cure for depression.

Consonant with their helplessness-centred views of the etiology of depression, Bibring (1957), Beck (1967), and Melges and Bowlby (1969) all stressed that reversing helplessness alleviates depression. For example, Bibring (1953) has stated:

> The same conditions which bring about depression (helplessness) in reverse serve frequently the restitution from depression. Generally, one can say that depression subsides either (I) when the narcissistically important goals and objects appear to be again within reach (which is frequently followed by a temporary elation) or (ii) when they become sufficiently modified or reduced to becoming realizable, or (iii) when they are altogether relinquished, or (iv) when the ego recovers from the narcissistic shock by regaining its self-esteem with the help of various recovery mechanisms (with or without any change of objective or goal).

In their review of therapies for depression, Seligan, Klein, and Miller (1976) indicated that most of the therapies have strong elements of inducing the patient to discover that responses produce the reinforcement he desires. In antidepression milieu therapy (Taulbee and Wright, 1971), for example, the patient is forced to emit one of the most powerful responses people have for controlling others—anger—and when this response is dragged out of his depleted behaviour repertoire, he is powerfully reinforced. Beck's (1970) cognitive therapy is aimed at similar goals. He sees success manipulations as changing the negative cognitive set ('I'm an ineffective person) of the depressive to a more positive set, and argues that the primary task of the therapist is to change the negative expectations of the depressed patient to more optimistic ones. Even so, both Burgess's (1968), therapy and the graded task assigned (Beck, Seligman, Binik, Schuyler, and Brill, unpublished data), the patient makes instrumental responses of gradually increasing complexity, and each is reinforced. Similarly, all instrumental behaviour therapy for depression (Hersen, Eisler, Alford, and Agras, 1973; Reisinger. 1972), by definition, arrange the contingencies so that responses control the occurrence of reinforcement; the patient's recognition of this relationship should alleviate depression. Lewinsohn's therapy also has this element; participation in activity and other nondepressed behaviour controls therapy time. (Lewinsohn, Weinstein, and Shaw, 1969). In assertive training (Wolpe, 1968), the patient must emit social responses to bring about a desired change in his environment. Such that the study provides a useful method fo r testing the effectiveness of any therapy for depression in the laboratory because we can bring depression into the laboratory, in that, both in its naturally occurring state and in the form of learned helplessness, we can now see what reverses it in the laboratory. Will assertive training, emotive expression or atropine given to helpless and depressed subjects in the laboratory reverse the symptoms of depression and helplessness?

In order to explain depression, Burgess (1968) and others have relied heavily on the reinforcement the patient gets for his depressed behaviour, it is tempting to seek to remove this reinforcement during therapy, but caution is in order, so to explain the persistence or maintenance of some depressive behaviours, but it does not explain how they began. Helplessness suggests that failure to initiate active responses originates in the perception that the patient cannot control reinforcement. Thus, there can be two sources of a depressed patient's passivity: (a) patients are passive for instrumental reasons, because they think staying depressed brings them sympathy, love and attention, and (b) patients are passive because they believe that no response at all will be effective in controlling their environment. In this sense, it means that there is at least some response that believes he can effectively perform. Maier (1970) found that dogs who were reinforced for being passive by shock termination were not nearly as debilitated as dogs for whom all responses were independent of shock termination. Similarly, patients who use their depression in a way of controlling reinforcement are less helpless than those who have given up. Nonetheless, depression may be directly antagonized when patients come to see that their own responses are effective in alleviating their suffering and produced gratifications.

Nonetheless, many therapies, from psychoanalysis to cognitive understandings, claim to be able to cure depression. the evidence presented is selective as only those treatments that seemed compatible with helplessness were such that was possible that when other therapies work it. It is, because they reinstate the patient's sense of efficacy. However, evidence on the effectiveness of therapy in depression that is less anecdotal and selective is sorely needed. The recent study of Klein and Seligman (1976) may provide a laboratory procedure for evaluating the effectiveness of any therapy suggested for learned helplessness and depression.

All the same, a behavioural self-control model for the study of depression is focussed on different subsets of depressive phenomena. Such that the self-control model organizes and relates these phenomena and has its own implications for symptomatology, etiology, and therapy. Depression has certain properties which make the development of a model particularly difficult, however, the term depression refers to a syndrome which encompass a broad set of symptoms with diverse behavioural referents (Beck, 1972; Levitt and Lubin, 1975; Mendels, 1970; Woodruff, Goodwin and Guze, 1974). Especially notable is the diversity among cognitive symptoms. Aside from manifest subjective sadness, depressed persons show clinical symptoms such as quilt, pessimism, low sel-esteem, self-derogation, and helplessness. Accounting for these distinctive cognitive behaviours and integrating them with the various overt-motor behaviours characteristic of depression are limited to verbal-cognitive and overt-motor variables is appropriate since no reliable physiological index has been clearly identified as a symptom of depression (Bruder, 1970).

A recent resurgence of interest in psychological aspects of depression has become evident, and, with it, new and innovative models have been advanced. Behavioural and cognitive modes proposed by Lewinsohn (1974), Seligman (1974) and Beck (1974) have been most prominent and influential in behavioural research and clinical application.

Lewinsohn (1974; Lewinsohn, Weinstein, and Shaw, 1969) has developed a clinical and research program which looks at depression as an extinction phenomenon. A loss or lack of response contingent positive reinforcement results in reduced rates of common overt-motor behaviour and also elicits a basic dysphoria. All other cognitive-verbal symptoms of depression are secondary elaborations of these basic dysphoria. Susceptivity to depression and ability to overcome depression are related to social skill, the range of events which are potentially reinforcing to the person, and reinforcement availability. The etiology of depression is therefore, the joint function of external environmental changes and individual differences in reinforcement potential and social skills. Therapy procedures are aimed at identifying potential sources of reinforcement in the person's environment and developing strategies to increase their frequency of occurrence (Lewinsohn, 1976. Lewinsohn and Shaffer, 1971; Robinson and Lewinsohn, 1973) In other instances, therapy consists of isolating deficits in social interaction and training subjects in modifying these socially skilled behaviours (Lewinsohn, Biglan and Zeiss, 1976); Lewinsohn and Shaw, 1969; Lewinsohn, Weinstein and Alper, 1970).

Also, Seligman has proposed a model of depression based on a laboratory paradigm of learned helplessness (Seligman, 1974, 1975). A situation in which the probability of the consequence given a response is equal to the probability of the consequence given no response produces the phenomenon of learned helplessness. Noncontingent punishment has been the situation most studied. Learned helplessness has properties which parallel the symptoms of depression: (1) lowered response initiation (passivity), (2) negative cognitive se t (belief that one's actions are doomed to failure; (3) dissipation over time, (4) lack of aggression, (5) loss of libido and appetite, and (6) norepinephrine depletion and cholinergic activity

(Seligman, Klein, and Miller, 1974). Cognition is given a central position in this model in that of the 'depressive retardation is caused by a brief in response-reinforcement independence'; (Seligman. 1974). Other cognitive symptoms are held to be elaborations on this central belief. No therapy studies have been directly generated by this model to date, however, Klein and Seligman (1976) have demonstrated the reversibility of learned helplessness and depression following experience with solvable problems.

From a different perspective, Beck (1970, 1972, 1974) has evolved a cognitive model of depression which holds that depression consists of a primary triad of cognitive patterns or schema (1) a negative view of the world; (2) a negative view of the self, and (3) a negative view of the future. These views are maintained by distorted models of cognition such as selective abstraction, arbitrary inference, and overgeneralization,. The over—behavioural symptoms of depression follow from cognitive distortion. Distorted schema develop in early childhood and leave individuals susceptible to depression in the face of stress. Therapy involves the identification of distortions and their confrontation with the evidence of objective experience. Case studies employing these modifications have been described by Beck (1972) and Rush, Khatami, and Beck (1975). Group studies have shown that therapy based on a Beck's cognitive behaviour modification model is superior to a program based on Lewinsohn's model, a nondirective control therapy and a waiting list control and is more effective than treatment with imipramine hydrochloride (Rush, Beck, Kovacs, and Hollon).

The severe disorders of mood or effect are among the most common of the major psychiatric syndromes. Lifetime expectancy rates for such disorders are between 3 and 8 percent of the general population. Only a minority are treated by psychiatrists or in psychiatric hospitals and about 70 percent of prescriptions for antidepressants are written by nonpsychiatrist physicians. These and other modern medical treatments of severe mood disorders have contributed to a virtual revolution in the theory and practice of modern psychiatry since the introduction of mood-altering drugs three decades ago. These agent s include lithium salts (1949), and monoamine oxidase (MAO) inhibitors (1952), and the antimanic and antipsychotic (neuroleptics) agents such as chlorpromazine (1952), and the tricyclic or heterocyclic (imipramine-like) antidepressants (1957). In addition, electroconvulsive therapy (ECT) continues to have a place in the treatment of very severe and acute mood disorders, especially life-threatening forms of depression.

The development of these modern medical therapies has had several important effects. First. These agents have provided of a relatively simple specific effect and safe forms of treatment with a profound impact on current patterns of medical practice, for example, many depressed or hypomanic patients can be managed adequately in outpatient facilities to avoid prolonged, expensive, and disruptive hospitalization which were formerly common. Second, partial understanding of the pharmacology of the psychotropic drugs has led to imaginative hypotheses concerning the pathophysiology or etiology of severe mood disorders. These, in turn, have encouraged a revolution on experimental psychiatry in which the hypotheses have been tested in clinical research. Many of the earlier hypotheses have been found wanting or simplistic, nevertheless, they have led to increased understanding of the diagnosis, biology, and treatment of mood disorders and to newer research that represents a third level of development. this is the focus of the practical clinical benefits of now and in the near future.

In the light of this some characteristics of infant development during this holding phase can be enumerated. It is at this stage that:

(1) primary process, (2) primary identification, (3) auto-erotism, (4) primary narcissism, and (5) living realities.

In this phase the ego changes over from an unintegrated state to a structure integration, and so the infant becomes able to experience anxiety associated with disintegration. The word disintegration begins to have meaning which it did not possess before go integration became a fact. In healthy development at this stage the infant retains the capacity for re-experiencing unintegrated states, but this depends on the continuation of reliable maternal care or on the built-up in the infant of memories of material care beginning gradually to be perceived as such. The result of healthy progress in the infant's development during this stage is that he attains to what might be called 'unit status'. The infant become a person, an individual in his own right.

Associated with this attainment is the infant 's psychosomatic existence which begins to take on a personal pattern: that is, that the basis for this for this indwelling is a linkage of motor and sensory and functional experience with the infant's new state of being a person. As a further development there comes into existence what might be called a limiting membrane, which to some extent (in health) is equated with the surface of the skin, and has a position between the infant's 'me' and his 'not me'. So the infant comes to have an inside and an outside, and a body-scheme. In this way meaning comes to the function of intake and output, moreover, it gradually become meaningful to postulate a personal or inner psychic reality for the infant.

During the holding phase other processes are initiated; the most important is the dawn of intelligence and the beginning of a mind as something distinct from the psyche, and, from this, the secondary processes and symbolic functioning, and of the organization of a personal psychic content, which forms a basis for dreaming and for living relationships.

At the same time there starts in the infant a joining up of two roots of impulsive behaviours. The term 'fusion' indicates the positive process whereby diffuse elements that belong to movement and to muscle erotism become fused with the orgiastic functioning of the erotogenic zones. This concept is more familiar as the reverse process of defusion, which is a complex and complication defence in which aggression becomes separated out from erotic experience after a period in which a degree of fusion has been achieved. All these developments belong to the environmental condition of 'holding', and without a good enough holding the stages cannot be attained, or once attained cannot become established,

A further development in the capacity for object relationships. In that, the infant changes from relationship to objectively conceived object to a relationship to a object objectively perceived. This change is closely bound up with the infant's change from being merged with the mother to being separate from her, or to relating to her as a separate and 'not-me', This development is not specifically related to the holding, but is related to the phase of 'living with' . . .

In the holding phase the infant is maximally dependent. One can classify dependence thus:

(I) Absolute Dependence: In this state the infant has no means of knowing about the maternal care, which is largely a matter of prophylaxis. He cannot gain control over what is well and what is badly done, but is only a position to gain profit or to suffer disturbances,

(ii) Relative Dependence: The infant can become aware of the need for the details of maternal care, and to a growing extent relate them to personal impulse, and then later, in a psychoanalytic treatment, can reproduce them in the transference,

(iii) The infant develops the means for doing without actual care. This is accomplished through the accumulation of memories of care, the projection of personal needs and the introjection of care details, with the development of confidence on the environment, and must be added that, the element of intellectual understanding with its tremendous implications.

Nonetheless, in borderline cases the analyst does not always wait in vain, that in the course of time the patient becomes able to make use of the psychoanalytic interpretations of the original traumatic projection. It may even happen that he is able to accept what is in the environment as a projection of the simple and stable going-on-being elements that derive from his own inherent potential.

Such that it is necessary to attempt to state briefly what happens to the inherented potential if this is to develop into an infant, and thereafter onto a child reaching towards independent existence, because if the plexuity of the subject such a statement must be made in the assumption of satisfactory material care, which means parental care. Satisfactory parental care can be classified roughly into three overlapping states.

1. Holding.
2. Mother and infant living together, as the father's function (on dealing with the environment for the mother) is not known to the infant
3. Father, mother, and infant, all three living together.

The term 'holding' is used to denote not only the actual physical holding of the infant, but also the total environmental provision prior to the concept of living with. In other words, it refers to a three-dimensional or space relationship (spatiality) with time gradually added. This overlaps with, but initiate prior to, instinctual experiences that in time would determine the object relationships. It includes the management of experiences that are inherent in existence, such as the completion (and therefore, the noncompeting) of processes, such ss the completion and, the noncomcompletion of specific processes which from the outside may seem to be purely physiological but which belong to infant psychology and take place on a complex psychological field, particularly, by determining the awareness and the empathy of the mother.

The term 'living with' implies object relationships, and the emergence of the infant from the state of being merged with the mother, or his perception of objects external to the self.

The paradox is that what is good and bad in the infant's environment is not in fact a projection, but in spite of this it is necessary, if the individual infant is to develop healthily, that everything will seem to him to be a projection. We find omnipotence and the pleasure principle in operation, as they certainly are in earliest infancy; and to this observation we can add that the recognition of a true 'not-me' is a matter of the intellect; it belongs to extreme sophistication and to the maturity of the individual.

In the writings of Freud most of the formulations concerning infancy derive from a study of adults in analysis. At first sight it would seem that a great deal of psychoanalytic theory is about early childhood and infancy, but in one sense Freud can be said to have neglected unfancy as a stare. This is brought out by a footnote in 'Formulations of the Two Principles of Mental Functioning,' of which he shows that he knows he is taking for granted the very things that are under discussion, as in the text he traces the development from the pleasure-principle to the reality-principle, following his usual course of reconstructing the infancy of his adult patients. The note runs as follows:

It will rightly be objected that an organization which was a slave to the pleasure principle and neglected the reality of the external world could not maintain itself alive for the shortest time, so that it could not have come into existence at all. The employment of a fiction like this is. however, justified when one considers that the infant—provided one includes with it the care it receives from its mother—does almost realize a psychical system of this kind.

Freud paid full tribute to the function of maternal care, and it must be assumed that he left this subject alone only because he was not ready to talk about its implications. The note continues:

> It probably hallucinates the fulfilment of its internal needs; it betrays its unpleasure, when there is an increase of stimulus and absence of satisfaction, by the motor discharge of screaming and beating about with its arms and legs, and it then experiences the satisfaction it has hallucinated. Later, as an older child, it learns too employ these manifestations of discharge intentionally for which of methods for expressing its feelings. Since the later care of children is modelled in the care of infants, the dominance of the pleasure principle can really come to an end when a child has achieved complete physical detachment from its parents.

The words: 'provide one includes with it the care it receives from its mother' have of a great importance in the immediate contextual presentation. The infant and the maternal care together from a unit. certainly if one is to study the theory of the parent-infant relationship one must come to a decision about these matters, which concern the real meaning of the word dependence or dependency. It is not enough that it is acknowledged that the environment is important if there is to be a discussion of the theory of the parent-infant relationship, then we are divided into two of the same who do not allow that at the earliest stages the infant and the maternal care belong to each other and cannot be disentangled. These two things, the infant and the maternal case, disentangle and dissociate themselves in health, which means as to do many things, to some extent it means a disentanglement of maternal care from something which we then call the infant, or the beginning of a growing child. This idea is covered by Freud's words at the end of the footnote, explaining that: The dominance of the pleasure principle can really come to an end only when a child has achieved complete physical detachment from its parents.

It is axiomatic in these matters of maternal care of holding variety that when things go well the infant has no means of knowing what is being properly provided and what is being prevented. Such, that when things do not go well that the infant becomes aware, not of the failure of maternal care, but of the results, whatever they may be, of that failure: That in saying, as a result of success in maternal care there is built up in th infant a continuity of being which is the basis of ego strength' of being interrupted by reactions to the consequences of that failure, The resultant of ego-weakening. Such interruptions constitute annihilation, and are evidently associated with pain of psychotic quality and intensity. In the extreme case the infant exists only on the basis of a continuity of reactions to impingement and of recoveries from such reactions. This is in great contras t to the continuity for being that which is our conception of ego strength.

In any individual it is possible to observe different patterns of loving and varieties of object choice, for example, the typical oedipal evolution of the patient traumatized by the primal scene who develops a persistent unconscious rescue fantasy together with a need for a degraded love object. A concomitant persistent wish may be to wreak vengeance upon surrogates for the betraying, unfaithful mother. Furthermore, in response to the fear of castration generated by the anticipation of retaliation for hostile wishes against the father. The same individual may develop a pattern of passive, submissive, feminine orientation toward men. In such a patient a variety of patterns of loving and object choices toward members of both sexes, characterized by patterns of instinctual gratification that represented both aim-inhibited and aim-fulfilled wishes. In derivatives of several types of unconscious fantasies, representing wishes derived from different moments in his relations to the important objects of, his past, the patient identified himself with different objects—his father, his mother the crucified Christ, certain figures from mythology and fairy tales. Each identification found expression in some form of loving. The identifications were the vehicles for drive derivatives, part of an unconscious fantasy of being either the father, the fathers sexual partner, or some conqueror: His patterns of loving relations with both men and women were determined by the nature of the persistent unconscious fantasies. Loving involves identification, but identification at many levels and at many different times with different objects. It is not necessarily a regressive reactivation of the primitive fusion with a love object or regression to a phase where there is no distinction between the self and the object world.

Within the analytic situation closer examination of the phenomenon of love demonstrates how certain aspects of the real person and of the self are rigorously excluded in the sense of oneness. What is experienced is determined by a fantasy or a se t of wishes centring about specific mental representations deriving from selected memories of experiences with the earlier object or objects—the father, the mother, and in the unusual cases, oneself or parts of one's body.

By way of comparison, one may observe another patient, in whom there were several distinct patterns of love relations. He was, first of all, a very successful Don Juan who typically won. Seduced, and then abruptly dropped his partner. The abruptness with which he terminated these relationships was parallel by the urgent intensity with which he pursued them in the beginning. If one concentrated only on the opening phases of his relationships, he would seem to epitomize the romantic ideal of the love-intoxicated, heartsick young swan. In these affairs, however, the culmination of the relationship was represented not by the successful libidinal gratification, but rather by the gratification of aggression directed toward the women, the promiscuous, disappointing oedipal and post-oedipal mother, but also an abandoning nursemaid who had abruptly left the family's employment when the patient was three and a half years of age.

In contrast, the same patient also had long-lasting devoted sexual attachments to older women, relationships that were regularly stormy, but compulsively maintained, remarkably ambivalent and characterized by vehement mutual recriminations. These relationships recapitulated a clandestine affair he had with a housekeeper-nursemaid, an affair that lasted through the oedipal and latency periods and parallelled in time the disillusioning experiences with his mother. The parallel's love relations with older women were sadomasochistic in quality and articulated specific forms of anal-erotic gratification that could be traced to the character of the housekeeper-nursemaid. Residue of this attachment could be seen in the aim-inhibited love relationship he had with his secretary. A much older women, as well as in the nature of his character structure, which reflected an identification with the clandestine lover through the compulsive and behaviour he pursued in identification with her. The active, phallic nature of this women undoubtedly predisposed the patient to make subsequent oedipal and post-oedipal object choices of women who were active and sensual and whose behaviour corresponded to his fantasy of the women possessing a penis. The Don Juan behaviour was multiple, and determined of a mixture of the fulfilment of erotic and aggressive impulses, an identification with the faithless, promiscuous mother, the abandoning love object, together with elements of defence against castration anxiety. while much more could be said about the determinants of the specific and complex patterns of loving in this case, however, it clearly illustrates the complicated interrelationship of identifications, defence, object relations, and instinctual gratification, all of which play a role in determining the nature of the patient's love. It would be impossible to reduce the plexuity of object-finding and gratification to any of the simple basic formulas proposed by several of the proponents of object relations theory.

The subject of identification quite naturally leads to the topic of the internalization of object relations. This is a concept which is very difficult to differentiate from identification. Does it mean more than the fact that the personality or psychic structure of an individual is transformed as the result of his or her interaction with others? Or do internalized object relations imply the positing of a persistent structure in the psychic apparatus which has a dynamic thrust of its own, a thrust to repeat and reproduce the original experience in a way that is independent of the drive representation? Is there a developmental thrust which asserts itself along predetermined lines through a hierarchical distinction in stages, beginning with the earliest relation and progressing toward an ideal endpoint, commonly known as the mature or genital form of object relationships, which presumably leads to the "highest" stage of love? The discoursing dialogue concerning the internalization as to the object relations theory and love, it seems that this developmental eventuality is considered as the 'sine qua non" of true love.

It would seem that, however surreptitiously, elements of value judgements infiltrate analytic considerations of love. this is a trend which can be traced to the early history of psychoanalysis. It is difficult to avoid a tendency to judge psychological phenomena in terms that essentially mean "good" or "bad". Some such tendency may be discerned in Abraham's (1924) study of the development of the libido. Abraham evaluated the nature of love relationships in terms of biology. The quality of the libidinal tie with any individual, he maintained, is determined by the level of psychosexual development which it reflects the development of sexuality evolved in precise stages and subdivisions by way of a normal, orderly succession of dominance by oral, and phallic instinctual drives. The nature of the object chosen was determined by the drive dominant at that particular stage when the choice was made. The highest stage of development, the mature form of love, was genital love. By way of contrast, choices effected at the pregenital level, Abraham considered the pre-ambivalent or ambivalent, a quality which offered poor prognostic outcome because it conveyed the potentiality for conflict and neurosogenesis. genital love, in it post-ambivalent form, and typified, no t at all surprising, in those qualities which society regards as both desirable and commendable in the relationship between two people of the opposite sex. To be sure, these qualities have unquestioned social utility, in so far as they strengthen the ties which make for a stable marriage and foster the solidarity of the family, the basic unit of society. from society's point of view an ideal post-ambivalent genital relationship is desirable, useful, and therefore "good."

Today, more than half a century later, the terminology and leading conceptualizations may have changed, but the problem remains the same. Formulations are now couched in terms of object relations instead of biology. The distinctions between the self and the object world have become the touchstones. Instead of an orderly, biological predetermined succession of libidinal stages, what is emphasized today is the developmental evolution of an orderly set of stages of object relations.

According to Friedman (1978), this process is considered by many to be equally predetermined as an inexorable developmental thrust, much in the same spirit as Abraham's formulation concerning libidinal phases and the concomitant object choices. While Abraham emphasized the developmental aspects of libidinal drive over the nature and vicissitudes of experience with the object, more recent formulations in terms of object relations theory tended to emphasize the vicissitudes of experience with the object, as well as the resultant cognitive and affective consequences. Thus, certain authors maintain that true love is possible only by culture. In our daily work with patient's, we are constantly passing judgement on whether the patient" s affective response is in keeping with, i.e., appropriate to, of his or her experience. We make such judgements in terms of standards relevant to our culture and to the individual's background. Cultural ambience influences not only how love is expressed, but also how it is experienced. the cultural influence may transcend the specific set of interactions characteristic of the relation s with the infantile love object. The fusion of the tender and the sensuous steams of the libidinal impulse and the idealization of the love object is a notion that was canonized during the romantic period. it is not always the model for the choice of a partner; and even today, it represents a notion as often honoured in the breach as in the observance. Other times and other levels of society had, in fact, institutionalized the distinction between these various components of what we call "being in love." they have done so by distinction of marriage, customs, property arrangements, and sanctioned extramarital liaisons. There have been and still are many polygamous societies. The significance of institutionalisms practice of predominant social patterns for courtship and for choosing a mate can hardly be lost on the younger members of our society. "Love at first sight," "falling head over heels in love," "loving in despair, from afar," "the attraction of the unattainable object." All represent styles of experiencing and expressing love. They are styles that had their ascendancy and decline. in yesteryear, the idealization of the love object and its public expression were encouraged by social norms.

Nonetheless, we face a dilemma. One contributor to the psychology of love from the point of view of object relations that love represents a re-emergence of the earliest, mo t primitive mother-child relationship. While another asserts that love reflects the most developed, most mature form of object relations.

All the same, as analysts, we pass judgement on the phenomenology of love we observe in our patients, we do so in terms of phase-specific anticipations, for example, we accept but hardly ever really analyze reports of impulsive patterns of loving that patients present concerning the adolescent scene. We relate this to the clearly patient psychological transformations of puberty, as we may look disapprovingly at the middle-aged man, and certainly at an elderly man, who falls in love following the adolescent pattern. In the same spirit, one has to note the social bias against older women having liaison with younger men; the reverse pattern is more acceptable. these are subtle, but definitive value judgements as couched in term s of normal, that is, statistical anticipations. Unconsciously, they dictate to us what and how we choose to analyze.

In actual practice we are concerned with what has keep a particular patient to love in her or his particular way; how, among the myriad patterns of love, the patient has come to select the one he or she actually did choose. How well we are able to determine this depends in large measure upon how close the distance is between the choice of object and the pattern of loving, and the central nexus of the patient's unconscious conflicts. the consequence of conflict make it possible for us to analyze the nature of the love relationship, but in those instances in which the pattern of loving is ego-syntonic, but have less of an opportunity to penetrate deeply into the psychology of loving and are therefore, not in a very good position to grasp some understanding of the precursors of the particular patterns of loving. Under such circumstances, the temptation is greatly interpretive, as only to speculate phenomenologically than dynamically. What we do, in effect, is conjecture on the bias of history about what might have been the individuals psychological experience, since we seem unable to trace out the interpretational inferentially from the data in the dynamic context of the analytic situation.

In practice, we deal with how the individual comes to choo s someone to love and how this love is expressed. This is a complex process involving the integration of the individual's total experience. I t is usually organized in terms of a few leading, unconscious fantasies which dominate an individual's inherent perceptions of the world and create the mental set by which she or he perceives and interpret their individual experience.

The existing stage during which there is no differentiation between the self and the object, of which appeals to those who view a good segment of psycho pathology as reflecting a "loss of boundaries", that, between the self and the object. Often associations for being in love as well as with loss of the sense of self of or of "boundaries" the overwhelming sense of time, that from detailed presentations on the material derivatives, is that of the sensations as warranted within the paradigms of the "timelessness" of an unconscious continuum. It should be noted that feeling at one with something, being completely identified with someone, thinking that someone experiences and feels everything that another person seems to feel, is not necessarily a recapitulation of the vague, undefined state that precedes the distinction between the self and the object world.

According to Freud and Abraham, the fundamental process in melancholia is the loss of the loved object. The real loss of a real object, or some similar situation having the same significance, resulting in the object becoming installed within the ego. Owing, however, to an excess of cannibalistic impulses in the subject, this introjection miscarries and the consequence is illness.

Now, why is it that the process of introjection is so specific for melancholia? Perhaps, that the main difference between incorporation in paranoia and in melancholia is connected with changes in the relation of the subject to the object, though it is also a question of a change in the constitution of the introjecting ego. But, according to Edward Glover, the ego, at first but loosely organized, consists of a considerable number of ego-nuclei. In his view, in the first place an oral ego-nucleus and later an oral ego-nucleus predominates over the other. In this ver y early phase, in which oral sadism plays a prominent part and which it seems the basis of schizophrenia, the ego's power of identifying itself with its objects is as yet small, partly because it is itself still uncoordinated and partly because the introjected objects are still mainly partial objects, which it equates with fæces.

In paranoia the characteristic defences are chiefly aimed at annihilating the "persecutor," while anxiety on the ego's account occupies a prominent place in the picture. As the ego becomes more fully organized, the internalized imagos will approximate more closely to reality and the ego will identify itself more fully with "good" objects. The dread of persecution, which was at first felt on the ego's account, now relates to the good object as well and from now on preservation of the good object is regarded as synonymous with the survival of the ego.

The combinality with this development goes a change of the highest importance, namely, from a partial object-relation to the relation to a complete object, through this step the ego arrives at a new position, which forms the foundation of that situation called the "loss of the love object." Not until the object is loved as a whole can it loss be felt as a whole.

With this change in the relation to the object, new anxiety-contents make their appearance and a change takes place in the mechanisms of defence. The development of the libido also is decisively influenced. Paranoid anxiety, lest the objects sadistically destroyed should themselves be a source of poison and danger inside the subject's body, causing him, in that, in spite of the vehemence of his oral-sadistic onslaughts, at the same time to be profoundly mistrustful of them yet, incorporating them.

This leads to a weakening of oral fixations. One manifestation of this may be observed in the difficulties very young children often show in regard to eating, which, in all probability, have a paranoid root. As a child (or an adult) identifies himself more fully with a good object. The libidinal urges increase as he develops a greedy love and desire to devour this object and the mechanism of introjection is reinforced. Besides, he finds himself constantly impelled to repeat the incorporation of a good object partly because he dreads that he has forfeited it by his cannibalism—i.e., the repetition of the act is designed to test the reality of his fears of the internalized persecutors against whom he requires a good object to help him. Nonetheless, the ego is more than ever driven both by love and by the need to introject the object.

When the analysis progressed and distrust in the analyst had diminished as the patient became very much concerned about the him. He had always worried about his mother's health, but he had not been able to develop real love toward her, though he did his best to please her. Now, together with the concern for therapist, strong feelings of love and gratitude came to the fore, together with feelings of unworthiness, sorrow and depression. The patient had never felt really happy, his depression had been spread out, one might say, over his whole life, but he had not suffered from actual depressive states. In hi s analysis he went through phantasies of deep depression with all the symptoms characteristic of this state of mind. Yet, the feelings and phantasies connected with his hypochondriacal pains changed. For instance, the patient felt anxiety that the cancer would.

Wherever a state of depression exists, be it in normal, the neurotic, in manic-depression o in mixed cases, there is always in this specific grouping of anxieties, distressed feelings and different varieties of the defences. If this point of view proves correct, should be able to understand those very frequent cases where we are presented with a picturer of mixed paranoiac and depressive trends, since we could then isolate the various elements of which it is composed.

The considering aspects about the depressive states may lead us to a better understanding of the still rather enigmatic reaction of suicide. According to the findings of Abraham and James Glover, a suicide is directed against the introjected object. but, while in committing suicide the ego intends to murder its bad objects, that is to say, that it alway aims at saving its loved objects, internal or external. To put it shortly; in some cases the phantasies underlying suicide aim at preserving the internalization of good objects and that part of the ego which is identified with good objects, and also at destroying the other part of the ego which is identified with the bad object and the id. Thus, the ego is enabled to become united with its loved object.

Freud has stated that mania has for its basis the same contents as melancholia and is, in fact, a way of escape from that state. That is to suggest, that in mania and ego seeks refuge not only from melancholia but also from a paranoiac condition which it is unable to master. Its torturing and perilous dependence on its loved objects drives the ego to find freedom. In that, its identification with these objects is too profound to b e renounced. On the other hand, the ego is pursued by its dread of bad objects and the id and, in its effort to escape from all these miseries. It has recourse to many different mechanism as, some of which, since they belong to different phases of develop phases of development, are mutually incompatible.

In the sense of omnipotence, is what, first and foremost characterizes mania and, further (as Helene Deutsch has stated) mania is bases on the mechanism of denial, as Helene Deutsch in the following point. She holds this "denial" is connected with the phallic phase and the castration complex (in girls it is a denial of the lack of the penis)"; which observations have led to conclude that this mechanism of denial originates in that every early phase which the development of denial endeavours to defend itself from the most overpowering and profound anxiety of all its dread of internalized persecutors and the id. That is to say, that which is first of all denied is psychic reality and the ego may then go on to deny a great deal of external reality.

We know that scotomization may lead to the subject's becoming entirely cut off from reality, and to his complete inactivity. In mania, however, denial is associated with an overactivity, although this excess of activity, as Helen e Deutsch points out, often bears no relation to any actual results achieved. Hence is to explain that in this state the source of the conflict is that the ego is unwilling and unable to renounce its goo internal objects and yet endeavour to escape from the perils of dependence on them as well as from its bad objects. its attempt to detach itself from an object as well as from its bad objects. It s attempt to detach itself from bad objects is without the same time of its completion. It is renounced, but it seems to be conditioned by an increase in the ego's own strength it seems in this compromise by denying the importance of its good objects and also the dangers with which it is a menace from its bad object and the id. All and all, it endeavours ceaselessly to master and control of it s objects, and the evidence of this effort is its hyperactivity

Implications that ego identity is the highest level organization of the world of object relations in the broadest sense, and also of the self. This is a very complex development, because while object relations are continuously internalized (as such internalization take place at gradually higher, more differentiated levels). At the same time, the internalized object relations are "depersonified" (Jacobson, 1964) and integrated into higher level ego and Superego structures such as the "ego ideal," character constellations, and autonomous ego functions. Simultaneously, with these processes of internalization and depersonification, internalized object relations are also organized into persistent object images which come to represent internally the external world as experience by the developing ego, which corresponds roughly to what Sandler and Rosenblatt (1962) have called the "representational world." It has to be stressed, however, that this internal world of objects such as seen in conscious, preconscious and unconscious fantasies never reproduced the actual world of real people with whom the individual has established relationships in the past and in the present; it is at most an approximation, always strongly influenced by the very early object images of introjection and identifications. It should be noted, however, it is also, that the "world of inner objects, as used by Klein, which gives the impression of remaining as free floating object images in the psychic apparatus rather than being related to any specific structures, does not do justice to the complexity of integration of object relations, organization of object images takes place both in the object relationships. Organization of object images takes place both in the sector of depersonified ego structures and in the sector of developing identity. Such object images which remain relatively unmodified, the repressed unconscious are less affected by structuralization; in this sense very primitive, distorted object images certainly continue to exist in the unconscious mind. Nevertheless, by far, the greater part of internalized object images is normally integrated into higher level structure, and those which remain as object representations experience important, modifications over the years were under the influence of ego growth and later object relationships. The normal outcome of identity formation is that identifications are gradually replaced by selective, partial, sublimatory identification, in which only those aspects of object relations are internalized to which are in harmony with the individual identity formation.

Actually, the enrichment of one's personal life by the internal presence of such selective, partial identifications representing people who are loved and admired in a realistic way without indiscriminate internalization, constitutes a major source of emotional depth and well being. The normal process of individualization is marked by the shift from identifications to partial, sublimated identifications under the influence of a well-integrated ego identity. One might say, that depersonification of internalized object relations, reshaping of part of them so that they come to resemble more then the real objects, and individualization are closely relate processes.

The world of inner objects, then, gradually changes and comes closer to the "external" perceptions of the reality of significant objects throughout childhood and later life, without ever becoming an actual copy of the environmental world. "Confirmation," intrapsychically speaking, is the ongoing process of reshaping the world of inner objects under the influence of the reality principle, of ego maturation and development, and through the cycle of projection and introjection. The persistence of "non-metabolized" early introjection is the outcome of a pathological fixation of severely disturbed, early object relationships. A fixation which is intimately related to the pathological development of splitting that which interferes with the integration of self and object images and the depersonification of internalized object relationships in general. Under the pathological circumstances, early, non-integrated object images come to the surface; but even then, as is being stressed throughout, as we never do have "free-floating" internal objects but are always confronted with the specific ego structures which they have crystalized.

Keeping in mind, our reservations about the concept of the "representational world" as a close reproduction of the external world of objects, we might say, that ego identity is the highest level of organizational presentations of the world of object relations in the broadest sense and comprises the concept of the representational world and that of the self on the other.

The concept of instinct, Freud defines as a stimulus; a stimulus not arising in the outer world but "from within the organism," he adds that a better term for an instinctual stimulus is a "need," and says further, that such 'stimuli are the signs of an external world." Freud lays explicit stress on one fundamental implication of his whole consideration of instinct, is, namely that it implies the concept of purpose in the form of what he calls a biological postulate. This postulate runs as follows: The nervous system is an apparatus which has the function of getting rid of the stimuli that reaches it, or of reducing them to the lowest possible level. An instinct is a stimulus from within reaching the nervous system. Since an instinct is a stimulus arising within the organism and acting "always as a constant force," it obliges the nervous system to renounce its ideal intention of keeping off stimuli and compels it "to undertake involved and interconnected activities by which the external world is so changed as to afford satisfaction to the internal source of stimulation.

As instinct brings an inner stimulus reaching the nervous apparatuses, the object of an instinct is "the thing in regard to which or through which the instinct is able to achieve its aim. This aim for being sufficiently satisfactory as convincing properties are adequately satisfied. Nonetheless, the object of an instinct is further described as "what is most variable about an instinct", "not originally connected with it," and as becoming "assigned to it, only in consequence for being peculiarly fitted to make satisfaction possible." It is here that we see instinctual drives being conceived of as "intrapsychic," or originally not related to objects.

In the later of Freud's writings, he gradually moves away from this position. Instincts are no longer define as (inner) stimuli which the nervous apparatuses' deals in accordance with the scheme of the reflex arc, but instinct as found, in, "Beyond the Pleasure Principle," is seen as "an urge inherent in organic life to restore an earlier state of things which the living entity has been obliged to abandon under the pressure of external disturbing forces. He defines instinct in terms equivalent to the terms he used earlier in describing the function of the nervous apparatuses itself. The nervous apparatuses, the "living entity" in its interchange with "external disturbing forces." Instinct is no longer an intrapsychic stimulus but, an expression of the function of the "urge" of the nervous apparatuses to deal with the environment. The intimate and fundamental relationship of instinct s, especially in so far as libido (sexual instinct, Eros) is concerned with objects is more clearly brought out in "The Problem of Anxiety," until originally, in "An Outline of Psychoanalysis," "the aim of the first of these basic instincts [Eros] is to establish ever greater unities and to preserve them thus—in short, to bind together." It is worthy of note, that the relatedness to objects is implicit; the aim of the instinct Eros is no longer formulated in terms of a contentless 'satisfaction," or satisfaction in the sense of abolishing stimuli, but the aim is clearly seen in terms of integration. it is "to bind together." And while Freud feels that it is possible to apply his earlier formula, "to the effect that instinct tended toward a return to an earlier [inanimate] state, to the destructive or death instinct," we are unable to apply the formula to Eros (the love instinct).

The basic concept Instinct has thus changed its contentual representation, since Freud wrote, "Instincts and Their Vicissitudes." In his later writings he does not take as his starting point and model the reflex-arc scheme of a self-contained, closed system, but bases his considerations on a much broader, more modern biological framework. And it should be clear from the last quotation that it is by no means the ego alone to which he assigns the function of no synthesis, of binding together. Eros, one of the two basic instincts, is itself an integrating force. This is in accordance with his concept of primary narcissism as first formulated in "On Narcissism: an Introduction," and further elaborated in his later writings, in, "Civilization and Its Discontents," where objects, reality, are far from being originally not connected with libido, and, are seen as becoming gradually differentiated from a primary narcissistic identity of "inner" and "outer" worlds. Nonetheless, one of Freud's proudest achievements was the transformation of the therapeutic relationship which takes place in psychoanalysis into a tool of scientific investigation. Freud also believed that "the future will probably attribute far greater importance to psychoanalysis as the science of the unconscious than as a therapeutic procedure (Freud, 1926).

You may question whether such a wide variety of differing symptomatic syndromes can be brought together under a single heading. If we consider the issue not in terms of presenting symptoms but in terms of the similar nature of their object relationships, we find many threads united these seemingly disparate disorders.

But, in actual practice we are concerned with what has kept a particular patient to love in her in his particular way; how, among the myriad patterns of love, the patient has come to select the one he or she actually did choose. How well we are able to determine this depends in large measure upon how close the distance is between the choice of an object and the pattern of loving, and the central nexus of the patient's unconscious conflicts. the consequences of conflict make it possible for us to analyze the nature of the love relationship, but in those instances in which the pattern of loving is ego-syntonic, but have less of an opportunity to penetrate deeply into the psychology of loving and are therefore, not in a very good position to grasp some understanding of the precursors of the particular patterns of loving. Under such circumstances, the temptation is greatly interpretive, as only to speculate phenomenologically than dynamically. What we do, in effect, is conjecture on the bias of history about what might have been the individuals psychological experience, since we seem unable to trace out the interpretational inferentially from the data in the dynamic context of the analytic situation.

Having interpreted the hysterical and paranoid technique in terms of the acceptance and rejection of objects, we can now obtain interesting results by applying a similar interpretation to the phobic and obsessional techniques. The conflict underlying the phobic state may be concisely formulated as one between flight to the object

835

and flight from the object. In the former case, is, of course, the object is accepted, whereas, in the latter case the object is rejected. In both cases, the object is treated as external, in the obsessional state, the conflict presents itself as one between the exclusion and the rejection of content. In this case, accordingly, both the accepted and the rejected objects are treated as internal. If in the case of the phobic state both the accepted and the rejected objects are treated as external and in the obsessional state both are treated as internal, the situation as regarding these hysterical and paranoid states is that one of these objects is treated as an externalized object and the other as an internalized object, in the hysterical state. It is the accepted object that is externalized, and the paranoid state, the object which is externalized is the rejected object.

The chief features of the stage of transition between infantile and adult dependence may now be briefly summarized. The transition period is characterized by a process of development, whereby object—relationships based upon identification gradually give place to relationships with differentiated objects. Satisfactory development during this period, therefore, depends upon the success which attends the process of differentiation of the object, and this in turn depends upon the issue of a conflict or separation from the object—a situation which is both desire d and feared. The conflict in question may call into operation any or all characteristic techniques—the obsessional, the paranoid, the hysterical and the phobic: and, if object—relationships are unsatisfactory, these techniques are liable to form the basis of characteristic psychopathological developments in later life. The various techniques cannot be classified in any order corresponding to presumptive levels of libidinal development. On the contrary, they must be regarded as alternative techniques, all belonging to the same stage in the development of object-relationships. Which of the techniques is employed, or to what extent each is employed would appear to depend on large measure upon the nature of the object-relationships established during the preceding stage of infantile dependence. In particular, it would seem to depend upon the degree which have been established between the developing ego and its internalized objects.

The infant is completely dependent upon his object not only for his existence and physical well-being, but also for the satisfaction of his psychological needs. It is true, nonetheless, that mature individuals are likewise dependent upon one another for the satisfaction of their psychological, and, no less than their physical, needs. Nevertheless, on the psychological side, the dependence of mature individuals sufficient to render him dependent in an unconditional sense. We also notice that, whereas in the case of the adult object-relationship has a considerable spread, in the case of the infant it tends to be focussed upon a single object. The loss of an object is thus, much more devastating in the case of the infant. If a mature individual loses an object, least of mention, he still has some objects remaining. His eggs are not all in one basket. Further, he has a choice of objects and can desert one for another. The infant, on the other hand, has no choice. He has no alternative but to accept or to reject his object—an alternative which is liable to present itself to him as a choice between life and death. His psychological dependence is further accentuated by the very nature of his object-relationship, for, as we have seen, this is based essentially upon identification. Dependence is exhibited in its most extreme form, in the intra-uterine state, and we may legitimately infer that on its psychological side this state is characterized by an absolute degree of identification. Identification may thus be regarded as representing the persistence into extra-uterine life of a relationship existing before birth. In so far as, identification persists after birth, the individual's object constitutes not only his world, but also himself; and it is this fac t, as has already been pointed out, that we must attribute the compulsive attitude of many schizoids and de repressive individuals toward their objects.

Normal development is characterized by a process whereby progressive differentiations of the object is accompanied by progressive decreases in identification. So long as infantile dependence persists, however, identification remains the most characteristic feature of the individual's emotional relationship with his object. Infantile dependence is equivalent to oral dependence—a fact which should be interpreted, not in the sens that the infant is inherently oral, but in the sense that the breast is the original object. During the oral phases, accordingly, identification remains the most characteristic feature of the individual's emotional relationship with his object. The tendency to identification, which is so characteristic of emotional relationships during these phases, also invade s the cognitive sphere, with the result that certain orally fixated individuals have only to hear of someone else suffering from any given disease in order to believe that they are suffering from it themselves. In the conative sphere, that identification has its counterpart in oral incorporation. And it is the merging of emotional identification with oral incorporation that confers upon the stage of infantile dependence its most distinctive feature. These features are based upon the fundamental equivalence for the infant of being held in his mother's arms and incorporating the contents of her breast.

The phenomenon of narcissism, which is one of the most prominent characteristics of infantile dependence, is an attitude arising out of identification with the object. Such that primary narcissism may be simply defined as just such a state of identification with the object, secondary narcissism being a state of identification with an object which is internalized. While narcissism is a feature common to both the early and the late oral phase, the latter phase differs from the former in virtue of a change in the nature of the object. In the early oral phase the natural object is the breast; but in the later oral phase, the natural object becomes the mother. The transition from one phase to the other is thus marked by the substitution of a whole object (or person) for a part-object. Nevertheless, the object continues to be treated as a part-object (the breast) with the result that the person of the mother becomes an object for incorporation. The transition from the early to the late oral phases are also characterized by the emergence of the biting tendency. Whereas in the early oral phase the libidinal attitude of incorporation monopolizes the field, in the late oral phase it is in competing with an accompanying attitude of biting. Now biting must be regarded for being essentially of all differentiated aggression. Consequently, the dawn of the late oral phase heralds the emergence of emotional ambivalence. The late oral phase is well described as pre-ambivalent. Nonetheless, one which aggression has not yet been differentiated from the libido. The early urge to incorporate is essentially a libidinal urge, to which true aggression makes no contribution, even as a component factor. The recognition of this fact is of the very greatest importance for an understanding of the essential problem underlying schizoid states, it is understanding. It is true that the incorporation urge is destructive in its gross effect, in the sense that the object which is eaten disappears. Nevertheless, the urge is not destructive in aim. When, as a child says that he 'loves' cake, it is certain to imply that the cake will vanish, and then consumingly destroyed. At the same time the destruction of the cake is not the aim of the child's 'love'. On the contrary, the disappearance of the cake is, from the child's point of view. A most regrettable consequence of his 'love' for it. What he really desires, is for himself, is to have his cake and eat it to. If the cake proves to be 'bad' he either spits it out or is sick. As this spiting out is specifically characteristic of the early oral phase, in that he rejects the bad cake, least of mention, he does not bite the cake with intentions for its being bad. This type of behaviour is specifically characterized of the early oral phasing, then, what is, so far as the object presents itself as 'good', it is incorporated, and, presents itself as 'bad', it is rejected, but, even when it appears to be bad, no attempt is made to destroy it. Again, it is the good object that is 'destroyed.' Albeit only incidentally and not by intention. In the late oral phase the situation is foreign, in that things are done differently, for in this phase the object may be bitten as well as incorporated. This mean that a direct aggression, as well as libidinal forces, are such that may be directed toward the object. Hence the appearance of the ambivalence which characterizes the late oral phase.

It soon becomes evident that the emotional oral phase takes the form of the alternative, that to incorporate or not to incorporate, i.e., 'to love or not to love.' This is the conflict underlying the depressive state. It will be seen, accordingly, that the problem of the schizoid individual is how to love without destroying by love, whereas, the greater of problems is for the depressive individual, is how to love without destroying by hate. These are two very different problems.

The conflict underlying the schizoid state is, of course, much more devastating than the conflict underlying the depressive stat e, and, since the schizoid reaction has its roots in an earlier stage of development than the depressive reaction, the schizoid individual is less capable of dealing with conflict than is the depressive. It is owing to these two facts that the disturbance of the personality found in schizophrenia is so much more profound than found in depression. The devastating nature of the conflict associated with the early oral phase lies in the fact that, if it seems a terrible thing for an individual to destroy his object by love. It is the great tragedy of the schizoid individual that it is his love which seems to destroy; and it is because his love seems so destructive that he experiences such difficulty in directing his libido toward objects outer reality. He becomes afraid to love, and therefore he erects barriers between his objects and himself. He tends both to keep his objects at a distance and to make himself remote from them. He rejects his objects, and at the same time, he withdraws his libido from them. This withdrawal of libidinal energies may be carried to all lengths. It may be carried to a point at which all emotional and physical contacts with other persons are renounced; and it may even go so far that all libidinal links with outer reality are surrendered, all interest in the world around fades and everything becomes meaningless. In proportion as libido is withdrawn from outer objects it is directed toward the internalization with its accompanied objects; and in proportion as this happens, the individual becomes introverted. And, incidentally, it is on the observation that this process of introversion is co characteristic on the onset of schizoid states that are themselves based on the conclusion that the introvert is essentially a schizoid. It is essentially in inner reality that the values of the schizoid are to be found. So far as he is concerned, the world of internalized objects is always encroaching upon the world of external objects; and in proportion as this happens his real objects become lost to him.

If loss of the real objects were the only trauma of the schizoid state the position of the schizoid individual would not be so precarious. It is necessary, nonetheless, to bear in mind the vicissitudes of the ego, which accompany loss of the object. Reference has already been made to the narcissism which results from an excessive libidinalization of internalized objects; and such narcissism is specially characteristic of the schizoid. Accompanying it, we invariably find an attitude of superiority which may manifest itself in consciousness to a varying degree as an actual sense of superiority. It should be of note, in that, this attitude of superiority is based upon an orientation toward internalized objects, and that in relation to objects in the world of outer reality the attitude of the schizoid is essentially one of inferiority. It is true, that the externally oriented inferiority may be masked by a façade of superiority, as based upon an identification of external with internalized objects. Nevertheless, it is invariably present, and it is evidence of a weakness in the ego. what chiefly compromises the development of the ego. In the case of the schizoid individual is the apparently insoluble dilemma which attends the direction of libido toward objects. Failure to direct libido toward the object is, of course, equivalent to loss of the object: But since, from the point of view of the schizoid, the libido is itself destructive, the object is equally lost when libido is directed toward it. It can thus readily be understood that, if the dilemma becomes sufficiently pronounced, the result is a complete impasse, which reduces the ego onto a state of utter impotence. The ego becomes quite incapable of expressing itself; and, in so far as this is so, its very existence become s compromised. This can be exemplified by the following, as: 'I can't say anything. 'I have nothing to say' I'm empty'. 'There's nothing of me,' . . . 'I feel quite useless' 'I haven't done anything,'"I've gone cold and hard' 'I don't feel anything' . . . 'I can't express myself' 'I feel futile.' Such descriptions are well illustrated, not only the state of impotence to which the ego is compromised in the schizoid dilemma. The last quoted remark of this is, perhaps, as drawing attentions to the characteristic affect of the schizoid state: For the characteristic affect of the schizoid state is undoubtedly a sense of futility.

The libido may be withdrawn in varying degrees even from that part of the psyche which is, so to speak, nearest to external objects. It may be withdrawn from the realm of the conscious into the unconscious. When this occasions, the effect is as if the ego itself had withdrawn into the unconscious: But the actual position would seem to be that, when the libido deserts the conscious part of the ego (such as it is), the unconscious part of the ego is all that is left to behave as a functioning ego. In extreme cases the libido would seem to desert even the unconscious part of the ego and relapse into the primal id, leaving both surface only the picture with which Kraepelin has familiarize us in his account of the last phase of dementia præcox. Whether such a mass-withdrawal of the libido can properly be ascribe d to repression is a debatable question, although where the process is restricted to a withdrawal from object-relationships, it may give that impression. At any rate, the effectual withdrawal of the libido 'feels quite different' from that of simple repression. There can be no doubt, nonetheless, that withdrawal of the libido from the conscious part of the ego has the effect of relieving emotional tension and mitigating the danger of violent outbursts of precipitate action. There can be equally little doubt that much of the schizoid individual's anxiety really represents fear of such outbursts occurring. This fear commonly manifests itself as a fear of going insane or as a fear of imminent disaster. It is possible, therefore, that massive withdrawal of the libido has the significance of as desperate effort on the part of an ego threatened with repression of the basic impulse which urge the individual on to make emotional contacts. In the case of the schizoid, of course, these impulses are essentially oral impulses. It is when this effort is within measurable distance of succeeding that the individual begins to tell us that he feels as if there were nothing of him, or as if he had los t his identity, or as if he were dead, or as if he had ceased to exist. The fact is that in renouncing the libido the ego renounces the very form of energy which holds it together—and the ego thus becomes lost. Loss of the ego is the ultimate psychopathological disaster which the schizoid individual is constantly struggling, with more or less success, too avert by exploiting all available techniques (including the transitional techniques) for the control of his libido. In essence, therefore, the schizoid state is not a defence, although evidence of the presence of defences may be detected in it. It represented the major disaster which may befall the individual who has failed to outgrow the early stage of dependence.

If the problem which confronts the individual in the early oral phase is how to love the object without destroying it by love, the problem which confronts the individual in the oral phase is how to love the object without destroying it by hate. Accordingly, since the depressive reaction has its roots in the late oral phase, It is the disposal of his hate, rather than the disposal of his love, that constitutes the difficulty of the depressive individual. The formidable as this difficulty is, the depressive is at any rate spared the devastating experience of feeling that his love is bad. Since his love, at any rate, seems good, he remains inherently capable of a libidinal relationship with outer objects in a sense in which the schizoid is not. his difficulty in maintaining such a relationship arises out of his ambivalence. This ambivalence in turn arises out of the fact that during the late oral phase, he was more successful than the schizoid in substituting direct aggression (biting) for simple rejection of the object. While his aggression has been differentiated, that, nonetheless, he has failed in some degree to achieve that further step in development which is represented by dichotomy of the object. This further step, had he taken it, would have enabled him to dispose of his hate by directing it, predominantly at least, towards the rejected object and he would have been left free to direct toward his accepted object love which was relatively unaccompanied by hate. In so far as he failed to take such a step, the depressive remains in that state which characterized his attitude toward his object during the late oral phase. His external object during that phase, of course, a whole object (his mother); and his libidinal attitude toward it was incorporative. The incorporated object to the depressive thus comes to be an undivided whole object, which he adopts an ambivalent attitude. The presence of such an inner situation is less disabling so far as outer adjustments are concerned than is the corresponding inner situation, in the case of the schizoid, for in the case of the depressive there is no formidable barrier obstructing the outward flow of libido. Consequently, the depressive individual readily establishes libidinal contacts with others; and, if his libidinal contact with others appear satisfactory with others, and if his libidinal contacts are satisfactory to him, his progress through life may appear fairly smooth, as the inner situation is always present, and it is readily reactivated if his libidinal relationships becomes disturbed. Any such disturbance if his libidinal relationships become disturbed, such disturbances immediately calls into operation the hating element in his ambivalent t attitude; and, when his hate becomes directed toward the internalized object, a depressive reaction supervene s any frustration in object-relationships is, of course, functionally equivalent to loss of the object. Whether partial or complete, since severe depression is so common a sequel to actual loss of the object (whether by the death of a loved person or things as severally otherwise). Loss of the object must be regarded as the essential trauma which provokes the depressive state.

Physical injury or illness is obviously represents himself, that is to any, that such a loss, e.g., the loss of an eye or a limb, represent the symbolic castration as taken that we no further, for it still remains to be explained why a reaction which is characteristically provoked by loss of the object should also b e provoked by loss of par t of the body. the true explanation lies in the fact that the depressive individual still remains to a be a distinctive feature of degrees to an actual state of infantile identification with his object. To him, is, therefore, bodily loss is functionally equivalent to loss of the object, and this equivalence is reinforced by the presence of an internalized object which, so speak, suffuses the individual's body and imparts it to narcissistic value.

A brief dispositional representation as the presentation for which of 'narcissism', is to mean, that the cathexis of the own 'self' with libido, is used in the term 'self' because the state of primary narcissism exists only prior to any ego differentiation, a point made by Hartmann. What is called the secondary narcissism is the late return of object cathexis to the own person.

There still remains to be explained is the phenomenon of involutional melancholia. According to Freud and Abraham, the functional process in melancholia is the loss of the loved objects, the real, or some similar situation having the same significance, result in the object becoming installed within the ego. Owing, however, to an excess of cannibalistic impulses in the object, this introjection miscarries and the consequence is illness.

All the same, are those who tend to regard the etiology of this condition as entirely different from that of 'reactive depression', nonetheless, the two conditions have sufficiencies in common clinical standpoints, to justify, as to invoke the principle of, 'entia non sunt multicanda præter necessitate.' It is not really melancholia is by definition closely associated with the climacteric; and the climacteric would seem to be in itself evidence of a definite waning of libidinal urges. It cannot be said, nonetheless, that there is any equivalent diminution of aggression. The balance between the libidinal and the aggressive urges is thus disturbed, and, further, It is disturbed in the same direction as when the hate of any ambivalent individual is activated by loss of the object. Accordingly, in an individual of the depressive type the climacteric has the effect of establishing the same situation as does actual loss of the object where object-relationships are concerned; and the result is a depressive reaction. If the prospect of recovery in the case of involutional melancholia is less hopeful than in cases of reactive depression, This is not difficult to explain: For, whereas the latter case a libido is still available for a restoration of the balance in the former case, it is not. Involutional melancholia is thus seen to conform to the general configuration of the depressive state, and it imposes upon as holding of no necessity to modify the conclusion already envisaged—that loss of the object is the basic trauma underlying the depressive state. As in the case of the schizoid state, this state is not a defence, on the contrary, it is a state against which the individual seeks to defend himself by means of such techniques (including the transitional techniques) as are available for the control of his aggression. It represents the major disaster which may befall the individual who failed to outgrow the late oral stage of infantile dependance.

We find ourselves confronted with two basic psychopathological conditions, each arising out of a failure in the past of the individual to establish a satisfactory object-relationship during the period of infantile dependence. the first of these conditions, by which the schizoid state, is associated with an unsatisfactory object-relationships during the early oral phase; and the second of these conditions, stem from or are directed in the depressive state, is associated with an unsatisfactory object-relationship during the early oral phase. It emerges quite clearly, however, from the analysis of both schizoid and depressive individuals that unsatisfactory object-relations hips during the early and late oral phases, only give rise to their characteristic psychopathological effects when object-relationships continue to be unsatisfactory during the succeeding years of early childhood. The schizoid and depressive states must, accordingly, be regarded as dependent upon a regressive reactivation, during early childhood of situations arising, respectively, during the early and late oral phases. The traumatic situation in either case is one in which the child feels that he is not really loved. If the phase in which infantile object-relationships have been pre-eminent, this phase in which infantile object-relationships have been pre-eminently unsatisfactory, is the early oral phase, this trauma provides in the child a reaction conforming to the idea that he is not loved because his own love is bad and destructive, and this reaction provides the basis for a subsequent schizoid tendency. If, the phase in which infantile object-relationships have been pre-eminently unsatisfied, as to a later idea that he is not loved because he presents of his badness and destructiveness, in that he is not loved because he presents of these distortions. This reaction provide the basis for a subsequent depressive tendency. Whether in any given case a schizoid or depressive state depends, in par t, of course, upon the circumstance which the individual is called upon to face in his later life But the most important determining factor is the degree to which objects have been incorporated during the oral phase. The various defensive techniques which characterize the transition period, i.e., the obsessional, paranoid, hysterical and phobic techniques. All represent attempts to deal with difficulties and conflicts attending object-relationships in consequence of the persistence of corporatised objects. These defensive techniques are accordingly seen to resolve themselves into differing methods of controlling an underlying schizoid or depressive tendency, and thus averting the onset of a schizoid or depressive state, as the case may be. Where a schizoid tendency is present, they represent methods designed to avert the ultimate psychopathological disaster which follows from loss of the ego, and, where a depressive tendency is present, they represent methods designed to avert the ultimate psychopathological disaster, in which follows from loss of the object.

It is so fortunate as to enjoy a perfect object-relationship during the impressionable period of infantile dependence, or for that matter during the transition period of infantile dependence. Consequently, no one ever becomes completely emancipated from the state of infantile dependence, or from some proportionate degree of oral fixation; and there is no one who has completely escaped the necessity of incorporating this early enacting of objects. It may consequently be inferred that there is present in every one either an underlying schizoid or an underlying depressive tendency, according as it as in the early or in the late oral phase that difficulties chiefly attended infantile object-relationships. We are thus introduced to the conception that every individual may be classified as falling into one or two psychological types—the schizoid and the depressive. It is not necessary to regard these two types as having more than phenomenological significance, nevertheless, it is impossible to ignore the fact that in the determination of these two types some part may be played by a hereditary factor—such that the relative strength of the inborn tendencies of sucking and biting.

Of these, we are reminded of Jung's dualistic theory of psychological types. According to Jung, is, of course, the 'introvert' and the 'extravert' representation to the fundamental types, into the constitution of which psychopathological factors do not primarily enter. There is, however, another essentially dualistic conception of psychological types, with which a conceptual representation prolonging the conception with which is expounded by Kretschmer in his works entitled 'Physique and Character' and 'The Psychology of Men of Genius' and according to which the two basic psychological types are the 'schizothymic' and the 'cyclothymic.' As these terms themselves infer from questions that we must take or come to reach a conclusion read between the lines. However, the reverential inference of cyclothymic individuals, as predisposed to circular or manic-depressive psychoses, and the schizothymic individual to schizophrenia, there is thus, a striking agreement between Kretschmer's conclusions and explanations that are envisaged types—an agreement all the more striking since the envisaged types of alternative operatives. The only significant divergence between the two analytic approaches arises out of the fact that Kretschmer regards the temperamental differences between the types as based essentially upon constitution factors and attributes to the psychopathological propensities to this temperamental differences. Whereas in viewing the psychopathological factors used during the period of infantile dependence making of any rate a considerable contribution to the temperamental difference. The sufficient agreement between Kretschmer's views and those as provided some independent support for autonomously unconfined study, however, Kretschmer's views also provide some independent support or an underlying depressive tendency, as presented at some level in every individual, and that all individuals may be classified upon this basis, so, as far as their psychopathological propensities are concerned.

Every theory of basic types is inevitably confronted with the problem of 'mixed types'. Kretschmer freely acknowledges the existence of mixed types, and he explains their occasioned occurrence on the grounds that the incidence (and perhaps, hormonic) groups of factors, which it may be usually of some mixed types is to be explained not so much in terms of fixations in developmental phases. Where difficulties over object-relationships assert themselves pre-eminently during the early oral phase, a schizoid tendency is established, and, where difficulties over object-relationships assert themselves pre-eminently during the late oral phase, the establishment of a depressive tendency is the result. In so far, is that, nonetheless, that such difficulties are fairly distributed between the two phases, we may expect to find a fixation in the late oral phase superimposed upon one in the early oral phases, and in that case a deeper schizoid tendency will be found underlying a superimposed depressive tendencies, that such a phenomenon may occur admits of no doubt whatsoever, and even the most 'normal' person must be regarded as having persuasions toward schizoid potentialities at the deepest levels. It is open to equally little question that even the most normal person may on certain circumstances become depressed. Similarly, schizoid individuals are not wholly immune to depression, and depressed individuals are sometimes grounded by displaying certain schizoid characteristics. Whether a depressive or a schizoid state will declare itself in any given case doubtless depends in part upon whether the precipitating circumstances take the form of the real object or of difficulties in object-relationships assuming in some other form; and where there is a fairly even balance between fixation in the early and the late phases, this may be the determining factor. Even so, the most important factor must always remain the degrees of regression, which is provoked; and this is determined primarily by the relative strength of fixation. In the last instance the degree of regression must depend upon whether the chief problem of the individualities, that lies in the disposal of his love or in the disposal of his hate and there must be few individuals in whom the disposal of love and the disposal of hate are attended by equal difficulty.

When we use as primary source not our own clinical data but the experience and insights of other fields., we betray a sese of our unease. Such behaviour indicates that our understanding of the clinical phenomena or of the analytic theory that we adduce to interpret them is not as firmly based as we would want it to be. Thus, Altman (1977), after an erudite and charming discourse on the vicissitudes of love ends by saying, . . . the vicissitudes of love are so interrelated with every aspect of human development, its ambiguities so numerous and persuasive, that we may still be obliged to ask, 'What is this thing called love?'

Altman observed, for instance, that when psychoanalysts are asked about love, they respond as cultured lay people, rather than as professionals. They do no t couch their responses in the language of scientific psychology. This should make us aware that from the very beginning, psychoanalytic discussion of love has been burdened by the analyst's entailment in his own culture, in its values and its social structure. In Western society, love is put forward as the 'summum bonun' of human relations. All moral teaching whether founded in faith in the supernatural or not, sanctifies love. Dealing fairly with one's neighbour and curbing one's aggression toward others ultimately involve an essential compassionate attitude toward people, that is, a capacity for positively-tinged affective identification with others. Since love is sanctified and regarded as sacred, it falls within the realm of the taboo. Accordingly, objectivity may be inhibited and curiosity curbed when we attempt to study love scientifically. An analyze love, especially the creative, 'nonconflictual' aspects of the phenomenon, may even imply a certain degree of sacrilege, a desecration of what should be revered rather than understood, of what should e cherished rather than analysed.

The high moral value we place on loving strengthens the Superego's influence on how we treat the subject during therapy and how we conceptualize love scientifically. 'What's wrong with a good love relationship?' Essentially, it is a rhetorical question, we almost always take a good love relationship for granted. Such a question constitutes a moral rather than an intellectual challenge.

The most recent literature concerning the phenomenology of love has emphasized the importance of early object love. In large measure, this has been occasioned by the stage of interest in narcissistic character disorder, and the so-called borderline condition. The connection between loving and these conditions arising from the fact that identification and narcissistic object choice is common to all of them, investigation of the etiology, therefore, has centered on the vicissitudes of the early mother-child as the matrix out of which identification and individuation are affected. Moreover, these are conditions in which vulnerability of self-esteem is of major significance. Freud (1914) placed variation of self-esteem in the centre of his discussion of falling in love and being in love, explaining the phenomenon in economic terms—in shifts of libidinal investment from the self-representation to the object-representation and back. According to object relations theorists, the nature of the earliest interaction between the child and the mother determines the quality of the child's subsequent love relationships. Bak (1973) states that fallng in love is an attempt to undo the original separation from the mother, and Bergmann (1971) says, that love revived if not direct memories, then . . . archaic ego states that were once active in the symbiotic phase. He cites Mahler (1967) to the effect in the symbiosis is to be understood as 'hallucinatory of delusional, somatopsychic, omnipotence fusion with the representation of the mother. In other words, the state of being in love reactivates or reflects the state of object relations that prevailed before the distinction between the self and the object developed. During the symbiotic phase, fusion with the mother is supposedly experienced as unalloyed bliss, while separation is tantamount to its annihilation and death.'

It was connection with Feud's revolutionary approach to the subject of sex and love that he developed the concept of the object. Discussing the nature of the energy of the erotic drive, the libido, Freud (1905) distinguished between the zone of origin of the libido, the aim of the libidinal instinct that the libido as the object of the instinct. It is upon the object that the libido is discharged and this process of discharge is experienced as pleasure. He said that the object is the mental representation of something which is the source of intense libidinal gratification, something highly cathected with the libido. The mental representation grows out of a mnemic image, a recollected set of sensory impressions accompanied by a pleasurable feeling, in that which, according to the dominant principle, one's wishfully attempt to reconstitute as a sensory impression. Accordingly, the object may be the representation of something which is part of one's own person—the lips, skin. mouth, and so forth, for example—or, it may be the mental representation of something inanimate which at a certain stage of cognitive development is still regarded as par t of one's own person. Fenichel (1945) observed that at particular stages in the child's development, the faecal mass is viewed sometimes as part of the self and sometimes as part of the external world. This is a striking parallel to Winnicott's (1953) concept of the transitional object. at a later stage the object may be an external representation of another person existing independently of the self. In each stag e of this development, it should be emphasized, we are dealing with a technical term, the concept of a mental representation. According to libido theory, it is no t the external thing which is vested with energy, It is the metal representation of the thing or person so cathected. The mental representation bears a special relationship to processes of instinctual discharge.

Emphasizing the representational aspect of the object highlights two kind s of confusion that pertain to the use of the object concept. The firs t of these confusions is shown by the theories of Wilhelm Reich (1942). Basing his views on Freud's earlier neurophysiological concept of the set or in the body of another person. This approach has perpetuated the confusion between what is internal and what is external. that is, where in the physical world the material libido is to be found. It disregards the fact that at all times we are dealing with a psychological experience, the mental representation of an object, a persistently 'internal' experience.

The second confusion is illustrated by the concept of a part object, as opposed to a whole object. Whatever it is that is represented mentally as instinctually cathected constitute an object. Instinctual wishes of an aggressive or libidinal nature may centre on mental representations of parts of one's own body, parts of someone else's body, or on mental representation of one's own or some other person's whole body. Any one of these may be taken as an object. The type of unconscious fantasy involved determines whether or not the person's body is regarded as a penis or whether the person as a whole is regarded as a breast or, as in the case of narcissistic object choice, whether another person is regarded as a representation of one's own self. When we make judgements about psychological experiences, whether for the purpose of clinical interpretation or a theory building, what we try to determine is the nature of the unconscious fantasy which underlies the thought or behaviour of the individual, either in regard to other persons or things or in regard to that individual (Arlow, 1969). In such fantasies of a real external person or, conversely, one's whole body in an unconscious fantasy may be conceived as a representation of one's own or someone else's penis, breast, or faeces. In any event, we are dealing with mental representations of an object in the sense as defined by itself, as whether that mental representation corresponds to the totality of another person' s body or to a part of one's own or another person's body.

A consequence of the confusion, it may be observed in the tendency to use the term's interpersonal relations and object relations interchangeably. They are not identical. In fact, they represent two different realms of discourse. A young man, for example, disappointed in his beloved, does not search for a new object. he is really looking for another woman, who may in time become the source of pleasurable cathected mental representations. Fundamentally, it is the effect of unconscious fantasy wishes, connected with special mental representations of objects, that colour, distorts and affects between the person and the object. this is essentially the core of transference, in which the person in the real world is confused with a mental representation of a childhood object, a mental representation of what once was either a person or a thing. These issues are no t simply semantic ones. They bear directly on any discussions of love and narcissism and the role of object relation s in ego development.

According to Freud (1911), the operation of the pleasure principle is expressed through a tendency to reestablish and experience a set of sensory perceptions of a pleasurable nature identical with the memory of earlier experience or pleasure. Thus, the first and fundamental categorization of experience is in terms of pleasant or unpleasant. (Brenner [1974], in his study, the development of affects, has demonstrated the fundamental role that this categorization plays in all subsequent affective structure.) This is t e abiding principle by which perceptions are integrated and organized in memory according to the quality of similarity with or differences from earlier memory traces. On the basis of how the memory of earlier perceptions has been organized, subsequent experience in interpreted metaphorically (Arlow, 1979) note once again, Freud (1925) wrote in, 'Negation'

. . . The function of judgement is concerned in the main with two sorts of decisions. It affirms or disaffirms the possession by a thing of a particular attribute; and it asserts or disputes that a presentation has an existence in reality. The attribute to be decided about may originally have been good or bad, useful or harmful. Expressed in the language of the oldest—the oral—instinctual impulses, the judgement is: 'I should like to eat this', or 'I should like to spit it out.' that is to say: 'I shall be inside me;, or, 'It shall be outside me.' The original pleasure-ego want is to introject into itself, such that everything that is good and to eject from itself everything that is bad. What is bad, what is alien to the ego and what is external are, to begin with, identical.

. . . The other sort of decision made by the function of judgement—as to the real existence of something of which there is a presentation (reality-testing)—is a concern of the definitive reality-ego, which develops out of the initial pleasure-ego. It is now no longer a question of whether what has been perceived (a thing) as a presentation can be rediscovered in perception (reality) as well. It is, we see, once more a question of external and internal. What is unreal, merely a presentation and subjective, is only internal; what is real is also there outside. In this stage of development regard for the pleasure has been set outside. experience has shown the subject has it is not only important whether a thing (an object of satisfaction for him) possesses the 'good' attribute and so deserves to be taken into his ego, but also whether it is there in the external world, so that he can get hold of it whenever he needs it. In order to understand this step forward we must recollect that all presentations or origin from perceptions are repetitions of them. Thus originally the mere existence of a presentation was a guarantee of the reality of what was presented. The antithesis between subjective and objective does not exist from the first. It only comes into being from the fact that thinking possesses the capacity to bring before the mind once more, something that has once been perceived, by reproducing it as a presentation without the external object having still to be there. The first and immediate aim, therefore, of reality-testing is, not to find an object in real perception which corresponds to the one presented, but to refined such an object, to convince oneself that it is still there.

We can see in this quotation from Freud that there is an all-pervasive series of equivalents which come to serve as the background for all judgements and interpretations of stimuli. What is pleasurable is at first treated as part of the self, and in keeping with the pleasure principle, the psychic apparatus operates toward trying to institute a repetition of these perceptions. It is not hard to understand how reality testing and the interpretations of sensory data, Functions acquire with such effort, and easily and readily set aside in the compulsive wishful strivings of dreams, fantasies, and neurotic symptoms, as well as under the influence of great passion or prejudice, and, of course, in love. The fundamental tendency to seek an identity of pleasurable perceptions goes far in explaining the persistent influence of unconscious childhood fantasies.

What is later organized and conceptualized as the need-gratifying object originates out of the memories of repetitive sensory impressions accompanied by feelings or gratification. Object seeking is predominantly oriented by the needs to try to achieve the identity of pleasurable perceptions remembered but not independently attained by infants. The disparity between infant's wishes and their limited capacity to achieve them in reality is a fundamental fact of human development connected with an external person become organize into a coherent memory structure, a mental representation of a person, which we call 'object.' The term, object, therefore, represents a concept pertaining to a persistent, that is, a structural experience in parallel fashion a coherent organization of memory traces of representations connected with pain may serve as the basis for the concept of another kind of object representation. Thus, it happens that two sets of memories of sensory impressions may be organized as mental representations, one associated with pain, the other pleasure. The pleasant representation of such memories may be labelled as 'good', the unpleasant one's as 'bad.' It is in this sense that we can understand what the Kleians mean when they talk about 'good' objects and 'bad' objects in referring to the psychic events in the earliest months of life.

It is only later in the course of development that the seemingly disparate mental representations of objects having identical sensory impressions are fused into the concept of an external person whose mental representations psychologically may be vested or associated with memories of pain as well as pleasure. From a psychological point of view the individual's concept of a person is a conglomerate of many earlier object representations. This coherent, organized concept may be dissolved regressively into its antecedent object representations. It is not necessarily the re-emergence of an earlier structure, but rather the reactivation of memory traces of the good object representation that is distinct from the good object representation, thus, the splitting of the representation of a person does not necessarily occur only in case of severe personality regression. When there is a painful interaction between two people, one can observe in the dreams and fantasies of the patient how the qualities o f goo d and bad become sharply dissociated in the mental representation of the object. the individual, in turn, may respond to the other pers on as if that person were the repetition of the earlier mental representation of the bad object. At the same time, such an individual may be functioning at an advanced level of mental development: The ease with which the coherent concept of the object may regressively dissolve into earlier separate mental representations is a measure of ego weakness. The tendency to split the object representations int a good and bad antecedent expressions is usually reversible. In severe pathology, however, the process is irreversible and the split of the object representation becomes fixed and persistent.

Mahler's (1975) concepts of separation-individuation and the observational base for these concepts has been well established. Her ideas are frequently invoked to explain certain phenomena observed on the borderline states, the psychosis, falling in love, and the experience of the orgasm. The stages prior to the phases of separation-individuation have been associated with the period of primary identification—the stage during which there is no differentiation between the self and the object. Regression to primary identification is a hypothesis which appeals to those who view a good segment of psychopathology as reflecting a 'loss of boundaries' between the self and the object. According to some, this is the condition which is regressively reactivated in the psychopathological formations. However, it should of note, that feeling at one with something, being completely identified with someone, thinking that someone experiences and feels everything that another person seems to feel, is not necessarily a recapitulation of the vague, undefined state that precedes the distinction between the self and the object world. When poets describe the ecstasy of love or orgasm by saying that they feel completely united and indissolubly fused with the beloved, there is, nonetheless, some concomitant awareness of the existence of the other person as an independent object. This is equally true for descriptions of timelessness and the so-called 'oceanic' feeling, two states of mind often associated with being in love as well as with loss of the sens e of self or of 'ego boundaries.' In a study of distortions of the sense of time (Arlow, 1974, in that, the ability to demonstrate, from detailed presentations of the material of the analysis was not that of fusion of self and object.; in one instance, the fantasy expressed a woman's wish to have the oedipal love object forever. In the case of a male patient, it represented an overcoming of the fear of castration, a wish for immortality to counteract the pressing awareness off the danger of castration as represented by a fear of death.

Freud (1914), in his work titled 'On Narcissism' emphasized that in severe, regressive narcissistic disorders, there is not only a break with reality and withdrawal from objects of the external world, but at the same time, one is unable to find any trace of cathexis of mental representations of objects in fantasy, conscious or unconscious. It should be emphasized that it is not the clinical phenomenon of relations or withdrawal from people which indicates a break of object relations, but rather the evidence if withdrawal of cathexis from mental representations of objects. This is an important distinction to bear in mind: Otherwise one is tempted to make extrapolations from phenomenology without appreciating the characteristic feature of psychoanalysis, namely, the nature of the unconsciously psychological experience. It is possible for certain individuals to have very poor or few relations with people, but at the same time to maintain a very high quality of object constancy in fantasy life. One has to avoid judging the significance of an experience by externally observable phenomena alone.

After, at least a beginning attempt at individuation and after the phase of the transitional object, the different constellations of the memories of sensory experiences of pleasure and pain may be organized around the inherent perceptions of the world of which is a common source of perceptions into the concept of the good or bad mother, the good and bad object. One aspect of the child's growing ability to master ambivalence resides in the capacity too integrate the two contradictory concepts into a specific, unified concept of a person in the external world. Developmental psychologists differ as to exactly when this achievement is attained—probably sometimes in the second year of life. It is an attainment however, that is easily and regularly undone by regression. The concept of the object, as well as the concept of the self and even of the Superego, may undergo regressive dissolution into their antecedent identifications. This may be observed and dreams and in psychopathology, especially in patients suffering from depression, both in the borderline states and the psychosis.

The self-control of depressed persons can be characterized as maladaptive in two ways within the self-evaluation phase. First, depressed persons frequently fail to make accurate internal attributions of causality. Second, depressed persons tend to set stringent criteria for self-evaluation.

From an attrbutional point of view, a depressed person and be 'helpless' in either of two ways. In the first, the person make excessive external attributions of causality and thus generally believes that there is a high degree of independence between performance and consequences. Such a person as helpless in Seligman's sense of the word and would seldom engage in self-control behaviour even in an aversive environment. Such a person would be passive and apathetic but would not necessarily be self-derogating. Since aversive consequences are seen as uncontrollable, performance is neither commendable nor condemnable. In the second form of helplessness, the person makes accurate or even excessively internal attributions of causality but perceives himself or herself to be lacking in ability to obtain positive consequences. Thus, the person believes that the world does contain lawful performance-consequence relationships but that she or he is incompetent and ineffective. This person would be self-derogatory and would express inappropriate guilt, e.g., excessive internal attribution of causality for past aversive consequences. The use of the term helpless is this latter instance is somewhat different from Seligman's use of the term.

The work on learned helplessness in depression can be interpreted as support for either type of inaccurate attribution. For example, Miller and Seligman (1973) found that following success on a skill-defined task, depressed students did not raise their expectations of success as the nondepressed students did. No differences in expectancy change were found after failure of in chance defined tasks. As it is to interpret, that this finding in terms of a generalized perception by depressed persons that reinforcement is response independent. From an attributional framework subjects either perceived the task outcome to have been due to external causes, i.e., chance, not skill, or perceived sustaining their success, i.e., lacking skill. The data admit equally to either interpretation.

Stringent self-evaluative criteria as a characteristic of depression has been previously suggested by Marston (1965) and Bandura (1971). Self-evaluative standards may be stringent in the sense of a high threshold requiring great quantitative or quantitative excellence for self-approval. Golin and Terrel found that depressed college students tend to set higher goal levels for themselves. This deficit together with selective monitoring of negative events result in very few perceived successes. Depressed persons may also have low thresholds for negative self-evaluation. Although these criteria may be relatively independent, clinical observation, (e.g., Beck, 1972) suggests that for some depressed persons they may be almost reciprocals, depressed persons may have 'all or none' self-evaluative criteria, i.e., an effort is either a smashing success or a dismal failure.

Self-evaluative criteria may also be stringent in the sense of excessive breadth, failure in one instance is taken as failure in the entire class of behaviour. for example, failure on one exam is taken as evidence for failure as a student and, perhaps, as a person. Beck (1972) describes overgeneralization as one of the primary mechanisms of cognitive distortion in depression.

The self-reinforcement phase of self-control is particularly importance in accounting for depressive behaviour. Depression can be characterized by the self-administration of relatively low rates of self-reward and of which rates of self-punishment. low rates of self-reward can be associated with the slowed rates of overt behaviour which typify depression. Lower general activity level, few responses initiations, lower latencies, and less persistence may be interpreted as resulting from low rates of self-reward.

Self-punishment in normals serves to control behaviour reward, e.g., 'kicking oneself' for going off a diet. Self-punishment may also serve as a cue initiating alternative behaviour for approaching a goal (Kanfer and Karolly, 1972), Because and set stringent self-evaluation criteria, potentially effective behaviour may also be supposed by excessive self-punishing. Vacillation between responding strategies may also result because each alternative is self-punished early in the response chain, e.g., indecisiveness.

Correlational evidence for self-reinforcement deficits in depression was obtained by Rozensky, Rehm, Pry and Roth. Their study demonstrated differences in rates of self-reward and self-punishment between depressed and nondepressed hospital patients. Nevertheless,. The former did not differ in correct responses, so that, a replicated procedure with college students varying in degree of depression. Depressed students gave themselves more self-punishment and less self-reward than n nondepressed students although only the former difference obtained statistical significance. The failure to replicate the self-reward finding maybe due to the fact that the latter population was by definition a relatively active group of normals capable of working for long term rewards.